FUNDAMENTALS OF COLLECTION DEVELOPMENT AND MANAGEMENT

FUNDAMENTALS OF COLLECTION DEVELOPMENT AND MANAGEMENT

Third Edition

Peggy Johnson

An imprint of the American Library Association

Chicago   2014

PEGGY JOHNSON is a frequent speaker and trainer on collection development and management. She has published several books, including ALA Editions' *Developing and Managing Electronic Collections: The Essentials,* and numerous journal articles. She edited the peer-reviewed journal *Library Resources & Technical Services* for more than nine years and continues to edit *Technicalities: Information Forum for the Technical Services Professional.* She teaches as an adjunct professor in the MLIS program at St. Catherine University. Prior to retiring from the University of Minnesota Libraries, she served as associate university librarian. A past president of the Association for Library Collections and Technical Services, she received the ALCTS Ross Atkinson Lifetime Achievement Award in 2009. She has a master's degree from the University of Chicago Graduate Library School.

Printed in the United States of America

18 17 16 15 14   5 4 3 2 1

Extensive effort has gone into ensuring the reliability of the information in this book; however, the publisher makes no warranty, express or implied, with respect to the material contained herein.

ISBNs: 978-0-8389-1191-4 (paper); 978-0-8389-1959-0 (PDF); 978-0-8389-1960-6 (ePub); 978-0-8389-1961-3 (Kindle). For more information on digital formats, visit the ALA Store at alastore.ala.org and select eEditions.

Library of Congress Cataloging-in-Publication Data
Johnson, Peggy, 1948–
    [Fundamentals of collection development & management]
    Fundamentals of collection development and management / Peggy Johnson. — Third edition.
       pages   cm
    Includes bibliographical references and index.
    ISBN 978-0-8389-1191-4 (alk. paper)
    1. Collection development (Libraries) 2. Collection management (Libraries) 3. Collection development (Libraries)—United States. 4. Collection management (Libraries)—United States. I. Title.
    Z687.J64 2014
    025.2'1—dc23   2013049725

Cover design by Kim Thornton. Images © Shutterstock, Inc.

Composition by Dianne M. Rooney in the Janson Text and Helvetica typefaces.

♾ This paper meets the requirements of ANSI/NISO Z39.48-1992 (Permanence of Paper).

CONTENTS

 Supplemental materials, including reading lists and case studies from the first two editions, are available online at www.alaeditions.org/webextras.

My goal in writing this book remains the same as that for the first and second editions—*Fundamentals of Collection Development and Management* is intended as a comprehensive introduction to the topic for students, a primer for experienced librarians with new collection development and management responsibilities, and a handy reference resource for practitioners as they go about their day-to-day work. Coverage is intended to reflect the practice of collection development and management in all types of libraries. Although the focus is on libraries in the United States, references to practices and initiatives in Canada have been expanded. The history of collection development and management is provided to set the context for current theory and practice. I draw from the literature outside library and information management when pertinent.

When I wrote the preface to the first edition in the summer of 2003, I observed that the work of collection development and management was being profoundly changed by the Internet and increasing options for resources in digital format. This is even truer today. Nearly all aspects of collection development and management in all types of libraries are being reshaped by technology and the ubiquity of the Internet. These powerful forces on the work we do and how we do it are made more challenging by sociological, educational, economic, demographic, political, regulatory, and institutional changes in our user communities and the parent organizations and agencies that fund libraries. Library users' needs and expectations are evolving concurrently. I have sought to reflect this rapidly changing environment with updated examples and data.

This edition follows the same structure as the second edition. Chapter 1 presents an introduction to and an overview of collection management and development, including a brief history of the evolution of collection development and management as a specialty within the profession. Chapter 2 explores the organization and assignment of collection development and management responsibilities in libraries. An important section in chapter 2 discusses ethical issues associated with building and managing collections. Chapter 3 addresses formal library planning and two important library planning tools—collection development and management policies and library budgets. Chapter 4, "Developing Collections," introduces topologies for types of materials that librarians select and explores the selection process, selection criteria, the acquisition process, and acquisition options. Chapter 5 examines the collection management responsibilities of librarians after they have developed collections through purchases, subscriptions, leases, and licenses. Topics include weeding for withdrawal and storage; preservation and conservation; subscription review, renewal, and cancellation; and protection of collections from deterioration, theft, mutilation, and disasters. "Marketing, Liaison Activities, and Outreach," chapter 6, defines marketing, places it in the library setting, and explores the importance of and techniques for building and maintaining community relationships. Chapter 7 covers approaches to collection analysis and how to answer questions about quality and utility using quantitative, qualitative, and use- and user-based methods. Chapter 8 on cooperative collection development and management addresses this increasingly important topic in today's environment of constrained budgets and limited space to house collections.

The final chapter takes on the complicated topic of scholarly communication and the impact of the open-access movement. Although some may not consider the process of reshaping scholarly communication equally pertinent to all types of libraries and the librarians who work in them, I encourage you to read this chapter. The potential that open access offers and the policies that foster it should be of concern to all librarians.

All chapters have new supplemental reading lists, and these contain no sources published before 2008. Reading lists from the first two editions can be accessed as supplemental resources at www.alaeditions.org/webextras. The case studies that supplement chapters 2–9 also are new. Although fictional, these stories represent real challenges that librarians encounter regularly. I hope that practitioners as well as students will view them as catalysts for discussion. Case studies from the previous editions also can be accessed at www.alaeditions.org/webextras.

The glossary and appendixes have been updated. The appendixes are A, "Professional Resources for Collection Development and Management"; B, "Selection Aids"; and C, "Sample Collection Development Policy Statements."

A book, by its nature, is bounded and, although each chapter and many topics addressed here could be and often have been explored in far greater depth, I have been constrained by time and space. The supplemental reading lists are intended to offer readers sources through which they can explore topics of particular interest.

Many sources referenced may be found as preprints or postprints in digital repositories, as well as in the journals cited. All URLs provided in this book were valid as of late fall 2013. References to products, companies, projects, and initiatives are intended as examples only and not endorsements of particular options among many possibilities. Commercial offerings, business models, and companies change; thus, some information in this book may not reflect the current environment.

I depend on the expertise of professional colleagues and their generous assistance whenever I undertake a writing project. They may answer a single question or several, point me to a key resource, or review a few paragraphs or a chapter. As I revised this book, I tried to note everyone who helped me and I am delighted to thank them here; all errors and omissions in the text are solely my responsibility. In grateful appreciation, I thank (in alphabetical order): Natalie Bernstein, Paideia School, Atlanta, Georgia; Julia Blixrud, Association of Research Libraries; Elise Calvi, Indiana University Libraries; Katie Clark, University of Rochester River Campus Libraries; Kirsten Clark, University of Minnesota Libraries; Lynn Silipigni Connaway, OCLC; Lisa German, Pennsylvania State University Libraries; Heidi Hammond, St. Catherine University Masters of Library and Information Science program; Michelle Jeske, Denver Public Library; Brian Karschnia, St. Paul Public Library; Robert H. Kieft, Occidental College; Michael Levine-Clark, University of Denver Libraries; Judy Luther, Informed Strategies; Bonnie MacEwan, Auburn University Libraries; Eric Novotny, Pennsylvania State University Libraries; Jan Price, Metropolitan Council Library, St. Paul, Minnesota; Becky Ringwelski, Minitex, Minnesota; Nancy Sims, University of Minnesota Libraries; Betsy Simpson, University of Florida Libraries; Sarah Simpson, Tulsa City-County Library; Peter Suber, Harvard University Berkman Center for Internet and Society and Harvard University Library Office for Scholarly Communication; Barry Trott, Williamsburg Regional Library, Williamsburg, Virginia; Liza Weisbrod, Auburn University Libraries; and Karen Williams, University of Arizona Libraries.

I am exceedingly fortunate to have ready access to the excellent library collections at the University of Minnesota and St. Catherine University, but—as you learn in this book—no library collection is complete and resource sharing is vital. Efficient interlibrary loan is essential, and I am privileged to receive wonderful service from the endlessly patient interlibrary loan staff at the University of Minnesota Libraries: Melissa Eighmy Brown, Guy Peterson, Emily Riha, Alice Welch, and Cherie Weston.

I want to acknowledge the support and encouragement my parents gave me as I grew up, went to school, and learned my craft. With deepest thanks, I dedicate this book to Odell "Swede" Johnson and Virginia M. Johnson.

CHAPTER ONE

Introduction to Collection Development and Management

A book devoted to collection development and management should begin with a shared understanding of what this phrase means. For the purposes of this book, a *collection* consists of the materials in all formats and genres that a library owns or to which it provides remote access, through either purchase or lease. Collection development is the thoughtful process of developing or building a library collection in response to institutional priorities and community or user needs and interests. *Collection development* covers several activities related to the development of library collections, including selection, the determination and coordination of selection policy, assessment of the needs of users and potential users, budget management, identification of collection needs, community and user outreach and liaison, planning for resource sharing, and perhaps e-resources contract review and negotiation. Although *collection management* has been proposed as an umbrella term under which collection development is subsumed, this book distinguishes the two. In this construct, collection management covers decisions about weeding, serials cancellation, storage, and preservation and the activities that inform these decisions such as use studies and cost/benefit assessment. Also of concern in collection development and management are the organization and assignment of responsibilities for its practice.

This chapter begins with an introduction to concepts, followed by a capsule history of libraries and their collections, focusing on the United States. It concludes with an exploration of the evolution of collection development and management as a specialty within the profession. A brief look at the history of collection work, the libraries in which collections were developed, and external forces influencing collections is useful because contemporary practice builds on that of the past. Today's librarians work with library collections that have been created over time in accordance with earlier practices and conventions. In addition, many challenges faced by librarians have remained constant over time. Topics introduced in this chapter are explored in more depth in subsequent chapters.

Components of Collection Development and Management

Many librarians use the terms *collection development* and *collection management* synonymously or in tandem. For example, the professional organization within ALA's Association for Library Collections and Technical Services that focuses on this topic is called the Collection Management Section. The Reference and User Services Association's comparable section is called the Collection Development and Evaluation Section (CODES). The Medical Library Association has a Collection Development Section, and the Association for Library Service to Children has a Children's Collection Management Discussion Group. The professional literature also uses the terms interchangeably. Nevertheless, librarians generally have a common understanding of the practice and purpose of collection development and management, namely:

> The goal of any collection development organization must be to provide the library with a collection that meets the appropriate needs of its client population within the limits of its fiscal and personnel resources. To reach this goal, each segment of the collection must be developed with an application of resources consistent with its relative importance to the mission of the library and the needs of its patrons.[1]

Those who practice collection development and management are variously called selectors, bibliographers, collections librarians, subject specialists, liaisons or subject liaisons, collection development librarians, collection managers, and collection developers. In smaller libraries, the individual developing and managing collections may simply have the title of librarian or, in schools, school librarian or media specialist. Additional titles for those who build and manage collections also are used. This book uses these terms interchangeably to mean a library staff member who is responsible for developing, managing, and teaching about collections.

In many libraries, collections responsibilities are part of a suite of duties that librarians are assigned. Collection development and management responsibilities include the following:

- selecting materials in all formats for acquisition and access
- reviewing and negotiating contracts to acquire or access e-resources
- managing the collection through informed weeding, cancellation, storage, and preservation

- writing and revising collection development policies
- promoting, marketing, and interpreting collections and resources
- evaluating and assessing collections and related services, collection use, and users' experiences
- responding to challenges to materials selected
- carrying out community liaison and outreach activities
- preparing budgets, managing allocations, and demonstrating responsible stewardship of funds
- working with other libraries in support of resource sharing and cooperative collection development and management
- soliciting supplemental funds for collection development and management through grants and monetary gifts.

Although the assignment and importance of these responsibilities vary from library to library and librarian to librarian, they are found in all types of libraries. For that reason, this book does not contain separate chapters for various types of libraries.

All these responsibilities imply a knowledge of the library's user community and its fiscal and personnel resources, mission, values, and priorities along with those of the library's parent organization. Collection development and management cannot be successful unless integrated within all library operations; thus, the responsible librarians must have an understanding of and close relationship with other library operations and services. Important considerations for the collections librarian include who has access to the collection on-site and online, circulation and use policies, types of interfaces the library supports, and ease of resource discovery. A constant theme throughout this book is the importance of the environment, both internal and external to the library, within which collection management librarians practice their craft.

Historical Overview

Selection of materials for libraries has been around as long as libraries have, though records of how decisions were made in the ancient libraries of Nineveh, Alexandria, and Pergamum are not available. One can assume that the scarcity of written materials and their value as unique records made comprehensiveness, completeness, and preservation guiding principles. The library at Alexandria, which flourished between the third century BCE and the first or second century CE, held more than 600,000 scrolls, reportedly acquired through theft as well as purchase.[2] In the 800s, Al-Mamun, caliph of Bagdad, collected as many classical works from the Byzantine Empire as he could, had them translated into Arabic, and kept them in the House of Wisdom. Libraries served primarily as storehouses rather than as instruments for the dissemination of knowledge or sources for recreational reading. Comprehensiveness, completeness, and preservation have continued as library goals through the growth of commerce, the Renaissance, the invention of movable type, expanding lay literacy, the Enlightenment, the public library movement, and the proliferation of electronic resources.

Systematic philosophies of selection were rare until the end of the nineteenth century, although a few early librarians wrote about their guiding principles. Gabriel Naudé, hired by Cardinal Mazarin to manage his personal library in the early 1600s, addressed selection in the first modern treatise on the management of libraries. He stated, "It may be laid down as a maxim that there is no book whatsoever, be it never so bad or disparaged, but may in time be sought for by someone."[3] Completeness as a goal has been balanced by a desire to select the best and most appropriate materials. In 1780, Jean-Baptiste Cotton des Houssays, librarian at the Sorbonne, stated that libraries should consist only of books "of genuine merit and of well-approved utility," with new additions guided by "enlightened economy."[4] Appropriate criteria for selectivity have been a continuing debate among librarians and library users for centuries.

Academic Libraries

Libraries developed first in the American colonies as private collections and then within institutions of higher education. These early libraries were small for three reasons: relatively few materials were published in the New World, funds were limited, and acquiring materials was difficult. Even as late as 1850, only six hundred periodicals were being published in the United States, up from twenty-six in 1810.[5] Monographic publishing was equally sparse, with most works being religious in nature.

Academic libraries seldom had continuing budget allocations in their first centuries and, therefore, selection was not a major concern. Most support for academic libraries' collections came from gifts of books or donations to purchase them. Less than a tenth of the holdings of colonial American college libraries were added through direct purchase.[6] Most gifts were gladly accepted. Any institutional funds came from the occasional actions of the trustees or boards of regents rather than from recurring allocations. Student library fees were charged at several institutions, either on a per-annum or a per-use basis.[7] Even by 1856, when John Langdon Sibley became librarian of Harvard, the total fund for library acquisitions and binding was only $250 per year—about $6,366 in 2012 CPI dollars. In comparison, Harvard spent $45,220,000 on acquisitions and access in fiscal year 2012.[8] Even with funds in hand, acquiring materials was challenging. Everything had to be purchased on buying trips to book dealers in large East Coast cities and Europe.

Collections grew slowly. By 1790, Harvard's library had reached only 12,000 volumes. It had averaged eighty-two new volumes per year in the preceding 135 years. At the same time, the College of William and Mary's library collection numbered only 3,000, and it was the second largest. Academic libraries added, on the average, only 30–100 volumes per year before 1800. Most additions, because they were donations, were irrelevant to the educational programs of the time.[9] By 1850, only one U.S. academic institution had a collection larger than 50,000 volumes: Harvard College collections had reached 72,000 volumes.[10] At mid-century, total holdings for the approximately seven hundred colleges, professional schools, and public libraries in the United States were only 2.2 million volumes.[11]

Academic libraries reflected American education's priorities of the time: teaching rather than study, students rather than scholars, and maintaining order and discipline rather than promoting learning and research. Reflective thinking and theoretical considerations were unusual in any college discipline before the American Civil War. As a consequence, academic libraries had only limited significance in their institutions and still functioned as storehouses.

After the American Civil War, academic libraries and their parent institutions began a period of significant change. Libraries gained greater prominence as universities grew. The period from 1850 to 1900 witnessed a fundamental change in the structure of American scholarship, influenced by ideas and methods imported from German universities, which had become centers for advanced scholarship. The move to lectures and seminars as replacements for textbooks, memorization, and recitation and the increasing importance of research had far-reaching consequences for libraries. Passage of the Morrill Act in 1862, which created the land grant universities, introduced the concept that universities were obligated to produce and share knowledge that would advance society. A direct result was a tremendous increase in scholarly journals and monographs. The needs and working habits of the professionalized and institution-centered scholars were quite different from those of their predecessors. Scholars' attitudes toward the academic library experienced a basic reorientation, and the institutional academic library became a necessity. The scholarly profession was no longer confined to those who had the private wealth to amass extensive personal collections. A mounting flood of publications meant that even those few scholars with private means could not individually keep up with and manage all the new information available. They needed the institutional library to consult and to have access to the growing number of materials necessary for research. As the library became increasingly important to higher education, the process of creating collections gained a higher profile.

College libraries began to diverge from university libraries as their parent institutions' missions evolved in the second half of the 1800s. As universities expanded to support graduate and professional programs and major research initiatives, their libraries, in response, sought to develop comprehensive collections that would support both current and future programs and research. College libraries, on the other hand, retained a focus on supporting undergraduate teaching programs and the needs of undergraduates, a focus that continues today.[12] They did not seek to build the comprehensive collections that have come to characterize university libraries.

Well into the 1900s, most selection in both university and college libraries was handled by faculty members. When Asa Gray was hired as an instructor at the University of Michigan in 1838, he went first to Europe to acquire books for the library. The president at Ohio Wesleyan traveled to New York and Europe in 1854 to purchase library books.[13] German university libraries were unique in placing selection as the direct responsibility of librarians and staff, with less faculty input. A primary and early advocate of the role of librarians in developing library collections was Christian Gottlob Heyne, the librarian at the University of Göttingen in Germany from 1763 to 1812.[14] In 1930, faculty members in the United States still were selecting as much as 80 percent of total university library acquisitions, and librarians were choosing a modest 20 percent.[15] This ratio began to shift in the 1960s at universities and had reversed by the late 1970s, although faculty continue to have an important selection role in many smaller institutions. These teaching faculty often collaborate with librarians, who may have responsibility for some types of materials and portions of the collection. The change can be linked to an increasing professionalism among librarians, the burgeoning volume of publications, a growing number of librarians with extensive subject training, and the expanding pressure of other responsibilities, including research and publication, on faculty. As the responsibility for building library collections shifted from faculty to librarians—or to a shared responsibility—selection emphasis changed from selecting materials primarily to meet the needs and interests of specific faculty members to building a unified collection to meet both current and future institutional priorities.

The period between 1945 and 1970 has been called higher education's "golden age" and paralleled post–World War II economic expansion.[16] Unemployment was low for most of this period, and tax revenues at the local, state, and federal levels increased. Many of these dollars flowed into higher education, and libraries benefited directly. A series of federal programs, beginning with the Servicemen's Readjustment Act—the G.I. Bill—in 1944 subsidized student tuition.[17] The G.I. Bill, which allowed World War II veterans to attend college at no cost, resulted in an influx of funds that colleges and universities directed to new faculty positions and programs, and to infrastructure including libraries. The 1958 National Defense Education Act (NDEA) was a response to the Soviet Union's launch of Sputnik and fear that the United States was falling behind in technology and the sciences. The NDEA authorized funding for higher education loans and fellowships, vocational teacher training, and programs in the K–12 schools, including math, science, and foreign-language activities. In 1965, the Higher Education Act (HEA) was enacted to strengthen educational resources in colleges and universities and provide financial assistance for students. The HEA has been reauthorized at four-year intervals and is the basis for many of today's postsecondary education subsidies, including student loan and grant programs, direct funding for college and university libraries, and teacher training programs. Title VI of the HEA supports infrastructure building in colleges and universities for foreign-language, international, and area studies with often significant funding directed to building library collections in support of these initiatives.

The golden age of higher education was also a golden age for libraries. College and university library budgets grew rapidly. Rider made his famous prediction that research library collections would double every sixteen years. In 1953, Braugh wrote that the mission of Harvard's library was the "collection and preservation of everything printed."[18] The seemingly endless possibilities for growth broadened the librarian's collection responsibilities. Moving beyond individual book evaluation and selection, librarians began to view building coherent collections as an important responsibility. They began to seek and acquire materials from around the world. The scope of collections expanded to include Asia, Africa, the Middle East, and Eastern Europe as well as Western Europe.[19]

The emphasis during this period was on growth and handling it effectively. Collections theory began to focus on who should be selecting materials for the library, how selection decisions were made and the appropriate criteria, and alternatives to individual title selection for building collections. During the 1950s, vendors began offering services that freed librarians from ordering directly from publishers. Many of these service agencies began supplying materials through approval and blanket plans, freeing academic librarians to concentrate on identifying and obtaining more esoteric resources.

By the 1970s, budgets in academic libraries began to hold steady or to shrink. Fiscal constraints were coupled with increasing materials costs. In the 1980s, the escalating cost of journals led librarians to decry a "serials crisis." The Association of Research Libraries (ARL) began tracking serials and monograph unit costs, expenditures, and number of titles purchased against the CPI. Between 1986 and 2011, ARL, often a bellwether for all sizes of academic libraries, documented a 402 percent increase in serial expenditures.[20] Monograph unit costs increased 99 percent, those for monographs 71 percent. The result was only a 10 percent increase in the number of monographs purchased in ARL member libraries during the twenty-five years. These large academic libraries continue to invest a major portion (70 percent, on average) of their budgets in serials, including electronic resources, and a lesser portion in monographs.

The consolidation of publishers and vendors has changed the marketplace in which collection development librarians make their decisions. Six groups (Reed Elsevier, Taylor and Francis, Wolters Kluwer, Candover and Cinven, Wiley-Blackwell, and Verlagsgruppe George von Holtzbrinck) now control more than forty major commercial scholarly publishers, with Reed Elsevier controlling more than 30 percent of this market.[21] With mergers have come price increases: when Elsevier Reed purchased Pergamon, Pergamon's journals prices increased 27 percent; when Kluwer purchased Lippincott, Lippincott's prices increased 30 percent.

Initially, librarians hoped that electronic journals would provide an alternative to the high cost of serials facing libraries. The end of the 1990s introduced the Big Deal, in which commercial publishers bundled packages of e-journals for a single price with the promise that cost increases would be controlled if libraries accepted the package, often with conditions prohibiting cancellations for a specified number of years. Before long, academic librarians began to question the advantages of signing a Big Deal agreement because of the limitations on cancellations.

Academic librarians became preoccupied with journal pricing projections, serial cancellation projects, electronic publishing ventures that might affect pricing, and perceived unfair pricing practices. How best to allocate limited funds among different subject areas and formats and demonstrate financial account-ability concerned collections librarians, and they began to look for guidance in how they could make responsible decisions with less money. The goal of autono-mous, self-sufficient collections became less realistic. Collection development policy statements became more common as libraries sought guidance in manag-ing limited financial resources amid conflicting demands.

Interest grew in increasing library cooperation. OCLC (Online Computer Library Center), established in 1967 for academic libraries in Ohio, opened its membership to all types of libraries regardless of location and facilitated the sharing of resources as well as bibliographic records. The Research Libraries Group was founded in 1974 as a "partnership to achieve a planned, coordinated interdependence in response to the threat posed by a climate of economic retreat and financial uncertainty."[22]

Library consortia became increasingly important as academic libraries sought to negotiate the best price for e-content. Most early efforts at securing discounted subscriptions came from academic library consortia, but consortia now may represent all types of libraries and be based on geography, type of library, subject specailization, or a combination of these.

Librarians questioned the older idea of building comprehensive collec-tions in large libraries "just in case" a particular item might be needed and sug-gested that a more responsible use of budgets might be supplying materials to meet users' need "just in time." *Just-in-time* is a business phrase that describes a means of inventory control. The goal of just-in-time inventory management is to reduce the use of buffer inventories and to synchronize the movement of materials through the production process so that materials are delivered only just before they are needed. *Just-in-case* management is the opposite, meaning that large inventories of production materials are held on-site so they are always on hand whenever they are needed. Librarians often framed this as a debate between ownership versus access.

Increased use of interlibrary loan became an obvious option to building comprehensive local collections. In 1988, Line wrote, "Before World War 2, interlending was regarded as an optional extra, a grace and favour activity, to be indulged in sparingly; any research library considered it an admission of failure to have to obtain any item from elsewhere. Now every library, however large, accepts that it cannot be self-sufficient, and some of the largest obtain the most from elsewhere."[23]

Additional options for providing materials at the point of need have been embraced by many academic libraries. One option is to provide articles via pay-per-view. Libraries may cancel selected journal subscriptions and rely on purchasing articles when their users request them. Reallocating funds previously directed to subscriptions may be a reasonable way to use limited funds and yet meet user need. Another option, patron-driven acquisitions, has become increasingly popular in the twenty-first century. In this model, selection decisions are based on input from library users.

The 1990s introduced the idea of scholarly communication as an information food chain in which academic libraries purchase the resources that researchers use, researchers write up their findings and give them to journal publishers, who then publish the research in journals that they sell to libraries. Librarians began to question this system, which placed libraries at the low (and expensive) end of the food chain and potentially reduced the dissemination of scholarship. ARL started the Scholarly Publishing and Academic Resources Coalition (SPARC, www.arl.org/sparc), an alliance of universities, research libraries, and professional organizations, in 1997 as a constructive response to market dysfunctions in the scholarly communication system. The growth of the open-access movement, which seeks to make scholarly articles available online, free of charge, and free of many copyright and licensing restrictions through self-archiving and open-access journals, began in the early twenty-first century. Collections librarians in academic libraries joined together to raise the consciousness of their faculties about their own roles and responsibilities in the creation and dissemination of knowledge.

E-journals have come to dominate academic journal collections. The ARL statistics for 2010–2011 reported that 84 percent of paid serial subscriptions were for e-journals.[24] Scholarly e-books are rapidly obtaining a similar dominance in academic libraries. A 2012 study by *Library Journal* reported that 95 percent of academic libraries offered e-books.[25] The widespread adoption of e-books has presented challenges to the traditional practice of resource sharing, which depends on physical items delivered to requesting libraries. This has been less a problem with journal articles because e-journal publishers usually permit the lending library to print a copy of the article and then deliver it electronically to the borrowing library. ARL reported that member libraries were spending an average of 65 percent of their materials budgets on electronic resources in 2010–11.[26] Non-ARL academic libraries are rapidly approaching this figure, and it will continue to increase in all academic libraries. In response to the shift to e-content, collections librarians have developed new approaches to their responsibilities for selecting, licensing, evaluating, and managing these materials.

Another initiative, mass digitization of print materials, has affected the nature of collection development and management. The Google Books Library Project was launched in 2004 with the goal of scanning fifteen million volumes. As of March 2012, more than twenty million books had been scanned and were searchable. Books not protected by copyright (approximately 20 percent of the total) are available in full and can be read online.[27] Those not in the public domain are searchable, but not fully available. The nonprofit Internet Archive had a collection of nearly nine million items (video, music, audio, and texts) in November 2013. Project Gutenberg (www.gutenberg.org) offered more than 42,000 free e-books that could be read online or downloaded in HTML, as an EPUB book, or to a Kindle. Collections librarians began to consider the extent to which they could rely on these digital collections and perhaps reduce local holdings.

To address this concern about permanent access, HathiTrust, a partnership of large research institutions and libraries, was established to preserve and provide access to digitized materials deposited by members. Content comes from various sources, including Google, the Internet Archive, Microsoft, and partner institution in-house scanning. Anyone can search the HathiTrust Digital Library, but full viewing and downloading of public domain materials is limited to HathiTrust partners, all of which are academic libraries.

These massive projects are increasing national interest in what has been called the "collective collection," an initiative that seeks to foster cooperative management of the aggregate print collection.[28] As larger libraries face space constraints and decisions about retention and preservation of their collections, collections librarians consider the implications of these enterprises.

Another significant change in academic libraries in the twenty-first century has been the shift away from "pure" bibliographers—subject specialists whose sole responsibility is collection development and management. Libraries have emphasized outreach and liaison roles within the context of subject responsibilities. Conversely, many librarians (reference librarians and technical services librarians) who had not selected materials and managed collections were assigned these responsibilities.

Hazen proposed one possible future for academic libraries when he wrote,

> Looking to the future, research libraries will in some areas continue to build enduring collections of record. In others, they will settle for use-driven holdings while seeking neither comprehensive coverage nor long-term retention. The

availability of digital surrogates or of remotely maintained archival copies may also affect local choices. Ideally, libraries will seek to ensure that some institution is providing ongoing preservation and care for everything they hold—but there may be instances in which current-use materials are acquired and discarded regardless of provisions for persistence. The continuum of curation will become more diverse.[29]

Public Libraries

Academic libraries preceded public libraries in the United States. Established in 1833, the Peterborough Town Library in New Hampshire is usually identified as the first free publicly owned and maintained library in the United States. A library established in Franklin, Massachusetts, through funds from Benjamin Franklin to purchase 116 volumes was opened to all inhabitants of the town in 1790. Though public, it was not supported by public funding.[30]

Social libraries, limited to a specific clientele and supported by subscriptions, had existed in the colonies for more than a century. One of the better known is the Philadelphia Library Company, founded by Benjamin Franklin in 1731 and supported by fifty subscribers to share the cost of importing books and journals from England. Mercantile libraries were membership libraries founded by and for merchants and clerks both to educate and to offer an alternative to immoral entertainment.[31] They often featured presentations by prominent writers and thinkers. Examples were found in Boston (1820), Philadelphia (1821), and Cincinnati (1835). Lesser known are the literary society libraries formed by free African Americans in the northeast United States between 1828 and 1860. One of the earliest, the Colored Reading Society of Philadelphia founded in 1828, directed that all income from initiation fees and monthly dues (excluding that devoted to rent and light) be spent on books. The Phoenix Society of New York, established in 1933, aimed to "establish circulating libraries in each ward for the use of people of colour on very modest pay—to establish mental feasts."[32]

Other social libraries were established and supported by philanthropists and larger manufacturers to teach morality, provide a more wholesome environment, and offer self-education opportunities to the poor and uneducated drawn to cities. Circulating libraries were commercial ventures that loaned more popular materials, frequently novels, for a fee. When considered together, these early libraries were furnishing the collections that libraries provide today—materials that are used for information, education, and recreation.

Boston was the first major community to establish a public library, in 1852. The trustees defined the purpose of the public library as education and, though they had no plans to acquire novels, they were willing to include the more popular respectable books. In their first report, the trustees wrote, "We consider that a large public library is of the utmost importance as the means of completing our system of public education."[33] The responsibility of libraries to educate their users and to bring them to the better books and journals remained a topic of debate in public libraries for many years. Controversies persist about the appropriateness of some types of materials such as romance novels, graphic novels, juvenile audiobooks, and materials for diverse populations and on controversial subjects.

Trustees or committees appointed by trustees selected materials in early public libraries. By the end of the 1800s and as librarianship evolved as a profession, John Cotton Dana was advising that book selection in public libraries be left to the librarians, directed by the trustees or a book committee.[34] The present practice of assigning collections responsibility to librarians is the result of a slow transformation. In the United States, public librarians generally acquired selection responsibilities before those in academic libraries. The shift happened in public libraries earlier because the faculties of colleges and universities retained a more active interest in library collections than did the members of public library boards or trustees. The rise of library schools and the professionalization of librarianship led librarians to expect expanded responsibilities for selection and made public library trustees and boards more willing to transfer them to librarians.

Librarians' responsibilities for managing collections and access to content have been questioned as the U.S. federal government has sought to protect children from harmful materials on the Internet. The Communications Decency Act (Title V of the Telecommunications Act of 1996) sought to regulate both obscene and indecent materials on the Internet but was ruled unconstitutional by the U.S. Supreme Court for violating the First Amendment. Eventually, the attempt to regulate obscenity was addressed in the Children's Internet Protection Act (CIPA), which became law in December 2000.[35] CIPA requires schools and public libraries to use Internet filtering software on computers with Internet access to protect against access to visual depictions that are obscene, child pornographic, or harmful to minors. If a library receives federal E-rate funds (discounts to assist most schools and libraries to obtain affordable telecommunications and Internet access), this provision applies only to children; if a library receives only Library Services and Technology Act (LSTA) grant funds, the provision applies to all patrons.[36] Public librarians protested against CIPA, which they viewed as infringement on the right to read and a form of censorship. ALA challenged the law as unconstitutional in 2001, but the Supreme Court upheld it in 2003.

Funding for public libraries has largely depended on local and state appropriations. After World War II, economic growth resulted in increased tax revenues and thus increased funds for public libraries. Much of this money supported collections growth. Funding for public libraries began to hold steady or to decline in the late 1970s. Pressures to contain taxes at all levels of government reduced the flow of funds to libraries as municipalities began to make difficult choices about how to allocate limited resources. Libraries, in turn, faced choices about their priorities and where scarce funds should be directed—to hours of operation, staffing, services, or collections. Many public libraries closed branches and reduced the purchases of duplicate copies of popular titles. Book vendors began to offer rental collections that provided a rotating collection of popular titles, often with multiple copies, to help libraries manage limited collections budgets.

The Great Recession that began in late 2007 has compounded libraries' fiscal problems.[37] Nearly 60 percent of public libraries reported flat or decreased operating budgets in 2010–2011.[38] The *Public Libraries in the United States Survey* for fiscal year 2010 reported that collections expenditures decreased by 10.4 percent between 2000 and 2010.[39] In 2011, 43 percent of the states reported that local funding for a majority of public libraries declined.[40] The 2012 *Public Library Data Service Statistical Report* reported that library income continued to decline and average per-capita expenditures dropped 7.8 percent.[41] Simultaneously, use of public libraries, in both visits and circulation, continued to increase between 2000 and 2010, although visits dipped slightly in 2011.

A significant collections area of concern for public libraries is provision of e-books, which has several troubling components. E-books cost more than print books, often as much as 100 percent more. Libraries have limited access to e-books because of restrictions placed on their use by publishers. Some publishers have refused to sell to libraries and some have placed limitations on the number of loans per e-book license. Most e-book access is through aggregators, and libraries usually pay for access but do not own the book. Coupled with these unresolved issues is an increasing demand for e-books in public libraries. A 2011 *Library Journal* survey that explored user behavior and preferences reported that 77 percent of library e-book patrons wanted to see more e-books available at their libraries. Public libraries have been redirecting their funds in response. In 2012, *American Libraries* reported that 76 percent of public libraries offered e-books and 39 percent loaned e-readers. Librarians are challenged to provide digital content in an uncertain environment that is changing nearly daily.[42]

Levien describes the challenges facing public libraries in *Confronting the Future: Strategic Visions for the 21st Century Public Libraries:*

American libraries will confront formidable challenges during the next few decades of the 21st century. Both the media and technologies they deploy will continue the digital transformation that has already eroded or swept away in years what had lasted for decades or centuries. Nor is the rate of change slowing. The new media and technologies are enabling a steady flow of genre- and usage-changing innovations, and institutions drawing on these disruptive changes are competing with the library in its most fundamental roles. Libraries also are challenged by the financial constraints facing the agencies that support them, as well as shifts in the nature and needs of library users. If libraries are to evolve rapidly enough to meet these challenges, they will have to make careful and difficult strategic decisions and persevere in implementing those decisions.[43]

School Libraries

McGinnis traces the origins of school libraries and the idea that these centers should provide a variety of media to 1578, when an ordinance passed in Shrewsbury, England, directed that schools should include "a library and gallerie . . . furnished with all manner of books, mappes, spheres, instruments of astronomye and all other things apperteyninge to learning which may be either given to the school or procured with school money." School libraries were present in the early private schools in New England in the late eighteenth century.[44] Their collections were primarily composed of reference books and supported by donations. Public school libraries in the United States were first proposed in legislation recommended to the New York state legislature by governor DeWitt Clinton in 1827 with funds finally appropriated in 1839. By 1876, twenty-one states had passed legislation to support public school libraries.[45] Books were selected by school board members, superintendents, trustees, and occasionally those directly responsible for the school libraries. The debate over appropriate materials seen in public libraries was also present in school libraries. School superintendents were complaining about the presence of novels in New York school libraries in 1843. The emphasis was on acquiring materials that would further students' education and excluding "pernicious publications."[46]

The roles and responsibilities of school librarians began to be formalized with the establishment in 1896 of the School Library Section within the National Education Association.[47] Mary E. Kingsbury was appointed as librarian at the Erasmus Hall High School, Brooklyn, in 1900, and has been identified as the first library school graduate appointed to a high school library position as well as the first professionally trained librarian to be employed full time in a school. In 1914, the ALA Council approved a petition from the ALA Roundtable of Normal and High School Librarians to form the School Libraries Section, which held its first meeting at the June 1915 ALA annual conference. In 1951, this section became the American Association of School Librarians (AASL), a separate division in ALA. Despite this recognition within the profession of school librarianship as a specialty, lists prepared by state education boards governed most materials added to school libraries into the 1950s.

For many years, library collections in classrooms were the norm in elementary schools, and a collection of fifty selected books was regarded as sufficient for an individual classroom. In the early 1940s, only 18 percent of public schools nationwide reported having a centralized library.[48] By 1953, 36 percent of all public schools had libraries. School libraries were more common in secondary schools, with 95 percent having them, whereas libraries were found in only 24 percent of public elementary schools.[49] Early standards supported the creation of a separate library within schools, but elementary school libraries did not exist in most states until the 1958 NDEA and the 1965 Elementary and Secondary Education Act (ESEA).[50] Initially, libraries were not specifically mentioned in the NDEA. Though books and materials (especially in sciences, foreign language, and mathematics) could be purchased with NDEA funds, often these were not placed in libraries. Some school administrators did not see libraries as having a primary instructional role, and selection of materials often was not handled effectively. Program guidelines were issued and changes were made to the NDEA which, over time, strengthened the role of school libraries and librarians, including ensuring that librarians were responsible for selecting materials.

The second half of the twentieth century saw a change in the nature of school library collections, which were beginning to include nonprint. *Standards for School Media Programs*, a 1969 revision of school library standards, signaled a shift from the terms *school library* and *school library program* to *school media center* and *school media program* and stressed the importance of providing a variety of formats to support instruction and learning.[51] At the same time, school library media centers saw increasing emphasis on providing resources for teachers and often parents.

ESEA Title II provided $100 million in direct federal assistance for the acquisition of school library resources and other instructional materials. As a result, school library media staff were expected to provide leadership in selecting, acquiring, organizing, and using instructional materials. The ESEA had a profound effect on the establishment of school media centers. During the years 1965–1968, 12 percent of all public schools established a school library, and approximately 193,600 library expansion projects were funded during the same period.[52]

The ESEA was reauthorized at five-year intervals until 1981, when ESEA Title IV was consolidated with other educational programs in the Education Consolidation and Improvement Act (ECIA) to create one funding block program, the Chapter II block grant. The resulting block grants were distributed to states, which allocated funds to school districts that determined their own priorities. The result has been a decrease in grant funds specifically targeted at school libraries. By 1984/85, only 29 percent of the local block grant funds were being used for library and media center support.[53] The consistent growth in library media centers' collections seen over the previous twenty years had ended.

The No Child Left Behind Act of 2001 was intended to address a portion of the lost funding by providing grants to local school districts in which at least 20 percent of the students are from families with incomes below the poverty line. In the first year of the program (fiscal year 2002), $12.5 million was available for grants and ninety-four were awarded.[54] This amount seems modest compared to the $100 million made available annually in the early days of ESEA II. The situation became grimmer when the U.S. Department of Education eliminated fiscal 2011 funding for the Improving Literacy through School Libraries program, the only federal program solely for school libraries in the United States. The effects were soon felt at the state and local levels, although $28.6 million was returned to the Fund for Improvement of Education (FIE) and half of that was earmarked for libraries. President Obama's proposed 2013 budget again removed dedicated funding for school libraries, and the final appropriations for fiscal year 2013 did not include it. At the time of this writing, the Strengthening America's Schools Act of 2013, a bill that would reauthorize ESEA, was being considered by Congress.

Farmer describes the budgets in school library media centers as bleak in her survey of 2010/2011 spending, although she notes signs that the worst of the budget cuts might be over. AASL reported that the average expenditure on information resources (i.e., print and nonprint materials, licensed databases, and other electronic access to information) in school media centers rose from $11,390 in 2008 to $13,525 in 2009 but declined to $11,827 in 2012.[55] E-books continue to increase in school libraries and media centers.[56] In 2012, 40 percent of school libraries offered e-books, an increase of 33 percent from 2010. The higher the grade, the more likely school libraries were to provide e-books, with 63 percent of high school libraries, 50 percent of middle schools, and 33 percent of elementary schools offering them in 2012. Of the 60 percent of school libraries without e-books, 26 percent reported plans to purchase them during the next two years, and 55 percent might do so.

The profession has stepped back from using size of collections as a key measure of a school library media center's success, yet these and other numerical data are tracked nationally. The National Center for Education Statistics reported that only 62 percent of schools had a full-time certified library media specialist in fiscal year 2008. The average holdings per 100 students was 2,439 books and 107 audio and video items.[57] This works out to approximately twenty-five items per student—of interest when compared to the 1975 quantitative goal of forty items per student in schools with less than five hundred students.

Special Libraries

Special libraries are found in hospitals, churches and synagogues, commercial firms, museums, correctional institutions, government agencies, and trade and professional associations—to name only a few. Some special libraries are maintained within larger libraries, such as a business library within a public library. Because of this diversity, providing a history of special libraries and their collecting practices presents unique challenges. What special libraries have in common is a focus on meeting the specialized information needs of their host organizations and, usually, a narrow and focused user community. Many special libraries are characterized by a need to provide current or historical information as quickly as possible to solve a pressing problem and facilitate decision making. An obvious example is the medical library associated with a hospital.

Professional groups, such as doctors and architects, were among the first to establish special libraries. One of the first special libraries in the United States was the medical library at the Pennsylvania Hospital, established in 1763.[58] Common interest groups such as scientific and historical societies also founded libraries early. For example, the American Philosophical Society, founded in 1743, had a library. A third category of special libraries that began in the eighteenth century served state and federal legislative bodies. The Pennsylvania Assembly Library was one of the first, opening in 1745.

The Special Library Association was founded in 1909 to support those working in special libraries. It now has numerous divisions ranging from biomedical to business to military, museums, legal, and transportation. Many professional associations focus more narrowly on library types, such as the American Association of Law Libraries, Medical Library Association, and Church and Synagogue Library Association. Some specialties are served by divisions within larger organizations, such as the Engineering Libraries Division in the American Society for Engineering Education and the Museum Library Division within the Art Libraries Society of North America.

Early special libraries built their collections through donations, similar to academic libraries. Many were started by a gift of a single donor's collection. The Pennsylvania Hospital library charged medical students a library fee. As special libraries became more central to the operations of their parent organizations, they received continuing allocations to develop their collections. By their nature, collections in special libraries are limited to materials of interest to their parent organizations. Some libraries retain historical collections, others have limited retention policies. Some have been responsible for resources kept current through loose-leaf additions and technical reports. Part of managing the collection was ensuring that these materials were up-to-date and accessible. Some special libraries, especially those supporting commercial entities or government agencies, may be charged with maintaining historical archives that document the work of the organization. Some may be responsible for acquiring resources not physically housed within the library, such as print copies of handbooks and other ready reference tools kept in offices and laboratories.

Standards are not as common in special libraries as in other library types. Those that exist usually apply to libraries associated with educational institutions, such as law and medical schools and other professional programs. The history of these standards is intimately involved with accreditation standards for the parent schools, and most have been and continue to be developed by the accrediting bodies, like the American Bar Association and the Accrediting Board for Engineering and Technology. Early standards included quantitative measures and, in some cases, lists of materials that should be provided. Academic law library standards are one of the few that continue to contain title lists.[59] Most standards have shifted their focus to stressing the ability to meet the needs of faculty and students and to provide for research and other scholarly activities.

The advent of e-resources has profoundly affected many special libraries, especially corporate, legal, and medical libraries. Print is being cancelled as e-resources present viable alternatives and to the extent that special libraries can afford them. As in other types of libraries, users prefer online access for ease of use and accessibility. Many special librarians negotiate and contract for access to e-resources on behalf of their parent organization. Balancing print and electronic resources is as compelling an issue among special librarians as it is with other categories of librarians.

Theories of Selection

The origins of collection management and development can be traced to theories of selection. The first American guide to selection was prepared by Thaddeus M. Harris, Harvard librarian, in 1793. In his introduction to a catalog of books suggested for a "small and cheap" library to serve common readers at a distance in the country, he wrote that "books have become so exceedingly numerous . . . that the greatest caution is necessary in selecting those of established reputation from the many that are indifferent or useless."[60] Until the 1960s, most theories of selection promoted in the United States focused on choosing materials for public libraries. Libraries of all types have experienced a continuing tension between demand and value, and much of the literature on selection has focused on this tension between what people want and what librarians believe is good for them. This has been particularly true in public libraries, which have seen the education of citizens as a primary goal. Part of the demand-value controversy has been the question of what to do about fiction. The public's preference for novels was troubling to early library leaders, in part because of the long-term effects of Puritan condemnation of fiction reading. In 1899, Lucius Page Lane (New York State Library School, class of 1899) wrote to the *Library Journal* and quoted a school principal who stated that "the voracious devouring of fiction commonly indulged in by patrons of the public library, especially the young, is extremely pernicious and mentally unwholesome."[61] Many early librarians took a paternalistic and high, even elitist position about selection and collection building.

Librarians as Arbiters of Quality

Such legendary characters in American librarianship as Melvil Dewey, John Cotton Dana, Herbert Putnam, and Ainsworth Spofford insisted that libraries' primary role as educator implied that their responsibility was to provide only the highest-quality materials—with *quality* defined, of course, by librarians. Many librarians were proud of their role as censors, by which they meant arbiters of quality. Arthur E. Bostwick explained the positive role of public librarians as censors in his 1908 ALA presidential address. He stated that they had a responsibility to censor anything that was not Good, True, and Beautiful.[62] In contrast, other leading librarians of the time, including William F. Poole, Justin Winsor, and Charles Cutter, supported the selection and provision of more popular materials.

One of the most powerful early statements in support of popular reading materials in public libraries was written by Poole, the first director of the Chicago

Public Library. He voiced the still widely held view that reading less sophisticated materials leads readers to more cultivated works. In 1876, Poole wrote,

> To meet, therefore, the varied wants of readers there must be on the shelves of the library books which persons of culture never read, although it is quite probable they did read such books in some stage of their mental development. Judged from a critical standpoint, such books are feeble, rudimentary, and perhaps sensational; but they are higher in the scale of literary merit than the tastes of the people who seek them; and, like primers and first-readers in the public schools, they fortunately lead to something better.[63]

Not all librarians were confident they could select the Good, True, and Beautiful or identify the primers that would lead readers to a higher level. As the profession of librarianship developed, librarians turned to their professional associations and librarian authorities for guidance in selecting individual titles. Several reviewing tools appeared in the early 1900s to help select the best books, including *ALA Booklist* (1905), *Book Review Digest* (1906), *Fiction Catalog* (1908), and *The Children's Catalog (1909)*. The first edition of *Guide to the Study and Use of Reference Books* (now *Guide to Reference*) was published in 1902 by ALA.

Despite the theoretical debate among library leaders over value versus demand, the volume of fiction in American public libraries continued to increase. By 1876, practically all American public libraries offered at least some fictional materials, though it was often of the "better" kind. During World War I, opponents of fiction felt that the serious mood of the country provided a logical argument against the frivolity of popular fiction. Cornelia Marvin, state librarian of Oregon, suggested a new librarian's slogan: "No new fiction during the war." However, many librarians selected materials for military camp libraries and were not hesitant about choosing fiction to entertain and distract the troops. ALA was active in providing books and magazines in camp libraries through the Committee on Mobilization and War Services Plans (later the War Service Committee). Herbert Putnam, then head of the Library of Congress and of the War Service Committee, initially opposed women leading the camp libraries operated by ALA, but by the summer of 1919 women were in charge of several camp libraries and instrumental in building popular reading collections.[64]

After the war, the controversy about the role of fiction in public libraries continued. Many wanted libraries to be as attractive as possible to returning soldiers. Nevertheless, with the Great Depression resulting in a declining economy and reduced library funding, fiction continued as a point of contention. Some library leaders felt that the 1930s were a time for libraries to focus on educational reading. Carl Roden of the Chicago Public Library asked, "Who among us would not rather supply the books and competent guidance for ten self-students than the latest novels for a thousand fiction readers?"[65] Others felt that libraries had an obligation to provide fiction as part of their public mission. The debate over suitable library materials is documented in Carrier's two volumes on fiction in U.S. public libraries, which give a detailed picture of the arguments for and against fiction and its rise as part of collections.[66]

Evolution of Selection Theory

When Melvil Dewey founded the School of Library Economy at Columbia University in 1887, "Selection of Books and Periodicals" was one of the courses.[67] One of the first books on the theory of selection, written by Lionel McColvin and published in England in 1925, begins: "Book selection is the first task of librarianship. It precedes all other process . . . and it is the most important."[68] The first comprehensive American works on book selection were textbooks written by Francis Drury (1930) and Helen Haines (1935). These early works are reflections of their times—with statements such as Haines's "Consider what books mean in individual development: in the formation of character, in the activation of intelligence, in the enrichment of resources, and in the deepening of sensitivity"—and a testament to the continuity of guiding principles in collection management.[69] Drury's goals have relevance today, with a few exceptions that seem amusingly dated. He stated that the purposes of a course in book selection and, by implication, the goals of selectors were

- to analyze the nature of a community
- to recognize the various uses to which books of varied types are to be put
- to consider the character and policy of a library in adding books
- to cultivate the power of judging and selecting books for purchase, with their value and suitability to readers in mind
- to become familiar with the sources of information
- to renew acquaintance with books and writers from the library angle
- to develop the ability to review, criticize, and annotate books for library purposes
- to decide where in the library organization book selection fits
- to learn how to perform the necessary fundamental tasks of book selection
- to scrutinize the mental and personal fitness of the selector

According to Drury, "A qualified selector, acquainted with the demand from his community and knowing the book and money resource of his library, chooses the variety of books he believes will be used, applying his expert knowledge."[70]

The continuing tension between demand and value was a recurring theme in the professional literature on selection. A vigorous proponent of value was Leon Carnovsky, who framed his position by saying that public libraries should provide materials that were true.[71] Before World War II, he offered a scholarly position supporting internal censorship. He held a strong conviction that the public library should be a force for truth on vital issues. He advocated censorship of local prejudice and opinion and said the library is "acting democratically when it sets up the authority of reason as the censor."[72] The political implications of the coming war, combined with a loss of confidence in librarians' knowledge and ability to choose what is true and what is not, caused Carnovsky to moderate his position in the 1950s and 1960s.

The debate over popular materials in public libraries continued through much of the twentieth century. The Public Library Inquiry of the late 1940s once again raised serious questions about the place of light fiction. Funded by the Carnegie Corporation and conducted by the Social Science Research Council, the inquiry focused on describing libraries, their services, collections, and users. Bernard Berelson wrote the summary volume, in which he held to an elitist view of public libraries, recommending that the library's purpose be "serious" and its proper role to serve the culturally alert community members rather than to try to reach all people.[73]

Other librarians responded that a public library's duty was to supply its users with the books of most interest to them. They believed that democratic principles should operate in libraries as well as society. These librarians were increasingly conscious of the importance of the freedom to read and the right of all readers to find what they like best. In 1939, ALA adopted the first Library Bill of Rights to provide an official statement against censorship and to oppose pressures on the freedom of citizens to read what they wished. Lester Asheim, in his 1953 paper "Not Censorship but Selection," stressed the concept of selection as choosing good books instead of excluding bad ones.[74]

Librarians in the second half of the twentieth century began promoting the ideal that subjects should be covered evenly or equally within collections. Balanced coverage has meant seeking to select materials representing all viewpoints on important and controversial issues. Librarians have become increasingly aware of their responsibilities to be attentive to both content and format in selection of library materials.

Collection Development and Management as a Specialization

As selection of materials shifted to librarians, the responsibility often fell to acquisitions librarians. These early acquisitions librarians found their professional home in the ALA Board of Acquisition of Library Materials, created in 1951. The ALA Resources and Technical Services Division (RTSD) was created in 1957, and the Board of Acquisition of Library Materials became the Acquisitions Section within RTSD.

A preconference held before the ALA annual conference in Detroit in 1977 is often identified as the landmark event recognizing collection development as a new specialization separate from acquisitions work. A group of forward-looking librarians including Juanita Doares, Sheila Dowd, Hendrik Edelman, Murray Martin, Paul H. Mosher, and David Zubatsky created the new Collection Development Committee of the Resources Section of RTSD and were instrumental in developing the preconference.

The volume of new publications was increasing rapidly, the publishing world was becoming more complex, and acquisitions budgets had slowed libraries' expansion. Part-time faculty selectors and librarians without special expertise could no longer manage selection adequately in larger academic and public libraries. The planners, primarily academic librarians, of the 1977 preconference saw a need to develop research collections in a more conscious, planned, and documented manner. They called this new specialization *collection development* to distinguish it from acquisitions. The goal of the 1977 preconference was to educate the library profession about this new subdiscipline of collection development, its nature, components, and functions. The first *Guidelines for Collection Development*, published by the Collection Development Committee, followed soon after the preconference.[75] This 1979 publication has been revised and published as several numbers with narrower foci in the Collection Management and Development Guides series.

The first Collection Management and Development Institute, sponsored by RTSD's (now Association for Library Resources and Technical Services) Collection Development Committee, was held at Stanford University in 1981. Planners were increasingly aware that the management of collections—not just their development and growth—was the primary issue for the future of this new specialization. They focused on boundary-spanning aspects, including the integration of collection management with acquisitions and other internal library operations and services, and on working closely with interested constituents. They sought to define collection management in ways that had meaning to librarians in all types of libraries.

Many professional groups were focusing on collection development and management in the early 1980s. The Public Library Association sponsored a preconference in 1984.[76] ARL established a Collection Development Committee, the Research Libraries Group initiated a Collection Management and Development Committee, and other divisions within ALA, including the Reference and Adult Services Division (now Reference and User Services Association, RUSA), the Public Library Association, and the Association of College and Research Libraries, formed committees that concentrated on collection development and management. Whereas collection development has always been closely associated with acquisitions, these two functions began to be separated in larger libraries, with acquisitions more typically associated with technical services units and collection development and management as separate or, perhaps, allied with public services.

In the late 1970s and 1980s, the profession took up collection development and management as a cause célèbre. Numerous textbooks, manuals, overviews, and journal articles were published. Specialized journals, including *Collection Management* (1976), *Collection Building* (1983), and *Library Acquisitions: Practice and Theory* (1977, now *Library Collections, Acquisitions and Technical Services*), began publication. Several textbooks on collection development, which was more broadly defined than acquisitions or selection, appeared in the 1970s. Research in the field was summarized in the important publication *Collection Development in Libraries: A Treatise*.[77] By the mid-1980s, most professional library schools were offering one or more courses focusing on collection development and management. Kryzs identifies the topics covered in a basic collection development course of the time; these include the historical background of books and libraries, types of libraries and their communities, library materials, publishers and publishing, selection of materials, acquisition of material, and collection evaluation, which covers storage, weeding, preservation, and replacement decisions.[78] By the mid-1980s, the position of collection development librarian was firmly established.[79]

Future of Collection Development and Management

Several pressures in addition to financial stringency have buffeted libraries since the early 1990s. Rapid changes in user community expectations and the makeup of those communities, the publishing industry, telecommunication technology, copyright law, and scholarly communication are among the most significant. Collections librarians in all types of libraries are seeking to cope with scarce financial resources; preservation and conservation needs; cooperation in collection building and resource sharing; serials cancellation projects; and retention, weeding, and storage decisions. The growth of the Internet and omnipresent access have added online resources to the choices to be considered. Consumer adoption of e-books and e-readers has added another element to a complicated content environment. Options for purchasing e-content en bloc in large e-book packages and the ability to activate open patron-driven acquisition complicate the decisions collections librarians face. Librarians selecting electronic resources face decisions about licenses, software, technical support, operating systems, interfaces, and hardware. User expectations about ease of access and ubiquity have continued to increase. Financial austerity, which has characterized libraries for more than three decades, coupled with the need to readjust priorities continually, is a primary reason the term *collection management* has become more meaningful to the profession.

Nevertheless, this is an exciting time to work in libraries, especially for those charged with developing and managing their collections. Users continue to visit libraries in person and online to meet their information and recreational needs. OCLC reported that 68 percent of the U.S. population had a library card in 2010. ALA reported in 2012 that circulation continued to rise in many major city public libraries.[80] A study released by the Pew Research Center in 2013 found that 53 percent of Americans ages sixteen and older visited a library or bookmobile in the twelve months prior to the survey. This survey of 2,252 Americans explored the changing world of library services, focusing on the library activities in transition and the kinds of services and collections citizens would like to see. Results pertinent to collection development and management include these:

- 80 percent identified borrowing books as a very important library service.

- 77 percent said that free access to computers and the Internet is a very important library service.

- 53 percent stated that the library should definitely offer a broader selection of e-books.[81]

An Institute of Museum and Library Services (IMLS) survey released in 2008 looked into how people search for information in the online age and how this affects the ways they interact with public libraries and museums, both online and in person.[82] Drawing on data collected in five surveys of 1,000–1,600 individuals each, researchers found that libraries and museums were the most trusted sources of online information among adults of all ages, education levels, races, and ethnicities. Both the Pew Research Center and IMLS reports provide evidence that libraries continue as valued providers of information and recreation for Americans. Selecting and managing collections that meet library users needs and expectations is the goal of collection development and management.

Notes

1. Bonita Bryant, "The Organizational Structure of Collection Development," *Library Resources and Technical Services* 31, no. 2 (Apr. 1987): 118. For other examples, see Paul H. Mosher, "Collection Development to Collection Management: Toward Stewardship of Library Resources," *Collection Management* 4, no. 4 (Winter 1982): 45; Mary W. Ghikas, "Collection Management for the 21st Century," *Journal of Library Administration* 11, no. 1/2 (1989): 119–35; Michael R. Gabriel, *Collection Development and Evaluation: A Sourcebook* (Lanham, MD: Scarecrow, 1995), 3; Wayne Disher, *Crash Course in Collection Development* (Westport, CT: Libraries Unlimited, 2007), 2–3.

2. Kanwal Ameen, "Developments in the Philosophy of Collection Management: A Historical Review," *Collection Building* 24, no. 4 (2005): 112–16.

3. Gabriel Naudé, *Advice on Establishing a Library*, with an introduction by Archer Taylor (Berkeley: University of California Press, 1950), 17.

4. Jean-Baptiste Cotton des Houssays, *The Duties and Qualifications of a Librarian*, English translation (Chicago: A. C. McClurg, 1906), 43.

5. Howard Clayton, "The American College Library, 1800–1860," *Journal of Library History* 3, no. 2 (Apr. 1968): 120–37.

6. Louis Shores, *Origins of the American College Library, 1638–1800* (Nashville, TN: George Peabody College, 1934).

7. Arthur T. Hamlin, *The University Library in the United States* (Philadelphia: University of Pennsylvania Press, 1981).

8. Orvin Lee Shiflett, *Origins of American Academic Librarianship* (Norwood, NJ: Ablex, 1981); Martha Kyrillidou, Shaneka Morris, and Gary Roebuck, comps. and eds., *ARL Statistics 2011–2012* (Washington, DC: Association of Research Libraries, 2013).

9. Shores, *Origins of the American College Library*.

10. George Livermore, *Remarks on Public Libraries* (Cambridge, MA: Boils and Houghton, 1850), 17.

11. Michael K. Buckland, "The Roles of Collections and the Scope of Collection Development," *Journal of Documentation* 45, no. 3 (Sept. 1989): 213–26.

12. Mary F. Casserly, "Collection Development in College and University Libraries: A Comparison," in *Collection Development in College Libraries*, ed. Jeanne Schneider Hill, William E. Hannaford, and Ronald H. Epp, 3–14 (Chicago: American Library Association, 1991).

13. Shiflett, *Origins of American Academic Librarianship*.

14. Margaret Ann Johnson, *Christian Gottlob Heyne as Librarian* (master's thesis, Univ. of Chicago Graduate Library School, 1973).

15. U.S. Office of Education, *Survey of Land-Grant Colleges and University*, Bulletin no. 9, 2 vols. (Washington, DC: Government Printing Office, 1930).

16. John R. Thelin, "Gilt by Association: Higher Education's 'Golden Age,' 1945–1970," in *A History of American Higher Education*, 2nd ed., 260–316 (Baltimore: Johns Hopkins University Press, 2011).

17. Nancy L. Ruther, *Barely There, Powerfully Present: Thirty Years of U.S. Policy in International Higher Education* (New York: RoutledgeFalmer, 2002).

18. Fremont Rider, *The Scholar and the Future of the Research Library* (New York: Hadham, 1944); Kenneth J. Braugh, *Scholars Workshop: Evolving Concepts of Library Service* (Urbana: University of Illinois Press, 1953), 99.

19. Edward G. Holley, "North American Efforts at Worldwide Acquisitions since 1945," *Collection Management* 9, no. 2/3 (Summer/Fall 1987): 89–111.

20. Kyrillidou, Morris, and Roebuck, *ARL Statistics 2010–2011*; see graph 2, "Monograph and Serials Costs in ARL Libraries, 1986–2011."

21. University of California–Berkeley, Library, Library Collections, "Hot Topics—Publisher Mergers" (updated 2/16/12), www.lib.berkeley.edu/scholarlycommuni cation/publisher_mergers.html.

22. Jeanne Sohn, "Cooperative Collection Development: A Brief Overview," *Collection Management* 8, no. 2 (Summer 1986): 4.

23. Maurice B. Line, "Interlending and Document Supply in a Changing World," in *Interlending and Document Supply: Proceedings of the First International Conference Held in London, November, 1988*, ed. Graham P. Cornish and Alison Gallicao (Ballston Spa, England: IFLA Office for International Lending, 1989), 1.

24. Kyrillidou, Morris, and Roebuck, *ARL Statistics 2010–2011*.

25. *2012 Ebook Usage in U.S. Academic Libraries, Third Annual Survey* (New York: Library Journal, 2012), www.thedigitalshift.com/research/ebook-usage-reports/academic.

26. Kyrillidou, Morris, and Roebuck, *ARL Statistics 2010–2011*.

27. Jennifer Howard, "Google Begins to Scale Back Its Scanning of Books from University Libraries," *Chronicle of Higher Education* (Mar. 9, 2012), http://chronicle.com/article/Google-Begins-to-Scale-Back/131109.

28. Jim Michalko and Constance Malpas, "Managing the Collective Collection," *Next Space: The OCLC Newsletter* no. 12 (June 2009), www.oclc.org/nextspace/012/research.htm.

29. Dan Hazen, "Rethinking Research Library Collections: A Policy Framework for Straitened Times, and Beyond," *Library Resources and Technical Services* 54, no. 2 (Apr. 2010): 118.

30. Jesse H. Shera, *Foundations of the Public Library: The Origins of the Public Library Movement in New England, 1629–1855* (Chicago: University of Chicago Press, 1949), is the classic history of public libraries and the source of information presented here; James C. Baughman, "Sense Is Preferable to Sound," *Library Journal* 111, no. 17 (Oct. 1986): 44.

31. Edwin G. Borrows and Mike Wallace, *Gotham: A History of New York City to 1898* (New York: Oxford University Press, 1999).

32. Elizabeth McHenry, "'An Association of Kindred Spirits': Black Readers and Their Reading Rooms," in *Institutions of Reading: The Social Life of Libraries in the United States*, ed. Thomas Augst and Kenneth Carpenter, 99–108 (Amherst, MA: University of Massachusetts Press, 2007); *Address and Constitution of the Phoenix Society of New York, and the Auxiliary Ward Association* (1833), reprinted in Dorothy Burnett Porter, comp., *Early Negro Writing, 1760–1837* (Boston: Beacon Press, 1971), 144.

33. Boston Public Library, *Upon the Objects to Be Attained by the Establishment of a Public Library: Report of the Trustees of the Public Library of the City of Boston, July, 1852* (Boston: J. H. Eastburn, City Document no. 37, 1852; reprint, Boston: Hall, 1975), 8–9.

34. John Cotton Dana, *A Library Primer* (Chicago: Library Bureau, 1899).

35. Telecommunications Act of 1996, 104th Cong., 2nd sess. (1996), Public Law 104–104, 110 Stat. 56 (Feb. 8, 1996); Children's Internet Protection Act, 106th Cong., 2nd sess. (2000), Public Law 106–554, Stat. 2763 (Dec. 21, 2000).

36. The Library Services and Technology Act is Title II of the Museum and Library Services Act of 2003, 108th Cong., 2nd Sess. (2003), Public Law 108–81, 117 Stat. 991.

37. David Wessel, "Did 'Great Recession' Live Up to the Name?" *Wall Street Journal* (Apr. 8, 2010), http://online.wsj.com/article/SB10001424052702303591204575169693166352882.

38. "Public Library Funding and Technology Access Study 2011–2012," *American Libraries Digital Supplement* (Summer 2012), http://viewer.zmags.com/publication/4673a369#/4673a369/1.

39. Institute of Museum and Library Services, *Public Libraries in the United States Survey Fiscal Year 2010* (Washington, DC: Institute of Museum and Library Services, 2013), www.imls.gov/assets/1/AssetManager/PLS2010.pdf.

40. "2012 State of America's Libraries: A Report from the American Library Asso-ciation," *American Libraries Special Issue* (2012), www.ala.org/news/sites/ala.org .news/files/content/StateofAmericasLibrariesReport2012Finalwithcover.pdf.

41. "The State of American's Libraries; A Report from the American Library Association 2013," *American Libraries Special Issue* (2013), 16, 17, http://viewer .zmags.com/publication/33759128#/33759128/1.

42. "2012 State of America's Libraries"; Steve Paxhia and John Parsons, "Library Patrons and Ebook Usage Analysis," *Library Journal Patron Profiles* 1, no. 1 (Oct. 2011); "Public Library Funding and Technology Access Study 2011–2012," *American Libraries Digital Supplement* (Summer 2012), www.ala.org/research/ plftas/2011_2012.

43. Roger E. Levien, *Confronting the Future: Strategic Visions for the 21st Century Public Libraries*, Policy Brief no. 4 (Chicago: ALA Office for Information Technology Policy, 2011).

44. Dorothy McGinnis, "Instructional Materials Centers—Something New?" *California School Libraries* 34, no. 1 (1962): 4; Cheryl Ann McCarthy, "Progress in School Library Media Programs: Where Have We Been? Where Are We Now? And Where Are We Going?" *Advances in Librarianship* 30 (2006): 271–97.

45. Tim J. Cole, "The Origin and Development of School Libraries," *Peabody Journal of Education* 37, no. 2 (Sept. 1959): 87–92; U.S. Bureau of Education, *Public Libraries in the United States of America: Their History, Condition, and Management Special Report* (Washington, DC: U.S. Government Printing Office, 1876).

46. Frank Hermann Koos, *State Participation in Public School Library Service* (New York: Columbia University Teachers College, 1927); Josiah W. Leeds, *Concerning Printed Poison* (Philadelphia: Printed by the author, 1885), 7.

47. Cole, "Origin and Development."

48. Ibid.; Joan Michie and Barbara Holton, *Fifty Years of Supporting Children's Learning: A History of Public School Libraries and Federal Legislation from 1953–2000* (Washington, DC: National Center for Education Statistics, U.S. Department of Education, Institute of Education Sciences, 2005).

49. National Center for Education Statistics, *American Public School Libraries: 1953–2000* (Washington, DC: National Center for Education Statistics, 2005).

50. McCarthy, "Progress."

51. American Association of School Librarians and National Education Association, Department of Audiovisual Instruction, *Standards for School Media Programs* (Chicago: American Library Association, 1969).

52. U.S. Department of Health, Education, and Welfare, *An Evaluative Survey Report on ESEA Title II: Fiscal Years 1966–1968* (Washington, DC: U.S. Government Printing Office, 1972); U.S. Department of Health, Education, and Welfare, *School Library Resources, Textbooks, and Other Instructional Materials; Title II, Elementary*

and Secondary Education Act of 1964, Third Annual Report, Fiscal Year 1968 (Washington, DC: U.S. Government Printing Office, 1971).

53. Michael S. Knapp et al., *The Education Block Grant at the Local Level: The Implementation of Chapter 2 of the Education Consolidation and Improvement Act in Districts and Schools* (Menlo Park, CA: SRI International, 1986).

54. Michie and Holton, *Fifty Years.*

55. Lesley Farmer, "Expenditures for Resources in School Library Media Centers: 2010–2011," in *Library and Book Trade Almanac 2012,* 57th ed., ed. Dave Bogart (Medford, NJ: Information Today, 2012), 463–71; American Association of School Librarians, *2012 School Libraries Count! National Longitudinal Survey of School Library Programs* (Chicago: American Association of School Librarians, 2012), www.ala.org/aasl/sites/ala.org.aasl/files/content/researchandstatistics/slcsurvey/2012/AASL-SLC-2012-WEB.pdf.

56. *2012 Ebook Usage in U.S. School (K–12) Libraries, Third Annual Survey* (New York: Library Journal, 2012), www.thedigitalshift.com/research/ebook-usage-reports.

57. National Center for Education Statistics, *Characteristics of Public and Bureau of Indian Elementary and Secondary School Library Media Centers in the United States: Results from the 2007–08 Schools and Staffing Survey* (Washington, DC: U.S. Department of Education, 2009), http://nces.ed.gov/pubs2009/2009322.pdf; National Center for Education Statistics, "Digest of Education Statistics," Table 431. Selected Statistics on Public School Libraries/Media Centers, by Level of School: 1999–2000, 2003–04, and 2000–08, http://nces.ed.gov/programs/digest/d12/tables/dt12_431.asp.

58. Ada Winifred Johns, *Special Libraries: Development of the Concept, Their Organizations, and Their Services* (Metuchen, NJ: Scarecrow, 1968); Kathryn S. Thompson, "America's Oldest Medical Library: The Pennsylvania Hospital," *Bulletin of the Medical Library Association* 44, no. 4 (Oct. 1956): 428–30.

59. Cindy Hirsch, "The Rise and Fall of Academic Law Library Collection Standards," *Legal Reference Services Quarterly* 31, no. 1 (2012): 65–103.

60. Thaddeus M. Harris, *Seleced* [sic] *Catalogue of Some of the Most Esteemed Publications in the English Language. Proper to Form a Social Library, with an Introduction upon the Choice of Books.* (Boston: I. Thomas and E. T. Andrews, 1793), [ii].

61. "Monthly Report from Public Librarians upon the Reading of Minors: A Suggestion," *Library Journal* 23 (Aug. 1899): 479.

62. Arthur E. Bostwick, "Librarian as a Censor," *Library Journal* 33 (July 1908): 257–59.

63. William F. Poole, "The Organization and Management of Public Libraries," in *Public Libraries in the United States: Their History, Condition, and Management,* Part I, 479–80 (Washington, DC: U.S Government Printing Office, 1876).

64. Cornelia Marvin, "No New Fiction during the War," *Public Libraries* 23, no. 6 (June 1918): 269; American Library Association, "Our Libraries and the War," *Library Journal* 42 (Aug. 1917): 606–11; Arthur P. Young, *Books for Sammies: The American Library Association and World War I* (Pittsburgh, PA: Beta Phi Mu, 1981).

65. Carl B. Roden, "The Library in Hard Times," *Library Journal* 56 (Dec. 1, 1931): 984–87.

66. Esther Jane Carrier, *Fiction in Public Libraries, 1876–1900* (New York: Scarecrow, 1965), and Carrier, *Fiction in Public Libraries, 1900–1950* (Littleton, CO: Libraries Unlimited, 1985). For explorations of the manner in which librarians' cultural and social attitudes and biases have affected their theories of selection and service, see Lee Garrison, *Apostles of Culture: The Public Librarian and American Society, 1876–1920* (New York: The Free Press, 1979); Evelyn Geller, *Forbidden Books in American Public Libraries, 1879–1939: A Study in Cultural Change* (Westport, CT: Greenwood, 1984).

67. Sarah K. Vann, *Training for Librarianship before 1923: Education for Librarianship prior to the Publication of the Williamson Report* (Chicago: American Library Association, 1961).

68. Lionel Roy McColvin, *The Theory of Book Selection for Public Libraries* (London: Grafton, 1925), 9.

69. Helen Haines, *Living with Books: The Art of Book Selection* (New York: Columbia University Press, 1935), 3.

70. Francis K. W. Drury, *Book Selection* (Chicago: American Library Association, 1930), xii–xiii, 2.

71. Leon Carnovsky, "The Role of the Public Library: Implications for Library Education," in *The Intellectual Foundations of Library Education*, ed. Don R. Swanson (Chicago: University of Chicago Press, 1965), 13–23.

72. Leon Carnovsky, "Community Analysis and the Practice of Book Selection," in *The Practice of Book Selection*, ed. Louis R. Wilson, 20–39 (Chicago: University of Chicago Press, 1940), 27.

73. Bernard Berelson, *The Library's Public* (New York: Columbia University Press, 1949).

74. Lester Asheim, "Not Censorship but Selection," *Wilson Library Bulletin* 28, no. 1 (Sept. 1953): 63–67. See also Asheim, "Selection and Censorship: A Reappraisal," *Wilson Library Bulletin* 58, no. 3 (Nov. 1983): 180–84.

75. David L. Perkins, ed., *Guidelines for Collection Development* (Chicago: Collection Development Committee, Resources and Technical Services Division, American Library Association, 1979).

76. Judith Serebnick, ed., *Collection Management in Public Libraries: Proceedings of a Preconference to the 1984 ALA Annual Conference, June 21–22, 1984, Dallas* (Chicago: American Library Association, 1986).

77. Robert D. Stueart and George B. Miller Jr., eds., *Collection Development in Libraries: A Treatise*, 2 vols., Foundations in Library and Information Science 10 (Greenwich, CT: JAI Press, 1980). A second collection of essays updated this publication: Charles B. Osburn and Ross Atkinson, eds., *Collection Management: A New Treatise*, 2 vols., Foundations in Library and Information Science 26 (Greenwich, CT.: JAI Press, 1991).

78. Richard Kryzs, "Collection Development Courses," in *Internationalizing Library and Information Science Education: A Handbook of Policies and Procedures in Administration and Curriculum*, ed. John F. Harvey and Frances Laverne Carroll, 201–24 (New York: Greenwood, 1987); John M. Budd and Patricia L. Brill, "Education for Collection Management: Results of a Survey of Educators and Practitioners," *Library Resources and Technical Services* 38, no. 4 (Oct. 1994): 343–53; Paul Metz, "Collection Development in the Library and Information Science Curriculum," in *Recruiting, Educating, and Training Librarians for Collection Development*, ed. Peggy Johnson and Sheila S. Intner, 87–97 (Westport, CT: Greenwood, 1994).

79. Karen Schmidt, "Past Perfect, Future Tense: A Survey of Issues in Collection Development," *Library Collections, Acquisitions, and Technical Services* 28, no. 4 (2004): 360–72.

80. OCLC, *Perceptions of Libraries, 2010: Context and Community* (Dublin, OH: OCLC, 2011), www.oclc.org/us/en/reports/2010perceptions/2010perceptions_all _singlepage.pdf; "2012 State of America's Libraries."

81. Kathryn Zickuhr, Lee Rainie, and Kristen Purcell, *Library Services in the Digital Age* (Washington, DC: Pew Research Center's Internet and American Life Project, 2013), http://libraries.pewinternet.org/2013/01/22/Library-services.

82. José-Marie Griffiths and Donald W. King, *InterConnections: The IMLS National Study on the Use of Libraries, Museums and the Internet: Public Libraries Report* (Washington, DC: Institute of Museum and Library Services, 2008), http:// interconnectionsreport.org; José-Marie Griffiths and Donald W. King, *InterConnections: The IMLS National Study on the Use of Libraries, Museums and the Internet: Conclusions Summary* (Washington, DC: Institute of Museum and Library Services, 2008), http://interconnectionsreport.org/reports/ ConclusionsSummaryFinalB.pdf.

Suggested Readings

Albitz, Rebecca S., Christine Avery, and Diane Zabel, eds. *Rethinking Collection Development and Management*. Santa Barbara, CA: Libraries Unlimited, 2014.

American Association of Law Libraries, Private Law Libraries Special Interest Section. *Collection Rebalancing for Law Libraries*. Resource Guide no. 4. Chicago: American

Association of Law Libraries, 2011. www.aallnet.org/main-menu/Publications/products/Law-Librarians-Making-Information-Work/pll-guide-4.pdf.

Association of Research Libraries. *21st-Century Collections: Calibration of Investment and Collaborative Action.* Washington, DC: Association of Research Libraries, 2012. www.arl.org/bm~doc/21stctfreport_11may12.pdf.

Bishop, Kay. *The Collection Program in Schools: Concepts and Practices.* 5th ed. Westport, CT: Libraries Unlimited, 2013.

Brumley, Rebecca. *Electronic Collection Management Forms, Policies, Procedures, and Guidelines Manual with CD-ROM.* New York: Neal Schuman, 2009.

Budd, John M. "Collections." In *The Changing Academic Library: Operations, Culture Environments,* 2nd ed., 199–332. Chicago: Association of College and Research Libraries, 2012.

Casserly, Mary. "Research in Academic Library Collection Management." In *Academic Library Research: Perspectives and Current Trends,* ed. Marie L. Radford and Pamela Snelson, 82–135. ACRL Publications in Librarianship no. 59. Chicago: Association of College and Research Libraries, 2008.

Clement, Susanne K., and Jennifer M. Foy. *Collection Development in a Changing Environment: Policies and Organization for College and University Libraries.* Chicago: College Library Information Packet Committee, College Libraries Section, Association of College and Research Libraries, 2010.

Cole, Louise. *Challenges in E-resource Management: A Practitioner's Guide.* London: Facet, 2013.

Council on Library and Information Resources. *The Idea of Order: Transforming Research Collections for 21st Century Scholarship.* Washington, DC: Council on Library and Information Resources, 2010.

"Digital Content: What's Next?" *American Libraries E-Content Supplement* (June 2013), http://viewer.zmags.com/publication/7d9e3366.

Evans, G. Edward, and Margaret Zarnosky Saponaro. *Collection Management Basics.* 6th ed. Santa Barbara, CA: Libraries Unlimited, 2012.

Fieldhouse, Margaret, and Audrey Marshall, eds. *Collection Development in the Digital Age.* London: Facet, 2012.

Garvin, Peggy, ed. *Government Information Management in the 21st Century: International Perspectives.* Farnham, Surrey, UK: Ashgate, 2011.

Gregory, Vicki L. *Collection Development and Management for 21st Century Library Collections: An Introduction.* New York: Neal-Schuman, 2011.

Havey, Carl A. *The 21st Century Elementary Library Media Program.* Santa Barbara, CA: Libraries Unlimited, 2010.

Hazen, Dan. "Lost in the Cloud: Research Library Collections and Community in the Digital Age." *Library Resources and Technical Services* 55, no. 4 (Oct. 2011): 195–204.

Healy, Ciara, ed. *Current Trends in Academic Media Collections and Services.* Baltimore. MD: Johns Hopkins University Press, 2010. Special issue of *Library Trends* 58, no. 3 (Winter 2010).

Hibner, Holly, and Mary Kelly. *Making a Collection Count: A Holistic Approach to Library Collection Management,* 2nd ed. Oxford, UK: Chandos, 2014.

Holder, Sara. *Library Collection Development for Professional Programs: Trends and Best Practices.* Hershey, PA: Information Science References, 2013.

Horava, Tony. "Challenges and Possibilities for Collection Management in a Digital Age." *Library Resources and Technical Services* 54, no. 3 (July 2012): 142–52.

Johnson, Peggy. *Developing and Managing Electronic Collections: The Essentials.* Chicago: American Library Association, 2013.

Kaplan, Richard B., ed. *Building and Managing E-book Collections: A How-to-Do-It Manual for Librarians.* How-to-Do-It Manuals for Libraries 184. Chicago: Neal-Schuman, 2012.

Kelsey, Sigrid E. W., and Marjorie J. Porters, eds. *Best Practices for Corporate Libraries.* Santa Barbara, CA: Libraries Unlimited, 2011.

Kohl, David F. "Collection Development in the ARL Library." In *Encyclopedia of Library and Information Sciences,* 3rd ed., ed. Marcia J. Bates and Mary Niles Maack, 1106–23. New York: Taylor and Frances, 2010.

Kovacs, Diane K. *The Kovacs Guide to Electronic Library Collection Development: Essential Core Subject Collections, Selection Criteria, and Guidelines.* 2nd ed. New York: Neal-Schuman, 2009.

Martin, Barbara Stein, and Marco Zannier. *Fundamentals of School Library Media Management: A How-to-Do-It Manual.* How-to-Do-It Manuals 171. New York: Neal-Schuman, 2009.

Morris, Betty J. *Administering the School Library Media Center.* 5th ed. Santa Barbara, CA: Libraries Unlimited, 2010.

Morrison, Andrea Marie, ed. *Managing Electronic Government Information in Libraries: Issues and Practices.* Chicago: American Library Association, 2008.

Nebraska Education Media Association. *Guide for Developing and Evaluating School Library Programs.* 7th ed. Santa Barbara, CA: Libraries Unlimited, 2010.

Organisation for Economic Co-operation and Development. *E-books: Developments and Policy Considerations.* OECD Digital Economy Papers, no. 208. Paris: Organisation for Economic Co-Operation and Development, 2013. www.oecd.org/sti/ieconomy/e-booksdevelopmentsandpolicyconsiderations.htm.

Orr, Cynthia. "Collection Development in Public Libraries." In *Encyclopedia of Library and Information Sciences,* 3rd ed., ed. Marcia J. Bates and Mary Niles Maack, 1097–1105. New York: Taylor and Frances, 2010.

Ross, Lyman, and Pongracz Sennyey. "The Library Is Dead, Long Live the Library: The Practice of Academic Librarianship and the Digital Revolution." *Journal of Academic Librarianship* 34, no. 2 (Mar. 2008): 145–52.

Rinaldy, Caroline. *Trends in Rare Book and Documents Special Collections Management.* New York: Primary Research Group, 2008.

Sheehan, Kate. *The eBook Revolution: A Primer for Librarians on the Front Lines.* Santa Barbara, CA: Libraries Unlimited, 2013.

Stephens, Claire Gatrell, and Patricia Franklin. *School Library Collection Development: Just the Basics.* Santa Barbara, CA: Libraries Unlimited, 2012.

Vasileiou, Magdalini, Jennifer Rowley, and Richard Hartley. "The E-book Management Framework: The Management of E-books in Academic Libraries and Its Challenges." *Library and Information Science Research* 34, no. 4 (Oct. 2012): 282–91.

Webster, Peter M. *Managing Electronic Resources: New and Changing Roles for Libraries.* Oxford, UK: Chandos, 2008.

Woodward, Jeannette. *Transformed Library: E-books, Expertise, and Evolution.* Chicago: American Library Association, 2013.

CHAPTER TWO

Organizational Models, Staffing, and Responsibilities

Collection development and management involve many responsibilities. Despite constant changes in technology, user communities, and user expectations, collection development and management remain essential in twenty-first century libraries. As Gorman observes, "Libraries exist to make the connection between their users and the recorded knowledge and information they need and want."[1] This chapter offers an overview of these responsibilities and how collection development and management may be organized within a library. Subsequent chapters explore tasks, functions, and responsibilities in greater depth. Also addressed in this chapter are desired skills and competencies, learning and mastery, on-site training for collections librarians, performance evaluation, digital technology's influence on skills and work assignment, and ethical issues associated with the practice of collection development and management.

Collection Development and Management Responsibilities

A librarian with collections responsibilities may be called a selector, subject or area specialist, liaison or subject liaison, bibliographer, collection development or collection management librarian, or collections librarian—or simply librarian. In many libraries, especially smaller libraries, an individual may handle collections responsibilities along with various others, including placing orders, receipting and cataloging materials, providing reference service, teaching information literacy, circulating materials, collaborating with teachers, and instructing in technology use. A comprehensive list of possible collection development and management responsibilities follows:

Selecting
- choosing current materials in one or more formats for acquisition and access
- using an online book vendor system to select materials
- selecting access methods for digital resources
- negotiating contracts for e-resources
- deciding on retrospective materials for acquisition and access
- choosing which gift materials to accept
- evaluating free websites and web-based resources for possible inclusion in a library's catalog or made accessible through a library's website
- responding to users' suggestions for materials to be added
- selecting materials to withdraw, store, preserve, replace, digitize, or cancel
- identifying and soliciting materials for inclusion in a digital depository
- designing an approval plan
- designing a patron-driven acquisitions plan

Budgeting
- requesting and justifying budget allocations
- expending and managing allocated funds
- working with donors and potential donors of in-kind and cash gifts
- writing grant proposals and managing grants

Planning and organizing
- coordinating collection development and management activities with others in the library and with partner libraries
- monitoring and reviewing approval plans
- monitoring and reviewing exchange agreements
- monitoring and reviewing patron-driven acquisitions plans
- generating and evaluating reports using a local integrated library system and publisher- or vendor-supplied data
- using an electronic resources management system to extract pertinent data for analysis

- evaluating and assessing collections and related services, including identifying gaps that should be addressed
- fostering cooperative collection development
- writing and revising collection development policies

Communicating and reporting

- serving on internal and external committees dealing with collections issues
- keeping administrators (school principals, library directors, etc.) and other stakeholders informed about library challenges, accomplishments, and activities through reports and presentations
- promoting, marketing, and interpreting collections and resources
- performing liaison and outreach activities in the user community
- connecting with other libraries and librarians
- responding to challenges to materials in the collection
- advising community members on intellectual property rights, open access, scholarship communication, and other issues
- advising readers, often called readers' advisory service, and giving booktalks

Not listed in this summary is the preparation of bibliographies, once routinely taught in library school courses. Although some collections librarians do prepare both analytical and enumerative bibliographies of varying lengths, this function is not as common as those identified above.[2] Developing a dynamic library website or portal that is subject- or user-based and lists or points to related resources is replacing the preparation of static bibliographies. Sometimes called pathfinders, these tools are increasingly found online and guide users in researching a particular topic by pulling together various resources in a range of formats. One commercial tool often used by librarians to create and maintain subject guides is LibGuides (www.springshare.com/libguides).[3] Such tools may be customized to support specific courses in academic and school libraries or address the specific needs of researchers in special libraries.

Few collections librarians have all the responsibilities listed here. Assignment of responsibilities and placement of collections activities within an organization vary with the size of the library and its budget, mission, and user community. In small libraries, all activities may be handled by one individual. In larger libraries, responsibilities may be centralized or dispersed according to subject responsibility, user community, physical location of staff members, or subset of functions within the many that are considered collection development and management activities.

The contemporary understanding of collection development and management as an inclusive set of coherent activities mandates close coordination between activities when they are handled by different individuals or different units. When a single individual does not perform all functions identified in the list above, he or she usually works closely with those who handle these related tasks. For example, a preservation unit may identify items in need of treatment and recommend alternatives but rely on a collections librarian to decide if the item should be withdrawn, replaced, preserved, or conserved. Choosing an approval plan vendor may be the joint responsibility of the acquisitions unit and collections librarians. In-depth knowledge of activities elsewhere in the library affecting the collection is important for effective collection development and management.

Assignment of Responsibilities

Public Libraries

Public libraries vary in their approaches to collections work. Most larger public libraries use of some form of centralized selection. Research studies have shown that the variations between user interests and circulation at different branches are minimal because so much of contemporary reading is influenced by popular media, which reaches a wide audience.[4] Some have questioned the benefits of centralized selection, approval plans, and other forms of packages, which are seen to foster narrow and homogenous collections.[5] Public librarians may feel that the centralized collection librarian is too removed from the day-to-day business of working with the public and understanding their needs and interests. Nevertheless, centralized selection and ordering of multiple copies can speed the delivery of new materials to the branches, increase branch collection diversity, and reduce biases in individual collections. Many library systems with several branches have daily or biweekly delivery service to the branches, facilitating the movement of materials to the pickup location requested by patrons. In these libraries, branch librarians continue to make recommendations and, occasionally, to make some selection decisions locally. Orr suggests that public libraries are increasingly instituting centralized collection development as a cost-saving measure.[6]

All librarians are more likely to participate in collection development and management in medium-size and smaller public libraries to distribute the work and take advantage of librarians' formal education and interest areas. Selection and collection management typically are coordinated by the head librarian, who has direct budgetary responsibility. Of course, the smaller the budget, the less is expended on collections, though selection decisions require more scrutiny. In smaller public libraries, collection development and management are normally handled by a single individual, usually the head librarian. In the past, a small acquisitions budget also meant limited access to print review sources. Now a host of online review and discovery sources can be at the librarian's fingertips.

Larger public libraries may use full-time or part-time collections librarians or a combination of both. Large public libraries usually have a centrally located collections coordinator, collections officer, collection management supervisor, or collection development officer who manages the collections budget and either coordinates or directly supervises the work of several subject specialists located in a central library and branches, if they exist. Many public library collections librarians also have responsibilities for reference work and other public services and may manage a major subject- or user-based unit (e.g., music, children's services, or a branch library). Subject specialists and unit heads may have responsibility for monitoring review tools and selecting materials in their specialty. Another frequent division of selection responsibilities is according to publisher or format, or both. For example, one librarian may be responsible for selecting materials from major publishers and another may be responsible for small presses. Some large public libraries have one or two individuals who handle all selection work, while collection management (such as weeding) is handled at the service points. A common approach is to assign responsibility for e-resources to one librarian. Many public libraries have a selection committee with rotating membership.

Public libraries with one or more branches may assign some responsibility for selecting materials to branch librarians so that a collection can be developed that meets the needs of a particular user community. For example, a branch library patronized by senior citizens may have more large-print materials or more materials on health care. A branch library patronized by an immigrant population may have more materials in a language not extensively collected in the main library. Even in libraries with centralized selection or a selection committee, librarians not charged with selection or not members of the committee usually can make suggestions for new titles. In public libraries in which selection

responsibilities are widely distributed, the centrally located coordinator is usually charged with managing the collection budget, monitoring e-book packages,
and coordinating approval plans (if they are used). This individual also may
negotiate and sign licenses for e-content, although this responsibility may lie
with the library director or an e-resources librarian.

School Library Media Centers

The assignment of collections responsibilities in school library media centers
mirrors that found in public libraries. Large systems usually have a district coordinator who supervises the activities of librarians in the several schools that constitute the system. In some systems, one person or a committee selects items
that go to all schools, with variations depending on grade level (i.e., elementary,
middle, and high school). This can relieve some of the demands on individual
librarians but does not permit addressing the unique needs within each school.
In some school systems, especially smaller ones, without district media services,
each librarian may have responsibility for developing collections within his or
her school, in consultation with the school's teachers and in response to student needs and interests. For example, a librarian in a Spanish immersion school
selects resources tailored to meet the needs of this program. A typical process in
school districts is to place orders and receipt and process items centrally at the
district office, even when selection is handled at the school level. If the school
librarian is not part of a system or works in a school system without a district
office, then these responsibilities fall to the individual.

One aspect of collection development and management in school library
media centers not present in other types of libraries is the number and variety of
groups that may be engaged in decisions, including teachers, school administrators, school boards, parents, students, individuals in the community, and community organizations. As Lukenbill notes, these varied stakeholders both help
and hinder logical, well-considered selection decisions.[7] He goes on to advise
school media center librarians to accept this involvement and recognize the
inherent complexity this brings to the selection process. Educating others about
the selection process, stressing the professional nature of making good selection
decisions, and using generally accepted selection tools and aids can strengthen
the position of the school media center librarian.

Some schools have a standing curriculum and media committee to deal with
library selection and collections issues. A typical committee might consist of
a teacher from each grade level, a student representative, a special education

teacher, an ESL teacher, and perhaps other faculty members. If the school media center has a selection policy, the standing committee may be responsible for reviewing it and setting goals and priorities for the media program. The committee may be involved with other media center policies, including those that address Internet use, copyright, gifts, weeding, intellectual freedom, and responding to challenges to materials. In addition, the committee may preview suggested media, discuss requests for materials and equipment, make recommendations for purchases and online access, and evaluate and review challenged materials.

An important trend in collection management in school library media centers is a shifting of some responsibility for access to e-resources to state-wide programs. The 2011 *School Library Journal* spending survey reported that almost all states provided school libraries with statewide database subscriptions.[8] Frequently, the databases available through these initiatives are selected by an advisory group of librarians representing various types of libraries, including those in K–12 schools.

Special Libraries

Special libraries present a unique environment for collection development and management for several reasons. Special libraries have a specific mission and narrow user community. Often the need is for very current information. They may be staffed by only one librarian, who is responsible for all functions. In larger special libraries with several librarians, the librarians may have clear and narrow areas of specialization within which they manage a collection and provide associated services. Axtmann notes that most law libraries have moved away from centralizing all collections activities with a director and toward using committees or assigning selection responsibilities to several librarians.[9]

Often called information professionals, librarians in special libraries have moved rapidly into the digital environment to meet the need of their users to have information delivered to the desktop and laboratory. The Special Library Association explains that "information professionals have expertise in total management of information resources, including identifying, selecting, evaluating, securing and providing access to pertinent information resources. These resources may be in any media or format."[10] In many organizations, information professionals have moved away from a physical library space to delivering content and services electronically or to being part of work teams and specialized departments.[11] In this role, special librarians provide research assistance, not just reference answers. Housewright reports that corporate librarians who have maintained their relevance are those who have moved away from traditional roles no longer valued by their parent companies and have focused on innovative functions and existing functions of higher value.[12] Many special librarians assist with their parent organization's content management systems, supporting the development of taxonomies and methods for document version control and advising on document retention policies. Like all collections librarians, those in special libraries select resources in appropriate formats and manage them in the context of their user communities' needs and interests, and in light of available funds. Negotiating for access to e-content is an important responsibility. Funding constraints mean that many special libraries are moving to cost-per-use delivery of journal articles, mirroring the "just-in-time" approach found in other types of libraries.

Academic Libraries

The idea of subject specialist positions responsible for portions of the collection was developed in Germany in the 1800s. German academic libraries began the practice of placing selection in specific fields in the hands of library staff with academic credentials in those areas.[13] U.S. academic libraries did not begin to employ subject specialists (sometimes called area specialists) widely until after World War II, when selection in large libraries began to shift from faculty members to academic librarians.[14] Subject specialists were seen to be most appropriate in libraries with complex bibliographic, linguistic, acquisition, and processing problems that required specialized expertise.

In many smaller academic libraries, teaching faculty continue to play a major role in selecting materials, though collection management activities are generally handled by librarians. Faculty may identify new materials for acquisition through their work in a discipline and through review of approval plan notifications (print or electronic) and new approval plan receipts.[15] They may make recommendations with final authority for approving orders residing with the library. Smaller academic libraries seldom have the breadth and depth of specialized subject expertise found in larger libraries, so relying on the proficiency of faculty members active in the field is logical. The success of faculty-based selection depends on faculty members' interest in and involvement with the library. Because of their size, small and mid-size academic libraries often have one staff member—the director, an acquisitions librarian, or one charged with oversight of collections—responsible for authorizing purchases. This librarian typically has responsibility for developing and revising policies, developing and monitoring approval plan profiles, negotiating licenses for e-content, and setting up criteria for patron-driven acquisition. Librarians in smaller academic libraries usually carry several responsibilities in addition to those related to collections.[16] These might include providing reference service, teaching information literacy, or cataloging.

For a time, the titles *subject specialist* and *subject bibliographer* were understood to mean a librarian who was assigned full time to collections activities. Although such narrowly defined positions still exist in a few libraries, most librarians with collections responsibilities have many other assignments. Full-time academic bibliographer positions were, from their beginning, perceived as a special class of scholar-librarians, intended both to replace faculty selectors and to appease faculty members with appropriate replacements within the library.[17] The independent and solitary nature of a full-time bibliographer's work can result in internal cultural and organizational problems and in positions that do not fit comfortably into the library's organizational structure.[18] Such positions have fallen out of favor in most academic libraries as they seek to engage more directly with their user communities.

Rapidly changing technologies, a flood of digital content in a decentralized information environment, better understanding of how students learn, and changes in how scholars communicate and disseminate research and creative work have prompted libraries to focus on active engagement in the work of students, scholars, and community users. *Liaison* is now commonly used to denote this broader outreach role of subject librarians, but the transition to positions with multiple responsibilities has been under way for some time.[19] The contemporary understanding of the liaison model involves activities that enhance scholar productivity, empower learners, and actively engage these librarians in the research, teaching, and learning processes. A central goal is to integrate academic librarians and libraries into the workflows of students and scholars—or, as Dempsey suggests, "putting the library *in* the flow."[20]

Rodwell and Fairbairn propose a list of skills and attributes relevant to liaison work:

- confidence
- communication and presentation skills of a high order
- risk taking
- flexibility and comfort with ambiguity
- networking skills; being able to build coalitions and cultivate clients and supporters

- relationship or account management skills
- negotiation, persuasion, and influencing skills
- reflection on practice and ability to learn and play
- project management skills
- promotional and marketing skills
- high-level technical knowledge for production and publishing work and for facilitating or mediating between parties to achieve outcomes[21]

The RUSA "Guidelines for Liaison Work in Managing Collections and Services" makes clear that liaison work is important in all types of libraries. Liaison work is defined as "the process by which librarians involve the library's clientele in the assessment of collection needs and services and the measurement of user satisfaction with the collection." Further,

> Liaison work includes identifying user needs, evaluating existing collections, removing extraneous materials, and locating resources that will enhance the collections.
>
> Liaison work enables the library to communicate its collection policies, services, and needs to its clientele and to enhance the library's public relations.
>
> Liaison work enables the library's clientele to communicate its library needs and preferences to the library staff and governing body.
>
> Librarians functioning as liaisons have various titles and job descriptions.[22]

These guidelines describe the nature of liaison work in public, academic, and special libraries.

A study of liaisons supporting chemistry, English, and psychology departments in U.S. colleges and universities identifies several frequently assigned activities.[23] The most commonly held responsibilities are responding to departmental requests, selecting books and journals, consulting with faculty and students on their research, providing in-class library instruction, facilitating faculty participation in collection development and cancellation decisions, updating the department about library services and future plans, and teaching workshops on library resources.

Having many responsibilities can be challenging as academic librarians try to balance competing demands on their time. One successful project to develop a pragmatic, objective, and quantitative means of estimating collection development workload in an academic library is described by Metz, who proposes a formula of weighted parameters, with weights to be assigned different values according to the library in which the formula is applied.[24] The five parameters are number of academic departments and key centers for which a collections librarian is responsible; number of full-time tenure-track faculty in assigned departments or centers; number of orders in all the librarian's firm order budget accounts for the previous fiscal year; call number responsibilities measured as total inches in the shelf list or via automated title count; and the number of standing orders, serials, and continuations in all the librarian's accounts.

Skills and Competencies

ALA offers a set of core competences expected of all graduates from master's programs in library and information studies.[25] A section addressing information resources states that graduates should know and be able to employ

> concepts and issues related to the lifecycle of recorded knowledge and information, from creation through various stages of use to disposition

> concepts, issues, and methods related to the acquisition and disposition of resources, including evaluation, selection, purchasing, processing, storing, and deselection

> concepts, issues, and methods related to the management of various collections

> concepts, issues, and methods related to the maintenance of collections, including preservation and conservation

Many library organizations have similar lists of competencies. For example, the Special Librarian Association states that an information professional

> manages the full life cycle of information from its creation or acquisition through its destruction, including organizing, categorizing, cataloguing, classifying, disseminating; and creating and managing taxonomies, intranet and extranet content, and thesauri

builds a dynamic collection of information resources based on a deep understanding of clients' information needs and their learning, work, or business processes

demonstrates expert knowledge of the content and format of information resources, including the ability to evaluate, select, and filter them critically

provides access to the best available externally published and internally created information resources and deploys content throughout the organization using a suite of information access tools

negotiates the purchase and licensing of needed information products and services

develops information policies for the organization regarding externally published and internally created information resources and advises on the implementation of these policies[26]

The Association for Library Service to Children (ALSC) lists these "Knowledge of Materials" competencies for librarians serving children up to age fourteen in public libraries:

demonstrates a knowledge and appreciation of children's literature, periodicals, audiovisual materials, websites and other electronic media, and other materials that contribute to a diverse, current, and relevant children's collection

provides a wide and diverse variety of electronic resources, audiovisual materials, print materials, and other resource materials to best serve the needs of children and their caregivers

keeps abreast of new materials and those for retrospective purchase by consulting a wide variety of reviewing sources and publishers' catalogs, including those of small presses, by attending professional meetings, and by reading, viewing, and listening

keeps up-to-date on adult electronic and print reference sources that may serve the needs of children and their caregivers

develops a comprehensive collection development policy consistent with the mission and policies of the parent library and the ALA Library Bill of Rights considers the selection and discarding of materials according to collection development, selection, and weeding policies

maintains a diverse collection, recognizing children's need to see people like and unlike themselves in the materials they access

understands and applies criteria for evaluating the content and artistic merit of children's materials in all genres and formats

addresses materials against community challenges

demonstrates a knowledge of cataloging, classification, indexing procedures, and practices to support access to children's materials[27]

Libraries expect newly hired librarians to have gained these competencies and specific skills in a graduate school program. These are supplemented with on-the-job training and experience gained through the practice of collection development and management over time. Library and information schools provide the conceptual learning. These are the skills, principles, and concepts of librarianship and provide the building blocks or mental models for its practice. They represent the theory that lies behind the practice of collection development and are important to the master as well as the novice. For masters, they are points of reference that aid them in continually refining practice and in explaining it to others. For novices, they give an understanding of the rationale that guides collection development and management.

A library school curriculum should include basic functional principles. Soete calls these "assumed competencies."[28] They include knowing

- reasons for building library collections and a commitment to resource sharing
- importance of knowing the library's users
- factors that make for effective selection and collection management decisions
- tenets of intellectual freedom and respect for diverse points of view
- importance of building and preserving collections for the future as well as the present

Conceptual learning also involves skills and practices—basics that are as important as the philosophical underpinnings. Collections librarians need knowledge of the subjects, formats, and users for whom they select materials.

They need a basic understanding of the targeted user community and of the techniques necessary to learn about the specific local community being served. This means, at a minimum, expertise in the literature if the librarian is not an expert in the subject or discipline. Ideally, a subject specialist is familiar with specialized terminology, understands the basic concepts and importance of the field, is aware of current controversies, recognizes the names of prominent researchers and authors, knows of historical milestones and the names associated with them, and understands how the field relates to other fields and disciplines. A librarian who plans to work with collections used by children and teenagers is familiar with the history of children's fiction and nonfiction, understands children's interest and reading levels and the types of materials that match these, is aware of current theories about the use of literature in the curriculum, and knows the names of prominent authors, illustrators, and award-winning books.

A library expects a new collections librarian to understand the publishing industry and the factors a publisher considers in making decisions about what to publish, the types of materials in which major publishers specialize and the quality of their publications, and major publishers' reliability, pricing practices, and general reputation. The new librarian should have studied publishing trends, production statistics, and pricing behavior. Equally important is knowing how materials are provided to libraries and how to select the appropriate means of acquisition for various materials types. This includes familiarity with distribution and acquisitions mechanisms (vendors, agents, scholarly societies, aggregators, approval plans, firm orders, standing orders, etc.). The librarian should have a basic understanding of intellectual property rights, copyright law, and licensing agreements and the roles they play in the acquisition of and access to resources. Those who plan to become academic librarians should understand the changing nature of scholarly communication and academic research.

Budd and Bril found that collection development practitioners rank the ability to identify and use key materials as selection sources as the most important skill gained in graduate education. A similar study by Buttlar and De Mont asked practicing librarians in all types of libraries to rate the usefulness of fifty-nine competencies in eight categories.[29] Collection management skills (development, selection, deselection, preservation) ranked second in a list of ten competencies most frequently rated as essential; first was knowledge of sources in all formats to answer typical reference questions. Selecting and evaluating print/nonprint materials ranked seventh, applying appropriate principles to weed and to inventory materials and equipment ranked eighth, and developing selection policies ranked tenth.

Automation and emerging information technologies are affecting how collections librarians do their work as well as the resources with which they work. Being comfortable in an increasingly technology-driven environment is essential. Library automation and access to bibliographic networks, Internet resources, and vendor sites support collections activities such as selecting materials, verifying individual items, preparing orders, claiming, evaluating and assessing collections, managing budgets, fostering cooperative collection development, and communicating with library staff members and others outside the library, including publishers, vendors, and other suppliers. In-house automated library systems often can produce various useful reports and provide information on demand about fund balances, units and cost, circulation activity, use of online products, supplier performance, and other statistical compilations that can be manipulated on personal computers. Vendors, aggregators, and agents provide various reports that can help librarians evaluate their performance and use of their products. Most of these reports can be accessed online at no cost and are part of the services provided by the supplier.

Some libraries and librarians are creating web-based resources or locally designed online tools specifically to aid in the practice of collection development and management. A locally developed site for collections librarians typically provides links to local policies, procedures, forms, and reports; home pages of vendors and publishers frequently used by the library; and useful external sites prepared by other librarians. AcqWeb (www.acqweb.org), a resource for acquisitions and collection development librarians, provides links to resources of interest, including verification tools and directories of publishers and vendors. Some local sites include links to bibliographic tools, like *Books in Print*, to which the library has contractual access, and to relevant professional association pages. Other types of information often provided are budgets and fund allocation, a directory of librarians with their subject responsibilities, a currency converter, and management and statistical data.

Working with electronic information resources requires additional skills and expertise. Collections librarians must understand licensing and contract negotiation for electronic resources, copyright in the digital environment, and consortial agreements for cooperative purchasing. E-journal subscription packages, e-book collections, and other bulk purchases require new expertise to assess their appropriateness for and cost/benefit in the local environment. Much of selection activity moves to the macro level. More library staff members may be involved in evaluation and selection decisions because of the boundary-spanning nature of managing and servicing both local and online electronic information.

The importance of e-resources has resulted in the creation of positions charged primarily with managing the library's e-resources in larger libraries. These librarians, often appropriately called e-resources librarians, may have a background in collections, serials, or acquisitions work. They may combine the work of an e-resources librarian with other duties or focus solely on these responsibilities. Typical assignments include

- coordinating electronic resources, establishing and renewing licenses, and maintaining records for contracts
- negotiating new licenses and renewals with vendors and content providers, including consulting with legal counsel
- administering new and existing licenses for electronic products
- maintaining records of licenses and contracts
- applying knowledge of copyright and intellectual property principles to ensure that library users' rights are protected
- working closely with librarians to identify, select, and acquire new e-resources, assess needs of the user community, and adjust resources to fit these needs
- monitoring vendor services and performing vendor evaluations
- compiling and analyzing electronic resource use statistics
- working with acquisitions staff to ensure that e-resources are ordered and with cataloging staff to ensure that e-resources are cataloged as appropriate
- overseeing the operation of citation linkers and knowledge bases
- troubleshooting and resolving e-resource access problems

In a larger library, an e-resources librarian also may supervise and manage the workflow of an e-resource unit in which many of these functions are handled.

A new collections specialist position is appearing in large libraries and consortia. These individuals are responsible for managing legacy print collections and may have titles such as collections strategist or print collections analyst. Typically these librarians have a background in collections development and management or preservation or both. Driving issues are availability of digital surrogates and local space constraints. These individuals guide libraries is making decisions about retention, storage, and withdrawal. They work with partner libraries in shared print collection projects including managing storage facilities. An important aspect of this work is gathering and analyzing local collections data, such as use, and understanding the changing national environment of shared print collections, sometimes called the "collective collection." Key questions include how many copies of a title are needed and where should they be located. Collections development and management librarians have always managed collections; the difference today is that these decisions are made within a much larger context.

Various authors and professional associations have identified additional competencies that new collections librarians should bring to their first jobs:[30]

- knowledge of general business practices, including financial analysis and budget management
- knowledge of and ability to analyze currency fluctuations around the world, economic trends, and world market forces
- abilities in critical analysis, problem solving, and critical decision making
- commitment to continuous learning and professional development
- negotiation skills and diplomacy
- managerial and supervisory skills
- ability to work collaboratively
- understanding of organizational behavior, power, and politics
- effective written and verbal communication skills
- knowledge of grant writing and administration
- proficient use of current and emerging information technologies.

Many of these competencies are not normally part of a library school curriculum. Students should consider taking courses in other professional school programs, such as a business school, education department, or public policy program, to gain the skills needed in contemporary collection development and management practice.

Learning after School

The previous section identifies a set of core or assumed competencies consisting of principles, concepts, and skills that libraries expect a newly hired collections librarian to have learned in a course of graduate study. Not all librarians will have taken courses that cover each of these topics, and certain ingredients in successful collections work cannot be taught in library school. Much is mastered while on the job. Some skills are specific to the individual's library and are learned in the new position. These include learning the librarian's responsibilities (which depend on the job description), the library's collection (on-site and online), and local procedures. In the latter category are how to prepare orders, how to interact with various library units, and how the local budget and financial system operate. To this can be added learning about the local culture or organizational environment, including what is acceptable behavior and what is not, how decisions are made, and how autonomously individuals operate.

Learning and Mastery

Senge explores the difference between *learning* and *mastery* in his work on learning organizations, which succeed by continuously adapting and improving.[31] Successful collections work can be mastered only by practice—by actually doing the work. The distinction rests on the difference between theory, which can be learned, and practice. Practices are the most evident aspect of any profession in the sense that they are what define the field to those outside it. Practices are also the primary focus of individuals when they begin to follow a new career or discipline. The novice requires discipline in the sense of conscious and consistent effort because following the practices is not yet second nature.

New collections librarians working with mental models of how to develop and manage a collection must make an effort to identify their own assumptions and the skills and competencies that guide them. Over time and with experience, the practices of a discipline become more and more automatic. This is why it is sometimes hard for an experienced librarian to explain what goes into a selection or collection management decision and how one weighs pros and cons to select or not to select, replace, repair, withdraw, or cancel a title.

The novice is tempted to think that understanding certain principles means one has learned all about the discipline. This confuses intellectual understanding with mastery. A student of the French language may know French grammar and vocabulary but has not mastered the language until he or she speaks French automatically and without first mentally translating every word from English to French. Senge calls this the essence of a discipline, which cannot be gained by focusing conscious attention and effort on learning it. The essence of a discipline is the state of being that is experienced naturally by individuals with high levels of mastery in the discipline.

This perspective suggests that the successful collections librarian *is* a collection librarian instead of one who *does* collections development and management.

It means moving from a linear understanding (knowing the building blocks) to a nonlinear, internalized understanding of collection development and management as a whole. This is the mastery that cannot be learned in library school. New collections librarians may have learned everything they can through an educational program, but only through experience does the whole become greater than the sum of its parts.

Bolman and Deal use the term *artistry* instead of *mastery*, but they are equally concerned about the dangers of overemphasizing the rational and technical side. They state, "Artistry is neither exact nor precise; the artist interprets experience, expressing it in forms that can be felt, understood, and appreciated. Art fosters emotion, subtlety, and ambiguity."[32] Much in the practice of collection development and management is ambiguous and uncertain, and most decisions are revisited. Collection development is sometimes called both an art and a science. It combines creativity with empirical knowledge. Practice gives meaning to theory, refines performance, and builds mastery.

Training On-Site

If fortunate, a newly hired collections librarian is provided with a formal on-site training program, supported by a policies and procedures manual. A manual provides the documentation necessary for carrying out collection development and management activities in a specific library.[33] It documents local practices in a systematic way and provides a planning tool for individual librarians to measure the progress of their work or improve its quality. Other in-house training materials may include library-specific collection development policies, procedures for the acquisition process, guidelines for collection analysis, procedures for using an automated library system, and goals for collection development work.

A collections librarian should be prepared to develop a training program, because not all libraries offer one. The new librarian might consult the *Guide for Training Collection Development Librarians*, which lays out the skills and expertise specific to a library in which a new librarian will need training.[34] Even with a formal on-site program, a newly hired librarian should develop a personal self-education plan in consultation with the supervisor. It should include learning

- how the library and its parent organization are organized and the scope and emphasis of its programs
- who the library's staff members are and what they do
- the individuals and groups outside the library with whom the new librarian will work

- the library's holdings and their strengths and weaknesses
- how patrons use the collections
- how the materials budget is allocated, monitored, and spent
- reports available from the local automated system or generated manually
- reports available from vendors, publishers, and aggregators
- the library's collection development policies
- who is responsible for negotiating licenses and contracts
- existing agreements for access to online collections provided by publishers, vendors, and aggregators
- any cooperative collection development agreements and who has oversight
- how the library chooses, uses, and evaluates vendors and the vendors used
- local procedures for selection, ordering, and processing materials

As libraries move toward assigning staff members multiple duties, many librarians who have not handled collections responsibilities previously are being asked to assume them. This is a particular challenge for two reasons. For librarians who completed their graduate library school program some time ago, even if they remember the content of collection management courses, that information has likely become dated. Additionally, supervisors and coworkers may assume erroneously that the librarian with newly assigned collections responsibilities has a familiarity with in-house collection development and management policies, procedures, and performance expectations. A carefully designed training program is as important for an existing staff member who assumes collections responsibilities as it is for a newly hired librarian.

Effective performance of collection management and development activities requires continual learning, both in the theories and practices of this specialty and in the areas for which one is responsible. A commitment to self-education along with intellectual curiosity, energy, and time are essential.

Performance Evaluation

The natural follow-up to training is performance evaluation, an important aspect of any position. This may involve an annual formal performance review and should include frequent informal contacts with a supervisor that address performance goals, accomplishments, and problems. This continuous dialogue ensures that the librarian has a clear understanding of expectations and the extent to which they are being met. Performance appraisals, whether formal or informal, should provide constructive guidance and set clear future direction. Ideally, performance evaluation begins with an individual's job description, which reflects the relative importance of and anticipated percentage of time devoted to collection activities. The job description may be responsibility based or outcome based.

Evaluations of collection development librarians are complicated because of the difficulty of developing performance standards and measuring outcomes. If the librarian has multiple assignments and multiple supervisors, compiling and preparing the evaluation can be challenging. If more than one supervisor is involved, the librarian and supervisors must be in agreement about the priorities of multiple assignments and the effort to be devoted to each. Academic libraries may use peer reviews in place of or in addition to supervisor reviews. Librarians being reviewed should work with their supervisors to develop explicit goals within each review period. A clear understanding of performance criteria and what is being measured is important.

The newly hired collections librarian should know from the first day on the job how performance evaluation is handled. Many libraries require supporting documentation, and the librarian should be assembling this information on an ongoing basis. Some libraries require monthly reports prepared by the staff member. Academic libraries may solicit comments from faculty in academic departments.[35] Part of the annual review process may be the preparation of a self-review reporting on the individual's success or failure in meeting certain specific goals agreed upon at the beginning of the review cycle.

Performance expectations should be consistent with the library's overall mission and goals. They may be very specific and delineate every area of the job description such as quantity and quality of liaison contacts with users, success in managing budget allocations, quality of new acquisitions, and contributions to the library as a whole. Librarians in academic libraries and some school media centers also may have to meet performance expectations in order to be promoted or granted tenure or continuous appointment. Academic librarians often have performance expectations that are similar to those of teaching faculty, involving research, publication, instruction, and contributions to the profession. Increasingly, public librarians are expected to be actively engaged in the profession. Because most tenure and promotion decisions are based on a cumulative history of performance, the new librarian must work closely with supervisors and the tenure committee or its equivalent to begin building a persuasive dossier from the point of hire.

Technology's Influence on Skills and Work Assignment

Many changes in the work of collections librarians are effects of contemporary information technologies on the nature of collections; on the nature of work in acquiring, accessing, and managing these collections; and on user expectations. Braverman introduced the concept of *deskilling* in the 1970s and explored it in his *Labor and Monopoly Capital.*[36] He suggested that capitalism, combined with technology, results in degradation of work by pushing the skills necessary for doing a job down in the organization or profession. Some analyses of the effects of computerized technology on work have characterized them as a continuation of the deskilling process described by Braverman. More recently, economists, sociologists, and historians have seen new technologies as having reskilling, upskilling, and enskilling effects as well—that is, automation changes the nature of a position by requiring more sophisticated knowledge and skills.[37] The increasingly sophisticated responsibilities assigned to nurse practitioners and physician's assistants, who handle many medical practices previously performed only by physicians, are examples. One result of this shift is that physicians are freed to focus on more complicated medical conditions.

Heisig suggests that Braverman's view of deskilling is outdated because the proportion of lower-level jobs in general is declining and many clerical jobs have become redundant because of computers and information technology. Further, management is more interested in using the "productive capabilities that result from higher qualifications and knowledge by offering participation and cooperation" than in controlling work behavior.[38] The introduction of computers during the past few decades coupled with higher general education levels and higher skill levels means than many positions have become more technical and varied. The effect of these changes in collections work has led to questions about what defines a professional collections librarian.

Professions are generally distinguished by a central body that sets and maintains standards in education and practice; a professional code of conduct or ethics; self-governing professional associations of practitioners; careful management of knowledge in relation to the expertise that constitutes the basis of the profession's activities; certification and credentialing; legal and social recognition; relative autonomy in performance of work; and control of numbers, selection, and training of new entrants.[39] The professions of medicine and law, for example, have all of these characteristics. Library science has many of them, but not all. Nevertheless, most librarians consider librarianship a profession even though librarians and their professional associations have been unable to maintain exclusive control over the qualifications needed to perform library work and, consequently, to whom various types of work are assigned.

This lack of rigidity in how positions are defined and how work is assigned has been beneficial in numerous libraries. Many activities are moving downward in the library hierarchy as a result of advances in technology, reduced budgets and reduced staffing, and increasing demands on professional staff. Library paraprofessionals and support staff have taken on more diverse and higher levels of responsibilities.[40] One result is that professionals are able to devote time to more complex activities that meet the changing needs of their libraries and user communities.

The distinctions between professionals and paraprofessionals are blurring. Zhu's 2011 study surveyed 820 academic library professionals and paraprofessionals and examined duties assigned to each employee group.[41] The findings confirmed a lack of consistency in collections task assignment but also identified some collections responsibilities that remain primarily assigned to professionals: establishing collection development policies; taking the lead in or making major contributions to negotiating licensing for e-resources; and signing licenses for e-resources. In addition, professionals were much more frequently expected to be actively engaged in the profession of librarianship.

Zhu found that some collections duties, though primarily assigned to professionals, were held by 11.5–23.1 percent of paraprofessionals surveyed: selecting and deselecting materials; performing collection analysis, assessment, and evaluation; managing collections budgets (e.g., planning, allocating, tracking, balancing, setting cancellation targets); taking the lead in or making major contributions to the management of e-resources; and identifying or testing e-resources, including subscription, purchase, and open-access titles. One assumes that few paraprofessionals learned these duties through a formal undergraduate degree program and that most acquired the necessary expertise through on-the-job training and experience.

Academic libraries may assign collection development and management and liaison responsibilities to a staff member without a graduate library degree if that individual has extensive subject knowledge gained either through formal study (often a PhD) in the discipline or extensive experience with the local collections and their users.[42] Most academic libraries consider these employees as professionals although they do not have a master's degree in library and information science. As is the case with paraprofessionals who have collections responsibilities, these individuals acquire the necessary library skills through on-the-job training and experience.

The collections-related areas that remain the responsibility of professionals are distinguished by their complex and abstract nature, broad perspective, significant impact on the future of the library, and influence on how the library is perceived by its user community, stakeholders, partners, and services and materials providers. Veaner calls these *programmatic responsibilities*.[43] Such areas include planning and articulating collection development programs; serving as departmental and community liaisons; allocating and managing budgets; preparing and revising collection development policies; developing and reviewing approval plans and patron-driven acquisitions plans; assessing and evaluating collections; setting parameters for materials to be withdrawn or moved to storage; cancelling journal subscriptions; and negotiating with suppliers, vendors, aggregators, and consortia.

Organizational Models

Who performs various functions or activities, how these individuals are coordinated, and how they communicate among themselves and with others define the library's collection development and management organizational structure. Libraries with larger staffs, collections, and budgets are more likely to develop large, complex, and variant organizational structures.

No single collection development organizational model predominates. Defining the components of an optimal structure that assures successful accomplishment of goals has proved impossible. No model is perfect. Variations, as with the assignment of collections responsibilities, are influenced by the size of existing collections, staffing levels, available budget, local assumptions about the goals of collection management and development, and preferences of the current library administrators.

Bryant suggests that one or more of three conditions make some sort of collection management organizational structure necessary: when the decision of what to purchase and the responsibility for expenditure of the materials budget are no longer the direct responsibility of the library director; when the library acknowledges that neither technical services (where funds have been managed) nor public services (where selection and user liaison have occurred) allows the necessary combination of fund management and patron contact for systematic

Organizational Models, Staffing, and Responsibilities **61**

collection development and management; and when inconsistencies among collection growth, collection use, and patron needs are discovered.[44]

Libraries handle reporting lines and assignment of responsibilities in various ways, depending on their size, history, and individuals on their staffs. Two models predominate. They can be seen as two ends on a continuum, with variations falling in between. In the *functional model,* staff members with collection development and management responsibilities are grouped in a single organizational unit. This unit may be called a department, division, or team. The subject specialists may then be subdivided into subunits according to subject responsibilities, user community, or physical location of their offices, collections, or libraries.

In the *geographic* or *client-based model,* collection development librarians are part of a unit that consists of staff members with various responsibilities who are grouped according to the user community they serve or a common geographic location shared by members of the unit. Again, librarians may be assigned full or part time to collections work. As with the functional model, members of a geographic or client-based unit may be subdivided into smaller units. In this case, the smaller units may be functional or subject based.

The functional model has the advantage of improved communication and coordination among librarians with similar responsibilities, which can enhance the development of a coherent collection and make working on shared projects, such as serials cancellations or collection analysis, easier. The role of the collection development officer is less complicated because it implies direct authority as well as responsibility for the collections librarians. Disadvantages include the potential of isolation from other librarians and distance from the user community.

The geographic or client-based model can be particularly effective in focusing on the needs and expectations of a specific user group. In addition, these collections librarians work more closely with staff members, including catalogers, circulation units, and interlibrary loan staff, whose work is integral to effective collections work. Planning and problem solving may be easier. The main difficulty with this model is in coordinating collections activities across a large library with many geographic or client-based units. Balancing needs and goals can be a challenge.

Few libraries are organized into either of these "pure" models. Most fall somewhere between them. For example, a large public library system may have a central division of collection development librarians with system-wide responsibilities and several branch libraries with librarians who have multiple responsibilities including collection development and management. Hybrid models can have all the advantages of each of the pure models and all of their problems as well. Regardless of the organizational structure employed, the most important consideration is coordination of collection activities and their proper attention within the library's mission and priorities.

Many libraries have one or more standing committees to improve communication across departmental or divisional lines. Typical committees are a general collection development and management coordinating committee, a serials review committee, a discipline- or user-based committee (e.g., a committee of science librarians or of children's librarians), and a committee that addresses electronic resources. Many of these committees include staff members from other library units because of the boundary-spanning nature of collections work. A general coordinating committee may include, for example, representatives from the library's fiscal office, cataloging unit, or interlibrary loan operation. Committees that deal with electronic resources almost always include members from throughout the library—acquisitions and cataloging staff members, automation librarians, reference librarians, an individual charged with managing and monitoring contracts—whose expertise is essential in making responsible, informed decisions about acquisition and access. Libraries with distributed selection responsibilities may have a standing committee or working group that pulls together everyone with selection responsibilities for regular meetings to address shared concerns and pertinent topics. Ad hoc committees may be appointed to address a finite issue or project, such as choosing a new subscription agent or approval plan vendor or managing a large cancellation project. The goal of all these groups is to improve communication and decision making by drawing together the individuals and library units with appropriate expertise and who will be affected by the decisions.

Quinn explored the psychology of group decision making in collection development, drawing on research in the field of psychology.[45] He notes that the common perception that groups make better, more objective, and more rational decisions than individuals is not always correct. Group decision making has its own limitations and weaknesses because of group history, interpersonal dynamics, and social status of group members. Quinn offers several suggestions to improve group decisions, including process awareness, thorough research of the titles being considered, avoiding premature consensus, and effective management of meetings and participant behavior. Being attentive to these issues can improve the outcomes of collections committees.

Libraries in which several staff members have collections responsibilities generally have an individual who coordinates their activities. Public libraries may call these individuals collection coordinators. In academic libraries these individuals are often called collection development officers (CDOs). By 1994, 82 percent of ARL member libraries responding to a survey reported they had a senior collection development officer reporting directly to the head librarian.[46] In other types of libraries, this person may be called coordinator, team leader, head or director of collection development, assistant or associate librarian for collection development and management, assistant director for collections, media coordinator, or a variation of one of these. A separate senior position is found most commonly in large and medium-size public, academic, and research libraries. This person generally coordinates collection development activities, manages the overall collections budget, and may or may not have direct supervisory responsibility for all staff members with collection management and development assignments.

In large libraries of all types, the collections officer often has senior administrative responsibility for additional operations or services, such as information services, public services, technical services, reference, planning, document delivery and interlibrary loan, development of external funding sources, all aspects of electronic resources, or preservation. A direct linkage with acquisitions, through either placing acquisitions within the collection development and management division or combining senior administrative responsibility for technical services (of which acquisition is a subunit) and collection development and management, is seen frequently.[47] This arrangement provides direct control over budget expenditures. These alignments reflect both the boundary-spanning nature of collection development and management and a reduction in the number of senior administrators through consolidation of responsibilities. The collections officer is often a member of the library's administrative group and participates in library-wide policy development and planning, working with other administrators and unit heads to develop mutually agreed-upon processing priorities.

The collections officer's role varies depending on the span of control and responsibilities within the library and the library's collection development and management operation. As the administrator responsible for library-wide collection development and management, the collections officer is normally charged with preparing budget requests for staffing and collections, and allocating and monitoring the budget—expenditure and balances in the funds assigned to various librarians with selection and collection management responsibilities. Additional responsibilities may include recruiting, training, assigning responsibilities, supervising, and evaluating librarians and support staff engaged in collections work.

The collections officer oversees all aspects of collection building and management for all formats. Under this heading fall coordinating the creation and revision of collection development policies and ensuring those policies are upheld; coordinating collection assessment and evaluation; overseeing preservation and conservation decisions and withdrawals, transfers, and journal cancellations. The collections officer is one of several library administrators who may be charged with negotiating contracts and licenses for acquisition of and access to electronic resources. Primary responsibility for and coordination of cooperative collection development and consortial activities and fund raising through development activities and grant writing are usually assigned to the collections officer, and negotiating with individual donors and reviewing gifts and exchanges may be as well. The collections officer frequently represents the library's collection development program to user groups, governing agencies, and external forums.

Schad stresses the leadership role of the collections officer in academic libraries.[48] He lists team building, articulation of vision and values, continuous formal and informal training, and controlling workload as the four key challenges for a collections officer. These four responsibilities, which can apply to all types of libraries, enable librarians to know what to do and how to do it, realize why it is important, help reduce frustration, and enhance feelings of competence. The collections officer has an important role in helping set a realistic agenda that allows librarians with collections responsibilities to establish priorities, regulate work flow, and accomplish their work. Communication and interpersonal skills are particularly important.

In some libraries, the collections officer may not have direct authority for librarians with collections responsibilities. In this environment, those selecting and managing collections report to another administrator, such as a public library's assistant director responsible for technical services or public services, a public library branch head, an associate university librarian or director, or the school principal.

Ethical Issues

Normative ethics are the principles of conduct or standards of behavior governing a group, organization, or profession. Ethics seek to provide a context for determining what is right and wrong. *Primum non nocere* (first, do no harm) is one of the principal ethical precepts in the medical profession and is taught to all medical students. Professional ethics, an applied form of normative ethics, seeks to apply ethical principles to decisions made every day. Professional ethics is sometimes called professional values—an explicit concept of what an individual or group regards as desirable. Gorman identifies eight professional values for the library profession: stewardship, service, intellectual freedom, rationalism, literacy and learning, equity of access to recorded knowledge and information, privacy, and democracy.[49] He notes that these values are not absolutes, are often in conflict, and must be weighed against each other.

The difference between ethics and morals can seem somewhat arbitrary, and not all theorists make the distinction. One view is that morals are understood to apply to a person's character, whereas ethics stress a social system in which those morals are applied; in this construct, ethics point to standards or codes of behavior expected by the group to which the individual belongs. Thus, whereas a person's moral code is usually unchanging, the ethics and individual practices can be dependent on the group to which he or she belongs.

Ethical behavior is the result of a personal code of morality and an external ethical context provided by institutional and professional principles. A personal code may develop out of civic and religious convictions. People do what makes them feel good about themselves and avoid what makes them feel bad. They also are influenced by the frame of reference for behavior developed by the groups of which they are members. In other words, behavior can be a consequence of how one feels others around him or her perceive this behavior. People understand and react to what happens according to the particular frame of reference they are using for ethical behavior. Professional ethical considerations paired with personal moral convictions influence how librarians make decisions about their collections (what to add, withdraw, preserve, etc.) and interact with their user community, coworkers, materials sellers, suppliers, and service agents. In the latter area fall issues of bias, neutrality, confidentiality and privacy, and access to information.

Bolman and Deal identify four principles found in moral judgments: mutuality (all parties to a relationship are operating under the same understanding about the rules of the game), generality (a specific action follows a principle of conduct applicable to all comparable situations), openness (willingness to make one's thinking and decisions public and confrontable), and caring (for the legitimate interests of others).[50] These theorists stress the need for organizational dialogue about ethical choices. Taking a stance on values, ethical choices, and appropriate behavior is a reflection of principled judgment.

Professional ethics is an additional frame of reference for behavior and the decisions a librarian makes on a daily basis. Professional ethics are standards of behavior set forth, either formally or informally, by the profession of librarianship. Ethical concerns for collections librarians address

- censorship (intentional and unintentional)
- intellectual freedom and freedom of expression
- intellectual property and copyright
- privacy of individuals
- relationships and business practices with vendors, publishers, and subscription agents and avoiding conflict of interest
- compliance with library and parent institution requirements and applicable legislation

Several formal statements of ethics for librarianship have been developed. ALA first provided a "Code of Ethics" in 1938, which was most recently revised in 2008. It is supplemented by "The Freedom to Read Statement" and "The Freedom to View Statement."[51] The Association for Library Collections and Technical Services (ALCTS) has developed a set of guidelines for its members to supplement the ALA code, according to which,

> Within the context of the institution's missions and programs and the needs of the user populations served by the library, an ALCTS member:
>
> 1. strives to develop a collection of materials within collection policies and priorities;
> 2. strives to provide broad and unbiased access to information;
> 3. strives to preserve and conserve the materials in the library in accordance with established priorities and programs;
> 4. develops resource sharing programs to extend and enhance the information sources available to library users;
> 5. promotes the development and application of standards and professional guidelines;
> 6. establishes a secure and safe environment for staff and users;
> 7. fosters and promotes fair, ethical and legal trade and business practices;
> 8. maintains equitable treatment and confidentiality in competitive relations and manuscript and grant reviews;
> 9. supports and abides by any contractual agreements made by the library or its home institution in regard to the provision of or access to information resources, acquisition of services, and financial arrangements.[52]

Other groups of librarians have developed standards for ethical conduct, such as rare book, manuscript, and special collections librarians; acquisitions librarians; law librarians; medical librarians; special librarians; and the International Federation of Library Associations and Institutions (IFLA).[53]

An individual's response to situations is guided by a mix of standards or principles from various frames of reference. For example, one may operate within a set of religious or moral principles, legal requirements at the organizational level, and professional ethical standards. When these different frames lack coherence, the individual must decide which should predominate and guide behavior. When different sources or frames of reference for ethical behavior suggest different decisions or responses, the librarian must resolve the conflict in order to act. This is an individual decision. Occasionally, one may feel compelled to take an ethical stand that conflicts with one's employer. Situations in which the parent institution or community prescribes censorship of one form or another yet the librarian believes that intellectual freedom is being compromised are examples of personal and professional ethics in conflict with institutional ethics. Conversely, many libraries and librarians find personal and institutional values in conflict with tenets set forth in the Library Bill of Rights. One area of controversy is the bill's Article V: "A person's right to use a library should not be denied or abridged because of origin, age, background, or views." Research by Aiken published in 2007 found that nearly 51 percent of 110 public libraries responding to a survey did not permit free access for minors to nonprint materials.[54]

The challenge for librarians is dealing with what Adams calls the messy mix of local culture, local policies and procedures, competing community values, and administrators trying to be responsive to stakeholders.[55] Ethical dilemmas do not always have perfect solutions. The realities of day-to-day decisions and service policies should not be disconnected from the values and principles promoted by the library profession, but librarians should recognize that ethical principles must be applied "with a strong dose of reality."[56]

Censorship and Intellectual Freedom

Chapter 1 traces how the ideal of freedom to read came to replace a quite different ideology between 1876, when ALA endorsed the librarian as moral censor, and the 1940s, with ALA's first Library Bill of Rights. Librarians' attitudes toward censorship have changed in line with changing concepts of the public interest and of the library's democratic function. Intellectual freedom and free access to ideas are embodied in the First Amendment to the U.S. Constitution as a basic human right. The Library Bill of Rights continues to be an important statement for American librarians:

> The American Library Association affirms that all libraries are forums for information and ideas, and that the following basic policies should guide their services.

> I. Books and other library resources should be provided for the interest, information, and enlightenment of all people of the community the library serves. Materials should not be excluded because of the origin, background, or views of those contributing to their creation.

> II. Libraries should provide materials and information presenting all points of view on current and historical issues. Materials should not be proscribed or removed because of partisan or doctrinal disapproval.

> III. Libraries should challenge censorship in the fulfillment of their responsibility to provide information and enlightenment.

> IV. Libraries should cooperate with all persons and groups concerned with resisting abridgment of free expression and free access to ideas.

> V. A person's right to use a library should not be denied or abridged because of origin, age, background, or views.

> VI. Libraries which make exhibit spaces and meeting rooms available to the public they serve should make such facilities available on an equitable basis, regardless of the beliefs or affiliations of individuals or groups requesting their use.[57]

Ensuring intellectual freedom is a major focus of ALA, which maintains an Office for Intellectual Freedom and publishes the *Intellectual Freedom Manual*.[58] The Freedom to Read Foundation, a sister organization to ALA, was created to protect the freedoms of speech and press, with emphasis on First Amendment protection for libraries and library materials. The Foundation provides support and legal counsel to libraries whose collections are challenged.

An added challenge to intellectual freedom facing librarians is the public's concerns about ease of accessing questionable materials via the Internet.[59] ALA and many of its divisions have developed statements and various documents to address intellectual freedom and free access to information, particularly in relation to electronic information, including "Access to Digital Information, Services, and Networks: An Interpretation of the Library Bill of Rights," "Intellectual Freedom Principles for Academic Libraries: An Interpretation of the Library Bill of Rights," and "Access to Resources and Services in the School Library Media Program: An Interpretation of the Library Bill of Rights."[60]

ALA's "Freedom to Read" statement is a further iteration of librarians' commitment to free access to information and ideas:

1. It is in the public interest for publishers and librarians to make available the widest diversity of views and expressions, including those that are unorthodox, unpopular, or considered dangerous by the majority.

2. Publishers, librarians, and booksellers do not need to endorse every idea or presentation they make available. It would conflict with the public interest for them to establish their own political, moral, or aesthetic views as a standard for determining what should be published or circulated.

3. It is contrary to the public interest for publishers or librarians to bar access to writings on the basis of the personal history or political affiliations of the author.

4. There is no place in our society for efforts to coerce the taste of others, to confine adults to the reading matter deemed suitable for adolescents, or to inhibit the efforts of writers to achieve artistic expression.

5. It is not in the public interest to force a reader to accept the prejudgment of a label characterizing any expression or its author as subversive or dangerous.

6. It is the responsibility of publishers and librarians, as guardians of the people's freedom to read, to contest encroachments upon that freedom by individuals or groups seeking to impose their own standards or tastes upon the community at large; and by the government whenever it seeks to reduce or deny public access to public information.

7. It is the responsibility of publishers and librarians to give full meaning to the freedom to read by providing books that enrich the quality and diversity of thought and expression. By the exercise of this affirmative responsibility, they can demonstrate that the answer to a "bad" book is a good one, the answer to a "bad" idea is a good one.[61]

Librarians are charged with preventing censorship of collections and simultaneously ensuring freedom to read and access to diverse viewpoints within collections. Hauptman defines censorship as "the active suppression of books, journals, newspapers, theater pieces, lectures, discussions, radio and televisions programs, films, art works, etc.—either partially or in the entirety—that are deemed objectionable on moral, political, military, or other grounds."[62] In the name of intellectual freedom, librarians are encouraged to select, collect, and disseminate information without regard to race, sexual orientation, and other potential discriminators. Ideally, the guidelines for selecting materials are presented in a library's collection development policy, which can protect the library in the face of challenges. The goal is a diverse collection, representing all points of view, including the extreme. A collection is not diverse if it includes only majority, noncontroversial, inoffensive opinions.

Foerstel writes that the history of book censorship has consisted of the suppression of naughty stories.[63] Challenges on the grounds of immoral, obscene, or pornographic content are the most common, but other justifications, such as subversive political or social content, have been presented over the years. Challenges are more frequent in schools and school and public libraries. From 2000 through 2009 (the most recent compilation available), ALA recorded 5,099 attempts by groups or individuals to have books removed from library shelves and from classrooms.[64] Of these, 3,450 were in schools or school libraries, 1,217 in public libraries. In 2012, ALA logged 464 challenges and estimated that four or five times that number were made but not reported. The following list, compiled by the ALA Office for Intellectual Freedom, identifies the ten most frequently challenged books in 2012:

1. Captain Underpants (series), by Dav Pilkey
2. *The Absolutely True Diary of a Part-Time Indian*, by Sherman Alexie
3. *Thirteen Reasons Why*, by Jay Asher
4. *Fifty Shades of Grey*, by E. L. James
5. *And Tango Makes Three*, by Peter Parnell and Justin Richardson
6. *The Kite Runner*, by Khaled Hosseini
7. *Looking for Alaska*, by John Green
8. Scary Stories (series), by Alvin Schwartz
9. *The Glass Castle*, by Jeanette Walls
10. *Beloved*, by Toni Morrison

Types of Censorship

The first documented case of censorship in the American colonies resulted in a book burning in 1650. William Pynchon's *The Meritorious Price of Our Redemption*,

Justification, &c. was condemned as heresy by the Massachusetts General Court and ordered burned on the Boston Market Place.[65] Censorship comes in three varieties: mandated by the law, demanded by individuals or groups, and exercised by the librarian. Legal censorship occurs when national, state, or municipal legislation forbids access to materials deemed immoral or unacceptable (perhaps incendiary or subversive) under the law. Laws in the United States, notably the 1865 Mail Act and the 1873 Federal Anti-Obscenity Act, known as the Comstock Law, have sought to control access to "obscene," "lewd," "filthy," or "lascivious" publications by controlling the mailing and receiving of such materials. The problem lies in defining these terms. Such Supreme Court cases as *United States v. One Book Called "Ulysses"* (1934), *Roth v. United States* (1957), and *Miller v. California* (1973) have considered obscenity in relation to contemporary community standards and whether a work may be seen to have serious literary, artistic, political, or social value.[66] The Supreme Court has ruled that the states may prohibit the printing and sale of works that portray sexual conduct in an offensive manner. The emphasis has shifted to local standards. An important court case on book banning and the first heard by the Supreme Court involved books that the New York Island Tress School District Board of Education ordered removed from high school and junior high school libraries. The Court ruled in favor of the students who brought the suit, stating that the First Amendment protects the freedom of students of students to read and that "local school boards may not remove books from school libraries simply because they dislike the ideas contained in those books."[67] When librarians are presented with legislation requiring the removal of materials, they are seldom in a position to contest the law in court. More often, organizations such as the American Civil Liberties Union or ALA press a case.

Individuals and groups who challenge library materials may be parents, concerned citizens, school and library boards, religious and political organizations, or local politicians and police; in the early 1970s, for example, the Minneapolis city administration demanded that the public library remove the children's book *Sylvester and the Magic Pebble* (a Caldecott Medal winter) because the police were pigs, although the book showed anthropomorphic animals in other professions. Those objecting may seek to censor by banning books, severely limiting access, or labeling materials for special handling and restricted use. Most challenges revolve around sexual propriety, political views, religious beliefs, and the rights of minority groups (gays, lesbians, persons of color, atheists, etc.). Library publications such as *American Libraries, Library Journal*, and *Newsletter on Intellectual Freedom* regularly report on challenges to libraries around the United States.

Censorship frequently becomes an emotional issue and can divide a community because it develops out of personal beliefs, convictions, and value systems.

Censorship of material, particularly that of a pornographic or violent nature, available for children continues to have strong and articulate proponents.[68] A strong case grows out of the position that children are different from adults in their abilities to analyze conflicting visions of society and the extent to which they are affected by materials such as pornography or depictions of violence. Much of the discussion revolves around society's responsibility to protect minors and when legislation should be enacted to do so. The complication that attends this issue, as with all questionable materials, is reaching agreement on what constitutes pornographic and violent content and what has the potential to be harmful to minors.

Some censorship is unintentional and results from failure to select materials representing a pluralistic and diverse society. Librarians can protect against unintentional self-censorship by being conscious of and sensitive to diverse communities and viewpoints. Monitoring bibliographic tools, selection sources, and reviews can improve the multicultural and comprehensive nature of collection building. Quinn explores the role of bias, particularly cognitive (thought) and affective (feeling) aspects, which may affect librarians as they engage in collection development. He suggests that librarians can overcome their biases by "avoiding superficial thinking, challenging one's assumptions, actively seeking titles that disconfirm one's conventional beliefs, and avoiding associations from memory that may conform to one's biases."[69]

Intentional censorship or self-censorship by librarians is more troubling. Self-censorship can range from deciding not to buy a book to using book labeling, parental control requirements, or restricted rooms and shelves.[70] Personal values and standards, fears about potential challenges, or user complaints can lead a librarian to decide not to purchase a title, to limit access to an item, or to remove an item from the collection. When one's employment and source of income are at risk, pragmatism has a way of modifying one's values. Research over the years has demonstrated that, although librarians support the concept of intellectual freedom, many do not stand by these principles in the face of censorship pressures. Coley found that 82 percent of the high school librarians in his study group practiced self-censorship.[71] Some scholars writing on this dilemma have sought to get around it by emphasizing the selection process instead of the rejection process.[72] The challenge for librarians is distinguishing between self-censorship and careful selection of materials consistent with appropriate selection criteria.

Censorship should not be confused with refusing to spend limited funds unwisely, select materials inappropriate to the user community, or provide illegal or socially detrimental information. One easily can insist that a librarian should never censor or refuse to disseminate information. Nevertheless, all librarians are constrained to exclude some materials by their budgets, their professional values, and legislation. What is the judicious response when a high school student wants books on building pipe bombs, a white supremacist offers a free subscription of a racist newsletter to a public library, or those who deny the Holocaust insist the academic library purchase materials proving their point of view? When making decisions about material that is sexually explicit, racist, or dangerous to society, few librarians can take a neutral stance. They can only seek to exercise informed judgment. Free expression, intellectual freedom, and access to information must be protected, yet some materials are inappropriate and detrimental to certain user groups. The tension arises in determining what falls within these categories.

Censorship and the Internet

Providing Internet access in libraries brings new concerns about censorship and debates over the responsibility of librarians to select what users can and cannot access. School and public libraries receive frequent demands that blocking or filtering software be installed on library computers that access the Internet. One problem with filtering software is that useful sites can be blocked along with objectionable ones. State and federal legislation has been passed and court cases have been filed on both sides of the issue. A significant judgment was made in 1997 in *Reno v. American Civil Liberties Union* (Reno I), when the Supreme Court unanimously declared that the federal Communications Decency Act (CDA) was unconstitutional.[73] That law made it a crime to send or display indecent material online in a way available to minors. The Court held that the Internet is not comparable to broadcasting and instead, like books and newspapers, receives the highest level of First Amendment protection. Following Reno I, Congress passed the Child Online Protection Act (COPA), which sought to avoid the constitutional issues raised in the CDA. A federal district court in the case *American Civil Liberties Union v. Reno* (Reno II) determined that COPA was flawed in similar ways to CDA.[74]

The Children's Internet Protection Act (CIPA) and the Neighborhood Internet Protection Act (NCIPA) went into effect in 2001.[75] These laws place restrictions on the use of funds available through the LSTA, Title III of the Elementary and Secondary Education Act, and the Universal Service discount program known as the E-rate (Public Law 106-554). They require public libraries and schools to install filters on their Internet computers to retain federal funding and discounts for computers and computer access. Because CIPA directly affected libraries and their ability to make legal information freely available to their patrons, ALA and the Freedom to Read Foundation filed a lawsuit to overturn CIPA. In 2002, the Eastern District Court of Pennsylvania held CIPA to be unconstitutional and ruled Sections 1712(a)(2) and 1721(b) of CIPA to be facially invalid under the First Amendment. The court permanently enjoined the government from enforcing those provisions. Public libraries thus are not required to install filters on their computers in order to receive federal funds. The court held the CIPA statute to be unconstitutional because mandated filtering on all computers results in blocked access to substantial amounts of constitutionally protected speech. The Justice Department, acting on behalf of the Federal Communications Commission and the U.S. Institute of Museum and Library Sciences, appealed this ruling.

In June 2003, the Supreme Court reversed the district court's decision and rejected the plaintiffs' facial challenge to CIPA.[76] The stakes of ALA's case were lowered when the government promised, in the course of litigation, that libraries could, and would, remove the filters if users asked them to do so. It also promised that users would not have to explain why they were making the request. Although six justices voted to uphold CIPA, there was no majority opinion for the Court. The plurality opinion, authored by Chief Justice William Hubbs Rehnquist, was joined by three other justices (Sandra Day O'Connor, Antonin Scalia, and Clarence Thomas). Because it did not have the support of five justices, the reasoning of the plurality opinion is not controlling. Justices Anthony M. Kennedy and Stephen Breyer each wrote concurring opinions upholding CIPA against the plaintiff's facial challenge but on narrower grounds than those stated in the plurality opinion. In cases where no single opinion has the support of the majority of the justices, the narrow concurring opinions typically govern future interpretations and the precedential effect of the case.[77]

The dilemma is that filters can both overblock (block access to protected speech) and underblock (allow access to illegal or unconstitutional speech). The latter is of particular concern when libraries are perceived as violating obscenity, child pornography, and harmful-to-minors statutes or permitting user activities that create a hostile work environment. Libraries can face liability for installing content-based filtering software or for failing to install it. When librarians specifically select and point to Internet resources, they apply the appropriate criteria for quality, authenticity, and so forth. However, "open" Internet access is a much more complex issue.[78] As the Internet expands and the number of public and school libraries with Internet access increases, this issue will continue to trouble librarians and their user communities.

Responding to Complaints and Challenges to Materials

The best defense against challenges to a library collection is prior preparation. This begins with a written collection development policy. Many libraries post the ALA Library Bill of Rights in a public place and use additional methods to promote their commitment to intellectual freedom. ALA's Office for Intellectual Freedom (www.ala.org/oif) and many organizations provide advice and assistance in case of attempted censorship. These include the National Council of Teachers of English Anti-Censorship Center (www.ncte.org/action/anti-censorship), state educational and library associations, and the American Civil Liberties Union (www.aclu.org). Notifying the material's publisher may be helpful, because the publisher may have assembled information in response to previous challenges.

The library should have a process for handling complaints, and staff members should be familiar with it. ALA's *Intellectual Freedom Manual* contains guidelines for developing a local process.[79] Many libraries provide a template or form that can be used to request an item be removed from the collection. The form provides space for an individual's name and contact information, title and bibliographic information about the item, and what the concerns are. It also may ask if the individual is representing him- or herself or an organization. Some forms ask if the individual can suggest alternative resources that provide additional information or other viewpoints.

Dickinson makes a careful distinction between "questioned" and "challenged" materials.[80] A library item is questioned when a parent, citizen, administrator, teacher, or staff person expresses concern. This is often an emotional stage and requires a calm response by the librarian, who should notify the school principal or library director. Sometimes an informal complaint can be resolved by referring to the collection development policy or selection criteria, or by suggesting alternative materials. Only when the proper form (sometimes called a "Request for Reconsideration Form") is submitted is an item considered officially challenged. Ideally, this initiates a formal review process by a committee, which may be at the school level, the school district level, and in the case of public libraries the library or library system level. Following the authorized and board-approved process for reviewing challenges is critical in order to treat all challenges fairly and to avoid legal consequences. The librarian role at this point is to present the facts for the committee's deliberation, including criteria for selecting the item, how it meets these criteria, and (when pertinent) quotations from reviews—and let the committee complete its work.

Working with Suppliers and Vendors

Collections librarians can face ethical issues in their relationships with suppliers and vendors. Librarians often develop a congenial relationship with supplier and vendor representatives, fostered by pleasant lunches and conference receptions. This is one reason many libraries and their parent institutions prohibit or place financial limits on the gifts and personal benefits librarians may accept. Librarians should not permit a personal desire to be nice to representatives interfere with an ethical obligation to manage institutional resources as effectively as possible. Though librarians have an obligation to be honest and fair and to act in good faith with suppliers, they have no obligation to help them succeed. Librarians should keep the financial and service interests of their libraries foremost, seeking to obtain the maximum value for each purchase, license agreement, and service contract.

Another frame of reference may be explicitly or implicitly provided by the library and its parent institution. One university has issued a document called "Code of Ethics for Department Staff Responsible for Buying," which makes explicit the institution's expectations and values when negotiating with an external supplier. In the terms of this agreement, the employee agrees to "support and uphold the values, policies, and procedures of the University in all my purchasing activities . . . , maintain a high level of ethics, have no financial or personal beneficial interest directly or indirectly with vendors when I am in a position to influence the University decision to purchase from those vendors, . . . [and] strive to obtain the maximum value for each purchase."[81] Implicit guidance supplements explicit guidelines and codes and is modeled through the behavior of administrators, managers, and peers. Values are conveyed through actions as well as written statements.

A history of friendly relations between librarian and vendor or supplier is not the issue. Each service and purchase agreement must be reviewed while evaluating all available information. Each agreement must be continually assessed as a business decision, and the needs of the library must be placed first. A librarian must keep in mind the long-term interests of the communities these purchasing decisions affect. One must have the ethical convictions and courage to place these interests above any personal short-term preoccupations. A binder who cannot provide high-quality binding at market prices should not be retained as the library's binder, no matter how long the relationship has continued. A subscription agent who has a cash flow problem and fails to pay publishers is not a reliable agent with a promising future. No matter how gracious and charming a service agency's representatives are or how competently the agency has performed in the past, future performance and financial viability are the deciding factors.

Librarians' ethical obligations are twofold: to conduct business with mutual respect and trust, and to serve their own organizations as best they can. Explicit and implicit codes aim for high standards of professional conduct and integrity and value honesty, trustworthiness, respect, and fairness in dealing with other people and loyalty toward the ethical principles, values, policies, and procedures espoused by a librarian's institution. Librarians have an obligation to consistently demonstrate and carefully maintain a tradition of ethical behavior.

CASE STUDY

Stacy is responsible for collection development and technical services in the library at Smallville College. The library serves 3,000 undergraduates, 225 full-time faculty, and 115 part-time faculty. Stacy has oversight of the collections budget and works diligently to be a good steward of an allocation that never seems to be quite sufficient. The library uses a large domestic book vendor, with which it has an approval plan. This vendor supplies most of the libraries' monographs, either as part of the approval plan or through individual orders. This vendor gives a predetermined discount on most books it supplies to the Smallville library. The discount is based on total expenditures in the previous year. Occasionally, out-of-print (OP) books are ordered from a dealer, who also sells new imprints. The OP dealer does not give a discount. Eric, a paraprofessional in the technical services unit, places the book orders with the appropriate supplier. Stacy has just discovered that Eric is directing a portion of orders for new books to the OP dealer. When questioned, Eric's justification is that the OP dealer works conscientiously to provide the OP books, which can be challenging to locate. Eric feels the OP dealer deserves a break and sending orders for easy-to-supply current imprints is a way to reward the OP dealer for hard work. Eric takes pride in his fair treatment of suppliers, which he sees as ensuring continuing good service. Stacy has scheduled a meeting with Eric to discuss appropriate order placement.

Activity

Describe the professional ethics and personal values in conflict in this situation. What is at stake if Eric continues his current practice of sending a few easy orders to the OP dealer? What is at risk if he stops? Describe the appropriate course of action for Stacy and suggest the issues she should address in her meeting with Eric.

Notes

1. Michael Gorman, *Our Enduring Values: Librarianship in the 21st Century* (Chicago: American Library Association, 2000), 23.

2. See Robert B. Harmon, *Elements of Bibliography: A Guide to Information Sources and Practical Applications*, 3rd ed. (Lanham, MD: Scarecrow, 1998), for an introduction to the art of bibliography.

3. Sara E. Morris and Darcy Del Bosque, "Forgotten Resources: Subject Guides in the Era of Web 2.0," *Technical Services Quarterly* 27, no. 2 (2010): 178–93; Jim M. Kapoun, "Re-Thinking the Library Pathfinder," *College and Undergraduate Libraries 2*, no. 1 (1995): 93–105; Nancy R. Glassman and Karen Sorensen, "From Pathfinders to Subject Guides: One Library's Experience with LibGuides," *Journal of Electronic Resources in Medical Libraries* 7, no. 4 (2010): 281–91.

4. Catherine Gibson, "'But We've Always Done It This Way!' Centralized Selection Five Years Later," in *Public Library Collection Development in the Information Age*, ed. Annabel K. Stephens (Binghamton, NY: Haworth, 1998), 33–40; Phyllis Sue Alpert, "Effect of Multiculturalism and Automation in Public Library Collection Development and Technical Services," in *Current Practices in Public Libraries*, ed. William Miller and Pita M. Pellen (Binghamton, NY: Haworth, 2006), 91–104.

5. Juris Dilevko, "An Alternative Vision of Librarianship: James Danky and the Socio-cultural Politics of Collection Development," *Library Trends* 56, no. 3 (2008): 678–704.

6. Cynthia Orr, "Collection Development in Public Libraries," *Encyclopedia of Library and Information Science*, 3rd ed., ed. Marcia J. Bates and Mary Niles Maack (New York: Taylor and Francis, 2010), 1097–1105.

7. W. Bernard Lukenbill, *Collection Development for a New Century in the School Library Media Center* (Westport, CT: Greenwood, 2002).

8. Lesley Farmer, "SLJ's Spending Survey: As the Economy Limps Along and Federal Dollars Dwindle, School Librarians Are Turning into Resourceful Survivors," *School Library Journal* 57, no. 3 (2011): 42–47.

9. Margaret Maes Axtmann, "The Best of Times, the Worst of Times: Collection Development in the 21st Century," *AALL Spectrum* 6, no. 3 (Nov. 2001): 6–7.

10. Special Library Association, "Competencies for Information Professionals of the 21st Century," rev. ed. (June 2003), www.sla.org/about-sla/competencies.

11. Susan S. DiMattia, "Special Librarianship," *Encyclopedia of Library and Information Sciences*, 3rd ed., ed. Marcia J. Bates and Mary Niles Maack (New York: Taylor and Frances, 2011), 4956–65.

12. Ross Housewright, "Themes of Change in Corporate Libraries: Considerations for Academic Libraries," *portal: Libraries and the Academy* 9, no. 2 (2009): 253–71.

13. J. Periam Danton, "The Subject Specialist in National and University Libraries, with Special Reference to Book Selection," *Libri* 17, no. 1 (1967): 42–58.

14. Russell Duino, "Role of the Subject Specialist in British and American University Libraries: A Comparative Study," *Libri* 29, no. 1 (1979): 1–19.

15. See Robert Neville, James Williams III, and Caroline C. Hunt, "Faculty-Library Teamwork in Book Ordering," *College and Research Libraries* 59, no. 6 (Nov. 1998): 523–32, for a comparison of how faculty in different disciplines are involved in selection.

16. Susanne K. Clement and Jennifer Foy, *Collection Development in a Changing Environment: Policies and Organization for College and University Libraries*, CLIP Note no. 42 (Chicago: Association of College and Research Libraries, 2010).

17. John Haar, "Scholar or Librarian? How Academic Libraries' Dualistic Concept of the Bibliographer Affects Recruitment," *Collection Building* 13, no. 1/2 (1993): 18–23.

18. Eldred R. Smith, "The Impact of the Subject Specialist Librarian on the Organization and Structure of the Academic Research Library," in *The Academic Library: Essays in Honor of Guy R. Lyle*, ed. Evan Ira Farber and Ruth Walling (Metuchen, NJ: Scarecrow, 1974), 71–81.

19. Gail F. Latta, *Liaison Services in ARL Libraries*, SPEC Kit no. 189 (Washington, DC: Association of Research Libraries, 1992).

20. "A Special Issue on Liaison Librarian Roles," *Research Library Issues: A Bimonthly Report from ARL, CNI, and SPARC*, no. 265 (Aug. 2009), http://publications.arl .org/rli265; Janice Jaguszewski and Karen Williams, *New Roles for New Times: Transforming Liaison Roles in Research Libraries* (Washington, DC: Association of Research Libraries, 2013), www.arl.org/storage/documents/publications/NRNT -Liaison-Roles-final.pdf. Lorcan Dempsey, "In the Flow," *Lorcan Dempsey's Weblog* (blog), June 24, 2005, http://orweblog.oclc.org/archives/000688.html.

21. John Rodwell and Linden Fairbairn, "Dangerous Liaisons? Defining the Faculty Liaison Librarian Service Model, Its Effectiveness, and Sustainability," *Library Management* 29, no. 1/2 (2008): 123.

22. References and User Services Association, "Guidelines for Liaison Work in Managing Collections and Services" (rev. approved by the RUSA Board of Directors, March 2010), www.ala.org/rusa/files/resources/guidelines/liaison -guidelines-3.pdf, 1.

23. Julie Arendt and Megan Lotts, "What Liaisons Say about Themselves and What Faculty Say about Their Liaisons, a U.S. Survey," *portal: Libraries and the Academy* 12, no. 2 (Apr. 2012): 155–77.

24. Paul Metz, "Quantifying the Workload of Subject Bibliographers in Collection Development," *Journal of Academic Librarianship* 17, no. 5 (1991): 284–87.

25. American Library Association, *ALA's Core Competences of Librarianship* (final version approved by the ALA Executive Board, Oct. 25, 2008; approved and adopted as policy by the ALA Council, Jan. 27, 2009), www.ala.org/ala/educationcareers/careers/corecomp/corecompetences/finalcorecompstat09.pdf.

26. Special Library Association, "Competencies for Information Professionals."

27. Association for Library Service to Children, "Competencies for Librarians Serving Children in Public Libraries" (created by the ALSC Education Committee, 1989; revised by the ALSC Education Committee: 1999, 2009; approved by the ALSC Board of Directors at the 2009 American Library Association Annual Conference), www.ala.org/alsc/edcareeers/alsccorecomps.

28. George L. Soete, "Training for Success: Integrating the New Bibliographer into the Library," in *Recruiting, Educating, and Training Librarians for Collection Development*, ed. Peggy Johnson and Sheila S. Intner (Westport, CT: Greenwood, 1994), 160–69.

29. John M. Budd and Patricia L. Bril, "Education for Collection Management: Results of a Survey of Educators and Practitioners," *Library Resources and Technical Services* 38, no. 4 (Oct. 1994): 343–53; Lois Buttlar and Rosemary Du Mont, "Library and Information Science Competencies Revisited," *Journal of Education for Library and Information Studies*, 37, no. 1 (1996): 44–62.

30. See, for example, Christopher Cipkin and David Stacey, "Reflecting Roles: Being a Successful Subject Liaison Librarian in a Changing Environment," *SNOLUL Focus* 45 (2009): 27–30; Jim Martin and Raik Zaghloul, "Planning for the Acquisition of Information Resources Management Core Competencies," *New World Library* 112 (2011): 313–20; Sandy Hirsh, "Preparing Future Professionals through Broad Competency Planning," *Information Outlook* 16, no. 1 (Jan./Feb. 2012): 9–11.

31. Peter M. Senge, *The Fifth Discipline: The Art and Practice of the Learning Organization*, rev. ed. (New York: Doubleday, 2006).

32. Lee G. Bolman and Terrence E. Deal, *Reframing Organizations: Artistry, Choice, and Leadership*, 4th ed. (San Francisco: Jossey-Bass, 2008). ix–x.

33. Collection Management and Development Committee, Resources and Technical Services Division, American Library Association, *Guide for Writing a Bibliographer's Manual*, Collection Management and Development Guides 1 (Chicago: American Library Association, 1987).

34. Susan L. Fales, ed., *Guide for Training Collection Development Librarians*, Collection Management and Development Guides 8 (Chicago: Association for Library Collections and Technical Services, American Library Association, 1996).

35. Jack Siggins, comp., *Performance Appraisal of Collection Development Librarians*, SPEC Kit no. 181 (Washington, DC: Association of Research Libraries, 1992).

36. Harry Braverman, *Labor and Monopoly Capital: The Degradation of Work in the Twentieth Century* (New York: Monthly Review, 1974).

37. Shoshana Zuboff, *In the Age of the Smart Machine: The Future of Work and Power* (New York: Basic Books, 1988); Jannis Kallinikos, "The 'Age of Smart Machine': A 21st Century View," *Encyclopedia of Software Engineering*, ed. Phillip A. Laplante (Boca Raton, FL: Auerbach, Taylor, and Francis, 2011), 1–7, http://personal.lse .ac.uk/kallinik/NEW/IntheAgeof_the_SmartmachineFinal.pdf.

38. Ulrich Heisig, "The Deskilling and Upskilling Debate," in *International Handbook of Education for the Changing World of Work: Bridging Academic and Vocation Learning*, ed. Rupert MacLean and David Wilson (New York: Springer, 2009), 1639–65, quote 1642.

39. John Scott and Gordon Marshall, *A Dictionary of Sociology*, 3rd rev. ed. (Oxford, UK: Oxford University Press, 2009); Craig Calhoun, ed., *Dictionary of the Social Sciences* (Oxford, UK: Oxford University Press, 2002).

40. See Gillian S. Gremmels, "Staffing Trends in College and University Libraries," *Reference Services Review* 41, no. 2 (2013): 233–52, for an analysis of this movement in academic libraries.

41. Lihong Zhu, "The Role of Paraprofessionals in Technical Services in Academic Libraries," *Library Resources and Technical Services* 56, no. 3 (Apr. 2012): 127–54.

42. Michael A. Keller, "Late Awakenings: Recruiting Subject Specialists to Librarianship and Collection Development," in *Recruiting, Educating, and Training Librarians for Collection Development*, ed. Peggy Johnson and Sheila S. Intner (Westport, CT: Greenwood, 1994), 45–68.

43. Allen B. Veaner, "Paradigm Lost, Paradigm Regained? A Persistent Personnel Issue in Academic Librarianship, II," *College and Research Libraries* 55, no. 5 (1994): 393–94.

44. Bonita Bryant, "The Organizational Structure of Collection Development," *Library Resources and Technical Services* 31, no. 2 (Apr. 1987): 111–22.

45. Brian Quinn, "The Psychology of Group Decision Making in Collection Development," *Library Collections, Acquisitions, and Technical Services* 32, no. 1 (2008): 10–18.

46. Rowley and Rounds, *Organization of Collection Development*, from unpaged prefatory materials.

47. Nancy Courtney and Fred W. Jenkins, "Reorganizing Collection Development and Acquisitions in a Medium-Sized Academic Library," *Library Acquisitions: Practice and Theory* 22, no. 3 (1998): 287–93; Kathleen Wachel and Edward Shreeves, "An Alliance between Acquisitions and Collection Management," *Library Acquisitions: Practice and Theory* 16, no. 4 (1992): 383–89.

48. Jasper G. Schad, "Managing Collection Development in University Libraries That Utilize Librarians with Dual-Responsibility Assignments," *Library Acquisitions: Practice and Theory* 14, no. 2 (1990): 165–71.

49. Gorman, *Our Enduring Values*.

50. Bolman and Deal, *Reframing Organizations*.

51. American Library Association, "Code of Ethics of the American Library Association" (adopted at the 1939 Midwinter Meeting by the ALA Council; amended June 30, 1981; June 28, 1995; and January 22, 2008), www.ala.org/advocacy/proethics/codeofethics/codeethics; American Library Association, "The Freedom to Read Statement" (adopted June 25, 1953, by the ALA Council and the Association of American Publishers Freedom to Read Committee; amended January 28, 1972; January 16, 1991; July 12, 2000; June 30, 2004), www.ala .org/advocacy/intfreedom/statementspols/freedomreadstatement; American Library Association, "The Freedom to View Statement" (endorsed January 10, 1990, by the ALA Council), www.ala.org/advocacy/intfreedom/statementspols/freedomviewstatement.

52. Association for Library Collections and Technical Services, "Guidelines for ALCTS Members to Supplement the American Library Association Code of Ethics" (developed by the ALCTS Task Force on Professional Ethics and adopted by the ALCTS Board of Directors, Midwinter Meeting, February 7, 1994), www.ala.org/alcts/resources/alaethics.

53. Association of College and Research Libraries, Rare Books and Manuscripts Section, "ACRL Code of Ethics for Special Collections Librarians" (first appeared in 1987; a second edition of the Standards was approved by ACRL in 1993. This version was approved by ACRL in Oct. 2003), www.rbms.info/standards/code_of_ethics.shtml; Association for Library Collections and Technical Services, "Statement on Principles and Standards of Acquisitions Practice" (developed by the ALCTS Acquisitions Section Ethics Task Force; endorsed by the ALCTS Acquisitions Section and adopted by the ALCTS Board of Directors Feb. 7, 1994), www.ala.org/advocacy/proethics/explanatory/acquisitions; American Association of Law Libraries, "AALL Ethical Principles" (approved by the AALL membership, Apr. 5, 1999), www.aallnet.org/main-menu/Leadership-Governance/policies/PublicPolicies/policy-ethics.html; Medical Library Association, "Code of Ethics for Health Sciences Librarianship" (2010), www.mlanet.org/about/ethics.html; Special Libraries Association, "SLA Professional Ethics Guidelines" (approved by the SLA Board of Directors, Dec. 2010), www.sla.org/about-sla/competencies/sla-professional-ethics-guidelines/; International Federation of Library Associations and Institutions, "IFLA Code of Ethics for Librarians and Other Information Workers (full version)," (Aug. 12, 2012), www.ifla.org/news/ifla-code-of-ethics-for-librarians-and-other-information-workers-full-version.

54. Julian Aiken, "Outdated and Irrelevant? Rethinking the Library Bill of Rights—Does It Work in the Real World?" *American Libraries* 38, no. 8 (Sept. 2007): 54–56.

55. Helen R. Adams, "Reflections on Ethics in Practice," *Knowledge Quest* 37, no. 3 (Jan./Feb. 2009): 66–69.

56. Carol Simpson, "School Library Ethics: A Battle of Hats," *Library Media Connection* 22, no. 4 (Jan. 2004): 23.

57. American Library Association, "Library Bill of Rights" (adopted June 19, 1939, by the ALA Council; amended Oct. 14, 1944; June 18, 1948; Feb. 2, 1961; June 27, 1967; Jan. 23, 1980; inclusion of "age" reaffirmed Jan. 23, 1996.), www.ala.org/advocacy/intfreedom/librarybill.

58. American Library Association, Office for Intellectual Freedom, *Intellectual Freedom Manual*, 8th ed. (Chicago: American Library Association, 2010).

59. Barbara A. Jones, *Libraries, Access, and Intellectual Freedom: Developing Policies for Public and Academic Libraries* (Chicago: American Library Association, 1999).

60. American Library Association, "Access to Digital Information, Services, and Networks: An Interpretation of the Library Bill of Rights" (adopted Jan. 24, 1996, amended Jan. 19, 2005; and July 15, by the ALA Council), www.ala.org/advocacy/intfreedom/librarybill/interpretations/accessdigital; Association of College and Research Libraries, "Intellectual Freedom Principles for Academic Libraries" (approved by ACRL Intellectual Freedom Committee June 28, 199; approved by ACRL Board of Directors June 29, 1999; adopted by ALA Council July 12, 2000), www.ala.org/acrl/publications/whitepapers/intellectual; American Library Association, "Access to Resources and Services in the School Library Media Program: An Interpretation of the Library Bill of Rights" (adopted July 2, 1986 by the ALA Council; amended Jan. 10, 1990; July 12, 2000; January 19, 2005), www.ala.org/advocacy/intfreedom/librarybill/interpretations/accessresources.

61. American Library Association, "The Freedom to Read Statement" (adopted June 25, 1953, by the ALA Council and the Association of American Publishers Freedom to Read Committee; amended January 28, 1972; January 16, 1991; July 12, 2000; June 30, 2004), www.ala.org/advocacy/intfreedom/statementspols.

62. Robert Hauptman, *Ethical Challenges in Librarianship* (Phoenix, AZ: Oryx, 1988), 66.

63. Herbert N. Foerstel, *Banned in the Media: A Reference Guide to Censorship in the Press, Motion Pictures, Broadcasting, and the Internet* (Westport, CT: Greenwood, 1998), 2.

64. American Library Association, "Frequently Challenged Books of the 21st Century," www.ala.org/bbooks/frequentlychallengedbooks/top10#2012.

65. Samuel Eliot Morison, *William Pynchon, the Founder of Springfield* (Boston: Massachusetts Historical Society, 1932).

66. *United States v. One Book Called "Ulysses,"* 5 F. Supp. 182 (S.D.N.Y. 1933), affirmed 72 F. 2d 705 (2d Cir. 1934); *Roth v. United States,* 354 U.S. 476 (1957); *Miller v. California,* 413 U.S. 15 (1973).

67. *Board of Ed., Island Tress Union Free School Dist. No. 26 v. Steven A. Pico et al.* 457 US. 853 (1982).

68. Kevin W. Saunders, "The Government Should Help Parents Shield Children from Obscene and Violent Materials," in *Censorship*, ed. Julia Baudered (Detroit: Thomson Gale, 2007), 164–187.

69. Brian Quinn, "Collection Development and the Psychology of Bias," *Library Quarterly* 82, no. 3 (July 2012): 277–304, quote 300.

70. Rebecca Hill, "The Problem of Self-Censorship," *School Library Monthly* 27, no. 2 (Nov. 2010): 9–12.

71. See Frances B. MacDonald, *Censorship and Intellectual Freedom: A Survey of School Librarians, Attitudes, and Moral Reasoning* (Metuchen, NJ: Scarecrow, 1993); Andrea E. Niosi, "An Investigation of Censorship and Selection in Southern California Public Libraries," *Public Libraries* 37, no. 5 (Sept./Oct. 1998): 310–15; Ken P. Coley, "Moving toward a Method to Test for Self-Censorship by School Library Media Specialists," *School Library Media Research* 5 (2002), www.ala.org/aasl/aaslpubsandjournals/slmrb/slmrcontents/volume52002/coley.

72. Lester E. Asheim, "The Librarian's Responsibility: Not Censorship, but Selection," in *Freedom of Book Selection: Proceedings of the Second Conference on Intellectual Freedom, Whittier, California, June 20–21, 1953*, ed. Fredric J. Mosher (Chicago: American Library Association, 1954), 90–99.

73. *Reno v. American Civil Liberties Union*, 521 U.S. 844 (1997).

74. *American Civil Liberties Union v. Reno*, 31 F. Supp. 2d 473 (E. D. Pa. 1999).

75. Children's Internet Protection Act, 106th Cong. 1st sess. (2000), Public Law 106–554, Title XVII (Dec. 21, 2000), www.sos.mo.gov/library/cipa/106_cong_public_laws.pdf; Neighborhood Children's Internet Protection Act (NCIPA) is Subtitle C of the Children's Internet Protection Act.

76. *United States v. American Library Association*, 539 U.S. 1903 (2003).

77. Opinions on CIPA can be found at the American Library Association website devoted to the Children's Internet Protection Act, www.ala.org/advocacy/advleg/federallegislation/cipa.

78. For in-depth analyses of censorship and Internet access, see Marjorie Heins, Christina Cho, and Ariel Feldman, *Internet Filters: A Public Policy Report*, 2nd ed., Brennan Center for Justice, NYU School of Law, 2006), www.fepproject.org/policyreports/filters2.pdf; American Library Association, Office of Intellectual Freedom, "Filters and Filtering," www.ala.org/advocacy/intfreedom/filtering.

79. American Library Association, *Intellectual Freedom Manual*.

80. Gail Dickinson, "The Challenges of Challenges: Understanding and Being Prepared." *School Library Media Activities Monthly* 23, no. 5 (Jan. 2007): 26–8l; and Dickinson, "The Challenges of Challenges: What to Do?" *School Library Media Activities Monthly* 23, no. 6 (Feb. 2007): 21–24.

81. University of Minnesota, "Code of Ethics for Department Staff Responsible for Buying," www.policy.umn.edu/prod/groups/president/@pub/@forms/ @procurement/documents/form/codeofethics.pdf.

Suggested Readings

General

Arendt, Julie, and Megan Lotts. "What Liaisons Say about Themselves and What Faculty Say about Their Liaisons: A U.S. Survey." *portal: Libraries and the Academy* 12, no. 2 (Apr. 2012): 155–77.

Besnoy, Amy L., ed. *Ethics and Integrity in Libraries*. London: Routledge, 2009.

Bogel, Gayle. "School Librarian's Bill of Responsibilities and the ALA Core Competences." *Knowledge Quest* 38, no. 2 (Nov./Dec. 2009): 66–68.

Buchanan, Elizabeth. *Case Studies in Library and Information Science Ethics*. Jefferson, NC: McFarland, 2009.

Chu, Heting. "Library and Information Science Education in the Digital Age." *Advances in Librarianship* 32 (2010): 77–110.

Cooker, Louise, et al. "Evaluating the Impact of Academic Liaison Librarians on Their User Community: A Review and Case Study." *New Review of Academic Librarianship* 17, no. 1 (2011): 5–30.

Crawford, Alice. *New Directions for Academic Liaison Librarians*. Oxford, UK: Chandos, 2012.

Crossno, Jon E., et al. "A Case Study: The Evolution of a 'Facilitator Model' Liaison Program in an Academic Medical Library." *Journal of the Medical Library Association*." 100, no. 3 (July 2012): 171–75.

Dobbs, Aaron W., Ryan L. Sittler, and Douglas Cook, eds. *Using LibGuides to Enhance Library Services: A LITA Guide*. Chicago: American Library Association, 2013.

Dole, Wanda V., and Jitka M. Hurych. "Using Kidder's Dilemma Paradigm to Resolve Conflicts in Library Core Values." *New Library World* 110, no. 9/10 (2009): 449–56.

Ehrlich, Evelyn, and Angela Carreño. "The Changing Role of the Subject Specialist Librarian." In *Interdisciplinarity and Academic Libraries*, ed. Daniel C. Mack and Craig Gibson, 145–66. ACRL Publications in Librarianship 66. Chicago: American Library Association, 2012.

Foster, Catherine, and David McMenemy. "Do Librarians Have a Shared Set of Values? A Comparative Study of 36 Codes of Ethics Based on Gorman's *Enduring Values*." *Journal of Librarianship and Information Science* 44, no. 4 (2012): 249–62.

Hales, Karen, Randall Ward, and Annalaura Brown. "Liaison Efforts at a Small Business College." *Community and Junior College Libraries* 15, no. 4 (2009): 204–11.

Henry, Jo. "Academic Library Liaison Programs: Four Case Studies." *Library Review* 61, no. 7 (2012): 485–96.

Holden, Jesse. *Acquisitions in the New Information Universe: Core Competencies and Ethical Practices*. New York: Neal-Schuman, 2010.

Hooper, Brad. *Writing Reviews for Readers' Advisory*. Chicago: American Library Association, 2010.

Jackson, Millie. *Subject Specialists in the 21st Century*. Oxford, UK: Chandos, 2010.

Kendrick, Kaetrena Davis, and Echo Leaver. "Impact of the Code of Ethics on Workplace Behavior in Academic Libraries." *Journal of Information Ethics* 20, no. 1 (Spring 2011): 86–112.

Lenz, Connie, and Helen Wohl. "Does Form Follow Function? Academic Law Libraries' Organizational Structures for Collection Development." *Law Library Journal* 100, no. 1 (2008): 59–116.

Maatta, Stephanie L. *A Few Good Books: Using Contemporary Readers' Advisory Strategies to Connect Readers with Books*. New York: Neal Schuman, 2010.

Martin, Ann M. "Leadership: Integrity and the ALA Code of Ethics." *Knowledge Quest* 37, no. 3 (Jan./Feb. 2009): 6–11.

Martin, Jim, and Raik Zaghloul. "Planning for the Acquisition of Information Resources Management Core Competencies." *New Library World* 112, no. 7/8 (2011): 313–20.

Mathiesen, Kay, and Don Fallis. "Information Ethics and the Library Profession." In *The Handbook of Information and Computer Ethics*, ed. Kenneth Einar Himma and Herman T. Tavani, 221–244. Hoboken, NJ: John Wiley, 2008.

Morrisey, Locke J. "Ethical Issues in Collection Development." *Journal of Library Administration* 47, no. 3/4 (2008): 163–71.

Moyer, Jessica E., and Amanda Blau, eds. *Research-Based Readers' Advisory*. Chicago: American Library Association, 2008.

Moyer, Jessica E., and Kaite Mediatore Stover, eds. *The Readers' Advisory Handbook*. Chicago: American Library Association, 2010.

Noddings, Nel. "The Language of Care Ethics." *Knowledge Quest* 40, no. 4 (May/June 2012): 52–56.

Peck, Penny. *Readers' Advisory for Children and 'Tweens*. Santa Barbara, CA: Libraries Unlimited, 2010.

Preer, Jean. *Library Ethics*. Westport, CT: Libraries Unlimited, 2008.

Rodwell, John, and Linden Fairbairn. "Dangerous Liaisons? Defining the Faculty Liaison Library Service Model, Its Effectiveness, and Sustainability." *Library Management* 29, no. 1/2 (2008): 116–24.

Roth, Dana L. "The Future of Librarianship in Science and Technology Libraries." *Sci-Tech News* 64, no. 3 (2010). http://jdc.jefferson.edu/scitechnews/vol64/iss3/4.

Rubin, Richard, and Thomas J. Froehlich. "Ethical Aspects of Library and Information Science." In *Encyclopedia of Library and Information Sciences*, 3rd ed., ed. Marcia J. Bates and Mary Niles Maack, 1743–57. New York: Taylor and Francis, 2011.

Ryan, Mary L. "Does It Really Matter Who's Paying for Dinner?" *Journal of the Medical Library Association* 98, no. 1 (Jan. 2010): 1–3.

Shen, Lan. "Improving the Effectiveness of Librarian-Faculty Collaboration on Library Collection Development." *Collaborative Librarianship* 4, no. 1 (2012). www.collaborativelibrarianship.org/index.php/jocl/article/download/168/126.

Thomas, Joseph. "A Beginner's Guide to Working with Vendors." In *The E-resources Management Handbook*. Oxford, U.K.: UK Serials Group, 2006– (continually updated). http://uksg.metapress.com/content/j5387n5h756wk562/fulltext.pdf.

Wisneski, Richard. "Collection Development Assessment for New Collection Development Librarians." *Collection Management* 33, no. 1/2 (2008): 143–59.

Censorship and Intellectual Freedom

Adams, Helen R. "The Materials Selection Policy: Defense against Censorship." *School Library Media Activities Monthly* 24, no. 7 (Mar. 2008): 28.

———. "Preparing for and Facing a Challenge in a School Library." *Catholic Library World* 81, no. 2 (Dec. 2010): 113–17.

———. *Protecting Intellectual Freedom and Privacy in Your School Library*, 2nd ed. Santa Barbara, CA: Libraries Unlimited, 2013.

———. "Solo Librarians and Intellectual Freedom: Perspectives from the Field." *Knowledge Quest* 40, no. 2 (Nov./Dec. 2011): 31–35.

Auguste, Margaret. *VOYA's Guide to Intellectual Freedom for Teens*. Bowie, MD: VOYA, 2012.

Boyd, Fenice B., and Nacy M. Bailey. "Censorship in Three Metaphors." *Journal of Adolescent and Adult Literacy* 52, no. 8 (May 2009): 653–61.

Curwood, Jen Scott, Megan Schliesman, and Kathleen T. Horning. "Fight for Your Right: Censorship, Selection, and GLBTQ Literature." *English Journal* 98, no. 4 (Mar. 2009): 37–43.

Dell, Pamela. *You Can't Read This! Why Books Get Banned*. Mankato, MN: Compass Point Books, 2010.

DiMarco, Scott R. "Why I Banned a Book: How Censorship Can Impact a Learning Community." *College and Research Libraries News* 74, no. 7 (July 2013): 368–69.

Doyle, Robert P. *Banned Books: Challenging Our Freedom to Read*. Chicago: American Library Association, 2013.

Duthie, Fiona. "Libraries and the Ethics of Censorship." *Australian Library Journal* 59, no. 3 (Aug. 2010): 86–94.

Fletcher-Spear, Kristine, and Kelly Tyler. *Intellectual Freedom for Teens: A Practical Guide for Young Adult and School Librarians*. Chicago: American Library Association, 2013.

Heins, Marjorie. *Not in Front of the Children: "Indecency," Censorship, and the Innocence of Youth*. Piscataway, NJ: Rutgers University Press, 2008.

Hill, Lawrence. *Dear Sir, I Intend to Burn Your Book: An Anatomy of a Book Burning*. Edmonton: University of Alberta Press, 2013.

Intner, Shelia S. "Censorship versus Selection: It's déjà Vu All Over Again." *Technicalities* 32, no. 5 (Sept./Oct. 2012): 1, 9–11.

Jenkins, Christine. "Book Challenges, Challenging Books, and Young Readers: The Research Picture." *Language Arts* 85, no. 3 (Jan. 2008): 228–36.

Jones, Barbara M., for the Office for Intellectual Freedom. *Protecting Intellectual Freedom in Your Academic Library: Scenarios from the Front Lines*. Chicago: American Library Association, 2009.

Karolides, Nicholas J. *Literature Suppressed on Political Grounds*. New York: Facts on File, 2011.

Karolides, Nicholas J., Margaret Bald, and Dawn B. Sova. *120 Banned Books: Censorship Histories of World Literature*. New York: Checkmark Books, 2011.

Kemper, Mark. "Book Banning and Book Removals." *Encyclopedia of American Civil Liberties* (Sept. 1, 2012), http://american-civil-liberties.com/historical-overview/3225-book-banning-and-book-removals.html.

Kidd, Kenneth. "'Not Censorship but Selection': Censorship and/as Prizing." *Children's Literature in Education* 40, no. 3 (2009): 197–216.

Lankford, Ronald D. *Book Banning*. Detroit: Greenhaven, 2008.

Lent, ReLeah Cossett. "Facing the Issues: Challenges, Censorship, and Reflection through Dialogue." *English Journal* 97, no. 3 (Jan. 2008): 61–66.

McNicol, Sarah, ed. *Forbidden Fruit: The Censorship of Literature and Information for Young People*. Boca Raton, FL: Brown Walker Press, 2008.

Moellendick, Cora McAndrews. "Libraries, Censors, and Self-Censorship." *PNLA Quarterly* 73, no. 4 (Summer 2009): 68–76.

Nye, Valerie, and Kathy Barco, eds. *True Stories of Censorship Battles in America's Libraries*. Chicago: American Library Association, 2012.

Pelman, Amy, and Beverly Lynch. "The School Library versus the School Board: An Exploration of the Book Banning Trend of the 1980s." *Journal of Research on Libraries and Young Adults* (Feb. 14, 2011), www.yalsa.ala.org/jrlya/2011/02/

the-school-library-versus-the-school-board-an-exploration-of-the-book-banning
-trend-of-the-1980s.

Pinnell-Stephens, June. *Protecting Intellectual Freedom in Your Public Library: Scenarios from the Front Lines*. Chicago: American Library Association, 2009.

Rickman, Wendy. "A Study of Self-Censorship by School Librarians." *School Library Media Research* 13 (2010), www.ala.org/aasl/sites/ala.org.aasl/files/content/aaslpubsandjournals/slr/vol13/SLR_StudyofSelf-Censorship_V13.pdf.

Riggs, Thomas, ed. *Book Banning*. Detroit, MI: Greenhaven, 2012.

Scales, Pat R., for the Office of Intellectual Freedom. *Protecting Intellectual Freedom in Your School Library: Scenarios from the Front Lines*. Chicago: American Library Association, 2009.

Thomas, R. Murray. *What Schools Ban and Why*. Westport, CT: Praeger, 2008.

Whelan, Debra Lau. "A Dirty Little Secret: Self-Censorship Is Rampant and Lethal." *School Library Journal* 55, no. 2 (2009): 27–30.

CHAPTER THREE

Planning, Policy, and Budgets

Planning increases organizational efficiency and effectiveness by guiding allocation of resources, coordinating activities and initiatives, and reducing risk. Having a plan means being prepared. Formal or systematic planning and goal-setting activities, along with assessment and evaluation techniques to measure progress toward those goals, are standard practice in many libraries. Planning would not be necessary in a static environment, but the environment in which every library exists is changing constantly. These changes are on many fronts—sociological, educational, economic, demographic, political and regulatory, technological, and institutional. Collections policies and budgets are types of formal planning that should be developed in the context of overall library planning. This chapter introduces planning as an organizational responsibility, examines the reasons for and components of collection development and management policies, and discusses library budgeting, particularly in relation to collection development and management.

Planning in Libraries

Formal planning should not be viewed as solely the responsibility of managers and administrators. Planning should be part of all activities in the library, and all librarians have planning responsibilities. Planning means devising a method for accomplishing something. Planning occurs every day because outcomes are sought, decisions are made to reach those outcomes, and actions are taken based on those decisions. The distinction is between informal planning, which people do daily, and formal planning, which has a structure within which conscious, intentional planning occurs.

Drucker has written that formal planning is improving the "futurity" of present decisions.[1] In an environment of rapid change, formal continuous planning becomes essential. Libraries need to anticipate change and decide how to handle it. Formal planning examines both the probable and the possible future. Ideally, a library identifies several possible futures and then decides which are the most likely. The future is unpredictable, and alternatives need to be on hand so that plans can be modified as needed. Uncertainty is the reason planning is continuous. Planning is the process of allocating and reallocating resources in response to change in the environment within the context of the library's evolving mission and priorities.

Consider, for example, information in digital formats. Librarians recognize increasing user expectations to access e-resources through libraries and understand the financial implications of providing access. A librarian should consider several possible futures. What percentage of information resources will be available electronically five, ten, twenty years from now? How would these different conditions affect the current and projected acquisitions budgets? What percentage of the budget might be spent on e-resources five, ten, twenty years from now, and how would this affect acquisition of other formats? What percentage of current and potential library users will have e-readers? Given the forces at play, where would the library like to go and what does it need to do to get there? Laying out alternative scenarios allows the library to project funding needs and service implications.

Formal planning is a form of organizational learning. Planning for the future requires understanding what the library is doing now and what it would like to be doing in the future given certain probable conditions, then choosing the most reasonable path to that future. People involved in planning—and, ideally, planning is broad-based in an organization—learn a tremendous amount about their library, their parent organization, the external environment, and their user community.

Planning is also a communication tool. Information is shared within the library as part of the planning process. Equally important, information about present services and programs and future needs, expectations, and hopes is gathered and shared with the library's clientele and funding bodies. Planning sets a course for the future. It provides a mechanism to inform people about that future and an opportunity for them to buy into it.

Keller identifies several caveats to consider when planning.[2] Planning is not the production of a blueprint to be followed rigorously. A formal plan is not a set of platitudes and buzzwords. It should not be the personal vision of one individual or a statement by a particularly vocal individual or group. Planning does not work if it is an attempt to avoid or outwit the future. Plans do not eliminate risks, nor are they a surrender to external forces. Planning should not be limited to a once-a-year organizational exercise. Planning is continuous and benefits from course corrections over time. Planning will not solve all a library's problems, and it cannot address all issues at once. Formal planning is a library's guide for continuity. It provides a structured way to envision and move toward a future. Careful planning anticipates change and offers a roadmap to maximize its positive effects and minimize its negative ones.

Planning Models

No single style, method, or model of planning is best. Several types of planning may be in use simultaneously in the same library. The following discussion presents various planning approaches but is not exhaustive.

Master planning is top-down planning that begins in the administrative offices. In a college or university, the president's or provost's office begins with an institutional mission and sets out goals, objectives, and timelines with which each academic unit must adhere. City government master planning through the mayor's office or school district planning through the superintendent's office can take the same approach. Libraries prepare their plans consistent with the master plan. This model is simple because the initiative for planning is centralized and nothing changes unless mandated by the governing body or administrative office. Units and individuals within the organization or institution are seldom satisfied with such an approach. Their knowledge and expertise do not contribute to the planning process, and plans may be crafted in isolation from the reality in which librarians work.

Contingency planning is directed toward preparing for one possible and usually undesirable future. For examples, libraries prepare disaster contingency plans. Such a plan begins by identifying the possible disaster, such as a flood, and consequences for facilities, services, and collections. Contingency plans identify appropriate steps to respond to those circumstances. Collections librarians should ensure that a disaster response plan is prepared and kept up-to-date for the library collection.

Formal democratic planning is a cyclic planning process in which all units are requested to formulate their plans for program development on a regular schedule. Plans are reviewed simultaneously to arrive at a complete and coherent plan for the library, school system, or other organization. In this style, the source of ideas rests primarily with individuals and individual units. Contributing units and individuals may be given one or more themes or priorities on which to focus.

Strategic planning is a systematic, formal process that determines a desired future and develops goals, objectives, and tactics to reach this future. It is broad-based and attentive to changes in the environment in which the organization operates. Environmental scanning is an important component of strategic planning but equally useful in all types of planning. Strategic planning constantly reviews changing external and internal conditions and devises appropriate responses. It usually begins with a vision of the organization's future that serves as a guide to planning the goals, objectives, and strategies that form the plan. This is often articulated in a mission or vision statement. Strategic planning is broadly participative and often uses small groups to generate strategies that are incorporated into a coherent plan. Strategic planning, although it may look at one- or three- or five-year increments, does not produce a final, static plan. It remains an open-ended, continuous process that seeks to keep the organization in step with its environment. Strategic planning is employed widely in all types of libraries.[3]

In *scenario planning*, the library develops scenarios that describe alternative futures and formulates plans or strategies for the library in those various futures. Scenario planning can be used in strategic planning and in more focused planning as well. It provides an opportunity to be creative in envisioning the library's future and to consider what is probable, possible, and preferable. In 2010, ARL developed four possible scenarios for North American research institutions and invited libraries to envision their role in each possible future.[4] The intent was to aid libraries in their strategic planning processes.

Entrepreneurial planning, also called opportunistic planning, is a laissez-faire, individual approach to program planning that relies on individuals to come forward whenever they have an idea for altering or expanding programs. No planning constraints, timetables, or formal requests for ideas constrain this approach. Entrepreneurial planning implies acting immediately while the opportunity presents itself. The process of choosing remotely accessed e-resources in libraries is often entrepreneurial. If a new resource is suddenly available, the price is favorable, and the user demand is high, the library may choose to purchase access, even though that particular resource or subject focus was not identified as a priority in library planning.

Incentive planning has not been as prevalent in nonprofit organizations as in the corporate sector, though it is being seen more often in higher education, where it may be called *responsibility-centered management*. The institution is viewed as an economic organization with cost centers, within which revenue is attributed where it is earned. Institutional leaders develop performance benchmarks and an incentive structure that rewards particular types of activities. Each center, usually a functional unit or academic department, selects programs to be developed based on the incentive structure. For example, units may retain revenue generated through tuition or sales. Since a library has little opportunity to produce income, it is often defined for the purposes of incentive planning as a public or common good. Academic units may be taxed to support the library. In this scenario, the academic library faces pressures to justify its contributions to the institution.

Environmental Scanning

Environmental scanning, a formal method developed in the for-profit sector, can gather information and enhance understanding of the library's environment. It is a key component of strategic planning. Strategic environmental scanning aims at anticipating long-term environmental shifts and analyzing their potential effects.[5] Abels explains that "all organizations need to monitor at some level what goes on in their environments and recognize their strengths and weaknesses in relation to it. The importance of environmental information depends on the degree to which the success of the organization itself depends on its environment."[6] The purpose of environmental scanning is to detect, monitor, and analyze trends and issues in the environment, both internal and external, in which an organization operates. It is a key component in planning because it positions an organization to set goals and make plans within the framework of an emerging future.

Environmental scanning first received widespread attention in the late 1960s as businesses sought a way to avoid unexpected crises and to prepare for startling and increasingly rapid change. The American auto industry did not anticipate the consequences of smaller families, increasing fuel prices, and declining interest in new car models as status symbols. Consequently, U.S. companies lagged behind foreign car manufacturers in entering the small car market. Ultimately, these companies realized the necessity of preparing for significant changes in their market and the forces that governed that market. This realization evolved into an awareness that tracking external forces and issues that have great impact on an organization can provide a competitive advantage. An organization that analyzes alternative futures and effectively monitors potential threats and opportunities can take advance action. It can modify present decisions and adapt quickly.

Environmental scanning is distinguished from simple monitoring by a systematic approach. Its four elements are scanning, analyzing, reporting, and crafting an appropriate organizational response. Formal environmental scanning requires the creation of a scanning team, which collects and analyzes information. The environmental scanning team selects the resources to scan, chooses criteria by which to scan, and develops categories of trends to monitor. Team members have individual scanning assignments and meet regularly to review trends. After selecting key trends, they interpret these trends' strategic importance to the organization. The team is responsible for producing reports and briefings that can inform planning and decision making throughout the organization.

The corporate sector continues to rely on formal environmental scanning, but it is less widely used in nonprofit organizations because its complexities can be overwhelming. Environmental scanning is not, however, an all-or-nothing proposition. A modified approach can provide benefits to the library. Recognizing trends and analyzing their impact can position libraries to assign priorities and make decisions about budget, personnel, and facilities before crises force them into a corner. As planning for alternative futures becomes increasingly important, libraries need all the resources they can marshal to make informed decisions. Anticipating future user community needs, wants, and demands helps the library to design collections, services, and spaces to meet them.

Many libraries already monitor their internal and external environments, using techniques that can be applied more widely. When these monitoring techniques are combined with analysis and a commitment to link this analysis to planning activities, the library is engaging in strategic environmental scanning. Typical techniques are reading source materials, monitoring electronic discussion lists and blogs, tracking issues through personal contacts, and directly soliciting comments from the user community. Source materials may include newsletters and reports from peer and local libraries; pertinent articles and editorials; announcements and newsletters from the college or university, school district, or local or national government; federal and foundation grant announcements; vendor and publisher announcements; and publications from consortia, organizations, and agencies with whom the library has regular contact. Many library science journals have sections devoted to tracking important developments and issues of interest to librarians.

These information sources should be seen as more than providing current awareness. Classic environmental scanning includes developing a set of categories or a mental model within which trends or issues are organized. This helps draw together dispersed information to form a more complete picture of trends. One approach to organizing information gathered in an environmental scan is PESTLE, which categorizes findings from environmental scanning as political, economic, social, technological, legal, and environmental factors. Another approach might be to identify categories tied to local library concerns. Librarians often already use mental models as they scan the information that crosses their desks. For example, children's librarians in public libraries pay particular attention to information in the local media regarding trends in home-schooling or changes in competency requirements for advancing to the next elementary grade; they note which books are on banned book lists or the focus of parent challenges. Tracking popular topics for local school assignments, local trends in school age population, or growth in non-English-speaking families is important in planning library collections and services that address the needs of children.

One aspect of environmental scanning often neglected in libraries is analysis. The question is, What do these trends mean for our programs, services, and collections? A SWOT analysis is a popular technique that looks at strengths and weaknesses (usually internal) and opportunities and threats (usually external). Assessing factors as positive (strengths and opportunities) or negative (weaknesses and threats) can inform planning and goal setting. Analysis does not have to be addressed by a special team with the permanent responsibility of collecting and analyzing information. Individuals or small groups of staff members can prepare briefings that will guide planning and goal setting. In addition, occasional meetings of the management team and other library committees or teams can be devoted to a review and analysis of hot topics that should be monitored and incorporated into planning.

The goal of environmental scanning is to identify and analyze trends that can inform planning. Just as the corporate sector seeks a competitive advantage through environmental scanning, so, too, libraries can better position themselves to meet a changing future. Identifying the trends, events, and ideas on which the library might capitalize can guide the management of financial and personnel resources. Simultaneously, libraries can identify possible events outside their control that are threats and for which they need to plan and seek ways to mitigate. If issues and trends are identified early, librarians can incorporate them in planning. Recognizing and reacting to environmental change before it becomes a crisis is the goal of strategic environmental scanning.

Why Undertake Formal Planning?

The earlier an issue is identified and analyzed, the more successful the response. Planning does not eliminate uncertainty. It does suggest ways the organization can prepare for and respond to possibilities. Foresight, manifested in a plan, can lead to organizational actions that might prevent problems and provide positive opportunities for the organization. Refusing to prepare or delaying preparation of plans does not delay the future or minimize its impact. Such behavior only hinders the ability to respond effectively. Planning should not be viewed only as contingency planning for worst-case scenarios. Proactive planning gives the library a measure of control over the future. Planning offers an opportunity to influence the environment. Preparing plans is more than being prepared.

Planning, by focusing on goals along with the objectives or steps to reaching those goals, provides desired outcomes against which to measure progress. Accountability is increasingly important in nonprofit organizations like libraries. The library must be in a position to demonstrate and document how it is using its financial resources effectively. By pointing to what it has accomplished and positive outcomes, the library can justify continued and perhaps increased funding. Library plans often have subtitles such as "The Library in the Twenty-first Century" or "A Vision for the Future." These should not be seen as grandstanding. A plan with goals, objectives, and strategies is only one result of formal planning. The process of systematic planning creates its own benefits by creating a vision of the library and engaging people in that vision.

Collection Development Policy Statements

Any planning activity in a library affects collection development and management, and collection development and management planning must occur within the context of the library's overall planning. A collection development policy statement can be written and revised within various planning models. A collection policy is most effective if it has aspects of democratic planning—it should be prepared by the individuals who best understand the issues and will apply the plan.

Libraries without collection development policies are like businesses without business plans. Without a plan, an owner and the employees lack a clear understanding of what the business is doing now and what it will do in the future, and potential investors have little information about the business's prospects. The owner has no benchmarks against which to measure progress. Daily decisions are made without context. Even a library with written policy statements suffers if those statements are not consulted, reviewed, revised, and updated regularly. Collection development policies also are called selection policies, collection statements, or collection development plans—reflecting the reality that they serve as the plan for building and maintaining a collection, both locally held and accessed remotely. Selection, deselection, and priority setting throughout the library occur in isolation and without coordination if the library has no recorded rationale for decisions.

Spohrer states that a collection development policy "is the embodiment of a kind of social contract between the library and its clienteles, both local and extramural, and like all such contracts, its currency is an essential feature of its validity." Myall and Anderson explain that "collection plans synchronize the library's collection activity with the mission of the library and its parent institution and relate this activity to the needs of identified clientele." Pappas declares that "one of the most important policy documents for a school library media center is the selection policy or the collection development policy."[7] A collection development policy describes the collection (on-site and remotely accessed) as it is now, sets out a plan for how it will be developed, and defines the parameters guiding that development. It is a systematic document, both comprehensive and detailed, that serves multiple purposes as a resource for public planning, allocation, information, administration, and training.[8]

Written collection policies became more widespread, particularly in academic libraries, after World War II and the tremendous growth of academic libraries' collections. In the decades that followed, libraries of all types began to prepare polices that documented practices and goals. By the mid-1950s, ALA recommended that every public library have a written selection and collection maintenance policy. In 1961, the American Association of School Librarians endorsed collection policies in school libraries.[9]

Collections policies in special libraries, unless affiliated with academic institutions, are not as common because of the narrow focus of these libraries. When present, policies in special libraries tend to be succinct, as the following examples make clear.

> *Policy for a government library*
>
> The Minnesota Legislative Reference Library is committed to maintaining a print and electronic collection of current and historical materials to support effective public policy development, and to document the work of the Minnesota Legislature.[10]

> *Policy for an association library*
>
> The American Library Association Library
>
> • Collects materials on the history of and issues within libraries and librarianship
>
> • Serves as the repository for publications from ALA and its units

- Responds to reference and information requests supported by its collection scope
- Works closely with the ALA Archives[11]

Policy for a law firm library

> The Library acquires publications and services to support the practice of law at Debevoise & Plimpton. Materials include books, periodicals, newsletters, treatises and subscription services in a variety of formats that include print, CD-ROM, Web sites and fee-based databases, electronic subscriptions, audio and video.[12]

During the past fifty years, some have questioned the value of collection development policies. Snow views them as unnecessary, and Hazen finds them to be "of little practical utility." Vickery points out their theoretical and practical drawbacks, including a tendency to be overly idealistic, not grounded in the library's current context, and too complex and detailed and consequently difficult to change.[13]

Given these criticisms, what makes a collection policy relevant and meaningful? As Disher notes, "Having a collection development policy is not the same as having a *useful* collection development policy."[14] A useful policy is not general, idealistic, theoretical, rigid, or vague, but it should not be so detailed and ponderous that it is impractical to use. Policy statements are not static. Preparing, reviewing, and revising policy statements should be a continuous process, because the community served, the financial resources available, and the information resources produced are always changing. *Guide for Developing and Evaluating School Library Programs* states that "the school librarian needs to ensure that there is an approved selection policy for the school library program [and] that it is updated regularly."[15] Collections policies should have a clear purpose that is obvious to those who write, revise, and consult them.

Moran, Stueart, and Morner identify four characteristics of good policies: they are consistent; they are flexible and change as new needs arise; they allow some discretion and latitude (unlike rules and procedures, which are firm); and they are written.[16] No policy, however well crafted, is a substitute for good collection development and management. A policy statement defines a framework and provides parameters, but it never tells how to select or reject a specific title. No matter how specific and detailed the collection development policy statement is, personal judgment is still necessary.

Purposes and Audience

The many purposes that collection policies serve can be divided into two broad categories: to inform and to protect. The audience to whom the policy is directed also must be considered when creating a policy.

INFORMING

Collection development policy statements inform by first presenting the library's mission and then describing current collections in terms of strengths and weaknesses and setting future goals. By identifying future collecting levels, policies provide a benchmark against which to measure success in reaching those levels. To the extent that policies match collections to mission, they can guarantee that the collection being developed serves the educational, entertainment, and research mission of the parent institution or community. A policy "provides a theoretical overview that explains the educational, social, and cultural rationale for the development of the collection."[17]

By establishing collection priorities, policy statements can guide libraries in establishing staffing needs and allocating available personnel. Typically, a collection policy outlines who is responsible for collection development and management. In addition, collection policies can inform decisions about cataloging, space allocation, budgeting, and fund-raising priorities. They can guide those individuals responsible for managing personnel, fiscal resources, space, and other resources in support of collections.

Policy statements help with budgeting by providing information for external and internal budget preparation and allocation. A well-crafted policy demonstrates accountability by presenting a plan for careful management of fiscal resources and describing the results of funding decisions. It can improve the library's ability to compete for resources within a complex and competitive institutional or government environment, providing supporting information for the preparation of grant proposals, budget requests, and fund-raising and development plans. Policy statements can be used to respond to accreditation surveys and to inquiries about the impact of new academic and research programs or new service mandates.

Policy statements serve as a vehicle for communication with the library's staff, administration, and constituencies. While describing the library collection and its strengths and weaknesses, they also formally document practice. They are contracts recording the library's commitment, and they express this commitment in writing. Within the library, policy statements serve to coordinate selection when responsibility for selection is dispersed among many librarians and geographically among several physical locations. Policies provide control and consistency.

Policy statements are used to educate and train librarians responsible for collections. As new collections librarians, subject liaisons, and school librarians are hired or collections responsibilities reassigned, policy statements can serve as a training tool. If the policy statement is current in describing community service priorities, academic programs and research interests, school curricula, criteria for selection and deselection, collecting levels, and other pertinent areas, it provides the newly assigned collections librarian with a baseline of information from which to begin developing and managing the collection.

Policy statements serve a particularly important function to the extent that they document and support cooperative collection development and management. The policy statement should explicitly identify all current cooperative programs in which the library participates: collection building, resource sharing, shared agreements to purchase or lease e-content, regional storage, commitments to retention, and so on. Demas and Miller stress the critical importance of individual libraries addressing collaborative collection management in their policies and note that this is an essential component of shaping the collective collection nationally.[18] By reporting what the library does and what it plans to do with collecting levels by discipline or user group, a policy can facilitate cooperative collection development and resource-sharing programs. Using the same policy format and descriptive measures or terms within a consortium or other resource-sharing group can expedite cooperation and coordination.

PROTECTING

Collection development policy statements protect the library against external pressures. Policy statements can serve to protect intellectual freedom and prevent censorship. Many libraries' statements repeat or reference the Library Bill of Rights and other intellectual freedom statements. A library is best served by preparing a statement that is tailored to its own environment. The policy may include the procedures for handling a challenge to material held by a library. This does not mean that a statement about censorship is totally negative. The policy can be written to affirm the library's commitment to intellectual freedom. The process of creating a statement on intellectual freedom provides staff with the opportunity to think through these issues and to clarify their position. The presence of a carefully prepared and board-approved policy does not decrease the likelihood of a challenge to a specific controversial title but does increase the likelihood that challenged materials will be fairly reviewed. When the library is challenged, the policy ensures that librarians are prepared to respond. They have, in effect, rehearsed their response through the writing of a policy. Many school media center collections policies include a section that lays out the process for requesting reconsideration of materials and the steps followed in responding to a reconsideration request. They may include a template or form that students, parents, and legal guardians can use to challenge resources available in the library media center. Having a policy and process in place protects the library from being accused of inconsistency in responding to challenges.

At the same time that a policy resists the exclusion of certain materials, it can protect against pressure to purchase inappropriate and irrelevant materials. A policy makes clear that materials are rejected because of collection guidelines, not because of who may or may not wish their acceptance.

Policies can protect by guiding the handling of gifts. The policy specifies the conditions under which the library accepts and rejects gifts. The gift policy should address the economic, social, and political situation in which a library exists. Libraries are advised not to appraise gifts but to refer potential donors to one or more external appraisers. Gift policies may be written for specific collections within a larger library or library system. For example, special collections may have their own policies for gifts.[19] By defining policy and procedures for accepting or declining, appraising, accessioning, acknowledging, and processing gifts, both the library and the potential donor are protected legally and practically.

In times of decreasing budgets and increasing materials costs, libraries need protection as they plan weeding, deselection, collection moves to storage, and serials cancellations. Making clear the operating principles under which these decisions are made protects the library from charges of bias and irresponsible behavior. A policy should define the process through which materials identified for withdrawal, transfer to storage, and cancellation are reviewed and evaluated and by whom. Any processes for involving members of the user community should be described. This portion of the policy statement should include guidelines for disposal of unneeded materials.

A policy statement can identify issues of confidentiality. By specifying the types of information that are private—for example, about donors, budgets, costs and value of materials, and users of the collection—a policy protects the library and its users, the parent institution, and donors.

AUDIENCE

Just as collection development policy statements serve many purposes, they serve many audiences. The library's collection policy is usually designed for use by staff members. The better the policy is, the more frequently it will be consulted. Copies should be available for all library personnel, not just those with selection responsibilities. Many libraries post their policies on the library's website, where they can be consulted easily by staff and other stakeholders.[20]

A collection policy statement often serves a wider audience as well. It can be designed to be meaningful to library users, teachers and parents of students who use a school library media center, and external funding and governing bodies. Collections policies may be official governing board policies, especially in public libraries and schools. Though usually crafted by or in consultation with librarians, the collection management policy carries the imprimatur—and thus the authority—of the governing board. This credence can be useful in the face of challenges to materials held and accessed by the library. If well written, the policy tells administrators and the user community what the library is doing with its allocated funds and makes clear that the library materials budget is not a "black hole" without definition or dimension. Other libraries also can be part of the policy's audience. If the policy is intended to identify and develop cooperative collection building and use initiatives, then it must be shared with actual and potential partners.

Writing the Collection Development Policy Statement

A policy should be considered in terms of format, content, and style. A policy usually conforms to a standard appearance and arrangement. *AcqWeb's Directory of Collection Development Policies on the Web* provides example policies from public libraries, community college libraries, college libraries, university libraries, academic library special collections, national and state government libraries, and school libraries.[21] Authors, whether individuals or committees, should keep in mind their primary purpose and audience while writing the policy and tailor the document appropriately. For example, a policy that will be shared within a consortium and used for cooperative collection development planning is more meaningful if it matches the style of others in the consortium. A policy statement intended to inform teaching faculties or the parents of K–12 students might incorporate terminology from the curriculum. Format, content, and style can be crafted to meet specific ends and speak to specific audiences. Well-researched and well-written policy statements can address multiple purposes and audiences effectively.

Effective collection development policies have standard elements and include sections that address

- purpose
- background or history
- responsibility for collection development
- library mission, goals, and objectives
- target audiences
- budgeting and funding
- selection criteria
- patron-driven acquisitions (if used)
- pay-per-use (if used)
- formats and genres (e.g., textbooks, repair manuals, independently published materials, games) included and excluded and the rationale for these decisions
- government publications
- treatment of specific resource groups
- special collections
- cooperative collection development and resource-sharing agreements
- services
- selection aids and handling of user recommendations
- copyright
- intellectual freedom
- acquisitions
- gifts and exchanges
- collection maintenance including weeding
- collection evaluation
- challenges to materials in the collection
- policy revision
- definition of terms or glossary

- bibliography
- appendixes[22]

Though all these components might be found in a single policy, such comprehensiveness is certainly not universal or always necessary. Developing and maintaining a policy with so many sections can be daunting and result in either the absence of a policy or failure to use or revise it as needed. Most libraries focus on those areas that most clearly speak to their own priorities and issues. For example, school library media centers and public libraries would be more likely to have a section dealing with challenges to materials in the collection than would special or academic libraries.

Policies often begin with an overview or introductory section. A common first element is a statement of the policy's purpose, followed by the library's (or the parent organization's) mission statement. This is followed by a brief description or profile of the user community, including numbers and types of users served and these users' needs. Types of users mentioned in an academic library may include undergraduates, graduate and special students, faculty, distance education students, and the general public. The policy for an academic library also might describes academic programs, degrees granted, and research centers. The policy of a public library describes the citizens and their needs. Types of users might include K–12 students, adult users, students at local higher education institutions and community colleges, ethnic communities, care facility residents, local businesses, elderly, visually impaired, and prison inmates. A library media center collection policy might identify the user community in terms of ESL students, special needs students, grade levels, teachers, and so on.

A description of the user community is followed by a general statement of library priorities related to primary and secondary users. The mission statement and community served provide information that sets the stage for the policies and guidelines that follow. Guidelines governing the appropriateness of materials, subjects, formats, and language must be coherent with the library's mission.

Limitations affecting collection development and management can be an important part of the policy's introduction. This is the place to note any factors that may limit the library in achieving its goals. New academic programs may have been added without additional library funding, meaning reduced support for all collection areas. The school enrollment or city's population may be increasing rapidly or changing significantly in ethnic composition. The impact of increasing need for access to e-resources, escalating monograph and serial prices, or reduced or steady-state budgets may be addressed in this section.

Often, a brief description of the library and the scope of its collections follows. This can consist of the history of the collection, broad subject areas emphasized or deemphasized, and collection locations. The quality and character of existing collections are evaluated in broad terms, as is current collecting practice. A general statement about criteria guiding selection and management decisions usually appears in the introduction. The policy introduction lists any cooperative collection development and resource-sharing agreements. Finally, the introduction describes the library's collection development organization. It locates responsibility for collection building and management. The specific tasks of evaluation, selection, collection maintenance, budget management, user community liaison, and so forth can be identified and assigned.

An overview of system-wide polices and guidelines follows the introduction. Collection development policy statements vary greatly in what they cover, though some areas are addressed more consistently. Policies usually enumerate types of materials that are selected and not selected, referencing those that apply only to certain subjects. A typical list might include statements about books, periodicals, newspapers, textbooks, juvenile materials, reprints, maps, dissertations and theses, textbooks, paperbacks, microforms, pamphlets, popular magazines, artworks, musical scores, audiovisual materials, software, games, and access to remote e-resources.

Many policies briefly describe the criteria that guide selection. For example, the St. Paul Public Library offers these basic selection principles:

> Selectors use their training, knowledge, and expertise along with following standard criteria to select materials. An item need not meet all criteria to be selected.

> *General Criteria*
> - Relevance to current and anticipated community needs
> - Suitability of subject and style for intended audience
> - Critical reviews
> - Reputation and qualifications of the author and/or publisher
> - Cost
> - Relation to the current collection and other materials on the subject
> - Local significance of the author or topic
> - Potential user appeal

Content Criteria

The selection of materials includes, but is not limited, to:

- Comprehensiveness of treatment
- Authority, competence, reputation and purpose of the author
- Currency and accuracy of the information
- Long-term significance or interest
- Representation of diverse points of view

Selectors decide how many copies to purchase based on anticipated demand, the interests of library users in our many neighborhoods, physical space available in branches and total cost of the materials. The library recognizes that users have differing abilities and backgrounds and thus provides materials on varying levels of difficulty and scholarship.[23]

Other issues briefly addressed in general policies might be special collections and archives, reference materials, and government documents. Policy statements dealing with languages and translations, popular and trade materials, handling of superseded materials, gifts, duplicate copies, and expensive purchases are common. Three topics frequently addressed in collections policies are intellectual freedom, access to collections materials, and challenges to library materials. For example, the Denver Public Library collection development policy and the Paideia School Elementary Library (Atlanta, Georgia) policy statement (both in appendix C) include procedures for reconsideration of materials.

With the tremendous increase in self-published materials, some libraries are addressing these in their policy statements. For example, the St. Paul Public Library collection development policy states:

All independently published materials are subject to the Library's Collection Development Policy. In general, an item is more likely to be added if it:

- Features regional connections, has relevance to the greater collection, and/or has wide audience appeal
- Has received a positive review in one or more library review journals or one of the local papers
- Is available for purchase through an established distributor.[24]

When e-resources became part of library collections, many libraries developed supplemental policies to address the complexities of selecting and managing them. Libraries have moved away from separate policies for e-resources and increasingly integrate e-resources into overall policy, assuming that the same guidelines, practices, and criteria apply to all resources regardless of format or delivery mechanism. Topics particular to e-resources are added as appropriate. These might address unique selection criteria, such as ease of use and availability to multiple users; situations in which duplication in multiple formats is appropriate; preference for e-versions, if the library has made that policy decision; and any licensing conditions that would exclude an e-resource from consideration, such as limitations on certain types of use or the absence of perpetual access. If a library has implemented a patron-driven acquisition model for e-books or encourages library users to participate in selection in other ways, the collections policy should reflect these practices. Some considerations in the selection of e-resources are more likely to be addressed in an internal procedures document, which describes how the library handles contracts and licenses, including who is responsible for their review and negotiation and the role of individual librarians in the process.

Many libraries find that a policy that contains the information described above is sufficient and can be presented in five or six pages—or less. Policies are often available and posted on libraries' public web pages. The Denver Public Library offers this brief summary of its collection development policy on the library's website:

> Collection Development Policy: The Denver Public Library collects materials, in a variety of popular formats, which support its function as a major information source for the demanding needs of a metropolitan population. The collection also serves the popular and recreational needs of the general public, and reflects the racial, ethnic and cultural diversity of the community.[25]

This is supplemented by an expanded version (also on the website), and the entire policy is available as a PDF file (see appendix C). Making policies easy to locate serves to both inform and protect.

General policies may be supplemented by more detailed policies focusing on subjects, user communities, or special collections. A public library may have a general policy augmented by policies for the children's collection, reference collection, and so on. An academic library or school media center may have supplemental policies addressing various subjects or disciplines. These supplemental collection development policies usually follow one of three formats: narrative, classed analysis, or a combination of elements of these two.

NARRATIVE MODEL

The *narrative model* is text-based. It includes a series of narrative descriptions, one for each subject, discipline, or subcollection. These are often called subject profiles. The sections may be defined broadly (e.g., social sciences, humanities, and sciences; or adult fiction, children's fiction, and reference), or each section may have a narrower focus (e.g., subdividing agriculture into animal science, agronomy, soil science, etc., or adult fiction into mysteries, romances, science fiction, etc.). The purpose is to give a focused view of subjects or subdivisions and of collection management as practiced in the library preparing the policy. An advantage of the narrative model is use of terms that are local and immediately familiar to describe programs and collections.

These focused policy statements generally follow the outline and content of the overview. Each discusses the specific user community, particular limitations or emphasis, types of materials collected or excluded, library unit or individual responsible for this collection, interdisciplinary relationships, additional resources, and other local factors. University of Minnesota Libraries' "Collection Development Policy for the Institute on the Environment" (see appendix C) is a narrative policy.

CLASSED MODEL

A *classed model* collection development policy describes the collection and current collecting levels in abbreviated language and numerical codes, most typically according to the Library of Congress or Dewey Decimal classification schemes. It also may describe preservation levels and proposed future collecting levels. Though often extensive, this model allows one to see the collection as a whole, displayed in tables. This format grew out of libraries' need to develop an effective, consistent way of defining subjects and levels of collecting. The Research Libraries Group was a leader in developing the classed analysis format as the Conspectus (examined in detail in chapter 7). Complemented by verification studies and supplemental guidelines, the Conspectus has done much to define concepts, standardize procedures and terminology, and offer consistent techniques for describing and managing collections.[26] The Conspectus model was adopted by ARL for its North American Collections Inventory Project in the late 1980s, was adapted by the National Library of Canada for use in that country, and is employed in many other countries.[27] IFLA has prepared *Guidelines for Collection Development Using the Conspectus Model* and makes it available in several languages.[28] Though initially intended for use by research libraries, the

Conspectus has been modified for use by libraries collecting at less than research intensity for state or regional resource sharing, fund allocations, space allocation and storage projects, accreditation, grant proposals, and preservation priorities. The Conspectus approach to defining both present collecting practice and future goals through the use of a standard vocabulary has become accepted as a tool that is both adaptable and widely applicable.

A library using the classed analysis model should use the same classification system for its collection development policy that is used to organize its collection. This allows the library to use title counts to verify existing levels and measure changes over time as described in the policy. The library can select the appropriate level of specificity to be used. The original Conspectus uses some 3,400 subject classifications; these are generally contracted into far fewer divisions to describe collections for which less fine distinctions between subjects are more appropriate.

In the Conspectus, subject categories are defined by classification range and subject descriptors. Each category is assigned a series of numbers for existing collection strength, current collecting intensity, and desired collecting intensity. The numbers, often called collection depth indicators, range from 0 (out of scope—nothing is collected in this subject) to 5 (comprehensive—collecting is exhaustive, inclusive, and intensive). Language codes can be assigned to each category. Scope notes can be used to describe special features of parts of the collection. Librarians should not become too preoccupied with levels. Levels do not imply value. Reporting a level of 4 or 5 does not mean a library is better. The most important part of using collection depth indicators is to understand how librarians are collecting and to reconcile practice with the library's mission, goals, objectives, and available funding. The classed analysis, through the use of standardized divisions and terminology, provides a vehicle for verification, comparisons and cooperation between libraries, clear division and coordination among selecting responsibilities, and measurement of progress, and it can define the context in which selection and collection management occur.

COMBINED NARRATIVE AND CLASSED MODELS

A combination of the two models takes the most useful features of each to describe the collecting plan. It can be useful when reviewed and updated as the environment in which the library operates and the resources available change. The Pennsylvania State University Libraries collection development policy for history (see appendix C) combines narrative with a variation of the classed model. Instead of classification numbers, it uses brief prose descriptions of the subject areas and assigns Conspectus levels for both collecting intensity and language coverage.

SUPPLEMENTAL POLICIES

Other policies can be written to deal with specific issues. These may address procedures for donor relations and other considerations in accepting and declining gifts. A preservation policy addresses principles for handling the collection's physical condition. It covers criteria for decisions about binding, conservation, reformatting, and other treatment options; priorities for allocating preservation resources are addressed here. A separate statement about weeding and deselection policy is useful. This defines how materials are reviewed for transfer between collections, transfer to remote storage, and withdrawal. It may include guidelines for cancelling periodical subscriptions and disposing of unneeded materials. If appropriate, this section addresses the library's responsibilities as a library of record or resource for the district, state, or region. Note, however, that policies addressing gifts, preservation, and weeding and deselection often can be addressed effectively within the general collection policy.

● ● ●

Regardless of the model employed, a collection development policy should be well organized, consistent from section to section in use of terminology and elements addressed, detailed, and literate without being wordy. A collection development policy is a formal, official, documented policy of the library, but it should be crafted to be easy to understand and practical to use. A policy that is well written will be used; one that is not will be put in a file and left there.

Budgeting and Finance

Budget Basics

One of the most important types of planning is the allocation of financial resources within the context of institutional priorities. Preparing a budget serves this purpose. The word *budget* denotes two things—a plan and an allocation. In the planning sense, the library's budget is its plan for the use of money available during a fiscal year and reflects allocations, expected revenues, and projected expenditures. A proposed budget is presented to funding authorities as both a request for funding and a plan for what the library will do with the money it receives. Allocations are the dollar amounts that are distributed to various fund lines in the budget. This budget also is called a budget document. Such a budget may include, in addition to allocations and other sources of revenue, fund balances and encumbrances brought forward from the previous year, if permitted by the parent agency. A fund balance consists of the dollars allocated but unexpended at the end of a fiscal year. Encumbrances represent the projected cost of orders that have been placed but for which the items have not yet been received. An encumbrance is recorded as soon as the obligation for payment is incurred, that is, when the order is placed. When the item is received, the encumbrance is cleared and the actual cost recorded as an expenditure. If encumbrances are present at the end of the fiscal year, unexpended funds must be held in escrow until payments for outstanding orders are made.

Budget also can mean the total amount of funds allocated to meet a library's expenditures over a fixed period of time. The budget varies from year to year. This use of the concept is at play when a librarian reports receiving an increase or decrease in the current year's budget compared to the previous year. Most libraries manage their budgets on a fiscal year, which may or may not parallel the calendar year. Parent institutions determine the fiscal year. Most colleges, universities, schools, public libraries, and many companies run on a July-to-July fiscal year, some follow a calendar year, and the U.S. government's fiscal year begins October 1 and ends September 30.

Once a library's goals and objectives are understood through the planning process, its budget serves both to document those decisions through allocations and to coordinate achieving those goals and objectives. Allocations are a measure of the financial commitment to support activities necessary to reach the goals outlined in a plan. A well-crafted budget becomes an internal control that can measure operating effectiveness and performance. The materials budget, also called the acquisitions budget, collections budget, or resources budget, is one portion of a library's total budget. Wiemers writes that "the materials budget is both the plan and the framework that sets the boundaries within which choice will be allowed to operate. The 'correct' budget will produce the optimal set of limits on choice that will reflect the library's collection goals and priorities, and provide a mechanism to track the library's efforts to reach those goals."[29]

The materials budget is one part of the overall library budget. A library also has an operating budget, which covers ongoing expenses necessary to operate the library. The library's personnel budget may be managed within the operating budget, or it may be a third separate budget within the total budget. For many libraries, the split is 20–30 percent for collections, 50–60 percent for personnel, and 10–20 percent for operating expenses. Another type of budget is the capital budget, which is devoted to proposed additions, replacements, and improvements to fixed assets (property and equipment) and the means of financing them. These budgets are long-term plans and are usually handled separately from annual budgeting activities.

The planning process should make clear which budget covers which types of expenses. The materials budget may cover the purchase of equipment to house collections, costs to support the technological infrastructure that provides access to electronic resources, binding and other preservation and conservation treatments, vendor service charges, catalog records, shelf-ready processing, shipping and handling fees, institution memberships, and shared digital repositories and storage facilities. Some libraries fund document delivery through the materials budget. In some libraries, once funds are appropriated to the library and allocated to the library's materials budget, operating budget, and personnel budget, they cannot be moved from one budget section to another.

A materials budget should be consistent with both the library's long-range and short-range plans. Budgets are most effective and most realistic if their preparation occurs within the context of organizational planning. Both the overall mission of the library and the goals and objectives of library departments should be considered. Because budgets generally parallel the accounting period, they may focus on short-range planning at the expense of the long-range view. Long-range fiscal planning is difficult because the library's future and that of its environment are so volatile. Libraries face problems in predicting materials costs and the effect of inflation, publication patterns, international currency fluctuations, and the funds that will be available. In addition, the parent agency may make unanticipated changes that affect the user community and user demands and expectations. Nevertheless, including long-range projections in the total budgeting process is important.

Materials budgets, both the request for funding and the allocations once funds are received, are usually prepared by the librarian with administrative responsibility for collections. In a smaller library, the head librarian may prepare the total budget, of which the materials budget is one portion. In school library media centers, librarians usually prepare an acquisitions budget within the context of the school's or the school district's budget. They may have modest input into the amount of funds allocated for acquisitions but usually have some responsibility for how it is allocated (e.g., amounts allocated by subjects, reading levels, discretionary and nondiscretionary purchases). In larger libraries, the individual with administrative responsibility for collection development and management usually prepares the materials budget, generally in consultation with individual collections librarians or, perhaps, with a coordinating committee.

Individual librarians with specific collections responsibilities are usually asked to present annual requests for the level of funding they wish to receive in their fund lines in the next fiscal year. The administrator with responsibility for the entire materials budget rolls these individual requests into the total amount requested for the library.

Budgeting Techniques

Approaches to the budgeting process vary from library to library. The parent institution may mandate the approach and, in some organizations, this may change from year to year. A *zero-based budget* requires a fresh start each year. The library is asked to begin with a blank page and determine how much to spend in each category of the budget. Each funding request is proposed and defended without reference to past practice. Few government and nonprofit organizations take this approach because of the amount of work involved. A *program* or *performance budgeting* approach looks at allocations for specific activities or programs and provides a very clear connection with planning documents and the objectives set each year. Some libraries' allocations are determined through *formula-based budgets*, which use a set of weighted variables to calculate allocations to each fund line.

Most libraries use a *historical* or *incremental budgeting* approach, which determines the needed incremental changes in various categories. This is sometimes called *line-item budgeting* (not to be confused with a line-item budget), because existing categories are increased or decreased by a percentage. Existing fund lines may be increased or decreased by a predetermined percentage. Combining incremental budgeting with program budgeting is a common practice. The library begins with the previous year's base budget and identifies programmatic priorities that should be funded at a higher level and, ideally, areas of lower priority where the allocation can be reduced.

The librarian should approach budget preparation in the manner required by the parent institution. An effective budget system provides the tools for making reasonable decisions about allocation or reallocation of resources.

A recurring theme in the budget process in today's libraries is accountability. Librarians are expected to be able to demonstrate effective stewardship of the funds they receive and expend. Effectiveness is usually measured by the degree to which the organization's stated goals and objectives are achieved. Though counting materials acquired and current serial subscriptions and e-resources has been a traditional measure of success, increased attention is given to demonstrated outcomes. If a library has set a goal of expanding large-print books to meet the increasing number of senior citizens, success would be a combination of the number of titles acquired and the number of circulations these materials have. Additional considerations reflecting responsible stewardship include balanced encumbrances and expenditures over the budget year and avoidance of financial misconduct.

Funding Sources

For most libraries, the largest part of the budget is funded through an appropriation from the parent organization. Prior to the end of the fiscal year, most libraries prepare a funding request and, just prior to or soon after the beginning of the fiscal year, receive an appropriation or budget allocation. In many organizations, the budget for library materials is treated as a protected category and may receive extra scrutiny and interest in how it is allocated and spent. This scrutiny underlines the need for linking the budget to a well-crafted and widely supported plan, and for being accountable for effective use of the allocated funds. Sources of funding, in addition to an appropriation, include gifts, endowment income, grants, fees and charges, and fines.

Supplemental funds are of increasing importance in most libraries. In the broadest sense, fund raising is the process of seeking additional moneys from sources other than the parent organization and includes seeking gifts, bequests, and grants. Collections librarians are becoming more involved in fund raising. They may be called upon to write or present proposals to donors to solicit collections, obtain funds to purchase collections, or create endowments that will generate income to maintain collections. As institutions become more dependent on these sources of funds, they have found that the librarians closest to the collection and its users often can make the most convincing cases to potential donors. Their enthusiasm and commitment can be infectious. A successful fund raiser knows the job, the institution, and the donor.[30]

Collections librarians are also critical to the stewardship process in that they ensure that gifts, whether dollars or collections, are managed well. Donors often mandate how the money is to be spent and expect that their gifts will be an addition to the amount currently allocated to that specific purpose. Most donors want to know that their gifts are being used to further the goals of the institution. Librarians are called upon to write letters or meet with donors to thank them, to let them know how their gifts are being used, and to encourage their continued involvement with the library.

Grants can provide additional funding for library collections. Collections librarians may be expected to seek grants from private and government agencies. Grant proposals draw upon the librarian's knowledge of the collection and its users and require special writing skills. Once a library receives a grant, tracking mechanisms and reporting procedures are specified in the grant guidelines. Many academic institutions have offices through which grants are managed, and libraries also must comply with their requirements. The reporting dates for the grant may be different from the library's fiscal year. Projects funded through grants should be consistent with the library's planning and reflect its goals.

Another option for leveraging the collections budget is to seek partnerships with stakeholders. Harris called this blended funding.[31] In a high school, the librarian might approach the English department for additional money to help support a new literary criticism resource. An academic librarian might approach the business school for supplemental funds to subscribe to an expensive source for corporate profiles and affiliations in which faculty are interested.

School library media centers have additional options for supplemental funds. Parent-teacher associations frequently view library media centers as a good investment because all students in a school benefit. Another possibility is book fairs, which bring in an outside vendor who displays books for purchase, with the library media center or sponsoring organization receiving a percentage of the profits.

Material Budget Requests

Before the fiscal year begins, the library is asked to submit a budget request. This is usually part of the overall planning process of the parent organization. The library can use this process for two purposes: to request funds and to inform. A well-crafted proposal begins by explaining a library's financial needs in reference to internal and external forces. Ideally, an environmental scan has assembled this information and informed the library's planning document. Through this explanation, the funding body or parent institution learns about pressures, constraints, and expectations the library faces. An initial summary of external and internal conditions sets the stage for a convincing proposal. This information must be presented clearly and succinctly but with enough detail to make a case.

Among the external and internal conditions that can affect the library's funding needs are changes in the population to be served. As their user communities become more diverse, some libraries are called upon to provide new resources to meet the needs of these changing populations. Special libraries may need resources for new product research and development or other new corporate foci. School library media centers may have increasing or declining enrollments or need to support new standards for grade advancement and graduation. Harvey notes that making clear how school library media center funding directly affects students and student learning and supports specific curriculum projects and initiatives is important.[32] An academic institution may be expected to serve new graduate programs, undergraduate degrees, or research centers. The needs of distance-education students place new demands on libraries. A budget proposal often has a programmatic basis, that is, a case is made for funding based on program areas such as recreational resources, information resources, or new areas of emphasis.

One internal influence on the budget is the collection mix, that is, the kinds of materials in the collection. A library with a higher ratio of serials to monographs can predict greater financial need because serials costs increase at a higher rate than monograph costs. Libraries with a higher proportion of foreign acquisitions are more vulnerable to fluctuations in foreign currency. Budgeting is forecasting future funding needs based on internal and external factors.

Changes in pricing trends in library materials and services, volume of materials published, impact of electronic information, CPI, and value of the dollar on the international market can all be relevant. Serials and book prices continue to increase at significantly greater rates than either the CPI or annual increases to most libraries' base allocations. Added pressures come from the increase in the volume of materials to be considered for purchase and the need to respond to user demand for e-resources. Librarians seeking to support user community needs and interests should ensure that funding agencies are aware of the many pressures on materials budgets.

Some academic libraries use the budgets of an agreed-upon set of peer libraries as benchmarks to support their own budget requests. In many cases, the parent institution may have determined a set of peers, and comparing the resources of the library to those held in the other members of the peer group can be useful.

Regardless of the strategy used, a materials budget proposal should make clear the consequences of various funding levels. Using statistical data and meaningful information strengthens the budget proposal and provides an opportunity to inform the parent institution of the library's short- and long-term plans. In the process, the library should take care to present consequences not as threats but as reality.

Several reliable sources provide statistical information about pricing, publishing, and population trends. These include professional library publications, trade publications, and library service vendors:

- *Library and Book Trade Almanac,* published by Bowker

- "Library Materials Price Index," prepared by the ALCTS Library Materials Price Editorial Board

- "Periodicals Price Survey," published annually by *Library Journal*

- *Publishers Weekly*

- *School Library Journal*, which usually publishes average book prices in the March issue

- reports and projections prepared by serials agents and monograph vendors, which can be found on their websites

Allocation of Funds

The allocation of funds within the collection development budget may absorb much of a head librarian's or collection development officer's time in larger libraries. The annual allocation process is an opportunity to create "a successful budget [that] translates competing demands into real levels of financial support."[33] The goal of the allocation process is to reflect the goals and priorities set out in the library's planning process and to create a mechanism to track the library's efforts to reach those goals. The method used to make allocations should be understood clearly by both those within the library and external stakeholders.

Most collections budgets are *line-item budgets*, with subdivisions or subaccounts within the larger budget. A line-item budget lists allocations and expenditures, classified by type, in a detailed line-by-line format. A line-item budget allows easy comparisons from year to year and promotes accountability. Large libraries may have one hundred or more lines in the materials budget. Libraries may allocate by one or more of the following: subject or discipline; location (main library, branch library, children's department, remote research site); type of user (children, adult); format or genre (monographs, serials, reference materials, fiction, microforms, e-resources, newspapers); or type of publishers (trade presses, academic presses, small presses). Very large libraries may further subdivide allocations. For example, funds allocated to purchase materials for children in a large public library might be subdivided to fund lines for nonfiction, fiction, picture books, and videos. School library media center budgets might be allocated according to curriculum areas, subjects, users, curriculum mapping, or formats. In this way, allocations mirror the organizational structure of the library, the community served, and the collection development policy. Collections librarians are responsible for one or more fund lines. The details represented in line-item budget divisions provide for accountability and convenience of reporting.

Line-item budgets have advantages and disadvantages. On the positive side, a line-item budget with many lines offers increased ability to track expenditures and collections librarian performance at a granular level. It simplifies the process of aligning the library's goals with those of the parent institution, but it also may heighten the political sensitivity of the process. Citizens, teachers, researchers, or faculty members may question why the library spends more money in one area than another when the funding is allocated into readily identifiable budget lines. Adding lines to a budget for new focus areas or changing an existing line item may be difficult. A very granular line-item budget may limit flexibility, though many libraries have the option of moving funds from one line to another during the fiscal year as surpluses and deficits develop.

Libraries, even those that do not use multiple fund lines, typically divide the annual budget between *discretionary* and *nondiscretionary* allocations. Discretionary purchases are individual orders for items. Nondiscretionary purchases reflect a known, ongoing financial commitment, typically subscriptions to journals and databases. Funds must be set aside at the beginning of the fiscal year to cover these expenses. Librarians have tended to think of books as discretionary expenses. This, however, is changing because many libraries purchase access to e-books on annual subscriptions and must budget for these expected expenses. If a library has purchased the e-content, it still may need to pay annual platform or hosting fees. An added wrinkle occurs when an e-book is added during the year. In theory, this is a discretionary purchase, but likely it needs to be considered as part of the next year's nondiscretionary allocation.

Libraries that have approval plans may have a third type of allocation under a subject fund line to cover these expenses. These are usually nondiscretionary in the sense that a certain amount is set aside to cover books that come through the approval plan and are not selected on a title-by-title basis.

Another challenge when allocating funds is patron-driven acquisition. Deciding the amount to allocate, the appropriate fund lines to use, and mechanisms for monitoring and controlling expenditures can be difficult. Users often treat unmediated patron-driven acquisitions as a never-ending buffet, and many libraries have found that use quickly outstrips the funds that have been allocated.[34] Allocations for patron-driven acquisition are usually redirected from discretionary budget lines. A subset may be created under an existing fund line, or the library may create a new fund line.

Annual allocations for approval plans and patron-driven acquisition are usually based on activity during the previous year. These data can be provided by the vendor or extracted from the library's year-end expenditure reports.

Some libraries create separate fund lines for formats (print, video and audio recordings, electronic resources, microforms) or genres (books, periodicals, musical scores, government documents), either as subsets within subject lines or as all-encompassing funds. For example, a library might have a fund line used to purchase all microforms regardless of subject. This approach may have utility in smaller libraries, but many libraries are moving to format- and genre-agnostic budgets to reflect an emphasis on viewing the collection holistically.[35] In this approach, materials are selected based on collecting priorities and need regardless of format or genre, and the budget allocations are also not constrained by format or genre. If the ability to report expenditures by format or genre is important, most acquisitions modules in integrated library systems allow libraries to create material type codes that are applied to orders as they are placed. These might include book (print), book (electronic), serial (print), serial (electronic), computer file, music score, realia, and many more, depending of the granularity of the data the library needs to track and report. Reports can be run that total expenditures and number of items by code.

Recent rapid increases in prices have made monitoring the balance between expenditures for discretionary and nondiscretionary materials especially critical. Inflating prices for nondiscretionary commitments can easily consume a library's budget within a few years, leaving little to spend on discretionary purchases. When materials acquired with nondiscretionary allocations were primarily serials, libraries could look at the ratio between serials and monographs and set targets. Although the collecting goals of each library affect this ratio, a common practice in academic libraries has been to maintain a ratio of no less than 30 percent of the budget spent on monographs and no more than 70 percent on serials. Public and school libraries generally have aimed for something closer to a 50:50 ratio. Some special libraries might set a target that accepts spending 80–90 percent of the budget on serials. All targets now need to be reviewed carefully in the face of continuing commitments for e-packages. Few libraries want to be in a position in which they have no or very limited funds for discretionary purchase.

Libraries use different approaches to determine allocation amounts. These range from using an allocation formula to zero-based budgeting to incremental adjustments to historical allocations. Ideally, the process of allocating annually is efficient, transparent, and repeatable. Cumbersome approaches can be difficult to administer and just as unwieldy as overly complex collections policies. No perfect solution exists, but libraries continue to tweak various approaches.

Allocation formulas are usually built on supply and demand factors.[36] The supply factors take into account the amount of material published in the subject area, the cost of those materials, and total library collections support. Demand factors include number of students, teachers, faculty, courses offered, circulation, registered borrowers, interlibrary activity, and library and parent organization priorities. Often, factors in the formula are weighted. For example, the number of doctoral students might be weighted three times the number of undergraduates in the formula to accommodate the specialized resource needs of doctoral candidates.

Formula-based budgeting is appealing because it appears impartial and objective, but its success depends on the factors used to create the formula and the data applied, both of which can be subjective and unreliable. Paris reports that the formula allocation model his library used "remained a perennial target of complaints and seemed impossible to revise to everyone's satisfaction." Cross calls budget allocation formulas inherently irrational. Shirk, while noting that formulas have been successful in some settings, considers them in many ways arbitrary conventions that lack a "defensible theoretical framework that relates objective variables to the collection's performance in a meaningful way."[37]

Many libraries have found formulas useful because they are data-driven and are appealing in settings where the budget is open to a highly interested constituency of users. However, formulas can be exceedingly complex to employ because of the extensive data required and the intricacy of calculations. Formula-based allocations are often adjusted on the basis of professional judgment and local factors that cannot be quantified completely in a formula.

Another method of collections budget allocation is *incremental* and based on historical—that is, prior—allocations. A senior collection development officer or the director of the library gathers information from collections librarians and the parent organization and adjusts the historical allocations based on this information. The collection development officer often takes into account the same factors used in the allocation formula but brings to bear a knowledge of the parent institution or agency, the user community, and the library's longer-term goals in a less rigid manner. One advantage of this method is that the effects of unexpected and short-term shifts in the parent body are diminished.

Regardless of the allocation method used, most libraries begin the process by allocating "off the top" for known annual expenditures and contractual obligations. This means that money is set aside for these expenditures before the rest of the money is allocated to fund lines. These might be memberships, consortial purchases, and perhaps multiyear subscriptions if the library has committed to a Big Deal. If the library uses patron-driven acquisitions, this also might be funded off the top.

Budget models vary in how they handle allocation of and responsibility for expending funds for e-resources. Some libraries have a single central fund line used for all e-resources. A single separate fund can emphasize the priority of e-resources to the organization and make tracking expenditures easier, but it can also stress their separateness from other selection and management activities. At the other end of the continuum is the model in which all funds are allocated to subject lines, and individual librarians manage these fund lines as they manage fund lines for more traditional library materials. Librarians may make cooperative purchases with other librarians by pooling funds, but no resources are funded centrally. A middle ground retains some money in a central fund for resources (perhaps a general periodical index and associated full-text file, an encyclopedia, or an aggregator package) of system-wide interest and allocates to the individual subject line level for more narrowly focused titles. If e-journals and e-books are part of a package from an aggregator or a publisher, separating and tracking costs of individual titles and aligning these costs with subject fund lines present challenges for collection development librarians and library accounting staff.

Most libraries hold some money aside in a *contingency fund*, which may be managed by the collection development officer, the library director, or a library committee. This fund can be used to meet unexpected needs, purchase expensive items, and balance unexpected fluctuations in user demand. Holding 5–10 percent of the total materials budget in a contingency fund is a common strategy.

Allocating and managing a collections budget require compliance with the parent organization's fiscal and accounting requirements as well as wise financial decisions. Most nonprofit organizations are required to use *fund accounting*, a procedure through which funds are classified for accounting and reporting purposes in accordance with the regulations, restrictions, or limitations imposed by the governing board or sources outside the library, or in accordance with activities or objectives specified by donors. Fund accounting is usually expressed in a line-item budget. Moving funds from the operating budget to the collections budget or using collections fund to acquire computer equipment or to support data lines for accessing remote resources may be prohibited. Though many libraries have accounting staff or rely on the resources of the larger organization for accounting activities, librarians with collections responsibilities should understand the regulations, restrictions, and limitations that apply.

Expending the Budget

Once the collections budget is allocated, it must be spent. Expenditures are tracked to inform the planning process and allow the library to report on its progress to the parent institution or governing body. Many libraries use this information to assess the performance of librarians and of the library as a whole. For example, the library may have a goal of meeting the needs of a multicultural population. The library could use the reports of funds expended combined with circulation data to show progress toward this goal. In addition, reports of expenditures are useful when preparing stewardship reports and thanking donors.

Most libraries set targets for expenditures and encumbrances during and at the end of the fiscal year. Institutions that operate on a cash accounting system require that the funds be fully expended by the end of the fiscal year and do not permit unexpended funds to be carried forward to the next year. Some organizations using a cash accounting system do permit carrying forward of encumbrances, with the funds held in escrow to cover payment when the ordered item is receipted. The accrual system of accounting allows a library to carry over unexpended funds and encumbered dollars, which are added to the new year's allocation. Some libraries and their parent organizations discourage developing large cash balances, often called reserves, which can suggest that the library or a particular budget line is overfunded. Figure 3-1 presents a sample budget cycle for an academic library that is able to carry forward encumbrances.

Figure 3-2 represents the midyear financial status of a public library that has allocated $820,000, with varying ratios in the allocations to discretionary and nondiscretionary categories, depending on the collection and user focus. This library has allocated off the top for multidisciplinary databases and packages for e-books and audio recordings. In addition, funds are allocated at the highest level for reference, adult, and young adult and children's materials, with subcategories under each. The library does not have an approval plan. Note that all invoices for multidisciplinary databases, e-book packages, audio packages, and electronic nondiscretionary materials under the primary budget divisions (reference, adult, and young adult and children) were paid early in the year. Nondiscretionary funds do not show encumbrances because the commitments for these resources are known when the initial allocations are made and orders are not placed during the fiscal year. A few invoices for print nondiscretionary materials (primarily serials) have not been received, so these fund lines show modest free balances. A few discretionary fund lines have free balances (initial allocation minus encumbrances and expenditures) that do not match the target of 50 percent of the allocation available at the midyear point. Apparently, the collections librarian

July	**Fiscal Year Closeout/New Year Startup**
	Open and partial orders and funds are rolled over for new fiscal year cycle.
	Preliminary allocations are made and selectors are advised to begin ordering, assuming they have 60% of previous year's allocation (all funds and endowments) and carryover and unexpended gift funds from previous year.
	Administration notifies libraries about new general funds available for collections.
	First half-year payment is made to vendor to ensure approval plan discount.
August	**New Fiscal Year Allocation Planning**
	Library Budget Advisory Group meets to determine distribution of general funds.
	Selectors are advised if serials cancellation required.
	Head of Collection Unit, in consultation with Collection Development Advisory Group, determines subject and collection allocations.
September	End-of-fiscal-year documentation is prepared for selectors, including summaries of allocations, outstanding encumbrances, and expenditures by category.
	Balance of current fiscal year funds (new general funds and endowment funds) is allocated to subject and collection fund lines.
	Serial title cancellations are due to Serials Department.
November	General monographic funds should be 66% committed.
January	General monographic funds should be 85% committed.
	All non-U.S. source orders should be submitted by January 31.
	Second half-year payment is made to vendor to ensure approval plan discount.
March	March 15: Deadline for submitting monographic orders (should be 100% committed).
	March 31: Uncommitted general funds are pooled for special purchases.
April	Special purchase requests are solicited, final decisions made, and orders placed.
June	June 30: Endowment funds should be fully committed.

FIGURE 3-1   Sample budget cycle for an academic library using an accrual accounting system

responsible for adult materials has been fixated on ordering media, leaving less than 2 percent of the allocation for the second half of the year. The adult print collection is suffering from lack of attention, with 75 percent of the allocation still available. The contingency fund allocation remains untouched and can be used for special purchases or to address clear needs.

Libraries can experience a significant lag—as much as ninety days—between the date an order is placed and the date the item is received and the invoice paid. The period between order placement and item receipt of highly specialized materials can be years. Librarians with collections responsibilities usually have encumbrance target dates that are based on the library's experience with receiving material and paying bills. The simplest way to accomplish this is to count

Fund Line	Initial Allocation 7/1/2013	Encumbrances 12/31/2013	Expenditures 12/31/2013	Free Balance 12/31/2013	% Remaining 12/31/2013
Electronic					
Multidisciplinary databases	125,000	0	125,000	0	0
E-book packages	50,000	0	50,000	0	0
Audio packages	25,000	0	25,000	0	0
Subtotal	200,000	0	200,000	0	0
Reference					
Discretionary	30,000	2,000	13,000	15,000	50.0
Nondiscretionary	70,000	0	60,000	10,000	14.3
Subtotal	100,000	2,000	73,000	25,000	25.0
Adult					
Discretionary					
Print	160,000	2,000	38,000	120,000	75.0
Media	15,000	400	14,400	200	1.3
Nondiscretionary					
Print	87,500	0	82,000	5,500	6.3
Electronic	87,500	0	87,500	0	0
Subtotal	350,000	2,400	221,900	125,700	35.9
Young Adult and Children					
Discretionary					
Print	70,000	5,000	30,000	35,000	50.0
Media	10,000	500	4,500	5,000	50.0
Nondiscretionary					
Print	30,000	0	26,000	4,000	13.3
Electronic	20,000	0	20,000	0	0
Subtotal	130,000	5,500	80,500	44,000	33.8
Contingency	40,000	0	0	40,000	100.0
TOTAL	820,000	9,900	575,400	234,700	28.6

FIGURE 3-2 Sample midyear budget report for a public library

backward from the end of the fiscal year and end the collection development year on the last day one can expect to receive and pay for the material. Setting interim dates to check the progress of the library toward its goal of fully expending the budget is important. The amount of material published can vary widely from year to year, and libraries may need to make midyear adjustments to ensure all funds are spent by the end of the fiscal year.

Most institutions require some separation of selection, acquisition, and payment responsibilities to guard against fraud and malfeasance. Depending on the size of the library, it may have three people or three departments. Within a large acquisitions department, separate units may order and receipt materials. In very small libraries, the same person may handle all functions. Even then, the three functions should be clearly defined and distinguished. Proper handling of these functions is necessary for a successful audit. Audits are reviews of financial records, usually conducted at regular intervals by parties external to the library. They serve to verify that financial records are accurate and orderly, that the library is in compliance with organizational and generally accepted accounting policies and procedures, and that units are operating effectively.

Monitoring the Materials Budget

Several individuals may have responsibilities for monitoring the materials budget. A librarian assigned one or more fund lines against which orders are placed is normally charged with monitoring these allocations and ensuring that funds are expended over the fiscal year in accordance with the collections policy and library goals. In libraries with a collections officer, collections coordinator, or someone else with oversight responsibility for the materials budget, this person monitors the total budget to track that balances are being spent down and, when necessary, to reallocate unspent funds. This person is charged with ensuring that the budget is being spent in a manner consistent with the library's planning documents. In libraries that have a financial officer or that rely on the parent organization's financial officer, this individual oversees procedures to ensure that encumbrances and payments are correctly recorded. If any funds are to be carried forward into the next year, either as encumbered or cash balances, the financial officer negotiates and monitors this process. Usually, the financial officer prepares year-end reports. These show balances by fund line and list expenditures and encumbrances. The librarian with overall collections responsibility uses this report to see if goals for the year were met, to prepare the next year's budget request, and to adjust allocations. Of course, in smaller libraries and those with one librarian, all these responsibilities rest with a single individual.

CASE STUDY

Cody was recently hired as collections coordinator at the Merryman County Public Library System, which has a central library, forty-five branch locations, and two bookmobiles serving a population of more than two million that is increasingly diverse. The system employs 752 FTE staff, of whom 216 are librarians. The collection includes 3.8 million items; it offers downloadable e-books, audiobooks, music, videos, and more than 150 databases. The system has allocated $3,158,000 for collections, with $1,990,500 for print materials, $580,000 for electronic materials, and $587,500 for "other materials." Funds allocated for other materials have been used to purchase films, audio recordings, and microforms. The system has continued to add databases and also has licensed access to downloadable collections of e-titles for children, e-books for adults, and music, but it has only rarely added circulating DVDs, Blu-ray discs, and CDs. The system is just starting to acquire video games. The budget model has not been adjusted to reflect the increasing expenditures for e-content or the formats in which acquisition is declining. The current budget uses both format and genre categories within an overarching distinction between materials for adults and youth (which includes children and young adults). The current fund lines are as follows:

Adult fiction
Adult nonfiction
Adult feature films
Adult nonfeature films
Adult periodicals
Adult music
Adult microfilm
Adult reference
Adult standing orders

Adult spoken word
Adult large print
Adult mass market
  paperbacks
Youth fiction
Youth nonfiction
Youth picture books
Youth films
Youth periodicals

Youth music
Youth reference
Youth spoken word
Non-English-language
  materials
Electronic
  subscriptions
Contingency

The director of the library system has asked Cody to propose a new budget model for her consideration.

Activity

Develop a new budget model for the Merryman County Public Library System. This new model should reflect the changing focus of the collection through the use of meaningful fund names and address the need for discretionary and nondiscretionary allocations. You may allocate dollars to each new fund line using the total available budget of $3,158,000 or indicate a percentage to be allocated to each fund line. Explain why you have chosen the new budget model and fund names along with your rationale for the amounts or percentages allocated to each fund line.

Notes

1. Peter Drucker, *Management: Tasks, Responsibilities, Practices* (New York: Harper and Row, 1974), 125.

2. George Keller, *Academic Strategy: The Management Revolution in American Higher Education* (Baltimore, MD: Johns Hopkins University Press, 1983).

3. See, for example, John D. Crowley, *Developing a Vision: Strategic Planning for the School Librarian in the 21st Century*, 2nd ed. (Santa Barbara, CA: Libraries Unlimited, 2011); Ken Roberts and Daphne Wood, "Strategic Planning: A Valuable, Productive and Engaging Experience (Honest)," *Feliciter* 58, no. 5 (2012): 10–11; David J. Staley, Scott Seaman, and Eileen Theodore-Shusta, "Futuring, Strategic Planning and Shared Awareness: An Ohio State University Libraries' Case Study," *Journal of Academic Librarianship* 38, no. 1 (Jan. 2012): 1–5; Joseph R. Matthews, *Strategic Planning and Management for Library Managers* (Westport, CT: Libraries Unlimited, 2005); Meredith Taylor and Fred Heath, "Assessment and Continuous Planning: The Key to Transformation at the University of Texas Libraries," *Journal of Library Administration* 52, no. 5 (July 2012): 424–35; Tracey Wong, "Strategic Long-Range Planning," *Library Media Connection* 31, no. 2 (Oct. 2012): 22–24.

4. Association of Research libraries, *The ARL 2030 Scenarios: A User's Guide for Research Libraries* (Washington, DC: Association of Research libraries, 2010).

5. Jörg H. Mayer et al., "More Applicable Environmental Scanning Systems Leveraging 'Modern' Information Systems," *Information Systems and e-Business Management,* 11, no. 4 (Dec. 2013): 507–40.

6. Eileen Abels, "Environmental Scanning," *Bulletin of the American Society for Information Science and Technology* 28, no. 3 (Feb./Mar. 2002): 16.

7. James H. Spohrer, "The End of an American (Library) Dream: The Rise and Decline of the Collection Development Policy Statement at Berkeley," *Acquisitions Librarian* 25, no. 30 (2003): 46; Carolynne Myall and Sue Anderson, "Can This Orthodoxy Be Saved? Enhancing the Usefulness of Collection Plans in the Digital Environment," *Collection Management* 32, no. 3/4 (2007): 235–58; Marjorie L. Pappas, "Selection Policies," *School Library Media Activities Monthly* 21, no. 2 (Oct. 2004): 41, 45.

8. Joanne S. Anderson, ed., *Guide for Written Collection Policy Statements*, 2nd ed., Collection Management and Development Guides no.7 (Chicago: American Library Association, 1996), 1.

9. American Library Association, Coordinating Committee on Revision of Public Library Standards, *Public Library Service to America: A Guide to Evaluation, with Minimum Standards* (Chicago: American Library Association, 1956); American Association of School Librarians, *Policies and Procedures for the Selection of School Library Materials* (Chicago: American Library Association, 1961).

10. Minnesota Legislative Reference Library, "About," www.leg.state.mn.us/lrl/about.aspx.

11. American Library Association, "About the ALA Library," www.ala.org/tools/about-ala-library.

12. Steven A. Lastres, "Collection Development in the Age of the Virtual Law Library," *AALL Spectrum* 15, no. 8 (June 2011): 20–23.

13. Richard Snow, "Wasted Words: The Written Collection Development Policy and the Academic Library," *Journal of Academic Librarianship* 22, no. 3 (1996): 191–94; Dan Hazen, "Collection Development Policies in the Information Age," *College and Research Libraries* 56, no. 1 (Jan. 1995): 29; Jim Vickery, "Making a Statement: Reviewing the Case for Written Collection Development Policies," *Library Management* 25, no. 8/9 (2004): 337–42.

14. Wayne Disher, *Crash Course in Collection Development* (Westport, CT: Libraries Unlimited, 2007), 46.

15. Nebraska Educational Media Association, *Guide for Developing and Evaluating School Library Programs*, 7th ed. (Santa Barbara, CA: Libraries Unlimited, 2010), 117.

16. Barbara B. Moran, Robert D. Stueart, and Claudia J. Morner, *Library and Information Center Management*, 8th ed. (Santa Barbara, CA: Libraries Unlimited, 2013).

17. W. Bernard Lukenbill, *Collection Development for a New Century in the School Library Media Center* (Westport, CT: Greenwood, 2002), 43.

18. Samuel Demas and Mary E. Miller, "Rethinking Collection Management Plans: Shaping Collective Collections for the 21st Century," *Collection Management* 37, no. 3/4 (2012): 168–87.

19. Elizabeth A. Sudduth, Nancy B. Newins, and William E. Sudduth, comps., *Special Collections in College and University Libraries*, CLIP Note no. 35 (Chicago: Association of College and Research Libraries, 2004).

20. Andy Corrigan, "The Collection Policy Reborn: A Practical Application of Web-Based Documentation," *Collection Building* 24, no. 2 (2005): 65–69.

21. *AcqWeb's Directory of Collection Development Policies on the Web*, www.acqweb.org/cd_policy.html. Several print resources on format, content, and style are available. Among these are Anderson, *Guide for Written Collection Policy Statements;* Frank W. Hoffman and Richard J. Wood, *Library Collection Development Policies: Academic Public, and Special Libraries* (Lanham, MD: Scarecrow, 2005); Frank W. Hoffman and Richard J. Wood, *Library Collection Development Policies: School Libraries and Learning Resource Centers*, Good Policy, Good Practice no. 2 (Lanham, MD: Scarecrow, 2007).

22. This list is an expansion of the list of elements offered in Hoffman and Wood, *Library Collection Development Policies: Academic, Public, and Special Libraries*.

23. St. Paul Public Library, "Collection Development Policy," www.sppl.org/about/
    policies-and-guidelines/collection-development.

24. St. Paul Public Library, "Collection Development Policy, Independently Published
    Materials," www.sppl.org/about/policies-and-guidelines/collection
    -development.

25. Denver Public Libraries, Library Policies and Resources, "Collection Development
    Policy," http://denverlibrary.org/content/library-policies-resources.

26. Dora Biblarz, "The Conspectus as a Blueprint for Creating Collection Develop-
    ment Policy Statements," in *Collection Assessment: A Look at the RLG Conspectus*, ed.
    Richard J. Wood and Katina P. Strauch, 169–76 (New York: Haworth, 1992).

27. David Farrell and Jutta Reed-Scott, "The North American Inventory Project:
    Implications for the Future of Coordinated Management of Research Collections,"
    Library Resources and Technical Services 33, no. 1 (Jan. 1989): 15–28; Mary C.
    Bushing, "The Evolution of Conspectus Practice in Libraries: The Beginnings and
    the Present Applications," Sborník ze semináře CASLIN 2001—Popis a zpřístupění
    dokumětů: nová výzva [Proceedings of the Seminar CASLIN 2001—Document
    Description and Access: New Challenge], Beroun, Czech Republic, May 27–31,
    2001, http://klement.nkp.cz/Caslin/caslin01/sbornik/conspectus.html.

28. International Federation of Library Associations and Institutions, Section on
    Acquisition and Collections Development, *Guidelines for a Collection Development
    Policy Using the Conspectus Model* (The Hague: International Federation of Library
    Associations and Institutions, 2001), www.ifla.org/files/assets/acquisition-collection
    -development/publications/gcdp-en.pdf.

29. Eugene L. Wiemers Jr., "Budget," in *Collection Management: A New Treatise*,
    ed. Charles B. Osburn and Ross Atkinson, 67–79, Foundations in Library and
    Information Science 26 (Greenwich, CT: JAI, 1991), 67.

30. David Farrell, "Fundraising for Collection Development Librarians," in *Collection
    Management and Development: Issues in an Electronic Era*, ed. Peggy Johnson and
    Bonnie MacEwan, 133–42 (Chicago: American Library Association, 1994).

31. Christopher Harris, "Enter 'Blended Funding': Schools Must Pool Money to
    Support Common Core," *School Library Journal* 58, no. 12 (Dec. 2012): 16.

32. Carl A. Harvey II, *The 21st Century Elementary Library Media Program* (Santa
    Barbara, CA: Libraries Unlimited, 2010).

33. Wiemers, "Budget," 68–69.

34. Erin S. Fisher and Lisa Kurt, presenters, Sarah Garner, recorder, "Exploring
    Patron-Driven Access Models for E-journals and E-books," *Serials Librarian* 62,
    no. 1/4 (2012): 164–69; Tian Ciao Zhang, "Pay-Per-View: A Promising Model of
    E-articles Subscription for Middle/Small Sized Academic Libraries in the Digital
    Age," *Libraries in the Digital Age (LIDA) Proceedings* 12 (2012), http://ozk.unizd.hr/
    proceedings/index.php/lida2012/article/view/8/18.

35. James P. Kusik and Mark A. Vargas, "Improving Electronic Resources through Holistic Budgeting," *Journal of Electronic Resources Librarianship* 21, no. 3/4 (2009): 200–205.

36. Charles B. Lowry offers an overview of formulas, including the limits they have as allocation tools in his "Reconciling Pragmatism, Equity, and Need in the Formula Allocation of Book and Serial Funds," *College and Research Libraries* 53, no. 2 (Mar. 1992): 121–38.

37. Terrence Paris, "Breaking the Mould: How Re-examining the Allocation Formula Led to the Creation of a Dynamic Role for the University's Librarians," *Partnership: The Canadian Journal of Library and information Practice and Research* 2, no. 2 (2007), http://condor.lib.uoguelph.ca/index.php/perj/article/view/302/566; Roger L. Cross, "Budget Allocation Formulas: Magic or Illusion?" *Bottom Line: Managing Library Finances* 24, no. 1 (2011): 63–67; Gary M. Shirk, "Allocation Formulas for Budgeting Library Materials: Science of Procedure?" *Collection Management* 6, no. 3/4 (Fall/Winter 1984): 46.

Suggested Readings

Albitz, Becky, and David Brennan. "Budgeting for E-books." In *Building and Managing E-book Collections*, ed. Richard Kaplan, 85–94. New York: Neal-Schuman, 2012.

Bishop, Kay. "Fiscal Issues Relating to the Collection." In *The Collection Program in Schools: Concepts and Practices*, 5th ed., 205–11. Santa Barbara, CA: Libraries Unlimited, 2012.

———. "Policies and Procedures." In *The Collection Program in Schools: Concepts and Practices*, 5th ed., 37–43. Santa Barbara, CA: Libraries Unlimited, 2012.

Bosch, Stephen, Kittie S. Henderson, and Heather Klusendorf. "Polishing the Crystal Ball: Using Historical Data to Project Serials Trends and Pricing." *Serials Librarian* 62, no. 1/4 (2012): 87–94.

Bryson, John M. *Strategic Planning for Public and Nonprofit Organizations: A Guide to Strengthening and Sustaining Organizational Achievement.* 4th ed. San Francisco: Jossey-Bass, 2011.

Burkett, Karen. "The Development of a Selection Policy for the School Library." *Literacies, Learning, and Libraries* 2, no. 1 (2009): 3–6.

Carpenter, Julie. *Library Project Funding: A Guide to Planning and Writing Proposals.* Oxford, UK: Chandos, 2008.

Chan, Gayle R. Y. C. "Aligning Collections Budget with Program Priorities: A Modified Zero-Based Approach." *Library Collections, Acquisitions, and Technical Services* 32, no. 1 (2008): 46–52.

Clement, Susanne K., and Jennifer M. Foy. *Collection Development in a Changing Environment: Policies and Organization for College and University Libraries.* CLIP

Note no. 42. Chicago: College Library Information Packet Committee, College Libraries Section, Association of College and Research Libraries, 2010.

Conrad, Suzanna. "Collection Development and Circulation Policies in Prison Libraries: An Exploratory Survey of Librarians in U.S. Correctional Institutions." *Library Quarterly* 82, no. 4 (Oct. 2012): 407–27.

Dinkins, Debbi. "Allocating Academic Library Budgets: Adapting Historical Data Models at One University Library." *Collection Management* 36, no. 2 (2011): 119–30.

Douglas, C. Steven. "Revising a Collection Development Policy in a Rapidly Changing Environment." *Journal of Electronic Resources in Medical Libraries* 8, no. 1 (2011): 15–21.

Dowlin, Kenneth E. *Getting the Money: How to Succeed in Fundraising for Public and Nonprofit Libraries*. Westport, CT: Libraries Unlimited, 2009.

Downs, Elizabeth. *The School Library Media Specialist's Policy and Procedure Writer*. New York: Neal-Schuman, 2010.

Evans, G. Edward, and Camila Alire. "The Planning Process." In *Management Basics for Information Professionals*, 3rd ed., 85–106. New York: Neal-Schuman, 2013.

Franklin, Pat, and Claire G. Stephens. "Gaining Skills to Write Winning Grants." *School Library Media Activities Monthly* 25, no. 3 (2008): 43–44.

Gregory, Vicki L. "Collection Development Policies." In *Collection Development and Management for 21st Century Library Collections: An Introduction*, 31–53. New York: Neal-Schuman, 2011.

Hall-Ellis, Sylvia D., et al. *Librarian's Handbook for Seeking, Writing, and Managing Grants*. Santa Barbara, CA: Libraries Unlimited, 2011.

Kirk, Rachel A. *Balancing the Books: Accounting for Librarians*. Westport, CT: Libraries Unlimited, 2012.

Landau, Herbert B. *Winning Library Grants: A Game Plan*. Chicago: American Library Association, 2011.

Lyons, Lucy Eleonore, and John Blosser. "An Analysis and Allocation System for Library Collections Budgets: The Comprehensive Allocation Process (CAP)." *Journal of Academic Librarianship* 38, no. 5 (Sept. 2012): 294–310.

MacKellar, Pamela H., and Stephanie K. Gerding. *Winning Grants: A How-to-Do-It Manual for Librarians with Multimedia Tutorials and Grant Development Tools*. How-to-Do-It Manuals for Librarians 173. New York: Neal-Schuman, 2010.

Mangrum, Suzanne, and Mary Ellen Pozzebon. "Use of Collection Development Policies in Electronic Resource Management." *Collection Building* 31, no. 3 (2012): 108–14.

Maxwell, Nancy Kalikow. *The ALA Book of Library Grant Money*. Chicago: American Library Association, 2014.

———. *Grant Money through Collaborative Partnerships*. Chicago: American Library Association, 2012.

Meyer, Nadean. "Collection Development and Budgets: Methods to Keep the Curriculum Center Current." In *Curriculum Materials Collections and Centers: Legacies from the Past, Visions of the Future*, ed. Rita Kohrman, 75–100. Chicago: Association of College and Research Libraries, 2012.

Nelke, Margareta. *Strategic Business Development for Information Centres and Libraries*. Oxford, UK: Chandos, 2012.

Nelson, Sandra, for the Public Library Association. *Implementing for Results: Your Strategic Plan in Action*. Chicago: American Library Association, 2009.

———. *Strategic Planning for Results*. PLA Results Series. Chicago: American Library Association, 2008.

O'Connor, Steve, and Peter Sidorko. *Imagine Your Library's Future: Scenario Planning for Libraries and Information Organisations*. Oxford, UK: Chandos, 2010.

Pickett, Carmelita, et al. "Revisiting an Abandoned Practice: The Death and Resurrection of Collection Development Policies." *Collection Management* 36, no. 3 (2011): 165–81.

Pomerantz, Sarah, and Andrew White. "Re-modeling ILS Acquisitions Data to Financially Transition from Print to Digital Formats." *Library Collections, Acquisitions, and Technical Services* 33, no. 1 (2009): 42–49.

Shaw, Wendy. "Collection Development Policies for the Digital Age." In *Collection Development in the Digital Age*, ed. Maggie Fieldhouse and Audrey Marshall, 165–80. London: Facet, 2012.

Smith, Debbi A. "Percentage-Based Allocation of an Academic Library Materials Budget." *Collection Building* 27, no.1 (2008): 30–34.

Stachokas, George, and Tim Gritten. "Adapting to Scarcity: Developing an Integrated Allocation Formula." *Collection Management* 38, no. 1 (2013): 33–50.

Staines, Gail M. *Go Get That Grant! A Practical Guide Libraries and Nonprofit Organizations*. Lanham, MD: Scarecrow, 2010.

Vandenbroek, Alicia. "Grant Writing without Blowing a Gasket." *Library Media Connection* 28, no. 6 (2010): 28–30.

VanDuinkerken, Wyoma, et al. "Creating a Flexible Fund Structure to Meet the Needs and Goals of the Library and Its Users." *Library Collections, Acquisitions, and Technical Services* 32, no. 3/4 (2008): 142–49.

Walters, William H. "A Fund Allocation Formula Based on Demand, Cost, and Supply." *Library Quarterly* 78, no. 3 (July 2008): 303–14.

Williams, Virginia Kay, and June Schmidt. "Determining the Average Cost of a Book for Allocation Formulas: Comparing Options." *Library Resources and Technical Services* 52, no. 1 (2008): 60–70.

CHAPTER FOUR

Developing Collections

This chapter covers the activities that develop or build collections. It might have been called "Selection" in earlier times. Selecting between two or more options is part of nearly every decision collections librarians make as they seek to implement collection development and management goals; as Carrigan puts it, "The essence of collection development is choice."[1] This chapter introduces various topologies for defining types of materials and explores the selection process and selection criteria; sources for identifying titles, evaluating materials, and assessing their value to the local user community; the importance of serving diverse users; the acquisition process; and acquisition options.

Universe of Published Materials

Selecting among the vast number of materials published each year can seem a daunting task. Book title output increases every year. UNESCO no longer collects data on the number of books published per country per year, but a Wikipedia entry, drawing from a variety of sources, estimates that more than two million titles are published annually.[2] Bowker reported that U.S. title output of traditional print books increased by 6 percent between 2010 and 2011 to a projected 347,178 titles.[3] Although this was the largest increase in more than four years, it was driven by tremendous growth in the self-publishing market. According to Bowker, self-published books in the United States grew 286 percent between 2006 and 2011—and this number reflects only books that were issued ISBNs.[4] Although data on the sales of e-books are available, the number of new e-books released each year is not. The number of active periodicals also continues to grow. When consulted in 2013, Bowker's Ulrichsweb.com listed more than 234,650 academic and scholarly journals (largely peer-reviewed titles including many open-access publications), popular magazines, newspapers, newsletters, and other types of periodicals in print and electronic versions from around the world.[5]

Librarians are challenged by increasing materials costs as well as the vast number of publications. The costs of materials have been increasing far in excess of U.S. inflation for more than twenty-five years and usually in excess of most libraries' acquisition budgets. Between 2007 and 2008, the CPI increased 0.1 percent and the average price of U.S. periodicals increased by 8.0 percent. The average price of North American academic books published in 2010 increased by 12.4 percent over 2009, compared to the CPI increase of 1.5 percent; during the same period hardcover books increased by 5.54 percent and mass market paperbacks 1.94 percent.[6]

As noted earlier, budgets in libraries of all types are constrained, sometimes increasing slightly, sometimes holding steady, and often declining. Libraries experience constant pressure to provide more digital resources and face a confusing array of e-content purchase and lease options. More materials from which to choose, increasing prices, limited budgets, and user interest in e-content mean that collections librarians must be increasingly discriminating in the choices they make.

Categorizing Materials

A frequent first step in selecting materials is separating them into categories. Larger libraries may assign selection responsibilities for these categories to different people. Several topologies, many of them overlapping, have been and continue to be used. Format is a typical topology and distinguishes, for example, between print, microforms, video and audio recordings, and e-resources. Format often guides how the material is handled in the library—if it is represented in the library's catalog, who catalogs it, and, if a physical object, how it is marked, shelved or stored, and circulated. Other formats are manuscripts and archives, maps, slides, pictures, globes, kits, models, games, and realia.

Genre is often mingled incorrectly with format when discussing types of materials. Genre categories include monographs, monographic series, manga and anime, zines, dissertations, musical scores, newspapers, application software, numeric data sets, exhibition catalogs, pamphlets, novels, plays, manuals, websites, encyclopedias, ephemera, gray literature, indexes and abstracts, directories, journals, magazines, textbooks, and government documents. A single genre may be presented in several formats. For example, serial publications can be acquired in print, microform, and digital formats.

Resources may be categorized by subject. These may be broad divisions (humanities, social sciences, sciences), narrower (literature, sociology, engineering), or very refined (American literature, family social science, chemical engineering). Often, the categories are described by divisions in a classification scheme, typically the Library of Congress or Dewey Decimal systems. Some genres are more frequently found within subjects and disciplines. For example, the sciences rely heavily on proceedings and research reports. Tests and other measurement tools are part of the education and psychology literature.

Materials can be subdivided by language in which they are produced or geographic area in which they are published or which they cover. They may be considered by the age of the reader to whom they are directed—children, young adult, adult. These, too, can be subdivided (e.g., picture books, early readers). Public libraries may subdivide materials by type of publisher, for example, adult hardcover, trade fiction, and mass market paperbacks. Academic and research libraries may distinguish between primary (source documents), secondary (reviews, state-of-the-art summaries, textbooks, interpretations of primary sources), and tertiary resources (repackaging of the primary literature in popular treatments, annuals, handbooks, and encyclopedias).

Topologies guide how reviews, publication lists, and introductions to the literature are organized or defined. These may reflect format, such as *Film and Video Finder*.[7] They may reflect subject areas ("Top Physics and Science Books of 2012"), reader groups (*Multiethnic Books for the Middle-School Curriculum*), or genres (*Public Library Core Collection: Nonfiction*).[8] Appendix B suggests bibliographic tools, directories, and review resources to aid in selection.

Many libraries merge some categories when assigning and managing selection responsibilities. Academic libraries might use a combination of subject or discipline specialists, geographic area studies librarians, and government documents librarians, each with associated collection responsibilities. Public libraries may categorize by reader group or subject area or a combination. School libraries may think in terms of fiction and nonfiction, age of reader, and subject area.

Rigidly following topological distinctions in performing collections responsibilities can result in important resources being ignored because they are in a format or genre outside a librarian's normal scope of collecting or not covered in a familiar catalog or selection tool. According to "Guidelines for Audiovisual and Multimedia Materials in Libraries and Other Institutions," issued by IFLA, "An ever-increasing amount of information—covering educational and recreational interests as well as information needs—is being produced in a wide range of audiovisual and electronic formats. Access to these materials should be as open and as free as access to print-based materials." Abram calls on librarians to be "container and format agnostic" to ensure that collections seamlessly offer users all relevant resources regardless of format and genre.[9] Graphic novels are one example of a format that may be unfamiliar and thus ignored. Graphic novels are book-length publications presented in comic format and, despite being called novels, can be fiction or nonfiction. They can fulfill various roles in school library media centers, from supporting the K–12 curriculum to meeting students' leisure reading interests. Being aware of the variety of formats and genres available and the various tools to review them can enhance developing the collection as a coherent whole. Failing to encompass all formats in collections ignores a tremendous wealth of information and artistic expression.

The Selection Process

Selection is both an art and a science. It results from a combination of knowledge, experience, and intuition. Experienced collections librarians may be hard-pressed to explain exactly how they decide what to add and what to exclude. Rutledge and Swindler propose a mental model that assigns a weighted value to each criterion considered.[10] They suggest that a collections librarian works through this mental model and reaches one of three conclusions: the title must be added, should be added, or could be added. Williams explores how the mind works in the decision process, citing the role of recognition, "an automatic or deliberative decision-making process whereby a cue is subjected to some kind of familiarity test and an affirmative or negative response is given."[11] Recognition guides the librarian to determining if the item is appropriate and helps answer questions about whether the content is relevant and whether the author, editor, publisher, or title is familiar. Williams notes that recognition capabilities are strengthened as a result of frequent, routine, and repeated collection building. Mastery comes through these activities.

Despite the central roles that experience, intuition, and sometimes emotion play in collection building, familiarity with selection tools and understanding their techniques, processes, and potential problems are essential building blocks for success. The librarian should know the appropriate resources for locating suitable materials and needs skills in choosing between various materials and formats, evaluating materials' quality, and balancing costs with funds available.

All selection decisions begin with consideration of the user community and the long-term mission, goals, and priorities of the library and its parent body. Long ago Drury stated, "The high purpose of book selection is to provide the right book for the right reader at the right time." About the same time, Ranganathan proposed his five laws of library science, which include "Every reader his or her book" and "Every book its reader."[12] In the ideal situation, a collections librarian has a written collection development policy that describes the library's mission and user community and provides guidance for developing and managing a collection and the subsection or category for which he or she is responsible. In the absence of a local policy, the librarian aims to understand the informal guidelines for collection building through a review of the collection and consultation with other librarians. Familiarity with the community and the collection guidelines or policy statement is one of the building blocks for good selection. To this is added knowledge of the literature for which the librarian is responsible. The librarian with a firm grasp of these elements is equipped to begin selection.

Selection can be thought of as a four-step process: (1) identification of the relevant; (2) evaluation (is the item worthy of selection?) and assessment (is the item appropriate for the collection?); (3) decision to purchase; and (4) order preparation and sometimes placement.

Identifying the Relevant: Selection Tools and Resources

Many tools and resources exist to help librarians find the basic, factual information about authors, titles, publishers, and topics required to identify possible items for selection. *Bibliographies* and *lists* may be issued by libraries, library publishers, school systems, professional societies, and commercial publishers. National bibliographies and trade lists have been standard tools in libraries for decades. Libraries often consult recent accession lists, prepared by other libraries. Recommended lists are prepared by library associations and other professional associations. Several sources list books that have received awards, such as the Pura Belpré Awards and the Newbery and Caldecott Medal Books.[13]

Bibliographies published by commercial publishers are usually available as an online resource (which is constantly updated), a print subscription (which may be updated annually or perhaps quarterly), or a monograph issued in revised editions. Bibliographies and lists provide guidance for filling gaps in existing collections. For example, a young adult librarian seeking to increase a collection of audiobooks could consult the "Amazing Audiobooks" lists issued annually by the Young Adult Library Services Association (www.ala.org/yalsa/amazing-audio books). Indexing and abstracting resources provide a list of the titles indexed, which can be checked against library holdings. Some resources identify specific types of publications, such as graphic novels.[14] Bibliographies and lists are not, however, inclusive, not available in every field, and not always annotated. Even well-respected and long-standing selection guides, such as the *Public Library Core*

Collection: Nonfiction, can lack balanced perspectives, because they are developed and maintained by individuals (who have their own points of view and expertise) working together.[15]

Librarians can use *directories* to identify a discipline's professional associations. *Yearbook of International Organizations* is one example.[16] Directory entries usually list the association's periodical publications and contact information to request catalogs and other information on current imprints.

Reviews appear in the library-oriented press, popular media, and discipline-based journals. Public librarians should keep up with popular media because they have a significant influence on reader interests. Titles reviewed in the *New York Times Book Review* and appearing on its best-seller lists are always in high demand. Booklist Online (www.booklistonline.com) is a free website containing reviews that appear in ALA's *Booklist* from 1992 forward. *Booklist* subscribers can access full reviews; abbreviated reviews are accessible without a subscription. Many discipline-specific journals provide scholarly and critical reviews of high quality, but these often follow publication by several months or years. Finding reviews of Internet sites is becoming easier. *College and Research Libraries News* (http://crln.acrl.org) has a monthly feature, "Internet Reviews," that reviews selected Internet sites on a specific topic. *The Scout Report* (http://scout.wisc.edu/scout -report), provided by the Internet Scout Project at the University of Wisconsin–Madison, offers thousands of critical annotations for carefully selected Internet sites and mailing lists. *Great Websites for Kids* (http://gws.ala.org) is sponsored by the Association for Library Service to Children.

A current problem with the traditional reviewing media is a tendency to ignore self-published books. The primary source of information about self-published books remains word of mouth.[17] One review source for self-published books is BlueInk Review (www.blueinkreview.com), which is fee-based but states that its reviews are honest, credible, and written by professionals. BlueInk Review is also collaborating with Publishing Perspectives (http://publishingper spectives.com), a project of the Frankfurt Book Fair, to offer free monthly lists of its starred reviews. Remember, however, that the total number of titles reviewed in all sources combined is only a small portion of the world's publishing output.

Publisher announcements (brochures, advertisements, catalogs, websites) provide detailed content descriptions, tables of contents, and author information. Sample chapters may be found on publishers' web pages. Evaluative statements in publishers' announcements should be viewed with caution because most of these are solicited by the publisher as part of the promotional process. Announcements are timely—often appearing before or simultaneously with the publication—and are widely used by all types of libraries.

Review copies and *e-resource demonstrations and trials* are ideal selection aids. Publishers often provide review copies at library conference exhibits and sometimes sell them at the same time. Journal publishers often provide a sample issue upon request. Many video suppliers provide a preview copy to be returned if the item is not selected for acquisition. Many electronic resources offer demonstrations and trial periods during which librarians and users can try the product.

Book fairs and *bookstores* provide an opportunity to examine materials before purchase. Book fairs bring together many publishers, who display and promote their publications. Book fairs may be local, regional, national, or international in scope. Among the best known are the books fairs in Frankfurt, Zimbabwe, Guadalajara, and Madrid. Many professional association conferences include publisher exhibitors. Though not book fairs in the true sense, they serve the same purpose of introducing new publications and, often, authors to attendees. Bookstores are particularly useful for finding alternative literature and materials from outside the predominant culture, which are less frequently reviewed in traditional sources.

Web-based tools provide several approaches to locating new and relevant older titles. Librarians can find reviews, out-of-print dealers who offer lists of available titles and will search for specific requests, vendor and publisher information, and online stores and catalogs covering all formats. Amazon.com is one of the more familiar online dealers and useful for subject-based searching, reviews, and speedy delivery of items. Alibris.com and AbeBooks.com offer similar services. Publishers frequently provide tables of contents and sample chapters of new books on their websites. Librarians can perform subject searches in national bibliographic utilities and in other libraries' catalogs. Electronic discussion groups and electronic newsletters directed toward collection development and acquisitions librarians can provide information about publishers and resources for specific subject areas and types of materials.

In-house information, such as interlibrary loan requests, can aid selection. Repeated requests from users for articles from a particular journal suggest that journal should be added to the collection. The same is true for repeated requests for a specific book title. Frequent recalls or a long waiting list for a book provides evidence that the title should be considered for duplication. Many libraries have added a service that purchases books requested through interlibrary loan for users and adds them to the libraries' permanent collection after the user's loan period.[18] Some libraries have implemented the Getting It System Toolkit (GIST, www.gistlibrary.org), free, open-source software developed at the State University of New York College at Geneseo to assist with using interlibrary loan to initiate a purchase decision.[19] GIST integrates with ILLiad interlibrary loan management software (a commercial product) and determines if a title requested is held locally, if a free online version exists, and how much the title costs. These data help users and library staff make informed decisions about the best option to meet users' needs. Most libraries accept purchase requests from users. These suggest specific titles that should be considered for addition and may recommend formats, subject areas, or genres to which the library should add materials.

IDENTIFYING GOVERNMENT DOCUMENTS

Locating information about *government documents* (the official publications of agencies at the international, national, regional, state, and local level) presents its own challenges. The aim in selecting documents is the same as that for all types of materials. As Ennis writes, "The goal is to develop the best [documents] collection possible, concentrating on the most appropriate content in the most appropriate formats for your user base."[20] The freely available Government Printing Office (GPO) online Catalog of U.S. Federal Documents (http://catalog.gpo.gov) has a "new title" search feature offering one way to identify new federal government documents.

The nature of U.S. federal document collecting has changed significantly because most of these publications are now available online. In 2013, the GPO estimated that approximately 97 percent of all U.S. federal government documents were born digital and many of these are never printed.[21] The GPO relies on agency websites for access and is also integrating preservation and archiving into the Federal Digital System (www.gpo.gov/fdsys). Librarians in libraries not part of the Federal Depository Library Program (FDLP, www.gpo.gov/libraries) are encouraged to be selective in choosing digital resources they wish to catalog locally because many users bypass the local catalog and go directly to the government website.

Some libraries are legally designated as U.S. federal depository libraries through the FDLP and as such are charged with ensuring that the public has free and open access to the government publications that are received without cost from the GPO. Regional depositories must acquire all FDLP federal government publications and also can acquire fugitive documents (unknown to the GPO and not in the *Catalog of U.S. Government Publications*) in addition to those received from the GPO. A portion of depository materials is available in multiple formats (print, CD-ROM, and online). Regional depositories can choose between multiple formats but cannot substitute an online format for a tangible format. A selective depository is permitted to replace tangible versions with online equivalents of depository materials provided the library has held the publication for at least one year; its regional depository has approved the disposal of the tangibles; and the online version is official, complete, and free of charge to the user.[22] Selective depository libraries build their collections through the creation of profiles, making selections for series and groups of publications. FDLP regional libraries and selective depository libraries are obligated to provide both intellectual access to the U.S. documents in their purview and services to the public. Many questions about the future of the FDLP are unanswered. What are these libraries' collecting preservation responsibilities, beyond including records in the catalog, in a digital environment where many publications are accessed and not acquired? What are the implications for a library and its users of selecting a freely available web-based resource? These questions and others are pushing the GPO and the depository library community to redefine what being a depository library means.[23]

Local government information has been called the "domestic intelligence gap" because of the problems libraries face in identifying and obtaining it.[24] This is compounded by the transition of state and local governments to digital publishing paralleling that of the federal government. Some states, such as California and Colorado, have state government depository programs through which designated partner libraries receive publications produced or distributed by state agencies. The Colorado State Publications Library publishes a monthly list of new state documents including links to the URLs for e-documents (www .cde.state.co.us/stateinfo/slstpnewt.htm). Regional and local government publications can be more difficult to identify. One of the most effective methods for identifying and acquiring nonfederal documents in the United States is through direct contact with the issuing agency, which may provide websites listing publications and links to online resources. Some commercial indexes, such as *Statistical Reference Index* and *Index to Current Urban Documents*, contain state and local documents, but no resource aggregates all local government publications.[25]

International government information may be produced by national and local governments of other countries and international government organizations (IGOs), such as the United Nations or European Union. These entities produce two types of information: documents pertaining to their operations, and documents compiling information intended for the general public.[26] Foreign documents are often listed in government and agency catalogs and on their websites; see, for example, the United Nations Publications website (http://unp .un.org). An increasing number of foreign and intergovernmental publications are available free via the Internet. Some agencies offer depository systems for libraries; one example is the United Nations depository libraries program (www .un.org/Depts/dhl/deplib/deplibsystem.htm). However, as Latham and Stevens note, "The increase in digital publications has caused a rethinking of the role of international depositories." As the IGOs move away from print, they may eliminate their depository systems. If this occurs, "it will engender the same questions with regard to preservation and maintenance of international digital publications that the U.S. federal government is currently attempting to address."[27] Many libraries purchase access to collections assembled by vendors.[28] Bernan (www.bernan.com), a commercial source for publications from U.S. government agencies and intergovernmental organizations worldwide, has an extensive online catalog.

Many publications released by state, regional, and local government agencies, foreign governments, and IGOs can be considered gray literature, because they are not available through regular market channels and are poorly represented in indexing and abstracting tools. Such materials present persistent problems for librarians trying to identify those that are appropriate to add to their collections. A librarian who decides to develop a collection of these materials must be diligent in seeking them.

Evaluating and Assessing Potential Selections

Evaluation and assessment assist the collections librarian in deciding if the title should be added. *Evaluation* looks at item-intrinsic qualities, and items are considered on their own merits. *Assessment* considers the ability of items to meet local needs. In practice, evaluation and assessment generally occur simultaneously. A collections librarian should not devote time to evaluating an item if that item is not appropriate for the user community being served.

EVALUATION

Evaluation criteria vary from item to item and between categories of materials but generally include several of the following considerations:

- content or subject
- language
- currency
- veracity (e.g., truthfulness, accuracy)
- writing style (e.g., well written, easy to read, aesthetic aspects)
- completeness and scope of treatment
- reputation, credentials, or authoritativeness of author, publisher, editor, reviewers

- geographic coverage
- quality of scholarship
- frequency the title is referenced in bibliographies or citations
- reading or user level to which content is directed
- frequency of updates or revisions
- access points (e.g., indexes, level of detail in the table of contents)
- ease of use
- external resources that index the publication
- physical quality (e.g., illustrations, paper and binding, format, typography, durability, visual and audio characteristics)
- uniqueness of content, capabilities, or features
- availability of equipment required for hearing or viewing audiovisual material
- cost in relation to quality of the item and its projected use

Some categories of materials have additional and unique evaluation criteria that should guide selection. For example, a librarian selecting pictures books should give special consideration to the nature and quality of the illustrations. Van Orden and Strong recommend that a librarian ask if the artwork extends or clarifies the text (or in a wordless book, if the story is clear through the pictures) and consider the artistic elements of color, line, shape, composition, and design.[29] The mission of the library and the user community can suggest supplemental considerations.

The nature of e-resources also suggests additional criteria for consideration:

- provider business model (e.g., special pricing considerations, including discounts for retaining or cancelling paper subscriptions, restrictions on cancellations, discounts for consortial purchase, access to content if subscription cancelled)
- licensing and contractual terms, limitations, and obligations
- ease of authentication
- completeness (if an e-version of a print resource, is the same content provided?)
- currency (is e-content added in a timely manner? Is the e-book available simultaneous with the print version?)
- ability to select and deselect individual titles or other content subsets, if offering is a package deal from an aggregator or publisher

- local service implications and local physical and logistical requirements
- compatibility with bibliographic and citation management software and course management software
- compatibility with mobile devices and e-readers
- accessibility for people with disabilities
- OpenURL compliance
- functionality of the end-user interface and accessibility
- output options
- option to transfer e-content to a different delivery platform
- availability of data to measure use and effectiveness
- response time
- vendor support and responsiveness
- availability of back files for formats such as e-journals and databases
- persistence of content and access to archival files
- availability of descriptive metadata for local use
- duplication or replacement of existing library resources

For electronic resources involving physical media (e.g., CD-ROMs), additional criteria should be considered:

- physical and logistical requirements within the library, including space, furniture, hardware, wiring, and telecommunication and data ports
- effective use of technology

Comparing the same e-content delivered several ways can be a challenge. A product may be available in print, CD-ROM, online from several suppliers, and with different pricing models. For example, *PsychINFO* can be acquired directly from the American Psychological Association and through EBSCO, Ovid, ProQuest, DIALOG, and other vendors. When possible, a library should arrange demonstrations and free trials and involve staff in public services and the library's information technology unit in reviewing the e-resource. One approach to evaluating similar products is to create a decision matrix in which comparative information is recorded for each product. The criteria listed earlier are a good starting point; the library should, at a minimum, compare those criteria it has decided are critical. This facilitates weighing similarities, differences, advantages, and disadvantages of the options being considered.

The process of selecting serials and other resources with ongoing commitments (regardless of format) parallels that for other types of publications. The differences are the need to consider the continuing financial commitment implicit in initiating a subscription or licensing access and the possible need to negotiate a contract for electronic resources. A serial is "a publication in any medium issued in successive parts bearing numerical or chronological designations and intended to be continued indefinitely."[30] Many librarians interchange the terms *serial* and *periodical*. Serials include general magazines, which provide recreational reading and popular sources of information on current social and political issues; scholarly and scientific journals, which are often specialized and directed to a narrow audience; annual reports and house organs of businesses; trade and technology-focused magazines; and "little magazines," which concentrate on literature, politics, or both and often fall within what is known as alternative literature.

The term *e-journal* is often used to describe any serial that is available electronically. *Continuing resource* is an umbrella term for serials (issued successively over time) and all types of integrating resources that continue over time (e.g., indexing and abstracting tools with and without associated full-text articles, online encyclopedias, directories, dictionaries, statistical compendia). According to *Resource Description and Access: RDA*, an integrating resource is "a resource that is added to or changed by means of updates that do not remain discrete but are integrated into the whole. An integrating resource may be tangible (e.g., a loose-leaf manual that is updated by means of replacement pages) or intangible (e.g., a Web site that is updated either continuously or on a cyclical basis)."[31]

The term *continuing resource* indicates the continuing financial obligation implicit in selecting it. The financial commitment incurred with a serial subscription or other continuing resource is significant. The library pays, usually on an annual cycle, for periodicals before they are published and for access to e-resources for a period of time into the future. A librarian needs to consider the library budget's ability to accommodate annual increases for these materials often in excess of normal collections budget growth. He or she must be prepared to cancel serials and other continuing resources to operate within available funds and as part of the selection process for new resources.

When selecting a serial, the collections librarian pays particular attention to the purpose of the publication and to where it is indexed. Magazines, trade journals, scholarly periodicals, and so on each have an intended audience, and the evaluation criteria set out in this chapter are generally applicable. For example, part of evaluating a scholarly journal is considering the credentials of the editors and reviewers to determine the rigor with which submissions are analyzed. A public library might consider whether a popular magazine is indexed in *Readers Guide to Periodical Literature*.[32]

Because of the continuing financial commitment, many libraries use selection committees to evaluate possible new serial titles and continuing resources. The committee can consider several titles at the same time, prioritizing them and seeking balanced coverage. School libraries may have a committee composed of teachers and the school librarian. Committees are not without problems; individual preferences, personality characteristics, and the social status of members can influence group decisions.[33] Academic libraries, school library media centers, and special libraries may seek evaluations from stakeholders.

Although monographic by definition, most commercial e-books involve a continuing financial commitment either through a subscription or for an annual hosting fee. An e-book is a digital object containing an electronic representation of a book, most commonly thought of as the electronic analog of a printed book. The term *e-book* now most often refers to digital objects designed to be accessible online and read on either a handheld device or a personal computer. E-books may be purchased, or the library may contract for access for a period of time. Another option frequently available is pay-per-view (sometimes called rental, short-term loan, or pay-per-use), through which a single user accesses the book for a set period of time for a fee, usually paid by the library. In this model, a library usually creates a deposit account with the supplier or purchases "tokens" that are traded for uses. Even when purchasing an e-book, the library usually incurs a continuing cost to support ongoing hosting of the e-content and provision of the interface.

E-books are a contentious topic for librarians for several reasons.[34] These include limitations imposed by digital rights management (DRM), limitations on lending and interlibrary loan, premium prices charged to libraries compared to that for the same titles sold to individuals, lag between appearance of print books and their e-counterparts, caps on e-book lending, unwillingness of some publishers to sell e-books to libraries, and concerns about reader privacy and equity of access. Variations in license terms and the multiplicity of e-book file formats complicate the decision process.

ALA created the Digital Content and Libraries Working Group (www.ala .org/groups/committees/special/ala-dcwg) in the fall of 2011 to address digital content from both a policy and a practical perspective. To date, much of its focus has been on e-books. ALA maintains a resource website, "Ebooks & Digital Content" (www.ala.org/transforminglibraries/ebooks-digital-content), which provides information to support libraries as they transition from print to digital content.

The criteria for evaluating e-books are consistent with those for all materials. When the same titles are available from multiple sources, special attention should be given to interface usability, type of DRM employed, supplier business model, and pricing.[35] DRM is the technologies, tools, and process that protect intellectual property by enabling secure distribution or disabling illegal distribution. DRM can limit the devices on which content can be loaded and prevent sharing of content between users even if they have the same type of device. The limitations on use of digital content and devices inherent in DRM are called "hard restrictions" because they strictly prevent specific uses. DRM often supplements the restrictions mandated in licenses. Various platforms have their own DRM, which is not consistent across platforms. Library users find DRM frustrating and confusing because the limitations are often not obvious. Individual publisher sites tend to be less restrictive because they are hosting only their own content. Librarians should understand the DRM employed when evaluating possible e-content suppliers. The ALA Digital Content and Libraries Working Group prepared a report for public libraries that describes e-book business models and developed a scorecard for evaluating them.[36] Aggregators present an additional complication: because they offer collections from various publishers having multiple authors, titles initially available may be withdrawn from the collection. For this reason, some libraries that acquire multiple e-books from the same publisher may prefer to work with the publisher directly instead of with aggregators.

ASSESSMENT

In an assessment, one considers the item in relation to user needs, the existing collection, the mission of the library, and consortial obligations. Does the item support the curriculum, community interests, faculty or teacher specialties, or areas of current research? Does it fall within the parameters of subjects or areas identified in the collection policy? Librarians need to consider if a title is being acquired to satisfy short-term needs and how it might relate to any long-term collection goals. Does the library need an additional work on this subject? Would the item fill a gap in the collection? Is a duplicate copy justified? Is it readily available from another library? If the item entails a contract, are the licensing terms consistent with local policies and practices? Does the library have the ability to handle the title? Would it get prompt cataloging? Does the library have appropriate housing (shelf space, microform or map cabinets, server capacity), equipment (microform readers, computers, printers, scanners), and electrical and telecommunication infrastructure? Are staff members who work with the public prepared to support the title's use and service needs? Does the library have a consortial obligation to purchase the item?

School librarians assess materials' ability to match curricular trends. They often find themselves playing catch-up as the curriculum and its emphasis and philosophy shift. Smith identifies three primary purposes of school library media center collections: supporting the curriculum, providing materials for recreational use, and providing professional aids for teachers, with primary emphasis on the first.[37] Achieving these aims requires understanding the intended user community. The current national emphasis on core competencies and meeting basic standards to be promoted to the next grade and to graduate are influencing selection activities. School librarians often seek to balance building collections that support curricular goals with building a core collection that meets more broad-based objectives. Learner-centered collection development, a concept and practice explored by Hughes-Hassell and Mancall, aims to accommodate the changing curricular needs and recreational interests of students through broad engagement with teachers and other stakeholders.[38] These authors developed a decision-making matrix for school librarians that asks whether the resource addresses the information needs of the learning community, matches learner characteristics, fits the teaching-learning context, is consistent with the current knowledge bases, and falls within budget parameters (or is available from partners). If the answer is no to any of these questions, the resource does not meet the requirements of the learning community and should not be selected.

Patron-Driven Acquisition

One approach to assessing and meeting local needs is to implement *patron-driven acquisition*, which is also known as demand-driven acquisition, user-driven collection development, patron-initiated purchasing, and books-on-demand. As the name implies, selection decisions are driven by library patron actions. Although related to both purchasing items when requested via interlibrary loan and using approval plans to streamline selection through macro-selection, patron-driven acquisition has been called a game changer for publishers, aggregators, vendors, libraries, and library users.[39] Depending on the model chosen, patrons can choose print or e-books, although patron-driven acquisition of e-books is more common. MARC records for books, often matching a profile determined by the library but sometimes an entire publisher's title list, are loaded into the library's catalog. Once a specific e-book has been discovered and viewed a predetermined number of times or for a specified length of time, it is purchased for the collection. Patron-driven acquisition, most commonly found in academic libraries, is also used in other types of libraries including schools.[40]

Patron-driven acquisition is offered by book vendors, aggregators, and publishers. The business models and licensing options vary from supplier to supplier.

Pay-per-view is an option that some libraries choose. In this model, the library rents or leases access to the e-book at a discounted price instead of purchasing perpetual access. Typically the library purchases the e-book when a set number of uses or rentals is reached. Not all suppliers offer pay-per-view, and those that do may not credit rental fees toward the actual purchase price. Nevertheless, pay-per-view may be appropriate for titles that meet an immediate and limited need but do not have lasting value.

Librarians can exercise control over patron-driven acquisition by setting parameters for the titles that are loaded into the catalog and thus eligible for patron selection and by identifying the users who are eligible to initiate such acquisition. Librarians can stipulate reader level, maximum price above which librarian review is needed, imprint date, language, and exclusions (e.g., textbooks, popular fiction, repair manuals, publishers) in the profile. Some libraries simply load records for items that would have been shipped on a books approval plan or identified in an online notification system. Another choice libraries make is setting the triggers needed to generate a purchase. Common triggers are number of continuous minutes of viewing, number of unique page views by a single user, number of "loans," printing of any pages, or a combination of these. Tables of contents and index pages are often not counted.

Patron-driven acquisition is extremely popular. Proponents see it as an extension of a common practice in libraries to purchase books requested via interlibrary loan and a way to identify materials missed in the usual selection processes. Patron-driven acquisition is valued because it quickly meets users' needs and is consistent with an increasing emphasis on acquiring materials just-in-time of need instead of just-in-case of some future need. Each title selected through patron-driven acquisition is guaranteed at least one use, unlike many titles selected by librarians. Problems can, however, arise, even when parameters are set by librarians. Some users, particularly undergraduates, can be voracious and often undiscriminating acquirers. One undergraduate at the University of Mississippi selected nearly 170 books in one year, equal to one quarter of the patron-driven acquisition titles acquired in that period.[41] One way to reduce indiscriminate selection is to limit the categories of users authorized to initiate orders. Options might be limiting authorized users to graduate students, faculty, and researchers in an academic library or to teachers in a school library.

Patron-driven acquisition is not universally endorsed in the profession. Walters warns that it may not support the broader educational mission of academic libraries. Hodges, Preston, and Hamilton raise similar concerns that patrons, in buying for immediate need, will change the nature of academic collections over time.[42] They foresee patron-driven acquisition generating excessive amounts of purchases in one area to the detriment of building a balanced collection, possibly polarizing collection levels between introductory works and narrowly focused research materials with less variation in between. Shen and colleagues recommend carefully crafting patron-driven programs to set caps on the price of titles and exclude older materials, journals, duplicates, and titles from publishers that offer bundled packages.[43]

With proper management, patron-driven acquisition can offer value to libraries by letting users assess their own need. To be effective, it should be understood as part of routine collection building and not viewed as a special initiative. It should be managed and monitored by librarians. It should be seen as part of the library's overall collection plan and be consistent with policies and practices that seek to build collections that match users' needs now and in the future.

Diverse Communities and Alternative Literatures

A key element is assessing the coherence between materials under consideration and local needs is understanding the community being served. The United States is a diverse and multicultural society, reflecting variations in race, religion, geographic origin, economic status, political affiliation, and personal preference. Professional associations stress the need to reflect diverse communities in library collections. For example:

> The American Library Association (ALA) promotes equal access to information for all persons and recognizes the ongoing need to increase awareness of and responsiveness to the diversity of the communities we serve. ALA recognizes the critical need for access to library and information resources, services, and technologies by all people, especially those who may experience language or literacy-related barriers; economic distress; cultural or social isolation; physical or attitudinal barriers; racism; discrimination on the basis of appearance, ethnicity, immigrant status, religious background, sexual orientation, gender identity, gender expression; or barriers to equal education, employment, and housing.[44]

ACRL affirms that "librarians and library staff shall develop collections and provide programs and services that are inclusive of the needs of all persons in the community the library serves."[45]

Demographic data make clear the pluralistic and diverse nature of the United States. In 2010, 12.9 percent of U.S. residents were foreign born and 36.6 of the U.S. population were minorities. In 2011, 47 percent of children were minorities, and minorities are projected to constitute more than half of all children by

2023.[46] A 2012 study reports that 3.4 percent of adults self-identified as lesbian, gay, bisexual, or transgender. As many as nine million children in this country have a gay or lesbian parent. Less than half of U.S. households consist of married straight couples with families.[47] The population of the United States is aging. In 2009, 12.9 percent of the U.S. population was 65 or older and was projected to increase to 19 percent by 2030.[48] U.S. Census Bureau data from 2011 indicated that 12.1 percent of the noninstitutionalized population had a disability.[49] Library collections should address and respond to the needs and interests of an increasingly diverse society, including individuals with disabilities; single-parent and other nontraditional families; gay, lesbian, bisexual, transgender, intersex, and questioning individuals; and foreign-born and nonnative English speakers.

The librarian's professional obligation is to develop balanced collections that reflect and meet the educational and recreational needs of these diverse user communities and are not biased by the librarian's own cultural identity and personal experiences. ALA provides guidance in "Diversity in Collection Development: An Interpretation of the Library Bill of Rights."[50] Agosto writes that school library collections representing a range of cultures "can serve as a form of advocacy on behalf of students from minority backgrounds by making them feel included in classroom and school environments."[51] In addition to meeting the needs and reflecting the perspectives and experiences of various populations, multicultural materials and materials representing different lifestyles present all library users opportunities to understand other people and cultures. Finding materials that are representative and age-appropriate can, however, present difficulties. For example, Kaiser describes the challenging and time-consuming nature of locating current books for children with disabilities and their families.[52]

Publications that are not part of the dominant culture and do not share the perspective and beliefs of that culture are often considered alternative literature. Generally, these materials are published by small presses, independent publishers, the radical right and left, and other dissenting groups. Many topics that dominate alternative literature are the same topics that are challenged in library collections.[53] These include critiques of public life and the mass media, environmental activism, peace and antimilitarism, human rights (including right to life and free choice), freedom of speech and censorship, creationism, anarchism, situationist literature, critical education and free schools, sexual politics, paranormal and fortean phenomena, and literature of extremist groups. Alternative literature includes works of nonfiction, fiction, poetry, art, and music.

Librarians are generally comfortable selecting works that represent diverse cultural and ethnic groups, because this is perceived as the sensitive and politically correct stance. They are less at ease when making selection decisions that are inconsistent with their own social, moral, and political interests. As Benton and Grimm observe, "It is very easy for librarians to avoid materials that seem different to them."[54] Being aware of the community served can help librarians assess materials being considered for the collection.

Licensing

The advent of e-resources brought librarians into a new era of selection and acquisition—one in which licensing and contractual terms, limitations, and obligations became another area requiring assessment. Libraries no longer purchase all materials outright for addition to a physical collection; they license access to digital content through contracts with providers. Nearly all publishers, aggregators, and vendors require a signed contract before permitting access to an online resource or providing CD-ROMs to a library. Contracts must be signed by individuals who have the authority and power to represent and legally bind a party to a written agreement.

At its most basic, a contract consists of an offer, an acceptance of the offer, and a consideration, which is the exchange of something of value in the eyes of the law (e.g., a good, a service, or money). The publisher, aggregator, or vendor (e.g., licensor) offers a product with terms and conditions set forth in the contract, the library accepts the offer, and the vendor provides access to the product for which the library pays a fee. The licensor is free to ask whatever price and set whatever conditions on use the market will bear. A license or license agreement is a legally binding form of a contract through which a library (the licensee) pays for the right to use or access a resource, usually for a fixed period of time. A lease is a contract by which one party grants access to another party to use a resource for a specified term and for a specified amount.

A contract is normally in writing, but an oral contract between parties can be legally binding in some jurisdictions. In libraries, a license or license agreement is the portion of a contract that presents the terms under which a vendor, aggregator, or publisher grants rights (powers or privileges) to use one or more proprietary bibliographic databases, e-journals, e-books, or other online resources, usually for a fixed period of time in exchange for payment. Often, the CD-ROMs must be returned and access to an online resource is terminated if the contract is not renewed. The selection process involves careful review of a contract and its conditions before a decision is made to choose the resource.

Many library services and traditional collections usage may be curtailed or disallowed in an e-resources contract, which spells out terms and conditions governing the resource. Because contracts are part of the legal system and subject to contract law, they use legal terminology. Frequently used contractual terms appear in this book's glossary. Contracts include clauses that

- identify the content being licensed
- name the parties to the agreement
- govern terms of use (e.g., prohibitions against using or permission to use the e-content in interlibrary loan and course reserves)
- define who authorized users are and any limitations on walk-in use and off-site access
- specify the process of authorizing and authenticating authorized users
- specify rights (permitted uses) granted and any restrictions on use
- set out the pricing model (which may be based on FTE users, pay-per-use, or number of concurrent users), often in an appendix
- specify the term or duration of the contract and any prohibitions against cancellation
- specify whether the library has access to the content after the contract ends, e.g., perpetual access
- list warranties and disclaimers made by parties to the contract
- lists penalties in response to a breach and the length of time available to cure a breach before penalties are enacted
- address indemnity and limitations of liability
- describe renewal and cancellation processes
- stipulate the contractual obligations of both parties and the penalties if obligations are not fulfilled
- identify the governing law under which a dispute relating to the contract would be adjudicated

Libraries are increasingly resisting *nondisclosure clauses*, which limit the ability to share information about contract terms and pricing information and thus limit libraries' ability to negotiate with suppliers.[55] Academic and many other types of libraries frequently seek *perpetual access rights* through a clause that ensures that the library retains access to e-content released during the term of the agreement.

In theory, everything within a contract can be changed through negotiation. By its nature, a contract must be mutually acceptable before it is signed. The librarian's goal is a contract that allows the user community to pursue its usual activities; renders a fair exchange of money for product and service; and balances the rights, responsibilities, and legal liabilities of all parties. Most libraries work with a list of desirable terms and conditions that they hope to negotiate in their favor (e.g., many libraries prefer to have the contract under the governing law of the state in which the library is located but do not consider alternatives to be deal breakers) and a list of terms or conditions that must meet the library's requirements (e.g., the ability to provide unaffiliated users walk-in, on-site access). Contract law is complex, and negotiating contracts can be time consuming. Librarians should be able to identify the issues that need to be addressed when negotiating a contract. They should know when to call for expert opinion and advice. They should understand the policies of the library and its parent body regarding contracts, leases, purchasing, and accountability to ensure that all contracts and their signings are consistent in these policies.

Audiovisual media is another area where law and licensing intersect and can be confusing to librarians selecting these materials.[56] Copyright is a particularly complex area for librarians who work with media, and licenses magnify the confusion.[57] According to U.S copyright law, the following educational uses are not infringements of copyright:

> performance or display of a work by instructors or pupils in the course of face-to-face teaching activities of a nonprofit educational institution, in a classroom or similar place devoted to instruction, unless, in the case of a motion picture or other audiovisual work, the performance, or the display of individual images, is given by means of a copy that was not lawfully made under this title.[58]

Thus, media purchased by a library (or made available through a library's contract for streaming media) for use in the classroom for "face-to-face teaching activities" should not require permission from the copyright holder or the distributor for instructional use. The issue for libraries is that media distributors often state on their websites or include in their licenses a prohibition against using their media in classroom instruction unless the library pays a higher price for what are sometimes called public performance screening rights. Unless the library plans to show movies, TV shows, and other audiovisual media to groups outside the classroom or provides videos to teachers who plan to show movies for purely entertainment purposes, the library should resist accepting contractual clauses that prohibit educational classroom use and not agree to pay more for public performance rights. Note that libraries also have the right to digitize and stream library DVDs to course management systems for educational purposes; this has been judged fair use by the court.[59] Not at issue is the right of libraries to loan or rent videos or make them available for viewing by one person or a very limited group on-site.

Several resources are available to help librarians with contracts and licensing for e-resources. Model licenses can be found at LibLicense (http://libli cense.crl.edu) and LicensingModels.org. IFLA and the University of California Libraries have developed licensing principles.[60] The ALCTS *Guide to Licensing and Acquiring Electronic Information* offers a comprehensive but not overwhelming starting point.[61] Additional sources are listed in the "Suggested Readings" for this chapter.

A new approach to acquiring electronic resources without negotiating license agreements is available—the NISO Shared Electronic Resources Understanding Best Practice (SERU).[62] SERU is not designed to replace all license agreements, but it can be convenient for inexpensive electronic resources, especially those from small publishers that do not have large staffs to negotiate license agreements. SERU is not a license agreement but rather a set of statements that reference existing law (e.g., copyright law) and describe some common practices in working with electronic resources. If both the library and publisher agree, a simple reference to SERU can be made in a purchase order and the library gains access when payment is made. No license agreement is signed, so no negotiation is needed. Libraries and publishers can register with NISO to indicate their willingness to consider using SERU for e-resource acquisitions.

National site licensing is another approach to simplifying licensing, one that involves a large number of libraries across a country, not confined by geographic proximity but often limited to a particular sector, such as higher education. Zhu suggests that national site licenses require a centralized education policy-making system and funding system, supportive political trends, and a tradition of cooperation. A large number of institutions, diversity, concerns about the Big Deal, and legal concerns about monopoly can work against a national site license.[63]

Decision to Purchase

Once the librarian has considered all relevant evaluation and assessment questions, he or she is ready to add or reject the item. The decision to add an item is generally considered a purchase decision, although the library may be paying to own an item or paying for the right to access an item or collection of materials. Atkinson refers to the universe of materials not selected locally as the anti-collection. He holds that selection is, "to a great extent, a continuous series of decisions about which items in the anti-collection should be moved into the collection" and suggests that the selection decision is relatively simple because the librarian has only two options: add or do not add.[64] Librarians employ a mental model that looks at the potential utility for current and future users.

For Atkinson, the line between accepting and rejecting materials is primarily dependent on the financial resources available. Given the volume of materials being published and the finite nature of library budgets, librarians will always face choices about what not to add as they choose what to add.

Order Preparation and Acquisition Options

Processes and systems for ordering and obtaining library materials after they are selected are called *acquisition*. The acquisition of materials is closely related to collection development, though in most medium-size and large libraries selection and acquisition are handled by different individuals who may be located in different library departments or units. Acquisitions responsibilities typically include placing orders (i.e., initiating purchase orders), claiming, cancelling, receipting, invoice processing, and preparing requests for proposals (RFPs) from monographic vendors and subscription agents, and they may include payment processing. Typical accounting guidelines require that the responsibility for approval for payment and payment processing be assigned to different individuals. Selection and acquisitions may be handled separately in smaller libraries if the number of staff members makes this reasonable; however, combining the functions of selection and acquisition is common. The ease with which librarians can work directly with suppliers' online databases is blurring the traditional division of work. Librarians may place orders directly online as part of the item identification process.

When placing orders, the selecting librarian is usually expected to verify title, author or editor, publisher, publication date, and cost. Ideally, he or she also identifies series, ISBN or ISSN, and perhaps information about the source from which the publication is available. Specifying the source is essential if the item is an e-resource, because many e-resources are available from multiple suppliers. In addition, e-resources usually require a contract, although an existing contract may apply if one has been negotiated with the supplier earlier. Many libraries request that librarians provide bibliographic information on forms that may be preprinted, retrieved and printed from an online template, or completed online (figure 4-1). These forms usually require the librarian to assign a fund or budget line, identify the collection or location to which the item will be added, request any special handling, and confirm, if appropriate, that a duplicate copy is desired. If the title being ordered is a serial, the librarian identifies the volume with which the subscription should begin and any back files that are to be ordered.

The selection and acquisition of e-resources add complexity to the interaction of collections librarians and acquisitions staff for many reasons. Many

Selector Name: [   ]

Title: [   ]

ISBN: [   ]

Author: [   ]

Publisher: [   ]

Budget code: [Select code from drop-down menu ↓]

Begin order with volumes/issue/year (if standing order): [   ]

Location: [   ]

Is a record in the catalog?   Yes [ ]   BIB ID#: [   ]   No [ ]

Price: [   ]

Comments:
[   ]

[Submit]   [Reset]

FIGURE 4-1   Sample online internal order form

e-resources are expensive and may require special approval processes. Standard systems that facilitate acquisition of print resources may be lacking for e-resources. Ordering e-resources commonly requires more direct interaction with the supplier. In addition to the information listed above, the selector likely will be asked to indicate

- URL, if available
- if the order is for a package of titles, whether all titles the package or only selected titles meeting certain criteria are desired
- contact information if the selector has been working with a sales representative
- type of resource (e.g., book, index, journal reference source, streaming media)
- if an existing print subscription is active, whether the subscription to print should be continued
- if the request is for a trial (with start and end date), one-time or back file purchase, subscription, or standing order
- any special information about cost and pricing, including such information as "free with print" or special discounts
- if a license with the content provider is already in place[65]

Supplemental information might include whether MARC records are available with an e-book package, whether additional software and hardware are needed, and the number of simultaneous users if the license does not allow unlimited access.

Many e-resources require the added step of negotiating license agreements, which must be signed or approved online by a designated individual with signing authority for the library. In some libraries, the librarian selecting the title shepherds license agreements through the institution's approval process. In others, a specified collections librarian or library administrator may be charged with the responsibility, or it may be handled by acquisitions staff members. In some school library media centers, especially in larger school systems, the selection and management of online resources may be handled centrally by procurement staff or by staff in an information technology department. Figure 4.2 presents a sample online form for initiating the order for an e-resource.

One challenge facing a library after signing contracts for e-resources is managing them and monitoring the terms and conditions specified. Electronic resources management (ERM) systems are automated systems used to manage

Selector Name:

Budget Code: Select code from drop-down menu ⬇

Title(s): If this is a package purchase, indicate if you want "all titles" or "selected titles" only. If you wanted selected titles from the publisher, list all titles on this form.

Publisher/Vendor: If you have been working with a particular sales representative, provide all relevant contact information.

Contract Information: Is a contract with this publisher or vendor on file?   Yes ☐   No ☐

Resource Type	**Print Duplication**	**Timing**
☐ Book	Do you want to retain an	☐ Trial only
☐ DVD	existing print subscription?	☐ One-time or back-file purchase
☐ Index	☐ Yes	☐ Subscription or standing order
☐ Journal	☐ No	
☐ Streaming media		

Cost: If the resource is "free with print," provide the cost of the print subscription.
   Also note any one-time or ongoing costs.

Additional Information: If unlimited access is not available, how many simultaneous users? Is extra software required, e.g., browser plug-ins, client program. If this is an e-book package, are MARC records available? If this is a trial, when should it start and end?

Submit   Reset

FIGURE 4-2   Sample online internal e-resource request form

the creation, use, and maintenance of information related to e-resource contracts. These systems may be developed in-house or purchased from a library system vendor, subscription agent, or third-party company. Initially developed to handle e-journal subscriptions and their licenses, ERM systems now also manage e-book and e-journal packages. Commercially available ERM systems link and manage a library's subscriptions through Open URL link resolvers and often A-Z listing services. They usually record information about selection, trials, status of contract negotiation, vendor, dates actions are taken, term of contract and renewal dates, cost and fund line billed, and contractual obligations and limitations. Because much of the information recorded in an ERM system duplicates that tracked in an automated acquisitions system, interoperability between the ERM system and the local automated system is desirable. The ERM system should be easily searchable by collections, acquisitions, and interlibrary loan staff.

SELECTING THE APPROPRIATE SUPPLIER

Libraries can place orders with vendors and agents, purchase from a retailer, order directly from publishers, or use aggregators. Selecting the appropriate supplier involves several considerations and careful weighing of the advantages and disadvantages.

Vendors and Subscription Agents

Libraries acquire materials through a third party because of the ability to consolidate orders, receive consolidated invoices, and rely on the third party to handle claims. Vendors (sometimes called wholesalers, dealers, or book vendors) may supply print books, e-books, music, audio, and video. They normally consolidate shipments and offer discounts. Baker and Taylor, Blackwell, Brodart, Coutts, Follett, Ingram, and YBP are familiar vendors in the United States. Numerous international vendors offer similar services. For example, Harassowitz handles materials from much of Europe; Casalini specializes in publications from Italy, France, Spain, Portugal, and Greece; and Touzot provides French-language materials from Europe, Canada, and other francophone regions. ALCTS maintains a "Foreign Book Dealers Directory" (www.ala.org/CFApps/bookdealers) listing dealers in Eastern Europe, Africa, Central Eurasia, Asia, the Middle East, and the Pacific region.

The difference between book vendors and subscription agents is becoming less distinct. Subscription agents now sell e-books and book vendors sell e-book collections. Bosch and colleagues identify the following support that libraries expect from vendors and agents:

> increased customer service and communication tailored to the specific library's needs
>
> a customer-friendly interface to a web-accessible catalog of the publications available, with the ability for the library to effect transactions in the vendor's database (plus training in the use of the database)
>
> bibliographic services (order confirmation records and catalog records)
>
> reporting capabilities to support collection development decision making, whether purchasing data or usage statistics
>
> ability to work with consortia (licensing, business processes, resource sharing, training, management of trials and introduction of new products)[66]

Vendors handle imprints from a variety of publishers. They may specialize in disciplines or subject areas (e.g., music, medicine, legal publications), publishers, materials for types of libraries (e.g., public, school, academic), and types of materials (e.g., audio and video media). Some types of materials, such as publications from small and alternative presses, may be available only by ordering directly from the publisher.[67] Items that are ordered title by title are called *discretionary purchases* or *firm orders*. A firm order is an order for a specific title placed with a dealer or publisher that specifies a time limit for delivery and a price that must not be exceeded without the library's approval. Selecting individual titles is considered *micro-selection*.

The alternative to micro-selection is *macro-selection*, which adds large numbers of materials to the library en masse. Macro-selection is managed through mass buying plans—approval plans, blanket orders, and standing orders (sometimes called nonperiodical continuations)—or the acquisition of large retrospective collections, either through purchase or as a gift. Macro-selection is more common in larger public and academic libraries, but it is also found in smaller academic libraries and in public libraries of all sizes. Several authors have argued convincingly that approval plans are desirable in smaller libraries for the same reasons they are used in larger libraries—efficiency, cost-effectiveness, and well-rounded collections. Jacoby observes that approval plans continue to be "an effective, time-saving tool for librarians who are increasingly pressured to devote their time to activities other than book selection."[68] Libraries usually select approval plan vendors through an RFP process.

Macro-selection does involve true selection because librarians must decide the criteria that will guide which titles the vendor supplies. Criteria for approval plans and blanket orders are specified in a library-developed profile. A standing order is an order placed by a library with a publisher or dealer to supply each volume or part of a specific title or type of publication as published, until further notice. Setting up approval plans and blanket orders may have substantial set-up costs and requires time to establish and monitor, but the upfront costs are offset by librarian time savings once this macro-selection plan is implemented.

Approval plans are business arrangements in which a wholesale dealer assumes responsibility for supplying, usually subject to return privileges, all new publications that match a library's collecting profile. Richard Abel is credited with the invention, in the early 1960s, of the approval plan as it is employed now.[69] Many books vendors also offer approval plans. An approval plan *profile* is defined by the library's collections librarians and specifies the subjects, levels of specialization and difficulty, formats, series, genres, prices, languages, publishers included and excluded, and so on to be provided. These parallel the criteria librarians use in micro-selection. Some libraries are implementing an additional condition to their approval plans—e-preferred. This means that the library prefers an e-book version of a title if it is available and meets certain conditions, for example, the e-book release must not lag more than six weeks behind its print counterpart.

The approval plan vendor sends materials (or activates access to e-books) that fit the profile on a regular basis. Librarians review the items received and decide which to buy. Sullivan notes that, "for children's items especially, the ability to hold the item, examine illustrations, glossaries, indexes, and the like is a great improvement over buying from a printed review."[70] Most vendors and libraries aim for a 2 percent or less return rate. Nearly all approval plan vendors offer online notification of titles that match the library's profile as an alternative to the publications themselves. An approval plan may provide a combination of online notification and books, with books automatically provided in some subjects and online notification provided for others. Librarians refine and revise the profile as the library's goals, priorities, and budget change.

Blanket order plans are an arrangement with an individual publisher or scholarly society, which will provide all its publications (or all publications below a specified price) each year, or with a vendor, who agrees to provide a copy of every book published in a particular country within certain parameters. A blanket order plan does not, in most cases, include return privileges.

The variety of services and enhancements provided by both approval plan vendors and firm order suppliers has grown to include electronic data interchange (EDI) through which digital order records and invoices can be loaded into a local library automated system, interactive access to the vendor or supplier online database, online order placement, cataloging records (which may be Library of Congress copy, Cataloging-in-Publication records, or original brief or full cataloging created by the vendor), and fully shelf-ready books. Shelf-ready books come to the library cataloged and processed with spine labels, book plates, and antitheft strips. Shelf-ready books cannot be returned, so the library needs to have confidence in the profile it has developed. In these ways, vendors are supplementing or replacing functions traditionally performed within libraries. Libraries that contract externally for services previously provided by internal library staff members are outsourcing those services. Librarians have viewed outsourcing as a way to contain costs when library staffing has been reduced and as a way to release staff members for other responsibilities perceived as more important. Approval plans are widely employed because they can provide discounted prices, faster delivery of newly published books, reliable coverage, and reports that enable selectors to monitor plans. They can free librarians to look for more esoteric materials and to do other types of work.

Approval plans are not without controversy. Some have criticized approval plans because they create homogeneous collections and generally do not provide extensive coverage of materials from small and alternative presses. Brantley notes that approval plans often miss materials that cross disciplinary boundaries, which can be overlooked in classification-based profiles.[71]

Approval plans were the source of a major flap in the library profession in the 1990s. In 1996, the Hawaii State Public Library System implemented a radical extension of approval plans and contracted with a vendor for purchasing, processing, cataloging, and 100 percent of selecting for its entire acquisitions budget and forty-nine branch libraries. Administrators saw this as way to manage a 25 percent budget cut without laying off employees and to release technical services librarians for direct public service. Most of Hawaii's librarians felt that they could not respond to users' needs and that collections deteriorated under the plan. They saw this kind of outsourcing as a challenge to the very heart of professional librarianship and moved the debate to a national forum. The Hawaii situation became an emotional issue for librarians across the United States, who resented the use of a vendor that caused "commodification, commercialization, and homogenization of books, information materials, and libraries."[72] The Hawaii contract with the vendor was terminated two years after it was begun and selection returned to the librarians.

Subscription agents provide centralized subscription services to relieve libraries of the time-consuming task of dealing with publishers individually. EBSCO is one of the best known subscription agents; many book vendors also serve as subscription agents. Libraries pay a service charge, usually 5–10 percent of total annual subscription cost. The greater the expenditure with a subscription agent, the lower the percentage used to determine the service fee. Many subscription agents also provide access to bibliographic and full-text databases. When possible, most libraries acquire as many subscriptions as possible through one or a few subscription agents because of efficiencies gained. Instead of dozens or even thousands of individual invoices coming from multiple publishers, the agent provides a single invoice for all the titles it handles. Often, the invoice is loaded directly into the library's automated system. Subscription agents typically offer centralized online ordering, claiming, renewal, cancellation, and reports. Libraries usually issue RFPs for a subscription agent at periodic intervals (perhaps every five years), soliciting proposals from their current agent and competitors. The transition to e-journals is changing the role of subscription agents, who are compensating for business lost to publishers' journal packages by offering additional services (such as A-Z titles lists, contract negotiation, and management of contract access rights and license terms) and reports tailored to the digital environment. For example, subscription agents often can collect, consolidate, and report usage data for e-content.

Retailers

Retail bookstores' primary goal is to sell directly to consumers. Libraries occasionally purchase from retailers if they need an item quickly and the retailer can guarantee speedy delivery or a library staff member can go to a local store. One frequently used retailer is Amazon.com. One complication for public institutions in dealing with retailers is ensuring that no tax is charged. Retailers generally do not offer discounts to libraries, but paying list price (plus shipping, if delivered) may be justified if the need is urgent.

Publishers

For many years, most book publishers did not consider libraries their primary market. The prevalent business model was to work through vendors. Although libraries could also buy directly from publishers, they did not receive the discount available from vendors. The advantages for publishers working through vendors paralleled those for libraries: avoiding the need to prepare individual item invoices and ship small packages. Book publishers offered deep discounts to vendors, a portion of which was passed on to libraries. The shift to e-content motivated publishers to sell to libraries actively because of the ease in selling packages or bundles of content.

Serial publishers were the first publishers to sell directly to libraries aggressively by offering packages of e-journals. A comprehensive package of e-journal titles from a single publisher, often referred to as a "Big Deal," generally includes a clause that locks in the total price or caps the annual rate of price increase for a specified number of years and also limits the dollar value of titles the library can cancel in a year. Traditionally, prices have been determined by a library's historic print subscriptions, although this history is increasingly distant.[73] Although this approach may offer differential pricing or a price discount and provide additional titles, it has disadvantages and has been viewed critically by some in the profession.[74] Librarians can lose the ability to select and deselect individual titles. Tracking titles by discipline and budget line can be difficult. Libraries may be locked into keeping titles that are no longer relevant or good value. When locked into a Big Deal and faced with a budget reduction, libraries are forced to cancel titles from smaller publishers not bound by multiyear subscriptions. In addition to consuming most of the serials budget, Big Deals can eat into money allocated for monographs. Some academic libraries have backed away from Big Deals, but 2012 research indicated that large research libraries generally retain their Big Deals although they often negotiate to reduce the titles to a subset of the original Big Deal title list.[75] On the other hand, Big Deal arrangements can offer a cost-effective approach to acquiring numerous titles for some institutions. Botero, Carrico, and Tennant used comparative data to demonstrate that the University of Florida reduced expenditures through Big Deals because the library no longer had to pay document delivery charges for articles in journals added through the licenses, and these arrangements also provided access to titles not previously represented in the university's print collection.[76] Other advantages may include a single search interface to multiple titles, a single order and license agreement for multiple titles, and consistent presentation of usage statistics.

Publishers also sell packages of e-books. By their nature, they consist of a single publisher's list, but they may be available as smaller subject-based collections. An advantage of working directly with the publisher may be more flexibility in negotiating an agreement that better meets the individual library's needs. Vendors are seldom in a position to handle these negotiations on behalf of multiple publishers with multiple libraries. DRM on publisher sites may be less restrictive. Many large publishers make book and serial digital content available on the same platform. Although e-book packages are usually cost-effective with lower prices per title, they have the same disadvantage as Big Deals—the inability to add and remove individual titles. Many publishers sell directly to libraries and also through vendors, but some e-book publishers do not sell individual titles to libraries.

Aggregators

Aggregators are third parties that offer access to the full text of periodicals, articles, books, or media originally published by multiple publishers and provide online access to the content through a common interface or platform. Aggregators such as Ebook Library (EBL), EBSCO eBooks (formerly Net Library), ebrary, OverDrive, and the 3M Cloud Library host the content of several publishers for online access. A survey of public, academic, corporate, legal, and government libraries conducted by the Primary Research Group in 2012 found that 81 percent of e-book contracts in the libraries surveyed were with aggregators.[77] Specialized aggregators offer a variety of content. For example, Recorded Books .com makes available for download more than 15,000 unabridged audiobooks to libraries and schools and distributes the Zinio digital collection of more than 5,000 popular magazines. Several aggregators (e.g., Library Ideas, OverDrive, Recorded Books) offer streaming video of movies and television shows and sometimes streaming music from a variety of sources. Producers of many indexing and abstracting databases also offer aggregated article collections and build hypertext links between the full-text electronic documents and the index records, combining index searching with full-text access. For example, as of November 2013, Academic Search Premier (from EBSCOhost) was indexing more than 13,600 journals and providing full text to 4,700 of them. Business Source Premier (also from EBSCOhost) was offering the full text of more than 2,200 business publications. An advantage of acquiring e-content through an aggregator is the provision of a single contract or licensing agreement.

Aggregators offer various pricing models for e-books. The most popular are selecting title by title and purchasing a bundled subject collection. Either may be available for single-user or multiple-user access. Subscription or perpetual-ownership models are available as well. Prices for individual titles are generally at or above the print list price. The cost of titles supplied in packages varies depending on the aggregator and number of users but is usually less than the cost of purchasing the titles separately. One drawback of e-book packages, as with journal packages, is the inclusion of titles of little value or interest to the library. Some publishers delay making new titles available through aggregators. Benefits of using an aggregator include a single contract, federated search compatibility, 24/7 access to full text, free MARC records, usage statistics, and often the ability to customize the interface or offer it in multiple languages. Many aggregators collaborate with vendors and agents. For example, ebrary, EBL, and EBSCO partner with YBP to offer their digital titles available to YBP customers within YPB's suite of services.

Aggregators' agreements with publishers have been volatile, with publishers signing on with an aggregator and then withdrawing from the agreement. The description of Academic Search Premier makes this clear in the statement "Publications included on this database are subject to change without notice due to contractual agreements with publishers."[78] Aggregators offering e-journals sometimes provide selected articles and may not include book reviews, editorials, and advertisements. High-quality illustrations may be missing. Embargoes on current journal content, from a few months to a few years, also are normal. Journal publishers that contribute to multiple aggregator collections may offer their e-journal subscriptions directly to libraries, which may find they are acquiring the same content from multiple sources. Libraries should compare to the extent they can to avoid paying twice or more for the same content. Aggregator collections can be a convenient and cost-effective approach to providing access to a sizable set of e-content, but they rarely offer a long-term guarantee of access to the titles in the package.

Project MUSE, BioOne, and JSTOR are three aggregators that focus on scholarly content, although their customers include public libraries, museums, secondary schools, and higher education and research institutions. Project MUSE (http://muse.jhu.edu) is a nonprofit collaboration of the Milton S. Eisenhower Library (Johns Hopkins University), other libraries, and more than 120 university presses and scholarly societies. Project MUSE provides access to resources in the humanities and social sciences. Journal publishers contribute the complete content of each journal as it is published. To supplement current issues, Project MUSE subscribers have access to back files for selected titles. Libraries can choose from interdisciplinary journal collections and two broad collections in the humanities or social sciences. If a publisher ceases contributing to Project MUSE, all issues currently online remain available to subscribing libraries. Project MUSE's e-book collection is offered in partnership with the University Press e-book Consortium (UPeC). Libraries purchase the e-books and have perpetual access right. E-books are available as full text, in PDF, and retrievable at the chapter level. Because the e-books have no DRM attached, users at libraries that have purchased them can print, copy, download, and save content. Books are available in packaged collections by date or subject for purchase or through access-only subscriptions.

BioOne (www.bioone.org) is another collaborative initiative among scientific societies, libraries, academe, and the private sector and offers a package of biological, ecological, and environmental science research journals. Most of

BioOne's titles are published by small societies and other not-for-profit organizational publishers and, like Project MUSE, BioOne provides the latest issues and full journal content for titles in its collection.

JSTOR (www.jstor.org) is a nonprofit organization that provides a somewhat different kind of journal collection. It creates and maintains a trusted archive of scholarly journals beginning with volume 1, issue 1. Content represents many disciplines from more than eight hundred publishers and is offered in several packages of journal titles on a subscription basis. JSTOR creates scanned images of journal issues and pages as originally published and offers full-text searching of the journals based on optical character recognition. Originally limited to back issues, JSTOR now also includes current issues of journals available through its Current Scholarship Program. In many cases, though, current issues are not available, because JSTOR employs a moving wall approach, meaning that the most recently published journal issues are embargoed for one to five years, and only the older issues are available. Some journals that participate in Project MUSE or BioOne for their current issues also work with JSTOR to provide access to their older issues. JSTOR also makes public domain content (journal content published before 1923 in the United States and before 1970 elsewhere) freely available online.[79] JSTOR began offering current and backlist books in June 2012, partnering with several scholarly publishers and university presses.

Selecting appropriate aggregators requires extensive research and comparison of options. Each library needs to evaluate and assess alternatives, examining content, business model, and licenses and DRM to find the best match for local needs that is affordable and sustainable.

EXCHANGE AGREEMENTS

Some academic libraries use exchanges as a form of en masse selection.[80] Exchanges are most frequently with foreign partners and can provide materials not available in other ways or more economically than direct purchase. The library supplies local publications to a foreign partner library or institution, which sends its publications from its own country to the library. Partners may be libraries, scholarly societies and associations, university academic departments, or research academies and institutes. Exchanges may be a viable means to acquire foreign documents, although U.S. trade embargoes against certain nations can restrict the importation and exportation of informational materials. In 2004, IFLA and the International Publishers Association issued a joint statement urging the U.S. government to removed repressive regulations that limit free exchange of information.[81] Exchanges should be established and monitored within the library's collections priorities. Some libraries are reducing their exchange programs, though many libraries continue exchange agreements because they serve as a cost-effective mechanism for obtaining publications, a cross-cultural activity, and a way of helping other libraries.

GIFTS AND OTHER FREE MATERIALS

Gifts may bring individual items or a collection of items to the library. A gift is transferred voluntarily without compensation. Any gift that is not cash is called a gift-in-kind and can be goods, services, and property. Gifts may be conveyed to the library through a *deed of gift*, a legal document that transfers title from the donor to the library without requiring payment; a deed of gift may contain conditions with which the library must comply.[82] Generous donors expect careful stewardship of their gifts. No payment to the donor does not mean the library has no costs associated with the gift. Costs arise when it is reviewed by the librarian, cataloged and processed, shelved and reshelved, and repaired and preserved. Gift serial subscriptions have ongoing costs just as paid subscriptions do. Most selection decisions about gifts can be reduced to a tradeoff between the cost of adding the item and its value to the library.

Gift materials are desirable because they can strengthen a library's holdings, fill gaps, supply replacements, and provide materials that are unaffordable or not available through purchase. A collection of many items from a single donor often focuses on a particular area or discipline. It may contain out-of-print items, serial runs in excellent condition, first editions, and other items of intrinsic value. Besides filling gaps, a gift collection can add both depth and breadth to a library's collection. Gift materials can enter the library unsolicited, through direct negotiations with potential donors, or through requests to publishers and distributors. Special collections librarians or library development staff members may target individuals with known collections and negotiate a gift. A library may ask to receive all publications of a corporation, a research center, or an academic institution—in effect, a gift standing order.

Many librarians are questioning the ultimate value of gifts-in-kind because of the costs associated with reviewing, storing, and processing gifts when the yield in materials added to the collection is low.[83] Some libraries feel that accepting gifts-in-kind increases the likelihood that donors will donate money in the future; Canevari de Paredes found this not to be the case.[84] As libraries begin to focus on just-in-time acquisitions, adding gift materials just in case they will be needed at some future time becomes less defensible.

When libraries curtail or eliminate gifts to the library, they often continue to accept gifts to archives and special collections. Some public libraries accept gifts with the understanding they may be sold in book sales with any revenue directed toward the collections budget. Managing gift inventory and sales is also an expensive undertaking. Book sales may generate community goodwill, but the revenue frequently does not cover their associated costs. For this reason, some libraries rely on Friends associations to manage gift sales.

The same criteria that guide selection of items for purchase should be considered when reviewing gifts. The first decision the librarian must make is whether the material fits the scope of the library's collecting policy or guidelines. The library may have policies about adding or not adding particular types of materials such as textbooks, laboratory manuals, duplicates, vanity press and self-published items, realia, reprints and preprints of individual articles, collections of reprinted journal articles, trade paperbacks, popular pamphlets, and commercial publications of a promotional nature.

Donors must be considered as part of the selection process. Some gifts are not worth adding to the library precisely because of special conditions insisted upon by the potential donor. Donors may offer gifts with conditions about use, housing, and special treatment. Even a library that does not have guidelines for the selection of gift materials may have guidelines that address acceptable and unacceptable donor restrictions. The librarian should weigh the value of the gift (and possible future gifts) to the library against any donor restrictions.

The library receiving gifts usually supplies the donor with a letter of acknowledgment. Under the U.S. Revenue Reconciliation Bill in 1993, which modified the 1984 Tax Reform Act slightly, donors are required to provide a written acknowledgment from the library for any noncash donation in which they are claiming a deduction of $250 or more. Libraries should not give appraisals or estimates of value to the donor.[85] A letter provides the donor with a record that may be used to claim a tax deduction, creates a permanent record of gifts received for the library, and graciously acknowledges the donor's gift to the library. Such a deed of gift eliminates any ambiguity regarding the library's right to use, retain, or dispose of materials received from donors.

If the donor's total deduction for all noncash contributions for the year is more than $500, the donor must file IRS Form 8283 (Noncash Charitable Contributions) and attach the receiving organization's acknowledgment letter of receipt. The donor is responsible for determining the fair market value of the gift; librarians should avoid estimating value. If the property being contributed is worth $5,000 or more, the donor must retain a qualified appraiser to determine the gift's fair market value. U.S. tax law requires a recipient institution to retain any gift valued at $500 or above for two years. If the library disposes of the gift or portions of it and thereby reduces the value of the original gift, it must file an IRS Form 8282 (Donee Information Return), which will affect the donor's original deduction.

Many librarians are selecting resources that are accessible without charge on the Internet. Nevertheless, like gifts, "free" online resources entail costs to the library. Librarians spend time evaluating and assessing them. The same librarians or others spend time creating access, though either the catalog or other finding tools. The persistence of these resources should be monitored, and they should be deselected if no longer relevant. Selection of such items is an extension of a librarian's normal collection-building activities. The nature and complexity of free web resources suggest an important role for librarians in their review, evaluation, selection, and cataloging for library users.[86] Micro-selection and management of free e-resources can be extremely time consuming, and each library should decide the extent to which the benefits gained justify the staff investment.

Several websites offer free online access to extensive collections of resources. Project Gutenberg (http://gutenberg.org) claims to be the first and largest single collection of free e-books. Bartleby.com offers transcriptions of literature, reference, and verse in the public domain. The Internet Archive (http://archive.org) provides free access to moving images (movies, films, and videos), books and texts, and audio files, and it archives web pages. The International Music Score Library Project (http://imslp.org), also called the Petrucci Music Library, offers public domain scores, works by contemporary composers willing to share their music, and MP3 files. The State University Libraries of Florida Literature for Children (http://susdl.fcla.edu/juv) collection offers digitized public domain titles published predominantly in the United States and Great Britain from the seventeenth through the twentieth century. The Digital Public Library of America (http://dp.la) aims to bring "together the riches of America's libraries, archives, and museums, and makes them freely available to the world. It strives to contain the full breadth of human expression, from the written word, to works of art and culture, to records of America's heritage, to the efforts and data of science." The DPLA provides a single portal to access digitized photographs, manuscripts, books, sound, and moving images held in numerous collections in the United States. Europeana (http://europeana.eu) serves a similar purpose for materials held in more than two thousand libraries, museums, archives, and other collections in Europe.

Any discussion of free access to e-content must include the Google Books (http://books.google.com) project, which is scanning millions of books held by libraries and partnering with publishers and authors to provide limited access to their books. Google Book Search is a tool from Google that searches the full text of books that Google scans and stores. Google Book Search lets the user view pages (if permitted by the publisher) or snippets from the book, offers links to the publisher's website and booksellers, and displays information about libraries that hold the book. If the book is under copyright, Google limits the number of viewable pages. If the book is out of copyright or the publisher has given permission, one can see a preview of the book and, in some cases, the complete text. If the book is in the public domain, one can download a PDF copy.

Many libraries selectively catalog items found in these collections; others do not because they are readily discoverable through the hosting site. Some free e-books suffer from lack of quality control. Deciding if a library should select and direct users to these resources and, if so, which ones and how to do so depends on the library's own missions, policies, and user community.

RETROSPECTIVE SELECTION

Retrospective selection is the process of selecting materials that are old, rare, antiquarian, used, or out of print (OP). It includes seeking replacements for missing or damaged materials and older materials not previously acquired. Many librarians develop desiderata files of titles to be purchased when funding is available or the item is located. These materials may be needed to fill gaps in the collection or to support new academic programs or community interests. Retrospective selection is more common in larger research libraries. The usual sources for materials are OP dealers' catalogs, auctions, and private owners.

OP titles are those that can no longer be obtained from the original publishers. This can happen rapidly as a result of the limited number of copies published in some fields. Many used and OP booksellers produce catalogs. These catalogs, either in print or online, usually list only single copies; therefore, the librarian must act quickly to ensure acquisition. Many OP dealers accept lists of titles the library is seeking. Dealers can be located through the *American Book Trade Directory.*[87] Additional suppliers can be found through the Antiquarian Booksellers Association of America (http://abaa.org) and the International League of Antiquarian Booksellers (www.ilab-lila.com). Many university press books no longer go out of print because of print-on-demand, a technology employed by publishers in which new copies of a book are not printed until an order has been received. This method is also used by smaller presses and academic publishers to maintain an active backlist of short-run titles.

A specialized area within retrospective selection is filling gaps in serial runs and replacing missing issues. Filling gaps with print issues is less common because of the ease with which articles are supplied through interlibrary loan and the option of purchasing digital back files. One source for print issues is the

Duplicates Exchange Union (www.ala.org/alcts/mgrps/ecoms/deu), sponsored by ALCTS. Libraries prepare lists of periodical issues and books they are willing to supply to, and those they want to obtain from, member libraries through a cooperative exchange. Receiving libraries are asked to cover shipping fees. Sometimes a publisher can provide missing issues for a price. If a library is unable to locate replacement issues, it may borrow and photocopy issues needed to complete a serial run.

Microforms, reprints, and digital collections are viable alternatives in retrospective selection. If the item is too costly to replace in print, the OP title or issues cannot be located, or the item will not see heavy use, microform is a reasonable solution. Some titles are available in reprint editions, which are usually photo reproductions of the original and satisfy most users' needs. Librarians can purchase extensive microform sets of retrospective titles on specific topics, and several publishers and vendors provide online access to important retrospective collections. *Early English Books Online* (wwwlib.umi.com/eebo) is one example of the latter. The more than 125,000 titles published from 1475 to 1661 in this collection are also available in microfilm format.

CASE STUDY

Kathryn is the collections coordinator for the urban Emeryville school district, which consists of twenty-five elementary (K–6) schools, fifteen middle schools, and ten high schools and serves 39,000 students. The district has 3,100 teachers, 900 paraprofessionals, 1,000 support staff, and 227 administrators. Seventy percent of teachers have a master's or other advanced degree. All schools have a library media center, but many schools share a school librarian and are staffed by aides when the librarian is at another school. The school district shares a union catalog and supports delivery of materials between schools. The school board has delegated responsibility for selecting learning materials and resources that support teachers to the collections coordinator. Kathryn has, in turn, delegated responsibility for selecting materials for individual schools to the librarians on site. Kathryn retains responsibility for selecting and managing e-resources that are available to all schools. She works with a representative committee of school librarians who advise her in this area. In addition to advice on selecting titles, this group recommends e-resources that should be available in specific schools.

One area of selecting responsibility that challenges Kathryn and the school librarians is materials that support teachers—both materials on pedagogical theory and practical resources for improving classroom instruction. For this job, Kathryn, with the support of the school librarians, has decided to explore patron-driven acquisition of e-books. Her goal is to provide a larger collection of books to teachers than was possible previously, reduce the number of duplicates currently being purchased, and provide 24/7 access. She believes that empowering teachers to take a direct role in selecting the resources they need will improve both the quality of materials selected and the service provided to teachers.

Activity

Develop a plan for patron-driven acquisition that Kathryn can implement; do not limit the plan to models currently available. Assume that bibliographic records for possible titles will be loaded in the shared catalog and that an "adequate" budget is available. Consider what options and limitations should be in place. For example, who should be able to initiate orders? Should a price cap be in place? Should publications be limited by imprint date, publisher, subject, or other criteria? Should selections made by teachers be reviewed? If so, by whom? Should Kathryn choose a purchase or subscription model? Is short-term rental a viable option? Should the model be for a single user or simultaneous users? If the latter, should Kathryn select a set number of users or unlimited simultaneous users? Explain the rationale behind your choices.

Notes

1. Dennis P. Carrigan, "Librarians and the 'Dismal Science,'" *Library Journal* 113, no. 11 (June 15, 1988): 22.
2. See data and sources at *Wikipedia*, s.v. "Books Published per Country per year," last modified Nov. 5, 2013, http://en.wikipedia.org/wiki/Books_published_per _country_per_year.
3. Bowker, "Publishing Market Shows Steady Title Growth in 2011 Fueled Largely by Self-Publishing Sector" (June 5, 2012), www.bowker.com/en-US/aboutus/press _room/2012/pr_06052012.shtml.
4. Bowker, "Self-Publishing Sees Triple-Digit Growth in Just Five Years, Says Bowker" (Oct. 23, 2012), www.bowker.com/en-US/aboutus/press_room/2012/ pr_10242012.shtml.
5. "Ulrichsweb: Global Serials Directory" (the subscription-based, online version of Ulrich's *Periodicals Directory*, Providence, RI: Bowker). The search, conducted July 22, 2013, was limited to "active" and applied the "Edition Type" filter to isolate "Primary" editions, which removed counts for multiple formats.
6. Narda Tafari, "Prices of U.S. and Foreign Published Materials," in *Library and Book Trade Almanac*, 57th ed., ed. Dave Bogart (Medford, NJ: Information Today, 2012). *Library and Book Trade Almanac* is a reliable source for pertinent data, with

a few caveats. The data reported are publishers' list prices and exclude publisher discounts or subscription agent service charges. Most serial pricing is based on the National Information Standards Organization, *Criteria for Price Indexes for Print Library Materials*, ANSI/NISO Z39.20 (Baltimore: NISO, 1999), and is only beginning to reflect e-journals.

7. *Film and Video Finder* (Medford, NJ: National Information Center for Educational Media).

8. Physics Database.com, "Top Physics and Science Books of 2012," http://physicsdatabase.com/2013/01/11/top-physics-and-science-books-of-2012; Cherri Jones and J. B. Petty, *Multiethnic Books for Middle-School Curriculum* (Chicago: American Library Association, 2013); *Public Library Core Collection: Nonfiction* (New York: H. W. Wilson).

9. International Association of Library Associations and Institutions, "Guidelines for Audiovisual and Multimedia Materials in Libraries and Other Institutions" (Mar. 2004), http://archive.ifla.org/VII/s35/pubs/avm-guidelines04.htm; Stephen Abram, "Social Libraries: The Librarian 2.0 Phenomenon," *Library Resources and Technical Services* 52, no. 2 (Apr. 2008): 21.

10. John Rutledge and Luke Swindler, "The Selection Decision: Defining Criteria and Establishing Priorities," *College and Research Libraries* 48, no. 2 (Mar. 1987): 128.

11. Lynn B. Williams, "Subject Knowledge for Subject Specialists: What the Novice Bibliographer Needs to Know," *Collection Management* 14, no. 3/4 (1991): 39.

12. Francis K. W. Drury, *Book Selection* (Chicago: American Library Association, 1930), 1; S. R. Ranganathan, *The Five Laws of Library Science* (Madras, India: Madras Library Association; London: Edward Goldston, 1931).

13. Rose Zertuche Trevino, *The Pura Belpré Awards: Celebrating Latino Authors and Illustrators* (Chicago: American Library Association, 2006); Association for Library Services to Children, *Newbery and Caldecott Medal Books: A Guide to the Medal and Honor Books* (Chicago: American Library Association, 2014 [updated annually]).

14. *Graphics Novels Core Collection* (New York: Wilson).

15. Juris Dilevko and Lisa Gottlieb, "The Politics of Standard Selection Guides: The Case of the *Public Library Catalog*," *Library Quarterly* 73, no. 3 (July 2003): 289–337.

16. *Yearbook of International Organizations* (Brussels: Union of International Associations).

17. Josh Hadro, "What's the Problem with Self-Publishing?" *Library Journal* (Apr. 11, 2013), http://lj.libraryjournal.com/2013/04/publishing/whats-the-problem-with-self-publishing; Barbara Hoffert, "Materials Mix: Investigating Trends in Materials Budgets and Circulation," *Library Journal* (Feb. 19, 2013), http://lj.libraryjournal.com/2013/02/publishing/materials-mix-investigating-trends-in-materials-budgets-and-circulation.

18. Margie Ruppel, "Tying Collection Development's Loose Ends with Interlibrary Loan," *Collection Building* 25, no.3 (2006): 72–77; Dracine Hodges, Cyndi Preston,

and Marsha J. Hamilton, "Patron-Initiated Collection Development: Progress of a Paradigm Shift," *Collection Management* 35, no. 3/4 (2010): 208–21; Judith M. Nixon and E. Stewart Saunders, "A Study of Circulation Statistics of Books on Demand: A Decade of Patron-Driven Collection Development, Part 3," *Collection Management* 35, no. 3/4 (2010): 151–61; David C. Tyler et al., "Just How Right Are the Customers? An Analysis of the Relative Performance of Patron-Initiated Interlibrary Loan Monograph Purchases," *Collection Management*, 35, no. 3/4 (2010): 162–79.

19. Kate Pitcher et al., "Point-of-Need Collection Development: The Getting It System Toolkit (GIST) and a New System for Acquisitions and Interlibrary Loan Integrated Workflow and Collection Development," *Collection Management* 35, no. 3/4 (2010): 222–36.

20. Linda A. Ennis, *Government Documents Librarianship: A Guide for the Neo-depository Era* (Medford, NJ: Information Today, 2007), 67.

21. U.S. Government Printing Office, *Customer Centric and Employee Driven: GPO Strategic Plan FY2013–2017* (Washington, DC: Government Printing Office, 2012).

22. FDLP Desktop, "Substituting Online for Tangible Versions of Depository Publications by Selectives" (last updated June 17, 2010), www.fdlp.gov/collections/collection-maintenance/141-substitution-guidelines.

23. See Steven L. Sowell et al., "Between a Rock and a Hard Place: Managing Government Document Collections in a Digital World," *Collection Management* 37, no. 2 (2012): 98–112, for a case study and recommendations for one FDLP library working to manage government documents during the transition from print to digital.

24. Bernard Fry, "Preface," in *Municipal Government Reference Sources: Publications and Collections*, ed. Peter Hernon et al. (New York: Bowker, 1978), vii.

25. *Statistical Reference Index: A Selective Guide to American Statistical Publications from Sources Other than the U.S. Government* (Washington, DC: Congressional Information Service, monthly, with annual cumulations); *Index to Current Urban Documents* (Fredericksburg, VA: ILM, annual).

26. Catherine Morse, "Managing Electronic International Government Information: Issues and Practices," in *Managing Government Information in Libraries: Issues and Practices*, ed. Andrea M. Morrison (Chicago: American Library Association, 2008), 195–208.

27. Bethany Latham and Kimberly Weatherford Stevens, "Managing the Digital Collection," in *Government Information Management in the 21st Century: International Perspectives*, ed. Peggy Garvin, 79–93 (Farnham, Surrey, UK: Ashgate, 2011), 91.

28. Andrea Morrison, "International and Foreign Government Publications: Collection Development Issues," *DttP: Documents to the People* 30, no. 2 (2002): 22–28.

29. Phyllis J. Van Orden and Sunny Strong, *Children's Books: A Practical Guide to Selection* (New York: Neal-Schuman, 2007).

30. Association for Library Collections and Technical Services, Serials Section, Acquisitions Committee, "Serials Acquisitions Glossary," 3rd ed. rev. (2005), www.ala.org/alcts/files/resources/collect/serials/acqglossary/05seracq_glo.pdf.

31. American Library Association, *RDA Toolkit: Resource Description and Access*, "Glossary" (Chicago: American Library Association, 2010–) [proprietary online resource].

32. *Readers' Guide to Periodical Literature* (New York: Wilson).

33. Brian Quinn, "The Psychology of Group Decision Making in Collection Development," *Library Collections, Acquisitions, and Technical Services* 32, no. 1 (2008): 10–18.

34. William H. Walter wrote several perceptive articles on the challenges e-books present for academic libraries. See his "E-books in Academic Libraries: Challenges for Acquisition and Collection Management," *portal: Libraries and the Academy* 13, no. 2 (2013): 187–211; "E-books in Academic Libraries: Challenges for Discovery and Access," *Serials Review* 39, no. 2 (June 2013): 97–104; and "E-books in Academic Libraries: Challenges for Sharing and Use," *Journal of Librarianship and Information Science* 46, no. 2 (2014), published online Jan. 10, 2013.

35. A useful source for required and desired e-book technical specifications, rights terms, and support services is "ARL E-book Requirements," www.arl.org/storage/documents/publications/arl-e-book-requirements-2012.pdf. This is Appendix C, "Detailed Evaluation Requirements and Desirables," in the RFP for selecting an e-book licensing agent developed by ARL.

36. American Library Association Digital Content and Libraries Working Group, "EBook Business Models for Public Libraries" (Aug. 8, 2012), http://connect.ala .org/files/80755/EbookBusinessModelsPublicLibs.pdf; "EBook Business Models: A Scorecard for Public Libraries" (Jan. 25, 2013), www.districtdispatch.org/wp-content/uploads/2013/01/Ebook_Scorecard.pdf.

37. Lotsee P. Smith, "The Curriculum and Materials Selection: Requisite for Collection Development," *Collection Management* 7, no. 3/4 (Fall 1985/Winter 1985–86): 39.

38. Sandra Hughes-Hassell and Jacqueline C. Mancall, *Collection Management for Youth: Responding to the Needs of Learners* (Chicago: American Library Association, 2005).

39. Rick Lugg, "Collecting for the Moment: Patron-Driven Acquisitions as a Disruptive Technology," in *Patron-Driven Acquisitions: History and Best Practices*, ed. Dave A. Swords (Berlin: Walter de Gruyter, 2011), 7–22.

40. Tom Corbett, "Patron-Driven Acquisitions in School Libraries: The Promise and the Problems," in *Patron-Driven Acquisitions: History and Best Practices*, ed. David A. Swords (Berlin: Walter De Gruyter, 2011), 95–105.

41. Gail Herrera and Judy Greenwood, "Patron-Initiated Purchasing: Evaluating Criteria and Workflows," *Journal of Interlibrary Loan, Document Delivery, and Electronic Reserves* 21, no. 1/2 (2011): 9–24.

42. William H. Walters, "Patron-Driven Acquisition and the Educational Mission of the Academic Library," *Library Resources and Technical Services* 56, no. 3 (July 2012): 199–213; Dracine Hodges, Cyndi Preston, and Marsha J. Hamilton, "Patron-Initiated Collection Development: Progress of a Paradigm Shift," *Collection Management* 35, no. 3/4 (2010): 219.

43. Lisa Shen et al., "Head First into the Patron-Driven Acquisitions Pool: A Comparison of Librarian Selections versus Patron Purchases," *Journal of Electronic Resources Librarianship* 23, no. 3 (2011): 203–18.

44. American Library Association, *ALA Policy Manual*, Section Two: Positions and Public Policy Statements, 60, Diversity, 45, www.ala.org/aboutala/files/governance/policymanual/updatedpolicymanual/ALA%20Policy%20Manual%20part%20two.pdf.

45. Association of College and Research Libraries, "Diversity Standards: Cultural Competency for Academic Libraries" (2012), www.ala.org/acrl/standards/diversity.

46. U.S. Census Bureau, *Foreign-Born Population in the United States: 2010* (May 2010), www.census.gov/prod/2012pubs/acs-19.pdf; U.S. Census Bureau, "Most Children Younger than Age 1 Are Minorities, Census Bureau Reports" (May 17, 2012), www.census.gov/newsroom/releases/archives/population/cb12-90.html; Annie E. Casey Foundation, Data Center Kids Count, Data across States, "Child Population by Race (Percent)—2011," http://datacenter.kidscount.org/data/acrossstates/Rankings.aspx?ind=103; U.S. Census Bureau, "An Older and More Diverse Nation by Midcentury" (Aug. 2008), www.census.gov/newsroom/releases/archives/population/cb08-123.html.

47. Gary J. Gates and Frank Newport, "Special Report: 3.4% of U.S. Adults Identify as LGBT: Inaugural Gallup Findings Based on More than 120,000 Interviews" (Oct. 18, 2012), www.gallup.com/poll/158066/special-report-adults-identify-lgbt.aspx; Wendell Ricketts, *Lesbians and Gay Men as Foster Parents* (Portland: University of Southern Maine, 1991); U.S. Census Bureau, "Households and Families: 2010" (Apr. 2012), www.census.gov/prod/cen2010/briefs/c2010br-14.pdf.

48. U.S. Department of Health and Human Services, Administration on Aging, "Aging Statistics," www.aoa.gov/Aging_Statistics.

49. U.S. Census Bureau, American Fact Finder, "Selected Social Characteristics in the United States," http://factfinder2.census.gov/faces/tableservices/jsf/pages/productview.xhtml?pid=ACS_11_1YR_DP02&prodType=table.

50. American Library Association, "Diversity in Collection Development: An Interpretation of the Library Bill of Rights" (adopted July 14, 1982, by the ALA Council; amended Jan. 10, 1990; July 2, 2008), www.ala.org/advocacy/intfreedom/librarybill/interpretations/diversitycollection.

51. Denise E. Agosto, "Building a Multicultural School Library: Issues and Challenges," *Teacher Librarian* 34, no. 3 (Feb. 2007): 27–31.

52. Crystal E. Kaiser, "Is Your Early Childhood Literature Collection Disability-Inclusive and Current?" *Children and Libraries* 5, no. 3 (Winter 2007): 5–12.

53. Chris Atton, "The Subjects of Alternative Literature: A General Guide," in *Alternative Literature: A Practical Guide for Librarians* (Aldershot, Hampshire, UK: Gower, 1996), 39–64.

54. Bleue J. Benton and Sharon Grimm, "When Collection Development Leads to Staff Development: The Transgender Resource Collection," in *Serving LGBTIQ Library and Archives Users: Essays on Outreach, Service, Collections and Access*, ed. Ellen Greenblatt (Jefferson, NC: McFarland, 2011), 310–18.

55. Karla L. Strieb and Julia C. Blixrud, "The State of Large-Publisher Bundles in 2012," *Research Library Issues: A Report from ARL, CNI, and SPARC*, no. 282 (Spring 2013): 13–20, http://publications.arl.org/rli282.

56. For a useful source of information, see American Library Association, "Video and Copyright," ALA Library Fact Sheet 7 (last updated Mar. 2012), www.ala.org/tools/libfactsheets/alalibraryfactsheet07.

57. Carrie Russell, "The Best of Copyright and VideoLib," *Library Trends* 58, no. 3 (Winter 2010): 349.

58. *Copyright Law of the United States and Related Laws Contained in Title 17 of the United States Code*, Circular 92 (Washington, DC: Library of Congress, Copyright Office, 2011), www.copyright.gov/title17/circ92.pdf, 24.

59. Marc Parry, "Judge Dismisses Lawsuit against UCLA over Use of Streaming Video," Wired Campus, *Chronicle of Higher Education* (Oct. 4, 2011), http://chronicle.com/blogs/wiredcampus/judge-dismisses-lawsuit-against-ucla-over-use-of-streaming-video/33513.

60. International Federation of Library Associations and Institutions, Committee on Copyright and Other Legal Matters, "Licensing Principles" (2001), www.ifla.org/publications/ifla-licensing-principles-2001; University of California Libraries, Collection Development Committee, "Principles for Acquiring and Licensing Information in Digital Formats" (July 2006), http://libraries.universityofcalifornia.edu/groups/files/cdc/docs/principlesforacquiring.pdf.

61. Stephen Bosch, Patricia A. Promis, and Chris Sugnet, with contributions by Trisha Davis, *Guide to Licensing and Acquiring Electronic Information*, ALCTS Acquisitions Guides 2 and Collection Management and Development Guides 13 (Lanham, MD: Association for Library Collections and Technical Services with Scarecrow, 2005).

62. National Information Standards Organization, *SERU: A Shared Electronic Resource Understanding*, NISO RP-7-2012 (Baltimore, MD: National Information Standards Organization, 2012), www.niso.org/publications/rp/RP-7-2012_SERU.pdf; Zachary Rolnik and Selden Lamoureux, with Kelly A. Smith, recorder,

"Alternatives to Licensing of E-resources," *Serials Librarian* 54, no. 3/4 (2008): 281–87; Todd Carpenter, "The Value of Standards in Electronic Content Distribution: Reflections on the Adoption of NISO Standards," *Journal of Electronic Publishing* 14, no. 1 (Summer 2011), http://quod.lib.umich.edu/cgi/t/text/idx/j/jep/3336451.0014.102/value-of-standards-in-electronic-content-distribution?rgn=main;view=fulltext#N10.

63. Xiaohua Zhu, "The National Site Licensing of Electronic Resources: An Institutional Perspective," *Journal of Library and Information Studies* 9, no. 1 (June 2011): 51–75.

64. Ross Atkinson, "Access, Ownership, and the Future of Collection Development," in *Collection Management and Development: Issues in an Electronic Era*, ed. Peggy Johnson and Bonnie MacEwan (Chicago: American Library Association, 1994), 92–109.

65. Peggy Johnson, *Developing and Managing Electronic Collections* (Chicago: American Library Association, 2013), 50.

66. Stephen Bosch et al., "Do Libraries Still Need Book Vendors and Subscription Agents?" (Oct. 2011), www.ala.org/alcts/resources/z687/vend.

67. Possible sources for identifying small presses and alternative publishers are Byron Anderson, *Alternative Publishers of Books in North America*, 6th ed. (Duluth, MN: Library Juice, 2006), and Len Fulton, ed., *The Directory of Small Press and Magazine Editors and Publishers* (Paradise, CA: Dustbooks). The latter is updated annually and available on CD-ROM and as an online subscription. Library Juice Press also provides a freely accessible online directory, Alternatives in Print (http://directory.libraryjuicepress.com), which lists alternative book publishers and periodicals.

68. Susan Mueller, "Approval Plans and Faculty Selection: Are They Compatible?" *Library Collections, Acquisitions, and Technical Services* 29, no. 1 (2005): 61–70; Clare Appavoo, "Size Doesn't Matter: Book Approval Plans Can Be Catered to Tight Budgets," *Feliciter* 53, no. 5 (2007): 238–40; Assako N. Hoyoke, "Getting the Best Out of an Approval Plan," *Journal of Hospital Librarianship* 10, no. 2 (2010): 115–22; Beth E. Jacoby, "Status of Approval Plans in College Libraries," *College and Research Libraries* 69, no. 3 (May 2008): 227–40, quote 235.

69. Ann L. O'Neill, "How the Richard Abel Co., Inc. Changed the Way We Work," *Library Acquisitions: Practice and Theory* 17, no. 1 (Spring 1993): 41–46.

70. Michael Sullivan, *Fundamentals of Children's Services* (Chicago: American Library Association, 2005), 55.

71. Juris Dilevko, "An Alternative Vision of Librarianship: James Danky and the Socio-cultural Politics of Collection Development," *Library Trend* 56, no. 3 (Winter 2008): 678–704; Charles Willet, "Consider the Source: A Case against Outsourcing Materials Selection in Academic Libraries," *Collection Building* 17, no. 2 (1998): 91–95; Audrey Fenner, "The Approval Plan: Selection Aid, Selection Substitute," *Acquisitions Librarian* 16, no. 31/32 (2004): 227–40; John S. Brantley,

"Approval Plans, Discipline Change, and the Importance of Human Mediated Book Selection," *Library Collections, Acquisitions, and Technical Services* 34, no. 1 (2010): 11–24.

72. Carol Reid, "Down and Outsourced in Hawaii," *American Libraries* 28 (June/July 1997): 56–58; Rebecca Knuth and Donna G. Bair-Mundy, "Revolt over Outsourcing: Hawaii's Librarians Speak Out about Contracted Selection," *Collection Management* 23, no. 1/2 (1998): 109.

73. Streib and Blixrud, "The State of Large-Publisher Bundles in 2012."

74. Theodore C. Bergstrom, "Librarians and the Terrible Fix: Economics of the Big Deal," *Serials* 23, no. 2 (July 2012): 77–82; Rickey D. Best, "Is the 'Big Deal' Dead?" *Serials Librarian* 57, no. 4 (2009): 353–63; Tina Feick, Gary Ives, and Jo McClamroch, "The Big E-package Deals: Smoothing the Way through Subscription Agents," *Serials Librarian* 50, no. 3/4 (2006): 267–70; Kenneth Frazier, "What's the Big Deal?" *Serials Librarian* 48, no. 1/2 (2005): 49–59.

75. Nancy J. Gibbs, "Walking Away from the 'Big Deal': Consequences and Achievements," *Serials* 18, no. 2 (July 2005): 89–94; Amy Carlson and Barbara M. Pope, "The 'Big Deal': A Survey of How Libraries Are Responding and What the Alternatives Are," *Serials Librarian* 57, no. 4 (2009): 380–98; Emma Cryer and Karen S. Grigg, "Consortia and Journal Package Renewal: Evolving Trends in the 'Big Package Deal'?" *Journal of Electronic Resources in Medical Libraries* 8, no. 1 (2011): 22–34; Streib and Blixrud, "State of Large-Publisher Bundles."

76. Cecilia Botero, Steven Carrico, and Michele Tennant, "Using Comparative Online Journal Usage Studies to Assess the Big Deal," *Library Resources and Technical Service* 52, no. 2 (2008): 61–68.

77. Primary Research Group, *Library Use of EBooks 2013 Edition* (New York: Primary Research Group, 2013).

78. EBSCOhost, "Academic Search Premier Magazines and Journals," www.ebscohost.com/titleLists/aph-journals.htm.

79. Laura Brown, "JSTOR—Free Access to Early Journal Content and Serving 'Unaffiliated' Users" (Sept. 07, 2011), http://about.jstor.org/news/jstor-free-access-early-journal-content-and-serving-unnaffiliated-users.

80. Kristi Ekonen, Päivi Paloposkim, and Pentti Vattulainen, *Handbook on the International Exchange of Publications*, 5th ed. (Munich: G. K. Saur, 2006).

81. "IFLA and IPA Deplore OFAC Regulations Limiting the Exchange of Information Materials," *IFLA Journal* 30, no. 3 (2004): 247.

82. Two model deeds of gift are available in *Research Library Issues: A Quarterly Report from ARL, CNI, and SPARC* no. 279 (June 2012), http://publications.arl.org/2ds247.pdf.

83. See, for example, John Ballestro and Philip C. Howze, "When a Gift Is Not a Gift: Collection Assessment Using Cost-Benefit Analysis," *Collection Management* 30, no. 3 (2006): 49–66; Janet Bishop, Patricia A. Smith, and Chris Sugnet, "Refocusing a

Gift Program in an Academic Library," *Library Collections, Acquisitions, and Technical Services* 34, no. 4 (2010): 115–22; Ruth Fisher, Rick Lugg, and Kent C. Boese, "Cataloging: How to Take a Business Approach," *Bottom Line: Managing Library Finances* 17, no. 2 (2004): 50–54.

84. Donna Canevari de Paredes, "Gifts-in-Kind in the Academic Library: The University of Saskatchewan Experience," *Library Collections, Acquisitions, and Technical Services* 30, no. 1/2 (2006): 55–68.

85. Omnibus Budget Reconciliation Act of 1993, 103rd Cong. 1st sess. (1993), Public Law 103–66, Stat. 312 (Aug. 10, 1993), www.gpo.gov/fdsys/pkg/BILLS-103hr2264 enr/pdf/BILLS-103hr2264enr.pdf.

86. Chuanfu Chen et al., "Assessing the Authority of Free Online Scholarly Information," *Scientometrics* 90, no. 2 (Feb. 2012): 543–60; Inga K. Hsieh, Kathleen R. Murray, and Cathy Nelson Hartman, "Developing Collections of Web-Published Materials," *Journal of Web Librarianship* 1, no. 2 (2007): 5–26; Karen Schmidt, Wendy Allen Shelburne, and David Steven Vess, "Approaches to Selection, Access, and Collection Development in the Web World: A Case Study with Fugitive Literature," *Library Resources and Technical Services* 52, no. 3 (2009): 184–91.

87. *American Book Trade Directory* (New Providence, RI: Bowker).

Suggested Readings

General

Alan, Robert, et al. "Approval Plan Profile Assessment in Two Large ARL Libraries: University of Illinois at Urbana-Champaign and Pennsylvania State University." *Library Resources and Technical Services* 54, no. 2 (Apr. 2010): 64–76.

Albitz, Becky. *Licensing and Managing Electronic Resources*. Oxford, UK: Chandos, 2008.

Anson, Catherine, and Ruth R. Connell. *E-books Collections*. SPEC Kit 313. Washington, DC: Association of Research Libraries, 2009.

Ashmore, Beth, Jill E. Grogg, and Jeff Weddle. *The Librarian's Guide to Negotiation: Winning Strategies for the Digital Age*. Medford, NJ: Information Today, 2012.

Association for College and Research Libraries. "Guidelines for Media Resources in Academic Libraries (2012)." www.ala.org/acrl/standards/mediaresources.

Austenfeld, Anne Marie. "Building the College Library Collection to Support Curriculum Growth." *Collection Management* 34, no. 3 (2009): 209–27.

Blummer, Barbara, and Jeffrey Kenton, "Best Practices for Integrating E-books in Academic Libraries: A Literature Review from 2005 to Present." *Collection Management* 37, no. 2 (2012): 65–97.

Brantley, John S. "Approval Plans, Discipline Change, and the Importance of Human Mediated Book Selection." *Library Collections, Acquisitions, and Technical Services* 34, no. 1 (2010): 11–24.

Bridges, Karl. *Customer-Based Collection Development: An Overview*. Chicago: American Library Association, 2013.

Buckley, Matthew, and Deborah Tritt. "Ebook Approval Plans: Integration to Meet User Needs." *Computers in Libraries* 31, no. 3 (Apr. 2011): 15–18.

Carr, Patrick L. "The Commitment to Securing Perpetual Journal Access: A Survey of Academic Research Libraries." *Library Resources and Technical Services* 55, no. 1 (Jan. 2011): 4–16.

Cassell, Kay Ann, et al. *Gifts for the Collections: Guidelines for Libraries*. IFLA Professional Reports 112. The Hague: International Federation of Library Associations and Institutions, 2008.

Cassell, Kay Ann, and Uma Hiremath. "Selecting and Evaluating Reference Materials." In *Reference and Information Services: An Introduction*, 3rd ed., 357–70. Chicago: Neal-Schuman, 2013.

Caudle, Dana M., Cecilia M. Schmitz, and Elizabeth J. Wiesbrod. "Microform—Not Extinct Yet: Results of a Long-Term Microform Use Study in the Digital Age." *Library Collections, Acquisitions, and Technical Services* 37, no. 1/2 (2013): 2–12.

Chadwell, Faye A. "What's Next for Collection Management and Managers? Good Gifts Stewardship." *Collection Management* 35, no. 2 (2010): 59–68.

Chuen, Wookjin, et al. *Collecting Global Resources*. SPEC Kit 324. Washington, DC: Association of Research Libraries, 2011.

Cornog, Martha, and Timothy T. Perper, eds. *Graphic Novels beyond the Basics: Insights and Issues for Libraries*. Santa Barbara, CA: Libraries Unlimited, 2009.

Crawford, Walt. *The Big Deal and the Damage Done*. [n.p.]: Cites and Insights Books, 2013.

Emery, Jill, and Graham Stone. "Acquisition of New Content." In *Techniques for Electronic Resource Management*, 16–20. *Library Technology Reports* 49, no. 2. Chicago: ALA TechSource, 2013.

———. "Investigation of New Content." In *Techniques for Electronic Resource Management*, 10–15. *Library Technology Reports* 49, no. 2. Chicago: ALA TechSource, 2013.

Eschenfelder, Kristin R., et al. "How Institutionalized Are Model License Use Terms? An Analysis of E-journal License Use Rights Clauses from 2000 to 2009." *College and Research Libraries* 74, no. 4 (July 2013): 326–55.

Esposito, Joseph J., Kizer Walker, and Terry Ehling. *PDA and the University Press*. [n.p.]: 2012. http://scholarlykitchen.files.wordpress.com/2012/10/pda-and-the-university-press-5-2-final.pdf.

Fagan, Bryan D., and Jody Condit Fagan. *Comic Book Collections for Libraries*. Santa Barbara, CA: Libraries Unlimited, 2011.

Farace, Dominc John, and Joachim Schöpfel, eds. *Grey Literature in Library and Information Studies*. Berlin: De Gruyter Saur, 2010.

Fischer, Karen S., et al. "Give 'Em What They Want: A One-Year Study of Unmediated Patron-Driven Acquisition of E-books." *College and Research Libraries* 73, no. 5 (Sept. 2012): 469–92.

Fletcher-Spear, Kristen, and Merideth Bowie Jenson-Benjamin. *Library Collections for Teens: Manga and Graphic Novels*. Bowie, MD: E. L. Kurdlay, in association with Neal-Schuman, 2010.

Forte, Eric J., Cassandra J. Hartnett, and Andrea L. Sevetson. *Fundamentals of Government Information: Mining, Finding, Evaluating, and Using Government Resources*. New York: Neal-Schuman, 2011.

Garvin, Peggy. *Government Information Management in the 21st Century*. Farnham, Surrey, UK: Ashgate, 2011.

Grover, Sharon, and Lizette Hannegan. *Listening to Learn: Audiobooks Supporting Literacy*. Chicago: American Library Association, 2012.

Handman, Gary. "License to Look: Evolving Models for Library Video Acquisition and Access." *Library Trends* 58, no. 3 (Winter 2010): 324–34.

Harris, Lesley Ellen. *Licensing Digital Content: A Practical Guide for Librarians*. 2nd ed. Chicago: American Library Association, 2009.

Hooper, Lisa. "And We're Back! Experiences in Quickly Building a Robust Sound Recording Collection." *Music Reference Services Quarterly* 15, no. 3 (2012): 173–79.

Jenemann, Laura. "Public Performance Rights Management in Academic Libraries." Paper presented at the World Library and Information Congress, 77th IFLA General Conference and Assembly, San Juan, Puerto Rico, Aug. 17, 2011. http://conference.ifla.org/past/ifla77/161-jenemann-en.pdf.

Jensen, Kristi. "Engaging Faculty through Collection Development Utilizing Online Survey Tools." *Collection Building* 28, no. 3 (2009): 117–21.

Johnson Sharon, et al. *Key Issues for E-resource Collection Development: A Guide for Libraries*. The Hague: International Federation of Library Associations and Institutions, Acquisition and Collection Development Section, 2012. www.ifla.org/files/assets/acquisition-collection-development/publications/Electronic-resource-guide.pdf.

Jones, Wayne. *E-journals Access and Management*. New York: Routledge, 2009.

Kairis, Rob. "A Subject-Based Approval Plan for Consortia Purchasing of U.S. University Press Books." *Library Collections, Acquisitions, and Technical Services* 36, no. 1/2 (Mar. 2012): 30–38.

Karp, Jesse. *Graphic Novels in Your School Library*. Chicago: American Library Association, 2012.

Koh, Rowena. "Alternative Literature in Libraries: The Unseen Zine." *Collection Building* 27, no. 2 (2008): 48–51.

Korat, Ofra. "Reading Electronic Books as a Support for Vocabulary, Story Comprehension, and Word Reading in Kindergarten and First Grade." *Computers and Education* 55, no. 1 (Aug. 2010): 24–31.

Krueger, Karla S. "The Status of Statewide Subscription Databases." *School Library Research* 15 (2012). www.ala.org/aasl/slr/volume15/krueger.

Lamothe, Alian R. "Factors Influencing the Usage of an Electronic Book Collection: Size of the E-book Collection, the Student Population, and the Faculty Population." *College and Research Libraries* 74, no. 1 (Jan. 2013): 39–59.

Lamoureux, Selden Durgom, Clint Chamberlain, and Jane Bethel. "Basics of E-resource Licensing." *Serials Librarian* 58, no. 1/4 (Apr. 2010): 20–31.

Laskowski, Mary S. *Guide to Video Acquisitions in Libraries: Issues and Best Practices*. ALCTS Acquisitions Guides 15. Chicago: American Library Association, 2011.

Lawrence, Amanda. "Electronic Documents in a Print World: Grey Literature and the Internet." *Media International Australia* no. 143 (2012): 122–31.

Lemely, Trey, Robert M. Britton, and Jie Li. "Negotiating Your License." *Journal of Electronic Resources in Medical Libraries* 8, no. 4 (2011): 325–38.

Lewis, David W. "From Stacks to the Web: The Transformation of Academic Library Collecting." *College and Research Libraries* 74, no. 2 (Mar. 2013): 159–76.

Lipinski, Tomas A. *The Librarian's Legal Companion for Licensing Information Resources and Services*. Chicago: Neal-Schuman, 2013.

Lowry, Charles B., and Julia C. Blixrud. "E-book Licensing and Research Libraries: Negotiating Principles and Price in an Emerging Market." *Research Library Issues: A Quarterly Report from ARL, CNI, and SPARC*, no. 280 (Sept. 2012): 11–19. http://publications.arl.org/rli280.

Masuchika, Glenn, and Gail Boldt. "Japanese Manga in Translation and American Graphic Novels: A Preliminary Examination of the Collections in 44 Academic Libraries." *Journal of Academic Librarianship* 36, no. 6 (Nov. 2010): 511–17.

Minčić-Obradović, Ksenija. *E-books in Academic Libraries*. Oxford, UK: Chandos, 2011.

Moeller, Robin A. "'Aren't These Boy Books?': High School Students' Readings of Gender in Graphic Novels." *Journal of Adolescent and Adult Literacy* 54, no. 7 (Apr. 2011): 476–84.

Moorefield-Lang, Heather, and Karen Gavigan. "These Aren't Your Father's Funny Papers: The New World of Digital Graphic Novels." *Knowledge Quest* 40, no. 3 (Jan./Feb. 2012): 30–35.

Moyer, Jessica E. "Audiobooks and E-books: A Literature Review." *Reference and User Services Quarterly* 51, no. 4 (2012): 340–54.

Nardini, Robert F. "Approval Plans." In *Encyclopedia of Library and Information Sciences*, 3rd ed., ed. Marcia J. Bates and Mary Niles Maack, 109–14. New York: Taylor and Frances, 2010.

Pattee, Amy S. *Developing Library Collections for Today's Young Adults*. Lanham, MD: Scarecrow, 2013.

Pickett, Carmelita. "Eliminating Administrative Churn: The 'Big Deal' and Database Subscriptions." *Serials Review* 37, no. 4 (2011): 258–61.

Pickett, Carmelita, Simona Tabacaru, and Jeanne Harrell. "E-approval Plans in Research Libraries." *College and Research Libraries*, forthcoming, accepted Nov. 2012; anticipated publication March 2014, available as a preprint, http://crl.acrl .org/content/early/2012/12/19/crl12-410.full.pdf+html.

Polanka, Sue. *The No Shelf Required Guide to E-book Purchasing*. *Library Technology Reports* 47, no. 8. Chicago: ALA TechSource, 2011.

Porcaro, JP. *Video Game Collection Development and Management*. Chicago: American Library Association, 2012.

Poynder, Richard. "The Big Deal: Not Price but Cost." *Information Today* 28, no. 8 (Sept. 2011). www.infotoday.com/it/sep11/The-Big-Deal-Not-Price-But-Cost.shtml.

Price, Kate, and Virginia Havergal, eds. *E-books in Libraries: A Practical Guide*. London: Facet, 2011.

Pyles, Christine. "It's No Joke: Comics and Collection Development," *Public Libraries* 51, no. 6 (Nov./Dec. 2012): 32–35.

Reynolds, Gretchen E., Cynthia Holt, and John C. Walsh. "Collection Development: Acquiring Content across and beyond Disciplines." In *Interdisciplinarity and Academic Libraries*, ed. Daniel C. Mack and Craig Gibson, 97–113. ACLR Publications in Librarianship 66. Chicago: American Library Association, 2012.

Reynolds, Leslie J, et al. "User-Driven Acquisitions: Allowing Patron Requests to Drive Collection Development in an Academic Library." *Collection Management* 35, no. 3/4 (2010): 244–54.

Roncevic, Mirela. *E-book Platforms for Libraries*. *Library Technology Reports* 49, no. 3. Chicago: ALA TechSource, 2013.

Schöpfel, Joachim, and Dominic J. Farace. "Grey Literature." In *Encyclopedia of Library and Information Sciences*, 3rd ed., ed. Marcia J. Bates and Mary Niles Maack, 2029–39. New York: Taylor and Frances, 2010.

Schöpfel, Joachim, and Claire Leduc. "Big Deal and Long Tail: E-journal Usage and Subscriptions." *Library Review* 61, no. 7 (2012): 497–510.

Serchay, David S. *The Librarian's Guide to Graphic Novels for Adults*. New York: Neal-Schuman, 2010.

———. *The Librarian's Guide to Graphic Novels for Children and Tweens*. New York: Neal-Schuman, 2008.

Shirkey, Cindy. "Taking the Guesswork Out of Collection Development: Using Syllabi for a User-Centered Collection Development Method." *Collection Management* 36, no. 3 (2011): 154–64.

Singer, Carol A. *Fundamentals of Managing Reference Collections*. Chicago: American Library Association, 2012.

Slater, Robert. "E-books or Print Books, 'Big Deals' or Local Selections—What Gets More Use?" *Library Collections, Acquisitions, and Technical Services* 33, no. 1 (2009): 31–41.

Staiger, Jeff. "How E-books Are Used: A Literature Review of the E-book Studies Conducted from 2006 to 2011." *Reference and User Services Quarterly* 51, no. 4 (Summer 2012): 355–65.

Stern, David. "Ebooks: From Institutional to Consortial Considerations." *Online* 34, no. 3 (2010): 29–35.

Strauch, Bruce, and Adam Chesler. "A Licensing Survival Guide for Librarians." *Journal of Electronic Resources in Medical Libraries* 6, no. 2 (2009): 123–37.

Street, Leslie A., and Amanda M. Runyon. "Finding the Middle Ground in Collection Development: How Academic Law Libraries Can Shape Their Collections in Response to the Call for More Practice-Oriented Legal Education." *Law Library Journal* 102, no. 3 (2010): 399–439.

Swords, Dave A., ed. *Patron-Driven Acquisitions: History and Best Practices*. Berlin: Walter de Gruyter, 2011.

Tappeiner, Elizabeth, and Catherine Lyons. "Selection Criteria for Academic Video Game Collections." *Collection Building* 27, no. 3 (2008): 121–25.

Toren, Beth Jane. "Bam! Pow! Graphic Novels Fight Stereotypes in Academic Libraries: Supporting Collecting, Promoting." *Technical Services Quarterly* 28, no. 1 (2010): 55–69.

Tyler, David C. "Patron-Driven Purchase on Demand Programs for Printed Books and Similar Materials: A Chronological Review and Summary of Findings." *Library Philosophy and Practice* (2011), http://dialnet.unirioja.es/servlet/articulo?codigo=3709395&orden=309367&info=link.

Tyler, David C., et al. "Patron-Driven Acquisition and Circulation at an Academic Library: Interaction Effects and Circulation Performance of Print Books Acquired via Librarians' Orders, Approval Plans, and Patrons' Interlibrary Loan Requests." *Collection Management* 38, no. 1 (2013): 3–32.

Vasileiou, Magdalini, Jennnifer Rowley, and Richard Hartley. "The E-book Management Framework: The Management of E-books in Academic Libraries and Its Challenges." *Library and Information Science Research* 34, no. 4 (2012): 282–91.

———. "Perspectives on the Future of E-books in Libraries in Universities." *Journal of Librarianship and Information Science* 44, no. 4 (2012): 217–26.

Wagner, Cassie. "Graphic Novel Collections in Academic ARL Libraries." *College and Research Libraries* 71, no. 1 (Jan. 2010): 42–48.

Ward, Suzanne M. *Guide to Implementing and Managing Patron-Driven Acquisitions.* ALCTS Acquisitions Guides Series 16. Chicago: American Library Association, 2012.

Weiner, Robert G., ed. *Graphic Novels and Comics in Libraries and Archives: Essays on Readers, Research, History, and Cataloging.* Jefferson, NC: MacFarland, 2010.

Weir, Ryan O. *Managing Electronic Resources: A LITA Guide.* Chicago: American Library Association, 2012.

Widzinski, Lori. "'Step Away from the Machine': A Look at Our Collective Past." *Library Trends* 58, no. 3 (Winter 2010): 358–77.

Wikoff, Karen. *Electronic Resources Management in the Academic Library: A Professional Guide.* Santa Barbara, CA: Libraries Unlimited, 2012.

Wiley, Lynn, and Elizabeth Clarage. "Building on Success: Evolving Local and Consortium Purchase-on-Demand Programs." *Interlending and Document Supply* 40, no. 2 (2012): 105–10.

Wilkinson, Frances C., and Linda K. Lewis. *A Guide to Writing RFPs for Acquisitions.* ALCTS Acquisitions Guides 14. Chicago: Acquisitions Section, Association for Library Collections and Technical Services, American Library Association, 2008.

Williams, Virginia K. "Building and Evaluating Juvenile Collections in Academic Libraries." *College and Undergraduate Libraries* 18, no. 1 (2011): 58–76.

Williams, Virginia K., and Kathy A Downes. "Assessing Your Vendors' Viability." *Serials Librarian* 59, no. 3/4 (2010): 313–24.

Williams, Virginia K., and Damen V. Peterson. "Graphic Novels in Libraries Supporting Teacher Education and Librarianship Programs." *Library Resources and Technical Services* 53, no. 3 (July 2009): 166–73.

Wolfson, Gene. "Using Audiobooks to Meet the Needs of Adolescent Readers." *American Secondary Education* 36, no. 2 (Spring 2008): 105–17.

Young, Terry. "Aligning Collection Development with Instructional and Learning Needs." *School Library Monthly* 25, no. 10 (June 2010): 20–22.

Diverse and Alternative Literatures and Communities

Avila, Salvador. *Serving Latino Teens.* Santa Barbara, CA: Libraries Unlimited, 2012.

Burke, Susan K. "Social Tolerance and Racist Materials in Public Libraries." *Reference and User Services Quarterly* 49, no. 4 (2010): 369–79.

Case, Mary, et al. *Report of the ARL Joint Task Force on Services to Patrons with Print Disabilities.* Washington, DC: Association of Research Libraries, 2012. www.arl.org/storage/documents/publications/print-disabilities-tfreport02nov12.pdf.

Farmer, Lesley S. J. *Library Services for Youth with Autism Spectrum Disorders.* Chicago: American Library Association, 2013.

Gilton, Donna L. "The Future of Multicultural Youth Literature." *Knowledge Quest* 40, no. 3 (Jan./Feb. 2012): 44–47.

Greenblatt, Ellen, ed. *Serving LGBTIQ Library and Archives Users: Essays on Outreach, Service, Collections, and Access*. Jefferson, NC: McFarland, 2011.

Hoffert, Barbara. "Immigrant Nation: How Public Libraries Select Materials for a Growing Population Whose First Language Is Not English," *Library Journal* 133, no. 14 (Sept. 1, 2008): 34–36.

Hughes-Hassell, Sandra, Elizabeth Overberg, and Shannon Harris. "Lesbian, Gay, Bisexual, Transgender, and Questioning (LGBTQ)–Themed Literature for Teens: Are School Libraries Providing Adequate Collections?" *School Library Research* 16 (2013). www.ala.org/aasl/sites/ala.org.aasl/files/content/aaslpubsandjournals/slr/vol16/SLR_LGBTQThemedLiteratureforTeens_V16.pdf.

Naidoo, Jamie Campbell. *Rainbow Family Collections: Selecting and Using Children's Books with Lesbian, Gay, Bisexual, Transgender and Queer Content*. Santa Barbara, CA: Libraries Unlimited, 2012.

Naidoo, Jamie Campbell, and Sarah Park Dahlen, eds. *Diversity in Youth Literature: Opening Doors through Reading*. Chicago: American Library Association, 2012.

Norton, Donna E. *Multicultural Children's Literature: Through the Eyes of Many Children*. 4th ed. Boston: Pearson, 2013.

Prater, Mary Ann, and Tina Taylor Dyches. *Teaching about Disabilities through Children's Literature*. Westport, CT. Libraries Unlimited, 2008.

Rajput, Toby. "Questioning Your Collection." *Knowledge Quest* 38, no. 1 (2009): 62–69.

Smallwood, Carol, and Kim Becnel. *Library Services for Multicultural Patrons: Strategies to Encourage Library Use*. Lanham, MD: Scarecrow, 2013.

Wopperer, Emily. "Inclusive Literature in the Library and the Classroom: The Importance of Young Adult and Children's Books That Portray Characters with Disabilities." *Knowledge Quest* 39, no. 3 (Jan./Feb. 2011): 26–34.

CHAPTER FIVE

Managing Collections

Much of the education and training for collection development focuses on building collections, which can seem the most stimulating and satisfying part of the work. An equally important and challenging responsibility is collection management or maintenance. This chapter explores making decisions that constitute collection management—weeding for withdrawal and transfer to storage and other locations; preservation and conservation; and subscription review, renewal, cancellation, and the transition to electronic-only access—and concludes with a section on protecting collections from deterioration, theft, mutilation, and disasters.

Collection management is an umbrella term covering all the decisions made after an item is part of the collection. These decisions often become critical because of condition, budget or space limitations, or shifts in the library's user community and parent organization priorities. Collection management often is more politically charged than collection development. User communities, administrative agencies, and funding bodies may be suspicious about the disposition of materials for which "good money" has been spent. Both users and librarians may have an emotional investment in the library's collections. Cancelling journals distresses at least part of the user group. Some preservation reformatting products are less comfortable to use and some are less permanent. Deciding what to retain and where to house it challenges libraries. Moving materials to remote storage sites usually delays access and frustrates patrons. The future of coordinated curation in storage facilities is complex and uncertain. Although many best practices for collection management exist, much is in turmoil.

Weeding

Weeding is the process of removing materials from the active collection for withdrawal or transfer. *Withdrawal* is the physical process of pulling materials from the collection and removing the location on the descriptive records from the catalog. Items withdrawn from the active collection may be discarded, offered for sale, or given to other organizations. Transferred items may be moved to another location within the library or library system, including into storage.

Other terms used for weeding are *deselection, pruning, thinning, culling, deaccession, relegation, deacquisition, retirement, reverse selection, negative selection,* and *book stock control.* The extensive list of euphemisms suggests the degree to which librarians are uncomfortable removing materials from collections even if the decision is not to dispose of them but to transfer them to storage. As Manley observes, "Next to emptying the outdoor bookdrop on cold and snowy days, weeding is the most undesirable job in the library. It is also one of the most important." Baumbach and Miller offer a succinct description of weeding and its importance in school library media centers:

> Simply put, weeding is selection in reverse. It is deselection. Weeding is the act of reevaluating items in the collection and removing any that are inaccurate, out of date, misleading, inappropriate, unused, in poor condition, or otherwise harmful to students. It is something all librarians and library media specialists must do regularly if they want to maintain the best possible collections for their school communities. It is a professional responsibility that cannot be taken lightly.[1]

Libraries have run into political problems when their communities have discovered withdrawn materials in dumpsters and landfills. Nicholson Baker attracted national attention with his 1996 *New Yorker* article on massive withdrawal and discard projects at the San Francisco Public Library.[2] The University of New Mexico Library made the news in 2001 when faculty members protested withdrawing back runs of 803 math journals.[3] The library faced severe space constraints and was, at the time of the withdrawal, providing online access to the titles through JSTOR. As a result of the protest, the library reacquired or replaced all withdrawn volumes. In 2004, East St. Louis citizens discovered 10,000 deselected books and albums in a decommissioned library building.[4] The items had been withdrawn and left behind when the library moved to a new, smaller building in 2001. The intention had been to sell the materials, but a new library director knew nothing about the collection or the intent to sell it. The discovery resulted in an imbroglio and bad publicity for the library and East St. Louis. Withdrawal projects in other countries have sparked similar outrage.[5]

Libraries did not give much attention to withdrawals until late in the 1800s. Library materials were so scarce and valuable that the emphasis was on building collections, not culling them. As the number of books in libraries increased and space grew more limited, withdrawing and discarding items in public and school libraries became more common. One early report from the Lunn Public Library in Massachusetts noted that five hundred books were withdrawn in 1883 because they were superseded or no longer useful.[6] A weeding plan proposed to address the overflowing Quincy Public Library (also in Massachusetts) caused a major flap at the ALA 1893 annual meeting.[7] William Frederick Poole, a leading figure in librarianship of the time, railed against weeding and said the solution was to build bigger libraries. Large academic and research libraries, which valued comprehensiveness and quantity, were less likely to discard materials, looking instead to transfer volumes to remote storage. In 1893, in one of the earliest documented examples, Harvard librarian Justin Winsor oversaw moving 15,000 volumes to storage because of space constraints.[8]

Reasons for Weeding

ALA explains that "the continuous review of library materials is necessary as a means of maintaining an active library collection of current interest to users. In the process, materials may be added and physically deteriorated or obsolete materials may be replaced or removed in accordance with the collection maintenance policy of a given library and the needs of the community it serves."[9]

Reasons for weeding usually are related to improving services and collections. More effective use of the library's space and staff required to maintain the collection represents one justification for weeding. Libraries dispose of materials that are no longer useful, current, or appropriate. Little-used materials can be sent to a site less expensive to maintain or put into compact storage in a less accessible area of the main library building. These tactics can alleviate collection space problems, provide options for repurposing existing spaces, and make collections more attractive and easier to maintain. An important reason is to assure continued quality in the collection. When weeding is justified on the grounds that user service will be improved, the rational is that borrowers will more easily find up-to-date materials; sexist, racist, out-of-date, and possibly inaccurate materials will be removed; the general appearance of the library will be improved; and browsing capability will be enhanced.

A library should have established criteria, documented in a written policy, guiding weeding and withdrawal decisions. The library then has a measure of protection in pointing to a systematic plan for not only building but also managing its collection. Criteria vary from library to library, depending on mission, priorities, users, physical facilities, staffing, and age and type of collection. Dilevko and Gottlieb found that circulation, physical condition, and accuracy of information were the three most common criteria for weeding in forty public libraries they surveyed.[10]

Successful Weeding

Weeding is not simple. It is time-consuming, involves many library units, and can be "the most politically charged responsibility any librarian will assume."[11] The important elements of successful weeding are a clear purpose (improving the collection, making materials more accessible, freeing space, etc.) and criteria, sound planning, sufficient time to do it well, careful consideration, and appropriate communication with administrators and constituents. The process should be conscientious, consistent with policy and institutional goals, attentive to consortial commitments, and sensitive to users.

Effective and timely communication with users, governing authorities, and library staff is critical. Information about the reasons for weeding and the benefits to be gained must be prepared as part of planning the project. A first step is to gain buy-in from staff, some of whom may be emotionally invested in collections they helped develop. Having talking points that librarians can use with their constituents is useful. Academic libraries can use their subject liaisons to cultivate acceptance with specific faculty groups. Metz and Gray recommend that a single librarian (the collections coordinator or perhaps the director) be designated as the individual to whom unresolved concerns be directed.[12] Senior library administrators in all types of libraries should always inform their supervisors of large weeding projects. Transparency is the best approach, and a willingness to reverse some decisions is desirable.

Ideally, libraries review materials in the collection with the same regularity that they add them. One technique is the use of periodic collection inventories or audits. An example of this approach is CREW (continuous review, evaluation, and weeding), which was developed by Segal and most recently revised and updated by Larson.[13] The CREW manual recommends establishing guidelines for weeding each part of the collection according to the classification into which it falls, building weeding into the year's work calendar, and combining inventory review with careful consideration of each item in the collection for discarding, binding, or replacement.

More frequently, a withdrawal project is a discrete project, forced upon the library by circumstances. The motivation may be a critical demand for more space, the need to review a portion of the collection prior to compacting or shifting it, an inventory or collection analysis project, a project to reclassify materials, or a physical disaster. Such a crash project can put pressure on several library units—circulation, cataloging, stack maintenance—as well as the collections librarians reviewing items. Planning a project should include comparing the costs of the effort with the costs of doing nothing. Costs associated with weeding include staff time to review materials, revise associated records, move materials, shift remaining materials within the space, educate users, retrieve materials if moved to storage, or obtain them from elsewhere if later requested. Costs resulting from doing nothing include ongoing collection maintenance (reshelving, shifting collections, maintaining catalog records, etc.), unavailable shelf space, unattractive and unappealing collections, and provision of dated and possibly inaccurate information.

Weeding Criteria

Most weeding processes combine mechanical, objective approaches (such as analysis of circulation data and citation frequency) with more judgmental, subjective considerations (such as local program needs and knowledge of the subject literature). Reviewing en masse depends more on objective data because each item is not considered individually. Criteria for weeding are similar to those used in selecting items, remembering that all libraries are different and criteria are more or less relevant depending on the subject area, format, and user community. The three most frequently asked questions are Has it been used? Is it worn, soiled, or damaged? Is it outdated? Although these are valid concerns, the following questions also should be considered.

- Is the content still pertinent?
- Is it in a language that current and future users can read?
- Is it duplicated in the collection—perhaps additional copies, a comparable item on the same topic, or available digitally?
- Is it available and easily accessible elsewhere?
- Is it rare or valuable or both?
- Has it been superseded by a newer edition?
- Was it selected originally in error?
- Is it cited in standard abstracting or indexing tools?
- Is it listed in a standard bibliography of important works?
- Does it have local relevance?
- Does it fill a consortial commitment or regional need?
- If available in electronic format and the library is considering withdrawing the print version, is continued access to the e-version ensured?

Specific types of materials have additional considerations when evaluated for weeding. For example, Smith notes that collections of music scores may need multiple versions and copies of a score (e.g., performance editions, miniature and study scores, and multiple copies if the work is for more than one performer). Hightower and Gantt address the need for currency in health science collections, where outdated resources can have critical consequences. Matlak suggests that obsolescence is a questionable criterion for withdrawing materials in the social sciences, where current research often uses outdated and discounted research. Libraries that are part of the Federal Depository Library Program must abide by this program's policies regarding government document retention and disposal.[14]

School library media centers often develop detailed guidelines to keep a collection fresh and current. Guiding principles are based on the length of time the content remains up-to-date and the frequency with which materials should be replaced. When materials become damaged or worn, they should be withdrawn and replaced, if appropriate. Figure 5-1 offers possible replacement guidelines for a school media center, recognizing that exceptions exist. For example, art and literature books generally do not become dated, so condition is of primary concern.

Slote recommends an objective, scientific approach to collection weeding in which the amount and time of use are the principal criteria for deciding what

Type of material	Replace after
Almanacs, yearbooks, statistical compilations	1 year or when new edition is received
Print journals	Keep only 1 year if not indexed
Computer science	3 years
Career	3 to 5 years
Pure science (except botany and natural history)	3 to 5 years
Technology and applied science	3 to 5 years
General encyclopedias	3 to 5 years
Atlases	3 to 5 years
Geography and history	5 to 7 years
Philosophy, psychology, and religion	5 to 7 years
Dictionaries	5 to 10 years
Language	7 to 10 years
Arts and recreation	7 to 10 years
Literature	10 years

FIGURE 5-1   Guidelines for replacing materials in a school media center

items to remove.[15] He proposes a macro methodology in which library materials are divided into two groups: a core collection that will serve 90–95 percent of current use, and a "weedable" collection consisting of a larger group of materials that provides the remaining 5–10 percent of use. Much of the literature on collection review has considered use as a primary criterion. Trueswell's study, conducted in the 1960s, determined that 20 percent of a collection accounts for 80 percent of the circulation and that one-half of the collection meets 99 percent of its users' needs. He suggested that "the last circulation date may be an ideal statistic to define and measure circulation requirements and patterns."[16] A famous study by Kent and colleagues at the University of Pittsburgh indicated that 40 percent of materials purchased never circulated.[17]

Relying on past use data as a predictor of future use has its problems. Programs, interests, and priorities change. The 1970s energy crisis produced interest in peat and wind as sources of energy and sent researchers after publications that had not been requested in sixty years. Most circulation data do not reflect in-house use. Librarians have not been able to predict accurately the use of materials before purchase and cannot be confident that they will do much better after the item is in the collection. Past use and predicted future use are seldom used as the sole criteria for withdrawing items.

Approaches to Weeding

CREW (continuous review, evaluation, and weeding) is one of most popular methods for weeding. The CREW method applies objective and subjective criteria in the evaluation of materials. The two main objective factors are the age of the materials and circulation or use. The CREW method uses another acronym, MUSTIE, to describe the subjective criteria: Misleading (factually inaccurate), Ugly (worn beyond mending or rebinding), Superseded (by a new edition or by a better book on the same subject), Trivial (of no discernible literary or scientific merit), Irrelevant (unrelated to the needs and interests of the library's community), and Elsewhere (it is easily obtainable from another library). A variation is MUSTY, in which the Y stands for "Your collection has no use for this book." Another easy-to-remember acronym for weeding is WORST, which stands for Worn out, Out of date, Rarely used, System (e.g., in-library equipment) cannot support, and Trivial (faddish).

A frequently applied technique for weeding is shelf scanning, which involves direct examination of volumes. Title-by-title review provides information about the condition, scope, depth, and currency of materials. It can, however, become a slow and tedious process if the librarian seeks to answer all possible questions.

Although success depends on the experience and knowledge of the librarians doing the work, they must balance available time against the desired outcomes. Sometimes, the weeder works in consultation with other librarians, teachers, or faculty members, making a preliminary identification of items to weed that teachers or faculty members then review. Title-by-title review requires knowledge of the collection and subject area, circulation activity, user community, curricular and research needs—and the library's collection development policy.

A straightforward approach to weeding is to work through the physical collection and place materials on a book truck, separating into categories such as to be withdrawn (sold, donated, disposed), repaired, transferred, and so on. Another technique is to insert decision forms in the items. Decision forms (figure 5-2) can be fairly brief, providing just a few options (e.g., withdraw, repair, replace, or transfer to storage). This type of form is used to record the decision made at the point of review. A more detailed form can be designed to record responses to questions that are answered later, such as when and how often the item circulates and whether the item is a duplicate copy. Answering an extensive list of review questions usually involves subsequent checking away from the stacks. Detailed

Title: _____

Call number: _____

      ☐ Rebind
      ☐ Repair
      ☐ Transfer to storage
      ☐ Withdraw
          ☐ Discard
          ☐ Donate to _____

      ☐ Replace with:
          ☐ Print
          ☐ Microform
          ☐ Digital resource
          ☐ New edition

Reviewer name: _____

Date: _____

FIGURE 5-2   Simple treatment decision form

forms may record all the information checked in reaching the decision or serve to track the item through the review and treatment process. They can include sections for a second person to approve the decisions and for dates that track routing the item through the library units that will process it. A detailed form (figure 5-3) offers the opportunity to compile data about the collection at large. For example, when a representative sample is in hand, several forms can be tallied to learn what percentage of the collection is in poor condition. The level of detail collected on a treatment decision form varies according to the purpose of the project, level of staff involved, and time available. Either sample form should be adapted to the needs of the library using it. For tracking purposes, librarians may record these data on a spreadsheet or possibly in a freetext field in the holdings record attached to the bibliographic record.

Another approach to weeding is to begin with reports generated by the library's integrated library system. Typical data extracted for each title are classification, date of publication, date of last check-in, number of circulations within a set period (perhaps the last five years), and number of copies held. These data can be configured and sorted by the various components. For example, a library might focus on a specific call number range and extract only data for titles in this range published earlier than ten years prior to running the report and that have not circulated in the previous five years. These reports can be used to generate a pick list of likely candidates for weeding, and the actual pulling from the shelves can be done by other staff, student workers, or, perhaps, volunteers. If materials are being transferred to the general collection or a storage facility, additional review by the librarian may not be needed. If the materials are to be withdrawn, good practice suggests that the librarian review the pick list to confirm the initial decisions. A critical step in weeding is to ensure that the bibliographic records are updated to reflect the disposition of the item.

Another option is the Getting It System Toolkit (GIST, www.gistlibrary .org), free open-source software that includes a Deselection Manager interface. In an automated process, GIST uses data from the local automated system, WorldCat, Amazon.com, HathiTrust, and Google Books to determine availability elsewhere and recommend retention or withdrawal. As with other automated methods, librarians should review the software-generated reports for final withdrawal decisions.

A commercial option is provided by Sustainable Collection Services (http:// sustainablecollections.com), which offers deselection decision support tools for academic libraries for a fee. Reports combine local circulation and item data with WorldCat holdings, HathiTrust Digital Library holdings, and authoritative title

Title: _____

Call number: _____

Number of times circulated in the past five years: _____

Duplicate? ☐ Yes ☐ No

Condition? ☐ Can no longer circulate ☐ Poor ☐ Acceptable

Out of scope? ☐ Yes ☐ No

Out of date? ☐ Yes ☐ No

Have later edition? ☐ Yes ☐ No

Recommended Treatment

☐ Rebind ☐ Repair ☐ Transfer to storage ☐ Withdraw

☐ Discard ☐ Donate to: _____

☐ Replace with:

☐ Print

☐ Microform

☐ Digital resource

☐ New edition

Reviewer name: _____

Date: _____

Treatment Approved By

Name: _____

Date: _____

Routing

Send to: ☐ Cataloging Unit: work completed (date) _____

☐ Binding/Repair Unit: work completed (date) _____

☐ Circulation Unit: work completed (date) _____

☐ Shipping Unit for disposal: work completed (date)_____

FIGURE 5-3 Detailed treatment decision form

lists and can be used by a library to develop lists of titles that can be withdrawn or placed in storage.

Some libraries do massive weeding projects every few years, some weed as worn or damaged materials cross the circulation desk or are reshelved, and some weed by collection segments. For example, a public library might weed picture books in the spring and young adult fiction in the fall. Other techniques are to divide the collection into equal parts and work through the entire collection in a year, month by month, or to develop a multiyear schedule in which portions of the collection are reviewed cyclically.

Most of the literature on withdrawals focuses on print items, but all formats deserve consideration. Media should be reviewed using the same criteria applied to print materials. Special attention should be given to visual and sound quality, physical condition, and availability of equipment to view or listen to the media. School librarians consult with teachers to ensure that media continue to satisfy instructional needs. E-books are easy to ignore because they do not take up physical space and their use does not appear in standard circulation activity reports. Many e-book providers do not making removing e-books from packages easy or even possible.[18] If records for e-books have been loaded into the local catalog, one option is to remove the bibliographic records from the catalog (and WorldCat holdings if the library reports these) and thus prevent their discovery. The same criteria should be applied (e.g., currency, scope of coverage, usage), and these materials should be reviewed along with the rest of the collection.

Because of the potential political consequences of disposing of materials, libraries should have a disposition policy that states the options and processes for disposing of materials and is consistent with the policies of the parent agency and legal considerations. Most libraries stamp the item "Discard" or "Withdrawn" and deface or remove ownership marks, including barcodes. If a card has been used to circulate the item, it should be removed and shredded to protect user privacy. Although the San Francisco Public Library acted within the governing laws in its infamous, massive weeding project, city auditors have cited libraries for illegally disposing of city property.[19] Best practices should guide the disposition of materials. Items that are outdated, inaccurate, offensive, or in very poor condition should not be sold, donated, or traded. Do not pass materials on to teachers if they have been withdrawn from the school library media center because they are no longer appropriate. Do not store withdrawn materials to avoid disposing of them properly. Be careful about piling large amounts of discarded materials in dumpsters, where they are easily seen and questioned. Consider locked recycling bins for materials that are being disposed. Before donating materials to other libraries and institutions, librarians should check the gift criteria of the potential recipient.

Some libraries sell withdrawn materials through on-site book sales or used book dealers. Local sales are usually expensive to run and often do not generate enough revenue to offset their cost in staff time. Sometimes Friends organizations manage the sales, which can reduce the overhead. In 2006, the San Francisco Public Library Friends group raised $247,000 for the library in a four-day sale, but one has to assume this was a massive undertaking with many volunteers.[20] If libraries sell items locally, they may be required to collect sales tax, adding another complexity to the process. Several companies (e.g., Better World Books and Thrift Books) partner with libraries to sell their withdrawn books, but usually with stringent requirements regarding both acceptability of materials and number of items that must be supplied. Libraries can sell withdrawn materials directly through online out-of-print dealer sites, but this, too, can be a labor-intensive process.

The public relations aspects of weeding should not be overlooked. Issues most often arise and controversy develops as the result of large projects, but even small projects that are not handled effectively can cause a commotion. Without a context, many people are affronted that libraries do not keep everything forever. The librarian provides the context—the need for space, availability of materials electronically, new materials replacing outdated materials, unacceptable condition (e.g., damaged, moldy), and so on. Metz and Gray describe the communications process used at Virginia Tech Libraries when 160,000 volumes were withdrawn and 270,000 volumes were moved to storage over a seven-year period.[21] They recommend advance and continuous information describing the project, the reasons for it, and the criteria guiding decisions as well as a speedy response to questions raised. Many libraries can provide opportunities for consultation with faculty, teachers, and other stakeholders. For example, an academic library moving extensive back runs of serials to a storage facility might ask faculty members to review the list of titles to ensure that no critical titles are relocated. Often the opportunity for consultation can diffuse anxiety while resulting in only a few titles being retained on site. Other library staff members or units need to be informed so that they can plan for the work—record updating, disposal, transport, shifting, repair, and so on. Library directors, principals, or other internal administrators should be part of the project planning and aware of ongoing weeding activities so that they can decide how or if the information should be shared.

Weeding Variations by Library Type

School and public libraries are more likely than large research libraries to withdraw and dispose of items. They need current nonfiction and fiction and attractive new items and often have severe space limitations. Out-of-date information disadvantages students and citizens who should have the most recent and relevant information. Much of the recreational reading material and popular reference material (e.g., travel books) in public libraries becomes dated within a few years. Multiple copies of once-popular novels seldom need to be retained as user demand for these titles declines. Small and branch public libraries usually concentrate on high-demand materials and can rely on a central library or state or regional interlibrary loan system to supply items that have little demand. Small public libraries should routinely review popular fiction, children's and young adult books, and reference collections.

College libraries may be weeded regularly and carefully because of limited stack and storage space. Focusing on a working collection for undergraduates reduces the need to maintain a constantly growing collection of all materials acquired. Increased online access to retrospective journal files and reference sources along with improved bibliographic and physical access to collections elsewhere have reduced the pressures on small academic libraries to retain everything.

Reference collections in all types of libraries usually are weeded more regularly than other portions of collections. Currency of reference materials is critical and space may be more constrained. Some libraries have a policy that a volume must be removed from the reference collection whenever a new volume is added. They may have a schedule for replacing reference books. For example, any title more than five years old would be reviewed for replacement with a new edition or more current work on the topic. Some libraries have a practice of using a database or putting a hash mark (using a different colored ink each year) on the inside cover to record whenever a volume in the reference collection is reshelved. These practices miss the use of items that patrons reshelve themselves but can give some indication of use and guide weeding.

A few guidelines can facilitate review and weeding of reference collections. Bibliographies and encyclopedias are of little use after ten years, with a few exceptions such as the famous *Britannica* eleventh edition. Almanacs and yearbooks should be withdrawn or transferred to the general collection or storage when they are superseded and a new edition is received. The rapid proliferation of online reference materials has dramatically transformed reference collections.[22] Because of the currency of online sources, many libraries find that retention of paper copies, even in the circulating collection or a storage facility, is not justified. Heintzelman, Moore, and Ward offer this advice: "A reference collection should evolve into a smaller and more efficient tool that continually adapts to the new era, merging into a symbiotic relationship with electronic resources."[23]

Special libraries serve many different clientele groups, from hospitals to law firms to corporations. Weeding and withdrawal policies must pay special attention to the particular user community being served. Many special libraries are expected to provide up-to-date technical information and to withdraw obsolete materials. The emphasis tends to be on an efficient core collection, providing additional materials at the point of need. Weeding is regular and constant.

Weeding with the intent to withdraw materials has not been as common in large academic and research libraries. Weeding a collection is more likely to be for the purpose of transferring materials—from a reference collection to the general collection, from the general collection to storage or to a special collection. The ACRL Rare Books and Manuscripts Section developed guidelines to inform the transfer of materials to special collections.[24] A few circumstances, such as unneeded duplicates or materials in very poor condition, prompt removal. The latter might be replaced or reformatted. Items considered outdated or less relevant usually are placed in storage instead of removed from the collection. Libraries have started to withdraw back runs of journals if they are confident that reliable access to this content is available through the library's e-journal back files. This access might be through the purchase of back files from publishers that guarantee perpetual access through either their own site or a service such as Portico, or through the library's participation in JSTOR. Relying on continuing access through aggregators is risky because of the volatility of their content.

Centralized, Cooperative Curation

A large question concerns the number of print copies that should be retained nationally in what is sometimes called the collective collection. *What to Withdraw? Print Collections Management in the Wake of Digitization*, authored by Schonfeld and Housewright in 2009, tackles this troubling topic and identifies five reasons for retaining some copies of the print version when a digital version is available: the need to fix scanning errors, insufficient reliability of the digital provider, inadequate preservation of the digitized versions, the presence of significant quantities of important nontextual material that may be poorly represented in digital form, and local political considerations.[25] The authors note that online versions can satisfy most access needs, leaving print versions to serve a preservation role. The issue then becomes determining how many copies of the print should be retained. This depends on the rationales for retention noted above. For example, Schonfeld and Housewright suggest that two copies of text-only, digitized JSTOR journals would be sufficient for the national collection. Large scale withdrawal of print journals must, of course, be subject to system-wide coordination to fulfill libraries' preservation mission.

Developing a coordinated, persistent archive (most likely a set of archives) is needed to protect and preserve print resources. Malpas reports that "effective shared print storage solutions will depend upon a network of providers who will need to optimize holdings as a collective resource." Without coordination, libraries face the risk of withdrawing the last copy held or failing to retain the number of copies needed to protect the historical record. Creating a network of trusted regional archives would allow libraries to withdraw both serials and monographs with the confidence that they are retained nationally. Dempsey observes, "I believe we are moving to a situation where network-level management of the collective collection becomes the norm, but it will take some years for service, policy, and infrastructure frameworks to be worked out and evolution will be uneven. The network may be at the level of a consortium, a state or region, or a country."[26]

One initiative that aims to assist with coordination is the Print Archives Preservation Registry (PAPR, www.crl.edu/archiving-preservation/print-archives/papr). PAPR currently focuses on print serials and provides comprehensive information about titles, holdings, and archiving terms and conditions of major print archiving programs.

Storage

Placing library materials in storage has been called "a necessary evil for which there are no obvious alternatives."[27] Storage may be remote or on-site with standard, high-density, or compact shelving and is generally not open for public browsing or retrieval.[28] Materials in a storage facility are usually paged upon request for users and delivered to a library site or perhaps campus office. Some facilities provide an on-site reading room to which materials are brought upon user request. Storage splits collections, limits browsability, and inconveniences users. Even the speediest delivery can annoy users, who want an item in hand immediately.

Library storage facilities have a long history. They have been traced to the ancient library in Alexandria, which is reported to have placed duplicate scrolls in a separate location.[29] When libraries run out of room for collections or want to repurpose space, librarians face the choice of withdrawal or storage. Larger American research libraries were coping with this problem by the end of the nineteenth century. Charles W. Eliot, president of Harvard in 1891, wrote, "What then can keep the shelves from encumbrance? Only constant elimination, convenient storage, frequent rearrangement. The books less wanted must be stacked away . . . and the books most valued must be brought forward."[30]

Despite a common perception that collections have stopped growing because "everything is electronic," libraries continue to build physical collections. The number of printed books increases annually. For many parts of the world, publications are available only in print-on-paper formats. Large academic and research libraries hold significant collections of rare and unique materials that are retained even if digital surrogates are available. Despite the opportunities that digitized content provide for drawing down print collections and efforts to develop a national coordinated preservation plan, libraries continue to seek space to store collections. In 2005, 60 percent of the more than 5,000 libraries responding to a Heritage Preservation survey reported a need for new or additional off-site storage.[31]

OFF-SITE STORAGE

By the middle of the twentieth century, several academic and research libraries were coping with limited space by building off-site storage facilities.[32] Many were shared by several institutions to gain further economies. The New England Depository opened in 1942 as a cooperative storage facility for seven academic and four nonacademic libraries. The Midwest Inter-Library Center (now the Center for Research Libraries, CRL) opened in 1951 to provide storage for member academic libraries as part of several cooperative programs. In the early 1980s, the University of California system opened the Northern and Southern Regional Library Facilities. The Washington Research Library Consortium, established in 1978, is a partnership of nine libraries in the Washington, DC, metropolitan area that operates a shared-collections high-density facility housing more than 1.8 million volumes and more than 40,000 archival boxes. The Minnesota Library Access Center, opened in 2000, provides a high-density, below-ground storage facility shared by academic, public, and government libraries in Minnesota. In 2013, the Texas A&M University System and the University of Texas System opened a joint library facility that can house more than a million volumes on Texas A&M University's Riverside campus. The State University System of Florida is planning a shared storage facility called Florida Academic Repository (FLARE) with the goal of completing the project in 2016 or 2017.

Most cooperative facilities have policies that address costs, criteria for placing materials in storage, duplicates, retrieval procedures, whether on-site use is permitted, requirements for condition of items and associated bibliographic records, and ownership of the materials after deposit.[33] The University of California Regional Library Facilities' policy of not accepting duplicates initially meant that some libraries were reluctant to withdraw local duplicates in fear that a library would recall a deposited item for return to its local collection. In response, the University of California developed "Persistent Deposits in UC Regional Library Facilities" to ensure that last copies in the facilities would be retained.[34]

Several institutions, including Cornell University, Penn State University, and Harvard, have their own storage facilities. Most academic storage facilities provide high-density shelving, in which items are arranged by size to maximize capacity.[35] Items frequently are stored in trays or bins. Item bar codes are linked to tray bar codes, and the trays are linked to shelf and stack range numbers. Shelving areas are normally closed to users. Some storage facilities provide a reading room; others have no on-site user services. Many storage facilities, such as the Joe and Rika Mansueto Library at the University of Chicago and the Methewson-IGT Knowledge Center at the University of Nevada–Las Vegas, use an automated storage and retrieval system, which supports higher-density storage and reduces labor costs.

Libraries place materials in storage because they lack sufficient collections space in their main facility or wish to free collections space for other purposes yet wish to retain the items. Little-used materials, as well as materials that need special protection, are moved to storage. Many libraries face an economic necessity to find more cost-effective ways to retain materials. Courant and Nielsen determined that the average cost of keeping a volume in open stacks was $4.26 annually compared to $0.86 annually for high-density storage (both figures in 2009 US$).[36] Their calculations combined six major cost elements—construction, maintenance, cleaning, electricity, staffing, and circulation.

More recently, storage facilities with optimum environmental conditions have been seen as a viable preservation strategy. Yale University Library's selection policy for its storage facility, which opened in 1998, states that "the new facility will be devoted principally to shelving infrequently-used library materials," and "the new facility will accommodate those library materials that will most benefit from the facility's singularly optimal environmental and security conditions." Other storage facilities (e.g., Indiana University, Cornell University, and ReCap, shared by Columbia University, Princeton University, and the New York Public Library) explicitly accept rare, fragile, and at-risk materials. These materials benefit not only from favorable environmental controls but also from reduced handling and enhanced security.[37]

Placing materials in storage can be as controversial as withdrawing them. When the Syracuse University Libraries determined that stacks in its main library were at 98 percent capacity in 2009, and Dean of Libraries Suzanne E. Thorin announced plans to put lesser-used and duplicate volumes in storage 250 miles from campus, students and faculty protested. In response, the university built the Syracuse University Library Facility, a high-density storage facility on campus that opened in 2012. When the New York Public Library announced plans to move most of the volumes from its Fifth Avenue research center to off-site storage as part of a major redesign, the public outcry (and an $8 million gift) motivated the library to change its plans, proposing to move forward with clearing and repurposing existing stack space but also to expand the existing below-grade on-site storage. This compromise was subsequently challenged in lawsuits filed by the group Citizens Defending Libraries and others.[38]

The type of storage used depends on funds the library and its parent organization have to invest, the probable costs of moving materials back and forth, the difficulty of changing library records to show location of materials, and estimates of how much users will be inconvenienced by remote materials. Criteria for storing materials may be influenced by the provision of a reading room at the storage facility and the speed with which items are delivered to users at the main library. Placing materials in storage can serve as a preservation treatment if the storage facility has optimum temperature and humidity conditions. The reduction in handling that is a consequence of storage can benefit collections. An additional benefit of placing materials in storage is an often increased ability to locate materials because the likelihood of misshelved materials is much lower in a building with controlled access.[39]

Selecting and processing materials for storage is labor intensive. Staff members throughout the library are involved. Collection management librarians define the criteria and review materials. Even with the most logical and defensible criteria, informed judgment is necessary. A librarian or communications officer from the library needs to prepare and disseminate communication to stakeholders. Technical services staff change the location on bibliographic records and mark items for storage. Materials are pulled from stacks and transported to the new location. Physical control at the storage site requires a finding and retrieval system. This may involve creating a parallel catalog and putting additional markings on the items.

Either a separate policy or a section in the library's general collection management policy should address criteria and rationale for storing items. A policy should define the process through which materials are reviewed and evaluated, by whom, and how. Making clear the operating principles under which these decisions are made protects the library from charges of bias and irresponsible behavior. For example, academic librarians who have a policy that references institutional priorities and to which they can direct constituents find it easier to explain that eliminating a degree program has led to transferring supporting materials to remote storage. By identifying the library's participation in cooperative collection building, resource sharing, and regional storage programs, the policy explains the manner in which the library and its partners support each other.

Many storage facilities began by accepting materials without prohibiting the deposit of duplicates in print and before many libraries began to purchase e-books and access to digital back files of journals. Some of these storage facilities are themselves running out of space. Consequently, some facilities have undertaken weeding projects.[40] The Florida Academic Repository is systematically removing duplicate monographs and journals.[41] The Washington Research Library Consortium implemented a policy of retaining only one copy of a serial in its Shared Collections Facility in 2008 and retains only two copies of any edition of a monograph. In addition, the Washington Research Library Consortium and the Association of Southeast Research Libraries agreed in 2013 to jointly identify and retain print journal titles until at least 2035. This single retention and access agreement creates the largest print journal distributed archive (300,000 volumes, or 8,000 journal titles) in the United States and reduces the number of volumes that member libraries need to retain either in storage facilities or on-site.[42] This agreement is a concrete step toward creating a planned collective collection.

CRITERIA FOR STORAGE

For many years, the primary criterion for moving materials to storage was little or no use. The simplest approach may be moving to storage all materials that have not circulated after a specified date or that have circulated fewer than a certain number of times within a specified period. This ignores in-library use and variations between disciplines' use of their literatures. Projected use is a variation of historical use criteria and is, obviously, more subjective. This approach presupposes a clear understanding of institutional priorities and detailed knowledge of the collection. Because it is based on perceptions of future utility and cannot be documented, justification is difficult.

One approach is to move all inactive serials or all bound serial volumes published before a specified date. This has the advantage of freeing up the most space with the smallest number of bibliographic record changes. Again, variations between disciplines are ignored. Splitting serial runs can cause user confusion and frustration. Another straightforward approach is to apply the criterion of date of publication to all formats. An advantage is that the pain of remote storage is spread across subjects. On the other hand, variations in literature use among disciplines are ignored. A date-of-publication criterion can also serve a preservation function. All older materials are moved to a facility where they have significantly less handling and usually benefit from environmental controls. Identifying blocks of materials for storage simplifies the review process and makes possible global changes to bibliographic records. This approach assumes knowledge of how the block of material is used—or not used. It also runs the risk of antagonizing an entire segment of users.

Refinements are added as required by users and as time and staffing permit. Typical additional criteria address superseded reference volumes, duplicates, print materials duplicated online and in microform, condition, and value. Criteria can be modified within subjects or disciplines. For example, date of publication may be considered inappropriate in the humanities but appropriate in the sciences, where, however, exceptions are still persistent. Older materials in botany are heavily used resources, for example. Each exception requires a staff member to intervene and apply judgment. Review for transfer to storage typically follows procedures similar to those used for other collection review decisions, such as use of decision forms, consultation with other units in the library, and—as appropriate—consultation with stakeholders in the user community.

Meeting the needs of a collection's users is a critical aspect of effective storage programs. Careful selection and good bibliographic control are meaningless without speedy and effective delivery of materials to users. A willingness to reverse storage decisions, sometimes called derelegation, can be desirable. Moving such items back to the main collection can reduce user dissatisfaction. All criteria will be scrutinized and questioned by the collection's users. Communicating with library users is a critical part of any storage initiative. Well-informed and well-prepared librarians can help defuse user anxieties and misconceptions.

Preservation and Conservation

Preservation encompasses activities intended to prevent, retard, or stop deterioration of materials; retain the intellectual content of materials no longer physically intact; or transfer content to a more appropriate format for use. Gorman describes preservation as part of librarians' stewardship responsibilities—"the preservation of the human record to ensure that future generations know what we know." ALA identifies preservation as a core value of librarianship and issued a policy affirming this.[43] Preservation includes selecting replacement copies, moving items to a protected area, and selecting materials for reformatting. Binding, rebinding, repairing, using protective enclosures, controlling use, monitoring environmental conditions, and conserving are preservation activities intended to prolong the useful life of materials.

An alternative to preservation is *planned deterioration.* The item is retained until it has deteriorated beyond use and then withdrawn or replaced. Maintaining collections in usable condition challenges all types of libraries, especially those whose mission includes permanent retention of materials. Federal funding, through the National Endowment for the Humanities (NEH) and, more recently, IMLS, has provided millions of dollars for preservation activities across the country. Grants have funded conservation projects, reformatting projects, preservation planning, research, and education.

Heavy use may result in wear on even the newest materials, but many libraries face the added burden of an aging collection. The greatest source of deterioration in large academic and research collections is the acidic paper manufactured after 1840 and the binding, glues, and other components of printed objects. Before 1840, most paper was made from linen and cotton rags and is much more stable than the paper made from wood pulp that replaced it. Chemicals used during the papermaking process result in chemical processes that also increase acidity and contribute to embrittlement. Brittle paper breaks when page corners are folded one or two times. Books have been known to crumble when moved on shelves, leaving debris compared to corn flakes. Deterioration is compounded by poor housing conditions in which temperature, excess light, and humidity extremes accelerate deterioration. Research conducted by Hayes in the mid-1980s determined that 25 percent of the volumes held in ARL member libraries were embrittled, and the percentage was increasing annually.[44]

Librarians and publishers became increasingly aware of the brittle books problem in the 1970s and 1980s and began calling it the "slow fires" eating away at library collections. Many scholarly publishers, government agencies, professional associations, and trade publishers now use alkaline papers and comply with the national standard for permanent paper, first issued in 1985 and subsequently revised. Standards are concerned with both performance (paper's shelf life) and durability (ability to withstand use).[45]

Libraries may undertake deacidification because an item has enduring value or is rare. Several methods of deacidification have been developed, including processes that treat large numbers of items (called mass deacidification) and techniques that can be applied individually.[46] During deacidification an alkaline agent is deposited in the paper to neutralize the acid, but this does not restore paper strength. Several commercial deacidification techniques are on the market. Most treatments are done in special plants, requiring that libraries send books off-site. BookKeeper, the only mass-deacidification process widely used in the United States, is available through Preservation Technologies, L.P. The CSC BookSaver is available through Conservación de Sustratos Celulósicos S.L. (Barcelona, Spain). Papersave was developed by Battelle Ingenieurtechnik GmbH and is, therefore, often called the Battelle process. Unlike Bookkeeper, it can be installed at libraries for on-site use. The Wei T'o process, developed by Richard Smith, is usually used for single items and less commonly for mass deacidification. BookKeeper, CSC BookSaver, Papersave, and Wei T'o are also available as hand-held sprays; all require special care in their use because of health and environmental concerns.

Before 1900, most techniques used to repair materials drew on traditional bookbinding practices and materials. As collections began to age and become worn, numerous detrimental treatments became common. Using adhesive tape, household glues and pastes, and flimsy, acidic pamphlet binders accelerates deterioration. Benign neglect has been more effective in preserving library materials, but many simple activities can extend the useful life of materials. At the top of the list is good housekeeping—keeping materials dusted and the library free of food and other wastes that attract pests and vermin. Controlling temperature, humidity, pollution, and exposure to light protects collections. Educating staff members and users in proper handling of materials is important. Shelves should be the proper height for the items placed on them and should not be packed too tightly. Storage containers and protective enclosures should be archivally sound. Book drops should be padded and emptied frequently.

Some materials may be appropriate for repair or binding, such as reference titles or other heavily used materials. In some instances existing covers can be repaired. Rebinding can be cost-effective and may be appropriate if the original cover is very worn and the original binding is not of value as an artifact. Libraries may have some soft-cover items bound on receipt if they expect heavy use. Most research libraries bind all the periodical titles they retain. Libraries rely on commercial library binderies. Binding should follow the library binding standard, developed by NISO and the Library Binding Institute.[47] Other options are to retain unbound periodical issues, to replace some or all periodicals with commercial microform or digital back files, or to rely on print volumes held in larger libraries.

Librarians have become more conscious of the consequences of poor repair techniques and materials. Commercial suppliers now offer a variety of archivally sound and reversible materials for cleaning, repairing, and storing materials. Materials, procedures, and techniques should meet the latest standards and be acid-free, nondamaging, and safe for workers. Cleaning supplies can remove ballpoint pen ink and crayon marks from book pages, residue from compact disks, and mold and mildew. Even removing surface dirt should be done carefully.[48] Many of these supplies are appropriate for extending the life of the item but are not true conservation techniques. Government and private organizations provide information, advice, and services.[49]

If an item is worn beyond repair or the cost of repair is too high, a library may replace it. Options are a commercial paper reprint or microform copy, a used copy through an out-of-print dealer, or a digital equivalent. Commercial publishers and distributors sell reprint paper facsimiles, microforms, and digital surrogates of titles and packages of specialized titles. The librarian should select a company that follows accepted guidelines and standards for permanence, durability, and fidelity.

If, however, the library plans to retain the item in perpetuity, specialized cleaning and repair should be done by a trained conservator. If the physical entity or artifact is of value, the library may choose *conservation*—the use of minimally invasive physical or chemical methods to ensure the survival of manuscripts, books, and other materials. The goal is to preserve items in their original condition and thus their historical integrity. Important aspects of conservation are initial examination of the item, determining the most appropriate treatment, and documenting the actions taken. Effective conservation treatment is costly, requiring specialized training and expensive supplies and equipment. In such cases, relying on professional conservators and regional conservation centers is the best option.

Nonprint collections also need preservation. Libraries holding unique or rare nonprint materials (audio recordings, photographs, etc.) may face special challenges. Several sources offer guidelines and best practices for preserving these items.[50] Libraries with commercially produced media often replace the item, if it is still available. Born-digital resources and digitized files present different problems because of various formats and the speed with which standards, software, and hardware change. Libraries with digital collections plan for refreshing and migrating the data or emulating obsolete software and hardware if they wish to retain the content beyond the life of the medium.

The mutability of the Internet has led some scholars and librarians to ponder how to preserve a medium that is constantly changing in content, location, and organization. The Internet Archive (www.archive.org) is building an Internet library to offer free and permanent access to historical collections that exist in digital format. Founded in 1996 by Brewster Kahle and John Gage, the Internet Archive is collaborating with institutions, such as the Library of Congress and the Smithsonian Institution, to collect and store web pages, texts, audio, moving images, and software and to prevent Internet content and other born-digital materials from disappearing. Part of this initiative is the Internet Wayback Machine, which allows people to surf nearly two petabytes (growing at a rate of 20 terabytes per month) of data collected from websites from 1996 to the present.

Preservation and conservation combine evaluating materials and selecting the appropriate action. Micro decisions often are made when an item in poor condition is discovered during circulation or when a staff member is working with materials on the shelves. Macro decisions treat large portions of a collection. The collections librarian reselects materials by selecting them for treatment. The questions to be answered are: Is treatment desirable? Suitable? Available? Affordable?

Preservation Reformatting and Copyright Law

Preservation reformatting of paper-based materials may involve photocopying an item, creating a microform copy, or creating a digital surrogate. If an item cannot be replaced from an external source or is of enduring value and needs reduced handling, the library may decide to reformat it. Reformatting on an item-by-item basis can be expensive. The collections librarian must decide if the intellectual content of an item has sufficient enduring value to justify reformatting and if the format selected will capture the content and support current and future use. A librarian who opts to reproduce an item should ensure that appropriate quality and permanence standards are met.

Preservation microfilming increased in popularity as a reformatting approach in the 1980s, though it has a long history. In the 1930s, the New York Public Library, Harvard University, and Columbia University began microfilming newspapers and fragile materials. As the library world became aware of the pervasive problem of embrittled paper and disintegrating collections, reformatting on a large scale became an attractive option. Many materials fell apart when handled, and reliable surrogates became desirable. In 1992, Patricia Battin, president of the Commission on Preservation and Access, wrote,

> We faced very painful and wrenching choices—we had to accept the fact that we couldn't save it all, that we had to accept the inevitability of triage, that we had to change our focus from single-item salvation to a mass production

process, and we had to create a comprehensive cooperative strategy. We had to move from the cottage industries in our individual library back rooms to a coordinated nationwide mass-production effort.[51]

Several developments fostered cooperative preservation microfilming projects, which were seen as the best option for dealing with a critical situation. National standards for microfilm durability and permanence were developed, and 35 mm silver halide film was accepted as a reliable medium. National bibliographic utilities provided access to holdings and helped libraries avoid duplication of effort, and the federal government began funding preservation microfilming projects. The Commission on Preservation and Access was created in 1986 to instigate and coordinate collaborative efforts, publicize the problem of brittle books, and provide national leadership; the Commission merged with the Council on Library Resources to form the Council on Library and Information Resources in 1997. Cooperative microfilming projects through consortia and the NEH United States Newspaper Program (1980–2007) coordinated national efforts to identify, describe, and preserve fragile resources. In 2007, the USNP was supplemented by the National Digital Newspaper Program, jointly sponsored by NEH and the Library of Congress. This project is developing a database of digitized U.S. newspapers published from 1690 to the present. The Library of Congress maintains the digitized files, which can be searched in Chronicling America: Historic American Newspapers (http://chroniclingamerica.loc.gov).

Nicholson Baker focused the nation's attention on preservation microfilming.[52] He lamented the destruction and disposal of items that were microfilmed. Baker's book has been called a "journalistic jeremiad" because of his relentless attack on libraries, librarians, and preservation microfilming. His critics maintain that the practices he described were in place for a limited period and that he misrepresented much of the history of library preservation.[53] Some statements he made regarding the durability of acidic paper remain under question. The routine disbinding and discarding of materials as part of microfilming are no longer done. In some cases, however, reformatting is the only option to preserve the content.

In recent years, digital preservation has outpaced microfilming as a reformatting option. The ALCTS Preservation and Reformatting Section explains that digital preservation "combines policies, strategies and actions to ensure the most accurate rendering possible of authenticated content over time, regardless of the challenges of file corruption, media failure and technological change. Digital preservation applies to content that is born digital or converted to digital form."[54] Libraries may decide to preserve items digitally in their collection for the same reasons they choose other preservation options: rarity and fragility. Like preservation microfilming, creating a digital surrogate can protect and prolong the life of the original item.

Digitizing is a viable preservation treatment for many libraries. A digitized surrogate can add value through enhanced description and searching capability. Digitization has the advantage of reducing handling of the original artifact and making it accessible to more people. The Digital Library Federation developed a "Benchmark for Faithful Digital Reproductions of Monographs and Serials," which provides standards for optimally formatted digital content that address quality, persistence, and interoperability.[55] Digitization often is combined with conservation of the original or with microfilm reformatting. Libraries that undertake local digitization as a preservation medium must have a robust hardware and software infrastructure and the resources to carry out the project and provide continuing access. Libraries should strive not to duplicate work done at other libraries. Most libraries that digitize works record this information in OCLC WorldCat.

Librarians who wish to make copies of a work for preservation purposes should understand copyright law, which has been described as "complicated, arcane, and counterintuitive."[56] The intended purpose of copyright is to balance the rights of the public for access to information and creative expression with the rights of its creator and to provide incentives for the advancement of knowledge and creativity. Copyright law gives authors and the owners of copyrighted materials several broad rights and also subjects these rights to expectations, such as "first sale doctrine" (copyright owners have no right to control the distribution of a copy of a work after they sell that copy), "fair use" (the legal privilege to make unauthorized use of a copyrighted work for good reason), and the right to make copies for archival and preservation purposes, for patrons, and for interlibrary loan.

United States copyright law appears in chapters 1–8 and 10–12 of Title 17 of the United States Code. The basic framework for current copyright law is contained in the Copyright Act of 1976, subsequently amended several times.[57] Works published in the United States before 1923 are in the public domain. Works are protected by copyright in the United States if created after 1922 and registered before 1978, or if created after 1978.[58] Section 108 ("Limitations on Exclusive Rights: Reproduction by Libraries and Archives") of the U.S. copyright law grants libraries and archives the right to create reproductions of their own holdings during the final twenty years of any term of copyright for purposes of preservation or replacing deteriorated materials if the item cannot be obtained at a reasonable price. In addition, a library can make copies of manuscripts, pictures, art, and other works for preservation purposes under Section 108 if the copies are solely for replacement of an item that is damaged, deteriorating, lost, or stolen, or if the format of the work has become obsolete; and if the library conducts a reasonable investigation to conclude that an unused replacement cannot be obtained at fair price.

The Digital Millennium Copyright Act of 1998 amended Section 108 to clarify libraries' rights to create digital copies for replacement and preservation. However, the law states that digital formats must be used within the library. The 1998 legislation also criminalizes production and dissemination of technology intended to circumvent measures taken to protect copyright, not merely infringement of copyright itself, and increases the penalties for copyright infringement on the Internet. It amended Title 17 of the U.S. Code to extend the reach of copyright while limiting the liability of online providers from copyright infringement by their users.[59]

The Copyright Term Extension Act of 1998 (CTEA)—also known as the Sonny Bono Copyright Term Extension Act or as the Mickey Mouse Protection Act—extended copyright terms in the United States by twenty years. Before the CTEA, copyright lasted for the life of the author plus fifty years, or seventy-five years for a work of corporate authorship. CTEA extends these terms to life of the author plus seventy years and ninety-five years, respectively. The act also affected copyright terms for copyrighted works published prior to January 1, 1978, increasing their term of protection by twenty years.[60] The library community expressed concerns that such protection of copyright holders disenfranchised libraries and their ability to digitize materials retrospectively for preservation and access.

If a work is protected within its term of copyright, but the author, creator, or copyright holder cannot be identified or located by someone (a library, another author, etc.) who wishes to use the work and is seeking permission to do so, that work is called an *orphan work*.[61] Under current law, anyone who uses an orphan work without permission runs the risk that the copyright owner may bring an infringement lawsuit unless a specific exception or limitation to copyright applies. A 2006 report prepared for the U.S. Office of Copyright recommended legislation to provide a meaningful solution to the problem of orphan works.[62] Maria Pallante, the federal register of copyrights, observed that the effort and expense of searching for owners of orphan works on a case-by-case approach cannot scale to accommodate mass digitization.[63] Several bills have been introduced seeking to limit the remedies in cases where the owner of the orphan work cannot be identified or located, but they have failed to pass. ALA monitors legislation regarding copyright, and all librarians should do likewise. Several useful books address copyright for librarians.[64]

Digital Repositories

Several initiatives are seeking to address the preservation of digital content on a larger scale in digital repositories. The Research Libraries Group and OCLC explored the concept of trusted digital repositories to "provide reliable, long-term access to managed digital resources to its designated community, now and in the future" in a 2002 report that defines digital preservation as "the managed activities necessary for ensuring both the long-term maintenance of a bitstream and continued accessibility of content."[65] The notion of a trusted digital repository implies an ethical obligation as well as the technical and organizational infrastructure to sustain it. Subsequently, OCLC and CRL issued *Trustworthy Repositories Audit and Certification: Criteria and Checklist (TRAC)*, a document that enables repository audit, assessment, and certification.[66] By 2013, CRL had conducted audits of Portico (www.portico.org), HathiTrust, Chronopolis (http://chronopolis.sdsc.edu), and the Canadian Scholars Portal (www.scholarsportal.info) and certified all as trustworthy digital repositories. In 2012, the International Standards Organization approved *Trusted Third Party Repository for Digital Records*, which specifies the authorized custody services of a trusted third-party repository to ensure integrity and authenticity of the clients' digital records.[67] Other initiatives include the European Framework for Audit and Certification of Digital Repositories, nestor (Network of Expertise in Long-Term Storage of Digital Resources) in Germany, and Digital Preservation Europe's Planning Tool for Trusted Electronic Repositories (PLATTER).[68]

Digital repositories also may be called digital archives or institutional repositories. Institutional repositories were defined in a SPARC position paper as "digital collections capturing and preserving the intellectual output of a single or multi-university community."[69] In this model, faculty and researchers at universities deposit digital copies of their articles, conference papers, research data sets, working papers, and course materials into a centrally managed electronic archive. Some institutional repositories include student works, such as dissertations, master's papers, and honors theses. Some include institutional digital resources that would have gone to an institutional archive, such as annual and committee reports, bulletins, and other publications. Collections librarians may be involved in defining the scope of institutional repositories and in soliciting deposits by faculty. Some institutional repositories limit access to affiliated users; others provide open access to all to promote the free exchange of scholarship.

One of the first institutional repositories was the Massachusetts Institute of Technology D-Space (http://libraries.mit.edu/dspace-mit). Other repositories are discipline-based, such as the ePrint archive (http://arxiv.org) established by

Paul Ginsparg and now hosted at Cornell University. Serving as an online pre-print archive and distribution server for research papers, this service has become a major forum for speedy dissemination of results in physics and related disciplines, mathematics, nonlinear sciences, computational linguistics, and neuroscience. The Florida Digital Archive (FDA, http://fclaweb.fcla.edu/FDA), a statewide digital repository, contains approximately 112 terabytes of archived materials deposited by libraries in the Florida State university system for long-term preservation. The success of digital repositories depends on individuals depositing content, tools that harvest content, and effective dissemination. The Open Archives Initiative (www.openarchives.org) develops and promotes protocols and standards for interoperability to facilitate the efficient dissemination of content.

Mass Digitization

Mass digitization is the scanning of print texts or images to digital format on a very large scale using user-operated equipment capable of scanning hundreds of pages per hour. Mass commercial digitization projects have created controversy since the arrival of the Google Libraries project in 2004, in which Google announced partnerships with libraries at the University of Michigan, Harvard, and Stanford, the Bodleian Library at Oxford, and the New York Public Library to digitize all or large portions of their print collections. The number of project partners continues to grow, although Google has scaled back the volume being scanned. In most agreements, Google digitally scans and makes searchable both public domain and copyrighted materials. For books protected by copyright, a search yields basic information (book title, author name, etc.) and a few lines of text (called "snippets" by Google) related to the search along with information about purchasing or borrowing the volume from a library. Public domain materials can be viewed, searched, or downloaded in their entirety from the Google site. Google provides partner libraries with a digital copy of their materials scanned in the project.

Much of the discussion has been around three topics: intellectual property and copyright, technical aspects, and the social impact of these projects. The copyright issues are made more complex by the variety of agreements Google has reached with the partnering university and research libraries. In some cases, Google scans only volumes that are out of copyright and in the public domain. In others, the library's complete holdings are scanned regardless of copyright status, although Google does not make these titles available online in their entirety.

Contention among publishers, authors, and Google has led to legal challenges. The Association of American Publishers, the Authors Guild, and the American Society of Media Photographers criticized the project's inclusion of snippets of copyrighted works as willful infringement of copyright. Google claims its project represents a fair use because it is providing only bibliographic information (the equivalent of a card catalog) and snippets. Of note is the fact that many publishers (including those who challenged the mass scanning projects) already partner with Google and provide digital versions of their publications, with the understanding that searchers will be directed to sites where they can purchase the books. McGraw-Hill, Pearson Education, Penguin, John Wiley and Sons, and Simon and Schuster filed a copyright infringement suit against Google in 2005. The plaintiffs and Google reached a confidential out-of-court settlement in late 2012.[70] Details are not known, but parties agreed that books scanned as part of the Google project can be included in Google Books and users can browse up to 20 percent of the content. Publishers retain the right to withhold books from digitization.

In November 2013, the federal district court for the Southern District of New York dismissed the class action suit, *Authors Guild et al. v. Google*, which questioned the legality of Google's book database and claimed copyright infringement. In his summary judgment, Judge Denny Chin stated, "In my view, Google Books provides significant public benefits. It advances the progress of the arts and sciences, while maintaining respectful consideration for the rights of authors and other creative individuals, and without adversely impacting the rights of copyright holders. It has become an invaluable research tool that permits students, teachers, librarians, and others to more efficiently identify and locate books."[71]

One remaining class action suit, *Society of Media Photographers et al. v. Google*, is stayed at the time of this writing, pending a procedural appeal.

The Google project has evoked both criticism and praise. Criticisms of the Google project have addressed problems with quality control (pictures of scanners' fingers, lost text from books held incorrectly, etc.), insufficient description (flawed metadata), handling of orphan works, and the nature of a commercial project that is digitizing millions of books. Duguid raises many of these concerns in "Inheritance and Loss: A Brief Survey of Google Books." Darnton explores "Six Reasons Google Books Failed."[72]

Others have seen more opportunities than problems. Dempsey suggests that the Google initiative is part of the "changing dynamic of discovery and delivery in a network environment." Courant writes, "The Google settlement provides a mechanism whereby the print works of the 20th century will be searchable, findable, readable and generally usable online, with large parts of the text readable online for free. All of this is of tremendous public and scholarly value, and no one other than Google has shown any willingness to make the investment necessary to get the job done."[73] The mass digitization of printed cultural heritage has the potential to contribute to the public good in unprecedented ways.[74]

Concerns have surfaced in the library community about Google's commitment to long-term preservation. Because libraries who partner with Google receive image files of their digitized volumes, they have the option of dealing with these locally (a daunting proposition, given the number and size of files) or seeking a cooperative solution. HathiTrust, a partnership of some sixty libraries and research institutions established in 2008, aims to ensure long-term curation of scanned content. The HathiTrust Digital Library stores and makes accessible digital files acquired by libraries through their partnerships with Google and other sources, including the Internet Archive, Microsoft, and in-house initiatives. Anyone can search the HathiTrust Digital Library, but full viewing and downloading of public domain materials (approximately 32 percent of its corpus in 2013) is limited to HathiTrust partners.[75] In addition, HathiTrust provides services for users with disabilities. Eligible patrons at HathiTrust partner institutions can receive special access to in-copyright materials in HathiTrust. The materials must be held currently or have been held previously by the institution's library. The HathiTrust Research Center enables computational access for published works in the public domain and plans to provide access on limited terms to in-copyright works.

In 2011, the Authors Guild and other parties filed suit against HathiTrust, the Regents of the University of Michigan, the Regents of the University of California, the Board of Regents of the University of Wisconsin System, the Trustees of Indiana University, and Cornell University, claiming copyright infringement in the loading of digitized books into the HathiTrust Digital Library. In October 2012, Judge Harold Baer rejected the case, ruling that the scanning program was clear fair use under the law.[76]

The Open Content Alliance (www.opencontentalliance.org), a nonprofit established in 2005, has sought to avoid many of the legal challenges directed at Google by digitizing only material that is in the public domain or has the copyright holders' authorization. One feature of the Open Content Alliance is the storage and maintenance of data in multiple repositories. Without the financial resources of Google and dependent on content contributors and donors, the Alliance is moving slowly to build a mass of scanned data. Another player on the mass scanning field was Microsoft and its Live Search Books, which also digitized works in the public domain. Microsoft ended this initiative in 2008, but books scanned remain available through the Internet Archive.

Preservation Plans

Many libraries prepare a systematic preservation plan.[77] Plans vary in scale and complexity depending on the size and nature of the library. A comprehensive preservation plan prepares the library to deal with complex preservation challenges on an ongoing basis. Initially, it increases knowledge among library staff members of existing condition and use issues, possible approaches, existing capabilities, and the financial and technical resources currently available. A preservation plan is also a political instrument. It can serve to raise awareness in the library and the parent organization about preservation problems and help develop a consensus on how to address them.

The first element of a preservation plan is a survey of the collection condition. This involves determining the extent to which all parts of the collection are at risk from acidic paper; embrittlement; loose or incomplete text blocks; deterioration of the text, image, or medium; damaged bindings; or lack of protective enclosures. A second component of a plan is gathering data on environmental conditions (temperature, relative humidity, cleanliness, potential exposure to pollution and particulate matter in the air, excessive light, and pests and vermin), disaster preparedness, and current practices for collection handling, storage, and use. This includes information about fire prevention, detection, and suppression systems and security measures. Identifying the protective measures in place allows the library to assess the degree to which collections are exposed to future deterioration and sudden damage.

Once librarians have an understanding of collection and environmental conditions, they can begin establishing preservation priorities. Priorities balance the importance of materials with treatment capacities within the context of available and potential funds, staffing, and equipment. Possible strategies for selecting materials for preservation might be to treat those materials at greatest risk, those that can be treated quickly and inexpensively, those that need a particular type of treatment, or those most important to the library.

Serials Review, Renewal, Cancellation, and the Transition to Electronic-Only Access

Libraries should regularly review the materials that are provided through subscriptions and leases because content and pricing of offerings change constantly. In addition, both the quality and appropriateness of subscribed content changes over time. Most libraries face continuing pressure on their budgets and must strive to make the most effective use of limited funds.

IFLA recommends the following considerations for cancellation decisions:

- Is the resource still relevant to users?
- Is usage increasing or decreasing compared to previous years or in comparison to similar products?
- How does cost per use of the resource compare to other resources?
- Does the resource continue to represent value for money?
- Are other options for access (e.g., pay-per-view, selected content versus a package deal) more cost-effective?
- Is the number of simultaneous users set appropriately?
- How does the usage of current content compare to that of back file content?[78]

In addition, libraries should consider the presence and effect of changes to the information provider, operation platform, business model, access provision, pricing, access to back files, license, and package and content available. Usage data and cost per use are important but should be assessed in concert with these other considerations. Finally, libraries that acquire serial titles as part of a Big Deal package need to determine the extent to which titles can be cancelled in a single year and the possible savings gained if the Big Deal is not renewed and selected titles are renewed individually.

The process of serials cancellation begins with a review that parallels that for other collection maintenance functions. Ideally, active subscriptions are reviewed regularly as part of ensuring that the collection continues to meet user needs and library goals and objectives. In reality, identifying subscriptions to cancel has become an annual activity in many—perhaps most—libraries for at least the past twenty years because of constant and rapid increases in prices in excess of budget increases. Although academic and research libraries have been hit harder because of their heavy concentration of expensive scholarly journals, all libraries have experienced subscription cost increases in excess of national inflation rates and budget increases.

Other reasons lead libraries to cancel serials and other continuing resources. A library may aim for a constant ratio between expenditures for serials and for monographs. Libraries may cancel titles because they seek to maintain expenditure ratios between disciplines or between user groups. For example, journals in the children's and young adult room do not cost as much or increase in price as rapidly as titles in the business section. Therefore, the library may opt to cancel more titles and set a higher dollar target when reviewing the business serials. Changes in curriculum focus or the user community may make some titles less relevant. A compelling reason to cancel a journal is declining quality or content that is no longer appropriate for the collection. Some libraries decide to cancel individual e-journal subscriptions if the titles are provided in aggregator packages, but this can be risky if continuing access is important, because packages frequently drop titles and rarely guarantee continued access.

Librarians use many techniques to make the cancellation process as logical and defensible as possible. Every library needs policies and procedures to guide cancellations and to keep user communities informed and involved to the extent that is reasonable and practical. The same criteria (quality and appropriateness) that guide the selection of a journal or other continuing resource are applied when considering it for cancellation. Use is a leading criterion. Data may be available from circulation and e-resource use statistics, interlibrary loan requests, user surveys, or records of in-house use.[79] See chapter 7 for more information on approaches to collecting and using e-resource use data. The difficulty with use studies of print resources is that many libraries do not circulate serials or indexing and abstracting tools, and in-house use data are notoriously unreliable.

Use data often are combined with cost of the title to determine a cost-per-use figure. Very expensive titles that get little use do not provide the benefits to the library and its users that cheaper titles with heavy use do. Journals in some disciplines, typically in the humanities and social sciences, may be more cost-effective. They are so low in price that subscribing to them may be cheaper than requesting them through interlibrary loan or document delivery. Cost may be the first criterion considered when a library faces a budget-driven cancellation project, because cancelling high-cost resources generates the greatest savings.

Availability of serial titles within a consortium and through interlibrary loan can influence decisions, as does the affordability of pay-per-view options. Libraries need to honor commitments made to partner libraries to retain titles and protect specific disciplines. Libraries first may cancel low-use titles to which convenient access is available regionally or through an established cooperative delivery service. In many cases, commercial document delivery services and full-text online pay-per-view services are viable and cost-effective alternatives to local subscriptions in libraries. Unlike interlibrary loan, pay-per-view access is instant.[80] In pay-per-view, a library creates an account with a content provider and authenticated users can purchase articles at the library's expense.

Academic librarians usually work closely with faculty when cancelling serials. Cancelling journals, like placing materials in storage and withdrawing items, has significant political implications. Many journal users in academic libraries remain oblivious to the extreme price increases that have challenged libraries for years. Librarians need to bring this problem before their user communities repeatedly. Consultation can prevent serious cancellation mistakes, though it can open heated debates in academic libraries as faculty members defend the importance of serial titles in their particular specialty. Nevertheless, surveying constituents is important because it both solicits their input and informs them of the continuing need for cancellations to operate within available budgets.[81]

Librarians have been seeking an ideal way to combine data assembled during the review and consultation process. Several approaches, including using weighted formulas, have been described in the literature. Use data often are the most heavily weighted element. Metz and Cosgriff recommend creating a serials decision database to track information collected.[82] An important benefit of having data readily at hand is being able to explain and justify cancellations to disgruntled users.

Academic libraries have generally moved to cancel print subscriptions and rely on the e-versions. On average, approximately 88 percent of current serials purchased in ARL member libraries in 2010/11 were e-serials.[83] Many libraries state that a contractual guarantee to access subscribed issues if the e-journal subscription is cancelled, if the journal ceases, or if the publisher goes out of existence is the deciding factor in whether to move to e-only. The reality is that few libraries make perpetual access a deciding factor.[84] Access via a journal aggregator service alone would not satisfy the requirement for perpetual access, because the aggregator as a third party usually does not hold permanent access to its constituent publishers' titles, and titles come and go with little or no notice.

Other typical criteria for retaining print subscriptions instead of moving to e-only may include these:

- user preference (e.g., print is needed for particular research practices, especially high-profile titles or those that are heavily used in print format)

- content (e.g., content of print differs from that of the electronic version; print has significant artifactual or aesthetic value; print journal functions better as a browsing journal or current awareness source; images and graphics are unavailable or of poorer quality in the electronic journal)

- current availability (e.g., the provider of the electronic journal is technically unreliable or does not provide prompt technical support; electronic issue are not made available promptly)

- cooperative resource sharing (i.e., the contract does not permit interlibrary lending or needed document delivery services using the e-format)

- consortial commitment (i.e., the library has agreed to retain the print format as part of a larger collaborative preservation effort)

Several options exist for perpetual access. A publisher may guarantee access on its own website, though libraries have been reluctant to place their confidence in publishers, who do not have the same commitment to long-term preservation as libraries and are subject to shifts in the changing marketplace. Some publishers have reached agreements with national libraries to preserve content. For example, Elsevier is partnering with the Koninklijke Bibliotheek (the national library of the Netherlands), through which the latter is the official digital archive for Elsevier Science journals. If Elsevier ceases to make these journals available on a commercial basis, the Koninklijke Bibliotheek will provide remote access to the entire archive.

Project MUSE provides subscribers with access to current and retrospective issues of scholarly journals and to books in the humanities and social sciences. At the conclusion of each year during which a library subscribes to Project MUSE, the library may request an archival digital file copy containing all of the articles published online during the previous subscription year. Libraries, therefore, own the material from the electronic files to which they subscribe, but they must decide what to do with the content if they receive a digital file of it. Project MUSE has committed to providing permanent maintenance and preservation of all the digital files in the MUSE database. All MUSE partner publishers are contractually bound to allow journal content published in MUSE to remain permanently in the database, even if they should discontinue their relationship with MUSE. Thus, libraries that continue their subscription to Project MUSE are assured access.

Some e-book and e-journal publishers have placed their content in Portico to ensure future access.[85] The mission of Portico, a nonprofit service with library and publisher partners, is to preserve scholarly literature published in electronic form and to ensure that these materials remain accessible to future scholars, researchers, and students. Many publishers participating in Portico have chosen to make their content available to subscribing libraries after cancellation. In keeping with this mission, Portico established an agreement with the Koninklijke Bibliotheek in 2008 through which the latter places a copy of the Portico archive in a secure access- and climate-controlled facility, in essence a dark archive, meaning that content is available only in the event of a "trigger event" (the publisher stops operations, ceases to publish a title, or no longer offers back issues, or the publisher's delivery platform suffers catastrophic and sustained failure). Library partners pay Portico an annual archive support payment. Publisher partners provide Portico with the original source files of electronic journals, and Portico normalizes the original source files to an archival format and assumes responsibility for future content migrations. When a title is no longer available from the publisher or any other source through a trigger event, Portico makes the content available to member libraries. The first trigger event was announced in late 2007, when the journal *Graft: Organ and Cell Transplantation*, published by SAGE Publications, was removed from SAGE's online offering and made accessible through Portico.

Tracking responsibility for long-term archiving of e-journals is another aspect of having confidence in their preservation and ongoing accessibility. The Keepers Registry (http://thekeepers.org) resulted from Piloting an E-journal Preservation Registry Service (PEPRS), which was funded by JISC (formerly the Joint Information System Committee) in the United Kingdom. Participating agencies archive e-journals and make metadata for the journals in their archives available to the Keepers Registry. Participants include the British Library, CLOCKSS, LOCKSS, HathiTrust, Portico, and others. Searching the Keepers Registry is free.

A library either individually or as part of a consortium may negotiate keeping and mounting licensed content locally, but it faces the challenge of migrating and refreshing the data over time. A 2011 study of ARL member libraries found that only 59 percent were planning to preserve licensed materials.[86] A few cooperative options have been developed to address this challenge. The OhioLINK Electronic Journal Center (EJC) contains more than 8,200 scholarly journals titles from more than one hundred publishers and is an optional service of OhioLINK for libraries in Ohio. OhioLINK intends to maintain the EJC content as a permanent archive and has perpetual archival rights through the consortial licenses from all publishers except the American Chemical Society. The LOCKSS (Lots of Copies Keep Stuff Safe, www.lockss.org) program, originated at Stanford University, offers an open-source software appliance that allows libraries to collect, store, preserve, and provide access to their own local copies of purchased content. Libraries manage their LOCKSS boxes and capture content from participating publishers. LOCKSS is a light archive, meaning that content is currently accessible, under the terms of applicable publisher agreements. CLOCKS (Controlled LOCKS, www.clockss.org) is a membership organization that holds digital assets on behalf of the larger community. CLOCKS is a dark archive.

Collection Protection and Security

Collection protection is another collection management responsibility. It encompasses proper handling of items by staff members and users, appropriate environmental conditions, security against theft and mutilation, protection of electronic resources, and planning for and responding to disasters. Some libraries hold regular training for staff members, covering such topics as how to remove volumes from shelves, the importance of not shelving volumes too tightly, and the need to use approved supplies for simple mending. Libraries often run publicity campaigns to educate users in the proper care of library materials and to protect against food and drink near collections and computers.

A proper environment protects collections. This encompasses sound shelving and storage containers, moderate temperature and humidity with minimal fluctuations in each, cleanliness including pest control, and the avoidance of excessive light and ultraviolet radiation. Ideal temperatures are 65–70°F for general collections and 35–65°F for special collections and archives.[87] Libraries generally make accommodations for personal comfort and increase temperatures slightly for areas in which users and collections share the same space. Optimum relative humidity (RH) is 30–50 percent. High RH encourages mold and pests. Low RH results in desiccation, shrinking, and cracking. Fluctuations cause materials to expand and contract and can result in warping. Regardless of the targets set for temperature and humidity, controlling fluctuations is critical. Temperature should vary no more than two or three degrees, and RH should fluctuate no more than 2–3 percent. Libraries frequently use data loggers to measure and record temperature and RH in collections where consistent conditions are required.

Mold outbreaks terrorize libraries because of the damage they do to collections and the potential harm to human health. The most important preventative measure is ensuring that no mold-infested materials are added to the collection. Gift materials are the most likely culprit, but mold has been found in purchased items as well. Staff handling materials that exhibit dry spores and mycelium should wear HEPA (high-efficiency particulate air) masks, goggles, and protective gloves. Mold outbreaks in collections can occur when RH increases to about 65 percent. Flooding naturally increases RH, and wet volumes are clearly at risk, but even moisture in floor coverings and walls migrates to collections that are not initially wet. Large-scale mold problems, especially active outbreaks, should be addressed by professionals, but inactive dry mold on a limited number of items can be addressed by trained staff using proper procedures, supplies, and equipment.[88]

Protection against theft is the issue that comes most frequently to mind when considering collection security. One of the most famous book thieves is Stephen Carric Blumberg, who, when apprehended in 1990, had amassed nearly 25,000 volumes valued at more than $5.3 million stolen during more than twenty years from 327 libraries across the United States.[89] People steal for different reasons—to build their own collections, to sell the items, because they are angry, to remove materials they find offensive. Both library patrons and staff members can be thieves. Theft and mutilation have legal implications under local and federal ordinances and laws. Libraries should work with their governing body and local law enforcement agencies when theft is suspected. Notifying other libraries, manuscript dealers, and rare and out-of-print book dealers of thefts is a useful tactic and has led to the identification and capture of repeat offenders.

Several steps help protect libraries from theft. Ideally, a library should have a written security policy and an individual charged with overseeing security. All holdings should be documented through a catalog or other means. All items should carry ownership markings, unless inappropriate to the items. The library should conduct regular inventories. The library should have limited entrances and exits with, ideally, some sort of monitoring. Book theft detection systems are common and a useful deterrent. Some libraries employ closed circuit surveillance camera systems. Others hire security monitors. Some libraries and most archives and special collections require users to show identification and register when entering, and they search bags and backpacks when patrons leave. Protecting against theft needs to be balanced with users' access to the collection and privacy rights. Useful safety and security guidelines have been developed by the Library Leadership and Management Association.[90]

Collections should be reviewed regularly to determine which materials should be transferred to special collections or to other more secure areas either because of value or vulnerability to mutilation. Rare book and special collections usually have more stringent security measures, such as excluding users from the stacks and prohibiting briefcases and bags in the reading room. The ACRL Rare Books and Manuscripts Section has developed guidelines for the security of special collections.[91] These guidelines contain an appendix of organizations and electronic discussion lists to which thefts can be reported.

Mutilation is frequently not discovered until someone uses a damaged item. Mutilation can result when patrons remove pages because they do not want to make a photocopy or in order to obtain a high-quality illustration, censor the collection, or make some other type of personal statement. Protecting collections from mutilation involves many of the same procedures as protecting them against theft. Libraries have found that having good, convenient, inexpensive photocopy machines and digital scanners reduces collection damage. School library media centers and academic libraries may want to reach agreements with instructors regarding illustrative matter in submitted reports and papers. Ideally, homework should not encourage students to cut material from original books and journals. Only photocopies, digitally generated images, or illustrations created by the student should be accepted by their teachers.

Natural disasters—earthquakes, fires, floods, burst pipes and building leaks, hurricanes, tornados, volcanoes, vermin and pest infestations, wind damage, chemical spills, and extended power failures—can be very costly. A 1997 flood at Colorado State University caused $100,000,000 in damages.[92] In the fall of 2005, Hurricane Katrina devastated libraries of all types in Louisiana and Mississippi.[93] Even modest leaks have significant potential to disrupt services and put collections at risk. In May 2013, 30,000 gallons of water were dumped into the Jimmie B. Keel Regional Library in Tampa, Florida, as a result of heavy rain flooding under a temporary wall.[94] Staff quickly moved books from bottom to upper shelves, and workers ran pumps and dehumidifiers to extract moisture and prevent mildew and mold. Natural disasters cannot be prevented, but libraries are well served if they know what to do when one strikes.

All libraries should have an up-to-date, comprehensive disaster preparedness plan. This document, also called a disaster response plan, provides a policy and procedures for responding to emergencies and specifies priorities and techniques for salvaging different types of material if damaged. It lists who should be notified, what the chain of command is, who is responsible for which steps, where equipment and supplies (e.g., buckets, plastic sheeting, gloves, dust masks) are kept, and safety considerations. It provides contact information for services needed to respond to different conditions, which may include collection transport, rapid freezing, and mold abatement. Several sources advise on planning for disasters and developing salvage plans.[95] A simple template for developing an emergency response plan is available through the Northeast Document Conservation Center.[96]

Ensuring security for electronic files and systems adds another dimension to collection protection. Issues of concern are protecting against unauthorized access, theft of resources, damage by hackers or viruses, unintentional damage, and compromise of patron information, and ensuring availability of electronic resources to legitimate users. Libraries may back up information resources and seek to negotiate replacement files from suppliers in the event of data destruction.

Several activities can help librarians protect their collections. A staff training program can address proper handling of library materials, monitoring security issues, and responding to emergencies. A security audit and risk assessment detects problem areas where the library and its collections are vulnerable. The library should have a clear reporting procedure and a designated leader for each situation. An individualized disaster preparedness plan provides specific procedures for dealing with different crises. Although librarians can do much to minimize risk to collections, equally important is knowing how to react when problems develop.

CASE STUDY

Erica has been a member of the reference staff in the agricultural sciences library at a large western university for twelve years. She was recently selected to replace the reference department head, who retired. Her predecessor, Ethel, led the reference unit for forty years, and the collection reflects her approach to providing reference service, which was to develop and maintain an extensive and comprehensive print collection to ensure resources were immediately at hand to assist patrons. Ethel examined every new book received for the general collection, and if she found information (particularly data represented in charts and graphs) that might be useful in answering a question she added the book to the reference collection. She never removed earlier editions of dictionaries, directories, or statistical compilations because she might want to consult them when helping a patron.

The reference collection contains all the print back runs of indexes to which the library now subscribes online and to which it has online access to complete back files. The reference collection is, needless to say, quite large and has encroached on space that the library wishes to repurpose for an expanded study commons. Much—perhaps most—of the print collection is not used by the reference staff and patrons. With the support of the library director and the reference unit staff, Erica will lead a comprehensive reference collection weeding project.

Activity

Develop a rationale and plan for weeding the print reference collection. The plan should have several components: (a) criteria to apply when deciding if items should be retained in the reference collection, transferred to the general collection, transferred to remote storage, or withdrawn; (b) a reference collection policy to guide developing and managing the collection in the future; (c) a list of staff and library units to be involved in the project; and (d) a work plan that identifies tasks and assigns responsibilities. Do not go into the details of how the processing is handled once decisions are made, but do note the steps involved in general terms.

Notes

1. Will Manley, "The Manley Arts: If I Called This Column 'Weeding,' You Wouldn't Read It," *Booklist 92* (Mar. 1, 1996), 1108; Donna J. Baumbach and Linda L. Miller, *Less Is More: A Practical Guide to Weeding School Library Collections* (Chicago: American Library Association, 2006), 3.

2. Nicholson Baker, "The Author vs. the Library," *New Yorker* 72, no. 31 (Oct. 14, 1996): 50–53, 56–62; and Baker, "A Couple of Codicils about San Francisco," *American Libraries* 30, no. 3 (Mar. 1999): 35–36.

3. "UNM Criticized for Decision to Give Away Journals," *Amarillo Globe News* (May 8, 2001), http://amarillo.com/stories/050801/usn_unm.shtml.

4. Terrence C. Miltner and Gordon Flagg, "10,000 Books Found in Abandoned East St. Louis Library," *American Libraries* 35, no. 9 (Oct. 2004): 13.

5. Hannah Edwards, "Students Lost over Shrinking Uni Library," *Sydney Morning Herald* (Apr. 8, 2007), www.smh.com.au/news/national/students-lost-over-shrinking-uni-library/2007/04/07/1175366530093.html, describes the reaction to a weeding project at the University of New South Wales in Australia; Bev Holder, "MP Calls for Probe into Book Binning Scandal," *Stourbridge News* (June 11, 2008), www.stourbridgenews.co.uk/news/2329272.MP_calls_for_probe_into_book _binning_scandal/, reports the investigation prompted when thousands of the town's library books were "binned in a skip" (loaded in a dumpster); Ingrid Peritz, "A Brouhaha in the Bookery," *Globe and Mail* (Sept. 17, 2008), www .theglobeandmail.com/news/national/a-brouhaha-in-the-bookery/article1349975, describes the uproar when the Literary and Historical Society of Quebec decided to weed 1,500 books that were duplicates or in poor condition from its collection and put them up for auction.

6. "Abstracts of and Extracts from Reports," *Library Journal* 8 (1883): 257.

7. Loriene Roy, "Weeding," in *Encyclopedia of Library and Information Science*, 54 (suppl. 15), ed. Allen Kent, 352–98 (New York: Marcel Dekker, 1994).

8. Kenneth J. Brough, *Scholar's Workshop: Evolving Conceptions of Library Service*, Illinois Contributions to Librarianship 5 (Urbana: University of Illinois, 1953).

9. American Library Association, "Evaluating Library Collections: An Interpretation of the Library Bill of Rights" (adopted Feb. 2, 1873, by the ALA Council; amended July 1, 1981; June 2, 2008), www.ala.org/advocacy/intfreedom/librarybill/interpretations/evaluatinglibrary.

10. Juris Dilevko and Lisa Gottlieb, "Weed to Achieve: A Fundamental Part of the Public Library Mission?" *Library Collections, Acquisitions, and Technical Services* 27, no. 1 (2003): 73–96.

11. Charles B. Osburn, "Collection Management in the *Library Quarterly*, 1931–2005," *Library Quarterly* 76, no. 1 (Jan. 2006): 41.

12. Paul Metz and Caryl Gray, "Public Relations and Library Weeding," *Journal of Academic Librarianship* 31, no. 3 (May 2005): 273–79.

13. Joseph P. Segal, *Evaluating and Weeding Collections in Small and Medium-Sized Public Libraries: The CREW Method* (Chicago: American Library Association, 1980); Jeanette Larson, *CREW: A Weeding Manual for Modern Libraries* (Austin: Texas State Library and Archives Commission, 2012), www.tsl.state.tx.us/sites/default/files/public/tslac/ld/ld/pubs/crew/crewmethod12.pdf. The 2012 revision includes a section on weeding e-books.

14. Shelley L. Smith, "Weeding Considerations for an Academic Music Collection," *Music Reference Services Quarterly* 15, no. 1 (2012): 22–33; Barbara E. Hightower and John T. Gantt, "Weeding Nursing E-books in an Academic Library," *Library Collections, Acquisitions, and Technical Services* 36, no. 1/2 (2012): 53–57; Jeffrey Matlak, "Weeding Older Social Sciences Journals," *Behavioral and Social Sciences Librarian* 29, no. 3 (2010): 169–83.

15. Stanley J. Slote, *Weeding Library Collections: Library Weeding Methods*, 4th ed. (Littleton, CO: Libraries Unlimited, 1997).

16. Ferdinand F. Leimkuhler, "The Bradford Distribution," *Journal of Documentation* 23, no. 3 (Sept. 1967): 199; Richard W. Trueswell, "A Quantitative Measure of User Circulation Requirements and Its Possible Effect on Stack Thinning and Multiple Copy Determination," *American Documentation* 16, no. 1 (Jan. 1965): 20–25; Richard W. Trueswell, "Some Behavioral Patterns of Library Users: The 80/20 Rule," *Wilson Library Bulletin* 43, no. 5 (1969): 458–61; Richard W. Trueswell, "Determining the Optimal Number of Volumes for a Library's Core Collection," *Libri* 16, no. 1 (1966): 58–59.

17. Allen Kent et al., *Use of Library Materials: The University of Pittsburgh Study* (New York: Marcel Dekker, 1979).

18. Alene E. Moroni, "Weeding in a Digital Age," *Library Journal* 137, no. 15 (Sept. 15, 2012): 26–28.

19. Evan St. Lifer and Susan DiMattia, "City Rebukes Philadelphia Library on Weeding Practices," *Library Journal* 121, no. 9 (May 15, 1979): 12.

20. San Francisco Public Library Commission, "Minutes of the Regular Meeting of Thursday October 5, 2006," http://sfpl.org/html/about/libcomm/minutes100506.htm.

21. Metz and Gray, "Public Relations and Library Weeding."

22. Carol A. Singer, "Weeding Gone Wild: Planning and Implementing a Review of the Reference Collection," *Reference and User Services Quarterly* 47, no. 3 (2008): 263.

23. Nicole Heintzelman, Courtney Moore, and Joyce Ward, "Are Reference Books Becoming an Endangered Species? Results of a Yearlong Study of Reference Books

Usage at the Winter Park Public Library," *Public Libraries* 47, no. 5 (Sept./Oct. 2008): 63.

24. Association for College and Research Libraries, Rare Books and Manuscripts Section, "Guidelines on the Selection and Transfer of Materials from General Collections to Special Collections," 3rd ed. (approved by the ACRL Board of Directors, July 1, 2008), www.ala.org/acrl/standards/selctransfer.

25. Roger C. Schonfeld and Ross Housewright, *What to Withdraw? Print Collections Management in the Wake of Digitization* (New York: Ithaka S+R, 2009), http://sr.ithaka.org/sites/all/modules/contrib/pubdlcnt/pubdlcnt.php?file=http://sr.ithaka.org/sites/default/files/reports/What_to_Withdraw_Print_Collections _Management_in_the_Wake_of_Digitization.pdf&nid=357.

26. Constance Malpas, *Cloud-Sourcing Research Collections: Managing Print in the Mass-Digitized Library Environment* (Dublin, Ohio: OCLC, 2011), http://oclc.org/research/publications/library/2011/2011-01.pdf, 9; Lorcan Dempsey, "Managing Down Collections," *Lorcan Dempsey's Weblog* (blog), Jan. 21, 2011, http://orweblog .oclc.org/archives/002151.html.

27. Dan C. Hazen, "Selecting for Storage: Local Problems, Local Responses, and an Emerging Common Challenge," *Library Resources and Technical Services* 44, no. 4 (Oct. 2000): 176.

28. Danuta A. Nitecki, ed., *Library Off-Site Shelving: Guide for High-Density Facilities* (Englewood, CO: Libraries Unlimited, 2001); Lizanne Payne, *Library Storage Facilities and the Future of Print Collections in North America* (Dublin, OH: OCLC, 2007); Bernard F. Reilly Jr., *Developing Print Repositories: Models for Shared Preservation and Access* (Washington, DC: Council on Library and Information Resources, 2003).

29. David Block, "Remote Storage in Research Libraries: A Microhistory," *Library Resources and Technical Services* 44, no. 4 (Oct. 2000): 184–89.

30. Eliot quoted in Kenneth I. Brough, *Scholars Workshop: Evolving Conceptions of Libraries Services*, Illinois Contributions to Librarianship 5 (Urbana: University of Illinois, 1953), 125.

31. Heritage Preservation, "Collections Storage," in *A Public Trust at Risk: The Heritage Health Index Report on the State of American's Collections*, 57–60 (Washington, DC: Heritage Preservation, 2005), www.heritagepreservation.org/HHI/HHIfull.pdf.

32. Willis E. Bridegam, *A Collaborative Approach to Collection Storage: The Five-College Library Depository* (Washington, DC: Council on Library and Information Resources, 2001); Scott Seaman, "Collaborative Collection Management in a High-Density Storage Facility," *College and Research Libraries* 66, no. 1 (Jan. 2005): 20–27; David Weeks and Ron Chepesiuk, "The Harvard Model and the Rise of Shared Storage Facilities," *Resource Sharing and Information Networks* 16, no. 2 (2002): 159–68.

33. See Center for Research Libraries, "Print Archiving Services Agreements," www.crl.edu/archiving-preservation/print-archives/service-agreements, for a list of service agreements or memoranda of understanding for print archiving initiatives. A few of these are for shared storage facilities.

34. University of California University Libraries, "Persistent Deposits in UC Regional Library Facilities" (May 6, 2004; revised Feb. 20, 2006), http://libraries .universityofcalifornia.edu/planning/SLFB_deposit_management_final.pdf.

35. Payne, *Library Storage Facilities*.

36. Paul N. Courant and Matthew "Buzzy" Nielsen, "On the Cost of Keeping a Book," in *The Idea of Order* (Washington, DC: Council on Library and Information Resources, 2010), 81–105, www.clir.org/pubs/reports/pub147/pub147.pdf.

37. Yale University Library, "Library Shelving Facility Yale University Selection Policy" (Dec. 1997), http://dagda.library.yale.edu/lsf/selection.html; Catherine Murray-Rust, "Library Storage as a Preservation Strategy," *Advances in Librarianship* 27 (2010): 159–83.

38. Jennifer Epstein, "A Win for the Stacks," *Inside Higher Ed* (Nov. 13, 2009), www .insidehighered.com/news/2009/11/13/syracuse; Robin Pogrebin, "New York Public Library Shifts Plan for 5th Ave. Building," *New York Times* (Sept. 19, 2012), www.nytimes.com/2012/09/20/books/main-library-revises-storage-plan-for -research-books.html?_r=0.

39. Stephanie S. Atkins and Cherié L. Weible, "Lost Is Found: The Impact of a High-Density Shelving Facility on a Library's Collection," *Collection Management* 31, no. 3 (2006): 15–32.

40. Suzanne M. Ward and Mary Aagard, "The Dark Side of Collection Management: Deselecting Serials from a Research Library's Storage Facility using WorldCat Collection Analysis," *Collection Management* 33, no. 4 (2008): 272–87; Scott Gillies and Carol Stephenson, "Three Libraries, Three Weeding Projects: Collaborative Weeding Projects within a Shared Print Repository," *Collection Management* 37, no. 3/4 (2012): 205–22.

41. Judith C. (Judy) Russell, "Update on Florida Academic Repository (FLARE), the Florida Statewide Shared Collection Activities," (Jan. 2013), www.crl.edu/sites/ default/files/attachments/misc/PANMidwinterUpdates.pdf.

42. Michael Kelley, "Kudos for Print Archiving," *Library Journal* (Apr. 4, 2013), http:// lj.libraryjournal.com/2013/04/opinion/editorial/kudos-for-print-archiving.

43. Michael Gorman, *Our Enduring Values: Librarianship in the Twenty-First Century* (Chicago: American Library Association, 2000), 58; American Library Association, "American Library Association Preservation Policy 2008," www.ala.org/alcts/ resources/preserv/08alaprespolicy.

44. Chandru J. Shahani and William K. Wilson, "Preservation of Libraries and Archives," *American Scientist* 75, no. 3 (May/June 1987): 240–51; Robert M. Hayes,

"Analysis of the Magnitude, Costs, and Benefits of the Preservation of Research Library Books," working paper, Council on Library Resources, Washington, DC, 1985.

45. Terry Sanders, *Slow Fires: On the Preservation of the Human Record* (video recording) (Santa Monica, CA: American Film Foundation, 1987); *American National Standard for Information Sciences—Permanence of Paper for Printed Publications and Documents in Libraries and Archives*, ANSI Z39.48-1992 (R2009) (Gaithersburg, MD: National Institute of Standards and Technology, 2011), www.niso.org/apps/ group_public/download.php/6549/Permanence%20of%20Paper%20for%20 Publications%20and%20Documents%20in%20Libraries%20and%20 Archives.pdf.

46. John W. Baty et al. "Deacidification for the Conservation and Preservation of Paper-Based Works: A Review," *Bioresources* 5, no. 3 (2010): 1955–2023, www.ncsu .edu/bioresources/BioRes_05/BioRes_05_3_1955_Baty_MMHJ_Deacidification _Conserv_Paper_Review_972.pdf.

47. National Information Standards Organization, *Library Binding: An American Standard*, ANSI/NISO/LBI Z39.78-2000 (Bethesda, MD: NISO, 2000), www .niso.org/apps/group_public/download.php/6565/Library%20Binding.pdf; see also Jan Merrill-Oldham and Paul Parisi, *Guide to the ANSI/MISO/LBI Library Banding Standard: ANSI/NISO/LBI Z39.78-2000* (Chicago: Association for Library Collections and Technical Services, 2009).

48. Caroline Bendix and Alison Walker, *Cleaning Books and Documents*, rev. ed. (London: British Library Preservation Advisory Center, 2011), www.bl.uk/blpac/ pdf/clean.pdf.

49. Among these are the American Institute for Conservation of Historic and Artistic Works (www.conservation-us.org), the Preservation and Reformatting Section of ALCTS (www.ala.org/alcts/mgrps/pars), and several regional conservation centers, such as the Northeast Document Conservation Center in Massachusetts (www .nedcc.org).

50. Mike Casey and Bruce Gordon, *Sound Directions: Best Practices for Audio Preservation* (Bloomington, IN: Trustees of Indiana University; Boston: President and Fellows of Harvard University, 2007), www.dlib.indiana.edu/projects/sounddirections/ papersPresent/index.shtml; Peter Z. Adelstein, *IPI Media Storage Quick Reference*, 2nd ed. (Rochester, NY: Image Permanence Institute, Rochester Institute of Technology, 2009); James M. Reilly, *IPI Storage Guide for Acetate Film: Instructions for Using the Wheel, Graphs, and Table: Basic Strategy for Film Preservation* (Rochester, NY: Image Permanence Institute, Rochester Institute of Technology, 1993); James M. Reilly, *Storage Guide for Color Photographic Materials: Caring for Color Slides, Prints, Negatives, and Movie Films* (Albany, NY: University of the State of New York, New York State Education Dept., New York State Library, New York State Program for the Conservation and Preservation of Library Research Materials, 1998). The Northeast Document Conservation Center offers several leaflets

addressing specific formats that can be downloaded at www.nedcc.org/resources/leaflets.list.php.

51. Patricia Battin, "Substitution: The American Experience," typescript, lecture in Oxford Library Seminar, "Preserving Our Library Heritage," Feb. 25, 1992, 9.

52. Nicholson Baker, "Deadline: The Author's Desperate Bid to Save America's Past," *New Yorker* 76, no. 29 (July 24, 2000): 42–61; and Baker, *Double Fold: Libraries and the Assault on Paper* (New York: Random House, 2001).

53. Robert Darnton, "The Great Book Massacre," review of *Double Fold: Libraries and the Assault on Paper*, by Nicholson Baker, *New York Review of Books* 48, i7 (April 26, 2001): 16–19; Richard J. Cox, *Vandals in the Stacks? A Response to Nicholson Baker's Assault on Libraries*, Contributions in Librarianship and Information Science 98 (Westport, CT: Greenwood, 2002), offers one of many thoughtful responses to Baker.

54. Association for Library Collections and Technical Services, Preservation and Reformatting Section, Working Group of Defining Digital Preservation, "Definitions of Digital Preservation" (June 18, 2009), www.ala.org/alcts/resources/preserv/2009def.

55. Digital Library Federation, "Benchmark for Faithful Digital Reproductions of Monographs and Serials, Version 1" (Dec. 2002), www.diglib.org/standards/bmarkfin.htm.

56. Jessica Litman, *Digital Copyright* (Amherst, NY: Prometheus, 2001), 112.

57. Copyright Act of 1976, 94th Cong., 2d sess. (1976), Public Law 94-553, Stat. 2541 (Oct. 19, 1976); see *Copyright Law of the United States and Related Laws Contained in Title 17 of the United States Code*, Circular 92 (Washington, D.C.: Library of Congress United States Copyright Office, 2011), D.C., www.copyright.gov/title17/circ92.pdf.

58. This is a somewhat simplified description of a complicated situation. A more detailed explication can be found in Kenneth D. Crews, "Duration and Formalities: How Long Do Copyrights Last?" in *Copyright Law for Librarians and Educators: Creative Strategies and Practical Solutions*, 3rd ed., 23–29 (Chicago: American Library Association, 2012).

59. The Digital Millennium Copyright Act, 105th Cong., 2d sess. (1998), Public Law 105-304, Stat. 2860 (Oct. 28, 1998). See U.S. Copyright Office, "The Digital Millennium Copyright Act of 1998, U.S. Copyright Office Summary" (Dec. 1998), www.copyright.gov/legislation/dmca.pdf.

60. Copyright Term Extension Act, 105th Cong. 2d sess. (1998), Public Law 105-298, Stat. 2827 (Oct. 27, 1998), www.copyright.gov/legislation/s505.pdf.

61. Prudence Adler, Johnathan Band, and Brandon Butler, "Resource Packet on Orphan Works: Legal and Policy Issues for Research Libraries" (Sept. 13, 2011), www.arl.org/bm~doc/resource_orphanworks_13sept11.pdf, issued by ARL, is a useful summary of issues concerning orphan works.

62. Library of Congress, U.S. Copyright Office, "Report on Orphan Works: A Report to the Register of Copyrights" (Jan. 2006), www.copyright.gov/orphan/orphan-report.pdf; "Copyright Office Notice of Inquiry: Orphan Works and Mass Digitization," *Federal Register* 77, no. 204 (Oct. 22, 2012): 64555–61, www.gpo.gov/fdsys/pkg/FR-2012-10-22/html/2012-25932.htm. See also Denise Troll Covey, "Response to Library of Congress NOI on Orphan Works and Mass Digitization," University Libraries Research, paper 92 (Jan. 1, 2013), http://repository.cmu.edu/lib_science/92.

63. Maria A. Pallante, "Orphan Works and Mass Digitization: Obstacles and Opportunities," Keynote address, Symposium on Orphan Works and Mass Digitization: Obstacles and Opportunities, Berkeley, CA, April 12, 2012, www.law.berkeley.edu/files/2012-04-12_Pallante_Orphan_Works_Speech-1(1).pdf.

64. American Library Association, "Copyright Legislation," www.ala.org/advocacy/copyright/copyrightlegislation. Useful sources for librarians include Crews, *Copyright Law for Librarians and Educators*; Carrie Russell, *Complete Copyright for K–12 Libraries and Educators* (Chicago: American Library Association, 2012); Carrie Russell, *Complete Copyright Guide for Everyday Librarians* (Chicago: American Library Association, 2004).

65. Research Libraries Group and OCLC, *Trusted Digital Repositories: Attributes and Responsibilities* (Mountain View, CA: RLG, 2002), www.oclc.org/content/dam/research/activities/trustedrep/repositories.pdf.

66. OCLC and Center for Research Libraries, *Trustworthy Repositories Audit and Certification: Criteria and Checklist* (Chicago: Center for Research Libraries; Dublin, OH: OCLC, 2007), www.crl.edu/sites/default/files/attachments/pages/trac_0.pdf.

67. International Standards Organization, *Trusted Third Party Repository for Digital Records*, ISO 16363:2012 (Geneva: International Standards Organization, 2012).

68. European Framework for Audit and Certification of Digital Repositories, www.trusteddigitalrepository.eu/Site/Trusted%20Digital%20Repository.html; nestor, www.langzeitarchivierung.de/Subsites/nestor/DE; Digital Preservation Europe's Planning Tool for Trusted Electronic Repositories, www.digitalpreservationeurope.eu/platter.

69. Raym Crow, "The Case for Institutional Repositories: A SPARC Position Paper," *ARL: A Bimonthly Report* no. 223 (Aug. 2001), 1, http://sparc.arl.org/sites/default/files/media_files/instrepo.pdf.

70. Dawn C. Chmielewski, "Google and Publishers Settle Longtime Dispute over Digitized Books," *Los Angeles Times* (Oct. 4, 2012), http://articles.latimes.com/2012/oct/04/entertainment/la-et-ct-google-publishers-settle-digitized-books-dispute-20121004.

71. For Chin's comments on *Authors Guild et al. v. Google*, see www.scribd.com/doc/184162035/Google-Books-ruling-on-fair-use-pdf, 26.

72. Paul Duguid, "Inheritance and Loss? A Brief Survey of Google Books," *First Monday* 12, no. 8 (Aug. 6, 2007), www.uic.edu/htbin/cgiwrap/bin/ojs/index.php/fm/article/view/1972/1847; Robert Darnton, "Six Reasons Google Books Failed," *New York Review of Books Blog* (Mar. 28, 2011), www.nybooks.com/blogs/nyrblog/2011/mar/28/six-reasons-google-books-failed.

73. Barbara Quint, "Who the Heck Is Tristram Shandy? Or What's Not Wrong with Google Book Search?" *Information Today* 24, no. 9 (Oct. 2007): 7–8; Anthony Grafton, "Future Reading: Digitization and Its Discontents," *New Yorker* 83, no. 34 (Nov. 7, 2007): 50–54; Lorcan Dempsey, "Systemic Change: CIC and Google," *Lorcan Dempsey's Weblog* (blog), June 6, 2007, http://orweblog.oclc.org/archives/001366.html; Paul N. Courant, "Google's Good Deal for Libraries," *Washington Post* (May 24, 2009), http://articles.washingtonpost.com/2009-05-24/opinions/36850402_1_google-libraries-brewster-kahle.

74. See Richard K. Johnson, "In Google's Broad Wake: Taking Responsibility for Shaping the Global Digital Library," *ARL: A Bimonthly Report* no. 250 (Feb. 2007): 1–15, for an exploration of what libraries can and should do in shaping mass digitization initiatives; see also Oya Y. Rieger, *Preservation in the Age of Large-Scale Digitization* (Washington, DC: Council on Library and Information Resources, 2008), http://clir.org/pubs/abstract/pub141abst.html.

75. HathiTrust, "Welcome to the Shared Digital Future," www.hathitrust.org/about.

76. Andrew Ablanese, "Google Scanning Is Fair Use Says Judge," *Publishers Weekly* (Oct. 22, 2012), www.publishersweekly.com/pw/by-topic/digital/copyright/article/54321-in-hathitrust-ruling-judge-says-google-scanning-is-fair-use.html. The full complaint, *The Authors Guild, Inc., the Australian Society of Authors Limited, Union des écrivians et des écrivvains Québécois, Pat Cummings, Angelo Loukakis, Roxana Robinson, Andre Roy, James Shapiro, Daniele Simpson, T.G. Stiles, and Fay Weldon v. Google, Inc., Defendant*, filed in October 2005, is available at http://thepublicindex.org/docs/cases/hathitrust/complaint.pdf.

77. The Northeast Document Conservation Center offers a series of useful, freely available leaflets on preservation planning and prioritizing; see "NEDCC Preservation Leaflets," www.nedcc.org/free-resources/preservation-leaflets/overview for the complete listing. See also Carolyn Morrow, "Defining the Library Preservation Program: Policies and Organization," in *Preservation: Issues and Planning*, ed. Paul Banks and Roberta Pilette, 1–27 (Chicago: American Library Association, 2000); Elise Calvi et al. *Preservation Manager's Guide to Cost Analysis* (Chicago: American Library Association, 2006).

78. Sharon Johnson et al., *Key Issues for E-resource Collection Development: A Guide for Libraries* (The Hague: International Federation of Library Associations and Institutions, 2012).

79. Carol French and Eleanor Pollard, "Serials Usage Study in a Public Library," *Public Library Quarterly* 16, no. 4 (1997): 45–53; Mariyam Thohiroa, Mary Beth

Chambers, and Nancy Sprague, "Full-Text Databases: A Case Study Revisited a Decade Later," *Serials Review* 36, no. 3 (Sept. 2010): 152–60; Kathryn Kennedy et al., "Evaluating Continuing Resources: Perspectives and Methods from Science Librarians," *Serials Librarian* 55, no. 3 (2008): 428–43; Diane Carroll and Joel Cummings, "Data Driven Collection Assessment Using a Serials Decision Database," *Serials Review* 36, no. 4 (Dec. 2010): 227–39.

80. Clint Chamberlain and Barbara MacAlpine, "Pay-per-View Article Access: A Viable Replacement for Subscriptions?" *Serials* 21, no. 1 (Mar. 2008): 30–34; Maureen Weicher and Tian Xiao Zhang, "Unbundling the 'Big Deal' with Pay-per-View of E-journal Articles," *Serials Librarian* 63, no. 1 (2012): 28–37; Patrick L. Carr, "Acquiring Articles through Unmediated, User-Initiated Pay-per-View Transactions: As Assessment of Current Practices," *Serials Review* 35, no. 4 (Dec. 2009): 272–77.

81. Paul Metz, "Thirteen Steps to Avoiding Bad Luck in a Serials Cancellation Project," *Journal of Academic Librarianship* 18, no. 2 (1992): 76–82.

82. Paul Metz and John Cosgriff, "Building a Comprehensive Serials Decision Database at Virginia Tech," *College and Research Libraries* 61, no. 4 (July 2000): 324–34; Judith M. Nixon, "A Reprise, or Round Three: Using a Database Management Program as a Decision-Support System for the Cancellation of Serials," *Serials Librarian* 59, no. 3/4 (2010): 302–12; Ronald A. Banks, "Decision-Making Factors Related to Bibliographic Database Cancellation," *Behavioral and Social Sciences Librarian* 25, no. 1 (2006): 93–110; Robin A. Paynter, "Commercial Library Decision Support Systems: An Analysis Based on Collection Managers' Needs," *Collection Management* 34, no. 1 (Jan. 2008): 31–47.

83. Association of Research Libraries, *ARL Statistics 2010–2011* (Washington, DC: Association of Research Libraries, 2012).

84. Patrick L. Carr, "The Commitment to Securing Perpetual Journal Access," *Library Resources and Technical Services* 55, no. 1 (2011): 4–16; Eugenia Beh and Jane Smith, "Preserving the Scholarly Collection: An Examination of the Perpetual Access Clauses in the Texas A&M University Libraries' Major E-journal Licenses," *Serials Review* 38, no. 4 (Dec. 2012): 235–42.

85. Eileen Gifford Fenton, "An Overview of Portico: An Electronic Archiving Service," *Serials Review* 32, no. 2 (June 2006): 81–86.

86. Gail McMillan, Matt Schultz, and Katherine Skinner, *Digital Preservation*, SPEC Kit 324 (Washington, DC: Association of Research Libraries, 2011).

87. Northeast Document Conversation Center, "Exploring Environmental Control," http://unfacilitated.preservation101.org/session4/expl_envi-temp_guide.asp.

88. See Northeast Document Conservation Center, Emergency Management, "Emergency Salvage of Moldy Books and Paper" (2012), www.nedcc.org/free-resources/preservation-leaflets/3.-emergency-management/3.8-emergency

-salvage-of-moldy-books-and-paper; R.E. Child, *Mould*, rev. ed. (London: British Library Preservation Advisory Centre, 2011.)

89. Susan M. Allen, "The Blumberg Case: A Costly Lesson for Librarians," *AB Bookman's Weekly* 88, no. 2 (Sept. 2, 1991): 769–73; Philip Weiss, "The Book Thief: A True Tale of Bibliomania," *Harper's Magazine* 288, no. 1724 (Jan. 1994): 37–56.

90. Library Leadership and Management Association, Building and Equipment Section, Safety and Security of Library Buildings Committee, *Library Security Guidelines Document* (Chicago: Library Leadership and Management Association, 2010), www.ala.org/llama/sites/ala.org.llama/files/content/conted/11-16-11 _LibrarySecurityGuide2010.pdf.

91. Association of College and Research Libraries, Rare Books and Manuscripts Section, "ACRL/RBMS Guidelines Regarding Security and Theft in Special Collection" (completed by the RBMS Security Committee in 2008 and approved by ACRL in 2009), www.ala.org/acrl/standards/security_theft.

92. "Flood Toll at Colorado State Could Reach $100 Million," *American Libraries* 28, no. 8 (Sept. 1997): 16.

93. Tom Clareson and Jane S. Long, "Libraries in the Eye of the Storm: Lessons Learned from Hurricane Katrina," *American Libraries* 37, no. 7 (Aug. 2006): 38–41; Jamie Ellis, "Lessons Learned: The Recovery of a Research Collection after Hurricane Katrina," *Collection Building* 26, no. 4 (2007): 108–11; "Hurricane Katrina Damage: A Summary," *Mississippi Libraries* 69, no. 4 (Winter 2005): 93–95.

94. Richard Danielson, "Inundated by 30,000 Gallons of Rain, Jimmie B. Keel Library to Reopen Tuesday," *Tampa Bay Times* (May 29, 2013), www.tampabay.com/news/localgovernment/inundated-by-30000-gallons-of-rain-jimmie-b-keel-library-to-reopen-tuesday/2123160.

95. See, for example, Miriam B. Kahn, *Disaster Response and Planning for Libraries*, 3rd ed. (Chicago: American Library Association, 2012); and Emma Dadson, *Salvaging Library and Archive Collections* (London: British Library Preservation Advisory Centre, 2012), www.bl.uk/blpac/pdf/salvage.pdf. Other sources are listed in this chapter's Suggested Readings.

96. Karen E. Brown, "3.4 Worksheet for Outlining a Disaster Plan," www.nedcc.org/free-resources/preservation-leaflets/3.-emergency-management/3.4-worksheet-for-outlining-a-disaster-plan.

Suggested Readings

Adams, Carolyn. "Managing Automated Storage in the 21st Century." In *Robots in Academic Libraries: Advancements in Library Automation*, ed. Edward Iglesias, 115–27. Hershey, PA: IGIG Global, 2013.

Allen, Melissa. "Weed 'Em and Reap: The Art of Weeding to Avoid Criticism." *Library Media Connection* 28, no. 6 (May/June 2010): 32–33.

American Library Association Map and Geography Round Table, Task Force on Library Security for Cartographic Resources. *Map Collection Security Guidelines*. Electronic Publication Series 8 (Chicago: American Library Association, 2010). www.ala .org/magirt/sites/ala.org.magirt/files/content/publicationsab/Map%20Coll%20 Security%20Guidelines.pdf.

Anderson, Mary Alice. "Weeding, from Alphabet Books to Zip Drives." *Multimedia and Internet @ Schools* 17, no. 3 (2010): 28–30.

Barnes, Michael, Robert G. Kelly, and Maureen Kerwin. "Lost Gems: Identifying Rare and Unusual Monographs in a University's Circulating Collection." *Library Collections, Acquisitions, and Technical Services* 34, no. 2/3 (2010): 57–65.

Berger, Sherri. "The Evolving Ethics of Preservation: Redefining Practices and Responsibilities in the 21st Century." *Serials Librarian* 57, no. 1/2 (2009): 57–68.

Bishop, Kay. "Maintenance and Preservation." In *The Collection Program in Schools: Concepts and Practices*, 5th ed., 117–26. Santa Barbara, CA: Libraries Unlimited, 2013.

Blecic, Deborah D., et al. "Deal or No Deal? Evaluating Big Deals and Their Journals." *College and Research Libraries* 74, no. 2 (Mar. 2013): 178–94.

Bradley, Kevin, ed. *Guidelines on the Production and Preservation of Digital Objects*. 2nd ed. IASA-TC04. Auckland Park, South Africa: International Association of Sound and Audiovisual Archives, 2009.

Bravender, Patricia, and Valeria Long. "Weeding an Outdated Collection in an Automated Retrieval System." *Collection Management* 36, no. 4 (2011): 237–45.

Britton, Scott, and John Renaud, comps. *Print Retention Decision Making*. SPEC Kit 337. Washington, DC: Association of Research Libraries, 2013.

Brown, Adrian. *Practical Digital Preservation: A How-to Guide for Organizations of Any Size*. Chicago: Neal-Schuman, 2013.

Brown, Josh. "Collection Development and Institutional Repositories." In *Collection Development in the Digital Age*, ed. Maggie Fieldhouse and Audrey Marshall, 149–62. London: Facet, 2012.

Brown, Karen E., and Beth Lindbolm Patkus. "Emergency Management, 3.11 Collections Security: Planning and Prevention for Libraries and Archives." [n.d.] www.nedcc.org/free-resources/preservation-leaflets/3.-emergency-management/ 3.11-collections-security-planning-and-prevention-for-libraries-and-archives.

Brush, Denise. "Preserving Last Copies in a Virtual Collection." *Technical Services Quarterly* 28, no. 1 (2010): 1–16.

Bruxvoort, Diane, John E. Burger, and Lynn Sorensen Sutton. "Like a Snowball Gathering Speed: Development of ASERL's Print Journal Retention Program." *Collection Management* 37, no. 3/4 (2012): 223–36.

Bülow, Anna E., and Jess Ahmon. *Preparing Collections for Digitization*. London: Facet, in association with the National Archives, 2011.

Burnhill, Peter. "Tales from the Keepers Registry: Serials Issues about Archiving and the Web." *Serials Review* 39, no. 1 (Mar. 2013): 3–20.

Caplan, Priscilla, ed. *The Preservation of Digital Materials. Library Technology Reports* 44, no. 2. Chicago: ALA TechSource, 2008.

Clement, Susanne, et al. "Collaboration and Organization for Successful Serials Cancellation." *Serials Libraries* 54, no. 3/4 (2008): 229–34.

Collier, Ginny. "The Reluctant Weeder: Embracing the Joy of Weeding." *Children and Libraries* 8, no. 2 (Summer/Fall 2010): 51–53.

Conway, Paul. "Measuring Content Quality in a Preservation Repository: HathiTrust and Large-Scale Book Digitization." In *iPres 2010: Proceedings of 7th International Conference on Preservation of Digital Objects, September 19–24, 2010, Vienna, Austria*, ed. Andreas Rauber, 95–102. Vienna: Computer Gesellschaft, 2010. http://141.213.232.243/bitstream/handle/2027.42/85227/C06%20Conway%20 Measuring%20Content%20Quality%20iPres%202010.pdf?sequence=1.

———. "Preservation in the Age of Google: Digitization, Digital Preservation, and Dilemmas." *Library Quarterly* 80, no. 1 (Jan. 2010): 61–79.

Crosetto, Alice. "Weeding E-books." In *No Shelf Required 2: Use and Management of Electronic Books*, ed. Sue Polanka, 93–101. Chicago: American Library Association, 2012.

Dadson, Emma. *Emergency Planning and Response for Libraries, Archives, and Museums.* Lanham, MD: Scarecrow Press, 2013.

Daigle, Bradley. "Stewardship and Curation in a Digital World." In *Collection Development in the Digital Age*, ed. Maggie Fieldhouse and Andrey Marshall, 93–107. London: Facet, 2012.

Detmering, Robert, and Claudene Sproles. "Reference in Transition: A Case Study in Reference Collection Development." *Collection Building* 31, no. 1 (2012): 19–22.

Ditzler, Pat, and JoAnn Dumas. *A Book Sale How-to Guide: More Money, Less Stress.* Chicago: American Library Association, 2012.

Dubicki, Eleonora. "Weeding: Facing the Fears." *Collection Building* 27, no. 4 (2008): 132–35.

Emery, Jill, and Graham Stone. "Annual Review." In *Techniques for Electronic Resource Management*, 30–34. Library Technology Reports 49, no. 2. Chicago: ALA TechSource, 2013.

———. "Cancellation and Replacement Review." In *Techniques for Electronic Resource Management*, 35–38. Library Technology Reports 49, no. 2 Chicago: ALA TechSource, 2013.

Farmer, Lesley S. J. "The Life Cycle of Digital Reference Sources." *Reference Librarian* 50, no. 2 (2009): 117–36.

Fleischer, S. Victor, and Mark J. Heppner. "Disaster Planning for Libraries and Archives: What You Need to Know and How to Do It." *Library and Archival Security* 22, no. 2 (2009): 125–40.

Ford, Patricia. *IPI's Guide to Sustainable Preservation Practices for Managing Storage Environments*. Version 2.0. Rochester, NY: Image Permanence Institute, Rochester Institute of Technology, 2012.

Forde, Helen, and Jonathan Rhys-Lewis. *Preserving Archives*. 2nd ed. London: Facet, 2013.

Francis, Mary. "Weeding the Reference Collection: A Case Study of Collection Management." *Reference Librarian* 53, no. 2 (2012): 219–34.

Graham, Warren Davis. *The Black Belt Librarian: Real-World Safety and Security*. Chicago: American Library Association, 2012.

Griffiths, Ross, and Andrew Krol. "Insider Theft: Reviews and Recommendations from the Archive and Library Professional Literature." *Library and Archival Security* 22, no. 1 (2009): 5–18.

Hellyer, Paul. "Reference 2.0: The Future of Shrinking Print Reference Collections Seems Destined for the Web." *AALL Spectrum* 13, no. 5 (Mar. 2009): 24–27.

Henderson, Jane. *Managing the Library and Archive Environment*, rev. ed. London: British Library, Preservation Advisory Centre, 2010. www.bl.uk/blpac/pdf/environment.pdf.

Hill, V. Elizabeth. "The Preservation of Sound Recordings." *Music Reference Services Quarterly* 15, no. 2 (2012): 88–98.

Hirtle, Peter B., Anne R. Kenney, and Judy Ruttenberg. "Digitization of Special Collections and Archives: Legal and Contractual Issues." *Research Library Issues: A Quarterly Report from ARL, CNI, and SPARC*, no. 279 (June 2012): 2–4.

Kahn, Miriam B. *The Library Security and Safety Guide to Prevention, Planning, and Response*. Chicago: American Library Association, 2008.

Katz, Linda S. *Weeding and Maintenance of Reference Collections*. 11th ed. New York: Routledge, 2013.

Keogh, Patricia. "Decisions in Resource Management: The Case of Microforms." *Library Collections, Acquisitions, and Technical Services* 36, no. 1/2 (2012): 8–17.

Kirchhoff, Amy. "E-book Preservation: Business and Content Challenges." In *No Shelf Required 2: Use and Management of Electronic Books*, ed. Sue Polanka, 71–91. Chicago: American Library Association, 2012.

Lavender, Kenneth. *Book Repair: A How-to-Do-It Manual*. 2nd ed., rev. How-to-Do-It Manuals for School and Public Librarians 178. New York: Neal-Schuman, 2011.

Lee, Marta. "Weeding Is Not Just for Gardeners: A Case Study on Weeding a Reference Collection." *Community and Junior College Libraries* 15, no. 3 (2009): 129–35.

The Library of Congress National Recording Preservation Plan. CLIR Publication 156. Washington, DC: Council on Library and Information Resources and the Library of Congress, 2012. www.clir.org/pubs/reports/pub156/pub156.pdf.

Maidabino, Abashe Atiku, and A. N. Zainab. "A Holistic Approach to Collection Security Implementation in University Libraries." *Library Collections, Acquisitions, and Technical Services* 36, no. 3 (2012): 107–20.

Mason, Nancy L., and Sarah Pickle. *Appraising Our Digital Investment: Sustainability of Digitized Special Collections in ARL Libraries*. Washington, DC: Association of Research Libraries; New York: Ithaka S+R, 2013. www.arl.org/storage/documents/publications/digitizing-special-collections-report-21feb13.pdf.

Matthews, Graham, Yvonne Smith, and Gemma Knowles. *Disaster Management in Archives, Libraries, and Museums*. Farnham, UK: Ashgate, 2009.

McNair, Ellen. "Print to Digital: Opportunities for Choice." *Library Media Connection* 30, no. 6 (May/June 2012): 28–30.

Meyer, Lars. *Safeguarding Collections at the Dawn of the 21st Century: Describing Roles and Measuring Contemporary Preservation Activities in ARL Libraries*. Washington, DC: Association of Research Libraries, 2009.

Mix, Vickie. "Documents Journey through Time: Weeding a History." *Collection Building* 29, no. 4 (2010): 131–36.

Morris, Patricia. "Achieving a Preservation Environment with Data Logging Technology and Microclimates." *College and Undergraduate Libraries* 16, no. 1 (2009): 83–104.

Mounce, Michael, and Patricia Mounce. "Internal Control Implications in a University Library Environment." *Library and Archival Security* 21, no. 1 (2008): 13–20.

———. "Investigation of Special Collections Library Theft." *Library and Archival Security* 25, no. 2 (2012): 99–118.

Murray-Rust, Catherine. "Library Storage as a Preservation Strategy." *Advances in Librarianship* 27 (2010): 159–83.

Nelson, Naomi L., et al. *Managing Born-Digital Special Collections and Archival Materials*. SPEC Kit 329. Washington, DC: Association of Research Libraries, 2012.

O'Connor, Steve, and Cathie Jilovsky, "Approaches to the Storage of Low Use and Last Copy Research Materials." *Library Collections, Acquisitions, and Technical Services* 32, no. 3/4 (2008): 121–26.

Ottaviani, Jim, and Carolyn Hank. "Libraries Should Lead the Institutional Repository Initiative and Development at Their Institutions." *Bulletin of the American Society for Information Science and Technology* 35, no. 4 (Apr./May 2009): 17–21.

Philpott, Don, and Paul Serluco, eds. *Public School Emergency Preparedness and Crisis Management Plan*. Lanham, MD: Scarecrow, 2010.

Pinniger, David. *Pests*. London: British Library Preservation Advisory Centre, 2012. www.bl.uk/blpac/pdf/pests.pdf.

Preserving Our Digital Heritage: The National Digital Information Infrastructure and Preservation Program 2010 Report: A Collaborative Initiative of the Library of Congress. Washington, DC: Library of Congress, National Digital Information Infrastructure and Preservation Program, 2011. www.digitalpreservation.gov/documents/ NDIIPP2010Report_Post.pdf.

Reiger, Oya Y. *Preservation in the Age of Large-Scale Digitization: A White Paper.* Washington, DC: Council on Library and Information Resources, 2008. www.clir .org/pubs/abstract/pub141abst.html.

Revels, Ira. *Managing Digital Projects.* Chicago: American Library Association, 2014.

Runyon, Amanda M. "The Effect of Economics and Electronic Resources on the Traditional Law Library Print Collection." *Law Library Journal* 101, no. 2 (Spring 2009): 177–205.

Samuelson, Todd, Laura Sare, and Catherine Coker. "Unusual Suspects: The Case of Insider Theft in Research Libraries and Special Collections." *College and Research Libraries* 73, no. 6 (Nov. 2012): 556–68.

Sare, Laura. "A Tale of Two Depositories: Weeding Federal Depository Collections." *DttP: Documents to the People* 37, no. 1 (Spring 2009): 37–40.

Smith, Debbi A. "A Journal Back File Overlap Analysis: Looking Back to Move Forward." *Library Collections, Acquisitions, and Technical Services* 33, no. 1 (2009): 25–30.

Smith, Kevin L. "Copyright Risk Management: Principles and Strategies for Large-Scale Digitization Projects in Special Collections." *Research Library Issues: A Quarterly Report from ARL, CNI, and SPARC* no. 279 (2012): 17–23.

Soma, Amy K., and Lisa M. Sjoberg. "More Than Just Low-Hanging Fruit: A Collaborative Approach to Weeding in Academic Libraries." *Collection Management* 36, no. 1 (2010): 17–28.

The State of Recorded Sound Preservation in the United States: A National Legacy at Risk in the Digital Age. Washington, DC: Council on Library and Information Resources and the Library of Congress, 2010.

Stross, Randall E. *Planet Google: One Company's Audacious Plan to Organize Everything We Know.* New York: Free Press, 2008.

Tabacaru, Simona, and Carmelita Pickett. "Damned If You Do, Damned If You Don't: Texas A&M University Libraries' Collection Assessment for Off-Site." *Collection Building* 32, no. 3 (2013): 111–15.

Teper, Jennifer Hain, and Eric Alstrom, eds. *Planning and Constructing Book and Paper Conservation Laboratories: A Guidebook.* Chicago: Association for Library Collections and Technical Services, 2012.

Thomas, Marcia L., and Anke Voss, comps., Marcia Thomas, ed. *Emergency Response Planning in College Libraries.* CLIP Note 40. Chicago: College Library Information

Packet Committee, College Libraries Section, Association of College and Research Libraries, 2009.

Thomas, William Joseph, and Daniel L. Shouse. "Rules of Thumb for Deselecting, Relocating, and Retaining Bound Journals." *Collection Building* 31, no. 3 (2012): 92–97.

Todaro, Julie Beth. *Emergency Preparedness for Libraries*. Lanham, MD: Government Institutes, 2009.

Urban, Jennifer M. "How Fair Use Can Help Solve the Orphan Works Problem." *Berkeley Technology Law Journal* 27, no. 3 (2012): 1379–1430.

Van Gompel, Stef, and P. Bernt Hugenholtz. "The Orphan Works Problem: The Copyright Conundrum of Digitizing Large-Scale Audiovisual Archives and How to Solve It." *Popular Communication* 8, no. 1 (Jan./Mar. 2010): 61–71.

Van Nort, Sydney C. "Theft, Vandalism, and Security in Libraries and Archives." In *Encyclopedia of Library and Information Sciences*, 3rd ed., ed. Marcia J. Bates and Mary Niles Maack, 5204–19. New York: Taylor and Frances, 2009.

Walters, Tyler, and Katherine Skinner. *New Roles for New Times: Digital Curation for Preservation*. Washington, DC: Association of Research Libraries, 2011.

Warner, Dorothy A. "Libraries, Archives, and Digital Preservation: A Critical Overview." In *Information Technology in Librarianship: New Critical Approaches*, ed. Gloria J. Leckie and John E. Buschman, 262–80. Santa Barbara, CA: Libraries Unlimited, 2008.

Wilkie, Everett C., Jr., ed. *Guide to Security Considerations and Practices for Rare Book, Manuscript, and Special Collection Libraries*. Chicago: Association of College and Research Libraries, 2012.

Wilkinson, Frances C., Linda K. Lewis, and Nancy K. Dennis. *Comprehensive Guide to Emergency Preparedness and Disaster Recovery*. Chicago: Association of College and Research Libraries, 2010.

CHAPTER SIX

Marketing, Liaison Activities, and Outreach

Every library seeks to build collections and develop services that satisfy its user community within the constraints of its financial resources and in a manner consistent with its mission. The issues for collection development librarians are learning about and keeping current with users' changing needs, wants, and demands; developing the appropriate collections and services in response; and communicating their availability to users. Effective marketing can help address these challenges. Kendrick explains that successful marketing "will identify what drives users and build products and services around their needs; enable a highly differentiated service, not 'one size fits all'; create value and inspiration to use the library; and do all this with as little cost as possible. It will . . . attract non-users and develop loyalty behaviours in existing users, and will clearly influence attitudes towards the library."[1] This chapter defines marketing, considers the concepts of market research, market segmentation, and marketing mix in the library context; and explores developing and implementing a marketing plan and assessing its effectiveness. Because effective marketing depends on building and maintaining relationships, this chapter also explores liaison and outreach activities, including the use of social media.

Understanding Marketing

Marketing is the process of determining the user communities' wants and needs, developing the products and services in response, and encouraging users and potential users to take advantage of the products and services. Regular communication with clientele is essential for gathering the information needed both to perform routine collection development and management activities and to plan for the future. Regular communication, formal and informal, is equally fundamental for sharing information about the library—new acquisitions, new programs and services, successes, and constraints. Baker and Wallace write, "In essence, marketing library collections involves using strategic planning techniques to both anticipate and respond to the short- and long-term collection-related needs and desires of the individuals and groups whom the library serves."[2] Equally important is relationship building—connecting the user to the library and developing a sense of loyalty. Regardless of library type, understanding and consulting with the library's community, governing and funding bodies, community leaders, and administrators are essential responsibilities of librarians.

Liaison activities, outreach, and *public engagement* are often used to denote aspects of the same activity—communication or linkages with the library's community to share and gain information. Communication is a two-way enterprise. Librarians need to learn about and listen to their constituents' concerns and ideas as well as share information. Academic libraries tend to use *liaison* to refer to librarians' intermediary role between their constituents and the library. Public and school librarians more commonly use the term *outreach* to describe the act of reaching out or extending services beyond current or usual limits. The ALA Office for Literacy and Outreach Services (www.ala.org/offices/olos) defines outreach more narrowly as those activities intended to reach traditionally underserved populations, including new adult readers and nonreaders; gay, lesbian, bisexual, and transgender people; incarcerated people and ex-offenders; older adults; people of color; people with disabilities; poor and homeless people; rural, native, and tribal library patrons of all kinds; and bookmobile communities. The term *public engagement* is increasingly used to describe activities and services a library pursues to engage its user communities actively with the library's collections, resources, and expertise. In this book, *outreach* is used in the broader sense of libraries and librarians reaching out to and engaging with their user (and nonuser) communities.

Marketing as a term and a concept is a significant concern in libraries of all types. Attention focuses on how to reach users and potential users effectively and how to make clear what the library has to offer—its value. Helping user communities, stakeholders, and funders understand libraries as both a common good (shared and beneficial for members of a community) and a public good (one not be diminished by consumer by use) is of increasing importance. Doing this well depends on understanding the community and determining the products and services to develop and then promote. Much of the outreach and liaison work librarians do includes the tasks traditionally associated with marketing, and all librarians can benefit from knowing basic marketing concepts.

In a library context, the aim of marketing is both to understand and satisfy the library user and to develop and achieve a set of articulated goals, which may be increased use, community support, more patrons, a larger budget, or increased donations. In other words, effective marketing strategically studies the needs of the community the library serves, provides services and collections to meet those needs, and ensures that users recognize the quality and value of what is provided. For the collection development librarian, marketing means understanding the library's community of users and then developing and promoting a product (the collection) and related services that serve that community. The success of that product and promotional activities is then evaluated to ensure that performance is responsive to the community and gains support. Library marketing should always occur within the context of the library's mission, goals, and objectives and is often part of a library's strategic planning. Germano and Stretch-Stephenson write that "value-driven strategic market planning requires connecting library business and operational goals to customer needs by conducting environmental scans and formal market research as well as gathering everyday customer reactions, responses and objections."[3]

Marketing as part of collection development in libraries is not a new idea. In 1969, Lopez wrote that marketing is one of the seven responsibilities constituting collection development. The other responsibilities Lopez identified are fiscal management, planning, evaluation, review, quality control, and resource sharing. The 1996 *Guide for Training Collection Development Librarians* contained a section on "Marketing, Outreach, and Communications with Constituencies," documenting the increasingly widespread acceptance of marketing as a core competency for collection development librarians. Marketing, in the narrower sense of promotion, in libraries has an even longer history. Briscoe's *Library Advertising*, published in 1921, suggested techniques like publishing library newsletters aimed at different groups and promoting books that related to popular movies.[4]

Professional library associations recognize the importance of marketing through several annual awards. The IFLA Management and Marketing Section awards the International Marketing Award annually. The Library Leadership and Management Association Public Relations and Marketing Section recognizes the best public relations materials produced in the annual Best of Show Awards. The American Association of Law Libraries honors outstanding achievement with its Excellence in Marketing Award. The prestigious ALA John Cotton Dana Library Public Relations Award honors outstanding public relations in all types of libraries.[5]

Many of these association awards focus on initiatives that increase public awareness and foster advocacy. Advocacy is public support for an issue, cause, or policy. Often advocacy for libraries involves supporting continuing or increased financial support. ALA's "@ your library, The Campaign for America's Libraries" is a multiyear public campaign that aims to increase community understanding of the value of public, school, academic, and special libraries and librarians—and to foster advocacy. ALA makes materials available to libraries so they can customize "@ your library" to local use. Other resources are ALA's "Advocating in a Tough Economy Toolkit" and *The Campaign for America's Libraries @ your library Toolkit for Academic and Research Libraries.*[6]

A common misconception is that marketing is the same as advertising, promotion, or public relations.[7] Developing a library brand (a name, term or tag line, design, symbol, or another feature that identifies the library as distinct from other libraries or competitors) is not marketing. Many of the suggested readings at the end of this chapter, despite having marketing in their titles, address promoting library collections and services and do not explore all the elements of marketing. Although marketing does include promotion, this is only one aspect. The aims of marketing in collection development and management are to understand the library's present and future users; develop and maintain a collection that satisfies their needs, wants, and demands; inform users about the resources and associated services available; and monitor success or failure in conveying the message. Once a library understands its potential market, it formulates marketing strategies. These include developing overall plans to maximize impact on the market in both the short and long terms, deciding which information resources and services to offer, and establishing standards and measures for performance. In other words, marketing is market research, planning, implementation, and control. These activities are increasingly important in the nonprofit sector. Social agencies, educational institutions, charities, museums, and libraries employ marketing to learn the needs and wants of their target markets and to deliver the desired satisfaction more effectively and efficiently than their competitors.

Marketing can challenge libraries because, without profit-and-loss figures found in the commercial sector, measuring the success of marketing efforts is often difficult. Yet performance measurement is an essential component of effective collection development and management, and various methods for evaluation and assessment have been developed over time (see chapter 7). Some of these techniques can help measure the success of a marketing initiative by looking at increased use of resources and changes in users' level of satisfaction.

The library's community—consisting of users, potential users, and its funding and governing bodies—is its *market*. Marketing is implicit in Osburn's analysis of the relationship between libraries and their communities: "Since . . . libraries depend upon their communities for support, the future of libraries does hinge very definitely on the priority and importance assigned to them by their respective communities. . . . For this reason alone, each library will be better off for defining its community, trying to understand it, and demonstrating to it the value that can be expected of the library."[8]

Marketing Concepts

In *Strategic Marketing for Nonprofit Organizations*, Andreasen and Kotler define marketing as the effective management by an organization of its exchange relations with various markets and publics. In their *Principles of Marketing*, the authors stress that marketing should be understood in the new sense of satisfying customer needs, not in the old sense of telling and selling.[9] Marketing begins with market research—understanding who the market is and what that market needs, wants, and demands. For example, I need information. I want the library to help me find this information, by either giving it to me or directing me to a resource that provides it. I demand, in the marketing sense of this word, to use an online resource because I have been influenced by marketing, either by the library or the commercial sector, to prefer online information resources instead of print. Most people who enter the library or access its resources online seek information or entertainment. The individual may want a suspense novel and might demand the newest Stephen King novel.

Collections librarians should be cautious about seeking to meet all their users' perceived needs and wants, which is usually too narrow an objective. Most libraries have long-range goals and objectives, articulated in a mission statement and mandated by a parent authority or agency. Kotler and Fox refer to keeping the bigger picture in mind as a "societal marketing orientation."[10] The librarian's task is developing and managing collections to enhance the current users' level of satisfaction and to increase user support while preserving the library's well-being and long-term interests.

Products and services are anything that can be offered to satisfy a need or want. Libraries provide products in the form of information, books, journals, multimedia, online resources, customized bibliographies, handouts, library web pages, and so on. Library services are reference, interlibrary loan, reader advisory, training, story hours, class visits, and any time a staff person comes in contact with a patron. Collection development librarians can view the collections they build and manage as the product. Every contact they make with their constituents is a service.

In addition to gathering information to understand needs better, the collections librarian works with users to identify and solve problems they have experienced with the library. This is an essential element of building relationships with the user community. User problems include both inadequacies with the collection and problems with library services. Often, librarians discover that a user's assessment of the collection is based on incomplete or inaccurate knowledge of resources held locally and of the means available to access online resources or to request materials through interlibrary loan. Law found that lack of awareness of library resources is a significant barrier for undergraduates, who are "confronted with a bewildering and overwhelming array of electronic resources, with little knowledge of what the resources are, and few ideas on how to best sort through them."[11] The librarian gains information that helps develop outreach activities that more clearly and completely convey to users what the library has and does.

When user dissatisfaction is based on real problems, not misunderstanding, librarians take on the role of advocate in trying to solve these problems within the context of available library and institutional resources. They solicit advice from constituents regarding specific collection issues. This form of consultation is more common in school library media centers and academic libraries, in which teachers and faculty members make recommendations about purchasing expensive items, adding and cancelling journal titles, replacing specific titles and materials in particular subject areas, placing materials in storage, and needing multiple copies of individual titles.

Value and satisfaction define how consumers choose between the products and services that might satisfy a given need. Value is a complicated concept with a long history in economic thought. Karl Marx thought that the value of an object depended on how much labor went into its production. Contemporary thought defines value as subjective and dependent on its capacity to satisfy wants. I value the library and its services to the extent my wants are met. Do I get the information I need? Does the library have the book I want? Did the librarian order the book I recommended? How long do I have to wait? Even if I am satisfied this time, I may not value the library. Reichheld, Markey, and Hopton observe that satisfaction is "an inherently unstable and temporary mental state and measuring genuine satisfaction is a tricky business."[12] Research indicates that satisfaction does not necessarily translate into customer loyalty.[13] Citizens may value the library, be satisfied with its collections and service, but be unwilling to approve a tax increase to support it. Academic libraries, frequently glibly called the heart of the university, are seldom funded to the financial level this "value" might suggest. Faculty members may proclaim the library essential for teaching and research but fail to protect its budget allocation. Parents and school boards may value their school library media centers but be willing to reduce the number of media specialists before they will cut back on coaching staffing.

The phrase *exchange and transactions* denotes the act of obtaining a desired product or service by offering something in return. The concept of exchange is central to marketing because it implies that—by agreeing to the exchange—the participating parties see themselves as better off after the exchange. Transactions consist of a trade of values between two parties. The commodity exchanged for the product or service may not be financial, though it often is. Time and effort may be equally valuable commodities. The teacher or faculty member, valuing students who use the library, may give classroom time to the librarian, who provides an orientation to library resources and services. Many public libraries are finding that citizens are willing to pay for specialized reference service and document delivery if it is speedier and easier than doing the research and retrieval themselves. Academic libraries may offer document delivery services to affiliated users on a cost-recovery basis, gaining in goodwill while the user feels the time savings is worth the fee charged.

The market consists of all the potential customers sharing a particular need or want who might be willing and able to engage in exchange, which may be money, time, effort, or all three, to satisfy that need or want. Libraries typically deal with a complex market over which they have no authority and only indirect influence yet to which they must respond effectively in an anticipatory mode. Even when they do not seek direct cost recovery, libraries seek support and loyalty in exchange for user satisfaction. A marketer is one who engages in marketing—who analyzes and understands the market, develops a valued product or service for that market, communicates the offering, and monitors satisfaction. Effective collections librarians have an important role as marketers.

Marketing Mix

Borden introduced the phrase *marketing mix* in the late 1940s to describe the creative mix of product, price, place, and promotion (referred to as the Four Ps) that inform marketing. Kotler and Armstrong recognize that the Four Ps take the seller's view of the market and acknowledge the value of a Four Cs model (customer solution, customer cost, convenience, and communication) because it focuses more on the customer's perspective.[14] Librarians might benefit from thinking about the Four Cs first and then developing the Four Ps on that platform.

In the library context, *product* refers to both library collections (on-site and online) and services. Consumers make choices about products based on perceived functionality, utility, and reliability. The library examines the needs, demands, and wants of all segments of its public and the long-term requirements of the communities it serves, then designs a product—library services and resources—to meet those needs. Does the public library's community want more electronic resources, more copies of popular novels, more large-print materials, or fewer books and more journals? What services and types of contact do faculty members want from academic librarians? Can the library or the librarian modify current practices to satisfy the public better? Libraries face challenges building collections that balance formats, monographs and serials, and immediate needs and long-term mission. Developing and modifying the collections and services the library provides are what librarians do constantly, though they seldom think of these as marketing activities. The contact between librarian and community is an important product. The librarian should develop, monitor, and modify these liaison or outreach activities so that they become a valued service, for which the user community member is willing to exchange time, effort, and support.

Modifying either *price* or *place* modifies the product and influences demand. Librarians should understand these components and can adjust them, when appropriate, to increase the likelihood a patron will use and be satisfied with the library's collections and services. Price is what it costs the library user to acquire and access the library's products and services. Price can be measured in financial cost or the time or effort needed to obtain the product—that is, its convenience. Price is determined by a variety of factors, including competition, input costs, product identity, and the customer's perceived value of the product or services. The librarian's goal is to set the price of using the collection and services as low as is feasible, given the constraints placed on the library by its budget and staffing. Generally, traditional or routine services have no direct financial cost for primary constituents. Fees are seldom charged to borrow books and audio recordings, read journals, consult reference materials and staff members, or use the library's electronic resources. Some libraries charge users fees for receiving interlibrary loans, borrowing videos and best-sellers, requesting recalls, being placed on a waiting list, or using reference services extending beyond a certain length of time. Most libraries charge for photocopying and scanning services, printing, and retrieval and delivery to a home or office, though special libraries may be budgeted to absorb or subsidize these costs.

Collection development librarians have more influence on the time and effort cost to users than they do on fees charged. Librarians aim to lower users' perception of cost by saving their time and effort, and they assume that this will increase user satisfaction. The user's perception of the ideal library is one in which everything a user seeks is not just owned by the library but easy to locate and ready to use. Libraries' decreasing ability to develop collections that meet most local user expectations directly affects the cost to users in time and effort.

Waiting to use a computer workstation, waiting to access an online electronic resource because the library must limit simultaneous users, waiting for an item requested through interlibrary loan request to arrive, and waiting on a list for a popular title all can decrease user satisfaction. Collection librarians are always seeking to satisfy users within the library's mission, priorities, and budget. Being unable to locate and access a resource results in user frustration and perceived cost of using the library.

Place is the point at which the exchange of value for product and service occurs and may be called the *distribution channel*. It can be in the library, media center, bookmobile, via a website or social networking, or in the user's office, home, or classroom. The librarian's goal is to design a place, point of contact, or distribution system that allows patrons to find and access or get what they want—which may be information, an item, the collections librarian's attention—as quickly and conveniently as possible. The academic library may offer free or minimal cost delivery of locally owned materials to on-campus offices. The special librarian may deliver items directly to the executive or researcher who requested them. The librarian, regardless of library type, may provide users with mechanisms to recommend materials for purchase. Academic and special librarians may schedule office hours within the departments and divisions to facilitate contact with users. The goal is to make it as convenient as possible for librarians to provide services to their constituents. Selecting between print and electronic resources when making collection decisions has obvious implications about place. Users value the time saved when they can access electronic resources from home or office.

All liaison and outreach activities—all of the library's and librarians' communication activities and formats—can be considered *promotion*. Many users have very little idea of what librarians do or what they and the libraries in which they work offer. Promotional activities are the librarian's chance to inform and educate. Librarians should take every opportunity to publicize the library's collections and services along with their own availability. Information about the library should not focus only on collections and information resources. Librarians should keep constituents aware of all relevant library services, programs, and policies, regardless of the librarian or library unit offering them. Options might include current awareness services, document delivery services, library handouts tailored to specific class needs, online references services, workshops offered by the library, guest lectures by librarians, and library tours and demonstrations. Relevant policies may address collection development and management, gifts, Internet use, user privacy, course reserves, copyright, authorized access to electronic information resources, and borrowing privileges. Keeping constituents informed about all aspects of the library is an important part of liaison and out-reach activities.

Promotional activities are both formal and informal. Formal activities are structured and planned interactions, such as scheduled presentations and meet-ings, preparation of print materials, and creation and maintenance of online websites and social media. Informal promotion can occur every time a librarian comes in contact with a member of the library's community. Advances in tele-communication options and the growth of social media are expanding opportu-nities for library outreach and liaison activities. These include sending e-mail messages to individuals and targeted groups and creating library web pages, with online opportunities for comments and questions and forms for suggesting materials for purchase.

The concept of the marketing mix (product, price, plan, and promotion) has a long history. It is not without critics, who have seen it as too inward-looking without sufficient customer focus. In response, a more customer-centered ap-proach to marketing, called *customer relationship management* (CRM), has devel-oped. The basic idea is that building relationships with customers is more effective than mass marketing. On the for-profit side, CRM has evolved into automated systems that manage and coordinate information and activities within the business to provide a consistent and coherent image to the customer. Within libraries, CRM can be seen as a coordinated strategy to use the information gathered about users and nonusers to attract and keep them—to build confi-dence, trust, and loyalty. Haglund builds on the concept of CRM and explores *relationship marketing*, which "involves establishment, maintenance and even the enhancement of customer and other library-related relationships" developed over time.[15]

Kotler and Lee describe this customer-centered focus as assuming that the target audience is constantly asking the question "What's in it for me?"[16] This "WIIFM" phenomenon, they argue, motivates marketers to understand the wants and needs of target customers better than competitors do. CRM is perti-nent in libraries because it looks out to the user community, rather than inward at what librarians think about libraries and library offerings, to develop what Kendrick calls a "mutually beneficial relationship" that can be sustained over time and leads to advocacy and support as well as user satisfaction.[17] In other words, marketing is more effective if it begins with what the community sees and thinks about libraries. Understanding the community's perspective provides a better foundation for library marketing.

One important aspect of marketing is knowing the competition. Understand-ing the library's competition can come through market research—learning where users and potential users seek the products and services to satisfy their needs, wants, and desires, and why. Competition can be direct or indirect. Direct competition is when products or services that perform the same function compete against each other. For example, airlines are direct competitors. Indirect competition is when products or services are close substitutes for each other. Buses and trains are indirect competitors with airlines. Companies use several approaches to come out ahead of the competition. These include adjusting the marketing mix (e.g., lowering prices, improving the product or services, or increasing promotion), differentiating the product or service from that offered by competitors, fostering customer loyalty through brand recognition, and maintaining a customer-centered focus. As libraries better understand their competition, they can take similar steps.

Even without intentional market research, libraries are aware that they face competition from bookstores and from direct online information sources and search engines, particularly Google. More in-depth research seeks to determine why competitors are perceived as more appealing, attractive, efficient, and convenient. Librarians have determined that coffee shops and comfortable seating can make bookstores more appealing and, in response, have been adding both to libraries. In response to user perceptions that search engines like Google make finding information easier, libraries have implemented new and larger-scale discovery services, many of which provide a single search box. These approaches seek to improve the library's competitive edge and to improve its position in the information discovery and delivery market. Many librarian activities have been directed to positioning the library, its collections, and services in the user community's awareness more effectively. Librarians do not want users to think only of books when they think about libraries; they seek to promote the benefits the library offers through its collections and services and to differentiate libraries from their competitors.

Another approach to improving the library's position in the information and entertainment marketplace is what Dempsey calls getting "in the flow." He suggests that the library needs to coevolve with users' behaviors—which can be monitored through market research. As information and entertainment resources are increasingly integrated (e.g., Google, Netflix online delivery of rented movies, courseware management systems), librarians need to think more about getting into that flow of the user environment and less about getting users into the library either physically or virtually. The challenge is to do so authentically. Dempsey concludes his blog posting by stating that "integration of library resources should not be seen as an end in itself but as a means to better integration with the user environment." Intentional positioning is essential.[18]

Managing the Marketing Cycle

Managing a marketing effort involves four related components: conducting market research, developing a marketing plan, implementing that plan, and exercising control (figure 6-1). Successful marketing is a cycle, with each component interacting with and driving the others. The librarian identifies and researches user groups (public) to track their needs, wants, and demands, using direct examination of the user community and information from secondary sources—demographic data, research foci, curricula standards, emerging programs, and so forth. A marketing plan is developed on the basis of the determined marketing mix of product, price, place, and promotion. The library collections and associated services (the products) are configured to meet needs, wants, and demands within the terms and limits of the library's mission and financial resources. The librarian implements the plan, which involves promoting the product and associated services to the library's user community. Control is monitoring users' perceptions of and response to the marketing mix—and adjusting the mix and promotional activities to improve user response. This may involve additional market research, a revised marketing plan, and so on through the cycle.

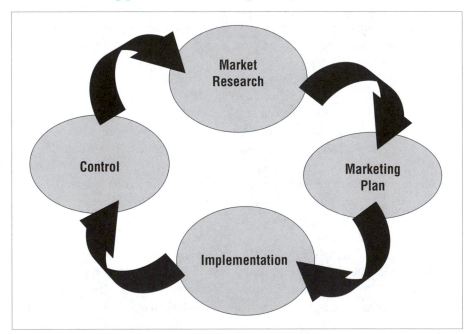

FIGURE 6-1 Interrelated aspects of marketing

Market Research

Marketing begins with market research. The American Marketing Association defines marketing research as

> the function that links the consumer, customer, and public to the marketer through information—information used to identify and define marketing opportunities and problems; generate, refine, and evaluate marketing actions; monitor marketing performance; and improve understanding of marketing as a process. Marketing research specifies the information required to address these issues, designs the method for collecting information, manages and implements the data collection process, analyzes the results, and communicates the findings and their implications.[19]

A librarian undertakes market research to define and understand the library's user community—its market. Market research establishes the overall size and structure of the community, identifies user characteristics, assesses needs of the users, and interprets trends. The terms *community analysis*, *needs assessment*, and *needs analysis* may be more familiar to librarians.[20] All are research through which librarians seek as much information as possible about their community or constituencies—users, potential users, supporters, and funding bodies.

MARKET SEGMENTATION

Market segmentation—dividing the market into categories in order to understand each one better—is one common strategy in market research. The library's user community can be understood in terms of its components, or segments. Librarians can gather secondary and primary data about each market segment and then develop collections and services that respond to these various user groups. The community can be segmented in many ways. Common approaches consider demographic characteristics (age, gender, income level, ethnic background, occupation, educational level), geographic characteristics (ability to travel to a library, the distance that must be traveled, residential or nonresidential status), past and present behavioral characteristics (extent and type of a patron's use—or nonuse—of the library in general or of specific collections and services), and sociological characteristics (socioeconomic class, lifestyle, personality, interests, opinions). All types of libraries can segment their user community for market research.

Fisher and Pride suggest the following demographic characteristics as useful in developing marketing strategies for public libraries:

- population density (rural, urban, suburban)
- population location (North, South, East, West)
- population size
- population growth pattern (e.g., stable, negative, positive)
- gender
- age, by ZIP code if possible
- family size
- family life cycle (e.g., bachelorhood, newly married, full nest, empty nest)
- income, by ZIP code if possible
- education
- race and nationality (ethnic groups), as defined by the U.S. census categories
- occupation
- number of public and private schools
- number of homeschooling families
- leading employers (industry types and number of employees)
- media outlets (local, regional, national)[21]

Another way to categorize public library users is suggested in the RUSA "Guidelines for Liaison Work in Managing Collections and Services" (not intended to be comprehensive):

- recreational readers
- civic groups
- government agencies
- businesspersons
- senior citizens
- persons with disabilities
- students
- teachers
- institutionalized populations
- non-English readers
- persons involved in literacy programs[22]

Chmelik stresses the importance of detailed information about the various market segments and their characteristics when one is developing and promoting collections and services in special libraries.[23] A corporate library might segment its users into researchers, marketers, sales people, legal staff, and management, with the aim of satisfying the information needs of each. Chmelik, a corporate librarian, determined that her most active user group consisted of individuals in middle to upper management who needed timely, concise responses to questions and had greater information needs at the beginning and end of each quarter. With this information in hand, she could look for the best matches with available resources and identify possible additions—and develop a marketing plan that would reach her target audience most effectively.

The academic library's community is often analyzed along the categories of faculty members, students, staff members, administrators, and external users. The first four groups usually are considered primary or affiliated users. External users, who might be segmented into categories such as alumni, citizens, and corporate researchers, are often called secondary or unaffiliated users. In many academic libraries, the same categories are employed when developing outreach and liaison activities. Faculty liaison responsibilities usually are divided between various librarians along subject or discipline lines. Outreach to students may be aligned according to subject foci or directed to undergraduate, graduate, and professional school student groups; on-campus and distance-education students; honors program students; and so on. How the market is segmented can determine how responsibilities are assigned. In addition, librarians may have liaison responsibilities with student government bodies and student organizations (ethnic, social, service, etc.). Information about each targeted group can aid the librarian in developing collections and services to meet that group's needs and interests.

School librarians usually think of their user community in terms of students, teachers, and—in some libraries—students' families. Students can be further segmented into, for example, age or grade groups, native English speakers and students for whom English is not their first language, or those with special needs or special abilities. Teachers can be categorized along similar lines, depending on their teaching responsibilities. School librarians might consider parent advisory groups and site councils, parent-teacher associations, school boards, and school administrators as part of the community for which their libraries are responsible and to whom they are accountable.

DATA GATHERING

The next step after defining the segments of the library's community is gathering data. Market research is conducted through analysis of secondary (existing) data and gathering and analysis of primary data. Many public sources provide useful secondary data. Census data can be a valuable resource. For example, the U.S. Census Bureau People and Household economic topics website (www .census.gov/people) provides information on ethnicity, income, education level, and other factors by city, town, county, state, or ZIP code. A useful tool for public libraries is the Public Library Geographic Database Mapping site, a research program of the Florida State University College of Communication and Information. The goal of this program is "to improve access to digital geographic information for library planning; and second, to create understanding of how systematic marketing can solve real-world library problems" by linking public library data and U.S. census data with a geographic information system.[24]

Bishop suggests the following information as useful for school librarians:

- enrollment
- grade levels
- ethnic makeup of the student body
- number of students whose second language is English
- socioeconomic status of the students
- number of students on free or reduced lunches
- dropout rate
- number of students enrolled in advanced courses
- percentage of students going to college
- special education population
- standardized test scores
- courses or units of study emphasized in the curriculum
- extracurricular activities available
- number of faculty members
- background of faculty members (Do the teachers live in local neighborhoods? Do they have advanced degrees? Do they have diverse backgrounds?)[25]

Many states have department of education websites that allow drilling down to specific schools and provide data about test scores, reading levels, percentage of students participating in free and reduced lunch cost programs, and more. Such data are often available in the school itself or from the central office of school systems. The school librarian should seek current information on special-needs students, including nonnative English speakers, attending the school.

Numerous secondary sources are available to help one understand local academic user communities. Academic institutions normally provide data on number of students by program and level, international students and scholars, faculty and researchers (by discipline, department, college), and staff. Many departments, research centers, and individual faculty members have web pages which, along with course catalogs, can be a resource for secondary information. Other sources are departmental promotional materials, newsletters, and reports, which may list new hires, faculty publications, and research grants.

Research projects conducted by other organizations are a rich source of secondary data. OCLC conducted two extensive market research projects that collected primary data exploring community perceptions of libraries and information resources.[26] For example, in 2005, 69 percent of Americans said books are the first thing that comes to mind when thinking about libraries. In 2010, this had increased to 75 percent and respondents identified the most important role of the library as providing books, videos, and music. These reports are a valuable source of data for all types of libraries and particularly useful because they break respondents down by age group: (e.g., teens, young adults, generation X, boomers, seniors).

A useful source of data from academic libraries is the work done by Ithaka S+R. This organization regularly surveys U.S. faculty members on various topics, including faculty perceptions of the roles and value of their institutional library and the roles the library plays in supporting their activities. The most recent research analyzed responses from more than 5,000 faculty.[27] Findings about the manner in which scholars use different types of materials in research and teaching, the way the changing digital environment affects scholars' discovery of and access to those materials, and scholars' perceptions of library collections in a changing environment can inform marketing activities in academic libraries.

An extensive research project conducted by the University of Rochester River Campus Libraries used anthropological methods to understand the work practices of undergraduates, graduate students, and faculty.[28] The goal was both to realign existing services and to develop new services to meet these behaviors. Other academic libraries also have studied the needs and wants of their communities.[29] Some studies look at characteristics of public library users and nonusers.[30] These studies use a variety of approaches to learn about users, including mining demographic data, conducting surveys and interviews, and observing users.

Primary data specific to the library's existing and potential user community must be collected by the library. This information is obtained through observational research, qualitative research (e.g., individual interviews and focus groups), and quantitative research (e.g., surveys). Some libraries collect data through their websites via one- or two-sentence surveys that simply ask "How are we doing?" and provide a text box for comments. Surveys range from the very simple to the very complex.

When librarians gather and analyze their own primary data, they seek specific answers that help guide collection development and pertinent services. Questions may address why an individual does or does not use a library resource, if a resource is easy to use or not, what the individual needed or wanted and was unable to obtain, how long the individual is willing to wait for the resource, and preferences for formats. Information gathered on these topics, in addition to guiding collection development, is useful in collection assessment. Information collected in these ways must be analyzed cautiously, however, because both user and researcher biases can skew results. User perceptions, memories, and understanding of collections and services may not always reflect reality. Researchers may have framed the questions in such a way that ambiguous responses result.

Academic librarians obtain information about their faculty members' needs and interests through conversations with individual faculty members and by attending departmental meetings. The lucky librarian has an established vehicle for communication—perhaps a departmental library committee or departmental faculty mailing list—through which information and requests for advice on general issues can be funneled. Less formal meetings, such as getting together with one or two faculty members over coffee or lunch, foster communication as well. The following list identifies information helpful for understanding academic user communities:

- faculty research interests and areas of concentration
- faculty language abilities
- grants and research centers
- number of faculty members and their ranks
- number of students and research assistants
- courses being taught and being planned
- special collection and resource needs
- requests for particular library services
- areas of crossover with other disciplines
- plans for future programs and degrees
- national standing of the department or program
- department's or program's priority in the institution

Academic librarians can begin by creating a list of faculty members in the subject areas for which they have collection development and management responsibilities. This list can be enhanced through the creation of faculty profiles and soliciting vitae. Many librarians regularly survey their constituents to learn their interest, needs, problems, and perceptions about library collections and services. Several examples of survey instruments and questionnaires are available.[31]

Figure 6-2 provides one example of a simple faculty questionnaire. This instrument collects information for the librarian's file on faculty members' interests. Information can be gathered through personal interaction instead of asking the individual to respond to a form. A librarian could expand the survey to

---

Faculty Profile

Name: _____

Office address: _____

E-mail address: _____

Phone: _____

Field(s) and geographical area(s) of interest:

_____

_____

Current research projects:

_____

_____

Courses currently taught or under development:

_____

_____

FIGURE 6-2 Simple faculty profile form

ask questions regarding perceptions about collections and services, both existing and desired, or ask these questions in a subsequent survey. A single survey
is never sufficient. Faculty members and their interests change, and librarians
need to resurvey their constituents periodically. A librarian should be cautious
about using a detailed form to collect data in an initial meeting. Faculty members
may be more receptive to survey questions that expand on the simple form after
they have developed rapport with the librarian. In addition to gathering data as
part of marketing research, this process can contribute to building relationships
between librarian and faculty members.

Using some form of user profile is beneficial in all types of libraries. In special libraries, profiles can help identify the needs and interests of specific library
and information center users by tracking individuals' research and development
activities and other areas of responsibility. School librarians may maintain profiles
for each teacher and his or her curriculum support needs. Turner and Riedling
propose creating what they call "instructional consultation assessment charts"
to track past interaction with teachers. The school librarian records the degree
of a teacher's involvement in several areas, including discussion of instructional
objectives and materials selection. Curriculum mapping also can provide data
to inform the development of teacher profiles. Another approach, suggested by
Langhorne, is to enter data into a spreadsheet that tracks monthly media center
use by teachers, their classes, activities, level of instructional support, and dates.
Not only does this help to develop a teacher profile, it can be correlated with the
curriculum map and local educational standards.[32]

A librarian's success in making and maintaining good user community relations depends on both enthusiasm and initiative. Only through constant attention can a librarian gain and supply the information needed to make liaison and
outreach work meaningful. The approaches librarians use to learn about their
constituents and their needs and interests vary with the situation. Even the most
dedicated librarian may run into a brick wall with some teachers and faculty
members, who fail to respond to any library initiative. Similar challenges exist
for school librarians. In these situations, the librarian should continue promotional activities, even if the communication remains one-directional.

Focus groups or group interviews are another way to gather data about users'
perceptions, values, and opinions. They are effective in creating an opportunity
to collect data from small numbers of people in an informal and relaxed setting.
Focus groups are led by a moderator and range in size from six to twelve participants. A focus group session is usually around two hours and may be shorter,
depending on the age of participants, the area of interest, and the time participants have available. Focus groups are a form of qualitative research. Focus

groups are appropriate for all types of libraries and often prove more informative than surveys when working with children and young people.[33]

The library itself can provide data on the ability of the existing collection to meet current needs. Such information can be found in interlibrary loan requests, circulation activity, e-resource use statistics, reference questions (answered and unanswered), and purchase suggestions from users. Library automation has the potential to produce a wealth of constituent use data that can guide collection development; however, not all systems live up to this promise, nor do librarians always make use of the available information. If the automated system is able to correlate use by various user categories (e.g., activity by adult and juvenile users in a public library or by student, staff, faculty, or unaffiliated users in an academic library), the librarian obtains hard data on market needs and wants that can help develop a responsive collection. Nackerud and colleagues at the University of Minnesota Libraries used individual student identifiers, called affinity strings, to investigate how students use the library.[34] Student privacy was protected while various demographic data were gathered, including level of student, college of enrollment, major, ethnicity, and GPA, which were then correlated with use. Use statistics should be weighed against categories of materials for which such data are not collected, such as noncirculating materials and those used on-site.

Developing and Implementing a Marketing Plan

After conducting market research, the next steps are planning the products (collections) and services that will meet the needs and expectations of the user community and then implementing these decisions. Kendrick defines an effective marketing plan as a process that

> will identify what drives users and build products and services around their needs; enable a highly differentiated service, not 'one size fits all'; create value and inspiration to use the library; and do all this with as little cost as possible. It will provide a process to ensure maximum use of the public libraries by the public, attract non-users and develop loyalty behaviours in existing users, and will clearly influence attitudes towards the library—our 'offer' as the best, the winning offer (in terms of use of time) in the scramble for their attention.[35]

This description applies to all types of libraries in their goal to understand and serve their communities.

The marketing plan is sometimes called the marketing strategy. Marketing plans are developed to introduce something new or fix an existing problem. In formulating a marketing plan, the library develops its market mix and marketing strategy, sets goals, and determines how to measure success in reaching them. A collections librarian cannot determine the marketing mix in isolation from the library's mission and goals but may have responsibility for developing portions of the mix and marketing strategy that relate to collections and associated services and also for developing a portion of the promotional plan.

Though libraries are more frequently developing library-wide marketing plans, collections librarians need to think about marketing in the context of their own responsibilities and goals. An individual librarian will not undertake something as large as a two-year campaign to introduce a new library brand and change the perceptions of the entire user community but can develop a marketing plan to increase awareness of an existing collection, resource, or service or introduce new ones.

A marketing plan contains several elements that cumulate in a strategy for action and methods for measuring effectiveness. For example, a marketing plan addressing the availability of a new collection of e-books might consist of the following:

- executive summary
- purpose, including a brief description of the product (e-books) to be introduced
- situational analysis of strengths, weaknesses, opportunities, and threats the library faces in the context of this e-content
- customer analysis, market segmentation, and target groups for the e-books
- competitor analysis and how the library's e-book offering is differentiated from competitors'
- goals of the marketing initiative
- marketing strategies (in the context of the marketing mix) with emphasis on the central marketing message and how the e-books will be promoted, including distribution channels and intended audiences (market segment) and objectives
- implementation plan detailing a timeline for the marketing campaign, the library staff who will be involved, and the budget for the campaign
- means to measure success in achieving the marketing initiative goals
- assignment of responsibility for assessing the success and date at which this will be done[36]

Assembling a marketing plan can sound overwhelming. As Dempsey writes, "The key to not panicking is to realize that, while you do need to go through every step in this cycle, you can make the process as big or as small as you want to by choosing which target market to work on."[37] The school librarian might decide that special education teachers are the right market for a particular initiative. The academic librarian might target undergraduate science majors or newly hired faculty. Marketing also can be made more manageable by limiting the product to be marketed. In the marketing plan outlined above, the product is limited to a new collection of e-books. This could be further narrowed by selecting teen readers as the target market. Even if the librarian is not presenting the plan for wide review within the library, its success depends on including all the elements.

Once a marketing plan is developed, it is implemented. This is the process through which the librarian turns plans into actions that will accomplish the marketing goals. If the plan has been carefully developed and strategies are well conceived, implementation should be straightforward.

Control

Control is performance measurement and the fourth element in the marketing cycle. In this phase, the librarian monitors and analyzes results and takes corrective actions where necessary. Developing a marketing program is pointless if the resulting performance is not measured. Marketing control involves analyzing where the original plan is falling short and then developing and implementing steps to correct problems. The range of techniques available for measuring the extent to which a library's collection satisfies its user community is expansive; see chapter 7 for a fuller review.

Put briefly, whereas control in the for-profit sector usually focuses on sales, profit, and market share, the control phase in libraries focuses on users and their activities and perceptions. Use statistics are an obvious measure. If the goal was to increase use of a particular product (e.g., e-books), the collections librarian should be able to compare use before and after implementing the marketing plan. If the goal was to develop better relationships with teachers, the school librarian might count personal contacts before and after implementing a marketing plan that focuses on the services provided. Surveys and focus groups may be used to assess satisfaction. The goal is to use these performance measurements to determine if the marketing plan is successful or if it needs to be revised. Performance measurement should occur as an integral part of working with the library's user community.

Liaison and Outreach Activities

Building relationships that connect users to the library, enhance their satisfaction, and develop loyalty and advocacy is an important responsibility of librarians. Liaison activities and community outreach are not only essential to successful collection development and management, they are both fulfilling and fun. This part of collection development work places the librarian at the heart of the community. As Gall observes, "Savvy librarians have long known the advantages of building relationships with library users, ensuring their satisfaction and encouraging not only return business but also their support with funding agencies."[38] The librarian has the chance to satisfy needs, respond to requests, answer questions, and solve problems. Helping a library's users, potential users, funding agencies, and governing bodies understand the library, its collections and services, and the constraints in which it operates benefits both the community and the library. Many liaison and outreach activities are promotional in the sense that they aim to increase awareness of the library, its collections and services, and the individual librarian.

Promoting one's self is an important aspect of outreach and liaison activities. Gall writes about using your personal brand to promote like a rock star. Ruddock explains,

> It is not just your organization and services that need promoting: you also need to promote yourself and for many of the same reasons. This isn't about boasting about how great you are, but about making people aware of your unique skills and expertise, so they can call on them as necessary.
>
> Just as your users won't know how your service can help them unless you specifically tell them, people won't know what you personally have to offer unless you make it obvious. In the workplace, you as a person can inspire trust and reliance in a way that your library or archive as a service can never do.[39]

The remainder of this section addresses outreach and liaison activities in various types of libraries; many of the strategies suggested can be used by all librarians regardless of the type of library in which they work. They serve to increase both the visibility of the librarian and the library's collections and services.

Public Libraries

The need for and value of public library marketing has been the topic of numerous recent books, particularly as a means of fostering advocacy.[40] The goal is to get public libraries into the lives of their users and potential users by identifying market segments and targeting the message to these various segments, based on their needs, wants, and desires. Kendrick stresses the need to identify the factors that will influence users and competitors, then to develop or identify existing products and services that are appropriate for user segments, and only then to develop the appropriate means to reach these segments. Some forms of communication are targeted and some are appropriate for general promotional activities. The following are representative options:

- Prepare bookmarks and handouts promoting specific collections, information resources, and services.
- Publish library newsletters or new acquisitions lists, which can be targeted to specific user groups.
- Provide public service announcements.
- Issue press releases.
- Prepare displays promoting new acquisitions and resources on a particular topic.
- Give booktalks in classes, in the library, to citizens' groups, and elsewhere.
- Create a library website (or subject- and age-specific sites) that promotes collections and services.
- Make book and journal request forms easily available online and at service desks.
- Participate in library Friends group meetings.
- Attend meetings of citizens' interest groups (e.g., League of Women Voters, Chamber of Congress, Urban League).

Special Libraries

Harrington suggests that librarians in special libraries need to supplement more familiar approaches with different techniques to reach their constituents. He emphasizes personal contact and recommends hand-delivering the book, article, or research report to the individual who requested it. Marketing the special library is about fostering personal relationships. Peros calls this person-to-person marketing and stresses the value of getting out of the library and "walking the halls," where every encounter with an individual builds and strengthens the relationship between librarian and user.[41]

Special librarians should participate in company, business, or agency departmental meetings and attend company social events. They can involve others when making decisions about the collection and services. This does not need to be a standing committee; it can consist of people who are interested in the issue being discussed. Keeping track of who is interested in which topics can prepare the special librarian to alert individuals about research or industry news that may be significant in their work. Some methods, such as a weekly e-mail list of new materials added, are equally valuable promotional vehicles for special librarians.

Bridges developed a list of suggestions for a hospital library, many of which are appropriate for other types of special libraries:

- Develop a brand (logo or slogan or both) and use it on all communications from the library—all forms, coversheets on articles, and so forth.
- Develop a flyer that explains library services and provides contact information.
- Attend informational meetings and ask how the librarian can support projects.
- Deliver items in person.
- Host brown-bag discussions and coffee hours on focused topics.
- Make presentations at regular meetings of various groups.
- Form partnerships, for example, with the information technology department.
- Host a vendor fair and invite companies to demonstrate new technologies.
- Ensure that the library is included in new employee orientation.
- Celebrate accomplishments and successes of others.[42]

School Library Media Centers

School librarians can promote school library media centers with many of the same approaches already suggested. Burkman identifies target groups for school librarians' promotional activities as administrators, teachers, students, parents, and the general community and notes that each audience requires a different strategy. She suggests that school librarians share data about circulation, numbers of students and classes using the library, and collaborative projects twice a year with school administrators. Schmidt and Reeve discuss the value of using data to foster advocacy on the part of various constituencies. Worley proposes assembling a portfolio that documents and can serve to promote the activities and contributions the library makes to the curriculum and to school life more broadly.[43]

AASL's *Empowering Learners: Guidelines for School Library Media Programs* makes clear that outreach is a key responsibility of school librarians and states, "The school library media program is guided by an advocacy plan that builds support from decision makers who affect the quality of the SLMP [school library media program]."[44] Helping administrators understand the value of school library media centers and trained librarians should be an important goal of marketing. Providing local data on use and information drawn from research can provide the tools for principals to advocate support for school library media centers, adequate budgets, and professional staff. For example, research by Lance and Loertscher has consistently demonstrated that the quality of the school library media center strongly correlates with student achievement and higher test scores, regardless of socioeconomic factors, teacher-pupil ratio, or amount spent per pupil.[45] The Library Research Service provides links to numerous school library impact studies.[46]

As appropriate, school librarians can try the following activities to promote collections and services:

- Participate in teachers' meetings.
- Be in the school library media center during school open houses and parent-teacher meetings.
- Become involved in the parent-teacher organization, site council, and similar venues.
- Hold book fairs a few times a year for parents and students.
- Celebrate National Book Week or Library Week.
- Create reading motivation programs for students.[47]
- Schedule regular classroom visits and collaborate with teachers in other ways.
- Prepare bookmarks and handouts promoting specific collections, information resources, and services.
- Prepare library newsletters or new acquisitions lists and distribute them electronically or in print to teachers.
- Prepare displays and bulletin boards promoting new acquisitions and resources on a particular topic.

- Give booktalks in classes.
- Create a library website that promotes collections and services.
- Make book and journal request forms easily available.
- Encourage visits to and use of the library media center by parents, administrators, elected officials, and other stakeholders.
- Form a "Friends of the School Library" program.
- Attend teacher and other school- and district-based meetings.[48]

Academic Libraries

Liaison activities in academic libraries encompass all contacts between librarians and individuals, academic departments and units, research centers, and committees within the institution and with individuals and organizations outside the college or university. Successful liaison activities provide a context in which to apply all other collection development and management skills. Liaisons promote the library's collections and services, provide improved visibility for the library, and increase advocacy. As when promoting school library media centers, one way to increase support for academic libraries is to demonstrate a correlation between academic library use and student success.[49] Effective liaison work gathers data about the user community and enhances a librarian's ability to build responsive collections. Todaro's *Power of Personal Persuasion* speaks to the important role that individual academic librarians can take in reaching out to user communities and offers tools to do so.[50]

Liaison work as defined in RUSA's "Guidelines for Liaison Work in Managing Collections and Services" sounds remarkably like marketing. This document explains that liaisons in academic libraries should "identify and define various constituencies (students, faculty, staff, and others) so that all can understand expectations of service . . . [and] involve clientele in collection services and issues as much as possible, in order to ensure that the materials satisfy the clients' needs and that the clients are aware of the materials and services available to them."[51]

Liaison activities are pervasive in academic libraries. A 2007 ARL survey reported that all but one of the sixty-six responding libraries provided liaison services to academic departments in their universities and that most provided outreach to faculty of all types, graduate assistants and other graduate students, administrative staff, and undergraduates.[52] A librarian in an academic library cannot develop and manage a collection without knowing the user community.

Faculty members are an important target or market segment because they depend on the library for research, give course assignments that use library resources, and can be important campus supporters of the library. Shen observes that personal connections are "especially critical in achieving library-faculty collaboration since ultimately all institutional strategies must rely on individual efforts."[53] Knowing and being known by faculty are important for success.

Each library liaison typically interacts with one or more groups of professors, usually defined by their affiliation with specific teaching departments or programs that parallel the subjects or disciplines for which the librarian is responsible. Liaisons assigned interdisciplinary responsibilities, including area studies, face a greater challenge in identifying who their constituents are and in reaching them. No matter their subject assignment, liaisons cannot depend solely on the knowledge they bring to the job. They must seek out their faculty user community and learn about them. By learning as much as possible about the specialties, needs, and interests of their assigned faculties, liaisons increase their ability to develop a collection that serves these specialties, needs, and interests. In addition to following individual faculty member's requirements and expectations, the liaison needs a collective understanding of the department's needs to balance collection development activities within this larger view.

Liaisons in academic libraries can assemble an informational packet of materials to give to each faculty member, ideally in person. This might include a collection development policy, information about services, relevant guides and bibliographies, and an information sheet about the liaison. E-mail is used frequently to share information. In addition, academic librarians can try some of the following faculty liaison activities:

- Attend academic departmental meetings and special events and let people know they are representing the library.
- Seek opportunities for collaborative teaching projects, research, and grants.
- Participate in university orientation programs for new faculty, students, teaching assistants, research assistants, and international and graduate students.
- Send notes of recognition when faculty members get grants and awards.
- Audit classes.
- Meet with new faculty members within their first academic term and tell them about the library collections and services.

- Meet regularly with department chairs and library-faculty liaison groups.
- Partner with faculty and other support units (e.g., writing centers, student services) on campus.
- Create a personal page or pages within the library's website with contact information and details about the liaison's areas of responsibility and interest.
- Develop a mailing list and send regular announcements of library activities, acquisitions, and events of interest.
- Post news and information on the library's web pages or in the library's newsletter, or both.[54]
- Create electronic discussion lists, blogs, and RSS feeds to share pertinent information about new resources, recent acquisitions, and programs.

Reaching out to and building relationships with college and university students can present different challenges. Possible market segments might be student category, program of study, affiliation with social and service organizations, and more. Age is seen as a powerful way to segment the student population in higher education. Berk writes that characteristics of the net generation (those born roughly between 1982 and 2003) have significant implications for connecting with and teaching these students, whereas Selwyn advises against making generalization about these "digital natives."[55] Cummings suggests partnering with campus organization and services (e.g., residency service, freshman orientation, athletics department) to target messages to various market segments.[56]

Benefits and Hazards of Liaison and Outreach Activities

A significant benefit that comes through liaison and outreach work is the information necessary to develop a collection that meets the needs of constituents. Other benefits accrue over time. An academic librarian armed with detailed knowledge about a department's programs, the research interests of faculty members, and the directions in which they are moving can make a case for appropriate support when library materials budgets are allocated. Developing public library collections and services that respond to and satisfy users builds community advocacy. Knowing the particular foci of special library users positions the librarian to respond appropriately and plan for the future. School librarians can position themselves to partner with teachers in class projects and contribute to improved student performance. The librarian has information at hand to explain needs and justify the resources required to meet them.

Effective liaison work saves time. Knowledge about individuals' interests prepares the librarian to contact the appropriate person for advice on particular topics. Knowing who specializes in decorative arts in the art department means that neither the librarian's nor other faculty members' time is wasted getting opinions on the value of a possible acquisition. Knowing the specific information needs of special library users means the librarian can anticipate and be proactive in providing resources. Developing teacher profiles and tracking student demographics help the school librarian develop responsive collections.

Ongoing liaison and outreach work gives librarians opportunities to establish credibility and trust. They can demonstrate their subject knowledge, understanding of the literature, and expertise in library activities through consistent, frequent contact. Individuals come to value the librarians' judgment and opinions. Good relationships with individual users and user groups are indispensable when subscriptions are cancelled or funds redirected to other collection areas. If the librarian has kept the library's community informed about pricing trends and library budgets, the need to cancel subscriptions will not come as a surprise. If the user community is aware of trends in the e-book marketplace and growing user interest in their availability through the library, increased expenditures for their access will be understood. A productive relationship means that the librarian is not seen simply as the bearer of bad news but as someone who understands user needs and will continue to work, despite constraints, to meet them.

Over time, librarians may come to personify the library to their constituents. Effectively handled, the relationship between librarian and users can enhance the library's image and reputation. Public librarians become a felt presence in their communities because they attend community meetings, sponsor exhibits and programs, provide reading lists, and serve on the boards of community and government organizations. Library professionals are seen as peers and colleagues by faculty members throughout the academic institution. Departments call on them to represent the library on departmental committees, contribute to accreditation studies, and sometimes participate in developing new courses, programs, and grant proposals. Teachers ask the school librarian to speak to their classes and help them with reference and curriculum needs. Schools and community groups invite public librarians to give booktalks. Users may begin to contact the librarian for help in solving any problems they perceive with the library, its collections, and services.

Strong personal relationships between librarians and constituents can also lead to a troubling pitfall—being perceived as a personal librarian. Academic liaisons must be cautious not to become connected more to academic departments than to the library and placed in a position in which department concerns take precedence over library priorities. Librarians should treat all members of the user community equally. A too-personal relationship between the school librarian and one or two teachers can be off-putting for other teachers. Perceptions of preferential treatment have negative consequences in fostering broad-based communication and outreach.

A parallel hazard is unreasonable or inappropriate requests by users for services or information the librarian cannot or should not provide. Some individuals and constituent groups can become extremely demanding, pressuring the librarian for personal services, special treatment, and purchases of out-of-scope materials. Again, the risk is becoming a personal or private librarian, caught between personal demands and library obligations. A fine line exists between supporting user needs and demands and allegiance to the library.

At the heart of successful liaison and outreach activities are excellent interpersonal and communication skills. Librarians need to work at building good working relationships with all members of their community. They must be skilled in dealing with demanding and unreasonable constituents as well as those who understand the librarian's responsibilities to the library. Librarians need to make these responsibilities clear while emphasizing their role in supporting users' needs and interests.

Social Media

A chapter on library marketing, liaison, and outreach would not be complete without a section on social media. The use of social media has become pervasive in libraries. Polger and Okamoto surveyed academic librarians in 2011 and found that 70 percent of respondents were using social media to reach library users and nonusers. Findings from a 2012 *Library Journal* survey of public libraries indicated that 86 percent of these libraries were using some form of social media.[57]

Numerous articles have been written about libraries using technologies such as Facebook, MySpace, Twitter, blogs, YouTube, Instagram, and even Pinterest.[58] Second Life, once trendy, seems to have faded from the library environment. Based on what librarians are reporting, libraries seek to use social media as a vehicle for communicating with users and other stakeholders, improving service, building relationships, and promoting the library, its collections, and services.

Research into the success of social media is sketchy and inconsistent. Few authors offer evidence to support claims of success. One persistent problem with library use of social media is a lack of clear goals and the absence of meaningful and validated measures of success.[59] Bodnar and Doshi observe that some libraries engage in social media simply because doing so "makes the library dynamic, modern, relevant, and vibrant." A study by Wan, which examined 159 active Facebook pages maintained by ARL member libraries in 2009, used number of "friends" as an indicator of popularity or ability to attract an audience and found that 67.2 percent of the pages had fewer than two hundred friends. If the goal of these libraries was simply to reach a large number of users, they were not particularly effective.[60]

Social media should be considered one of many communication channels (e.g., signage, press releases, newsletter, bookmarks) available to libraries. They should be used within the context of a marketing plan and strategically targeted at appropriate market segments. Connell found that some students resent a library or librarian's intrusion into their private space and that "a one-size-fits-all model does not work when it comes to using social network sites for library outreach."[61] A marketing plan sets goals and a means to measure success in reaching them. If one goal is increased use of a resource, the library should be able to measure use before and after introducing a particular social site as a marketing strategy. If a marketing goal is to strengthen relationships with teachers or faculty and the strategy is a blog, the librarian should be able determine if a particular blog post results in increased requests for consultation, classroom instruction, or some other service that is the focus of the message. Social media can be part of an effective marketing strategy if librarians clearly understand why they are using them and what the expected results are.

CASE STUDY

River City Public Library is located in a small town in New England. The library shares a facility with the county historical society, and the two agencies collaborate in the services they provide. The building has a large room that can be used for instruction and is available for local organizations' meetings. Both agencies are heavily used by genealogists, who consult materials in the library (microfilmed newspapers, local history books, city directories, etc.) and in the historical society, which has copies of county court records back to the early 1800s, extensive archives of personal papers, and a locally created database of birth and death certificates for the county. Both agencies track the number of visitors and the nature of the research they are doing or the type of reference questions asked. They find that they and their staff members are explaining the same genealogical research techniques and resources several times each week.

River City has a local chapter of the state genealogical society, and this group has occasionally met in the library/historical society meeting room. The public library has recently started a subscription to an online database that provides access to an extensive collection of resources of interest to genealogists. Amanda, director of the public library, and Luke, director of the historical society, are eager to work together to introduce this new resource to the community and have each allocated $500 (a combined budget of $1,000) for this purpose. Amanda has agreed to prepare a first draft of a marketing plan that she and Luke will review and revise together.

Activity

Develop the first draft of a marketing plan. Explain the purpose of the plan. Note that you might not want to limit the purpose to introducing the new online resource. You might wish to include its availability within a larger initiative. You will not be able to conduct the marketing research, but you should suggest how the market might be segmented and the type of data to be collected. Suggest the target market(s). Identify the goals of the initiative. Propose marketing strategies and develop an implementation plan. Develop methods to measure success of the initiative and assign responsibilities for doing the evaluation.

Notes

1. Terry Kendrick, *Developing Strategic Marketing Plans That Really Work: A Toolkit for Public Libraries* (London: Facet, 2006), 9.

2. Sharon L. Baker and Karen L. Wallace, *The Responsive Public Library: How to Develop and Market a Winning Collection*, 2nd ed. (Englewood, CO: Libraries Unlimited, 2002), 3.

3. Michael A. Germano and Shirley M. Stretch-Stephenson, "Strategic Value Planning for Libraries," *Bottom Line: Managing Library Finances* 25, no. 2 (2012): 82.

4. Manuel D. Lopez, "A Guide for Beginning Bibliographers," *Library Resources and Technical Services* 13 no. 4 (Fall 1969): 462–70; Susan L. Fales, ed., *Guide for Training Collection Development Librarians*, Collection Management and Development Guides 8 (Chicago: American Library Association, 1996); Walter Alwyn Briscoe, *Library Advertising: "Publicity" Methods for Public Libraries, Library-Work with Children, Rural Library Schemes, &c., with a Chapter on the Cinema and Library* (London: Grafton; New York, H. W. Wilson, 1921).

5. Dinesh K. Gupta, Christie Koontz, and Daisy McAdam, "In Search of Marketing Excellence in Libraries: The IFLA International Marketing Award," *IFLA Journal* 36 no. 2 (2010): 176–83; Library Leadership and Management Association, "LLAMA/PRMS 'Best of Show Awards'," www.ala.org/llama/awards/prxchange _bestofshow; American Association of Law Libraries, "Excellence in Marketing Award," www.aallnet.org/main-menu/Member-Resources/AALLawards/award -eim.html; American Library Association, "John Cotton Dana Library Public Relations Award," www.ala.org/awardsgrants/john-cotton-dana-library-public -relations-award-0.

6. Amerian Library Association, "@ your library, The Campaign for America's Libraries," www.ala.org/advocacy/advleg/publicawareness/campaign@yourlibrary/ aboutyourlibrary; American Library Association, "Advocating in a Tough Economy Toolkit" (updated Oct. 8, 2012), www.ala.org/advocacy/advleg/advocacyuniversity/ toolkit; *The Campaign for America's Libraries @ your library Toolkit for Academic and Research Libraries: Messages, Ideas, and Strategies for Promoting the Value of Our Libraries and Librarians in the 21st Century* (Chicago: American Library Association, 2007).

7. Christie Koontz, "Promotion Is Not the Same as Marketing," *Marketing Library Services* 20, no. 1 (Jan./Feb. 2006): 1–7.

8. Charles B. Osburn, "Toward a Reconceptualization of Collection Development," *Advances in Library Administration and Organization* 2 (1983): 188.

9. Alan R. Andreasen and Philip Kotler, *Strategic Marketing for Nonprofit Organizations*, 7th ed. (Upper Saddle River, NJ: Prentice-Hall, 2008); Kotler and Andreasen, *Principles of Marketing*, 15th ed. (Upper Saddle River, NJ: Prentice-Hall, 2014).

10. Philip Kotler and Karen F. A. Fox, *Strategic Marketing for Educational Institutions*, 2nd ed. (Englewood Cliffs, NJ: Prentice-Hall, 1995).

11. John Law, "Observing Student Researchers in Their Native Habitat," presentation at the VALA [Victorian Association for Library Automation] 2008 Conference: Libraries: Changing Spaces, Virtual Places, 14th Biennial Conference and Exhibition Feb. 5–7, 2008, Melbourne, Australia, www.valaconf.org.au/vala2008/ papers2008/45_Law_Final.pdf.

12. Frederick R. Reichheld, Robert G. Markey, and Christopher Hopton, "The Loyalty Effect: The Relationship between Loyalty and Profits," *European Business Journal* 12, no. 3 (2000): 137.

13. Svein Ottar Olsen, "Comparative Evaluation and the Relationship between Quality, Satisfaction, and Repurchase Loyalty," *Journal of the Academy of Marketing Science* 30, no. 3 (Summer 2002): 240–49; Anders Gustafsson, Michael D. Johnson, and Inger Roos, "The Effects of Customer Satisfaction, Relationship Commitment

Dimensions, and Triggers on Customer Retention," *Journal of Marketing* 69, no. 4 (Oct. 2005): 210–18.

14. Neil H. Borden, "The Concept of the Marketing Mix," in *Science in Marketing*, ed. George Schwartz, 386–97 (New York: Wiley, 1965); Kotler and Armstrong, *Principles of Marketing*.

15. Lotta Haglund, "Relationship Marketing Can Stimulate Library Development," presentation at Positioning the Profession: The Tenth International Congress on Medical Librarianship, Brisbane, Australia, Aug. 31–Sept. 4, 2009, http://espace .uq.edu.au/eserv/UQ:179791/n5_2_Thurs_Haglund_212.pdf, 1.

16. Philip Kotler and Nancy Lee, *Marketing in the Public Sector: A Roadmap for Improved Performance* (Upper Saddle River, NJ: Wharton School Publishing, 2007).

17. Kendrick, *Developing Strategic Marketing Plans*, 121.

18. Lorcan Dempsey, "In the Flow," *Lorcan Dempsey's Weblog* (blog), June 24, 2005, http://orweblog.oclc.org/archviesarchives/000688.html.

19. American Marketing Association, "Definition of Marketing" (approved Oct. 2004), www.marketingpower.com/aboutama/pages/definitionofmarketing.aspx.

20. David Nicholas, *Assessing Information Needs: Tools, Techniques, and Concepts for the Information Age* (London: Aslib Information Management, 2000), provides a concise introduction to data collection methods for user studies.

21. Patricia H. Fisher and Marseille M. Pride, *Blueprint for Your Library Marketing Plan: A Guide to Help You Survive and Thrive* (Chicago: American Library Association, 2006), 14.

22. Reference and User Services Association, Liaison with Users Committee, "Guidelines for Liaison Work in Managing Collections and Services" (1992, rev. 2001; approved by the RUSA Board of Directors, June 2001; rev. 2009 by the Liaison with User Committee of CODES; approved by the RUSA Standards and Guidelines Committee, Jan. 2010; approved by the RUSA Board of Directors, Mar. 2010), www.ala.org/rusa/files/resources/guidelines/liaison-guidelines -3.pdf.

23. Samantha Chmelik, "Market Research for Libraries," *Information Outlook* 10, no. 2 (Feb. 2006): 23–25.

24. "About GeoLib," Florida State University College of Information, www.geolib.org.

25. Kay Bishop, *The Collection Program in Schools: Concepts and Practices*, 5th ed. (Santa Barbara, CA: Libraries Unlimited, 2013), 23.

26. Cathy De Rosa, *Perceptions of Libraries and Information Resources: A Report to the OCLC Membership* (Dublin, OH: OCLC, 2005), www.oclc.org/content/dam/oclc/ reports/pdfs/Percept_all.pdf; De Rosa, *Perceptions of Libraries, 2010: Context and Community: A Report to the OCLC Membership* (Dublin, OH: OCLC, 2011), www.oclc.org/content/dam/oclc/reports/2010perceptions/2010perceptions_all _singlepage.pdf.

27. Ross Housewright, Roger C. Schonfeld, and Kate Wulfson, *Ithaka S+R US Faculty Survey 2012* (New York: Ithaka S+R, 2013), www.sr.ithaka.org/research -publications/us-faculty-survey-2012.

28. Susan Gibbons, "Techniques to Understand the Changing Needs of Library Users," *IFLA Journal* 39, no. 2 (2013): 162–67; Nancy Fried Foster and Susan Gibbons, *Studying Students: The Undergraduate Research Project at the University of Rochester* (Chicago: Association of College and Research Libraries, 2007).

29. See, for example, Lizah Ismail, "What Net Generation Students Really Want: Determining Library Help-Seeking Preferences of Undergraduates," *Reference Services Review* 38, no. 1(2010): 10–27; Diane Mizrachi, "Undergraduates' Academic Information and Library Behaviors: Preliminary Results," *Reference Services Review* 38, no. 4 (2010): 571–80; Melissa Kalpin Prescott and Jerilyn R. Veldof, "A Process Approach to Defining Services for Undergraduates," *portal: Libraries and the Academy* 10, no. 1 (Jan. 2010): 29–56; Lawrence T. Paretta and Amy Catalano, "What Students Really Do in the Library: An Observational Study," *Reference Librarian* 54, no. 2 (2013): 157–67.

30. See, for example, Sei-Ching Joanna Sin, "Modeling the Impact of Individuals' Characteristics and Library Service Levels on High School Students' Public Library Usage: A National Analysis," *Library and Information Science Research* 34, no. 3 (July 2012): 228–37; Sei-Ching Joanna Sin and Kyung-Sun Kim, "Use and Non-Use of Public Libraries in the Information Age: A Logistic Regression Analysis of Household Characteristics and Library Services Variables," *Library and Information Science Research* 30, no. 3 (2008): 207–15; Karla B. Collins and Carol A. Doll, "Resource Provisions of a High School Library Collection," *School Library Research* 25 (2012), www.ala.org/aasl/sites/ala.org.aasl/files/content/aaslpubsandjournals/slr/ vol15/SLR_Resource_Provisions_V15.pdf; Melanie Kimball et al., "Youth, Public Libraries, and the Internet: Part Three: Who Visits the Public Library, and What Do They Do There?" *Public Libraries* 46. No. 6 (Nov./Dec. 2007): 52–58; Andrea C. Japzon and Hongmian Gong, "A Neighborhood Analysis of Public Library Use in New York City," *Library Quarterly* 75, no. 4 (2005): 446–63.

31. Roger E. Stelk, Paul Metz, and Lane Rasmussen, "Departmental Profiles: A Collection Development Aid," *C&RL News* 54, no. 4 (Apr. 1993): 196–99; Doreen Kopycinski and Kimberley Sando, *User Surveys in College Libraries*, CLIP Note 38 (Chicago: Association of College and Research Libraries, 2007); Catherine E. Pasterczyk, "Checklist for the New Selector," *C&RL News* 49, no. 7 (July/Aug. 1988): 434–35.

32. Philip M. Turner and Ann Marlow Riedling, *Helping Teachers Teach: A School Library Media Specialist's Role*, 3rd ed. (Westport, CT: Libraries Unlimited, 2003); Mary Jo Langhorne, "Using Data in the School Library," in *Toward a 21st-Century School Library Media Program*, ed. Ester Rosenfeld and David V. Loertscher, 367–72 (Lanham, MD: Scarecrow, 2007).

33. Melissa L. Becher and Janice L. Flug, "Using Student Focus Groups to Inform Library Planning and Marketing," *College and Undergraduate Libraries* 12, no. 1/2 (2005): 1–18; Nancy Everhart and Kay Bishop, "Using Focus Groups with Young People," *Knowledge Quest* 30, no. 3 (Jan./Feb. 2002): 36–37; Sandra Hughes-Hassell and Kay Bishop, "Using Focus Group Interviews to Improve Library Services for Youth," *Teacher Librarian* 32, no. 1 (Oct. 2004): 8–12; Deborah K. Wilson-Matusky, "Implications of Using Focus Groups to Improve Library Services," *School Libraries Worldwide* 12, no. 2 (July 2006): 52–73.

34. Shane Nackerud et al., "Analyzing Demographics: Assessing Library Use across the Institution," *portal: Libraries and the Academy* 13, no. 2 (2013): 131–45.

35. Kendrick, *Developing Strategic Marketing Plans*, 9.

36. This list builds on that provided in Marie R. Kennedy and Cheryl LaGuardia, *Marketing Your Library's Electronic Resources: A How-to-Do-It Manual for Libraries* (New York: Neal-Schuman, 2013), 19.

37. Kathy Dempsey, *The Accidental Library Marketer* (Medford, NJ: Information Today, 2009), 147.

38. Dan Gall, "Librarian Like a Rock Star: Using Your Personal Brand to Promote Your Services and Reach Distant Users," *Journal of Library Administration* 50, no. 5/6 (2010), 632.

39. Ibid.; Bethan Ruddock, "Networking and Promoting Yourself," in *The New Professional's Toolkit* (London: Facet, 2012), 179.

40. Kendrick, *Developing Strategic Marketing Plans*; Ned Potter, *The Library Marketing Toolkit* (London: Facet, 2012); Carol Smallwood, Vera Bugnitskaia, and Kerol Harrod, eds., *Marketing Your Library: Tips and Tools That Work* (Jefferson, NC: McFarland, 2012); Nancy Dowd, Mary Evangeliste, and Jonathan Silberman, *Bite-Sized Marketing: Realistic Solutions for the Overworked Librarian* (Chicago: American Library Association, 2010); Susan Webreck Alman, *Crash Course in Marketing for Libraries* (Englewood, CO: Libraries Unlimited, 2007); Public Library Association, *Libraries Prosper with Passion, Purpose, and Persuasion! A PLA Toolkit for Success* (Chicago: American Library Association, 2007); Lisa A. Wolfe, *Library Public Relations, Promotions, and Communications: A How-to-Do-It Manual*, 2nd ed., How-to-Do-It Manuals for Librarians 126 (New York: Neal-Schuman, 2005).

41. Jim Harrington, "Get Out of Your Office and Practice In-Your-Face Marketing," *Information Outlook* 9, no. 2 (Feb. 2005): 19–20; Janet Peros, "Face Time: The Power of Person-to-Person Marketing," *Information Outlook* 9, no. 12 (Dec. 2005): 25–27.

42. Jane Bridges, "Marketing the Hospital Library," *Medical Reference Services Quarterly* 24, no. 3 (Fall 2005): 81–92.

43. Amy Burkman, "A Practical Approach to Marketing the School Library," *Library Media Connections* 23, no. 3 (Nov./Dec. 2004): 42–43; Cindy Schmidt and Frances

Reeve, "Prove It! Using Data to Advocate for School Library Media Programs," in *Educational Media and Technology Yearbook 34*, ed. Michael Orey, V. J. McClendon, and Robert Maribe Branch, 279–90 (New York: Springer, 2009); Wendy Worley, "Promoting the School Library: A Portfolio Is a Visual Record of Achievement," *School Librarian* 54, no. 4 (Winter 2006): 178–79.

44. American Association of School Librarians, *Empowering Learners: Guidelines for School Library Media Programs* (Chicago: American Association of School Librarians, 2009), 41.

45. Keith Curry Lance and David V. Loertscher, *Powering Achievement: School Library Media Programs Make a Difference: The Evidence Mounts*, 3rd ed. (Salt Lake City: Hi Willow, 2005); Lynn Barrett, "Effective School Libraries: Evidence of Impact on Student Achievement," *School Librarian* 58, no. 3 (Autumn 2010): 136–39; *School Libraries Work!* 3rd ed. (Danbury, CT: Scholastic Library, 2008), www.scholastic .com/content/collateral_resources/pdf/s/slw3_2008.pdf.

46. See Library Research Services, "School Library Impact Studies," www.lrs.org/data -tools/school-libraries/impact-studies.

47. Kay Bishop offers several ideas for reading motivation programs in *The Collection Program in School: Concepts and Practices*, 5th ed. (Santa Barbara, CA: Libraries Unlimited, 2013), 134–35.

48. Many of these activities are suggested in AASL, *Empowering Learners*.

49. Nackerud et al., "Analyzing Demographics"; Graham Stone and Bryony Ramsden, "Library Impact Data Project: Looking for the Link between Library Usage and Student Attainment," *College and Research Libraries* 74, no. 6 (Nov. 2013): 546–59; Rebekah Wong Shun Han and T. D. Webb, "Uncovering Meaningful Correlation between Student Academic Performance and Library Material Usage," *College and Research Libraries* 72, no. 4 (2011): 361–70.

50. Julie Beth Todaro, *The Power of Personal Persuasion: Advancing the Academic Library Agenda from the Front Lines: Toolkit* (Chicago: Association of College and Research Libraries, 2006), www.ala.org/acrl/sites/ala.org.acrl/files/content/issues/marketing/ advocacy_toolkit.pdf.

51. Reference and User Services Association, Liaison with Users Committee, "Guide- lines for Liaison Work in Managing Collections and Services."

52. Susan Logue et al., *Liaison Services*. SPEC Kit 301 (Washington, DC: Association of College and Research Libraries, 2007).

53. Lan Shen, "Improving the Effectiveness of Librarian-Faculty Collaboration on Library Collection Development," *Collaborative Librarianship* 4, no. 1 (2012): 20.

54. Susan J. Gardner, Johns Eric Juricek, and F. Grace Xu, "An Analysis of Academic Library Web Pages for Faculty," *Journal of Academic Librarianship* 34, no. 1 (Jan. 2008): 16–24.

55. Ronald A. Berk, "Teaching Strategies for the Net Generation," *Transformative Dialogues: Teaching and Learning Journal* 3, no. 2 (Nov. 2009), http://kwantlen .ca/TD/TD.3.2/TD.3.2_Berk_Teaching_Strategies_for_Net_Generation.pdf; Neil Selwyn, "The Digital Native: Myth and Reality," *Aslib Proceedings: New Information Perspective* 6, no. 4 (2009): 364–79.

56. Lara Ursin Cummings, "Bursting Out of the Box: Outreach to the Millennial Generation through Student Services Programs," *Reference Services Review* 35, no. 2 (2007) 285–95.

57. Mark Aaron Polger and Karen Okamoto, "Who's Spinning the Library? Responsibilities of Academic Librarians Who Promote," *Library Management* 34, no. 3 (2013): 236–53; Library Journal, *Public Library Marketing: Methods and Best Practices* (2013), http://lj.libraryjournal.com/downloads/public-library-marketing-methods -and-best-practices.

58. A few representative articles are Noa Aharony, "Twitter Use in Libraries: An Exploratory Analysis," *Journal of Web Librarianship* 4, no. 4 (2010): 333–50; Amy J. Chatfield et al. "Communicating with Faculty, Staff, and Students Using Library Blogs: Results from a Survey of Academic Health Sciences Libraries," *Internet Reference Services Quarterly* 15, no. 3 (2010): 149–68; Selene Colburn and Laura Haines, "Measuring Libraries' Use of YouTube as a Promotional Tool: An Exploratory Study and Proposed Best Practices," *Journal of Web Librarianship* 6, no. 1 (2012): 5–31; Darcy Del Bosque, Sam A. Leif, and Susie Skarl, "Libraries Atwitter: Trends in Academic Library Tweeting," *Reference Services Review* 40, no. 2 (2012): 199–213; Elaine Thornton, "Is Your Academic Library Pinning? Academic Libraries and Pinterest," *Journal of Web Librarianship* 6, no. 3 (2012): 164–75; Lee A. Vucovich et al., "Is the Time and Effort Worth It? One Library's Evaluation of Using Social Networking Tools for Outreach," *Medical Reference Services Quarterly* 32, no. 1 (2013): 13–25.

59. Paolo Gardois et al. "Implementation of Web 2.0 Services in Academic, Medical, and Research Libraries: A Scoping Review," *Health Information and Libraries Journal* 29, no. 2 (June 2012): 90–109.

60. Jonathan Bodnar and Ameet Doshi, "Asking the Right Questions: A Critique of Facebook, Social Media, and Libraries," *Public Services Quarterly* 7, no. 3/4 (2011): 103; Gang (Gary) Wan, "How Academic Libraries Reach Users on Facebook," *College and Undergraduate Libraries* 18, no. 4 (2011): 307–18.

61. Sara Ruth Connell, "Academic Libraries, Facebook and MySpace, and Student Outreach: A Survey of Student Opinion," *portal: Libraries and the Academy* 9, no. 1 (Jan. 2009): 33.

Suggested Readings

Affelt, Amy. "Best Practices for Aligning the Mission and Marketing the Services of the Corporate Library." In *Best Practices for Corporate Libraries*, ed. Sigrid E. Kelsey and Marjorie J. Powers, 153–66. Santa Barbara, CA: Libraries Unlimited, 2011.

Aharony, Noa. "Librarians' Attitudes towards Marketing Library Services." *Journal of Librarianship and Information Science* 41, no. 1 (Mar. 2009): 39–50.

Andrews, Sandra D. *The Power of Data: An Introduction to Using Local, State, and National Data to Support School Library Programs*. Chicago: American Association of School Librarians, 2012.

Ashcroft, Linda. "Marketing Strategies for Visibility." *Journal of Librarianship and Information Science* 42, no. 2 (2010): 89–96.

Baumann, Susana G. *¡Hola, Amigos!: A Plan for Latino Outreach*. Santa Barbara, CA: Libraries Unlimited, 2011.

Behrens, Jennifer L. "About Facebook: Change at the Social-Networking Juggernaut Creates New Opportunities for Law Library Outreach." *AALL Spectrum* 12, no. 6 (Apr. 2008): 14–17.

Bhatt, R. K. "Relevance of Ranganathan's Laws of Library Science in Library Marketing." *Library Philosophy and Practice* (2011). http://unllib.unl.edu/LPP/bhatt.pdf.

Blake, Barbara, Robert S. Martin, and Yunfei Du. *Successful Community Outreach: A How-to-Do-It Manual for Librarians*. How-to-Do-It Manuals 157. New York: New-Schuman, 2011.

Buxton, Karen. "Outreach to Scientists and Engineers at the Hanford Technical Library." Presentation at the Special Library Association Annual Conference, Seattle, Washington, June 15–18, 2008. http://scitech.sla.org/wp-content/uploads/2011/03/2008-Buxton.pdf.

Carpan, Carolyn. "The Importance of Library Liaison Programs." *College and Undergraduate Libraries* 18, no. 1 (2011): 104–10.

Carter, Toni, and Priscilla Seaman. "The Management and Support of Outreach in Academic Libraries." *Reference and User Services Quarterly* 51, no. 2 (2011): 163–71.

Chen, Dora Yu-Ting, Samuel Kai-Wah Chu, and Shu-Qin Xu. "How Do Libraries Use Social Networking Sites to Interact with Users?" *Proceedings of the American Society for Information Science and Technology* 49, no. 1 (2012): 1–10.

Chu, Melanie, and Yvone Nalani Meulemans. "The Problems and Potential of MySpace and Facebook Usage in Academic Libraries." *Internet Reference Services Quarterly* 13, no. 1 (2008): 69–85.

Comito, Lauren, Aliqae Geraci, and Christian Zabriskie. *Grassroots Library Advocacy: A Special Report*. Chicago: American Library Association, 2012.

Cox, Brina, and Margie Jantti. "Capturing Business Intelligence Required for Targeting Marketing, Demonstrating Value, and Driving Process Improvement." *Library and Information Science Research* 34, no. 4 (2012): 308–16.

David, Lourdes T., and Karryl Kim A. Sagun. "Increasing Awareness and Use of the Library's Resources and Facilities through Relationship Marketing Strategies." *Library Management* 33, no. 4/5 (2012): 292–96.

Dennis, Melissa. "Outreach Initiatives in Academic Libraries, 2009–2011." *Reference Services Review* 40, no. 3 (2012): 368–83.

De Rosa, Cathy, et al. *From Awareness to Funding: A Study of Library Support in America: A Report to the OCLC Membership.* Dublin, OH: 2008. www.oclc.org/content/dam/oclc/reports/funding/fullreport.pdf.

De Sáez, Eileen Elliott. *Marketing Concepts for Libraries and Information Services.* 3rd ed. London: Facet, 2013.

Dickson, Andrea, and Robert P. Holley. "Social Networking in Academic Libraries: The Possibilities and the Concerns." *New Library World* 111, no. 11/12 (2010): 468–79.

Dilger-Hill, Jeannie, and Erica MacCreaigh, eds. *On the Road with Outreach: Mobile Library Services.* Santa Barbara, CA: Libraries Unlimited, 2009.

Doucett, Elisabeth. *Creating Your Library Brand: Communicating Your Relevance and Value to Your Patrons.* Chicago: American Library Association, 2008.

Dubicki, Eleonora, ed. *Marketing and Promoting Electronic Resources: Creating the E-buzz!* London: Routledge, 2009.

Ganster, Ligaya, and Bridget Schumacher. "Expanding beyond Our Library Walls: Building an Active Online Community through Facebook." *Journal of Web Librarianship* 3, no. 2 (2009): 111–28.

Gardois, Paolo, et al. "Implementation of Web 2.0 Services in Academic, Medical, and Research Libraries: A Scoping Review." *Health Information and Libraries Journal* 29, no. 2 (June 2012): 90–109.

Germano, Michael A. "Narrative-Based Library Marketing: Selling Your Library's Value during Tough Economic Times." *Bottom Line: Managing Library Finances* 23, no. 1 (2010): 5–17.

Glazer, Harry. "Clever Outreach or Costly Diversion? An Academic Library Evaluates Its Facebook Experience." *College and Research Libraries News* 70, no. 1 (Jan. 2009): 11–19.

Gould, Mark R., ed. *The Library PR Handbook: High-Impact Communications.* Chicago: American Library, Association, 2009.

Gruenthal, Heather. "A School Library Advocacy Alphabet." *Young Adult Library Services* 11, no. 1 (Fall 2012): 13–18.

Gupta, Dinesh K., and Réjean Savard, eds. *Marketing Libraries in a Web 2.0 World.* IFLA Publications 145. Berlin: DeGruyter K.G. Saur, 2011.

Harriman, Joy H. P. "Creating a Marketing Plan." In *Creating Your Library's Business Plan: A How-to-Do-It Manual with Samples on CD-ROM*, 155–95. How-to-Do-It Manual 163. New York: New-Schuman, 2008.

Helinsky, Zuzana, and Colin Harrison. *A Short-Cut to Marketing the Library*. Oxford, UK: Chandos, 2008.

Horn, Laura Peowski. "Online Marketing Strategies for Reaching Today's Teens." *Young Adult Library Services* 9, no. 2 (Jan. 2011): 24–27.

Hristov, M. Nathalie, and Alan Wallace. "Marketing Music Library Services through Video Infomercial and Resource Guides: A Case Study from the University of Tennessee George F. DeVine Music Library." *Music Reference Services Quarterly* 10, no. 3/4 (2008): 1–24.

Jacobson, Terra B. "Facebook as a Library Tool: Perceived vs. Actual Use." *College and Research Libraries* 72, no. 1 (Jan. 2011): 79–90.

James, Russell D., and Peter J. Wosh, eds. *Public Relations and Marketing for Archives: A How-to-Do-It Manual*. How-to-Do-It Manuals for Libraries 176. New York: Neal-Schuman, 2011.

James-Gilboe, Lynda. "Raising the Library Profile to Fight Budget Challenges." *Serials Librarian* 59, no. 3/4 (2010): 360–69.

Johns, Sara Kelly. "What Can Teacher-Librarians Do to Promote Their Work and the School Library Media Program? Offensive Formula: P+M=A." *Teacher Librarian* 36, no. 2 (Dec. 2008): 30–31.

Jones, D. Yvonne, et al. "Simple Marketing Techniques and Space Planning to Increase Circulation." *Collection Management* 36, no. 2 (2011): 107–18.

Kaur, Kiran. "Marketing the Academic Library on the Web." *Library Management* 30, no. 6/7 (2009): 454–69.

Kennedy, Marie R. "Collaborative Marketing for Electronic Resources: A Project Report and Discussion." *Collaborative Librarianship* 5, no. 1 (2013): 42–51.

Kennedy, Marie R., and Cheryl LaGuardia. *Marketing Your Library's Electronic Resources: A How-to-Do-It Manual for Librarians*. New York: Neal-Schuman, 2013.

Kerr, George D. "Gaining and Retaining Customer Loyalty." *Public Library Quarterly* 29, no. 1 (Jan./Mar. 2010): 1–29.

Leonard, Elisabeth. "Librarian as Marketer: Learning to Promote Reference and Outreach Services." In *Reference Reborn: Breathing New Life into Public Services Librarianship*, ed. Diane Zabel, 143–53. Santa Barbara, CA: Libraries Unlimited, 2011.

Levitov, Deborah D., ed., *Activism and the School Librarian: Tools for Advocacy and Survival*. Santa Barbara, CA: Libraries Unlimited, 2012.

MacAdoo, Monty L. *Building Bridges: Connecting Faculty, Students, and the College Library*. Chicago: American Library Association, 2010.

Martin, Coleen Meyers. "One-Minute Video: Marketing Your Library to Faculty." *Reference Services Review* 40, no. 4 (2012): 589–600.

Mathews, Brian. *Marketing Today's Academic Library: A Bold New Approach to Communicating with Students*. Chicago: American Library Association, 2009.

Mathews, Brian, and Jon Bodnar. *Promoting the Library*. SPEC Kit 306. Washington, DC: Association of Research Libraries, 2008.

Merola, Marci. *Library Advocate's Handbook*. Chicago: American Library Association, 2008.

Pankl, Robert R. "Marketing the Public Library's Business Resources to Small Businesses." *Journal of Business and Finance Librarianship* 15, no. 2 (Apr./June 2010): 94–103.

Parsons, Allan. "Academic Liaison Librarianship: Curatorial Pedagogy or Pedagogical Curation?" *Adriane* 65 (Oct. 2010). www.ariadne.ac.uk/issue65/parsons.

Phillips, Loreen S. *Cruise to Success: How to Steer Your Way through the Murky Waters of Marketing Your Library*. London: Chandos, 2009.

Phillips, Nancy Kim. "Academic Library Use of Facebook: Building Relationships with Students." *Journal of Academic Librarianship* 37, no. 6 (2011): 512–22.

Potter, Ned. "Marketing Libraries Is Like Marketing Mayonnaise." *Library Journal* (Apr. 18, 2013). http://lj.libraryjournal.com/2013/04/opinion/advocates-corner/marketing-libraries-is-like-marketing-mayonnaise.

Ratzek, Wolfgang. "The Mutations of Marketing and Libraries." *IFLA Journal* 37, no. 2 (2011): 139–51.

Rhoades, James G., Jr., and Arianne Hartsell. "Marketing First Impressions: Academic Libraries Creating Partnerships and Connections at New Student Orientations." *Library Philosophy and Practice* Paper 202 (2008). http://digitalcommons.unl.edu/cgi/viewcontent.cgi?article=1207&context=libphilprac.

Robinson, Cynthia K. "Peter Drucker on Marketing: Applications and Implications for Libraries." *Bottom Line: Managing Library Finances* 25, no. 1 (2012): 4–12.

Rossiter, Nancy. *Marketing the Best Deal in Town: Your Library: Where Is Your Purple Owl?* Oxford, UK: Chandos, 2008.

Rowe, J., and J. J. Britz, "Strategies for Success: A Framework for the Development of a Marketing Plan for Information Services." *Mousaion* 27, no. 2 (2009): 36–50.

Ruddock, Bethan. "Marketing Your Services and Engaging Stakeholders." In *The New Professional's Toolkit*, 55–71 (London: Facet, 2012).

Sachs, Dianna E., Edward J. Eckel, and Kathleen A. Langan. "Striking a Balance: Effective Use of Facebook in an Academic Library." *Internet Reference Services Quarterly* 16, no. 1/2 (2011): 35–54.

Shen, Lan. "Improving the Effectiveness of Librarian-Faculty Collaboration on Library Collection Development." *Collaborative Librarianship* 4, no. 1 (2012): 14–22.

Singh, Rajesh. "Does Your Library Have an Attitude Problem towards 'Marketing'? Revealing Inter-relationships between Marketing Attitudes and Behaviour." *Journal of Academic Librarianship* 35, no. 1 (Jan. 2009): 25–32.

———. "Does Your Library Have a Marketing Culture? Implications for Service Providers." *Library Management* 30, no. 3 (2009): 117–37.

Smallwood, Carol, ed. *Librarians As Community Partners: An Outreach Handbook*. Chicago: American Library Association, 2010.

Smith, Debbi A. "Strategic Marketing of Library Resources and Services." *College and Undergraduate Libraries* 18, no. 4 (2011): 333–49.

Smith-Butler, Lisa. "Overcoming Your Aversion to the 'M' Word." *AALL Spectrum* 14, no. 5 (Mar. 2010): 7–8, 23.

Solomon, Laura. *Doing Social Media So It Matters: A Librarian's Guide*. Chicago: American Library Association, 2011.

———. *The Librarian's Guide to Nitty-Gritty Social Media*. Chicago: American Library Association, 2013.

Taddeo, Laura. "RU There? How to Reach a Virtual Audience through Affordable Marketing Strategies." *Internet Reference Services Quarterly* 13, no. 2/3 (2008): 227–44.

Vasileiou, Magdalini, and Jennifer Rowley. "Marketing and Promotion of E-books in Academic Libraries." *Journal of Documentation* 67, no. 4 (2011): 624–43.

Walters, Suzanne, and Kent Jackson. *Breakthrough Branding: Positioning Your Library to Survive and Thrive*. New York: Neal Schuman, 2013.

Welburn, William C., and Janice Welburn. *Advocacy, Outreach, and the Nation's Academic Libraries: A Call for Action*. Chicago: Association of College and Research Libraries, 2010.

Williams, Heather, and Anne Peters. "And That's How I Connect to MY Library: How a 42-Second Promotional Video Helped to Launch the UTSA Libraries' New Summon Mobile Application." *Reference Librarian* 53, no. 3 (2012): 322–25.

Woodward, Jeannette. "Sharing Our Vision: Marketing the Academic Library." In *Creating the Customer-Driven Academic Library*, 130–51. Chicago: American Library Association, 2009.

CHAPTER SEVEN

Collection Analysis: Evaluation and Assessment

In a collection analysis, the library considers its collection's use and its impact. Analysis provides information on various aspects of the collection, among them the number of pieces and titles in a particular subject; formats represented; age and condition of materials; breadth and depth of coverage; language in which the resources are available; patron use and nonuse of the collection; and resource sharing (what was loaned from the local collection and what was borrowed from elsewhere). Although librarians may think of collection analysis as measuring the collection's quality (an amorphous concept, at best), the real objective is to measure the collection's utility—how effective the collection is in satisfying the purpose for which it is intended and, by extension, how effective the library is in expending funds to develop and maintain that collection. The library profession is focusing increasing attention on identifying metrics that matter, that is, measurements that effectively monitor the library's performance in achieving its goals. Meaningful metrics can inform collection development and management decisions and demonstrate value to stakeholders. The challenging aspect of measuring and demonstrating value is using meaningful methods that are not overly onerous in their execution. This chapter explores the purposes of collection analysis and the difference between quantitative and qualitative and use- and user-based techniques, and offers advice on conducting collection analysis.

Collection Analysis as a Management Tool

Collection analysis is part of the effective and efficient management of resources. Several terms may be used in discussions of collection analysis. These include collection mapping, collection review, collection assessment, and collection evaluation. Although often used interchangeably, *assessment* and *evaluation* can be distinguished according to the intent of the analysis. The aim of assessment is to determine how well the collection supports the goals, needs, and mission of the library or parent organization. The collection (both locally held and remotely accessed materials) is assessed in the local context. The library's goals and purpose, therefore, must be stated clearly before any meaningful assessment of a library's collection can take place. Once collection goals (ideally, in a collection development policy statement) have been assigned to subject areas or user communities, the library can assess whether it has been collecting at the desired level. *Evaluation* seeks to examine or describe collections either in their own terms or in relation to other collections and checking mechanisms, such as lists. Though evaluation is a more abstract process because it does not consider the collection's use and users, findings are meaningless unless considered in the local context. For example, the extent to which a library has titles on a core list is meaningful only if the library has a goal to provide these materials.

Both evaluation and assessment provide a better understanding of the collection and the user community. Librarians gain information that helps them decide if a collection is meeting its objectives, how well it is serving users, in which ways or areas it is deficient, and what remains to be done to develop it. As librarians learn more about the collection and its utility, they are able to manage the collection—its growth, preservation and conservation, storage, withdrawal, and cancellation of serials and other continuing resources—in relation to users' needs and the library's and parent institution's mission.

Purposes of Collection Analysis

Collection analysis can also provide information that may be used for many other purposes. It can result in a detailed subject profile that informs new library staff members and users about the nature of the collection. It can assist in the writing or revision of a collection development policy and indicate an existing policy's effectiveness. It can help explain decisions and expenditures. For example, documented high use of e-resources during hours the library building is closed might explain allocating an increasing percentage of the total acquisitions budget for this format.

Information (e.g., on areas that need strengthening, weeding, updating) collected through collection analysis can be used in the planning process, including justifications for budget requests and funding referendums. It can guide and inform decisions and policymaking throughout the library, including budget and staffing allocations. Analysis projects that focus on the condition of materials and their availability can be used for disaster preparedness, inventory purposes, and space planning.

Reports from collection analysis projects can be used in accreditation reports and for other external purposes. Some academic libraries are involved in institutional planning for new degree programs. A specific and detailed collection analysis can demonstrate the degree to which a library can and cannot support a new program or major. Information about collection strengths can be used to recruit new faculty members and students. The results of collection analyses can give corporate libraries information to document their ability to support new research and development programs. School media centers can document the age of collections by subject area and compare circulation activity against titles held by subject, thus showing areas that may need strengthening. Information may be gathered through collection analysis that can be used in press releases, library reports and newsletters, and for grant proposals. Collection analysis positions a library to share information with other libraries with which it is involved through existing or proposed partnerships.

Collection analysis can be used to demonstrate accountability by tracking progress toward performance goals and showing how investments are being used effectively.[1] Being accountable to funding and governing bodies requires evidence that libraries are delivering the collections and services expected on investments. Collection assessment has received increasing attention in libraries since the late 1990s as part of growing emphasis on demonstrating accountability through positive outcomes, quality from the user's perspective, cost efficiencies and effectiveness, and responsible stewardship of resources. Creating a culture of assessment has been promoted as an important component in engaging everyone in a library in this critical activity. Lakos and Phipps define a culture of assessment as "an organizational environment in which decisions are based on facts, research, and analysis, and where services are planned and delivered in ways that maximize positive outcomes and impacts for customers and stakeholders."[2] One can broaden this definition to state that effective assessment results in services and collections that create positive outcomes for library users and stakeholders.

A common misconception is that collection assessment and evaluation determine how "good" a collection is. Earlier chapters in the book explore the debate over what defines a good book or other library resource. Contemporary theory advances the idea that a collection is considered good and appropriate to the extent that it matches the goals of the library and its parent institution. The collection developed to serve an elementary school is not an appropriate or good collection for a high school; a collection serving a two-year technical college is not a good collection for a university with many graduate programs and professional schools; and a collection developed to meet the needs of an electrical engineering firm is not a good collection for a teaching hospital. Even when evaluation techniques examine the collection in relation to an external measure, that measure must relate to the goals of the collection being considered. Deciding what not to collect is as important as deciding what to collect. Although analyses do identify collection areas that should be developed as well as strengths, intentional nonstrengths are equally valid.

Bushing describes collection review as "the ability to understand the specific strengths and weaknesses of information resources with statistical data as well as impressionistic judgments based on experience and knowledge of the discipline area under consideration."[3] *Learning for the Future* suggests that collection review in schools determines the effectiveness of the available information resources in meet the curricular and extracurricular needs and in contributing to improvement in student outcomes, as well as the effectiveness of the school's collection development strategies in attaining the policy priorities within budget targets.[4] Collection analysis also can serve as an internal control mechanism to measure individual performance. Decisions about other areas such as cooperative agreements, space limitations and needs, and ownership and access are informed through collection analysis.

Inputs, Outputs, and Outcomes

Historically, collection analysis has focused on inputs and outputs. *Inputs* are the resources available in a library, including staffing, allocations and expenditures, and collection size and growth. Inputs such as number of titles held in a specific subject area are common measures. *Outputs* are those activities the library provides, based on inputs. These include hours of service, availability and use of collections, reference transactions, and instructional sessions. A typical output measure might be usage statistics, such as number of print titles in circulation or e-journal article downloads. Use has been a popular way of defining value (e.g., the more books circulate, the better the collection; the more articles downloaded from an e-journal, the better that journal), but use should not be considered in isolation.

Outcomes have become increasingly important in the twenty-first century. Outcomes are the benefits to the user or user community as a result of a library's inputs and outputs. The question becomes how use can be connected to outcomes such as student learning, faculty productivity, or grants awarded. Hernon and Dugan write that outcomes assessment seeks to answer the question "How are users of our library changed as a direct result of their contact with our collections and services?"[5] In other words, outcomes assessment seeks to measure user achievements or changes in skill, knowledge, attitude, behavior, condition, or life status.

Developing meaningful outcome measures associated with collections is more challenging than developing input and output measures. Librarians first must develop clear and meaningful definitions of desired outcomes so that the correct questions can be asked and the appropriate data collected and analyzed. Second, they need to combine outcome assessments with other collections data to have a complete understanding of the collection, its use, and its users. Some outcomes are quantitative, calculating, for example, the relationship between library investment in collections and faculty research and teaching outcomes, or between student library material usage and student academic performance.[6] A 1993 study by Lance, Welborn, and Hamilton-Pennell conducted in Colorado linked student success on standardized tests with better-funded library media centers, larger and varied collections, and library media specialists who worked with teachers to select materials related to the curriculum or develop instructional units.[7] Some outcomes are qualitative. For example, surveys or focus groups could be used to determine if students "judge access to collections sufficient to support their educational and research needs," a sample outcome suggested in ACRL's *Standards for Libraries in Higher Education*.[8] Some outcomes are assessed by combining quantitative and qualitative data. Researchers at Minnesota State University–Mankato used circulation data and focus groups to explore the extent to which use of a library's foreign films collection by international students might ease acculturation and reduce anxiety about using the library.[9]

Techniques of Collection Analysis

Knowing the collection is a librarian's responsibility. Effective collection analysis leads to this knowledge. Collection analysis, therefore, is not a one-time project but an ongoing process defined by both individual analysis projects and constant attention to collection quality and its responsiveness to the user community. Assessment and evaluation provide, through specific analytical methods and continuous monitoring, information about the current collection and about progress toward collection goals. Each analysis project provides a snapshot of or baseline information about the existing collection. Various techniques can be used for collection analysis, leading one to assume that mastery of the methods always produces meaningful and useful findings, but this is not a given. As McClure notes, collection analysis "is an art, not a science, and the numbers that it generates are a means not an end."[10]

Methods and techniques of collection analysis range from impressionistic, descriptive assessments to complex statistical analyses. They can be labor-intensive and time-consuming and, as McClure observes, are sometimes exasperating.[11] All seek to provide organized, pertinent, specific, and accurate information about the collection. Two topologies are used in discussing the various approaches to analysis: techniques are either collection-based or use- and user-based and either quantitative or qualitative. Figure 7-1 represents these topologies as a matrix within which various techniques are organized; the commercial products listed are representative and not intended to be exhaustive.

Collection-based techniques examine the size, growth, depth, breadth, variety, balance, and coverage of library materials—often in comparison with an

	Use- and user-based	**Collection-based**
Quantitative	Interlibrary loan statistics	Collection size and growth
	Circulation statistics	Materials budget size and growth
	In-house use statistics	Collection size standards and formulas
	Document delivery statistics	Citation analysis and studies
	ILL transactions	Apply ratios (e.g., monographs
	"Hits" and downloads (e.g., transaction logs, vendor-supplied data)	expenditures to serial expenditures; expenditures compared to citizens)
	Cost per use	Content overlap studies
Qualitative	User opinion surveys (e.g., LibQual+, web-based, e-mail)	List checking (e.g., catalogs, bibliographies)
	User observation	Verification studies
	Focus groups	Citation analysis
	Usability testing	Direct collection checking
		Collection mapping (assigning conspectus levels)
		Brief tests of collection strength
		Commercial products (e.g., WorldCat Collection Analysis, Bowker's Book Analysis System, Ulrich's Serials Analysis System, Follett Library Resources TitleWise, Sagebrush BenchMARC, Sustainable Collection Services tools)

FIGURE 7-1   Methods of collection analysis

external standard or the holdings of one or more libraries known to be comprehensive in the relevant subject area. Techniques include checking lists, catalogs, and bibliographies; looking at materials on the shelf; and compiling statistics. Collection-based techniques provide information that can guide decisions about preservation and conservation treatments, withdrawals, serials cancellations, duplication, and storage.

Use- and user-based approaches look at who is using the materials, how often, and what their expectations are. Emphasis may be on the use or on the user. A use study focuses on the materials and examines individual titles or groups of titles or subject areas to determine user success in identifying and locating what is needed and in using these items. User studies focus on the individuals or groups using the collection and how they are using its various components. Use- and user-based studies include research into users' failure to locate and obtain materials locally and how alternatives, such as interlibrary loan, are used. Use and user studies collect information about user expectations, how users approach the collections, and the materials that users select from those available.

Quantitative analysis counts things. It measures titles, circulation transactions, interlibrary loan requests, access and download transactions with e-resources, and dollars spent. Some quantitative analyses compare measurements over time within a library and with other libraries. They consider ratios such as expenditures for serials in relation to expenditures for monographs and expenditures for print resources in relation to those for e-resources. An academic library may analyze total collection expenditures in relation to number of students, faculty members, and degree programs. A public library may consider annual expenditures or circulation transactions per user group or branch library. Quantitative methods demonstrate growth and use of collections by looking at collection and circulation statistics, electronic resource use, interlibrary loan requests, and budget information. Once a baseline is established, the size, growth, and use of a collection over time can be measured.

Automated systems have made the collection and analysis of collections data much easier. Librarians can extract data directly from a local system by using reports provided by the system or by writing customized report generators. Stowers and Tucker describe using link resolver reports generated by the University of Nevada–Las Vegas Libraries' automated system to inform collections decisions.[12] They used these reports to see which journal titles had full-text requests, to learn how users behave, and to discover access issues with specific journals.

Some commercial services, such as Follett Library Resources TitleWise Online Collection Analysis, Sagebrush BenchMARC, Bowker Book Analysis

System, and Ulrich's Serials Analysis System, generate library-specific reports using bibliographic data extracted from the library's automated system. Many of these services are free to current customers; others are not. OCLC's WorldCat Collection Analysis, a tool that libraries may purchase, relies on library holdings as recorded in the WorldCat database. Reports can analyze a collection from a single school or a school district, branch library or library system, individual academic libraries, and, in some cases, a group of libraries. Reports can provide counts and percentages of titles held by classification range, average date of publication for classification ranges, growth by classification range, and so on. Several services compare the collection to peer libraries or authoritative titles lists, such as *Choice Magazine's* Outstanding Academic Titles or grade-appropriate recommended school library collections. Reports generated by Sustainable Collection Services compare local holdings to WorldCat, HathiTrust Digital Library, and authoritative title lists to inform weeding and storage decisions. With information provided by one of these approaches, a librarian can make informed decisions about where weeding or further development may be needed. Several of these services evaluate a library's circulation activity (when a file of the library's circulation activity data is uploaded to the service provider) to help collection librarians identify areas that need attention.

Qualitative analysis is more subjective than quantitative analysis because it depends on perception, opinion, and the context in which the data are gathered. Gorman and Crayton offer this definition: "Qualitative research is a process of inquiry that draws data from the context in which events occur, in an attempt to describe these occurrences, as a means of determining the process in which events are imbedded and the perspectives of those participating in the events, using induction to derive possible explanations based on observed phenomena."[13]

The goal of qualitative analysis of a collection is to determine the collection's strengths, weaknesses, and nonstrengths, which reflect conscious decisions not to collect, and the degree to which the collection meets the needs and expectations of users. It depends on the opinion of local librarians and external experts and the perceptions of users. Even when collections are checked against external lists, these lists are themselves the result of informed opinion about what constitutes a good collection, what characterizes a collection designated as a specific collecting level, or what an appropriate collection is for a specific user group.

All collection analysis, whether qualitative or quantitative, should employ sound research practices. These require a clear understanding of what is being measured, how to measure it, and how to interpret the results. Collection analysis begins with an unambiguous question to be answered. A well-done research project produces information that is both reliable (likely to yield the same results when repeated) and valid (measures what it sets out to measure). In other words, the findings are repeatable and the conclusions are true. Several sources provide guidance for conducting research in libraries.[14] In addition to understanding and practicing sound research, librarians who plan to use survey instruments should consult with experts in their development and application.

Historical Overview of Collection Analysis

Until the end of the nineteenth century, collection analysis focused on description rather than assessment and evaluation. This was, in large part, a function of the manner in which collections were developed—through donations and what was available for acquisition, rather than intentional collection building to meet specific needs and goals. Around 1900, librarians began using selected bibliographies or lists against which individual library holdings were checked. These lists were prepared by ALA and its divisions, authoritative librarians, and subject specialists. Another form of list checking involved collecting favorable reviews and then determining if the library held the titles. Libraries also checked references and bibliographies in scholarly works against library holdings. List checking was the primary method of collection analysis until the middle of the twentieth century.

Quantitative Studies

In the 1960s, librarians began to promote more diverse and scientific methods of collection analysis. These included studying citation patterns, collection overlap and uniqueness, comparative statistics, and classification and curriculum relationships; developing formulas for collection size and acquisitions budgets; and employing sociological tools in the design and application of use and user studies. Much of the emphasis in this period was on the objectivity of analytical results. College and university librarians, particularly, sought quantitative measures that were both easy to apply and objective. Many studies focused on collecting and comparing collection size and expenditure statistics, both seen as measures of excellence.

Since the 1970s, both quantitative and qualitative collection analysis methods have been developed and promoted. Much of the impetus has been a desire to facilitate cooperative collection development in consortia and large library systems. Academic and research libraries have initiated several cooperative projects. The ARL Collection Analysis Project was begun in the 1970s to analyze collections within institutional contexts with the goal of increasing cooperative collection development among large research libraries.[15] The Ohio Library and Information Network (OhioLINK), a consortium of eighty-eight Ohio college and university libraries and the State Library of Ohio, conducted a project using circulation data to better understand how OhioLINK resources were being used.[16] The goals were to reduce duplication, allocate resources more effectively, and increase diversity in the collections. A similar project was conducted by the Five Colleges libraries (University of Massachusetts Amherst, Amherst College, Mount Holyoke, Smith College, and Hampshire College).[17]

Librarians have developed collection size formulas that use local variables to calculate the number of volumes required to meet local needs. The use of formulas depends on the notion of a minimum size for collections or budgets relative to the size of a library's user community or level of parent institution's programs. The Clapp-Jordan formula, which uses an acceptable core collection count plus volumes per student, per faculty, per undergraduate field, and per graduate field, is one model for this approach.[18] Others have been proposed over the years. Existing collections can be compared to the ideal specified by the formula. Some library standards provide formulas for deciding optimum collection size. Formulas have become less popular as libraries have moved away from relying solely on numbers (e.g., collection counts, dollars expended) as a measure of quality and begun to consider impacts and outcomes.

Collection analysis by studying collection use produced one of the more controversial statistical studies, which was conducted by Kent and colleagues at the University of Pittsburgh in the 1970s.[19] This study found that 26.8 percent of the monographs held in the University of Pittsburgh Library's collection accounted for 82.2 percent of the use and that only 60.1 percent of the collection circulated at all, leading researchers to suggest implications for past and future collection management practices. This finding confirmed earlier research on circulation of materials in public, special, and university libraries conducted by Trueswell, who suggested that the "80/20 Rule" (previously applied to business inventories in which 80 percent of business transactions involve only 20 percent of stocked items) also applies to libraries' holdings, in that 20 percent of the collection accounts for 80 percent of circulation.[20] Questions remain about whether frequency of book and journal use is an appropriate measure of academic library effectiveness. Nevertheless, circulation studies can provide guidance about which parts of the collection can be put in storage or withdrawn as well as which areas need to be developed.

Other quantitative use studies examine a collection by a collection profile, in-library use, shelf availability, document delivery, downloads from remote resources, or interlibrary lending and borrowing statistics. Budget-based quantitative studies—which, for example, measure growth of the materials budget, track changes in the ratio of expenditures for serials to those for monographs, or compare allocations between subject areas—are additional techniques for considering the relation of a library's operations to its goals and long-term mission.

Quantitative measures must be approached with some caution. Nisonger lists several weaknesses in such methods.[21] For example, all uses are counted equally, with no indications of benefit from the use. The data reflect success in locating an item but ignore failure. They measure what was used, not what should have been used. Use data do not take into account nonusers. Numbers can be skewed to emphasize a particular point or perspective.

Qualitative Studies

Qualitative studies seek to evaluate the intrinsic worth of the collection and are, by nature, subjective. They depend on the perceptions of librarians and library users. Qualitative studies were hampered initially by a lack of standard terminology. One of the first steps toward developing a shared vocabulary to describe collection strength or levels appeared in ALA's 1979 *Guidelines for Collection Development*.[22] This work designated five collecting levels, which were applied to existing collections ("collection density") and current collecting activity ("collection intensity"): (A) Comprehensive Level, (B) Research Level, (C) Study Level, (D) Basic Level, and (E) Minimal Level. This stratified view sought to analyze each collection according to its intended use.

These levels (with one additional level—Out of Scope) were inverted to form the basis of the Research Libraries Group (RLG) Conspectus, initiated in 1980. Though no longer maintained by it originators, the Conspectus has become a frequently used qualitative method and is employed worldwide in all types of libraries.[23] Generally speaking, a conspectus is a brief survey or summary of a subject. The RLG Conspectus is a comprehensive collection analysis tool intended to provide a summary of collecting intensities arranged by subjects, classification scheme, or a combination of both. The Conspectus method also is called *collection mapping* and *inventory profiling*. Ideally, the Conspectus provides a standardized procedure and terminology for sharing detailed descriptions of collections among libraries. Librarians apply numeric codes to identify five levels of existing collection strengths; 0 is used for areas in which no collection exists. Each level builds on the previous level.

The WLN Conspectus enhances the RLG Conspectus to meet the needs of small and medium-size libraries and added subdivisions for levels 1, 2, and 3, as follows:

0   Out of Scope (library intentionally does not collect materials in any format in this area)

1   Minimal (library collects resources that support minimal inquiries about this subject and includes a very limited collection of general resources)

      1a   Uneven
      1b   Focused

2   Basic Information (library collects resources that introduce and define a subject and can support the needs of general library users through the first two years of college instruction)

      2a   Introductory
      2b   Advanced

3   Study or Instructional Support (library collects resources that provide knowledge about a subject in a systematic way, but at a level of less than research intensity, and supports the needs of general library users through college and beginning graduate instruction)

      3a   Basic study
      3b   Intermediate
      3c   Advanced

4   Research (library very extensively collects the major published source materials required for doctoral study and independent research)

5   Comprehensive Level (library strives to collect as exhaustively as is reasonably possible in all pertinent formats, in all applicable languages, in both published materials and manuscripts).[24]

Conspectus level definitions were revised in the mid-1990s to reflect the emerging role of e-resources.[25] E-resources, both locally held and remotely accessed, are considered equivalent to print materials as long as the policies and procedures for their use permit at least an equivalent information-gathering experience.

Libraries also may apply language coverage indicators:

P   Primary language predominates

S   Selected other-language materials

W Wide selection of languages represented

X   Material is mainly in one language other than primary national language

D Dual languages or two primary languages

Finally, libraries have the option of indicating collecting activity and collection goal levels:

CL current collection level

AC acquisition commitment

CG collection goal

PC preservation commitment

The Conspectus grew out of RLG's interests in recording the collection depths of its members. Other groups around the world have adapted the Conspectus for their own use, both for individual library collection analysis and to provide a synopsis of a consortium's or network's coordinated collection development. Versions of the Conspectus permit use of the Library of Congress classification, the Dewey decimal classification, and the National Library of Medicine classification systems and can be adapted for use in all types of libraries. OCLC's WorldCat Collection Analysis Service presents holdings according to the OCLC Conspectus, a proprietary version of the tool. The software packages developed by WLN and RLG are no longer supported, but many of the functions of these packages can be duplicated using standard spreadsheet software.[26] The Conspectus approach to collection analysis has become accepted as a tool that can be adapted to local needs and is widely applicable. Its greatest strength is a shared vocabulary to describe collection levels.

The Conspectus has been criticized as being too subjective because it depends on the subject expertise and personal perceptions of the librarians using it.[27] In rebuttal, Munroe and Ver Steeg suggest that the question of external validity is irrelevant, because the Conspectus offers descriptive analysis, which by definition cannot have external validity, and seeks to assess the collection in relation to local needs. Osburn states that subjectivity is the key to effective evaluation because a "collection is of value only as it relates in subjective, cognitive ways to the community" it is intended to serve.[28]

"Brief tests of collection strength" is an empirical technique developed by White to verify the Conspectus levels that have been assigned to a collection.[29] Conducting a brief test of collection strength requires access to WorldCat. The method consists of five steps:

1. Choose a subject or area of the collection to evaluate.

2. Without reference to the collection being evaluated, create a list of ten or more titles that a library should have if it were collecting at the minimal level and additional lists for the basic, instructional, and research levels. All lists should be of equal length.

3. Search each title in WorldCat and list the number of holdings.

4. Arrange the master list of all titles according to the WorldCat holdings from minimal level (the most holding libraries) to research level (the fewest holding libraries). Divide the list into four equal parts, which correspond to the Conspectus levels. Thus, the group of titles (one-fourth of the total list) with the most holdings indicates a minimal level collection, and so on.

5. Search the titles in the local collection to determine which titles are held.

A collection is evaluated at the level in which half of more of the titles are held locally. For example, a library might hold all ten titles on the minimal list, nine of the ten titles on the basic list, eight of the ten titles on the instructional list, and three of the titles on the research list. This brief test would indicate that the library has an instructional level collection (in Conspectus terms) because it holds more than half the titles on the list.

In 2008, White proposed "coverage power tests" as an improvement on his brief tests of collection strength.[30] Presented as an empirical method for evaluating collections in all types of libraries by means of ranked holdings counts from WorldCat, coverage power tests permit objective comparisons of libraries and are potentially automatable. White developed this method to address problems (instability, inconsistencies due to relative counts, and problems with defining "ease of reading" on a meaningful scale) in the brief tests approach to collection evaluation, but some may find it more challenging than brief tests to employ.

The Conspectus also has been condemned because of its complexity. It offers between twenty-four and thirty-two divisions (broad disciplines), approximately five hundred categories (topics within disciplines), and as many as seven thousand subjects (the most detailed identification with a category). Applying all possible indicator levels to all possible subjects would be an impossible task. The reality is that most librarians choose a subset and select only the divisions, categories, and subjects that are relevant to the particular library and collection that are being analyzed.

Collection mapping is more commonly used as a qualitative approach to collection analysis in school media center than the Conspectus, though the latter also is used.[31] This approach begins with a curriculum map. The school library media specialist creates a chart that lists key topics divided by subject and grade level. Five to eight topics are selected for each subject and grade level. The curriculum map should reflect the school and district curriculum (and state curriculum, where appropriate). The media specialist should review the curriculum map with teachers to ensure that it reports what is actually being taught in the classroom. The library's collection is then mapped against the curriculum map to show areas of concentration and gaps visually, often in terms of core collections, general emphasis areas, and specific emphasis areas. The collection map also is shared with teachers to help set collection goals that match the curriculum and encourage teachers to be participants in collection development plans.

Electronic Resources and Collection Analysis

Assessment and evaluation of e-resources present their own challenges. The cost of these materials and the increasing percentage of library budgets going toward their acquisition and access mandate careful consideration of their value to users and their role within a library collection. Although e-resources always should be considered part of the collection being analyzed, many of the analytical methods described in this chapter cannot be applied to these formats easily. Many e-resources do not circulate through the library's automated system, nor are they consistently available to lend or borrow through interlibrary loan. E-books may circulate in the sense that the library licensed a book with limitations to the numbers of users who may simultaneously view it, but the circulation of these materials is not reflected in the library's circulation system; use data must be collected via the e-book supplier's reports. Not all e-resources are classified and represented in a shelf list. Direct collection checking and document delivery studies do not apply to most e-resources. The lists developed for checking local holdings may not include e-resources. Nevertheless, the library profession is developing new approaches to assessing and evaluating e-resources, their use, and the perspective of users.

The International Coalition of Library Consortia (ICOLC, www.icolc.net) has been a leader in identifying both the use statistics that are desirable and the obligations of remote resource providers to supply these statistics. ICOLC's "Revised Guidelines for Statistical Measure of Usage of Web-Based Information Resources" defines and creates a common set of basic use information requirements that all electronic products should provide.[32] These metrics permit libraries to analyze use within the individual library and in comparison with others. The data elements to be provided are

- number of sessions (logins)
- number of queries (searches)
- number of menu selections
- number of full-content units examined, downloaded, or otherwise supplied to user
- number of turn-aways, peak simultaneous users, and any other indicator relevant to the pricing model applied to the library or consortium

Project COUNTER (Counting Online Usage of NeTworked Electronic Resources, www.projectcounter.org) is an international initiative of librarians, vendors, publishers, and their professional organizations established to develop and maintain international codes to govern the recording and exchange of online usage data. COUNTER issued Release 4 of the "COUNTER Code of Practice for e-Resources" in April 2012. This version integrates existing codes of practice covering journals, databases, books, and multimedia content into a single code. In addition, it retires the earlier COUNTER metric "Sessions" because of duplication of results as a result of federated and discovery searches. Release 4 introduces "Results Clicks" and "Record Views" as metrics for databases. An important requirement of the COUNTER code is implementation of the Standardized Usage Statistics Harvesting Initiative (SUSHI) protocol. SUSHI is a NISO standard "that defines an automated request and response model for the harvesting of e-resources usage data utilizing a Web services framework." SUSHI replaces the need for libraries to download data by provider and manipulate them locally or contract with a third party, such as SerialsSolutions (www.serialssolutions.com) or ScholarlyStats (www.scholarlystats.com). To be COUNTER-compliant, vendors are required to demonstrate that they have implemented SUSHI and that customers can download usage reports using SUSHI. Many libraries require their e-resource providers to be COUNTER-compliant.[33]

One form of e-resource use statistics that can be collected locally is a transaction log, which measures use of information held locally and delivered via a local server.[34] Transaction logs can determine the type of user actions, percentage of users accessing the site from a specific domain, number of hits the server gets during specific hours, number of hits every page receives within a site, and path by which a user navigates through the site. Transaction log analysis can assist studies of user behavior and is an efficient technique for collecting longitudinal usage data. Nevertheless, it has limitations. Local transaction logs track hits but do not necessarily distinguish between hits and full-text downloads. Repeated hits on a site may indicate only failure to locate a desired or pertinent resource rather than extensive usage of the resource. In addition, extracting data, interpreting the data, and detecting trends and patterns can be difficult.

Tracing usage patterns across large and active populations of users is of critical importance as more funds are devoted to e-resources. Feeding data directly into reports designed to compare user behavior by discipline, status, time of day and year, preferred path to resources, turn-aways, failed searches, and other indicators of preference and satisfaction are important metrics for collection analysis.

One approach to assessing e-resources considers their cost-effectiveness.[35] Local cost-benefit analyses consider individual titles and packages and their utility. Cost-effectiveness means that the cost of providing resources is justified by the value they provide to the user. The more often that digital content is used, the lower the unit cost. Comparing the cost of providing full-text articles online to either print subscriptions or obtaining the articles via interlibrary loan or a commercial document delivery service is one means of assessing the cost-effectiveness of e-resources.[36] Libraries have compared usage of e-books and print books to determine user preferences and assess benefits of individual title selection versus e-books packages.[37] Evaluating use of titles in multiple e-book packages can provide data that inform selection of the most appropriate package.[38]

E-resources also are assessed to demonstrate how well they are satisfying the library's objectives and meeting the demands placed on them. One tool that explores user satisfaction is Measuring the Impact of Networked Electronic Services (MINES for Libraries, www.arl.org/focus-areas/statistics-assessment/mines-for-libraries), developed by Franklin and Plum.[39] MINES is a point-of-use, web-based survey that collects data on e-resource users and their purpose of use, information not documented in vendor and publisher use statistics. It can help a library explore its success in meeting user needs.

Methods of Collection-Based Analysis

Some collection-based analyses are quantitative, some are qualitative, and some have aspects of both approaches. If all e-resources (whether classified or not) are represented in the library's catalog, many of these methods are applicable.

Collection Profiling

The term *collection profile* is sometimes synonymous with *collection development statement*. In addition, the set of criteria a library prepares to guide the provision of materials by an approval plan vendor is typically referred to as a profile. When used in collection analysis, collection profiling is the process of assembling a numerical picture of the collection at one point in time—a statistical description. A collection profile may be as modest as a count of titles held within a specified set of classification ranges, or by broad categories such as picture books, young adult books, and adult books. A collection profile can report the distribution of titles by imprint years, perhaps arranged by decade—and this can be combined with title counts.

Creating a collection profile became much easier with automated library systems, which can be mined for desired data. The data can be manipulated in various ways to answer different questions and serve different purposes. Perrault and Dixon report on an analysis project that extracted data from a shared catalog in 1998 and 2002 and created a profile of the collective holdings of twenty-eight Florida community colleges.[40] These studies provide longitudinal data on counts of titles held by imprint date in twenty-nine broad LC classification ranges, cumulated percentages held by decade of publication, and individual collection-specific data. The 1998 collection profile, for example, revealed that more than 55 percent of the collective holdings were significantly out of date. Data from 2002 indicated that a majority of college librarians took advantage of the 1998 data to develop collections more responsive to the needs of their users, with fewer outdated materials retained and more current materials available.

Collection profiles can provide baseline data for future collection analysis, provide information for cooperative collection development and management, present a statistical description of the collection to stakeholders and funders, and identify areas that need improvement and, perhaps, warrant additional funding.

List Checking

In *list checking*, the librarian compares lists of titles appropriate to the subject area being analyzed against the library's holdings. The list may be another library's catalog, general list, specialized list or bibliography, publisher's or dealer's cata-log, annual subject compilation, list prepared by a professional association or government authority, course syllabi or required or recommended reading list, list of frequently cited journals, list of journals covered by an abstracting and indexing service, recent acquisitions list from a specialized library, or list pre-pared for a specific library, type of library, user group, or specific objective. One example is *Best Books for High School Readers, Grades 9–12*, now in its third edi-tion.[41] The commercial collection analysis tools are a form of list checking; they compare a library's holdings to the universe of titles and the holdings of peer libraries. A collection is studied by finding the percentage of the titles on the list that are owned by the library.

Verification studies are a variation of list checking, in which libraries carry out a collection analysis by checking their collections against a specially prepared list of titles, designed to encompass the most important works within a specific area. These lists are designed to verify that the libraries understand their collections' strengths. The brief tests of collection strength described earlier in this chap-ter are a form of list checking. Any list selected for checking should match the library's programs and goals and be appropriate to the subjects collected.

List checking is often used because it is easy to apply and lists are available that meet many different libraries' needs. Librarians usually can find a list that has credibility because of the authority and competence of those who compiled it. All or parts of the list can be checked. Many published lists are updated fre-quently and can be used to check the collection at regular intervals. List checking not only increases knowledge of the collection being analyzed but increases the librarian's knowledge of the subject's literature. A librarian also can use a list as a purchase guide to identify missing titles that should be acquired.

List checking combines both qualitative and quantitative techniques. The selection by the librarian of the list to be checked is a subjective decision, as was the development of the list, but the result is a statistical report of the number of titles on the list that the library owns. When analyzing the report, the librarian usually converts this percentage to a quality judgment about the collection. List checking also can identify gaps—titles not held and areas with low coverage.

List checking has disadvantages as well as advantages.[42] The library may have used the list as a selection tool in the past. Any list prepared by an individual or group reflects the biases and opinions of the compilers. Its validity rests on the assumption that those titles in the resource list are worthy and that the library needs them to satisfy patrons and support programs. A librarian may have dif-ficulty finding a list that matches the focus of the collection being analyzed and the mission of the library. Finding an up-to-date list also may present problems. Some items on a list may be out of print. Doll cautions about relying too heavily on standard bibliographies when evaluating school library media collections, because such lists are often seriously out of date.[43] Many lists cover materials for all ages and may not be useful for comparison to a collection developed to serve a specific age group. The librarian should recognize that a supplemental tool may be necessary to analyze the collection for materials published since the list was compiled.

Direct Collection Analysis

Direct collection analysis, sometimes called shelf scanning, means that someone with knowledge of the literature being analyzed physically examines the collection. That person then draws conclusions about the size, scope, depth or type of materials (textbooks, documents, paperbacks, beginning level, advanced level, professional level), and significance of the collection; the range and distribution of publishing dates; and the physical condition of the materials. The need for preservation, conservation, restoration, or replacement of materials also may be evaluated in this process. Direct collection analysis is most practical when the collection is small or the subject treated is narrowly defined. The evaluator's reputation must be sufficient to give credibility to the evaluation results. Physical analysis depends on labor, the time to do it, and personal judgment.

One advantage of this approach is its appropriateness to any discipline or library collection. Assuming that the collection being reviewed is of a manageable size, its strengths, weaknesses, and condition can be evaluated rapidly. Direct collection analysis is appropriate for a large collection if time is not a major consideration and if the librarian is interested in working through the collection one segment at a time. This method can serve several objectives simultaneously, because the items are physically handled. It is particularly useful as a learning tool for new librarians, who can gain an intimate knowledge of the collection.

Some problems with direct collection checking stem from its dependency on individuals' personal perspective. Local librarians may be less than objective as they review the collections they have built. External evaluators who know the subject and its literature, have time to devote to the project, and are affordable may be difficult to recruit. External evaluators may also lack the local context and, even if provided with the library's collection development policy, may be less effective than someone who knows the user community and local context. The subjective and impressionistic nature of this method does not provide comparable information. Only careful recording of findings can provide a quantitative report, and its accuracy may be suspect.

Another disadvantage is the reliance on hands-on examination. Because this approach examines only materials on the shelves, items not on the shelf (e.g., circulating items and most e-resources) cannot be examined; this weakness can be addressed if the evaluator also consults a shelf list, subject headings in the local catalog, and circulation records.

A variation of direct collection analysis involves working from the shelf list, which may be a paper or electronic file. Although physical items are not handled, this approach has the advantage of making all other information about the items immediately available. Detailed information about imprints—age, language of publication, percentage of duplication, and subject coverage—can be collected easily. Reports can calculate the distribution of a collection by determining the percentage of holdings by call number range and then by copyright date within these call number ranges. These data can be combined with circulation data. Such reports can be useful in identifying subject areas that need to be updated, weeded, or expanded. Qualitative information can be used to supplement the quantitative information collected in a shelf list title count. The primary drawback of this method is the potential absence of many items and formats from the classified shelf list. Portions of the collection, such as e-resources, media, and microforms, may not be classified, or the collection may be split between two or more classification schedules.

Comparative Statistics

Libraries have used *comparative statistics* on collection size and materials expenditures to determine relative strengths for many years, often under the assumption that bigger is better. Although depth and breadth of a collection are partly a function of collection size, numerical counts do not measure quality. The ARL member libraries submit comparative statistics in many areas, including several collection measures; these are maintained on the ARL statistics website (www.arl.org/stats). ARL annually calculates a weighted index formula and index for its university library members. Although member libraries frequently reference their annual ranking in this index, ARL states explicitly that the index does not measure a library's services, quality of collections, or success in meeting the needs of users. ARL, reflecting trends in the profession, seeks to assess outcomes, impacts, and quality, based on user satisfaction, and to develop comparative measures in these areas.

Nevertheless, numerical data for inputs and outputs remain important points of comparison for libraries of all types, and several sources are available.

For example, the National Center for Education Statistics (NCES) offers two websites that allow academic librarians to choose a peer institution or peer group and compare their libraries' data with that provided by others in the biennial NCES surveys and another that provides selected statistics on public school libraries and media centers through its Digest of Education Statistics program. IMLS provides statistics on the status of approximately nine thousand public libraries in the United States.[44] The *Annual Statistics of Medical School Libraries in the United States and Canada* provides comparative data, including characteristics of collections, for this type of library. AASL collects data and releases *School Libraries Count! National Longitudinal Survey of School Library Programs* annually.[45] Many states also have programs that collect and report data about school libraries, which allow librarians to compare their own library program to other similar libraries in the state.[46]

When libraries collect and compare a specific group of statistics, they must agree on the definition of each statistical component and implement identical measurement methods. Comparisons are meaningless without consistency. Libraries typically measure size of collections in number of volumes and titles and by format, rate of net growth, and expenditures for library materials by format and by total budget. Additional collection comparisons may include number of volumes bound and expenditures on preservation and conservation treatments. Another comparison frequently used is the degree of collection overlap and extent of unique holdings. This requires a mechanism, such as the OCLC Collection Analysis tool, to compare local holdings with that of one or more other libraries.

Statistics to be used for comparison can be gathered in various ways. Libraries' automated systems may generate counts based on cumulative transactions or through specially prepared programs run periodically. These reports count totals as well as activity (titles added and withdrawn, dollars expended, etc.) within a specified period. If the various measures are clearly defined, the statistics can be compared and have meaning to a wide audience. If the statistics are accurate, they can provide objective, quantifiable data. Nevertheless, statistical compilations are not without problems. If portions of a library's collection are not cataloged and not reflected in either online records or paper files, the statistics will not be accurate. Manual collection of statistics can be very labor intensive and data may not be recorded accurately. If definitions of categories are not consistently understood or applied, results many not be comparable. Finally, statistics cannot measure collection quality or, on their own, verify collection levels.

Application of Standards

Collection and resources standards, which have been developed by professional associations, accrediting agencies, funding agencies, and library boards, may be used by those types of libraries for which standards have been developed. These standards have moved away from prescriptive volume counts, budget sizes, and the application of formulas and now emphasize adequacy, access, and availability. ALA, its divisions, and other professional library associations have been leaders in developing standards and output measures for various types of libraries.

The first standards for school libraries were published in 1918 and were endorsed and republished by ALA in 1920 as *Standard Library Organization and Equipment for Secondary Schools of Different Sizes*. These and subsequent revisions provided quantitative standards for print materials and ultimately media. The 1998 revision, *Information Power: Building Partnerships for Learning*, was the first to drop quantitative recommendations. The current edition, *Empowering Learners: Guidelines for School Library Media Programs*, states succinctly, "The school library media program includes a well-developed collection of books, periodicals, and non-print material in a variety of formats that support curricular topics and are suited to inquiry learning and users' needs and interests."[47]

Some states have developed standards for school libraries that supplement national standards. For example, the Ohio Department of Education "Ohio Guidelines for Effective School Library Media Programs" advises schools to "provide students with age-appropriate fiction and nonfiction reading material and assist in the location and selection of reading materials based on student reading level, interests, and information needs" but sets no numerical benchmarks. The 2010 California Department of Education Model School Library Standards for California Public Schools: Kindergarten through Grade Twelve devotes most of its attention to school library standards for students but does briefly address school library program standards, including minimum numbers for various resources.[48]

The Young Adult Library Services Association (YALSA) has developed the YALSA Public Library Evaluation Tool, which defines essential elements in providing services to teens. Though not a standard per se, each element in this tool is accompanied by characteristics that define it as distinguished, proficient, basic, or below basic. For example, the essential element "Collection of materials in a variety of formats, reading levels, and languages" in a distinguished collection is characterized this way:

Young adult collection represents a wide variety of formats including print and digital. The entire collection is continually evaluated & weeded. Collection reflects languages other than English that reflect the library community. YA staff is familiar with all types of materials that teens consume in all types of formats.

The same element in a below basic collection:

YA collection consists mainly of print books and periodicals. The collection is out-of-date and hasn't been weeded in 3 or more years.[49]

The 2011 ACRL standards apply to all types of libraries in higher education and aim to help libraries "demonstrate their value and document their contributions to overall institutional effectiveness."[50] Instead of suggesting appropriate size as earlier ACRL standards did, the 2011 standards stress outcomes and suggest points of comparison with peers and for internal longitudinal analysis. Possible data for comparison might be ratio of volumes to combined student and faculty FTE, ratio of volumes added per year to combined total student and faculty FTE, ratio of circulation to combined student and faculty FTE, and ratio of interlibrary loan requests to combined student and faculty FTE.

Special libraries are so diverse in mission that the profession has developed specialized standards tailored to specific types of libraries. For example, the Medical Library Association has standards for hospital libraries and for chiropractic college libraries, among others.[51] The American Association of Law Libraries (AALL) has standards for many types of law libraries, ranging from county public law libraries to appellate court libraries and state law libraries.[52] Standards for special libraries generally stress having a collection that meets the needs of their users, although some AALL standards are specific to the point of listing a core collection of materials that can be used as a checklist for collection evaluation.

Standards developed by ALA and other professional associations and agencies usually are considered authoritative and widely accepted. Their credibility often means that they can be effective in securing library support. If a standard exists for the library type being studied, it generally relates closely to the library's goals. Standards provide a framework for comparing libraries of similar types. Still, the application of externally developed standards can present problems. Some standards are very general and difficult to apply to specific collections. As with any externally developed measure, standards are the product of opinion, and not everyone will agree with them. In addition, individuals may not agree with or accept the results reported. Some standards may set a minimum level of volumes, expenditures, or collection level, and the tendency is to view this minimum as the goal.

Methods of Use- and User-Centered Analysis

Use- and user-centered analysis may be quantitative, qualitative, or a combination of the two. A cardinal principle of librarianship is protecting the privacy of library users with respect to their information seeking. Collecting and analyzing use and user data must be done in a manner that protects and respects users' privacy. Most academic institutions have specific policies that must be followed when data are gathered from human subjects, ensuring that the privacy as well as the well-being of individuals are not at risk. Many states have statutes that protect the privacy of citizens.

The electronic environment makes collecting information about individuals and their information-seeking behavior much easier than in a solely print environment. Data can be captured as part of each online transaction. E-content providers have found this especially appealing because of the potential to redesign products in response to users and to target messages to individual users based on behavior. In July 2002, the ICOLC endorsed and released *Privacy Guidelines for Electronic Resources Vendors*, which includes this statement: "Publisher respects the privacy of the users of its products. Accordingly, Publisher will not disclose information about any individual user of its products . . . to a third party without the permission of that individual user, except as required by law."[53] Most libraries seek to include a clause in their contracts for e-resources that prohibits publishers and vendors from collecting and sharing personally identifiable information.

Citation Studies

Citation studies are a type of bibliometrics—the quantitative treatment of the properties that describe and predict the nature of scholarly literature use. Source publications are searched for bibliographic references, and these citations are used to analyze the collection. Citation studies assume that the more frequently cited publications are the more valuable, will continue to be used heavily, and, consequently, are more important to have in the library collections. Data from citation studies can guide cancellation and retention decisions. Citation analysis is closely related to list checking and consists of counting or ranking (or both) the number of times sources are cited (e.g., in footnote references, bibliographies, or indexing and abstracting tools) and comparing those figures to the collection.

One type of citation study examines citations in publications by scholars worldwide. Data compiled by Thomson Scientific (formerly ISI) and available through Thomson Scientific's *Journal Citation Reports* is a frequent source. Thomson Scientific evaluates leading journals and, through frequency of citation, their "impact factor" and influence in the research community. The validity of the data has been questioned by some.[54] Another approach to rating the importance of scientific journals uses Eigenfactor metrics (http://eigenfactor .org), developed by researchers at the University of Washington.[55] Some believe the Eigenfactor approach is more meaningful than impact factors because it considers the significance or influence of citations, not just their number, by using an iterative ranking scheme to weight top journals more heavily. A third metric, COUNTER Code of Practice for Usage Factors, is being developed by COUNTER and was released as a draft in 2012.[56] The concept of *usage factors* results from the Usage Factor project, which seeks to provide an alternative to citation-based measures of journal performance.[57] These global usage data, which provide information about the average use of items in an online journal, are intended to balance overreliance on impact factors.

A second type of citation study is local and examines the literature cited by the library's own user community and tracks sources cited in their research papers, theses, and dissertations. The emphasis is on determining relative importance of a journal to the local user community by counting and comparing the frequency with which a journal is cited. Wilde describes a project that used a customized service (Local Journal Utilization Report, from Thomson Reuters) to document local faculty publishing and citing trends to inform a journal cancellation project.[58]

School library media centers can use students' bibliographies to check citations and learn about the information needs of the local user. However, if the student uses only the collection being evaluated, the value of such citation studies is limited. In addition, these bibliographies are limited to the subjects on which students write papers, the number of students who write papers, and the number of teachers who require bibliographies.

Citation studies are particularly useful in collections where journals are important. They are most frequently used to determine the extent to which the collection responds to users' research needs, to develop core lists of primary journals, and to identify candidates for cancellation or storage. Data collected in citation studies can be arranged easily into categories for analysis. Citation studies also can identify trends in the literature. Online databases can make assembling a citation list efficient and rapid, and several published citation indexes exist. However, externally prepared citation lists may not match the bibliographic formats of the library, and developing a list of source items that reflect the subject studied or user needs can be challenging. Subsections of one discipline may have different citation patterns from the general subject. Citation studies are not appropriate to all disciplines. On the other hand, such approaches are viable in interdisciplinary fields, which can present unique problems for collection analysis because interdisciplinary study (e.g., bioethics, women's studies), teaching, and research require crossing the traditional discipline divisions reflected in library's classification schemes and subject headings.[59]

Another problem with citation studies is the inherent time lag in citations, which masks changes of emphasis in disciplines and the emergence of new journals. In addition, citation analysis is time consuming and labor intensive. Important materials for consultation or background work may not be cited frequently.

Circulation Studies

Circulation studies analyze local circulation transactions. Information can be collected for all or part of the circulating collection by user group, location, date of publication, subject classification, or type of transaction, such as loans, recalls and holds, reserves, and renewals. Circulation studies can identify those portions of the collections that are little used and perhaps appropriate for weeding, transfer, or storage. Information indicating less-used subject areas may suggest curtailing future acquisitions in these areas. The librarian may decide to duplicate titles that are heavily used or to select additional materials in the same subject area. Public libraries often set a limit on the number of holds that can be placed on a title; attempted holds in excess of that number prompt the library to order additional copies. Circulation statistics can be used to compare use patterns in selected subject areas or by types of materials against their representation in the total collection. This information may be used to modify collection development practices or fund allocations. Journal use statistics can be used to calculate cost per use and provide guidance in making journal cancellation decisions.

Circulation data can be arranged easily into categories for analysis, and these categories can be correlated in various ways. For example, a public library system can compare circulation of various categories of fiction in each of several branch libraries, leading to decisions about where to locate larger mystery, romance, and science fiction collections. A school library media center might use the automated system to provide statistics about the age of the collection broken down by classification number and include circulation data. If the automated system cannot provide this information or such a system is not in use, the library media specialist can pick random parts of the collection and average the publication dates of the books. Circulation data can determine how many items are checked out each month, what areas are most heavily used, and what areas get little or no use. For example, consider these findings from a school library using the Dewey

Decimal classification system. If 23 percent of the titles circulated are from the 500s and only 10 percent of the budget is designated for titles in the 500s, one might want to readjust that spending—remembering to consider areas emphasized by the curriculum when making these comparison. Circulation data usually can be collected easily and are objective. Automated circulation systems make data collection extremely efficient.

The prevalence of e-books is changing the nature of circulation studies. E-book circulation is reported by vendors and publishers, not through a library's automated system. To have a complete picture, libraries must combine multiple sources of data. Gray and Copeland examined e-book usage and cost in a public library by comparing popular e-books to their print counterparts and learned that e-book and print copies of the same title circulated at similar rates and had similar costs per circulation.[60] In 2012, *Library Journal* suggested that an apparent national decrease in circulation might be explained by reporting libraries' failure to combine circulation data for print and e-books and noted that some libraries oppose tracking circulation of materials they lease and do not own.[61]

The major problem with circulation data extracted from a library's automated system is that these data exclude in-house use (unless a mechanism is in place to capture in-house use) and use of most e-resources. Circulation statistics for materials that are heavily used do not reflect the true demand for these items unless the library has a means to include queued requests for materials in use. Also, circulation studies reflect only user successes in identifying, locating, and borrowing items. They provide no information on user failure to find materials or the collection's failure to provide them.

In-House Use Studies

Several techniques are available for recording the use of materials consulted by users in the library and reshelved by library staff. *In-house use studies* can focus on either materials used or the users of materials. They can look at the entire collection or a part of it, at all users or a sample of users. In-house use studies are most often used to measure usage in noncirculating collections, such as a reference collection. Combining an in-house use study with a circulation study gives more accurate information than either alone.

Use studies of noncirculating materials depend on users' willingness to refrain from reshelving materials after use. Materials must be set aside so their use can be tracked either manually or by scanning bar codes directly into an automated system. Because in-house use studies rely on users' cooperation, they may be less accurate. Most libraries use direct observation to correct for uncooperative users. If the study is conducted over a limited time, care must be taken to time the study appropriately so data do not reflect use only in peak or slow periods. Studies of in-house use report only users' success in locating materials; thus, user failures are not reported.

User Surveys and Focus Groups

User surveys seek to determine how well the library's collections meet users' needs and expectations and to identify those that are unmet. Surveys may be administered in various ways: verbally in person or on the phone, through guided discussion in focus groups, by e-mail, through pop-up screens on the library's catalog or web page, via web-based surveys, or as written questionnaires handed to users in the library either as they enter or exit or mailed to them at offices and homes. Information from user surveys can be used to assess quantitatively and qualitatively the effectiveness of the collections in meeting users' needs, help solve specific problems, define the makeup of the actual community of library users, identify user groups who need to be better served, provide feedback on successes as well as on deficiencies, improve public relations and assist in the education of the user community, and identify changing interests.

User surveys can improve the library's relations with its community and help educate users and nonusers. Such surveys are not limited to existing data, such as circulation statistics, but permit the library to study new areas—interdisciplinary fields, for example. They solicit direct responses from users and can collect opinions not normally shared with the library. A survey can range from short and simple to lengthy and complex.

LibQUAL+ (www.libqual.org), offered by ARL since 2000, is an online survey instrument within a suite of services that all types of libraries can use to solicit, track, understand, and act upon users' perceptions of library service quality. As of 2012, more than one thousand libraries including colleges and university libraries, community college libraries, health sciences libraries, academic law libraries, and public libraries have used LibQUAL+.[62] The LibQUAL+ survey instrument is a derivation of the SERVQUAL tool created to measure service quality in the private sector.[63] LibQUAL+ calculates gap scores between minimum and perceived expectations and desire and perceived expectations. Sections of the LibQUAL+ survey measure perceived quality in provision of collections and access to collections. Libraries can identify areas that users say are below their minimum expectation (e.g., access to e-resources) and begin to address problems of both library quality and user perception. A library that uses the LibQUAL+ instrument can collect longitudinal data and compare local findings with peer libraries. LibQUAL+, which has twenty-two core questions, has been criticized for being too lengthy. LibQUAL+ Lite (www.libqual.org/about/about_lq/LQ_lite) is an attempt to improve response rates by asking all users to answer a few, selected survey questions and randomly selecting a subsample of the users to answer the rest of the questions.[64]

Designing even the shortest survey instrument can be difficult. Crafting questions that yield the results sought often requires the help of an experienced questionnaire designer. The parent agency of some libraries may require prior approval of any research that involves human subjects, even a brief library user survey. Crafting surveys for young children can be challenging. Analyzing and interpreting data from an opinion survey can be difficult. Users are often passive about collections and so must be surveyed individually, increasing survey costs. Even with individual attention, some users may not cooperate in the survey, resulting in skewed results. Many users are uninformed or unaware of actual and possible library collections. They have difficulty in judging what is adequate or appropriate. User surveys may record perceptions, intentions, and recollections that do not reflect actual experiences or patterns of user behavior. Perceptions and opinions are not always quantifiable. By definition, surveys of users do not reach nonusers, who may have valuable observations.

Focus groups are a research tool in which a small representative group of people selected from the user community engages in a guided discussion in an informal setting.[65] The discussion is directed by a moderator who guides the discussion in order to obtain the group's opinions about or reactions to specific services or resources. Focus groups can provide in-depth information through facilitated conversation that explores topics and issues that cannot be covered in surveys. One difficulty is in measuring the results objectively. Nevertheless, focus groups can provide detailed comments, identification of issues, suggestions, and concerns. Other challenges include selecting participants and getting them to come, deciding how many focus groups are sufficient, facilitating a session effectively, avoiding interviewer bias that can skew discussion, taking good notes, and then analyzing and presenting findings.

Interlibrary Loan Analysis

Items requested through interlibrary loan represent a use of the collection because the requester has checked the collection, found the item lacking (either not owned or missing), and decided that he or she still needs it. *Interlibrary loan analysis* can identify areas in which the collection is not satisfying patron needs and may serve to identify books and journals that are appropriate to add. Statistical results often are readily available and can be analyzed by title, classification, date of imprint, or language. Analyses of subject classifications are best interpreted in conjunction with corresponding acquisitions and circulation data.[66] Results must be interpreted in relation to the collection development policy and existing resource-sharing agreements that rely on interlibrary loan. Requests can serve as indicators of change in the user community, new program needs, or a long-standing deficiency and can inform budget allocation and reallocation decisions. One approach is to look at interlibrary loan activity within a subject area and compare this to the level of collecting specified in the library's collection development policy. One problem with the use of interlibrary loan statistics is that their significance may be difficult to interpret. One library user might be skewing the data by requesting many items in one area of interest. Also, this type of study does not reflect users who go elsewhere instead of requesting resources through interlibrary loan.

Document Delivery Test

A *document delivery test* checks the library's ability to provide users with items at the time they are needed. Searching is done by library staff, who simulate users. Document delivery tests build on citation studies by determining first if the library owns a certain item and then if the item can be located and how long it takes to do so. The most frequent approach is to compile a list of citations that reflect the library users' information needs. Externally developed lists also can be used. The test determines both the number of items owned by the library and the time required to locate a specific item. Document delivery testing can provide objective measurements of a collection's capacity to satisfy user needs. This type of testing may identify service problems that then can be corrected. Benchmark data are gathered, and changes can be measured through subsequent testing. Compiling a list of representative citations can, however, be challenging. Because the testing is done by experienced library staff members, it can underestimate the problems encountered by users. To be meaningful, results require repeated tests.

Planning and Conducting a Collection Analysis Project

Although collection analysis should be an ongoing activity, it tends to be defined by discrete analysis projects. Ideally, the projects can be repeated and are part of a long-range analysis plan. An analysis can be all-inclusive or focus on specific areas, depending on the library's needs and available resources. Each project should be planned carefully to ensure efficiency and effectiveness. An analysis plan can be developed by the individual librarian or by a working group. The first step is to define the purposes of the study and the hypotheses that will be tested. What are the objectives of this project? Why is the information being collected? How will it be used? A plan identifies specific questions that will be answered.

The next step is to determine the data that will be gathered and the methods to be used to collect and analyze the data. Each method described in this chapter has advantages and unique benefits for analyzing collections. Each also has disadvantages. No single method of gathering data provides a complete understanding of a collection. Effective collection analysis requires a combination of techniques to gain a complete understanding of a collection and its users. For example, a project at Eastern Michigan University used three techniques—citation analysis, a survey, and interviews—to determine if the library owned the content that faculty cited in their research and if the collection was being used.[67]

Consider the format in which the results will be presented and the audience to which the report will be directed. Subject the choice of data to the same rigorous standards used in defining purposes, because each data element adds to the expense and complexity of the study.

The intended audience of the resulting report may be the library director, school principal, chief collection development officer, or a funding agency or governing board. An analysis project may generate information that will be used for more than one audience or purpose. The librarian decides which part of the collection or representative sample to study. All steps in an analysis project should be documented so that it can be repeated easily. The librarian should consider whether comparability of results with those of other libraries is desirable and what commonly used classification divisions, statistical categories, terminology, output measures, or survey questions may facilitate comparisons. Before undertaking an analysis project, the librarian should estimate the resources in staff time and funding needed to conduct the analysis. Many methods are time-consuming or require external experts or contracting for a commercial analysis product. The librarian should consult existing collection information, which may include a collection development policy, library mission or goal statement, and previously conducted analysis projects.

After the data are collected and analyzed, the report is prepared and disseminated. The report should follow generally accepted practices for reports. It should explain the purposes of the study, methods used, and problems encountered. It provides general comments on the collection analyzed and the purposes it is intended to serve. As part of the findings, the report summarizes specific strengths, nonstrengths, and weaknesses. A good report provides both textual and graphic representations of findings. Visualizations (charts and graphs) can provide "useful insights about how the collection compares to other collections, how it is developing over time, unintended gaps in the collection, strengths, and weaknesses in the support of interdisciplinary studies, the extent to which [the] collection contributes to the whole of the consortia in which you participate, the scatter of material needed for one discipline across the full subject scope of the library, and so on."[68]

An effective report both shares and interprets the data. It draws relevant conclusions, suggests a plan to improve collection in areas of undesirable weakness, and lists specific items or types of materials needed and cost estimates.

Wilde and Level offer useful guiding principles for collection analysis:

- Hard statistics must guide collection assessment and development, but they need to be supplemented by input from the user community and librarians.

- Data must be centrally archived and freely shared across library departments.

- Keep data up-to-date and maintain a data bank of collection assessment information.

- Consider only the relevant data.

- Usage patterns vary among the disciplines. Looking at science, engineering, and medicine separately from the humanities and social sciences may be useful.

- What worked last year might not work this year. Statistics that were available last year may not be available this year.

- Approach assessment from a philosophical framework, then create local solutions to fit the philosophy. The statistics and data the library receive may change, but the way the library uses the data should be stable.[69]

CASE STUDY

Marlys has worked for the Springfield Public Library System for several years. The system has a main central library and twelve branches. Recently, she was appointed the assistant librarian at a larger branch library located in a neighborhood with a diverse population, including many families in which English is not the primary language spoken at home. Marlys's responsibilities as assistant branch librarian include supporting children and young adults through programming and collections. New titles are selected by the head children's librarian in the central library. Marlys is responsible for ordering added copies and suggesting books to supplement those ordered centrally. The picture book collection, which totals approximately five thousand volumes (including numerous added copies), is heavily used. Previous practice has been a direct collection analysis of the picture books each fall to identify those items that are worn beyond simple mending and should be withdrawn. When Marlys's predecessor recognized a title to be withdrawn as a classic or award winner, he would order a replacement copy. Marlys understands the need to keep the picture book collection fresh and attractive, but she wants to use appropriate collection analysis techniques to decide which books to replace and where the collection might be strengthened.

Activity

Suggest at least two analysis methods Marlys can employ to determine which picture books to replace and areas that might be strengthened. Develop a plan for applying each method, including an explanation of why each approach is being used, what information will be collected, how the information will be used, who the audience is, and a schedule for the projects. Explain how the approaches proposed complement each other.

Notes

1. Sheila S. Intner and Elizabeth Futas, "Evaluating Public Library Collections: Why Do It and How to Use the Results," *American Libraries* 25, no. 5 (May 1994): 410–12.

2. See, for example, Amos Lakos, "The Missing Ingredient—Culture of Assessment in Libraries: Opinion Piece," *Performance Measurement and Metrics* 1, no. 1 (Aug. 1999): 3–7; Amos Lakos and Shelley Phipps, "Creating a Culture of Assessment: A Catalyst for Organizational Change," *portal: Libraries and the Academy* 4, no. 3 (2004): 345–61, quote 352.

3. Mary C. Bushing, "Collection Mapping: An Evolving Tool for Better Resources and Better Access," *Signum* 39, no. 3 (2006): 9, http://pro.tsv.fi/stks/signum.

4. Australian School Library Association and Australian Library and Information Association, *Learning for the Future: Developing Information Services in Schools*, 2nd ed. (Melbourne, Australia: Curriculum Corp., 2001).

5. Peter Hernon and Robert E. Dugan, *An Action Plan for Outcomes Assessment in Your Library* (Chicago: American Library Association, 2002), x.

6. Denise Pan, Gabrielle Wiersma, and Yem Fong, "Towards Demonstrating Value: Measuring the Contributions of Library Collections to University Research and Teaching Goals," in *Declaration of Interdependence: The Proceedings of the ACRL 2011 Conference, March 30–April 2, 2011, Philadelphia, Pennsylvania, 2011*, ed. Dawn M. Mueller (Chicago: Association of College and Research Libraries, 2011), 495–65, www.goeshow.com/acrl/national/2011/client_uploads/handouts/towards_demon strating_value.pdf; Shun Han Rebekah Wong and T.D. Webb, "Uncovering Meaningful Correlation between Student Academic Performance and Library Material Usage," *College and Research Libraries* 72, no. 4 (July 2011): 361–70.

7. Keith Curry Lance, Lynda Welborn, and Christine Hamilton-Pennell, *The Impact of School Library Media Centers on Student Achievement* (Castle Rock, CO: Hi Willow, 1993).

8. Association of College and Research Libraries, *Standards for Libraries in Higher Education* (Chicago: Association of College and Research Libraries, 2011), 20, www.ala.org/acrl/sites/ala.org.acrl/files/content/standards/slhe.pdf.

9. Jessica Schomberg and Barb Bergman, "International Students' Use of a Library's Media Collection," *Library Collections, Acquisitions, and Technical Services* 36, no. 3/4 (2012): 121–26.

10. Jennifer Z. McClure, "Collection Assessment through WorldCat," *Collection Management* 34, no. 2 (2009): 79.

11. Ibid.

12. Eva Stowers and Cory Tucker, "Using Link Resolver Reports for Collection Management." *Serials Review* 35, no. 1 (2009): 28–34.

13. G. E. Gorman et al., *Qualitative Research for the Information Professional: A Practical Handbook*, 2nd ed. (London: Facet, 2005), 3.

14. See Lynn Silipigni Connaway and Ronald R. Powell, *Basic Research Methods for Librarians*, 5th ed. (Santa Barbara, CA: Libraries Unlimited, 2010); Danny P. Wallace and Connie Van Fleet, *Knowledge into Action: Research and Evaluation in Library and Information Science* (Santa Barbara, CA: Libraries Unlimited, 2012); Douglas Cook and Lesley Farmer, eds., *Using Qualitative Methods in Actions Research: How Librarians Can Get to the Why of Data* (Chicago: American Library Association, 2011); Valeda Dent Goodman, *Qualitative Research and the Modern Library* (Oxford, UK: Chandos, 2011); Peter Clayton and G. G. Gorman, *The Information Professional's Guide to Quantitative Research: A Practical Handbook*, 2nd ed. (New York: Neal-Schuman, 2011); Alison Jane Pickard, *Research Methods in Information*, 2nd ed. (Chicago: Neal-Schuman, 2013).

15. Jeffrey J. Gamer and Duane E. Webster, *The Collection Analysis Project: Operating Manual for the Review and Analysis of the Collection Development Function in Academic and Research Libraries: CAP Manual* (Washington, DC: Association of Research Libraries, 1978).

16. Julie Gammon and Edward T. O'Neill, *OhioLINK OCLC Collection and Circulation Analysis Project 2011* (Dublin, OH: OCLC Research, 2011), www.oclc.org/content/dam/research/publications/library/2011/2011-06.pdf.

17. Leslie Horner Button and Rachel C. Lewellen, "Monograph Duplication Analysis to Inform Consortial Collection Development," in *Proceedings of the 2010 Library Assessment Conference: Building Effective, Sustainable, Practical Assessment, October 24–27, 2010, Baltimore, Maryland*, ed. Steve Hill et al., 715–20 (Washington, DC: Association of Research Libraries, 2011), http://libraryassessment.org/bm~doc/proceedings-lac-2010.pdf.

18. Verner W. Clapp and Robert T. Jordan, "Quantitative Criteria for Adequacy of Academic Library Collections," *College and Research Libraries* 50, no. 2 (Mar. 1989): 153–63. This article was originally published in 1965.

19. Allen Kent et al., *Use of Library Materials: The University of Pittsburgh Study* (New York: Marcel Dekker, 1979).

20. Richard W. Trueswell, "Some Behavioral Patterns of Library Users: The 80/20 Rule," *Wilson Library Bulletin* 43, no. 5 (Jan. 1969): 458–81.

21. Thomas E. Nisonger, *Management of Serials in Libraries* (Englewood, CO: Libraries Unlimited, 1998).

22. David L. Perkins, ed., *Guidelines for Collection Development* (Chicago: Collection Development Committee, Resources and Technical Services Division, American Library Association, 1979).

23. See, for example, Lolita Kwok, "Assessing Art Books Using the Conspectus Approach," *Art Documentation* 31, no. 1 (2012): 108–22, and Katie Lai, "A Revival of the Music Conspectus: A Multi-Dimensional Assessment for the Score Collection," *Notes* 66, no. 3 (Mar. 2010): 503–18, which report Conspectus use at Hong Kong Baptist University; and Madjid Dahmane and Zahir Yahiaoui, "Using the Conspectus Methodology in Algeria: Case Study of the University Library of Bejaia," *Against the Grain* 22, no. 1 (Feb. 2010): 42–44.

24. Mary Bushing, Burns Davis, and Nancy Powell, *Using the Conspectus Method: A Collection Assessment Handbook* (Lacey, WA: WLN, 1997).

25. International Federation of Library Associations and Institutions, Section on Acquisition and Collection Development, *Guidelines for a Collection Development Policy Using the Conspectus Model* (2001), Appendix 2: Conspectus Collection Depth Indicator Definitions, www.ifla.org/VII/s14/nd1/gcdp-e.pdf.

26. Tony Greiner and Bob Cooper, *Analyzing Library Collection Use with Excel®* (Chicago: American Library Association, 2007).

27. The Conspectus has been the subject of debate and numerous papers. The following are representative: Richard J. Wood, "The Conspectus: A Collection Analysis and Development Success," *Library Acquisitions: Practice and Theory* 20, no. 4 (1996): 429–53; Virgil L. P. Blake and Renee Tjoumas, "The Conspectus Approach to Collection Evaluation: Panacea or False Prophet?" *Collection Management* 18, no. 3/4 (1994): 1–31; Frederick J. Stielow and Helen R. Tibbo, "Collection Analysis in Modern Librarianship: A Stratified, Multidimensional Model," *Collection Management* 11, no. 3/4 (1989): 73–91.

28. Mary H. Munroe and Jennie E. Ver Steeg, "The Decision-Making Process in Conspectus Evaluation of Collections: The Quest for Certainty," *Library Quarterly* 74, no. 2 (2004): 181–205; Charles B. Osburn, "Collection Evaluation: A Reconsideration," *Advances in Library Administration and Organization* 22 (2005): 10.

29. Howard D. White, *Brief Tests of Collection Strength: A Methodology for All Types of Libraries*, Contributions in Library and Information Science no. 88 (Westport, CT: Greenwood, 1995). See also Jennifer Benedetto Beals and Ron Gilmour, "Assessing Collections Using Brief Tests and WorldCat Collection Analysis," *Collection Building* 26, no. 4 (2007): 104–7; Jennifer Benedetto Beals, "Assessing Library Collections Using Brief Test Methodology," *Electronic Journal of Academic and Special Librarianship* 7, no. 3 (Winter 2006), http://southernlibrarianship.icaap .org/content/v07n03/beals_j01.htm; David Lesniaski, "Evaluating Collections: A Discussion and Extension of Brief Test of Collection Strength," *College and Undergraduate Libraries* 11, no. 1 (2004): 11–24; Thomas M. Twiss, "A Validation of Brief Tests of Collection Strength," *Collection Management* 25, no. 3 (2001): 23–37; Sara Lowe and Sean M. Stone, "Testing Lesniaski's Revised Brief Test," *College and Undergraduate Libraries* 17, no. 1 (2010): 70–78.

30. Howard D. White, "Better Than Brief Tests: Coverage Power Tests of Collection Strength," *College and Research Libraries* 69, no. 2 (Mar. 2008): 155–74.

31. David V. Loertscher and Laura H. Wimberley, *Collection Development Using the Collection Mapping Technique: A Guide for Librarians* (San Jose, CA: Hi Willow, 2009). Debra E. Kachel applies the Conspectus approach to school libraries in her *Collection Assessment and Management for School Libraries: Preparing for Cooperative Collection Development* (Westport, CT: Greenwood, 1997).

32. International Coalition of Library Consortia, "Revised Guidelines for Statistical Measures of Usage of Web-Based Information Resources" (Oct. 4, 2006), www .icolc.net/statement/revised-guidelines-statistical-measures-usage-web-based -information-resources.

33. COUNTER, "Release 4 of the COUNTER Code of Practice for e-Resources (April 2012)," www.projectcounter.org/code_practice.html. See also National Information Standards Organization and American National Standards Institute, *The Standardized Usage Statistics Harvesting Initiative (SUSHI) Protocol*, ANSI/NISO Z39.93-2007 (Baltimore: National Information Standards Organization, 2007);

National Information Standards Organization, *NISO SUSHI Protocol: COUNTER-SUSHI Implementation Profile*, NISO RP-14-2012 (Baltimore: National Information Standards Organization, 2012).

34. An examination of transaction log analysis can be found in Denise Troll Covey, *Usage and Usability Assessment: Library Practices and Concerns* (Washington, DC: Digital Library Federation, Council on Library and Information Resources, 2002), www.clir.org/pubs/reports/pub105/contents.html.

35. See Jennifer Sweeney, "Cost/Benefit Comparison of Print and Electronic Journals in a University Library: A Progress Report," in *Proceedings of the 4th Northumbria International Conference on Performance Measurement in Libraries and Information Services: Meaningful Measures for Emerging Realities, Pittsburgh, PA, August 12–16, 2001*, ed. Joan Stein, Martha Kyrillidou, and Denise Davis, 345–48 (Washington, DC: Association of Research Libraries, 2002), www.libqual.org/documents/admin/sweeney.pdf; Brinley Franklin, "Managing the Electronic Collection with Cost per Use Data," (presentation, World Library and Information Congress: 70th IFLA General Conference and Council, August 22–27, 2004, Buenos Aires, Argentina), www.ifla.org/IV/ifla70/papers/098e-Franklin.pdf; Steve Block, "Impact of Full Text on Print Journal Use at a Liberal Arts College," *Library Resources and Technical Services* 49, no. 1 (Jan. 2005): 19–26; Cory Tucker, "Benchmarking Usage Statistics in Collection Management Decisions for Serials," *Journal of Electronic Resources Librarianship* 21, no. 1 (2009): 48–61.

36. Cecilia Botero, Steven Carrico, and Michele Tennant, "Using Comparative Online Journal Usage Studies to Assess the Big Deal," *Library Resources and Technical Services* 52, no. 2 (Apr. 2008): 61–68.

37. See, for example, Rusty Kimball, Gary Ives, and Kathy Jackson, "Comparative Usage of Science E-book and Print Collections at Texas A&M University Libraries," *Collection Management* 35, no. 1 (2009): 15–28; Robert Slater, "E-books or Print Books, 'Big Deals' or Local Selections—What Gets More Use?" *Library Collections, Acquisitions, and Technical Services* 33, no. 1 (2009): 31–41.

38. See James Cory Tucker, "E-book Collection Analysis: Subject and Publisher Trends," *Collection Building* 31, no. 2 (2012): 40–47; Nancy Sprague and Ben Hunter, "Assessing E-books: Taking a Closer Look at E-book Statistics," *Library Collections, Acquisitions, and Technical Services* 32, no. 3/4 (2009): 150–57; Terry Bucknell, "The 'Big Deal' Approach to Acquiring E-books: A Usage-Based Study," *Serials* 23, no. 2 (July 2010): 126–34; Catherine S. Herlihy and Hua Yi, "E-books in Academic Libraries: How Does Currency Affect Usage?" *New Library World* 111, no. 9/10 (2010): 371–80.

39. See Brinley Franklin and Terry Plum, "Assessing the Value and Impact of Digital Content," *Journal of Library Administration* 48, no. 1 (2008): 41–57; Terry Plum et al., "Measuring the Impact of Networked Electronic Resources: Developing an Assessment Infrastructure for Libraries, State, and Other Types of Consortia,"

Performance Measurement and Metrics 11, no. 2 (2010): 184–98; Martha Kyrillidou, Terry Plum, and Bruce Thompson, "Evaluating Usage and Impact of Networked Electronic Resources through Point-of-Use Surveys: A MINES for Libraries Study," *Serials Librarian* 59, no. 2 (2010): 159–83.

40. Anna H. Perrault and Jeannie Dixon, "Collection Assessment: Florida Community College Experience," *Community and Junior College Libraries* 14, no. 1 (2007): 7–20.

41. Catherine Barr, *Best Books for High School Readers, Grades 9–12*, 3rd ed. (Santa Barbara, CA: Libraries Unlimited, 2013).

42. For studies on the utility of list checking, see Robert N. Bland, "The College Textbook as a Tool for Collection Evaluation, Analysis, and Retrospective Collection Development," *Library Acquisitions: Practice and Theory*, 4, no. 3/4 (1980): 193–97; Anne H. Lundin, "List-Checking in Collection Development: An Imprecise Art," *Collection Management* 11, no. 3/4 (1989): 103–11.

43. Carol A. Doll, "Quality and Elementary School Library Media Collections," *School Library Media Quarterly* 25, no. 2 (Winter 1997): 95–102.

44. National Center for Education Statistics, "Compare Academic Libraries," http://nces.ed.gov/surveys/libraries/compare; National Center for Education Statistics, "Digest of Education Statistics," http://nces.ed.gov/programs/digest; Institute of Museum and Library Services, *Public Libraries in the United States Survey*, www.imls.gov/research/public_libraries_in_the_united_states_survey.aspx.

45. Association of Academic Health Sciences Libraries, *Annual Statistics of Medical School Libraries in the United States and Canada, 1978–*; American Association of School Librarians, *School Libraries Count! A National Survey of School Library Media Programs, 2007–*.

46. See, for example, Iowa Department of Education, School Library, "Iowa School Library Program Data," www.educateiowa.gov/pk-12/learner-supports/school-library#Iowa_School_Library_Program_Data; California Department of Education, "Statistics about California School Libraries," www.cde.ca.gov/ci/cr/lb/schoollibrstats08.asp.

47. Casper Carl Certain, *Standard Library Organization and Equipment for Secondary Schools of Different Sizes* (Washington, DC: National Education Association, Department of Secondary Education, 1918); American Association of School Librarians and Association for Educational Communications and Technology, *Information Power: Building Partnerships for Learning* (Chicago: American Library Association, 1998); *Empowering Learners: Guidelines for School Library Media Programs* (Chicago: American Association of School Librarians, 2009), 38.

48. Ohio Department of Education, "Ohio Guidelines for Effective School Library Media Programs" (2003), http://education.ohio.gov/getattachment/Topics/Academic-Content-Standards/Library-Guidelines/Library-Guidelines.pdf.aspx; California Department of Education, *Model School Library Standards for California Public Schools: Kindergarten through Grade Twelve* (Sacramento:

California Department of Education, 2010), www.cde.ca.gov/be/st/ss/documents/modellibrarystandards.doc.

49. "YALSA Public Library Evaluation Tool," *Young Adult Library Services* 10, no. 1 (Fall 2011): 39–51, quote 49, www.ala.org/yalsa/files/guidelines/yacompetencies/evaluationtool.pdf.

50. Association of College and Research Libraries, *Standards for Libraries in Higher Education* (Chicago: Association of College and Research Libraries, 2011), 5, www.ala.org/acrl/sites/ala.org.acrl/files/content/standards/slhe.pdf.

51. Margaret Bndy et al, "Standards for Hospital Libraries 2007," *Journal of the Medical Library Association* 96, no. 2 (Apr. 2008): 162–69, www.ncbi.nlm.nih.gov/pmc/articles/PMC2268237; Medical Library Association, Chiropractic College Libraries Section Standards Committee, "Standards for Chiropractic College Libraries" (1996), www.mlanet
.org/publications/standards/chiropractic/index.html.

52. American Association of Law Libraries, "County Public Law Library Standards" (July 2008), www.aallnet.org/main-menu/Leadership-Governance/policies/PublicPolicies/policy-county-standards.html; American Association of Law Libraries, "Appellate Court Libraries and State Law Libraries Standards" (March 2005), www.aallnet.org/main-menu/Leadership-Governance/policies/PublicPolicies/policy-appellate-standards.html.

53. International Coalition of Library Consortia, "Privacy Guidelines for Electronic Resources Vendors" (July 2002), http://icolc.net/statement/privacy-guidelines
-electronic-resources-vendors.

54. Mike Rossner, Heather Van Epps, and Emma Hill, "Show Me the Data," *Journal of Cell Biology* 179, no. 6 (Dec. 2007): 1091–92.

55. Carl Bergstrom, "Eigenfactor: Measuring the Value and Prestige of Scholarly Journals," *College and Research Libraries News* 68, no. 5 (May 2007): 314–16; Jevin D. West, Theodore C. Bergstrom, and Carl T. Bergstrom, "The Eigenfactor Metrics™: A Network Approach to Assessing Scholarly Journals," *College and Research Libraries* 71, no. 3 (May 2010): 236–44.

56. COUNTER, "Counter Code of Practice for Usage Factors: Draft Release 1," (Mar. 2012), www.projectcounter.org/documents/Draft_UF_R1.pdf.

57. Peter T. Shepherd, *Final Report on the Investigation into the Feasibility of Developing and Implementing Journal Usage Factors*, sponsored by the United Kingdom Serials Group (May 2007), www.uksg.org/sites/uksg.org/files/FinalReportUsageFactorProject.pdf; Peter Shepherd, *The Journal Usage Factor Project: Results, Recommendations, and Next Steps* (2011), www.projectcounter.org/documents/Journal_Usage_Factor_extended_report_July.pdf.

58. Michelle Wilde, "Local Journal Utilization Report: Supporting Data for Collection Decisions," *Collection Management* 35, no. 2 (2010): 102–107.

59. See Cynthia Dobson, Jeffrey D. Kushkowski, and Kristin H. Gerhard, "Collection Evaluation for Interdisciplinary Fields: A Comprehensive Approach," *Journal of Academic Librarianship* 22, no. 4 (July 1996): 279–84; Kristin H. Gerhard, "Challenges in Electronic Collection Building in Interdisciplinary Studies," *Collection Management* 25, no. 1/2 (2001): 51–65; Jeffrey D. Kushkowski and Charles B Shrader, "Developing a Core List of Journals in an Interdisciplinary Area," *Library Resources and Technical Services* 57, no. 1 (2013): 51–65.

60. David J. Gray and Andrea J. Copeland, "E-book versus Print: A Per-Title Cost and Use Comparison of a Public Library's Popular Titles," *Reference and User Services Quarterly* 51, no. 4 (Summer 2012): 334–39.

61. Barbara Hoffert, "Book Buying Survey 2012: Book Circ Takes a Hit," *Library Journal* (Feb. 14, 2012), http://lj.libraryjournal.com/2012/02/library-services/book -buying-survey-2012-book-circ-takes-a-hit.

62. LibQUAL+, General Information, www.libqual.org/about/about_lq/general_info.

63. A. Parasuraman, Valerie A. Zeitharnl, and Leonard L. Berry, "SERVQUAL: A Multiple-Item Scale for Measuring Consumer Perceptions of Service Quality," *Journal of Retailing* 64, no. 1 (Spring 1988): 12–40.

64. Bruce Thompson, Martha Kyrillidou, and Colleen Cook, "Equating Scores on 'Lite' and Long Library User Survey Forms: The LibQUAL+® Lite Randomized Control Trials," *Performance Measurement and Metrics* 10, no. 3 (2009): 212–19.

65. Pranee Liampottong, *Focus Group Methodology: Principles and Practice.* London: Sage, 2011.

66. See, for example, Jennifer E. Knievel, Heather Wicht, and Lynn Silipigni Connaway, "Use of Circulation Statistics and Interlibrary Loan Data in Collection Management," *College and Research Libraries* 67, no. 1 (2006): 35–49.

67. Susann deVries, Robert Kelly, and Paula M. Storm, "Moving beyond Citation Analysis: How Surveys and Interviews Enhance, Enrich, and Expand Your Research Findings," *College and Research Libraries* 71, no. 5 (Sept. 2010): 456–66.

68. Gary M. Shirk, "Towards a Topography of Library Collections," in *Digital Information and Knowledge Management: New Opportunities for Research Libraries*, ed. Sul H. Lee, 99–111 (Binghamton, NY: Haworth, 2007), 106.

69. Michelle Wilde and Allison Level, "How to Drink from a Fire Hose without Drowning: Collection Assessment in a Numbers-Driven Environment," *Collection Management* 36, no. 4 (2011): 217–36.

Suggested Readings

Adams, Brian, and Bob Noel. "Circulation Statistics in the Evaluation of Collection Development." *Collection Building 27*, no. 2 (2008): 71–73.

Armbruster, Chris. "Access, Usage, and Citation Metrics: What Function for Digital Libraries and Repositories in Research Evaluation?" *Online Currents 22*, no. 5 (2008): 168–80.

Bishop, Kay. "Evaluation of the Collection." In *The Collection Program in Schools: Concepts and Practices*, 5th ed., 139–55. Westport, CT: Libraries Unlimited, 2013.

Bleiler, Richard, and Jill Livingston. *Evaluating E-resources*. SPEC Kit 316. Washington, DC: Association of Research Libraries, 2010.

Bobal, Alison M., Margaret Mellinger, and Bonnie E. Avery. "Collection Assessment and New Academic Programs." *Collection Management 33*, no. 4 (2008): 288–301.

Borin, Jacqueline, and Hua Yi. "Assessing an Academic Library Collection through Capacity and Usage Indicators: Testing a Multi-Dimensional Model." *Collection Building 30*, no. 3 (2011): 120–25.

Brillon, Alicia. "Collection Analysis When the Budget Decreases." *Legal Reference Services Quarterly 30*, no. 4 (Oct./Dec. 2011): 289–98.

Carroll, Diane, and Joel Cummings. "Data Driven Collection Assessment Using a Serial Decision Database." *Serials Review 36*, no. 4 (2010): 227–39.

Cenzer, Pamela S., and Cynthia Gozzi. *Evaluating Acquisitions and Collections Management*. Hoboken: Taylor and Francis, 2012.

Chadwell, Faye A. "What's Next for Collection Management and Managers? Assessing the Value of Collection Services." *Collection Management 37*, no. 2 (2012): 58–64.

Champlin, Connie, David V. Loertscher, and Nancy A. S. Miller. *Sharing the Evidence: Library Media Center Assessment Tools and Resources*. Salt Lake City: Hi Willow Research, 2008.

Chrzastowski, Tina E., Michael Norman, and Sarah Elizabeth Miller. "SFX Statistical Reports: A Primer for Collection Assessment Librarians." *Collection Management 34*, no. 4 (2009): 286–303.

Ciszek, Matthew P., and Courtney L. Young. "Diversity Collection Assessment in Large Academic Libraries." *Collection Building 29*, no. 4 (2010): 154–61.

Conway, Martha O'Hara, and Merrilee Proffitt. "The Practice, Power, and Promise of Archival Collections Assessment." *RBM: A Journal of Rare Books, Manuscripts, and Cultural Heritage 13*, no. 2 (Fall 2012): 100–12. http://rbm.acrl.org/content/13/2/100.full.pdf+html.

Crosetto, Alice, Laura Kinner, and Lucy Duhon. "Assessment in a Tight Time Frame: Using Readily Available Data to Evaluate Your Collection." *Collection Management 33*, no. 1/2 (2008): 29–50.

Culbertson, Michael, and Michelle Wilde. "Collection Analysis to Enhance Funding for Research Materials." *Collection Building* 28, no. 1 (2009): 9–17.

Dando, Priscille. *Say It with Data: A Concise Guide to Making Your Case and Getting Results.* Chicago: Neal-Schuman, 2014.

Daniels, Kate. "Got Value? Journal Collection Analysis Is Worth the Effort." *Medical Reference Services Quarterly* 29, no. 3 (2010): 275–85.

Danielson, Robert. "A Dual Approach to Assessing Collection Development and Acquisitions for Academic Libraries." *Library Collections, Acquisitions, and Technical Services* 36, no. 3/4 (2012): 84–96.

De Bellis, Nicola. *Bibliometrics and Citation Analysis: From the Science Citation Index to Cybermetrics.* Lanham, MD: Scarecrow, 2009.

Dugan, Robert E., Peter Hernon, and Danuta A. Nitecki. *Viewing Library Metrics from Different Perspectives: Inputs, Outputs, and Outcomes.* Santa Barbara, CA: Libraries Unlimited, 2009.

Entlich, Richard. "Focus on Circulation Snapshots: A Powerful Tool for Print Collection Assessment." In *Proceedings of the 2010 Library Assessment Conference: Building Effective, Sustainable, Practical Assessment, October 24–27, 2010, Baltimore, Maryland,* ed. Steve Hiller et al., 703–13. Washington, DC: Association of Research Libraries, 2011.

Fleming-May, Rachel A., and Jill E. Gregg. "The Concept of Electronic Resource Usage and Libraries." *Library Technology Reports* 46, no. 6 (2010).

Franklin, Brinley, and Terry Plum. "Assessing the Value and Impact of Digital Content." *Journal of Library Administration* 48, no. 1 (2008): 41–57.

Gilliland, Anne T. "The OhioLINK OCLC Collection Analysis Project: A Preliminary Report." *Collection Management* 33, no. 1/2 (2008): 161–72.

Greiner, Tony. "Performing Collection Use Studies with Microsoft Excel 2007." *Collection Management* 35, no. 1 (2009): 38–48.

Grigg, Karen. "Assessment and Evaluation of E-book Collections." In *Building and Managing E-book Collections,* ed. Richard Kaplan, 127–37. How-to-Do It Manual 184. New York: Neal-Schuman, 2012.

Grigg, Karen S., et al. "Data-Driven Collection Management: Through Crisis Emerge Opportunities." *Journal of Electronic Resources in Medical Libraries* 7, no. 1 (2010): 1–12.

Henry, Elizabeth, Rachel Longstaff, and Doris Van Kampen. "Collection Analysis Outcomes in an Academic Library." *Collection Building* 27, no. 3 (2008): 113–17.

Hernon, Peter, Robert E. Dugan, and Danuta A. Nitecki. *Engaging in Evaluation and Assessment Research.* Santa Barbara, CA: Libraries Unlimited, 2011.

Hoffmann, Kristin, and Lise Doucette. "A Review of Citation Analysis Methodologies for Collection Management." *College and Research Libraries* 73, no. 4 (July 2012): 321–35.

Hughes, Lorna. *Evaluating and Measuring the Value, Use, and Impact of Digital Collections.* New York: Neal-Schuman, 2011.

Hughes, Michael. "Assessing the Collection through Use Data: An Automated Collection Assessment Tool." *Collection Management* 37, no. 2 (2012): 110–26.

Hyödynmaa, Merja, Aniita Ahlholm-Kannisto, and Hannele Nurminen. "How to Evaluate Library Collections: A Case Study of Collection Mapping." *Collection Building* 29, no. 2 (2010): 43–49.

Jensen, Karen. "Data-Driven Decisions for Library Liaisons: Exploring Strategies for Effectively Managing Diminishing Monograph Collections." *Collection Management* 37, no. 1 (2012): 9–22.

Kim, Pan Jun, Jae Yun Lee, and Ji-Hong Park. "Developing a New Collection-Evaluation Method: Mapping and the User-Side h-Index." *Journal of the American Society for Information Science and Technology* 60, no. 11 (2009): 2366–77.

Kinman, Virginia. "E-metrics and Library Assessment Action." *Journal of Electronic Resources Librarianship* 21, no. 1 (2009): 15–36.

Kohn, Karen C. "Usage-Based Collection Evaluation with a Curricular Focus." *College and Research Libraries* 74, no. 1 (Jan. 2013): 85–97.

Kolltay, Zsuzsa, and Xin Li, comps. *Impact Measures in Research Libraries.* SPEC Kit 318. Washington, DC: Association of Research Libraries, 2010.

Kurtz, Michale J., and Johan Bollen. "Usage Bibliometrics." *Annual Review of Information Science and Technology* 44, no. 1 (2010): 1–64.

Kyrillidou, Martha. "ARL Statistics: Redefining Serials Counts and Remaining Relevant in the 21st Century." *Research Library Issues: A Bimonthly Report from ARL, CNI, and SPARC*, no. 262 (Feb. 2009): 18–20. http://publications.arl.org/rli262/19.

———. "Statistics to Capture the New Environment." *ARL: A Bimonthly Report on Research Library Issues and Actions from ARL, CNI, and SPARC*, no. 256 (Feb. 2008): 9–11. www.arl.org/storage/documents/publications/avl-br-256.pdf.

LaFleur, LeRoy Jason. "Collection Action: Qualitative Methods for Library Collection Development. In *Using Qualitative Methods in Action Research: How Librarians Can Get to the Why of Data*, ed. Douglas Cook and Lesley Farmer, 225–35. Chicago: Association of College and Research Libraries, 2011.

Lamothe, Alain. "Electronic Book Usage Patterns as Observed at an Academic Library: Searches and Viewings." *Partnership: The Canadian Journal of Library and Information Practice and Research* 5, no. 1 (2010). https://journal.lib.uoguelph.ca/index.php/perj/article/view/1071/1696.

———. "Electronic Serials Usage Patterns as Observed at a Medium-Size University: Searches and Full-Text Downloads." *Partnership: The Canadian Journal of Library and Information Practice and Research* 3, no. 1 (2008). https://journal.lib.uoguelph.ca/index.php/perj/article/view/416/841.

Martin, Heath, et al. "Methods and Strategies for Creating a Culture of Collections Assessment at Comprehensive Universities." *Journal of Electronic Resources Librarianship* 21, no. 3/4 (2009): 213–36.

Mathews, Tansy E. "Improving Usage Statistics Processing for a Library Consortium: The Virtual Library of Virginia's Experience." *Journal of Electronic Resources Librarianship* 21, no. 1 (2009): 37–47.

McClure, Jennifer Z. "Collection Assessment through WorldCat." *Collection Management* 34, no. 2 (2009): 79–93.

Mentch, Fran, Barbara Strauss, and Carol Zsulya. "The Importance of 'Focusness': Focus Groups as a Means of Collection Management Assessment." *Collection Management* 33, no. 1/2 (2008): 115–28.

Metz, Paul. "Revisiting the Landscape of Literatures: Replication and Change in the Use of Subject Collections." *College and Research Libraries* 72, no. 4 (July 2011): 344–59.

Monroe-Gulick, Amalia, and Lea Currie. "Using the WorldCat Collection Analysis Tool: Experiences from the University of Kansas Libraries." *Collection Management* 36, no. 4 (2011): 203–16.

Nackerud, Shane, et al. "Analyzing Demographics: Assessing Library Use across the Institution." *portal: Libraries and the Academy* 13, no. 2 (2013): 132–45.

Neal, James G. "Stop the Madness: The Insanity of ROI and the Need for New Qualitative Measures of Academic Library Success." In *Declaration of Interdependence: The Proceedings of the ACRL 2011 Conference, March 30–April 2, 2011*, Philadelphia, Pennsylvania, ed. Dawn M. Mueller, 424–29. Chicago: Association of College and Research Libraries, 2011. www.ala.org/acrl/files/conferences/confsandpreconfs/national/2011/papers/stop_the_madness.pdf.

Oakleaf, Megan. *The Value of Academic Libraries: A Comprehensive Research Review and Report*. Chicago: Association of College and Research Libraries, 2010. www.acrl.ala.org/value.

Paynter, Robin A., Rose M. Jackson, and Laura Bowering Mullen. "Core Journal Lists: Classic Tool, New Relevance." *Behavioral and Social Sciences Librarian* 29, no. 1 (2010): 15–31.

Pesche, Oliver. "Perfecting COUNTER and SUSHI to Achieve Reliable Usage Analysis." *Serials Librarian* 61, no. 3/4 (Oct./Dec. 2011): 353–65.

Ralston, Rick, Carole Gall, and Frances A. Brahmi. "Do Local Citation Patterns Support Use of the Impact Factor for Collection Development?" *Journal of the Medical Library Association* 96, no. 4 (Oct. 2008): 374–78.

RBM: A Journal of Rare Books, Manuscripts, and Cultural Heritage 13, no. 2 (Fall 2012). Special issue devoted to special collections assessment. http://rbm.acrl.org/content/13/2.toc.

Ryder, Valerie J. "Measuring Value in Corporate Libraries." In *Best Practices for Corporate Libraries*, ed. Sigrid E. Kelsey and Marjorie J. Porter, 193–212. Santa Barbara, CA: Libraries Unlimited, 2011.

Schmidt, Jane. "Musings on Collection Analysis and Its Utility in Modern Collection Development." *Evidence Based Library and Information Practice* 5, no. 3 (2010): 62–67. https://ejournals.library.ualberta.ca/index.php/EBLIP/article/view/8971/7351.

Sivak, Allison, and Richard Hayman. "Interdisciplinary Collection Assessment Model." In *Proceedings of the 2010 Library Assessment Conference: Building Effective, Sustainable, Practical Assessment, October 24–27, 2010*, Baltimore, Maryland, ed. Steve Hiller et al., 663–76. Washington, DC: Association of Research Libraries, 2011.

Soria, Krista, Jan Fransen, and Shane Nackerud. "Library Use and Undergraduate Student Outcomes: New Evidence for Students' Retention and Academic Success." *portal: Libraries and the Academy* 13, no. 2 (2013): 147–64.

Stewart, Christopher. "The Next Chapter: Measuring the Pace of Change for Print Monograph Collections." *Journal of Academic Librarianship* 37, no. 4 (July 2011): 355–57.

Tenopir, Carol. "Beyond Usage: Measuring Library Outcomes and Value." *Library Management* 33, no. 1/2 (2012): 5–13.

Tenopir, Carol, and Richel Volentine, with assistance from Donald W. King. *UK Scholarly Reading and the Value of Library Resources; Summary Results of the Study Conducted Spring 2011*. University of Tennessee, Center for Information and Communication Studies, 2012. www.jisc-collections.ac.uk/Documents/Reports/UK%20Scholarly%20Reading%20and%20the%20Value%20of%20Library%20Resources%20Final%20Report.pdf.

Tenopir, Carol, et al. *University Investment in the Library, Phase II: An International Study of the Library's Value to the Grants Process*. San Diego, CA; Elsevier, 2010. http://libraryconnect.elsevier.com/sites/default/files/2010-06-whitepaper-roi2_0.pdf.

Todd, Ross J. "The Evidence-Based Manifesto." *School Library Journal* 54, no. 4 (2008): 38–43.

Tucker, Cory. "Benchmarking Usage Statistics in Collection Management Decisions for Serials." *Journal of Electronic Resources Librarianship* 21, no. 1 (2009): 48–61.

Walter, Virginia A. "Documenting the Results of Good Intentions: Applying Outcomes Evaluation to Library Services for Children." *Advances in Librarianship* 35 (2012): 47–62.

Walker, Mary. "E-resource Statistics: What to Do When You Have No Money." *Journal of Electronic Resources Librarianship* 21, no. 3/4 (2009): 237–50.

Wexelbaum Rachel, and Mark A. Kille, "The Relationship between Collection Strength and Student Achievement." *Advances in Librarianship* 35 (2012): 113–32.

Wilde, Michelle, and Allison Level. "How to Drink from a Fire Hose without Drowning: Collection Assessment in a Numbers-Driven Environment." *Collection Management* 36, no. 4 (2011): 217–36.

Wilson, Concepción A., and Carol Tenopir. "Local Citation Analysis, Publishing, and Reading Patterns: Using Multiple Methods to Evaluate Faculty Use of an Academic Library's Research Collection." *Journal of the American Society for Information Science and Technology* 59, no. 9 (July 2008): 1393–1408.

Wilson, Virginia. "Research Methods: Focus Groups." *Evidence Based Library and Information Practice* 7, no. 1 (2012): 129–31.

CHAPTER EIGHT

Cooperative Collection Development and Management

Cooperation (working together for mutual benefit) in libraries takes various forms and is a part of many collection development and management activities. Library cooperation requires more than being good citizens and behaving altruistically. For Atkinson, "Cooperation is, somewhat paradoxically, one of the few competitive advantages libraries have. Such cooperation does indeed entail significant risks for those libraries bold enough to engage in it—but those risks are in fact, negligible, in comparison with the dangers libraries will surely encounter by continuing to insist that they should each face the future alone."[1] Library cooperation has become even more essential in today's environment of constrained budgets and limited space to house collections. The ability to leverage funds through cooperative purchasing and shared storage facilities and to offer library users access to the world's vast information resources is a powerful force toward cooperation. This chapter presents an overview of cooperative collection development and management and identifies types of cooperation and elements that contribute to their success and work against them.

Overview

In one of the more elegant descriptions of library cooperation, Stam writes that "all libraries are linked in a great chain of access and what each has and does will have importance for the whole universe of libraries and their users."[2] He builds on the ancient concept of creation known as the Great Chain of Being—a theme that permeated science, literature, and philosophy in the time of Plato and was refined in the eighteenth century by Gottfried Wilhelm von Leibniz. This view held that all of existence is defined by plenitude, continuity, and gradation. These three elements can, as Stam implies, apply to libraries when *plenitude* is understood to mean abundance of the whole, *continuity* to mean uninterrupted connection, and *gradation* to mean variations between similar and related components.

Library cooperation is not a new idea. In 1886, Melvil Dewey listed one of the major needs of the modern library movement as "a practical means of bringing the enormous benefits of cooperation, which has been the watch word of the whole movement, into full play in the interests of the libraries." Effective library cooperation has challenged libraries for well more than a century, but most librarians believe, with Gorman, that "cooperation is as essential to a library as is water to a fish or air to a mammal."[3]

A working definition of cooperative collection development and management is "the sharing of responsibilities among two or more libraries for the process of acquiring materials, developing collections, and managing the growth and maintenance of collections in a user-beneficial and cost-beneficial way."[4] The umbrella term used into the mid-1980s was *resource sharing* and applied broadly to cooperative cataloging, shared storage facilities, shared preservation activities, interlibrary loan, and coordinated or cooperative collection development.[5] Today, resource sharing is generally understood to be the sharing of materials through interlibrary loan.

The phrase *cooperative collection development and management* is now understood to denote much more than resource sharing. It implies an overarching planning strategy that libraries employ to work together and provide materials and information that are not held on-site. The goal of cooperative collection development and management is to maximize use of resources regardless of where they reside and leverage available funding. In successful cooperative collection development and management three components must intersect (figure 8-1). The union of resource sharing (fulfillment), bibliographic access (discovery), and coordinated collection development and management makes cooperative collection development and management possible.

The Research Libraries Group (RLG), one of the most ambitious and energetic efforts to create a national cooperative library initiative in the United States, was formed in 1973 by Harvard University, Yale University, Columbia University, and the New York Public Library. RLG's goal was to provide the three components of cooperative collection development and management: physical access through a good delivery system and reciprocal borrowing privileges (the SHARES program), bibliographic access through a shared online catalog (RLIN, the Research Librarians Information Network) to facilitate coordinated acquisitions and resource sharing, and a program of coordinated collection development and management. RLG was described as "a partnership to achieve planned, coordinated interdependence in response to the threat posed by a climate of increasing economic restraint and financial uncertainty."[6] Although Harvard withdrew from the partnership, RLG membership expanded

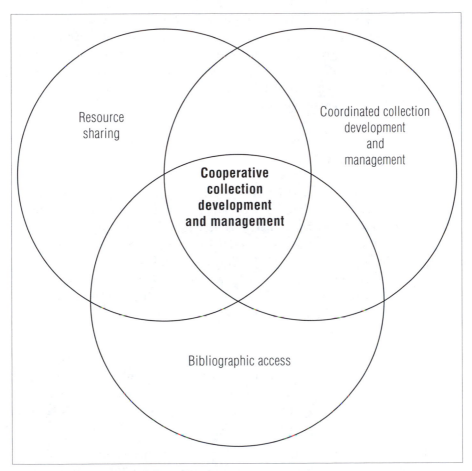

FIGURE 8-1   Components of cooperative collection development

to include many major academic and research libraries in the United States and abroad. In June 2006, RLG merged with OCLC. Its online catalog became part of OCLC's WorldCat and its programs joined with OCLC Research to become OCLC Programs and Research. SHARES (www.oclc.org/research/activities/shares.html) became an OCLC program and has expanded to serve research institutions worldwide.

Several RLG programs and projects had significant success and lasting impact. The Preservation Committee coordinated several cooperative microfilming projects. Cooperative collection development was the focus of RLG's Collection Management and Development Committee, which began with the realization that knowing the strengths, depth, and breadth of each library's collection was a first step toward coordination. To this end, the Collection Management and Development Committee developed the Conspectus, a systematic analysis and assessment tool using the Library of Congress classification scheme and a common language to describe collections.[7] The Conspectus (explored more fully in chapter 7) has been modified by other groups and applied internationally to all types of libraries.

Resource Sharing

Resource sharing is a library program for making requests and delivering resources, chiefly through the formal interlibrary loan process. *Interlibrary loan*, the reciprocal lending and borrowing of materials between libraries, has a long history. One of the earliest references dates from 200 BC, when the library in Alexandria is known to have lent materials to the Pergamum library.[8] Interlibrary lending did not become common in the United States until the last quarter of the nineteenth century. Ernest C. Richardson, librarian at Princeton University, promoted interlibrary loan and called for a national lending library in 1899. His rationale resonates in today's libraries:

> It is a matter of common observation that with the present limited facilities for our American libraries, students, whether dependent on college libraries or on general reference libraries, are constantly in lack of the books which they want. . . . We are duplicating, every year, a great many sets of periodicals, as we would not need to do under some system where all were free to borrow."[9]

Although the United States did not develop a national lending library, a formal process for managing lending and borrowing between libraries was in place early in the twentieth century. The Library of Congress issued its first policy governing interlibrary loan in 1917, and ALA adopted an interlibrary lending code in 1919.[10] The Code has been revised numerous times, the last in 2008. The 1993 revision recognized the important role of interlibrary loan by changing the 1980 statement "Interlibrary loan is an adjunct to, not a substitute for, collection development" to "Interlibrary borrowing is an integral element of collection development for all libraries, not an ancillary option."[11]

Interlibrary loan occurs between libraries, which manage the process for their users. It handles both returnables (items that must be returned to the lender) and nonreturnables (photocopies or digital transmissions). For much of its existence, interlibrary loan has been mediated—that is, a user submits a request for an item to local interlibrary loan staff, who then contacts potential lending libraries, which send the item to the borrower's library. Interlibrary loan may be strengthened by agreements among members of a consortium to expedite service. Consortia may charge members discounted lending fees and permit on-site use of collections by affiliated users of member libraries and reciprocal borrowing (the ability of a user affiliated with one library to borrow materials when visiting another member library). Interlibrary loan encompasses a protocol for making requests and acceptable methods of delivery. Most U.S. libraries submit requests electronically through OCLC or other interlibrary loan systems, although using an interlibrary loan form is an option.[12]

Interlibrary loan is the most pervasive form of library cooperation and links most libraries across the United States and Canada, and internationally as well. OCLC reported that member libraries worldwide used WorldCat to arrange 9.2 million interlibrary loans in 2011–2012. Academic library data collected by the U.S. National Center for Educational Statistics for 2011 (the last year for which data are available) reported that loans provided to other academic libraries totaled 10,157,182, and loans received from libraries totaled 11,213,645.[13] Of the loans received, 5,700,349 were returnables and 4,280,483 were nonreturnables. Public library data reveal the significant value that resource sharing offers to citizens. In fiscal year 2010 (the last year data are available), 8,952 libraries reporting data to IMLS loaned 65,114,000 items and borrowed 65,838,000. This is a significant increase compared to 2004 for 9,207 libraries: 30,158,000 items loaned and 30,471,000 borrowed (breakdown by returnables and nonreturnables not provided).[14] These numbers indicate that public libraries across this country shared more than 130 million items, a truly impressive number.

Information Power, published by AASL and the Association for Educational Communications and Technology, recommends that school librarians participate in networks that enhance access to resources outside schools.[15] Many school districts are members of multitype consortia or other networks through which they can share resources. Within a district sharing an online catalog, school librarians usually can submit interlibrary loan requests to other school library media centers within the district. The problem faced by school librarians, even within a school district with a rapid delivery, is that their students are seldom willing to wait for resource delivery.

Many special libraries participate in resource-sharing networks serving their specialized clientele. For example, the U.S. National Network of Libraries of Medicine (http://nnlm.org), coordinated by the National Library of Medicine, aims to provide all U.S. health professionals equal access to biomedical information. It consists of eight Regional Medical Libraries, more than 149 Resource Libraries (primarily at medical schools), and some 4,308 Primary Access Libraries (primarily at hospitals). Law libraries participate in numerous regional and state consortia. One example is the New England Law Libraries Consortium (www .nellco.org), which supports resource sharing among member academic, private nonprofit, and government law libraries in New England, the Northwest, and elsewhere across the nation.

Multiple consortia may unite to facilitate resources sharing. One example is an agreement between the Council of Prairie and Pacific University Libraries (www.coppul.ca; twenty-three libraries in Manitoba, Saskatchewan, Alberta, and British Columbia), the Ontario Council of University Libraries (www.ocul.on.ca; twenty-one university libraries in Ontario), the Council of Atlantic University Libraries (www.caul-cbua.ca; seventeen libraries in Atlantic Canada), and the Conference of Rectors and Principals of Quebec Universities (www.crepuq. qc.ca; all universities in Quebec), which supports reciprocal interlibrary loan and document delivery between the member libraries in each of these consortia.

Effective and speedy delivery is central to the success of resource sharing. Atkinson explains the quality of access—how well access is provided or achieved—in terms of time.[16] Users want prompt access to resources because their time is a valuable commodity. Improvements in telecommunications have had a significant impact on the transmission of requests, including unmediated borrowing, for books and articles. Unmediated borrowing (sometimes called direct borrowing) is the process in which a user places a request directly to the lending library. This typically decreases costs and increases fulfillment speed. Many libraries use OCLC ILLiad, resource-sharing management software that automates routine interlibrary loan functions through a single, Windows-based interface and supports an automated interlibrary loan subsystem that transmits requests to OCLC members and others. A library can configure its ILLiad software installation so that users who have created personal ILLiad accounts through the individual library can directly request items from within OCLC's WorldCat or an OCLC FirstSearch database at any time. Clio (www.cliosoft ware.com), Relais (www.relais-intl.com), and Auto-Graphics' SHAREit (www4 .auto-graphics.com/products-shareit-inter-library-loan-ill.asp) are additional ex-amples of resource-sharing management systems that also offer 24/7 access for users to initiate direct borrowing.

Implementing direct borrowing among groups of libraries that have sepa-rate integrated library systems adds complexity because an additional layer of technical infrastructure is necessary, but the ability of users to place unme-diated requests and speed the delivery process is significant. One example is Ohio Libraries Share: More (OLS: More, http://library.ohio.gov/IT/MORE), a state-funded program serving 2.5 million patrons at nearly one hundred public libraries in Ohio. This system uses the NISO Circulation Interchange Protocol.[17] Patrons from any participating library can request an item from another participating library and pick it up at the patron's home library. Another example is the MnLINK Gateway (www.mnlinkgateway.org), a statewide virtual library linking Minnesota libraries and managed by Minitex (www.minitex.umn .edu). The MnLINK Gateway searches the online catalogs of more than twenty Minnesota library systems representing some 515 libraries (public libraries and their branches; community, college, and university libraries; and government libraries). Interlibrary loan requests made within the MnLINK Gateway are automatically sent to the owning library for attention. Minitex, a regional network, provides the materials via daily deliveries to member libraries.

Breeding reports a trend toward larger consortia supported by large-scale integrated library systems with built-in resource-sharing capabilities.[18] The Massachusetts Library System (www.masslibsystem.org) and the Illinois Heartland Library System (www.illinoisheartland.org) are examples of the consolidation of previously separate consortia. Through the Massachusetts Library System's statewide catalog, MassCat, patrons take advantage of a statewide delivery system that serves approximately six hundred libraries of all types. The Illinois Heartland Library System "operates with the primary mission of support for resource sharing" and serves multitype libraries in southern and central Illinois; its shared automated library system, SHARE, provides a union catalog and manages resource sharing.[19]

The number of requests to borrow returnables has grown rapidly because of the ease of searching union catalogs and WorldCat. Minitex reports a 254 percent increase in interlibrary loan requests in the first year the MnLink Gateway was available, although volume of activity has stabilized in the past few years.[20] Fast delivery is essential to satisfy users. Many cooperative, consortial, and statewide systems use dedicated couriers to facilitate rapid delivery of returnables. The Center of Library Initiatives (www.cic.net/projects/library/home), a collaborative project of the Committee on Institutional Cooperation (CIC), is one example. CIC is a consortium of the Big Ten universities plus the University of Chicago, University of Maryland, and Rutgers University. Most CIC libraries participate in a program called UBorrow to support interlibrary lending of returnables, which typically arrive on campus within a week and can be checked out for twelve weeks. The system uses the Z39.50 protocol to search CIC library catalogs and sends requests to libraries where the materials are available for lending.[21] The relative proximity of CIC partners, as well as the commitments made by each institution, allows books to be delivered through UBorrow far more rapidly than through traditional interlibrary loan programs. Relais D2D

(Discovery-to-Delivery) supports UBorrow by passing the information for requests to each library's local ILLiad implementation.

The increasing availability of e-journal articles through individual library subscriptions, consortial purchase agreements, and state and regional programs is reducing interlibrary loan requests for nonreturnables. This ease of access has increased the importance of speedy delivery of articles and book chapters not available locally. Delivery of nonreturnables is facilitated by systems such as OCLC's Article Exchange (www.oclc.org/resource-sharing/features/article exchange.en.html) and Atlas's Odyssey (www.atlas-sys.com/odyssey), which are used worldwide with desktop computers, printers, and scanners to transmit documents as PDF files via the Internet, using either FTP (file transfer protocol) or e-mail. The scanned document can be delivered as an e-mail attachment or posted to a secure website, where it can be downloaded by the patron using appropriate credentials.

Atkinson observed in 2004 that "from the standpoint of [library] cooperation . . . the single most important development in the new era is the adoption of licenses that prohibit cooperation and define sharing as theft." Many publishers and vendors have changed their initial prohibition and now allow interlibrary lending of e-journal articles. Okamoto surveyed 129 libraries of all types in 2012 and found that 83 percent loaned e-journal articles.[22] However, libraries often must negotiate this permission in their licenses, and interlibrary lending staff must know what these rights are. One of the challenges for libraries seeking to borrow e-journal articles is determining if the lending library has permission to do so. Though various products and services manage, display, and communicate license information, they are not universally employed.

Lending e-books remains a problematic area because satisfactory models for e-book interlibrary loan have yet to evolve. Whereas the historical lending unit of a print book is the entire book, licenses frequently limit interlibrary lending to chapters, which is unsatisfactory for many users. Often the lending library is expected to make a printed copy of the chapter and then mail, fax, or use interlibrary lending software to send it to the borrowing library. Frederickson and colleagues published the results of a 2011 survey that explored interlibrary lending and borrowing of e-books in all types of libraries.[23] They found that only 2.4 percent of the 185 responding libraries reported that all their e-book licenses allowed interlibrary loan, and 26.6 percent reported that some e-book licenses permitted interlibrary loan. A significant problem for the 185 responding libraries was discerning what might be covered, permitted, restricted, or forbidden in e-book licenses.

A few examples demonstrate the challenges in tracking the variations in interlibrary loan permissions and prohibitions for e-content. Elsevier states, "The Interlibrary Loan Policy for electronic journals and books is included in each publicly funded institutional ScienceDirect subscription agreement. In short, the provision allows and provides for the use of electronic journal articles and book chapters as a source for the fulfillment of Interlibrary Loan (ILL) requests with some stipulations." JSTOR explicitly prohibits sharing e-books through interlibrary loan. With Project Muse, "a purchasing library may supply to an authorized user of another library (whether by post, fax or secure electronic transmission, using Ariel or its equivalent, whereby the electronic file is deleted immediately after printing) a single copy of an electronic original of an individual book chapter." E-book aggregators commonly used by public libraries, such as OverDrive and 3M Cloud Library, rarely allow e-book interlibrary loan.[24]

Increasingly, e-book publishers and aggregators are encouraging libraries to use what is known as *short-term lending* to provide complete e-books. In this model, a title is leased for a short time, with the borrowing library paying a percentage of the publisher's e-book list price. The aggregator ebrary observes, "Technically, the library may use portions of its ebrary ebooks in its customary ILL program under Section 108(g) of the Copyright Act," but it recommends that libraries use short-term loans as an alternative. This approach is a viable option when interlibrary loan of the entire e-book is prohibited and can provide a cost-effective alternative to purchasing the e-book locally.

The complexities of interlibrary loan in a increasingly digital environment led to the formation of the Rethinking Resource Sharing Initiative, an ad hoc group working to rethink the ways libraries share resources. This group is investigating delivery needs, interoperability, resource sharing policies, and user needs. A manifesto issued by the group begins:

> If libraries want to expand and promote information accessibility, and to continue to be valued resources, we believe that libraries must improve their information delivery system. Aligning resource sharing workflow, collection policies, and discovery-delivery systems by significantly reducing service barriers and cost and offering user service options are critical pieces that promote information access.[25]

Bibliographic Access

The second component in cooperative collection development and management is *bibliographic access*—discovering what is available from other sites through online catalogs, printed or microform catalogs, or bibliographic utilities. For many years, libraries depended on printed holdings information—records in the National Union Catalog, individual libraries' printed book catalogs, and union serials holdings lists. The first regional union catalog was developed at the California State Library in 1901, and the Library of Congress established the National Union Catalog in 1902. Checking such resources was tedious. The development of bibliographic utilities; multi-institutional, state, and regional online shared catalogs; and web-based access to online catalogs has allowed a tremendous step forward in bibliographic access for both library patrons and library staff.

Some states have statewide catalogs that allow users to search holdings and often enter unmediated interlibrary loan requests, regardless of the holding library's location. Examples are WISCAT (www.wiscat.net), a union catalog with an interlibrary loan management system for the state of Wisconsin, and the Montana Shared Catalog, a cooperative project in which more than 160 public, school, academic, medical, and special libraries share a single a integrated library system. Libraries seeking a grant to participate in the Montana Shared Catalog are required to have a current collection management policy, approved by the library board, school board, principal, or administrator, in place and on file at the Montana State Library.[26]

Libraries that use a shared catalog to discover resources rely on accurate, up-to-date bibliographic records and holdings information. This is true at the regional, state, and international level. Because bibliographic access is so essential, OCLC has developed "WorldCat Principles of Cooperation," which states that members make a commitment to "support prompt contribution of bibliographic records and related data to promote shared use of records and library resources."[27]

Coordinated Collection Development and Management

The third component in cooperative collection development and management is *coordinated collection development and management*. Ideally, coordinated collection development and management follow from a intentionally harmonized scheme of purchasing and maintaining collections that aims to create and sustain complementary collections on which the cooperating libraries can draw.

None of the components in cooperative collection development and management (resource sharing, bibliographic access, and coordinated collection development and management) works without some degree of success in the other two areas. Neither speedy delivery nor bibliographic access has meaning unless the resource the user wishes can be located in an identifiable library. If libraries have established partnerships to ensure coverage but collection gaps still exist, cooperation is not succeeding. A gap in one collection can be accommodated only if the same gap does not exist at a partner library. The ideal situation is equitable distribution of little-used titles. Collection overlaps (titles held by more than one library) can be justified because each library expects heavy use of these materials locally.

Coordinated collection development leverages available funds by increasing access to a wider collection of information resources. It enlarges the universe of titles available to library users and, when properly supported, speeds the delivery of materials through interlibrary lending and borrowing systems. It also can be viewed as cost containment through purchase avoidance. The libraries that participate in coordinated collection development reduce duplication to provide a stronger collective collection and increased user satisfaction.

Despite a few isolated coordinated collection development successes, libraries do not have a notable history of altering traditional collection development behaviors.[28] Libraries have not, in general, developed policies and practices that acknowledge or take advantage of being linked in a great chain of being. The extent to which meaningful and practical coordination has been implemented falls short of the enthusiasm with which it is proclaimed. Libraries are, however, beginning to demonstrate success in coordinated collection management because dealing with retrospective collections is easier than altering current collection development practices.

Coordinating Development

Several varieties of cooperating in collection development have been tried with varying degrees of success. These include the status quo approach, the synergistic or coordinated approach, shared approval plans, shared patron-driven acquisitions agreements, and cooperative funding.

STATUS QUO APPROACH

For many years, libraries have practiced what Mosher and Pankake call the *status quo approach*, which presumes that libraries' total collecting activities will build, on a national scale, reasonable depth in every area of interest.[29] In other words, every title that anyone might want now and in the future will be held somewhere simply as a result of serendipitous collection development and management. This assumes that libraries will select a certain number of titles that no other library is adding, yet research has shown that U.S. research libraries are acquiring fewer unique monographic titles.[30] The status quo approach, in which no intentional coordinated collecting activities are undertaken, is optimistic and increasingly unrealistic, given the financial constraints most libraries are experiencing.

One modest initiative that takes advantage of the status quo approach was implemented at Grasselli Library, John Carroll University, in Ohio, where faculty place most of the book orders.[31] Under a program implemented in 2006, orders are not placed for any title that has eight or more circulating copies recorded in the OhioLINK union catalog, unless the requesting faculty member submits an exception form. The program is considered successful because unspent funds can be redirected to acquiring other titles and reduced duplication results in a more heterogeneous collection.

SYNERGISTIC APPROACH

Atkinson refers to a second, *synergistic approach* in which different libraries take responsibilities for collecting different publications, according to some coordinated and collaborative plan. This is truly coordinated collection development because it is intentional with distributed responsibility for collection development. Underlying all efforts at cooperation is, in the words of Shreeves, a "widespread belief that cooperation in building collections can improve significantly the quality of library service by broadening and deepening the range of materials collectively available." Formal coordinated and collaborative collection development programs are normally guided by written agreements, contracts, or other documents outlining the commitments and responsibilities of the participants.[32]

The synergistic approach calls for dividing the information universe into core and peripheral materials and then dividing the periphery between the libraries that have agreed to cooperate. Librarians use the term *core* to mean two kinds of collections: a collection representing the intellectual nucleus of a discipline (consisting of the classic, synoptic, and most influential texts), and a nucleus of materials that is determined by heaviest use or meets certain criteria.[33] H. W. Wilson Company uses "core collection" in the latter sense in the titles of its selection tools, such as the *Public Library Core Collection: Nonfiction*, which "recommends reference and non-fiction books for the general adult audience."[34] Core collections, in this definition, are often considered the highest-quality, most important, and representative works on major subjects.[35] A library engaged in coordinated collection development develops collections of peripheral materials that respond to local needs and priorities but also serve consortial needs. This local collection, in turn, is backed up by the collections of consortial partners built through distributed responsibility for peripheral materials in complementary fields.

Defining *core* and *peripheral* in terms of collecting behavior has been a stumbling block to successful synergistic collection development projects in research libraries. Generally, materials in the periphery are considered to be research materials that will not be in heavy demand and will fall into Conspectus levels 4 (research collections) and 5 (comprehensive collections). One problem is that any research library's understanding of the core tends to shrink and expand in response to the funds available to that library during each budget cycle. Predicting what will constitute core materials is also a challenge. In 1989, Atkinson wrote, "Our effort to . . . distinguish core from non-core materials has been so far singularly unsuccessful, except through such retrospective methods as citation analysis or the use of circulation records. For purposes of planning, budgeting, or coordination, the concept of the core, for all its use, is practically useless."[36] Unfortunately, distinguishing core from noncore materials continues to test libraries that seek to coordinate collection development.

The only application of synergistic cooperation that is both logical and practical is one in which a library accepts responsibility for collecting in areas that also meet local needs and reflect local strengths. The history of cooperative initiatives has shown that libraries should not commit to developing and maintaining collections (or even subscribing to a particular journal title) for which local need and usage are not present. The key to success is building on the local imperative. One example might be found in a public library cooperative with member libraries serving different immigrant populations. One library might assume primary responsibility for building a collection to serve its large Hispanic population and another might assume responsibility for building a collection to serve a large group of Southeast Asian immigrants. Together, they have a coordinated collection which, through resource sharing, meets the needs of many. At the same time, a commitment by one library to a particular area does not obligate the other partners to give up supporting all needs in that area.[37] Coordinated collection development cannot substitute for adequate local collections.

Two early examples of synergistic coordinated collection development are the agreement between the Research Triangle University Libraries in North

Carolina and the Farmington Plan. The earliest is the Research Triangle (www
.trln.org), consisting of Duke University, University of North Carolina–Chapel
Hill, North Carolina State University, and North Carolina Central University,
which joined the group in 1995. In 1933, the University of North Carolina–
Chapel Hill and Duke University formed the Joint Committee on Intellectual
Cooperation in an effort to leverage limited financial resources during the Great
Depression. Library cooperation began in 1934 with a plan for systematic division of responsibility for publications in major disciplines. North Carolina State
University began participating in coordinated collection development programs in the 1950s. Over time, the program evolved into the area studies concept of dividing responsibilities by geographic coverage or language or both.
The Research Triangle has an enviable record of success in leveraging financial
resources and making unique materials available to its membership. A study in
2006 found that 71 percent of the 56,158,309 unique titles were held on only
one campus, and only 2 percent were held by all four universities. Much of the
success of the Research Triangle can be attributed to upper-level institutional
support; geographic proximity, which has meant easy and speedy access; and
bibliographic access to titles held in each of the member libraries.[38]

The Farmington Plan was less successful.[39] Launched in 1948 under the
sponsorship of ARL, it was a voluntary agreement on the part of approximately
sixty academic, special, and research libraries. The goal of the Farmington Plan
was to increase the nation's total resources for research. The participating libraries agreed to collect, for specified countries and subjects, one copy of each new
foreign publication in which a U.S. researcher could be presumed to be interested. The plan designed blanket order profiles that were placed with foreign
dealers. Libraries were expected to accept all materials within the scope of their
commitments.

The Farmington Plan was not concerned with the financial situations of its
participants and expected each library to provide the budgetary support needed
to accomplish the comprehensive plan goals. It ceased in 1972 primarily because
it failed to recognize the first condition of every successful cooperative plan—
libraries always give priority to local needs and priorities. Ideally, each participating library should be able to combine self-interest with the overarching aims
of the agreement. Each participant must be confident that it will receive benefits
that outweigh its sacrifices. Successful cooperation depends on a shared sense
of the common good. The tension between local needs and the needs of the
consortium underlies all cooperative collection development and management
ventures.

Smaller institutions in geographic proximity have more success with synergistic coordinated collection development. One example is found in the collections policy of the Tri-College Consortium (Haverford, Bryn Mawr, and Swarthmore Colleges) located in the Philadelphia area, which states that the libraries "will minimize *unnecessary* duplication of monographs and other easily-shared resources, in order to release funds to purchase materials that would not otherwise be bought."[40] Coordination is facilitated by a shared catalog, shared approval plan, and 24- to 48-hour delivery service.

Coordinated collection development can benefit school library media centers, though coordination in selection may be more of a challenge for these libraries. School library media centers in the same region are less likely to have diverse collections than in the past. They have a tendency to develop very similar collections because all are aiming to collect resources that support similar curricula and advancement and graduation standards. Variations in collections may be appropriate in schools that have a special focus or specialized programs. For example, the library media center in a Spanish immersion school has many more resources in Spanish, and a magnet school that offers special, supplemental classes in science and math has more resources in these areas; both can share their unique materials with other schools.

Kachel suggests several steps to better prepare school library media centers to engage in coordinated collection development. These include individual collection assessment, individual collection development policies, and regional resource mapping—a cooperative collection assessment to identify strengths and weaknesses across collections. She writes, "The view of a library operating self-sufficiently in isolation, with students and teachers having access only to what reside within the walls of the library, is outdated," and recommends that school librarians start by developing coordinated collection activities with other librarians in their own school district. Success at this level can be a building block to expanded coordinated collection development.[41]

ADDITIONAL OPTIONS FOR COORDINATING COLLECTION DEVELOPMENT

One intentional coordination approach is the use of a *shared approval plan*. Such plans present challenges because of the political and administrative costs of designing and maintaining them and the need to balance expectations of the larger group against the requirements of the individual partnering libraries. Shared approval plans must be designed to complement any existing approval plans and work best when the partner libraries are already using the same approval plan vendor. Collections librarians at each library work together with the vendor to develop the shared profile. One benefit may be a deeper discount from the vendor because of the increased volume of books sold. These plans usually require each partner library to make a financial commitment at the beginning of the fiscal year to expend a set dollar amount. Speedy delivery is essential for success. Eight Kent State University campuses developed a shared approval plan for nursing books. Each library committed dollars to the project based on an average of previous purchasing activity. Downey notes that the project was somewhat difficult to coordinate, but it was successful because it reduced duplication.[42]

A shared approval plan implemented in 2006 by eight members of the Colorado Alliance of Research Libraries was less successful.[43] The pilot project focused on undergraduate books in economics, mathematics, political science, and religion. Participating libraries established or revised profiles with two approval plan vendors (Blackwell and YBP), aiming to reduce duplication and buy more titles overall. Findings after two years indicated that duplication had increased slightly. The report's authors suggested that using two vendors and separating undergraduate- and graduate-level materials were primary causes of the plan's failure.

Four university libraries (Albany, Binghamton, Buffalo, and Stony Brook) in the State University of New York system have a shared collecting program that is press-based. Together they buy the complete publications of eight university presses and own the collection together, which is distributed across the four institutions. A similar initiative was proposed for Ohio academic libraries. In this initiative, all libraries (which use the same approval plan) would acquire unique copies of university press books. The goal in both programs is to reduce duplication and increase the depth and breadth of coverage across the libraries.[44]

A few libraries are experimenting with patron-driven acquisitions in a consortial environment. The Orbis Cascade Alliance began an e-book pilot with YBP and Ebook Library that transitioned to an ongoing program in fiscal year 2013.[45] Member libraries contribute to a central fund on a proportional basis, and all members in the Alliance own the purchased titles. The Alliance does not have a true union catalog and discovery is complicated by different local systems, WorldCat Group catalogs, and WorldCat Local. Once an e-book purchase is initiated by a user, the business model in place allows unlimited simultaneous user access and, within the Alliance, up to 1,625 unique accesses per year. The Ontario Council of University Libraries (OCUL) operated a patron-driven pilot with ebrary for e-books in 2010.[46] Again, the project was complicated by the absence of a union catalog; the twenty-one participating libraries had to load the bibliographic file for possible purchase into their own catalogs. Within a week, funds for the pilot were expended. Records for potential purchases then had to be removed from catalogs and replaced with records for the 467 titles purchased. The agreement with ebrary provided four copies of each title to share among the participating libraries. One significant problem was the degree of duplication with print and e-versions of titles already held within OCUL libraries.

A patron-driven print book acquisitions project at the Consortium of Academic and Research Libraries in Illinois (CARLI) was more successful, in part because bibliographic records for potential purchases were loaded into CARLI's I-Share union catalog.[47] Patrons at any participating library could initiate purchases, which were housed at the University of Illinois–Urbana Library. The success of the 2010 pilot led to a larger patron-driven acquisition project in fiscal year 2012. Key elements to the success of patron-driven acquisition in a consortium are a shared catalog and working with a single vendor.

One approach to coordination relies on cooperative funding for shared purchases. These may be print materials, microform, or e-content jointly owned by the cooperative. This approach, sometimes called *cooperative acquisition*, depends on a pool of shared monies used to acquire expensive items, less-used materials of general interest in the cooperative, or e-content that is accessible by all members. Purchased physical items are placed either in a central site or in the library with the highest anticipated local use. A still-successful program in the shared purchase model is the Center for Research Libraries (CRL; www.crl .edu).[48] Part of each library's annual membership fee goes to purchase materials that the membership agrees are important. CRL serves as a library's library—a complementary collection to extend the resources available to the membership.

CRL, established in 1949, is considered the nation's oldest cooperative research library and had more than 270 U.S. and Canadian members in 2013. The CRL facility in Chicago houses more than five million newspapers, journals, dissertations, archives, government publications, microform sets, and other traditional and digital resources for research and teaching, which are loaned to members. CRL members pay annual fees to support CRL and provide pooled funds to acquire, store, and preserve materials that would otherwise be too costly for a single institution. Many materials (e.g., major microfilm sets) are purchased through a member nominating and voting process. In addition, CRL negotiates favorable terms for the purchase of, or subscription to, major electronic resources, an activity that developed out of the major cooperative collection development efforts in area studies and other realms that have been CRL initiatives for some time. CRL has very clear objectives and been successful in leveraging investments to provide a collection of resources that no one library can afford on its own.

California is the site of a long-term cooperative funding program agreement among libraries of the University of California (UC) system. The Shared Print collections (www.cdlib.org/services/collections/sharedprint), begun in 1976, have a central pool of funds, to which member libraries contribute, to acquire resources and avoid duplication. Its goals (as of August 2013) are to

1. Facilitate the development of more comprehensive and diverse research collections available to UC library users throughout the system through efficient collaborative methods for the prospective acquisition of research resources.

2. Offer incremental economies to the campuses over time through space savings and other cost avoidances.

3. Begin to create long-term opportunities for the reallocation of library space to meet existing demands of current and retrospective collections and support new, transformative uses.

4. Preserve the scholarly printed record, where print remains the archival medium of choice, at the lowest possible unit cost.

Libraries use cooperative funding to acquire access to e-content that can be downloaded for patrons' use on personal computers, e-book readers, and media players. In one example, the Oregon Digital Library Consortium, a group of public libraries and public library federations, offers its patrons Library2Go (library2 go.lib.overdrive.com), a shared collection of e-books, audiobooks, and videos.

Collections librarians have a critical role in selecting cooperatively funded resources. Most of the cooperatives that engage in this activity rely on a group of librarians to propose and select the materials to be jointly acquired. For example, the UC program has a Shared Monographic Coordinating Group and twenty-six system-wide groups of bibliographers in specific subject areas who suggest shared purchases and coordinate collecting activities.

Coordinating Management

Coordinated collection management has been more successful than coordinated collection development. Libraries find that coordinated management of materials they already own is easier than agreeing on how to share responsibility for the collections they are developing. Areas with a history of success are coordinated preservation and coordinated weeding, retention, and storage.

COORDINATED PRESERVATION

Preservation microfilming projects have been some of the more successful approaches to coordinated preservation and have led to several cooperative projects over the years. Primarily funded through NEH grants, these projects have sought to develop a national collection of preserved documents while meeting agreed-upon archival standards for quality and storage and avoiding duplication. For example, the Committee on Institutional Cooperation coordinated several cooperative projects in the 1980s and 1990s that filmed many thousands of volumes. The nonprofit Law Library Microform Consortium (www.llmc.com) was founded in 1976 by law libraries to preserve historical legal texts, initially by microfilming and now by scanning. In addition, the Consortium preserves the original scanned volumes in a dark archive. The United States Agricultural Information Network and the National Agricultural Library coordinated a project that began in the early 1990s and, through a series of NEH grants, microfilmed important agricultural publications on a state-by-state basis. The United States Newspaper Program (www.neh.gov/us-newspaper-program), a cooperative national partnership among NEH, the Library of Congress, and state projects, was started in the early 1980s to locate, catalog, preserve on microfilm, and make available to researchers newspapers published in the United States from the eighteenth century to the present. This project has been supplemented by the National Digital Newspaper Program (www.loc.gov/ndnp), which is developing a database of digitized U.S. newspapers published from 1690 to the present.

State programs, regional systems, and consortia offer another venue for coordinated preservation activities. The University of California Libraries have had a collaborative and coordinated preservation program since the early 1980s. The Preservation Advisory Group (http://libraries.universityofcalifornia.edu/pag) reports to the University of California Libraries Collection Development Committee, with responsibilities that include coordinating system-wide preservation activities related to the preservation of digital collections, coordinating preservation policies among the campus library systems and the Committee, developing preservation services with the broadest possible cost savings for UC libraries, and serving as an education and discussion group for its members on preservation issues and innovations. Another example is LYRASIS (www.lyrasis.org), a library cooperative with more than 1,400 multitype members, which offers preservation services including information on library and archival preservation, advice on disaster preparedness and emergency response recovery, training in preservation methods and emergency response, and consultants.

Another cooperative approach to preservation is the use of shared storage facilities (discussed below). These becomes more than a cost-effective option for housing little-used materials if the depositing libraries commit to retention and the facility meets accepted environmental standards for preservation.

The mass digitization projects of recent years—Google Books Library Project, Microsoft's Live Search Books (which ceased in 2008), and the Open Content Alliance—are partnership projects primarily aimed to increase access to resources, yet they have a preservation component, as well. Although Google has made no commitment to long-term preservation, the Open Content Alliance (www.opencontentalliance.org) makes clear it is a collaborative effort to help build a permanent archive of digitized text and multimedia. Google makes its scanned files of print materials available to HathiTrust (www.hathitrust.org), a partnership of major research institutions and libraries committed to preserving the cultural record in the HathiTrust Digital Library.

COORDINATED WEEDING, RETENTION, AND SHARED STORAGE

Partners in *coordinated weeding and retention* programs seek to reduce the costs of maintaining local collections by distributing responsibilities and sharing costs. Coordinated weeding and retention require deliberate decision making and go hand in hand. They involve more than checking in a shared catalog to see that at least one other copy is held elsewhere before withdrawing the local copy. Just as coordinated collection development depends on identifying areas for which partner libraries have collecting responsibilities, coordinated weeding and retention rely on taking responsibility for retaining materials in certain areas or of certain types. Libraries that wish to withdraw materials because of condition issues or space limitations agree to check first whether the item is the last copy in the consortium or geographic area. This practice is often called *last-copy retention*, though usually more than a single copy is retained regionally and nationally to protect against catastrophic loss.

Efforts to achieve space economies through shared storage facilities date back more than seventy years. The New England Depository Library, founded in 1942 and the oldest shared storage facility in the United States, is used by libraries in the Northeast. CRL identified the provision of a permanent storage depository as one of its major goals. In addition to housing cooperative purchases, member libraries place lesser-used materials from their own collections in CRL's central storage building. Payne found that fourteen of the sixty-eight storage facilities in the United States and Canada were shared facilities in 2007; many of these did not, however, have an articulated commitment to perpetual retention and preservation.[49]

O'Conner, Wells, and Collier distinguish between cooperative storage, "essentially the sharing of a space within a facility," and collaborative storage, "a shared approach to the collection in terms of growth, shape, management, and access."[50] *Collaborative storage* can be seen as coordinated storage because it is intentional, planned, and focuses on sustaining a coordinated collection. Increasingly, libraries are implementing policies in their collaborative storage facilities in which they agree not to deposit duplicate copies and guarantee permanent access to the stored materials.

In the late 1990s, librarians in North America began to talk about creating a formal, large-scale cooperative program for shared print management, including coordinating the use of shared off-site storage facilities as "last copy" repositories. The North American Storage Trust (www.oclc.org/research/activities/nast .html) grew out of these discussions. This initiative aspired to provide a central registry for libraries to report which volumes they would retain and preserve either in storage facilities or in libraries, along with formal agreements that participating libraries could rely on access to the preserved copies if they withdrew their own. Payne likens this proposed voluntary distributed print retention and preservation system to LOCKSS (a voluntary distributed system to preserve electronic resources). She writes, "By leveraging this collective capacity, and building on existing networks of trust within the library community, we can begin to manage our physical inventories in ways that reduce unnecessary redundancy while preserving the world's print heritage as a shared public good."[51]

In 2007, the North American Storage Trust transitioned to an ongoing OCLC Shared Print Management program (www.oclc.org/services/projects/ shared-print-management.en.html), with the goal of collaborating with regional shared storage efforts. An early focus of this initiative was a pilot project in 2010–2012 to develop guidelines for shared print metadata.[52] These descriptive data are necessary to support

- preservation risk assessment (How many copies exist in the system? What is their condition? Are they subject to archival/persistence agreements?)
- collection management (Which copies in the local collection should be retained? How can space recovery be maximized? How can inventory be optimized?)
- resource sharing (Which retained copies can be accessed and by what means, under what terms and by whom?)

The pilot developed three key recommendations: create separate OCLC institution symbols to identify print archived titles in storage facilities and full-service libraries, enter holdings-level print archives data in MARC holdings records, and use MARC field 583 (Preservation Action Note) to describe specific characteristics of the print archive actions for each set of holdings.

CRL built on the OCLC recommendations in developing the Print Archives Preservation Registry (http://papr.crl.edu), an international consortium of university, college, and independent research libraries intended to support "archiving and management of serial collections by providing comprehensive information about titles, holdings, and archiving terms and conditions of major print archiving programs."[53] The Registry provides information about commitments to retain, gaps and condition, and institutions and programs (e.g., CLOCKSS and PORTICO) holding the titles.

Numerous collaborative storage and retention projects are under way. A survey of 328 libraries conducted in 2013 found 24 percent of respondents were participating in shared print programs, with 14 percent planning to participate within the next five years.[54] Participation is higher among academic libraries, with 58 percent of ARL members engaged in shared print programs and 24 percent of other academic libraries doing so. Ten percent of the 121 responding public libraries reported participating in shared print programs.

Kieft and Payne identify five categories of shared print programs, distinguished by type of selection that guides the deposit of materials: these programs may focus on materials already in shared storage that are redefined with retention commitment, library-nominated journal titles, journals selected by publisher, titles selected by domain or format, or materials selected through customized collection analysis.[55] Some collaborative programs use a shared storage facility and some rely on distributed retention, with materials held in the partner libraries. Some serve libraries that are close geographically and others serve more widely distributed libraries.

An example of the collaborative shared print facility is the Committee on Institutional Cooperation (CIC) Shared Print Repository (www.cic.net/projects/library/shared-print-repository/introduction), launched in 2011. The project's first host site was Indiana University's Auxiliary Library Facility, with participating libraries paying to support the initial shared collection of journal back files. Materials housed in this facility have a unique WorldCat institution symbol indicating their status in a print archive. The project's goals are to

> aggregate, secure, and preserve the rich print resources developed by CIC libraries over the past two centuries;
>
> ensure that CIC scholars and students have timely access to these archived resources;

> realize the economies of scale made possible through collective action that will allow CIC libraries to apply best practices for storing, preserving, servicing, and reflecting print holdings well into the future;

> help CIC campuses reclaim local resources, including space, funds, and staff time by relieving them of the obligation to store lesser-used redundant materials;

> integrate CIC libraries into an emerging national network of collectively managed research library resources.

The Council of Prairie and Pacific Libraries' Shared Print Archive Network (SPAN, www.coppul.ca/projects/SPAN.html), a retrospective print repository program serving university libraries in Manitoba, Saskatchewan, Alberta, and British Columbia, is an example of the distributed model. SPAN's goals are to provide access to shared print archives, create opportunities for the reallocation of library space, and preserve the print record for its members in a cost-effective way. SPAN emphasizes the role of archived print as part of an optimal copy network that includes other print archiving initiatives. Member libraries are consolidating and validating print journal back files and monographs at major library storage facilities and campus locations. Initial phases focus on journal back files, with a much less managed, optional process for retention and preservation of scarcely held monographs. Libraries select titles by using a risk management framework in which journals are categorized as low, moderate, or higher risk based on their availability electronically, rarity, and relevance to western Canada. Titles selected for archiving in phase 1 were low-risk titles—widely held in print with stable electronic versions. SPAN plans to report retention commitments in the Print Archives Preservation Registry.

Most coordinated print retention programs to date have focused on journals, in large part because many are widely held, removing local copies of long runs generates significant space, and many have been digitized and are in trusted repositories. As Kieft notes, monographs present the greatest challenges to shared print programs for several reasons, including

> their sheer number and the trivial amount of shelf-space gained per disposition decision. Local as opposed to collective sensibilities about "books," the difficulty of easily gathering and using data about holdings and circulation, and the lack of business models for large-scale retention and serving of monographs, together with a corollary uncertainty about how many copies are needed to serve foreseeable demand, are significant impediments to program development.[56]

A related issue is the extent to which digital surrogates are available in shared trusted repositories. Shared retention of print books, although more complex, will likely follow models similar to those for print journals, resulting in a network of regionally consolidated print book collections.[57]

A few initiatives are addressing coordinated print book retentions. One example is the Maine Shared Collections Strategy (www.maineinfonet.net/mscs), a three-year (2011–2014) demonstration project funded by IMLS that partners five academic libraries, two public libraries, the Maine State Library, and Maine Infonet, the state-funded collaborative that supports resource sharing and other initiatives.[58] Two of the project's goals are

1. to develop a strategy for a statewide, multitype library program for managing, storing, and preserving print collections among public and private institutions; and

2. to expand access to existing digital book collections by developing print-on-demand and e-book-on-demand services to support long-term management of a shared print collection, and the integration of digital resources with print collections.

The Maine project addresses books that should be retained and is using a proprietary collection analysis tool to identify unique and scarcely held titles.

The Michigan Shared Print Initiative (http://mlc.lib.mi.us/cms/sitem .cfm/library_tools/mi-spi) is taking a different approach by focusing on what to withdraw instead of what to retain. This project involves nine publicly funded Michigan universities and focuses on commonly held but little-used monographs.

As the examples above suggest, numerous initiatives to develop coordinated withdrawal and retention programs are under way across North America, most dealing with similar concerns and seeking best practices to address them. The Print Archive Network (PAN), an informal discussion group sponsored by CRL, offers a forum to share information among librarians involved in these programs. The group meets at the ALA midwinter meetings and annual conferences, and members post semiannual reports to the PAN website.[59]

A more recent approach to shared storage is the shared digital repository. Two examples of cooperative digital repositories are the HathiTrust Digital Library and the Alliance Digital Repository (http://adrresources.coalliance.org). Digital surrogates in the HathiTrust Digital Library represent an increasing percentage of print materials held in libraries and an important consideration as libraries draw down local print collections and develop shared print repositories. In 2011, HathiTrust approved the establishment of a distributed print archive of monographic holdings corresponding to volumes represented within the HathiTrust Digital Library, which requires print holdings information for digital surrogates.[60]

The Alliance Digital Repository (www.coalliance.org/software/digital-reposi tory), a consortial digital repository offered by the Colorado Alliance of Research Libraries, is a different model focusing on preserving digital content created at its member institutions and affiliates. The repository's stated purpose is to help its members "preserve and provide access to digital assets of enduring value that are critical to their work in research, education, and cultural heritage" by pre- serving and making accessible pre- and postprints, electronic theses and disserta- tions, datasets, publications, and learning objects; special collections and archival materials such as digitized documents, images, and audio/video files; and records and documents including policies, minutes, and contracts.

The HathiTrust Digital Library and the Alliance Digital Repository are examples of repositories that are viewed by their contributing members as single collections to be supported, shared, and used collectively. Centralized storage and management of digital collections are both practical and economical and have been easier for libraries to endorse and support financially than shared print collections, which remain linked to the perceived importance of local ownership and immediate physical access.

Infrastructures for Cooperative Collection Development and Management

The infrastructures through which libraries manage cooperative activities may be called cooperatives, networks, consortia, collaboratives, councils, federations, or alliances. These terms generally describe the same type of entity— a grouping of two or more libraries that have agreed to coordinate, cooperate in, or consoli- date some functions. NISO offers this definition:

> A *library cooperative* (network, system, and consortium) is an organization that has a formal arrangement whereby library and information services are supported for the mutual benefit of participating libraries. It must meet all of the following criteria:
>
> 1. Participants/members are primarily libraries.
> 2. The organization is a U.S. not-for-profit entity which has its own budget and its own paid staff.
> 3. The organization serves multiple institutions (e.g., libraries, school districts) that are not under the organization's administrative control.

4. The scope of the organization's activities includes support of library and information services by performing such functions as resource sharing, training, planning, and advocacy.[61]

The earliest regional library networks in the United States, which were developed to facilitate resource sharing, depended on the creation of union catalogs to facilitate resource discovery. Two early examples are the Bibliographical Center for Research (serving libraries in the Pacific Northwest), which was started in 1935, and PALINET (initially serving libraries in Pennsylvania), started in 1933. Each received grants to create union card catalogs. The number of library cooperatives grew rapidly with the spread of library automation and the resulting development of shared bibliographic databases. Ninety-six academic library consortia were established just between 1966 and 1970.[62] OCLC began as the Ohio College Library Center in 1967 with the purpose of creating a shared automated catalog network for Ohio libraries; it has grown into what Kopp called a megaconsortium, with more than 25,900 member libraries, archives, and museums around the world.[63] At the heart of OCLC is WorldCat, the world's largest bibliographic database, which is used by member libraries as a source for catalog records, a discovery tool, and a starting point for resource sharing.

The United States is covered by a complex arrangement of library networks, cooperatives, consortia, and the like. Some serve as OCLC service partners, contracting with OCLC to provide members with support and training for OCLC services. In addition, these organizations may offer

- consulting
- training
- contract cataloging
- reference service
- preservation support and disaster assistance
- discounted prices for library supplies through agreements with vendors
- preferential interlibrary loan and document delivery
- cooperative purchase of e-resources

Factors that affect organizational patterns include characteristics of individual members, administration of the program, kinds of cooperative activity, and sources of funding. Cooperating libraries, regardless of what they call their organization, may have a centralized or decentralized administrative structure.

A common feature of library cooperatives is the use of formal agreements that provide operating principles and, usually, define the goals of the organization.[64]

The 2013 *Library and Book Trade Almanac* listed nearly four hundred networks, consortia, and other cooperative library organizations in the United States and Canada.[65] Research conducted in December 2011 found that 89 percent of 730 responding libraries of all types (excluding schools) belonged to at least one consortium or library network, and 53 percent belonged to three or more.[66] These organizations have been merging to leverage their resources and collective power. For example, PALINET (serving the mid-Atlantic region and beyond), SOLINET (serving library and other information organizations in the Southeast and the Caribbean), and NELINET (serving libraries and cultural organizations of all types in New England) united to form LYRASIS (www.lyrasis.org) in 2009. In 2011, the Bibliographic Center for Research (which served eleven states in the Midwest and Northwest) joined LYRASIS, which is now the largest cooperative in North America.

Formal cooperative relationships with other libraries may be local, statewide, regional, national, or international. The cooperative may be focused on a particular type of library (e.g., academic, public) or may serve multiple types. OCLC surveyed leaders of 101 consortia in the United States in 2012.[67] Among the findings were the following:

> Fifty-six percent have more than forty member libraries, and 14 percent have more than one hundred.

> Fifty-two percent serve multiple types of libraries, 24 percent serve academic libraries, 16 percent serve public libraries, 5 percent serve school, federal, and other government libraries, and 3 percent serve special libraries.

> Twenty-six percent see facilitating resource sharing as their primary mission, and another 22 percent report that increasing efficiencies through collaboration is their primary mission.

> The three most used consortial services are interlibrary loan, resource sharing, and document delivery; shared online catalog or union list; and cooperative purchasing, with licensing of e-content being the top initiative.

Funding models and organizational strategies for cooperatives vary from simple to complex. OCLC found that 69 percent of the consortia surveyed had multiple sources of funding, with most of these being public taxes and state funding (29 percent) and membership fees (22 percent).[68] The membership fee may be a flat rate. Other consortia prorate the fee based on library operating budget or population served. Some consortia (called "virtual consortia")[69] exist primarily to serve as buying clubs, with no central office and modest budgets. Some statewide consortia are supported by state governments with members paying fees for additional services. Some cooperatives have central staffs of varying size; others rely on volunteers from the member libraries.

Many states have effective cooperative programs that provide a variety of services, including interlibrary loan, document delivery, and access to electronic resources. The programs are funded at the state level and do not require participating libraries to pay membership fees, although members may pay for supplemental services. They may be open to all citizens of the state or to individuals affiliated with member institutions and their libraries. A representative sampling of state programs is described here.

The Illinois Library and Information Network (ILLINET) (www.cyberdriveillinois.com/departments/library/libraries/illinet.html) formed in 1975 and is administered by the Illinois State Library.[70] More than five thousand academic, public, school, and special libraries are ILLINET members. A library becomes an member when it is accepted for membership in one of the twelve state-funded regional library systems. ILLINET provides a delivery service for interlibrary loan materials between libraries. It has an extensive program to provide access to electronic resources through E-RICH, a tiered set of offerings available to all ILLINET member libraries. Tier 1 e-resources are totally subsidized by the Illinois State Library and provided at no charge to all ILLINET member libraries. Tier 2 are e-resources partially subsidized by the Illinois State Library and available to all ILLINET member libraries, with a portion of the cost paid by the subscribing library. Tier 3 e-resources are not subsidized, but the Illinois State Library negotiates for favorable pricing for purchasing libraries.

OhioLINK is a statewide, state-funded network of eighty-nine Ohio college, technical school, and university libraries and the State Library of Ohio.[71] It provides access to more than 140 online research databases; more than seven thousand scholarly e-journals; approximately two thousand educational films, and thousands of digital images; a growing collection of e-books; and approximately fourteen thousand electronic theses and dissertations from participating colleges and universities. Patrons use a single online catalog that supports the submission of unmediated patron borrowing requests, and requested materials are delivered within 48 hours. A parallel initiative is INFOhio (www.infohio.org), a virtual K–12 library, which, like OhioLINK, is funded by the State of Ohio. It provides free access to a core collection of online, age-specific, curriculum-related resources for K–12 students, students' families, and educators. In addition, INFOhio provides a statewide online media catalog reservation and tracking system for educational materials through which teachers can book media for classroom use.

The Minitex Library Information Network is a publicly supported network of academic, public, state government, and special libraries. Minitex is funded by the Minnesota legislature through the Minnesota Office of Higher Education; programs for Minnesota public libraries are funded through a contract with Minnesota State Library Services and School Technology, a unit of the Minnesota Department of Education. Libraries in North Dakota and South Dakota participate in Minitex programs through contracts between the Minnesota Office of Higher Education and the North and South Dakota state libraries. Minitex began as a document delivery service and continues to deliver materials in the tristate region. In addition to many typical services associated with cooperatives (e.g., training, contract cataloging, OCLC support, discounted prices for library supplies and e-resources), Minitex provides statewide free access to Electronic Library for Minnesota (ELM), a suite of e-resources made available through state legislative funding. Minitex also manages MnLink and the MnLINK Gateway and operates the Minnesota Library Access Center (MLAC), a high-density storage facility for important but lesser-used items deposited by libraries throughout Minnesota.

Cooperative Acquisition of Electronic Resources

Collaborating in the acquisition of electronic resources has expanded rapidly among all types of libraries. Sometimes called *consortial cost sharing* or *buying clubs*, this is one of most successful areas of cooperation. All but one of seventy-three respondents to a 2010 ARL survey reported that they belonged to consortia for the primary purpose of acquiring commercially available e-resources.[72] A Primary Research Group survey published in 2012 reported that consortium purchases accounted for a mean of 40.84 percent of total licenses for electronic content in U.S. libraries sampled.[73] E-content acquired through consortia may be e-journals, e-books, online indexes, audiobooks, or other media.

Libraries that have not previously engaged in formal cooperative agreements are joining multiple organizations to gain savings and greater power in contract negotiations with suppliers or electronic information resources. The same Primary Research Group survey found that U.S. libraries were participating in an average of 2.1 licensing consortiums. When assured of a certain number of purchasers, vendors frequently offer discounted pricing. Often an added advantage for vendors is reduced operating costs. A publisher or vendor need negotiate the license only with the consortium, not with individual libraries, and billing is often handled through a single statement sent to the consortium office.

Advantages for libraries are access to a greater domain of materials than they can normally afford, the ability to leverage their acquisitions budgets and acquire access to more resources, reduced costs and time on the library side devoted to license negotiation since the consortium handles this, and increased likelihood that the collective clout of the consortium can negotiate more favorable licensing terms. The OhioLINK Electronic Journal Center and OhioLINK databases are examples of the expanded access to resources, offering access to more than forty-five million articles. Even Ohio's major universities hold an average of only 25 percent of the available scholarly journals, but users at those institutions utilize 80 percent of the available Electronic Journal Center titles.[74]

Libraries are leveraging investments through reductions in resource costs. This can be seen as cost avoidance because the library spends more than if it acquired nothing but less than if it paid the full price charged individual libraries. TexShare (www.tsl.state.tx.us/texshare), a consortium of 685 Texas libraries of all types and sizes, purchases online resources, shares print and electronic materials, and combines staff expertise. TexShare reported that the libraries participating in the TexShare database program in 2011–12 would have spent $101,982,797 to acquire access to the forty-nine database subscriptions that were purchased by the Texas State Library and Archives Commission for $5,977,061.[75]

Allocation of costs for products acquired through consortial licenses varies from consortium to consortium. When member libraries are of similar size, the consortium may divide the total cost of the licensed product equally among those libraries that opt to acquire access. Another typical approach is differential pricing—that is, dividing charges proportionally among participants according to projected use or the size of the institution, based either on enrollment (or enrolled students, plus staff and faculty/teachers) or on citizens served by the library. Noting that larger institutions may feel disadvantaged by this approach because vendors often discount their prices progressively according to the size of the user base, Anderson explores several alternatives, including hybrid models that take into account the savings gained through the consortium compared to what the library would pay if it licensed the content independently.[76]

Additional savings gained by working through a consortium to acquire e-resources can result from having a centralized staff to negotiate and administer the contracts. Individual libraries do not have to devote time to reviewing contracts and their negotiation. Another possible benefit is a multiyear contract that does not need to be negotiated as frequently and often guarantees reduced annual price increases.

Selection of e-resources is handled differently in each consortium and varies with the e-content being considered. Sometimes a vendor approaches the consortium and presents a proposal. Sometimes collections librarians in the consortium suggest a publisher or vendor whose package of e-resources is seen as attractive. In most cases, the proposal (regardless of its origin) is reviewed by collections librarians from the participating libraries, often through a committee of collection development officers that may include electronic resource librarians. If a library already has access to the content, the library's collections librarian reviews the existing terms and pricing to see if the consortial proposal is more attractive. Most vendors require a certain number of consortial participants to move forward with the offer. In general, member libraries—though they can opt in or opt out—do not have the ability to customize their selection. They are offered the entire package and cannot select components according to their local, intuitional preferences.

In some cases, the result of a consortial purchase agreement is separate subscriptions at each participating library. In other cases, consortia acquire access to e-resources that are shared across the membership. These might be statewide licenses in which all citizens have access to the content or consortium-wide licenses in which all members have access. One example of consortial buying is the Wisconsin Public Library Consortium, which collaboratively purchases e-books, audiobooks, videos, and music. Residents across Wisconsin, regardless of location, can download the content. The group purchase allows smaller libraries access to more materials than they could afford on their own. In 2012, all seventeen Wisconsin library systems and their 387 member public libraries contributed $700,000, which was combined with another $300,000 from LSTA funds to create an e-book buying pool.[77]

The role of consortia in acquiring electronic resources and access continues to expand. A potent illustration is the International Coalition of Library Consortia (ICOLC, http://icolc.net), organized in 1997. This informal group has a membership of approximately two hundred library consortia serving all types and sizes of libraries in several countries. Representatives from the various consortia meet twice a year with e-resource publishers, aggregators, and vendors to discuss new offerings, pricing practices, and contractual issues. Allen and Hirshon call ICOLC "a reverse cartel because these independent consortia come together not to limit competition or fix prices, but to leverage their collective power to open up the market."[78] In 1998, ICOLC released its "Statement of

Current Perspective and Preferred Practices for the Selection and Purchase of Electronic Information," which sought to establish an international perspective on consortial licensing and cooperative purchasing of electronic information by libraries. This was supplemented by two updates that address new developments in ejournal licensing and pricing and economics.[79]

Attributes of Successful Cooperative Collection Development and Management

Cooperating on collection development and management programs requires two or more partners—and most partnerships operate within the context of networks and consortia with several member libraries. As noted, successful cooperative collection development and management activities depend on the intersection of resource sharing, bibliographic access, and coordinated collection development and management. In addition, effective partnerships have several qualities that contribute to their success.

Self-knowledge—the capacity of a library to understand its own motives, abilities, and behaviors—is a key attribute of successful cooperation. Mark writes:

> Each library must have a clear idea of the community which it serves—its composition, its characteristics and its expectations. It should also know, of course, how it expects to meet these expectations in terms of collections, staffing and services. The needs of the home community are paramount. To neglect them is to do so at one's professional peril. If each library has its own clear vision as to its mission, guiding principles, goals and objectives then perhaps there will be less danger that the urgent questions will obscure the important ones.[80]

Once a library understands its mission, it must find an acceptable balance between local priorities and the priorities of the larger group to which the library belongs. This tension has defined the history of library cooperation. The library's obligation to provide materials to meet present and local needs is a more powerful force than any external agreement to acquire materials to meet the needs of unknown, remote users. One source of this tension is the reality that every library serves a local community, which may be a higher education institution, local citizens and governing body, school students, partners in a legal firm, or hospital staff members. Any cooperative program that requires a library to buy materials needed at another library at the expense of locally needed materials will fail. As entities accountable to their local communities and parent agencies and institutions, libraries must have a clear understanding of their institutional mission and be able to explain how resources are being used to meet the community's needs and desires along with the benefits gained through collaboration. The challenge of balancing local priorities and group commitments plagues every cooperative development initiative, but managing these counterpoints effectively is an attribute of successful cooperative initiatives.

Millard observes that "consortia tend to be cumbersome beasts . . . [and] there are various point where delays, misunderstandings and blame-shifting can and do occur."[81] Thus, cooperating successfully to develop and manage collections requires a high level of trust between the member libraries and the collections librarians. Equally important is effective consortium governance—a clear governing structure, organization mission and goals, and sufficient authority to make decisions. Members should agree and be committed to the mutual benefits of interdependence. A competent, strong consortium leader or administrator is necessary. All formal agreements and commitments must be flexible and permit modification. Clarity and adequate understanding among partners of the shared goals and intentions of the consortium are important. The consortium must have a reliable communication system to share decisions and changes quickly and widely. E-mail, electronic discussion lists, and consortium websites have lessened many communication barriers, especially between individual librarians. Both the consortium staff and the library representatives should fulfill their obligations (e.g., responding to queries, evaluating resources, returning purchase agreements) in a timely manner. Of critical importance are identifying measures of success that have meaning to the consortium members and their governing and funding bodies, then assessing success against these measures.

Enlightened self-interest of each institution in the consortium is important for success. Inculcating cooperation as a core value within the library can foster a willingness to make sacrifices and a belief that benefits will accrue. Success depends on respect for and recognition of the value of increased collaboration. One goal is to reach the stage at which the collections of cooperating libraries are no longer viewed as individual collections but as a single shared collection distributed in various locations and linked by shared discovery and delivery mechanisms. For cooperation to succeed, it must be considered a routine part of all work in the library.

Shelton identifies several best practices of successful cooperative collection development and management initiatives, including effective communication and consultation, clear goals and focus for initiatives, willingness to be flexible and adapt to changes, and a viable technological infrastructure. Kachel stresses the need for a written consortium policy that spells out commitments, responsibilities, goals, and objectives; the policy should be endorsed by signature of the appropriate administrators or perhaps (in the case of school library media centers) by the school board.[82]

Challenges to Cooperative Collection Development and Management

Cooperative collection development and management is difficult, with many forces pushing against it. Joycelyn Elders, former U.S. surgeon general, states, "Collaboration has been defined as an unnatural act between non-consenting adults. We all say we want to collaborate, but what we really mean is that we want to continue doing things as we have always done them while others change to fit what we are doing."[83] Unwillingness to change even when the reasons to do so are compelling is a persistent problem in effective cooperative collection development and management.

Desire for Local Autonomy

Librarians, since the beginning of collection building, have seen meeting current and future community needs as their goal. This has resulted in tremendous pride in being able to do so in a self-sufficient manner. This tradition of a strong local collection has been a defining characteristic of librarianship for centuries—fueled, suggests Runkle, by the heavy significance of property in our social and legal systems.[84] The dominant culture in the United States places tremendous value on ownership. In a material culture, the size of the local collection is a persistent measure of success. Many organizations, such as ARL, are using supplemental and alternative measures of library success, yet the need for local ownership with its implications of control and independence remains a potent force against cooperation.

The desire for independence and local autonomy is as powerful a force as the value associated with holding large collections. Branin suggests that cooperative collection development has had problems in the United States because of a long and deep-rooted tradition of local autonomy. Librarians and their libraries have had difficulty overcoming their parochialism in order to think more broadly—at the consortial, network, state, regional, or national level. Although cooperation and collaboration are considered good in the abstract, individual libraries' desire to be self-sufficient creates resistance to what is perceived as losing control. Consortia often stumble over the organizational and administrative aspects of establishing themselves. For Branin, "Cooperative collection development is at its most basic level a political, not a technical issue."[85]

Professional Pride

The culture of collection development and the persistent belief that the role of every librarian is to build the most complete collection possible also pull against cooperation. This form of turf professionalism leads subject specialists in research libraries to see themselves as developing competing collections rather than cooperating to build a shared resource. As Collins observes, "No single library wants to be the first to appear to be ceding their collecting duties to outside entities, even (or perhaps especially), peer institutions."[86] A major challenge facing cooperative collection development is to change these selection virtues of the past. Pride among all types of librarians has a tendency to focus on the quality of the local collection rather than the quality of the consortial or regional collection. A spirit of interdependence and trust among collection development librarians is a key element in successful cooperative collection development.

Attitudes of faculty members at academic institutions are equally constrained by the belief that large local collections equal academic status and prestige. Faculty fear that reductions in local collection growth, regardless of the wealth of resources readily available through resource sharing, will reduce their own program's reputation and negatively affect decisions about accreditation, joining the department, and faculty retention, promotion, and tenure. Local ownership of extremely expensive, esoteric items is a point of pride and prestige—even when such items are infrequently used. Changing faculty perceptions and expectations about the benefits of cooperative collection development remains a challenge as long as extensive local collections continue to hold such symbolic status. Nevertheless, library users who appreciate and have confidence in the mutual benefits that can result from cooperation are crucial for success.

Internal Barriers

Librarians often are unable to transcend organizational divisions and overcome communication barriers within their own libraries. If selection activities are too decentralized, they occur in isolation and efforts at cooperative policymaking cannot succeed. If coordinating selection activities within a library is difficult, coordinating with external partners is more so. Those involved in technical services, reference services, preservation activities, and interlibrary loan operations all must be aware of and support cooperative commitments and endeavors. If the library does not have a supportive internal organizational structure and clear authority for collection development, cooperation with other libraries is nearly impossible.

Lack of support, commitment, and leadership from governing boards and administrators, both within and external to the library, can be a significant problem. Strong leadership and constant support throughout the organization are important. CIC is an example of a consortium that benefits from strong institutional support. The members of the governing committee are the chief academic officers from each of the member universities. Programs and activities extend to all aspects of university activity except intercollegiate athletics. The CIC Center for Library Initiatives is one of several cooperating ventures, all of which are strongly supported by university administrators.

Dissatisfaction with the results of cooperation among library staff members creates difficulties. The absence of significant, observable accomplishments leads to self-defeating behaviors. Without some successes, momentum for progress is lacking. Thus, participants in cooperative collection development and management programs need a process for quantifying the cost benefits of cooperation and of regularly comparing the benefits of cooperation with those of independence.[87] Everyone must understand the consequences of ignoring consortial commitments. Documented evidence of the benefits of cooperation and the results of failing to cooperate are powerful incentives.

Local discontent with perceived lack of parity in partners' financial and time commitments can undermine effective participation in cooperative ventures. If library administrators or library staff members feel that the local library is carrying a disproportionate load (either financially or in time contributed to group initiatives), they are less motivated to fulfill other commitments. One solution might be a sliding scale of membership fees based on size of user community served. The cost of participating in consortial projects (e.g., shared storage or cooperative microfilming projects) can be prorated according the individual libraries' degree of participation. If a flat rate is charged, the library director should be able to explain the rationale for doing so.

Failures in Bibliographic Access and Physical Access

Failure to identify or locate resources undermines cooperative collection development and management. Success depends on an infrastructure that accurately reports the resources that are at hand and where additional resources are located. This, in turn, requires libraries to maintain accurate and current bibliographic and holdings records in their local catalogs and in any union catalogs, including WorldCat, to which they contribute records. Failure to do so thwarts discovery and defeats cooperation.

Any difficulties or delays in getting remote materials to users are barriers to cooperative collection development and management. Users want speedy request fulfillment. To succeed, a consortium needs dependable mechanisms for affordable, timely, efficient, and effective delivery of resources. These depend on effective use of suitable technology, sufficient library staff to handle the volume of interlibrary loan requests (both borrowing and lending), a rapid method to deliver both returnables and nonreturnables, and, ideally, the availability of systems to support unmediated user requests.

Evaluating Cooperative Collection Development and Management

Librarians assume that cooperative collection development and management programs are good, even essential, practices necessary to provide library users access to resources beyond the local collection. The issue, however, is developing measures to demonstrate how the user community and the library benefit (or not) when a library engages in cooperation with other libraries. Such areas as cost avoidance, cost savings, and user satisfaction can be challenging to quantify in meaningful ways, yet libraries need these data to monitor their performance, make course corrections, and report to stakeholders.

Cost-Benefit Analysis

Illustrating the positive cost-benefit ratio of specific collaborative collection development projects with concrete numbers can be difficult and elusive.[88] That does not mean that libraries have not tried and should not continue to do cost-benefit analyses. *Cost-benefit analysis* compares the various costs associated with an expenditure against the benefits that it proposes to return. Both tangible and intangible factors should be addressed and measured—to the extent possible. Cost-benefit analysis requires consistent measures. Traditional forms of these analyses calculate both present and future costs and present and future benefits (i.e., value) in monetary terms, then measure the benefits per dollar spent. Such an analysis helps a library determine which decisions are fiscally responsible.

Research in the 1990s looked at resource sharing and commercial document delivery services as alternatives to owning books and subscribing to print journals in academic libraries. In 1991 and 1992, Columbia University libraries compared costs for ownership with costs of borrowing the item from another library or using commercial document delivery.[89] The study found that the costs of owning a monograph used only once far exceeded the costs for accessing it through interlibrary loan, but the authors struggled with measuring and assigning values to intangibles such as the importance to researchers of being able to browse collections and materials. Louisiana State University, in a study reported in 1997, found that commercial document delivery was more economical for high-cost, low-use journals than local subscriptions, and that users accepted the service when it met promised expectations, including 24-hour turnaround.[90] Kingma applied cost-benefit analysis to access, ownership, and interlibrary loan and sought to assign a dollar value to all aspects of the analysis.[91]

Other researchers have investigated cost-benefit analysis of e-resources and various approaches to their acquisition. King and colleagues observe that the complex decisions surrounding e-resources "require a sound economic underpinning as well as good judgment in applying economic information and metrics."[92] This complexity involves deciding if the library should

- rely exclusively on electronic journals or purchase both electronic and print subscriptions and, if so, at what price
- subscribe to or rely on single-article demand for certain journals
- discard print issues or rely on them as backup for archival purposes
- negotiate site licenses
- deal directly with publishers or rely on intermediary services such as consortia, aggregators, or gateways, and, if so, at what price
- depend on information freely accessible on the web as a substitute for costly electronic resources

Cost-benefit analysis can help inform decisions about the best means of access. Determining the direct cost in dollars of a purchased book or print journal, e-book or e-journal licensed directly from the publisher or as part of a bundled package, e-book or e-journal licensed through a consortia, or provision through interlibrary loan or commercial document delivery is reasonably easy to do, but other aspects of the cost-benefit analysis are more challenging. A complete cost-benefit analysis calculates all costs in dollars on the library's side, including staffing costs associated with each task (selection, order placement, license negotiation and tracking, receipting physical items, invoice processing, cataloging, shelving, issue check-in, binding, reshelving, interlibrary loan processing, etc.) and benefits (money saved through reducing or eliminating tasks).

Additional cost components, such as equipment, depreciation, and telecommunication charges, might logically be part of an analysis. Few libraries have the capacity to do such a detailed and comprehensive cost-benefit analysis.

Calculating costs and benefits from the user's perspective is even less straightforward. How does one measure and assign a dollar value to user satisfaction, user effort, or a user's time to locate and obtain an item? If the item is held locally in print format, the user must locate it, note the call number or shelving location, look for it in the library, then check it out or make a photocopy. If it is held electronically, the user still needs to find it but does not always need to visit the library. Regardless of remote or on-site access, the user may incur printing costs. If not available in the library or online through a library license, the library user may use an unmediated interlibrary loan option or complete a form—and then wait for delivery.

Patron satisfaction or utility cost is equally difficult to assess. Economists use *utility* as a measure or expression of an individual's expected or anticipated satisfaction. Ideally, one would contrast the utility of on-site or online patron access to subscribed resources and interlibrary loan (or commercial document delivery, if the library offers this), in which at least some of the work is transferred to staff, access takes longer, and fees may be charged. One could add the option many publishers offer through which a customer orders an article directly and pays the publisher. Determining the *opportunity cost* (the true cost of choosing one alternative over another) from the user's perspective is difficult.

Library valuation research continues to gain attention as one means to demonstrate accountability.[93] Researchers have adopted valuation methods from the field of economics that allow libraries to assign a dollar value to their programs and services. Much of this work has focused on demonstrating through cost-benefit analysis the value that tax dollars spent on libraries bring to a community. One approach uses *stated-preference techniques* to estimate how much consumers would pay for a good or service if it were available for purchase. This technique is explicitly designed to provide value equivalents in situations where no market price can exist. The intent is not to determine what people will pay but to gather data that can be used in combination with cost data to calculate a cost-benefit ratio. One stated-preference technique is *contingent valuation*, in which users and nonusers are surveyed about their value perceptions and asked to respond to hypothetical scenarios. In contingent valuation surveys, individuals are asked how much they would be willing to pay for a good or service, or how much money they would accept in order to forgo the good or service—even though that good or service does not have a market price.[94] For example, library users and potential users could be asked to determine if they would assign a higher dollar value to having access to more materials with some delay in delivery (i.e., resource sharing and interlibrary loan) or a higher value to fewer materials that are readily available on-site.

Not many librarians or libraries are in a position to conduct a formal cost-benefit analysis when deciding whether to purchase a resource, to rely on resource sharing, or to purchase through a cooperative venture. Nevertheless, careful consideration is necessary and information can be gathered to make an informed decision. At its simplest, a cost-benefit analysis compares the pros and cons of alternatives. A librarian can supply direct costs where they are known and list staff tasks in general terms (without determining dollar costs) to compare costs and benefits on the library's side. Librarians can use existing library data where they are available, including circulation activity, interlibrary loan borrowing, and collection analyses about existing strengths and weaknesses. On the user side, the librarian can list any known fees or costs the user is expected to pay and then list benefits and costs from the user's perspective in general terms (i.e., without trying to assign dollar value). For example, one could confidently state that users assign proximity to physical collections a high value and 24-hour remote access to online resources a higher value. King and colleagues suggest using comparative terms (lower cost, low cost, moderate cost, high cost, higher cost) and descriptive terms (saves users time, less effort needed).[95] A fairly simple pro/con chart that lists costs and benefits from the library's perspective and from the user's perspective can effectively inform decision making.

Social Return on Investment and Balanced Scorecard

The outcomes-based tool *social return on investment* (SROI) expands on cost-benefit analysis to include explicitly the economic value of cultural and social impact. The Roberts Enterprise Development Fund (www.redf.org) pioneered the method for calculating SROI, which aims to use metrics to manage and measure impacts that are not included in traditional profit-loss accounts and to focus on outcomes instead of outputs. In the library context, SROI is user-community-focused, aims to understand value (i.e., benefits) from the users' perspective, and, where possible, uses monetary values for these indicators.[96]

One tool used in reporting SROI is the *balanced scorecard*, another performance metric borrowed from the for-profit sector and developed by Kaplan and Norton. It is intended to provide a context for the key measures chosen and permits expressing value in social as well as economic terms. It allows balancing successes across different types of financial and nonfinancial measures and recognizes their interaction. In 2003, Bosch, Lyons, and Munroe reported on work to develop a modified balanced scorecard that could measure the success of cooperative collection development activities. They developed four groups of performance measures: resources or input data (numerical data like staff numbers and hours of work, items purchased, items in collections), financial data (library/group expenditures, unit costs, etc.), use data (use of electronic, print, or near print; documents delivered; etc.), and user satisfaction data. A library using a balanced scorecard begins by identifying five or six key strategic objectives, maps causal links between them, and picks suitable measures for each objective. Unlike cost-benefit analysis, a formal comparison between cost dollars and benefit dollars (or value) is not the intended result. The goal is to find an equilibrium in which outcomes are equally positive without significant gains (or losses) in one area to the detriment (or undue benefit) of others.[97]

A library might, for example, select the following strategic objectives relating to collaborative collection development and management:

    a. access to more unique resources

    b. expansion of digital collections through leveraged investment

    c. increased availability in local shelf space through coordinated storage

    d. reduced user effort and time

    e. increased user satisfaction

    f. reduced library personnel costs

Corresponding measures assigned to these objectives might be

    a. title count of the shared universe of resources, or interlibrary loan activity

    b. title count of e-resources or cost savings through consortial purchases

    c. volumes withdrawn and local shelving space gained

    d. improvement in user perceptions about effort and time required for different tasks

    e. improvement in user satisfaction

    f. declining library personnel costs

The balanced scorecard is prepared and then revisited as new data are gathered at periodic intervals to track changes in each key measure. The purpose is to have quantitative and qualitative measures that can help the library determine if cooperating on collection development and management reduces costs, increases access to information resources, and results in increased use and user satisfaction—or if not, where it is failing.

CASE STUDY

The Colossal Center for Library Storage opened in 1995 as a high-density, closed storage center serving all types of libraries in a large metropolitan area. Construction was funded jointly by the state, public universities, private colleges, and city and county governments in a seven-county area, which saw a shared storage center as a cost-effective alternative to expanding or constructing new library buildings. Libraries that have materials in the Colossal Center pay both an annual flat fee and prorated annual charge based on the volume of materials in storage. These funds cover the salaries for the center's director and operating staff and support building overhead and maintenance. Staff manage ingest of materials and are responsible for retrieving, shipping, and reshelving paged materials. The Center has a governing board composed of the directors of the eight libraries with the largest deposited collections and three at-large members representing the other participating libraries.

Like many shared storage facilities established twenty to thirty years ago, the Center focused on the economies of sharing of space within a facility and not on a shared approach to shaping and managing the collection. For most of the Center's existence, the only criteria guiding deposit were that materials had to be cataloged fully with bibliographic records provided for loading into the inventory management system; all journals had to be bound; and all materials had to be mold- and pest-free. Libraries retain ownership of the items and indicate in their local catalogs that the items are in storage and will be paged upon request. They are free to remove materials from storage and relocate them in on-site circulating collections. No commitments to retention either in the shared storage or in individual libraries are in place. The Colossal Center is now 90 percent full, and participating libraries have become increasingly aware that they have four options: stop depositing materials, increase individual library collection space, build an additional facility, or develop a new operating model for the Center and its holdings. The governing board members agree that only the fourth option is viable and have hired Alex, a consultant, to develop and propose a new model for Colossal Center.

Activity

Alex has determined that 27 percent of the journals in the Center are duplicates, and three or more copies are on deposit for several of these back runs. Approximately 15 percent of the monographs are duplicates and, again, many of these are multiple-copy deposits. Approximately 30 percent of the materials have not been used since they were deposited. Develop a proposal for Alex to present to the governing board. Assume that the governing model will not change and that substantial one-time funds are available to implement the plan Alex develops. Funds might, for example, be used to employ a customized collection analysis tool, remove duplicates and compact the collection, turn the inventory management system into a publically accessible catalog for all materials in the Center, all of these—or other options, as well. Draft a mission statement for the Colossal Center's focus and develop a high-level strategic plan to implement this mission. Propose new policies (e.g., criteria for deposit, retention commitments, and shared ownership) necessary to implement the new model.

Notes

1. Ross Atkinson, "Uses and Abuses of Cooperation in a Digital Age," *Collection Management* 28, no. 1/2 (2004): 19.

2. David H. Stam, "Think Globally, Act Locally: Collection Development and Resource Sharing," *Collection Building* 5, no. 1 (Spring 1983): 21.

3. Melvil Dewey, *Library Notes* 1 (June 1886): 5; Michael Gorman, "Laying Siege to the 'Fortress Library,'" *American Libraries* 17, no. 5 (May 1986): 325.

4. Joseph J. Branin, "Cooperative Collection Development," in *Collection Management: A New Treatise*, ed. Charles B. Osburn and Ross Atkinson, 81–110 (Greenwich, CT: JAI, 1991), 82.

5. John R. Kaiser, "Resource Sharing in Collection Development," in *Collection Development in Libraries: A Treatise*, ed. Robert D. Stueart and George B. Miller Jr., 139–57 (Greenwich, CT: JAI, 1980).

6. Nancy E. Gwinn and Paul H. Mosher, "Coordinating Collection Development: The RLG Conspectus," *College and Research Libraries* 44, no. 2 (1983): 128.

7. See David H. Stam, "Collaborative Collection Development: Progress, Problems and Potential," *Collection Building* 7, no. 3 (1986): 3–9, for an analysis of the Conspectus's role in cooperative collection development.

8. John Fetterman, "Resource Sharing in Libraries—Why, How, When, Next Steps?" in *Resource Sharing in Libraries*, ed. Allen Kent, 1–31 (New York: Marcel Dekker, 1974), 3.

9. Ernest C. Richardson, "Co-operation in Lending among College and Reference Libraries," *Library Journal* 24, no. 7 (July 1899): 32–33.

10. Reference and User Services Association, "Interlibrary Loan Code for the United States" (prepared by the Interlibrary Loan Committee, Reference and User Services, 1994, revised 2001, revised 2008 by the Sharing and Transforming Access to Resources Section), www.ala.org/rusa/resources/guidelines/interlibrary. See also Reference and User Services Association, "Interlibrary Loan Code for the United State Explanatory Supplement," www.ala.org/rusa/resources/guidelines/interlibraryloancode.

11. "National Interlibrary Loan Code, 1980" (adopted by the Reference and Adult Services Division Board of Directors, New York 1980), *RQ* 20, no. 1 (Fall 1980): 29; "National Interlibrary Loan Code for the United States, 1993" (approved by the Reference and Adult Services Board of Directors, Feb. 8, 1994), *RQ* 33, no. 4 (Summer 1994): 477.

12. "ALA Interlibrary Loan Request Form," www.ala.org/rusa/files/resources/guidelines/illformprint.pdf.

13. OCLC, *Annual Report 2011/2012* (Dublin, OH: OCLC, 2012), www.oclc.org/content/dam/oclc/publications/AnnualReports/2012/2012.pdf; Tai Phan et al., *Academic Libraries: 2010: First Look*, NCES 2012-365 (Washington, DC: U.S.

Department of Education, National Center for Education Statistics, 2011), 4, http://nces.ed.gov/pubs2012/2012365.pdf.

14. Institute of Museum and Libraries Services, *Public Libraries in the United States Survey: Fiscal Year 2010: Supplementary Tables*, "Public Library Services and Resources, Table 9: Number of Interlibrary Loans Provided to, and Received from, per 1,000 Population, by Type of Services and State: Fiscal Year 2010," www.imls .gov/assets/1/AssetManager/FY2010_PLS_Tables_8-16A.pdf; Adrienne Chute et al., *Public Libraries in the United States: Fiscal Year 2004*, "Table 8. Number of Public Library Services and Library Services per Capita or per 1,000 Population, by Type of Service and State: Fiscal Year 2004" (Washington, DC: National Center for Education Statistics, 2006), http://nces.ed.gov/pubs2006/2006349.pdf.

15. American Association of School Librarians and Association for Educational Communications and Technology, *Information Power: Guidelines for School Library Media Programs* (Chicago: American Library Association; Washington, DC: Association for Educational Communications and Technology, 1988), 1.

16. Ross Atkinson, "Access, Ownership, and the Future of Collection Development," in *Collection Management and Development: Issues in an Electronic Era*, ed. Peggy Johnson and Bonnie MacEwan, 92–109 (Chicago: American Library Association, 1993).

17. National Information Standards Organization, *NISO Circulation Interchange Part 1: Protocol*, Version 2.02 (Baltimore, MD: National Information Standards Organization, 2012), www.niso.org/standards/z39-83-1-2012.

18. Marshall Breeding, "Resource Sharing in Libraries: Concepts, Products, Technologies, and Trends," *Library Technology Reports* 49, no. 1 (Chicago: ALA TechSource, 2013).

19. Illinois Heartland Library System, "Illinois Heartland Library System Resource Sharing Plan and Policy" (adopted July 5, 2011, revised July 24, 2012), www .illinoisheartland.org/sites/default/files/ResourceSharingPolicy_2012.pdf.

20. Elizabeth Ringwelski (Minitex associate director, Resource Sharing, Information Technology, and MnLINK), personal e-mail message to author, July 10, 2013.

21. *Information Retrieval (ANSI/NISO Z39.50): Application Service Definition and Protocol Specification* (Bethesda, MD: National Information Standards Organization, American National Standards Institute, 2003) specifies a client/server-based protocol for information retrieval and specifies procedures and formats for a client to search a database provided by a server, retrieve database records, and perform related information retrieval functions.

22. Atkinson, "Uses and Abuses," 11; Karen Okamota, "Licensed to Share: How Libraries Are Handling Electronic Journal Article Requests," *Journal of Interlibrary Loan, Document Delivery, and Electronic Reserve* 22, no. 3/4 (2012): 137–54.

23. Linda Fredericksen et al., "Ebooks and Interlibrary Loan: Licensed to Fill?" *Journal of Interlibrary Loan, Document Delivery and Electronic Research* 21, no. 3 (2011): 117–31.

24. Elsevier, "ScienceDirect Policies" (revised May 14, 2013), www.elsevier.com/about/publishing-guidelines/policies/sciencedirect-policies; JSTOR, "Terms and Conditions of Use" (updated Apr. 16, 2012), www.jstor.org/page/info/about/policies/terms.jsp#TCBooks; Project Muse, "UPCC Books Frequently Asked Questions," http://muse.jhu.edu/about/faq_books.html; ebrary, ebrary Support Center, "Interlibrary Loans (ILL)," http://support.ebrary.com/kb/interlibrary-loans.

25. Rethinking Resources Sharing Initiative, "A Manifesto for Rethinking Resource Sharing," http://rethinkingresourcesharing.org/?page_id=27; see also Beth Posner and Evan Simpson, "The Rethinking Resource Sharing Initiative: Education, Advocacy, and Inspiration for Libraries," *Interlending and Document Supply* 39, no. 3 (2011): 142–47.

26. Catalog at http://libraries.montanastatelibrary.org/statewide-projects/montana-shared-catalog; see also "Montana Shared Catalog Frequently Asked Questions (FAQ's) and Answers," http://msl.mt.gov/Statewide_Projects/Montana_Shared_Catalog/For_Members/Help&Guidelines/MSC%20FAQ.pdf.

27. OCLC, "WorldCat Principles of Cooperation" (amended and approved by Global Council, June 21, 2010), www.oclc.org/worldcat/community/principles.en.html.

28. Dan C. Hazen, "Cooperative Collection Development: Compelling Theory, Inconsequential Results?" in *Collection Management for the Twenty-First Century: A Handbook for Librarians*, ed. G. E. Gorman and Ruth H. Miller, 263–83 (Westport, CT: Greenwood, 1997).

29. Paul H. Mosher and Marcia Pankake, "A Guide to Coordinated and Cooperative Collection Development," *Library Resources and Technical Services* 27, no. 4 (1983): 417–31.

30. See, for example, Anna H. Perrault, "The Printed Book: Still in Need of CCD," *Collection Management* 24, no. 1/2 (2000): 119–36; John Budd and Katharine K. Craven, "Academic Library Monographic Acquisitions: Selection of *Choice's* Outstanding Academic Books," *Library Collections, Acquisitions, and Technical Services* 23, no. 1 (Spring 1999): 15–26; Rob Kairis, "Consortium Level Collection Development: A Duplication Study of the OhioLINK Central Catalog," *Library Collections, Acquisitions, and Technical Services* 27, no. 3 (2003): 317–26; Michael Levine-Clark, Margaret Jobe, and Sara Holladay, "Uniqueness and Collection Overlap in Academic Libraries," Presentation at Necessity Is the Mother of Invention, Charleston Library Conference, Nov. 4–7, 2009, Charleston, South Carolina, http://docs.lib.purdue.edu/cgi/viewcontent.cgi?article=1037&context=charleston; Levine-Clark provided supplemental slides, which contain the data tables, to the author in a personal e-mail message, June 26, 2013.

31. Ruth R. Connell, "Eight May Be Too Many: Getting a Toe-Hold on Cooperative Collection Building," *Collection Management* 33, no. 1/2 (2008): 17–28.

32. Ross Atkinson, "Crisis and Opportunity: Reevaluating Acquisitions Budgeting in an Age of Transition," *Journal of Library Administration* 19, no. 2 (1994): 33–55; Edward Shreeves, "Is There a Future for Cooperative Collection Development in the Digital Age?" *Library Trends* 45, no. 3 (Winter 1997): 376.

33. Charles B. Osburn, "Collection Development and Management," in *Academic Libraries: Research Perspectives*, ed. Mary Jo Lynch, 1–37, ACRL Publications in Librarianship 47 (Chicago: American Library Association, 1990).

34. H. W. Wilson, "Public Library Core Collection: Nonfiction," www.hwwilson inprint.com/pub_lib_non.php.

35. See, for example, Carol Alabaster, *Developing an Outstanding Core Collection: A Guide for Libraries*, 2nd ed. (Chicago: American Library Association, 2010).

36. Ross Atkinson, "Old Forms, New Forms: The Challenge of Collection Development," *College and Research Libraries* 50, no. 5 (Sept. 1989): 508.

37. Stam, "Think Globally," 21.

38. Gouri Dutta et al., "TRLN OCLC Collection Analysis Task Group: Report to the Committee on Information Resources (CIR) June 2006," www.trln.org/TaskGroups/CollectionAnalysis/TRLN_CollAnalysis_June2Report.pdf.

39. Hendrick Edelman, "The Death of the Farmington Plan," *Library Journal* 98, no. 9 (April 15, 1973): 1251–53; see also Ralph D. Wagner, *A History of the Farmington Plan* (Lanham, MD: Scarecrow, 2002).

40. "Appendix 1: Tri-College Collections Policy," www.haverford.edu/library/about/Trico_collection_development_policy_public.pdf.

41. Debra E. Kachel, "Look Inward before Looking Outward: Preparing the School Library Media Center for Cooperative Collection Development," *School Library Media Quarterly* 23, no. 2 (Winter 1995): 101–13; Debra E. Kachel, *Collection Assessment and Management for School Libraries: Preparing for Cooperative Collection Development* (Westport, CT: Greenwood, 1997), 77.

42. Kay Downey, "Cooperative Collection Development: Sharing Funds, Resources, and Responsibilities across Libraries: A Pilot Program in Nursing," presentation at Necessity Is the Mother of Invention: Charleston Library Conference, Nov. 4–7, 2009, Charleston, South Carolina, http://docs.lib.purdue.edu/cgi/viewcontent.cgi?article=1014&context=charleston.

43. Yem S. Fong et al., "The Alliance Shared Purchase Plan: A New Experiment in Collaborative Collection Development," *Technical Services Quarterly* 27, no. 1 (2010): 17–38.

44. H. Austin Booth and Kathleen O-Brien, "Demand-Driven Cooperative Collection Development: Three Case Studies from the USA," *Interlending and Document Supply* 39, no. 3 (2011): 148–55; Rob Kairis, "A Subject-Based Shared Approval Plan for Consortia Purchasing of U.S. University Press Books," *Library Collections, Acquisitions, and Technical Services* 35, no. 1/2 (2012): 30–38.

45. Greg Doyle and Cory Tucker, "Patron-Driven Acquisition—Working Collaboratively in a Consortial Environment: An Interview with Greg Doyle," *Collaborative Librarianship* 3, no. 4 (2011): 212–16; James Bunnelle, "Pilot to Program: Demand-Driven E-books at the Orbis-Cascade Consortium: 1 Year Later," *Against the Grain* 24, no. 5 (Nov. 2012): 24, 26, 28; Alliance Orbis Cascade Alliance, "FAQ: Orbis-Cascade's DDA Program," www.orbiscascade.org/index/cms-filesystem-action/collection_development/dda-faq-10-16-12.doc.

46. Kate Davis, et al. "Shared Patron-Driven Acquisition within a Consortium: The OCUL PDA Pilot," *Serials Review* 38, no. 3 (2012): 183–87.

47. Lynn Wiley and Elizabeth Clarage, "Building on Success: Evolving Local and Consortium Purchase-on-Demand Programs," *Interlending and Document Supply* 40, no. 2 (2012): 105–110.

48. See Donald B. Simpson, "Economics of Cooperative Collection Development and Management: The United States' Experience with Rarely Held Research Materials," *IFLA Journal* 24, no. 3 (1998): 161–65; Gay N. Dannelly, "The Center for Research Libraries and Cooperative Collection Development: Partnerships in Progress," in *Cooperative Collection Development: Significant Trends and Issues*, ed. Donald B. Simpson, 37–45 (New York: Haworth, 1998).

49. Lizanne Payne, *Library Storage Facilities and the Future of Print Collections in North America* (Dublin, OH: OCLC, 2007).

50. Steve O'Conner, Andrew Wells, and Mel Collier, "A Study of Collaborative Storage of Library Resources," *Library Hi Tech* 20, no. 3 (2002): 258.

51. Payne, *Library Storage Facilities*, 30.

52. "OCLC Print Archives Disclosure Pilot Final Report" (April 2012), www.oclc.org/content/dam/oclc/productworks/OCLCPrintArchivesDisclosurePilotFinalReport.pdf.

53. Center for Research Libraries, "Print Archives Preservation Registry," www.crl.edu/archiving-preservation/print-archives/papr.

54. Bill Carney, "OCLC Shared Print Study," presentation at the PAN (Print Archive Network) meeting, Chicago, June 28, 2013, www.crl.edu/sites/default/files/attachments/misc/PAN_OCLC_Carney_Ann2013.pptx.

55. Robert H. Kieft and Lizanne Payne, "Collective Collection, Collective Action," *Collection Management* 37, no. 3/4 (2012): 137–52.

56. Robert H. Kieft, "Beyond My People and Thy People, or the Shared Print Collections Imperative," in *Rethinking Collection Development and Management*, ed. Rebecca Albitz, Christine Avery, and Diane Zabel (Santa Barbara, CA: Libraries Unlimited, 2014), 305.

57. See Constance Malpas, *Cloud-Sourcing Research Collections: Managing Print in the Mass-Digitized Library Environment* (Dublin, OH: OCLC Research, 2011), for an examination of the feasibility of outsourcing management of low-use print books

to shared service providers, including print and digital repositories; see also Brian Lavoie, Constance Malpas, and J. D. Shipengrover, *Print Management at "Mega-scale": A Regional Perspective on Print Book Collections in North America* (Dublin, OH: OCLC Research, 2012), www.oclc.org/research/publications/library/2012/2012 -05.pdf.

58. Michael Kelley, "Major Maine Libraries, Public and Academic, Collaborate on Print Archiving Project," *Library Journal* (Mar. 15, 2013), http://lj.libraryjournal .com/2013/03/managing-libraries/major-maine-libraries-public-and-academic -collaborate-on-print-archiving-project.

59. Print Archive Network, "Shared Print Community Discussions," www.crl.edu/ archiving-preservation/print-archives/forum, offers information about PAN's meetings and pertinent presentations and webinars, including links to reports from shared repositories. See Robert H. Kieft and Bernard Reilly, "Regional and National Cooperation on Legacy Print Collections," *Collaborative Librarianship* 1, no. 3 (2009): 106–108.

60. HathiTrust, "Constitutional Convention Ballot Proposals," www.hathitrust.org/ constitutional_convention2011_ballot_proposals.

61. National Information Standards Organization, *Information Services and Use: Metrics and Statistics for Libraries and Information Providers—Data Dictionary*, NISO Z39.7-201-2013 (Baltimore, MD: National Information Standards Organization, 2013), 5, http://z39-7.niso.org.

62. Carlos A. Cuadra and Ruth J. Patrick, "Survey of Academic Library Consortia in the U.S.," *College and Research Libraries* 33, no. 4 (July 1972): 271–83.

63. James J. Kopp, "Library Consortia and Information Technology: The Past, the Present, the Promise," *Information Technology and Libraries* 17, no. 1 (Mar. 1998): 7–12.

64. See Library Success: A Best Practices Wiki, "Consortia," www.libsuccess.org/index .php?title=Consortia, for examples of documents from library consortia worldwide.

65. Dave Bogart, ed., *Library and Book Trade Almanac* (Medford, NJ: Information Today, 2013).

66. Joseph McKenrick, *The Digital Squeeze: Libraries at the Crossroads: The Library Resource Guide Benchmark Study on 2012 Library Spending Plans* (Providence RI: Unisphere Research, 2012), www.libraryresource.com/Downloads/Download .ashx?IssueID=3213.

67. OCLC, *A Snapshot of Priorities and Perspectives: U.S. Library Consortia* (Dublin, OH: OCLC, 2013), www.oclc.org/content/dam/oclc/reports/us-consortia/214986 -member-communication-survey-report-consortia-review.pdf.

68. Ibid.

69. Tim Bucknall, "The Virtual Consortium," *Library Journal* 130, no. 7 (Spring 2005): 16–19.

70. Nancy Chipman Shlaes, "Cooperative Collection Management Succeeds in Illinois," *Resource Sharing and Information Networks* 12, no. 1 (1996): 49–53.

71. Naomi J. Goodman and Carole L. Hinchcliff, "From Crisis to Cooperation and Beyond: OhioLINK's First Ten Years," *Resource Sharing and Information Networks* 13, no. 1 (1997): 21–38.

72. Richard Bleiler and Jill Livingston, *Evaluating E-resources,* SPEC Kit 316 (Washington, DC: Association of Research Libraries, 2010), 12.

73. Primary Research Group, *The Survey of Library Database Licensing Practices, 2012 Edition* (New York: Primary Research Group, 2012).

74. OhioLINK, "Fast Facts: OhioLINK Electronic Journal Center (EJC)" (updated May 2009), www.ohiolink.edu/about/news/ejcff.html.

75. Texas State Library and Archives Commission, "Costs Avoided by Local Libraries Due to the TexShare Database Program for the 49 Databases Provided for the Year July 1, 2011–June 30, 2012," www.tsl.state.tx.us/texshare/dbmtg/costsavings2011_2012.html.

76. Douglas Anderson, "Allocation of Costs for Electronic Products in Academic Library Consortia," *College and Research Libraries* 67, no. 2 (Mar. 2006): 123–35.

77. Wisconsin Public Library Consortium, For Patrons, "Wisconsin Libraries Contribute toward $1 Million E-book Buying Pool," www.wplc.info/about/welcome.

78. Barbara McFadden Allen and Arnold Hirshon, "Hanging Together to Avoid Hanging Separately: Opportunities for Academic Libraries and Consortia," *Information Technology and Libraries* 17, no. 1 (March 1998): 40.

79. International Coalition of Library Consortia, "Statement of Current Perspective and Preferred Practices for the Selection and Purchase of Electronic Information (Mar. 1998)," http://legacy.icolc.net/statement.html; International Coalition of Library Consortia, "Statement of Current Perspective and Preferred Practices for the Selection and Purchase of Electronic Information: Update No. 1: New Developments in Ejournal Licensing" (Dec. 2001 update), http://legacy.icolc .net/2001currentpractices.htm; International Coalition of Library Consortia "Statement of Current Perspective and Preferred Practices for the Selection and Purchase of Electronic Information: Update No. 2: Pricing and Economics" (Oct. 1, 2004), http://icolc.net/statement/statement-current-perspective-and-preferred -practices-selection-and-purchase-electronic.

80. Timothy Mark, "National and International Library Collaboration: Necessity, Advantages," *LIBER Quarterly* 17, no. 3/4 (2007): 124.

81. Ruth Millard, "Better Together: Some Reflections on Library Cooperation and Consortia with Special Reference to ANZTLA Consortia," *ANZTLA EJournal* no. 5 (2010), www.nla.gov.au/openpublish/index.php/ANZTLA/article/view/2935/3360.

82. Cynthia Shelton, "Best Practices in Cooperative Collection Development: A Report Prepared by the Center for Research Libraries Working Group in Best Practices in Cooperative Collection Development," *Collection Management* 28, no. 3 (2003): 191–222; Kachel, *Collection Assessment and Management.*

83. Quotation from Thomas E. Backer, "Evaluating Community Collaborations: An Overview," in *Evaluating Community Collaboration*, ed. Thomas E. Backer, 1–8 (New York: Springer, 2003), 10.

84. Martin Runkle, "What Was the Original Mission of the Center for Research Libraries and How Has It Changed?" in *CRL's Role in the Emerging Global Resources Program, 1997 Symposium, Chicago, Illinois, April 25, 1997, 1–4* (Chicago: Center for Research Libraries, 1997), 3.

85. Branin, "Cooperative Collection Development," 104.

86. Peter Collins, "Fear and Loathing in Cooperative Collection Development," *Interlending and Document Supply* 40, no. 2 (2012): 102.

87. Atkinson, "Crisis and Opportunity."

88. James Burgett, John Haar, and Linda L. Phillips, *Collaborative Collection Development: A Practical Guide for Your Library* (Chicago: American Library Association, 2004), 160.

89. Anthony W. Ferguson and Kathleen Kehoe, "Access vs. Ownership: What Is More Cost-Effective in the Sciences." *Journal of Library Administration* 19, no. 2 (1993): 89–99.

90. Jane P. Kleiner and Charles A. Hamaker, "Libraries 2000: Transforming Libraries Using Document Delivery, Needs Assessment, and Networked Resources," *College and Research Libraries* 58, no. 4 (July 1997): 355–74.

91. Bruce R. Kingma, "The Economics of Access versus Ownership: The Costs and Benefits of Access to Scholarly Articles via Interlibrary Loan and Journal Subscriptions," *Journal of Library Administration* 26, no. 1/2 (1998): 145–57.

92. Donald W. King et al., "Library Economic Metrics: Examples of the Comparison of Electronic and Print Journal Collections and Collection Services," *Library Trends* 51, no. 3 (2003): 377.

93. See, for example, Susan Imholz and Jennifer Weil Arns, *Worth Their Weight: An Assessment of the Evolving Field of Library Valuation* (New York: Americans for Libraries Council, 2007), www.actforlibraries.org/pdf/WorthTheirWeight.pdf; Svanhild Aabø, "Libraries and Return on Investment (ROI): A Meta-Analysis," *New Library World* 110, no. 7/8/ (2009): 311–24; Peter Edward Sidorko, "Demonstrating ROI in the Library: The Holy Grail Search Continues," *Library Management* 31, no. 8/9 (2010): 645–53.

94. Ian J. Bateman et al., *Economic Valuation with Stated Preference Techniques: A Manual* (Cheltenham, UK: Edward Elgar, 2002). See Christopher R. McIntosh, "Library

Return on Investment: Defending the Contingent Valuation Method for Public Benefits Estimation," *Library and Information Science Research* 35, no. 2 (Apr. 2013): 117–26, for a research project that uses a contingent value technique to estimate median annual household benefits for Minnesota public library services.

95. King et al., "Library Economic Metrics."

96. Peter Scholten, *SROI: A Guide to Social Return on Investment* (Amsterdam: Lenthe, 2006); Jeremy Nichols, Susan Mackenzie, and Ailbeth Somers, *Measuring Real Value: A DIY Guide to Social Return on Investment* (London: New Economics Foundation, 2007), www.scribd.com/doc/19678244/NEF-Measuring-Real-Value -Social-Return-on-Investment. See Joseph R. Matthews, "Assessing Organizational Effectiveness: The Role of Performance Measures," *Library Quarterly* 81, no. 1 (Jan. 2011): 83–110, for an in-depth review of performance measures, including SROI and the balanced scorecard.

97. Robert Kaplan and David Norton, "Using the Balanced Scorecard as a Strategic Management System," *Harvard Business Review* 74, no. 1 (1996): 75–85; Stephen Bosch, et al. "Measuring Success of Cooperative Collection Development: Report of the Center for Research Libraries/Greater Western Library Alliance Working Group for Quantitative Evaluation of Cooperative Collection Development Projects," *Collection Management* 28, no. 3 (2003): 223–39.

Suggested Readings

Ashmore, Beth, and Jill E. Grogg. "The Art of the Deal: Power and Pitfalls of Consortial Negotiation." *Searcher* 17, no. 3 (2009): 40–47.

Bailey, Jessica, and Mary C. Radnor. "Cooperative Remote Storage: Challenges for Resource Sharing." *Journal of Interlibrary Loan, Document Delivery and Electronic Reserve* 19, no. 3 (2009): 227–33.

Bailey-Hainer, Brenda. "The OCLC Network of Regional Service Providers: The Last 10 Years." *Journal of Library Administration* 49, no. 6 (2009): 621–29.

Beaubien, Anne K., et al. "White Paper: International Interlibrary Loan." *Research Libraries Issues*, no. 275 (June 2011): 7–14. http://publications.arl.org/1acgvq.pdf.

Bird, Gwen, and Gohar Ashoughian. "All Together Now: Planning for Shared Print Archiving in Canada's Western Universities." *Collection Management* 37, no. 3/4 (2012): 260–70.

Bruxvoort, Diane, John E. Burger, and Lynn Sorensen Sutton. "Like a Snowball Gathering Speed: Development of ASERL's Print Journal Retention Program." *Collection Management* 37, no. 3/4 (2012): 223–36.

Busby, Lorraine. "Our Friends Are Killing Us." *Serials Librarian* 61, no. 2 (2011): 160–67.

Butler, Brandon, et al. "White Paper: US Law and International Interlibrary Loan." *Research Libraries Issues*, no. 275 (June 2011): 15–18. http://publications.arl.org/1acgvq.pdf.

Button, Leslie Horner, and Rachel C. Lewellen. "Monograph Duplication Analysis to Inform Consortial Collection Development." In *Proceedings of the 2010 Library Assessment Conference, Building Effective, Sustainable, Practical Assessment, October 24–27, Baltimore, Maryland*, ed. Steve Hiller et al., 715–20 (Washington, DC: Association of Research Libraries, 2011.

Chadwell, Faye A. "Assessing the Value of Academic Library Consortia." *Journal of Library Administration* 51, no. 7/8 (2011): 645–61.

Clement, Susanne K. "From Collaborative Purchasing towards Collaborative Discarding: The Evolution of the Shared Print Repository." *Collection Management* 37, no. 3/4 (2012): 153–67.

Cook, Anita, and Dennis J. Smith, "The Ohio Library and Information Network: Resource Sharing at Its Best." *Journal of Interlibrary Loan, Document Delivery, and Electronic Reserve* 21, no. 5 (2011): 219–25.

Cryer, Emma, and Karen S. Grigg. "Consortia and Journal Package Renewal: Evolving Trends in the 'Big Package Deal'?" *Journal of Electronic Resources in Medical Libraries* 8, no. 1 (2011): 22–34.

Elguindi, Anne C., and Kari Schmidt. "Academic Library Consortia and the Evolving Role of Electronic Resources and Technology." In *Electronic Resource Management: Practical Perspectives in a New Technical Services Model*, 141–67. Oxford, UK: Chandos, 2012.

Gee, C. William, "Connecting K–12 School Media Centers to University Library Resources through Interlibrary Loan: A Case Study from Eastern North Carolina." *Journal of Interlibrary Loan, Document Delivery, and Electronic Reserve* 21, no. 3 (2011): 101–16.

Genoni, Paul. "An International Review of the Development and Implementation of Shared Print Storage." *Australian Academic and Research Libraries* 44, no. 1 (2013): 50–66.

Giesecke, Joan. "The Value of Partnerships: Building New Partnerships for Success." *Journal of Library Administration* 52, no. 1 (2012): 36–52.

Gillies, Scott, and Carol Stephenson. "Three Libraries, Three Weeding Projects: Collaborative Weeding Projects within a Shared Print Repository." *Collection Management* 37, no. 3/4 (2012): 205–22.

Godner, Matt, and Katie Birch. "Resource Sharing in a Cloud Computing Age." *Interlending and Document Supply* 40, no. 1 (2012): 4–11.

Gregory, David J., and Karen Lawson. "Small Scale: Using a Regional Pilot Project to Explore the Potential of Shared Print." *Collection Management* 37, no. 3/4 (2012): 188–204.

Guzzy, Judith E. "U.S. Academic Library Consortia: A Review." *Community and Junior College Libraries* 16, no. 3 (2010); 162–84.

Hales, Katharine Lareese. "Rebuilding Walls to Access and Service: The Impact of Electronic Resources on Resource Sharing." *Journal of Interlibrary Loan, Document Delivery, and Electronic Reserve* 22, no. 3/4 (2012): 123–36.

Kaufman, Paula. "Let's Get Cozy: Evolving Collaborations in the 21st Century." *Journal of Library Administration* 52, no. 1 (2012): 53–69.

Kinner, Laura, and Alice Crosetto. "Balancing Act for the Future: How the Academic Library Engages in Collection Development at the Local and Consortial Levels." *Journal of Library Administration* 49, no. 4 (2009): 419–37.

Knox, Emily. *Document Delivery and Interlibrary Loan on a Shoestring.* New York: Neal-Schuman, 2010.

Lamoureux, Selden Dourgom, and James Stemper. "White Paper: Trends in Licensing." *Research Libraries Issues* no. 275 (June 2011): 19–24. http://publications.arl.org/1acgvq.pdf.

Leon, Lars, and Nancy Kress. "Looking at Resource Sharing Costs." *Interlending and Document Supply* 40, no. 2 (2012): 81–87.

Maes, Margaret K., and Tracy L. Thompson-Przylucki. "Collaborative Stewardship: Building a Shared, Central Collection of Print Legal Materials." *Collection Management* 37, no. 3/4 (2012): 294–306.

Mak, Collette. "Resource Sharing among ARL Libraries in the US: 35 Years of Growth." *Interlending and Document Supply* 39, no. 1 (2011): 26–31.

Mallery, Mary, and Pamela Theus. "New Frontiers in Collaborative Collection Management." *Technical Services Quarterly* 29, no. 2 (2012): 101–12.

Maskell, Catherine A. "Consortia: Anti-Competitive or in the Public Good?" *Library Hi Tech* 26, no. 2 (2008): 164–83.

Maskell, Cathy, Jennifer Soutter, and Kristina Oldenburg. "Collaborative Print Repositories: A Case Study of Library Directors' Views." *Journal of Academic Librarianship* 36, no. 3 (May 2010): 242–49.

Massie, Dennis. "Interlending Trending: A Look Ahead from atop the Data Pile." *Interlending and Document Supply* 40, no. 2 (2012): 125–30.

———. *Tiers for Fears: Sensible, Streamlined Sharing of Special Collections.* Dublin, OH: OCLC Research, 2013. www.oclc.org/content/dam/research/publications/library/2013/2013-03.pdf.

Matthews, Joseph R. *Scorecards for Results: A Guide for Developing a Library Balanced Scorecard.* Westport, CT: Libraries Unlimited, 2008.

McGillivray, Sue, et al. "Key Factors for Consortial Success: Realizing a Shared Vision for Interlibrary Loan in a Consortium of Canadian Libraries." *Interlending and Document Supply* 37, no. 1 (2009): 11–19.

McMurdo, Thomas, and Birdie MacLennan. "The Vermont Digital Newspaper Project and the National Digital Newspaper Program: Cooperative Efforts in Long-Term Digital Newspaper Access and Preservation." *Library Resources and Technical Services* 57, no. 3 (2013): 148–63.

Neal, James G., et al. "Report of the Task Force on International Interlibrary Loan and Document Delivery Practices." *Research Libraries Issues*, no. 275 (June 2011): 1–6. http://publications.arl.org/1acgvq.pdf.

Pan, Denise, and Yem Fong. "Return on Investment for Collaborative Collection Development: A Cost-Benefit Evaluation of Consortia Purchasing." *Collaborative Librarianship* 2, no. 4 (2010): 183–92.

Posner, Beth. "The Ethics of Library Resource Sharing in the Digital Age." *Interlending and Document Supply* 40, no. 2 (2012): 119–24.

Radnor, Mary C., and Kristine Jo Shrauger. "Ebook Resource Sharing Models: Borrow, Buy, or Rent." *Journal of Interlibrary Loan, Document Delivery, and Electronic Reserve* 22, no. 3/4 (2012): 155–61.

Reilly, Bernard F., Jr. "Global Resources: How a Cooperative Collection Development Enterprise Keeps Pace with a Rapidly Changing World." *Journal of Library Administration* 52, no. 1 (2012): 70–77.

Roth, Karen L. "Shared Ownership: What's the Future?" *Medical Reference Services Quarterly* 32, no. 2 (2013): 203–208.

Russell, Carrie. "Threats to Digital Lending: Does the Durability of Ebooks Pose a Digital Danger to Libraries?" *American Libraries*, Jan./Feb. 2012 Ebooks Supplement. www.americanlibrariesmagazine.org/article/threats-digital-lending.

Sanville, Tom. "Do Economic Factors Really Matter in the Assessment and Retention of Electronic Resources Licensed at the Library Consortium Level?" *Collection Management* 33, no. 1/2 (2008): 1–16.

Steen, David. "Ebooks from Institutional to Consortial Considerations." *Online* 34, no. 3 (May/June 2010): 29–35.

Town, J. Stephen. "Value, Impact, and the Transcendent Library: Progress and Pressures in Performance Measurement and Evaluation." *Library Quarterly* 81, no. 1 (Jan. 2011): 111–25.

Wicht, Heather. "The Evolution of E-books and Interlibrary Loan in Academic Libraries." *Collaborative Librarianship* 3, no. 4 (2011): 205–11.

Wilt, Catherine C. "Regional Library Networks: United States." In *Encyclopedia of Library and Information Sciences*, 3rd ed., ed. Marcia J. Bates and Mary Niles Maack, 4492–97. New York: Taylor and Frances, 2010.

Wu, Michelle M. "Building a Collaborative Digital Collection: A Necessary Evolution in Libraries." *Law Library Journal* 103, no. 4 (2011): 527–51.

CHAPTER NINE

Scholarly Communication

Scholarly communication—the process of exchanging discoveries, ideas, and information—is being transformed through open access. Although these changes are critically important to academic and research librarians with collections responsibilities, they are important for collections librarians in all types of libraries. Libraries are in the knowledge business, with core functions to select and acquire resources, facilitate their discovery, support their access and dissemination, archive and preserve them, and support their community of users. Changes in the process of information dissemination have obvious effects in all these areas. The results of research and scholarship are increasingly perceived as both a public good and a common good that should be freely available and discoverable. The dissemination of these results and access to them should be of concern to all librarians because all library users, regardless of the type of library they use, are seeking, finding, and using information and resources located through the Internet.

One powerful example demonstrates the potential of opening information access to the community beyond research institutions and higher education. Jack Andraka was fourteen in 2011 when he decided he wanted to develop a new, simple, inexpensive way to detect pancreatic cancer, motivated by the death of a family friend. He began his research on the Internet and found numerous articles, but he could access only abstracts so he began paying for articles. Eventually, he was able to secure a position with a researcher at Johns Hopkins, where he had easy access to published research, and there he developed a revolutionary method to detect pancreatic, ovarian, and lung cancer. His independent research, ultimately assisted by a scholar and the ability to work in a laboratory, demonstrates the power of access to information. Andraka has written eloquently about "why science journal paywalls have to go."[1]

This chapter begins by exploring the scholarly communication system and its origins, changing nature, and role in the promotion and tenure system. Author copyright management is discussed. The open-access initiative and strategies and policies that support it are identified. The chapter concludes with issues for libraries and librarians, including changes in the library's role in the scholarly communication system.

Readers are strongly encouraged to view this chapter as a starting point for understanding a quickly changing landscape and then to monitor new events, initiatives, and publications on this topic.

What Is the Scholarly Communication System?

Scholarship is the craft of learning and teaching, activities encompassing research and creative expression.[2] *Scholarly communication* is the process of disseminating the results of these endeavors to the broader academic community formally in print and digital formats and informally through presentations, posters, blogs, online discussions, personal websites, and more. Scholarship is as much a process of communication as it is investigation and discovery. The *scholarly communication system* encompasses the interactions of participants who create, transform, distribute, collect, preserve, make available, and use the research of scholars and scientists for teaching, additional research, and other scholarly activities. *Scholarly publishing* is part of scholarly communication. Hahn defines scholarly publishing as "a subset of communication activities mediated through the use of a durable medium to fix knowledge."[3]

Through the Internet, scholarship has become a global activity conducted in real time. Computer technology can reduce barriers and result in increased access both to the scholarly literature and to the underlying research data and source materials. Courant writes that collaboration (across time and space) is the fundamental method of scholarship.[4] Through the Internet, researchers "have been able to expand the conversation at an earlier point in the research process and to explore the content of these exchanges to observers."[5] Scholarly communication via the Internet occurs through e-mail, blogs, online laboratory notebooks, electronic discussion groups, and websites as well as through e-journals, e-books, and digital repositories.

In the traditional scholarly communication system, publishing scholarly books and journals has provided an efficient way to disseminate scholarly findings, secure the final version of the work, and make it accessible to future generations. For scholars and researchers, publishing serves as a means of conferring qualitative evaluation and judgment on the scholar's or researcher's work through the practice of peer review and is an essential mechanism for establishing their reputation. Journal articles are the most common venue. As of November 2013, Ulrichsweb listed more than 35,103 peer-reviewed journals.[6] Formal publication in the journal literature and in scholarly monographs remains an essential component of promotion and tenure decisions in many academic disciplines.

Scholarly Publishing before the Internet

The traditional system of scholarly publishing can be viewed as a continuous cycle (figure 9-1). Universities and external funding agencies subsidize and pay the costs of research. Faculty members and researchers read earlier work, collect data, conduct research, and analyze their findings. They author journal articles and books that report their findings and analysis, and they transfer the intellectual property for their writings through copyright assignment to publishers. Faculty members, researchers, and recognized experts serve (seldom receiving financial compensation) on journal editorial boards and review papers submitted

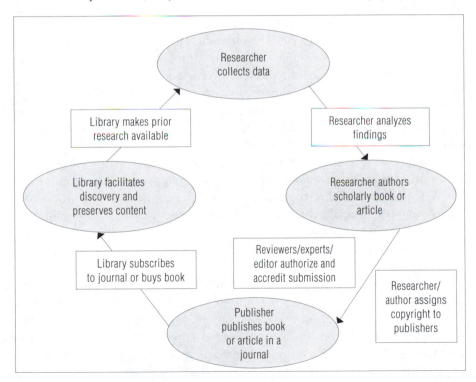

FIGURE 9-1 Traditional scholarly publishing cycle

for publication. Similar review boards at scholarly presses evaluate scholarly monographs for publication. Publishers usually handle copyediting and typography and are responsible for production and distribution of the printed work. Academic and research libraries buy the final publications to fulfill their role of organizing, disseminating, and archiving scholarly works. The cycle continues as researchers consult publications to advance new research.

Today's scholarly communication system has its roots in the 1600s, when European scholarly societies first were established. Their purpose was to provide a forum in which independent scholars could share and discuss their research. Scholarly publishing was born when these societies began to publish their findings in serial publications with names like *Comptes rendus*, *Transactions*, and *Abhandlungen*. These periodicals were issued by the society and their content was vetted by the society members or a small group selected to serve that role—the origins of peer review. In the United States, as in Europe, the original system of scholarly communication was in the realm of the wealthy; the creators and the consumers of scholarship were the same people, with virtually no middlemen involved.

This arrangement began to change in America with the Morrill Land-Grant Acts (1862 and 1890), which established funding for land grant universities and placed obligations on the faculties at these institutions to conduct research that would benefit society. A direct result was a tremendous increase in the publication of scholarly journals and monographs. After World War II, when college and university enrollments swelled and the U.S. government began to direct large amounts of money to higher education for research, the volume of scholarly publications grew exponentially. Unable to keep pace or absorb the expensive costs, many professional and scholarly societies turned to the for-profit sector to absorb the growth in publishing activities. Commercial publishers quickly saw the profit potential in controlling this unique content. Journal prices rose rapidly and commercial publishers began an ongoing program of consolidation. The result is a journal publishing system with a few large publishers of extensive journal lists and many professional and scholarly societies publishing single journals or small lists of titles.

Scholarly monographs have fared differently as the economics of scholarly publishing have changed. They have been published primarily by university presses and scholarly societies and associations with limited press runs (a few hundred to seldom more than two thousand copies). The market for scholarly monographs has suffered as academic and research libraries struggling to cope with increasing serials costs buy fewer books. Purchasing by academic and research libraries, the principal market for scholarly monographs, declined from as many as to 1,500 copies in the mid-1970s to around 250 by 2008.[7] Although universities and scholarly societies were once willing to subsidize the costs of publishing to advance scholarship, most now expect these presses to generate a profit or, at a minimum, sustain no losses. The result is that university, scholarly society, and scholarly association presses are more market sensitive, publishing fewer economically marginal books and charging more for those they do publish. Sales potential increasingly trumps scholarship in the decisions presses make about which books to publish. Many presses have been shut down by their universities. The result has been a significant decrease in opportunities for scholars to publish monographs.[8] Fisher compares the academic monograph to the Hapsburg monarchy because it seems to have been in decline forever.[9]

Rapidly escalating prices and libraries' financial difficulties in acquiring the materials needed to support their parent institution's research and teaching missions were seen initially as "the library's problem." Academic libraries started addressing increasing serials cost in the 1980s and began to talk about "the serials crisis." The serials crisis meant that libraries cancelled journal subscriptions and reduced monograph purchases. Over time, librarians realized that they alone could not bring about the changes needed in a publishing system driven largely by tenure considerations and profit-making concerns outside the control of libraries, and they began talking about the "crisis in scholarly communication." Librarians have sought to educate and involve faculty, college and university administrators, and government officials in understanding scholarly communication as a complex system with many stakeholders, each with responsibilities.

The Changing Nature of Scholarly Communication

The Internet and digital technology have had an equally powerful impact on scholarly publishing:

> Scholarly content is overwhelmingly born-digital, then digitally organized, digitally processed, digitally produced, and digitally disseminated (and in which print versions would play, at best, only a supplementary or niche role). Digital technology changed, in the course of only two decades, from a *sustaining innovation* within the scholarly publishing circuit to a *disruptive innovation* . . . ; from increasing productivity while supporting the traditional values and markets within the legacy print publishing system to an innovation that first suggested, then insisted on, a radically transformed system of scholarly publication, one

premised on digitally inspired and digitally mediated resources and perspectives introduced at every juncture of the system, as well as throughout all system flows and outputs.[10]

As the scholarly community began to understand the potential of the Internet and digital technology, its members began to consider a radical alternative to the traditional model of scholarly publishing—a new model without barriers, in other words, open access to the results of scholarship. One of the first events to give formal shape to the open-access movement was the Budapest Open Access Initiative (BOAI, www.soros.org/openaccess), born at an international conference convened by the Open Society Institute in December 2001. According to Suber, the BOAI "was the first [initiative] to offer a public definition of OA [open access], the first to use the term 'open access,' the first to call for OA journals and OA archives as complementary strategies, the first to call for OA in all disciplines and countries, and the first to be accompanied by significant funding."[11] The statement of principles defining the initiative was released on February 14, 2002, and begins:

> An old tradition and a new technology have converged to make possible an unprecedented public good. The old tradition is the willingness of scientists and scholars to publish the fruits of their research in scholarly journals without payment, for the sake of inquiry and knowledge. The new technology is the internet. The public good they make possible is the world-wide electronic distribution of the peer-reviewed journal literature and completely free and unrestricted access to it by all scientists, scholars, teachers, students, and other curious minds. Removing access barriers to this literature will accelerate research, enrich education, share the learning of the rich with the poor and the poor with the rich, make this literature as useful as it can be, and lay the foundation uniting humanity in a common intellectual conversation and quest for knowledge.[12]

Two further statements followed—the "Bethesda Statement on Open Access Publishing" (June 2003) and the "Berlin Declaration on Open Access to Knowledge in the Sciences and Humanities" (October 2003).[13] Both statements include the same definition of an open-access publication as one that meets the two following conditions:

> The author(s) and copyright holder(s) grant(s) to all users a free, irrevocable, worldwide, perpetual right of access to, and a license to copy, use, distribute, transmit and display the work publicly and to make and distribute derivative

works, in any digital medium for any responsible purpose, subject to proper attribution of authorship, as well as the right to make small numbers of printed copies for their personal use.

A complete version of the work and all supplemental materials, including a copy of the permission as stated above, in a suitable standard electronic format is deposited immediately upon initial publication in at least one online repository that is supported by an academic institution, scholarly society, government agency, or other well-established organization that seeks to enable open access, unrestricted distribution, interoperability, and long-term archiving.

Suber offers a more succinct definition—"Open access (OA) is digital, online, free of charge, and free of most copyright and licensing restrictions"—in his 2012 book *Open Access,* which (fittingly) became an open-access publication in 2013.[14]

To help scholars, librarians, and others in the scholarly publishing cycle identify scholarly journals' policies on various forms of open access, a color code has been developed. *Gold open-access* journals make their contents freely accessible online. Many gold open-access journals use a business model, sometimes called the dissemination-fee model, in which article processing fees (i.e., author-side fees) support journal publication. The fee may be paid by the author, the grant funding the research, or a third party. Fees may be waived in the case of financial hardship. A hybrid model, in which the publisher's main revenue stream continues to be based on subscriptions but authors may choose to pay a fee to have their article made openly accessible, is a way for toll-access publishers to experiment with open access, but it does not create a gold open-access journal.

Green open-access journals permit some form of author self-archiving, which may be postprint, preprint, or both. *Gray* is sometimes used to describe journals that allow no form of self-archiving. A work that is not open access and is available only for a price is called a *toll-access* publication. Suber introduced two additional terms to describe open-access publications: *gratis open access* and *libre open access.*[15] Gratis means "for zero price," and gratis open-access materials have no price barriers but do have permission barriers. *Libre* means "with little or no restriction," thus libre open-access materials remove both price barriers and unnecessary copyright and licensing restrictions.

The open-access model is sometimes seen as a simple solution to a simple problem—the need for researchers worldwide to have barrier-free access to information. However, both the problem and the solution are complicated by the importance of scholarly publication in the academy, the role publishers play in the scholarly publishing cycle, and ownership and management of copyright. A guide prepared by the Scholarly Publishing and Academic Resources Coalition and the Public Library of Science gives a sense of the complexity of issues from the author's perspective.[16] Authors are advised to consider several components—reader rights, reuse rights, copyrights, author posting rights, automatic posting, and machine readability—each of which can be more or less open or not open at all. For example, reader rights can range from free access to articles immediately upon publication (full open access) through free access after an embargo greater than six months (moderately open) to access only by subscription, membership, pay-per-view, or other fees (closed access).

Recognizing that a proactive approach to transforming scholarly publishing was needed, an international group of librarians, academic administrators, and representatives from professional associations met in Tempe, Arizona, in 2000 and agreed to a set of "Principles for Emerging Systems of Scholarly Publishing."[17] The Tempe Principles, as they came to be known, suggest three approaches: increased use of electronic capabilities, review of promotion and tenure practices, and responsible copyright management. These are not three separate strategies; rather, they are closely related. Increased use of electronic capabilities may seem an obvious approach to developing an efficient and effective communication system, but the relationships between tenure and promotion practices and author copyright management practices are less evident and complicate efforts to transform the system.

In 2012, the Budapest Open Access Initiative issued specific recommendations for advancing open access ten years after its original statement of principles.[18] These recommendations address policy issues, licensing and reuse, infrastructure and sustainability, and advocacy and coordination and conclude with these statements:

> OA benefits research and researchers, and the lack of OA impedes them.
>
> OA for publicly-funded research benefits taxpayers and increases the return on their investment in research. It has economic benefits as well as academic or scholarly benefits.
>
> OA amplifies the social value of research, and OA policies amplify the social value of funding agencies and research institutions.
>
> The costs of OA can be recovered without adding more money to the current system of scholarly communication.

OA is consistent with copyright law everywhere in the world, and gives both authors and readers more rights than they have under conventional publishing agreements.

OA is consistent with the highest standards of quality.

Though many endorse open access, not all agree. Osborne, for example, articulates many of the common criticisms:

Academic research is different in kind from industrial contract research, where the funder determines the activity and therefore is entitled to decide the use to which the results are put.

The inspiration for research-council projects comes from academics who therefore should retain the right to determine the form and location of the outputs.

There is no clear dividing line between projects funded by research councils and an academic's daily activities of thinking and teaching. If there are fees for access to teaching, there should be fees for access to research.

Under the current system, quality control is encouraged, and so is writing for a broader rather than a narrower readership.

Under gold open access there is a risk that the amount of work published increases and the quality decreases as publishers seek to maximize income from article processing charges.[19]

Even when open access is supported, controversy can surround selecting the most effective approach. One example, which ignited what Poynder called "a firestorm of protest," is *Accessibility, Sustainability, Excellence: How to Expand Access to Research Publications.*[20] Released in 2012, this report (commonly called the Finch Report) is the work of a committee appointed by U.K. Minister for Universities and Science David Willets and chaired by Janet Finch. Although the report recommends that the United Kingdom embrace the transition to open access and accelerate the process in a measured way that promotes innovation, the path to doing so created protest from many.[21] The Finch Report recommends relying on gold open access (the article processing fee model), in part because this avoids an embargo limiting access to self-archived articles. Further, the report recommends that institutional repositories (green open access) be limited to providing access to research data and gray literature and assisting with digital preservation. The U.K. government quickly accepted the report.[22]

One concern is that gold access will likely cost the U.K. research community an additional £50–60 million a year. A second more troubling consequence is that many researchers in developing countries and even those in more affluent countries with different funding models will be unable to pay article processing fees. Some subsequent reports in Britain recommended different approaches. The Research Councils UK (RCUK) updated its policy on open access, stating a preference for gold open access but reinstating green and gold open access as equal partners. In addition, RCUK announced its intention to award block grants to U.K. higher education institutions to meet the cost of article processing fees.[23] The European Commission also considers both the green and gold models as valid approaches to achieve open access.[24] In April 2013, the Canadian Association of Research Libraries (CARL) and the Canadian Research Knowledge Network (CRKN) endorsed a report and recommendations prepared by the Joint CARL-CRKN Open Access Working Group that include the need to investigate both gold and green open-access publication.[25]

Björk and colleagues take issue with the Finch Report's concern about embargoes, noting that "the top 100 publishers measured by output volume are surprisingly liberal and would in 62% of cases allow upload of accepted version manuscripts in institutional or subject repositories immediately upon publication, and a whole 79% within a year of publication." Swan and Houghton report that the cost of adopting green open access is much lower than the cost of gold open access—about one-tenth.[26]

Open access has been described as revolutionary, radical, and disruptive to traditional methods of scholarly communication, yet most agree that it is the future of scholarly communication. Uncertainty remains about how quickly change will happen, the best approaches to ensuring open access, and how various open-access models fit within or will change promotion and tenure practices: "An organized digital scholarly publishing system for monographs as well as for journal articles, different in kind from their print predecessors, is a certainty—although when and even where, much less how, they will coalesce is entirely and predictably obscure as yet."[27]

Scholarly Publication and Promotion and Tenure Practices

Scholarly publication in books and journals is a cornerstone of the current promotion and tenure system, yet this academic reward system in U.S. higher education is less than one hundred years old. In 1915, the American Association of University Professors (AAUP) formed and issued its "Declaration of Principles," which justified academic freedom and tenure. At that time, faculty members could be dismissed by trustees and presidents, who sought to control what faculty taught, said, and wrote. One key recommendation from the AAUP was that only committees of other faculty could judge a member of the faculty—a form of peer review. Colleges and universities were slow to adopt the AAUP's resolution, and the process for promotion and tenure varied from institution to institution until after World War II. After the war, the tremendous increase in students under the GI Bill resulted in faculty shortages. Only at this point did most higher education institutions begin offering formal tenure as a benefit and create an official process for promotion and tenure review.[28]

Scholarly publication quickly became a crucial component of the promotion and tenure process. A key element of scholarly publication is validating or certifying the research through a peer review process, intended to confirm that the publication is of high quality and scholarly merit. Scholars aspire to publish their research in the most prominent journals and with the most prominent presses, thereby signifying its merit as corroborated by equally prominent researchers in the discipline through the peer review process. Harley and colleagues call the peer review process "the coin of the realm," essential to ensuring quality.[29] Publication brings recognition to the authors and visibility to their institutions, and it supports future research.

"Publish or perish" is a phrase often used to describe the pressure on academics to advance their careers. Faculty members are usually evaluated in large part by their academic output, demonstrated in publications. Promotion and tenure decisions normally take into account the number of publications, the prestige of the journals in which a faculty member's papers are published, and (particularly in the humanities) the books a faculty member publishes and the prestige of the books' publishers. Research conducted by Harley and colleagues between 2007 and 2010 confirmed the importance of publication in the tenure process. They found that "the advice given to pre-tenure scholars was consistent across all fields: focus on publishing in the *right venues* [emphasis added] and avoid spending too much time on public engagement, committee work, writing op-ed pieces, developing websites, blogging, and other non-traditional forms of electronic dissemination (including online course activities)."[30]

At issue for scholars is determining the right venues for publication. A tension exists between the traditional system of scholarly publication, which provides what Friedlander calls "a collective trusted persistent record for multiple audiences," and the evolving new system, which is viewed with apprehension by some.[31] Harley and colleagues found that faculty members frequently perceive open-access models as having little or no means of rigorous quality control (e.g., peer review).

Faculty members have worried that publishing in open-access journals would not have the same credibility for measuring productivity or in promotion and tenure reviews that publishing in established, "brand name" (i.e., prestigious) journal titles does.[32] Most scholars can name the most prestigious journals in their fields, for example, *Cell* in the biological sciences, the *Journal of the American Medical Association* and the *New England Journal of Medicine* in general medicine, and *PMLA* (from the Modern Language Association of American) in literature in North America. Journals develop prestige over time, usually based on their impact factor, which measures the number of times an article is cited within a given time period divided by the number of articles published during that time period. Suber observes that "new journals can be excellent from birth, but even the best cannot be prestigious from birth," because they lack impact factors.[33]

To test the validity of the assumption that open-access journals are less highly cited, Björk and Solomon examined the impact of open-access journals and subscription journals in the sciences, controlling for journal age, country of publication, discipline, and business model.[34] They looked at two-year impact factors (average number of citations to the articles in a journal) and found that open-access journals indexed in Web of Science and Scopus had close to the same scientific impact and quality as subscription journals, particularly in the biomedical sciences and for journals funded by article processing fees. According to Björk and Solomon, open-access publishing is rapidly increasing its share of the overall volume of peer-reviewed journal publishing, and authors have no reason not to choose to publish in open journals just because of the open-access label, as long as they carefully check the quality standards of the journal they consider. Numerous studies report that scientific articles that are freely available on the Internet are cited more frequently than articles available only to subscribers.[35]

Additional research suggests that the attitude of scholarly authors toward open-access publication is changing. The Study of Open Access Publishing (SOAP) project surveyed 50,000 researchers in a variety of fields worldwide on their publishing practices.[36] Respondents tended to disagree with the statements "Open access undermines the system of peer review" and "Open access publishing leads to an increase in the publication of poor quality research." In total, 89 percent of more than 38,000 published researchers thought that journals publishing open-access articles were beneficial to their fields, yet 29 percent have not published open-access articles. Researchers perceived the availability of funding to pay publishing charges as the largest barrier to publishing in open-access journals. However, the second-largest barrier was the perception that high-quality open-access journals are lacking in particular fields—again, a concern about high impact.

Changing promotion and tenure processes, which Harley and colleagues describe as "inherently conservative," will require more than research into the impact factors of open-access journals.[37] The 2013 "San Francisco Declaration on Research Assessment" (DORA) is one effort to change and improve how research is evaluated by academic institutions, funding agencies, and others.[38] The declaration proposes that journal-based metrics should not be used as a surrogate measure of the quality of individual research articles; to assess an individual scientist's contributions; or in making hiring, promotion, or funding decisions. Signed by numerous organizations around the world and nearly 10,000 individuals (scholars, faculty, journal editors, heads of research institutions, directors of funding agencies, and more) within months of being issued, DORA may contribute to changing the promotion and tenure process.

Authors' Copyright Management

A major thrust of the movement to reform scholarly publishing focuses on authors' rights. In the traditional scholarly publishing system, authors routinely transfer all rights to the publishers. When authors retain some or all of their rights, they can keep control of how their work is distributed and used while maximizing their work's availability and impact by reducing access barriers. They can retain the legal rights to

- post their articles on their own websites
- deposit in institutional and disciplinary digital repositories
- distribute copies to students and use in classes
- distribute to colleagues for noncommercial purposes
- distribute copies at conference presentations and lectures
- use their work in future works (e.g., new books, revised editions, or studies building on the original work)

Copyright law defines the ownership of a work of intellectual property (published and unpublished) and the control that owners can exercise over access to and use of the work. Copyright owners can choose to keep their rights, give them over to another party, or share them as they see fit. U.S. copyright law defines copyright as a group of rights that can be individually granted or withheld.[39]

Copyright owner rights are the exclusive rights to reproduce the copyrighted work; prepare derivative works based on the copyrighted work; distribute copies to the public by sale or other transfer of ownership, or by rental, lease, or lending; perform or display the copyrighted work publicly (in the case of literary, musical, dramatic, and choreographic works, pantomimes, motion pictures, and other audiovisual works); and perform the work publicly by means of digital audio transmission (in the case of sound recording).

Authors can retain all or some rights; for example, an author can transfer to the publisher the single right of first publication. Publishers usually use a legal document (often called a copyright transfer agreement or publication agreement) to specify the rights the author transfers to the publisher and any rights the author retains. For decades, authors routinely assigned all copyrights to publishers, often not realizing what they were signing away. The 2003 RoMEO copyright transfer survey found that, even though 90 percent of responding authors assigned their copyright, 61 percent thought they still had ownership.[40] For example, many faculty authors assume they have the right to distribute copies of their articles to students in their classes or to post them on their websites when they have no legal standing to do so.

Authors seeking to manage their rights have several options. They can opt to publish only with publishers that have open copyright policies. An assertive author may find that some publishers offer multiple agreements; some are more restrictive (i.e., transferring all rights exclusively to the publishers) and some permit the author to assign specific rights to the publisher while retaining others. If the publisher has a single agreement that assigns, conveys, grants, or transfers all rights, copyright interest, copyright ownership, and title exclusively to the publisher, the author can seek to change the publisher's agreement by preparing an addendum to the publisher's standard agreement. Because the addendum is a proposed modification, the publisher can accept or reject it; many publishers are willing to negotiate publication terms when asked.

Various model addenda, prepared by lawyers, are available. One example is the Scholarly Publishing and Academic Resources Coalition author addendum.[41] This addendum assists the author in securing rights to reproduce, distribute, publicly perform, and publicly display the article for noncommercial purposes; prepare derivative works; make and distribute copies in the course of teaching and research; and post the article on personal and institutional websites and other open-access digital repositories.

Another source for model licenses is Creative Commons (http://creativecommons.org), a nonprofit organization that provides free tools to help authors, scientists, artists, and educators control their creative works. Creative Commons provides a set of copyright licenses that provides a simple, standardized way for authors to grant permission for others to share and use their works under the conditions they choose. These licenses do not replace copyright but work alongside it to enable authors to modify copyright terms to suit their needs. For example, creators can retain their copyright while licensing works as free for certain uses in certain conditions and prohibit commercial exploitation without the author's permission.

The GNU Free Documentation License (GFDL) also can be applied to e-books. It was originally created to make software and related documents freely available for copying and redistribution, with or without modification, as long as the author and publisher got credit for their work. The preamble explains, "This license is a kind of 'copyleft,' which means that derivative works of the document must themselves be free in the same sense."[42]

Open Access: Putting the Pieces Together

Open access to scholarly publications involves leveraging technology and author rights management to enhance the benefits of new knowledge and to reward scholars. Open-access literature is digital, online, free of charge, and free of copyright and licensing restrictions on access and use, and it ensures appropriate credit to authors and publishers for their efforts. Harnad and Brody concisely describe the benefits of open access: "OA dramatically increases the number of potential users of any given article by adding those users who would otherwise have been unable to access it because their institution could not afford the access-tolls of the journal in which it appeared; therefore, it stands to reason that OA can only increase both usage and impact." Willinsky and Alperin suggest that providing open access to research and scholarship is also a matter of academic ethics, which "have to do with recognizing people's right to know what is known, as well as the value to humanity of having . . . knowledge as widely shared as possible."[43]

Supporters of open access have based their case on the conviction that open access to scholarly communication is both a common good and a public good as well as an ethical responsibility. Some have looked at the economic benefits of open access. Houghton and colleagues conducted research that compared the costs and benefits of traditional (toll access) subscription publishing, open-access (gold) publishing, and self-archiving (green open access). Although the authors looked at implications for U.K. higher education, their findings have relevance beyond the United Kingdom. They modeled the impact of increased accessibility and efficiency resulting from more open access on returns to research and development over a twenty-year period and then compared costs and benefits. They concluded that the benefits of open-access publishing models will likely outweigh the costs:

> Preliminary analysis of the potential benefits of more open access to research findings suggests that returns to research can also be substantial, and that different scholarly publishing models can make a material difference to the returns realised, as well as the costs faced. . . . This suggests that there are gains to be realised from moving towards open access publishing models and, despite the lag between the costs and the realisation of benefits, the transition may be affordable within existing systemwide budgetary allocations.[44]

Open access does not mean forgoing peer review to obtain accessibility, nor does it mean the abandonment of copyright and its protections for authors. Despite many misconceptions, open access is entirely compatible with the peer review process. The same quality and control found in traditional scholarly publishing can apply. Peer review does not depend on the medium (print or digital) or on the means of access permitted.

Open access does not depend on putting online works into the public domain, although this does make them accessible. Works in the public domain have none of the rights that authors can retain through managing their copyrights. Among these are the rights to prevent plagiarism, prevent publication of corrupted versions of the work, protect the integrity of the work, and require appropriate citation of the source, thereby recognizing the creator or the work.

Open access should not be confused with open content. According to Wiley, open content is "content that is licensed in a manner that provides users with the right to make more kinds of uses than those normally permitted under the law—at no cost to the user."[45] Wiley goes on to identify the primary permissions or usage rights that apply to open content:

- reuse—the right to reuse the content in its unaltered/verbatim form (e.g., make a backup copy of the content)
- revise—the right to adapt, adjust, modify, or alter the content itself (e.g., translate the content into another language)
- remix—the right to combine the original or revised content with other content to create something new (e.g., incorporate the content into a mashup)

- redistribute—the right to share copies of the original content, your revisions, or your remixes with others (e.g., give a copy of the content to a friend)

The largest open-content project is Wikipedia (http://en.wikipedia.org), and even here there are copyright protections:

> The text of Wikipedia is copyrighted (automatically, under the Berne Convention) by Wikipedia editors and contributors and is formally licensed to the public under one or several liberal licenses. Most of Wikipedia's text and many of its images are co-licensed under the Creative Commons Attribution-Sharealike 3.0 Unported License (CC-BY-SA) and the GNU Free Documentation License (GFDL) (unversioned, with no invariant sections, front-cover texts, or back-cover texts). . . . The licenses Wikipedia uses grant free access to our content in the same sense that free software is licensed freely. Wikipedia content can be copied, modified, and redistributed *if and only if* the copied version is made available on the same terms to others and acknowledgment of the authors of the Wikipedia article used is included (a link back to the article is generally thought to satisfy the attribution requirement; see below for more details). Copied Wikipedia content will therefore remain free under appropriate license and can continue to be used by anyone subject to certain restrictions, most of which aim to ensure that freedom. This principle is known as copyleft in contrast to typical copyright licenses.[46]

Scholarly Publishing and Open-Access Strategies

The scholarly publishing cycle continues to evolve, and the options for facilitating open access have added variables to the process. Figure 9-2 builds on the cycle shown in figure 9-1 and adds the options of gold and green open access. This diagram makes clear that authors face a multitude of decision points as they consider how to make the results of their work available.

OPEN-ACCESS JOURNALS

Open-access journals are available online to the reader without financial or other barriers other than the ability to access the Internet. Regardless of whether the author or the publisher holds copyright, the copyright holder consents to open access for the published work. Different approaches to funding open-access journals are used—some are subsidized and some require payment on behalf of the author, paid by either the author or another party. Some publishers use a membership model in which authors' fees are removed or discounted if the

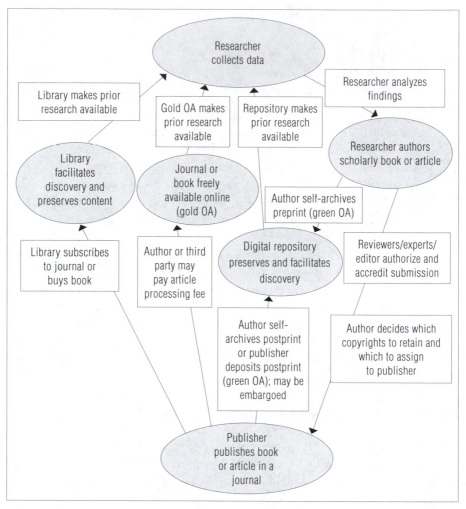

FIGURE 9-2 Evolving scholarly publishing cycle

author is associated with an institution or society that is paying the publisher a "membership" fee. Article processing fees are not new. Many academic journals, especially in the science, technology, and medicine (STM) disciplines, levy page charges to subsidize publication and have done so since before the open-access movement.

Suber notes that a minority of open-access journals charge article processing fees.[47] Citing several studies, he reports that 70 percent of open-access journals charge no upfront or article processing fees, and of the minority of those journals that do charge a fee, only 12 percent of the authors pay the fees themselves. The fees are waived or paid by sponsors (the author's institution or employer, or from the author's research grant) nearly 90 percent of the time. Some open-access journals that charge fees may waive the fee in whole or part in cases of financial hardship. According to Suber,

> Some no-fee OA journals have direct or indirect subsidies from institutions like universities, laboratories, research centers, libraries, hospitals, museums, learned societies, foundations, or government agencies. Some have revenue from a separate line of non-OA publications. Some have revenue from advertising, auxiliary services, membership dues, endowments, reprints, or a print or premium edition. Some rely, more than other journals, on volunteerism. Some undoubtedly use a combination of these means.[48]

Solomon and Björk examined article processing fees by surveying 429 authors who published in open-access journals.[49] In 2010, they found that leading scientific open-access journals using article processing fees tended to charge $2,000–$3,000 for publishing, but the average was $900 across all journals listed in the Directory of Open Access Journals. Björk and Solomon determined that the level of article processing fees charged is strongly related to the objective (impact factor) or perceived quality of the journal and that journals in disciplines where grant funding is plentiful charge higher article processing fees.

Suber suggests that gold open-access journals can cost less to produce than toll-access journals because publishers do not need to manage subscriptions or digital rights, can eliminate legal fees for licensing, and can reduce or eliminate marketing.[50] Production costs remain similar. Publishers must add the cost of collecting article processing fees and institutional subsidies. These fees and subsidies in turn support the gold open-access business model.

Several examples demonstrate the success of open-access journals. BioMed Central (www.biomedcentral.com) is a for-profit STM publisher that charges article processing fees to sustain its business model. BioMed Central offers more than 250 open-access, peer-reviewed research journals. Its article processing charges range from $660 to $2,330, with $1,985 being the average. Some discounts are available, including discounts if the author is involved in certain study protocols for trials or is affiliated with a BioMed Central supporting member institution, and waivers may be granted in cases of lack of funds.

SAGE Open (http://sgo.sagepub.com), a peer-reviewed gold open-access journal from SAGE Publications, is another example of the article processing fee model. *SAGE Open* publishes peer-reviewed, original research and review articles in the social and behavioral sciences and humanities and charges a flat

$99 article processing fee. SAGE announced three additional open-access journals in 2012—*SAGE Open Medicine, SAGE Open Medical Case Reports,* and *SAGE Open Engineering,* also using article processing fees, but with varying charges.

An example of a nonprofit publisher with article processing fees is Public Library of Science (PLOS) (www.plos.org), which was publishing seven peer-reviewed open-access journals as of November 2013. PLOS charges article processing fees ranging from $1,350 to $2,900 but charges no fee or a discounted fee if an author is in certain countries, and it waives or further reduces payment on a case-by-case basis. PLOS also generates revenue through individual and institutional members; authors affiliated with an institutional member are eligible for a fee discount. PLOS uses the Creative Commons Attribution License for all works it publishes and also deposits all articles in PubMed Central.

The Directory of Open Access Journals (DOAJ, www.doaj.org) listed 9,804 gold journals containing 1,573,847 articles in January 2014. Morrison reported in April 2013 that DOAJ was adding titles at the average rate of more than three per day.[51] DOAJ covers all open-access scientific and scholarly journals that use a quality control system, usually the traditional peer-review system, to guarantee the content's quality. In addition, it provides information on publisher fees. For example, in January 2014, 6,547 DOAJ journals charged no fees, 2,583 had article processing charges, 523 had conditional article processing charges, and 148 journals did not provide this information.[52]

Research in 2012 found that faculty members and researchers are consulting open-access journals more heavily than previously. Housewright, Schonfeld, and Wulfson surveyed 5,216 U.S. faculty members and learned that more than four-fifths of respondents often or occasionally looked for free online versions of materials not directly available through their local libraries.[53] Nevertheless, faculty continue to have concerns about the quality of open-access materials. Xia examined twenty years of research into scholars' attitudes about open-access journals. Although he found a steady increase in the number of scholars participating in open-access journal publishing and an increasing awareness of this form of scholarly communication, he did not detect a change in scholars' concerns about the low reputations of open-access journals or in their perception that these journal lack a peer review process.[54]

Addressing faculty members' persistent concerns about the quality of open-access publications is a responsibility of librarians and other advocates of open access. Because the quality of scholarly journals is a function of the quality of their editors, editorial boards, and referees, all journals (print or online, priced or free) can have the same quality controls. Open-access scholarly journals can, therefore, have the same commitment to peer review and quality and the same methods for ensuring it as priced journals.

One valid concern is the growth in what Beall calls predatory publishers, who "publish counterfeit journals to exploit the open-access-model in which the author pays."[55] These inferior publishers frequently invite an author's paper and then charge a high article processing fee. Unfortunately, authors may sign away their copyrights before they understand the fee to be charged and then are unable to submit their papers elsewhere. Others have written about this troubling trend, but even experienced scholars may be deceived.[56] Librarians can alert scholars to these unscrupulous publishers and their practices. Beall monitors predatory publishers and reports about them on his blog, Scholarly Open Access (http://scholarlyoa.com).

OPEN-ACCESS MONOGRAPHS

Although thousands of journals are fully open access and many more allow green open access for individual articles, publication of open-access monographs is developing more slowly. The Directory of Open Access Books (DOAB, www .doabooks.org), which records academic, peer-reviewed books that are open access, listed 1,603 titles from fifty-four publishers in November 2013. Morrison reports that more than one title was added per day during the first quarter of 2013.[57]

The challenges to developing effective open-access strategies for monographs appear to be greater than for journals. Hellman observes that cost is a significant challenge, noting that publication fees for mostly text-only books are around $10,000, and significantly more for a book with figures, photos, and equations.[58] Some book authors may fear the loss of royalties. In reality, though, most scholarly monographs earn modest royalties, and making a book open access has the potential of increasing sales of the print version.

Success in developing open-access monograph publishing models has been inconsistent. The National Academies Press (www.nap.edu), created in 1994 by the U.S. National Academies to publish reports issued by the National Academy of Sciences, the National Academy of Engineering, the Institute of Medicine, and the National Research Council, is one of the most enduring initiatives. This press provides free page-by-page online access to all of its books. Many books can be downloaded in their entirety or by chapter. Because the National Academies Press depends on a revenue stream to offset the cost of offering free PDF files, it continues to charge for some books in PDF format, print, and bundles of PDF and print. According to Michael Jensen, director of publishing technologies for the National Academies Press, online access capabilities boost print book sales by capturing the attention of potential purchasers.[59]

Less successful was the Gutenberg-e Project (www.gutenberg-e.org), launched in 1999 with a grant from the Andrew W. Mellon Foundation to explore and promote the electronic publication of scholarly writing. Between 1999 and 2004, the American Historical Association awarded Gutenberg-e prizes to high-quality dissertations in history. A panel of scholars judged the dissertations and selected award recipients based on scholarly merit. Each prize consisted of a $20,000 fellowship to be used by the author to convert the dissertation into an electronic monograph to be published by Columbia University Press. The goal of this project was to legitimize electronic publishing and change attitudes of academics toward e-books. Initially available through subscription, in late 2007 the thirty-six Gutenberg-e titles became open access because the original financial model was not sustainable without a significant revenue stream or outside support.[60]

Several university presses and academic libraries are publishing open-access monographs. One prominent example is the Scholarly Publishing Office (www.publishing.umich.edu) of the University of Michigan Library, which aims to provide academic publishing services that foster a sustainable economic model and support institutional control of intellectual assets. In addition to hosting and publishing open-access journals, the Scholarly Publishing Office publishes monographs in both print and online formats. Many publishing partners are affiliated with universities, but others are not, such as the Open Humanities (http://openhumanitiespress.org). The Scholarly Publishing Office is subsidizing the Open Humanities book production and distribution costs and providing its services without charge.[61] The goal of Open Humanities is to generate sufficient print-on-demand sales to cover production costs, pay author royalties, and subsidize the costs of its other titles.

Commercial publishers also are publishing open-access books. One example is SpringerOpen (www.springeropen.com/books), which publishes books under the Creative Commons Non-Commercial (CC BY-NC) license. An online book also can be purchased as a print book. SpringerOpen charges a publication fee (called an "open access fee"), which varies by the number of pages per book. Authors associated with institutional SpringerOpen members receive a 15 percent discount on the fee. Springer states that "SpringerOpen books are subject to the same high level peer-review, production and publishing processes followed by traditional Springer books."

SELF-ARCHIVING AND DIGITAL REPOSITORIES

Self-archiving is the deposit of articles, sometimes called e-prints, by authors (or directly by publishers as part of the agreement with an author) in free, open digital repositories, usually either discipline-based or institution-based, and was first formally proposed by Harnad in 1995. The history of self-archiving, however, dates to the 1980s when computer scientists were posting their papers on anonymous-FTP sites.[62] A *digital repository* is a library or archive where digital content is stored and made accessible to a user community. The development of digital repositories became possible with the decline in online storage costs, development and adoption of standard metadata harvesting protocols, and the maturity of digital preservation. To deposit articles (green open access), authors must retain the right to self-archive in their copyright agreements with publishers. Deposit can be in the form of a peer-reviewed postprint following publication in a journal or a non-peer-reviewed preprint.

Self-archiving in digital repositories does not simply provide for open access and permanent preservation. When these archives conform to the "Open Archives Initiative Protocol for Metadata Harvesting" (OAI-PMH, the interoperability standards created by the Open Archives Initiative), search engines can treat the separate archives as one and harvest data across a wide range of digital resources.[63] Searchers then do not need to know which archives exist or where they are located in order to find and use their contents.

OAIster (http://oaister.worldcat.org) is a catalog of digital resources that harvests data using OAI-PMH and is not limited to a single discipline or subject area. OAIster began at the University of Michigan in 2002 and is now managed by OCLC; thus OAIster records appear in WorldCat.org. In November 2013, OAIster included more than thirty million records from more than 1,500 contributors.[64] Resources include digitized books and articles, born-digital texts, audio and video files, photographic images, theses and research papers, and data sets (e.g., downloadable statistical information). Although OAIster serves to collocate resources through a single interface, much like a traditional library catalog, it has the same problems that library catalogs have: the information seeker needs to know to look in them. They are not necessarily in the flow where researchers do their work.

SHERPA RoMEO (www.sherpa.ac.uk/romeo) is a searchable database of publishers' policies regarding self-archiving of journal articles and certain conference series on the Web and in open-access repositories. It uses a four-color code to categorize publishers that differs slightly from the gold and green categories used for journals. RoMEO classifies publishers as green (authors can archive preprint and postprint or the publisher's version as a PDF), blue (authors can archive postprint, i.e., final draft postrefereeing or the publisher's version as a PDF), yellow (authors can archive preprint, i.e., prerefereeing), and white (archiving not formally supported). In November 2013, RoMEO listed copyright and self-archiving policies for 1,354 publishers, representing several thousand journals. Of them, 412 were green (30 percent), 443 blue, 103 yellow, and 3,967 white. In sum, 71 percent of the publishers in RoMEO allow some form of self-archiving.[65]

Nicholas and colleagues surveyed nearly 1,700 scientific researchers, mostly in the physical sciences, about their use and perspective on digital repositories.[66] Findings indicate high deposit rates with voluntary deposit as the main reason followed by mandates. Researchers perceived open access to their research materials as the greatest advantage offered by repositories. Younger researchers were more likely to deposit and to believe that repositories contribute to reform of scholarly communication and publishing.

In the early 2000s, several initiatives served as catalysts for digital repository development. The first OAI PMH-compliant software was designed for open-access archiving: EPrints, released by Southampton University in September 2000, and DSpace, released by MIT in November 2002. Also in 2002, the Consultative Committee for Space Data Systems released *Reference Model for an Open Archival information System (OAIS)*, on which the ISO-issued *Space Data Information Transfer—Open Archival Information System (OAIS)—Reference Model* (now in its second edition) is based.[67] These documents describe the requirements for an archive to provide permanent or indefinite long-term preservation of digital information and establish a common framework of terms and concepts that inform an open archival information system. EPrints and DSpace are used by more than half of the digital repositories in the Registry of Open Access Repositories (ROAR, http://roar.eprints.org). ROAR lists and categorizes open-access repositories of all types worldwide and reported 3,565 repositories in November 2013. Of these, 564 were in the United States and eighty-six in Canada.

Disciplinary repositories are subject based. Examples are PubMed Central (www.ncbi.nlm.nih.gov/pmc), which contains biomedical and life sciences journal literature, and arXiv (http://arxiv.org), which contains e-prints in the fields of physics, mathematics, computer science, nonlinear science, quantitative biology, quantitative finance, and statistics. High-energy physicists have been self-archiving in arXiv since 1991. Developed by Paul Ginsparg and now hosted at Cornell University, arXiv started as an archive for preprints in physics and later expanded to include additional disciplines. PubMed Central, developed and managed by the National Library of Medicine, was launched in 2000. Another early example is AgEcon Search (http://ageconsearch.umn.edu), developed and maintained by the University of Minnesota Libraries and Department of Applied Economics since 2001. The majority of items in AgEcon Search are working papers, conference papers, and journal articles in agricultural and applied economics. Full issues of more than fifty journals, some going back to volume 1, are also part of the archive.

An *institutional repository* is "a permanent, institution-wide repository of diverse, locally produced digital works (e.g., article preprints and postprints, data sets, electronic theses and dissertations, learning objects, and technical reports) that is available for public user and supports metadata harvesting."[68] Institutional repositories may offer several services: document ingest, storage, management, access, and preservation; descriptive metadata; system management; and user support. Some provide consultation, digitization of print materials, file conversion, and metadata services, and they may or may not charge fees for these functions. Many higher education repositories are maintained by the institution's library or by the library in partnership with an administrative unit, such as an office of research.

The earliest open-access institution-based repository that Suber has been able to identify is the IUBio-Archive (http://iubio.bio.indiana.edu), launched in 1989 at the Indiana University biology department and still serving as an open archive of biology data, open software, biology news, and documents.[69] Although not an institutional repository in the comprehensive sense, it is an institution-based repository focusing on a discipline. The IUBio-Archive "About" page states, rather charmingly, that "access to the archive is via HTTP (world wide web), Internet Gopher, anonymous FTP (file transfer), and e-mail programs that connect to computers on the Internet."

The early 2000s were a period of heightened interest in institutional repositories. The Scholarly Publishing and Academic Resources Coalition (SPARC, www.arl.org/sparc), an early proponent of institutional repositories, released the *SPARC Institutional Repository Checklist & Resources Guide* in 2002 to assist in their development and management. Also in 2002, Crow published "The Case for Institutional Repositories," which offered four characteristics of an institutional repository: it should be institutionally defined, contain scholarly content, be cumulative and perpetual, and support interoperability and open access.[70] A year later, Lynch suggested the comprehensive mission of an academic institutional repository, writing that

> a mature and fully realized institutional repository will contain the intellectual works of faculty and students—both research and teaching materials—also documentation of the activities of the institution itself in the form of records of events and performances and of the ongoing intellectual life of the institution. It will also house experimental and observational data captured by members of the institution that support their scholarly activities.[71]

Most definitions of institutional repositories, including Crow's above, state that an institutional repository provides open access to its content. Findings reported in *The Survey of Institutional Digital Repositories, 2012–13 Edition*, show that some repositories do not meet this criterion.[72] The survey reported that 18.37 percent of the responding repositories restricted access to the repository's institution or a limited group of institutions; restriction was more common in repositories not affiliated with higher education institutions. Obviously, digital repositories that limit access do not facilitate the open-access movement.

The Confederation of Open Access Repositories (COAR, www.coar-reposi tories.org), representing more than one hundred institutions worldwide, is seeking to foster a global network of open-access digital repositories and develop a community of practice. It is working to address barriers to populating repositories, increase interoperability among repositories, and support regional and national repository initiatives and the role of repository managers. Among U.S. members of COAR are the Coalition for Networked Information (www.cni .org) and OCLC, and members in Canada include the Canadian Association of Research Libraries.

In 2013, the Association of American Universities, the Association of Public and Land-Grant Universities, and ARL proposed Shared Access Research Ecosystem (SHARE), a plan to develop federated or cross-institutional digital repositories of public access research publications.[73] Under SHARE, each U.S. university or research institution receiving federal research funding would designate a digital repository as the site where its articles will be deposited, thus meeting the requirements of the February 2013 Obama administration directive to make the results of federally funded research openly available. Those institutions without repositories would have the opportunity to designate an existing institutional repository where its articles could be deposited for public access and long-term preservation.

Institutional repositories may be associated with a college, university, or research facility, or a department within one of these; federal or state agencies; historical societies; museums; library consortia; or other nonprofit organizations.

The NELLCO Legal Scholarship Repository (http://lsr.nellco.org), maintained by the New England Law Library Consortium, is an example of a consortium digital repository. It contains scholarly materials produced by faculty members, and in limited cases students, at consortium member law schools. OCLC Research Publications (www.oclc.org/research/publications) is an institutional repository that provides access to the publication output of OCLC, although some items are not openly available. The Smithsonian Digital Repository (http://si-pddr .si.edu/dspace) is the Smithsonian Institution's institutional repository and provides access to the institution's research output. Digital Commonwealth (http:// digitalcommonwealth.org) is a digital repository for cultural heritage materials (manuscripts, images, historical documents, sound recordings, etc.) held by Massachusetts public and academic libraries, museums, historical societies, and archives that are members of the Digital Commonwealth.

Digital repositories associated with public libraries are less common than those associated with other types of institutions. Most serve as repositories of digitized historical and cultural materials. For example, the Broward County Library, Fort Lauderdale, Florida, hosts "Education by Design" (http://digilab .browardlibrary.org/wpa), an online exhibit and digitized images of educational visual aids produced by the Works Progress Administration. The Detroit Public Library E. Azalia Hackley Collection (www.thehackley.org) houses more than six hundred pieces of digitized sheet music. Boss suggests that public libraries might serve a larger role, perhaps as a repository for the digital output of their parent government entity.[74] The critical first step for a public library is a needs assessment and analysis of the benefits to be obtained and the implementation and maintenance costs, especially to serve the preservation goals of a digital repository. The challenge for most public libraries is funding. Boss concludes that the most likely sources of funds are grants, leaving sustainability as a significant issue.

The most frequent content types in institutional repositories are journal articles, theses and dissertations, unpublished reports and working papers, and conference and workshop papers. Some contain multimedia and audiovisual materials, learning objects, datasets, and software.[75]

The deposit of electronic theses and dissertations can be controversial, although they are found in more than 1,200 higher education institutional repositories worldwide.[76] Many repositories permit a time-limited embargo, in part to protect research that may be patentable. In addition, some doctoral students are concerned about their ability to repurpose their dissertations as books. Howard interviewed individuals at several university presses and found varying practices: some editors are reluctant to consider publishing these works, others see doing so as a marketing boost. Ramirez and colleagues surveyed university press directors and journals editors to determine if providing open access to dissertations and theses reduces publishing opportunities in the social sciences and humanities. They found that 72 percent of university press directors and journal editors always welcomed or considered on a case-by-case basis the submission of works based on theses and dissertations that are openly accessible online.[77] Smaller presses seemed somewhat less likely to publish these materials, probably because of concerns about revenue. Nevertheless, in July 2013 the American Historical Association issued a statement strongly encouraging graduate programs and university libraries to adopt a policy that allows the embargo of history doctoral dissertations in digital form for as long as six years, to permit young historians time to revise their dissertations and obtain a publishing contract from a press.[78] Response to the American Historical Association's statement was negative and rapid, with many questioning the assumption that open-access theses and dissertations limit the ability to secure book contracts.[79]

POLICIES SUPPORTING OPEN ACCESS

Open-access publishing and self-archiving can result from decisions individual scholars and researchers make about where to publish their works and how to make them accessible. An effective strategy to advance open access and self-archiving has been the development of open-access policies. As Blixrud observes, "One important component for a robust and open scholarly communication system is the existence of public policies that promote the development of a barrier-free system."[80]

A historic step toward large-scale self-archiving in the United States occurred when Public Law 110-161 (consolidated Appropriations Act, 2008) was signed by President George W. Bush on December 26, 2007. The law states:

> The Director of the National Institutes of Health ("NIH") shall require that all investigators funded by the NIH submit or have submitted for them to the National Library of Medicine's PubMed Central an electronic version of their final, peer-reviewed manuscripts upon acceptance for publication, to be made publicly available no later than 12 months after the official date of publication: Provided, That the NIH shall implement the public access policy in a manner consistent with copyright law.[81]

With this law, which was made permanent in the Omnibus Appropriations Act of 2009, the NIH voluntary public access policy became mandatory.[82] Prior to its passage, fewer than 5 percent of researchers complied with the voluntary policy. Under the new policy, NIH grant recipients and their institutions (as the grantees) must ensure that any agreements made with publishers grant them the right to make their work publicly accessible via PubMed Central—the NIH publicly accessible, digital repository of full-text, peer-reviewed journal articles. Compliance is a statutory requirement. Anyone submitting an application, proposal, or progress report to NIH must include the PubMed Central or NIH manuscript submission reference number when citing articles that arise from their NIH-funded research. The policy permits an embargo of up to twelve months following publication. According to English and Joseph, the NIH public access mandate was "the largest such policy—both in terms of the size of the research budget it covers and the number of articles that result from funded projects—to be implemented by any government agency in the world."[83]

Numerous journals automatically deposit articles in PubMed Central on behalf of their authors. In addition, some publishers that do not participate in PubMed Central submit manuscripts for authors if the author completes a release form with the publisher. When contracting to publish with other journals, the author must retain the rights necessary to comply with the law when signing a publisher's agreement, either through the use of an addendum or by negotiating a revised agreement.[84]

Although NIH was the first funding agency with a deposit mandate based on U.S. law, it was not the first to require open-access archiving. For example, the United Kingdom's Wellcome Trust, which funds biomedical research, began requiring open-access archiving in 1995. SHERPA Juliet (www.sherpa. ac.uk/juliet) lists a summary of policies given by more than 120 research funders worldwide as part of their grant awards and covers open-access archiving, open-access publishing, and data archiving. ROARMAP: Registry of Open Access Repositories Mandatory Archiving Policies (http://roarmap.eprints.org) collects information about institution, funder, and thesis mandates worldwide.

A second historic development in the United States, also in 2008, was the unanimous approval of a motion by the Harvard University Faculty of Arts and Sciences mandating that Harvard faculty and researchers in the Faculty of Arts and Sciences deposit their scholarly articles in an open-access repository to be managed by the library and to be made freely available via the Internet. Faculty members can opt out of compliance by obtaining a waiver from the dean or dean's designee. The motion states, "In legal terms, the permission granted by each Faculty member is a nonexclusive, irrevocable, paid-up, worldwide license to exercise any and all rights under copyright relation to each of his or her scholarly articles, in any medium and to authorize others to the same, provided that the articles are not sold for profit."[85]

Stuart M. Shieber, professor of computer science at Harvard who put forth the motion, cited the astronomical increase in serials costs that have forced libraries to cancel subscriptions and reduce access to scholars' works and stated that the motion was intended to "be a very powerful message to the academic community that we want and should have more control over how our work is used and disseminated."[86] This first motion at Harvard was followed by similar motions approved in Harvard's graduate and professional schools and by numerous other institutions that mandate open-access archiving.

Various U.S. initiatives have sought to pass legislation that would extend the NIH mandate, but these have stalled in Congress. In response, the Obama administration issued a memorandum to the heads of executive departments and agencies in February 2013 that "directs each Federal agency with over $100 million in annual conduct of research and development expenditures to develop a plan to support increased public access to the results of research funded by the Federal Government. This includes any results published in peer-reviewed scholarly publications that are based on research that directly arises from Federal funds."[87] The directive also applies to digital research data.

In Canada, the Canadian Institutes of Health Research (CIHR) strengthened its "Open Access Policy," formerly known as the Policy on Research Outputs, in 2013. All researchers receiving funds from CIHR are required to make their peer-reviewed publications accessible at no cost within twelve months of publication—at the latest.[88] The National Sciences and Engineering Research Council of Canada (NSERC) is developing a similar policy.

Numerous organizations are advocating open access. One of the oldest is SPARC, first proposed at an ARL meeting in 1997. Now an international alliance with partner organizations SPARC Japan (www.nii.ac.jp/sparc/en) and SPARC Europe (http://sparceurope.org), SPARC has nearly eight hundred academic and research library members. Its goal is to create a more open system of scholarly communication, and it focuses on open access to scholarly and scientific research articles, open digital data, and open educational resources.

In a 2011 statement of open access, IFLA affirmed that it will

> work with global organizations and fora such as UN, UNESCO, WHO, WIPO, WSIS and others in promoting and advocating open access to publicly funded research, educational resources and cultural heritage. In its contacts and cooperation with these organizations, IFLA will explicitly state that open access in its authoritative meaning is required for the progress of science, the

development of society and true citizenship. Open access will provide users with the access they desire and enable libraries to maximize their role, thus improving global health and human well-being.[89]

UNESCO released *Policy Guidelines for the Development and Promotion of Open Access* in 2012.[90] The overall objective of these guidelines is to promote open access in member states by facilitating understanding of all relevant open-access issues and to assist in developing open-access policies at the government, institutional, and funding agency level. Though not prescriptive, these guidelines endorse open access regardless of the approach taken.

The Alliance for Taxpayer Access (www.taxpayeraccess.org) is a U.S. coalition of patient groups, physicians, researchers, educational institutions, publishers, and health promotion organizations that support barrier-free access to taxpayer-funded research. The Alliance advocates U.S. government–wide public access policies that support the sharing of research.

The Right to Research Coalition (www.righttoresearch.org) is composed of local, national, and international student organizations that promote "an open scholarly publishing system based on the belief that no student should be denied access to the articles they need because their institution cannot afford the often high cost of access." The Coalition promotes campus and national policies that require research results be made freely available in a timely manner and educates the next generation of scholars and researchers about open access as the new norm.

Issues for Libraries and Roles for Collections Librarians

As the previous sections make clear, reforming scholarly publishing is extremely complex and far beyond what was once called "the library's problem." Nevertheless, librarians can have an important role in reshaping scholarly communication. Carpenter and colleagues observe that "the changing landscape of research open access, data mining, and managing information and intellectual property rights have added urgency to the need to define the library's role in scholarly communication."[91]

Education

Librarians have a responsibility to inform their communities about the changing nature of scholarly communication, especially scholarly publishing. Many academic libraries are already taking a leadership role. A study by Radom,

Feltner-Reichert, and Stringer-Stanback found that 95 percent of responding ARL member libraries identified their libraries as responsible for scholarly communication leadership on their campuses.[92]

Librarians can advise and educate authors about options for rights retention. A key component is helping authors understand what copyright is, the protections copyright provides, and the types of materials subject to copyright. Equally important is knowing the rights, such as the right to distribute copies of one's own works to students, that authors sign away under most standard publisher agreements. Librarians can explain rights transfer and retention language commonly used in publishing contracts and provide information about options for modifying rights transfer, such as addenda and Creative Commons licenses.

Librarians can explain what open access is and describe the green and gold open access options. They can educate their community about the role of peer review in open access and counter misperceptions about the authority and credibility of open-access publications by explaining that the process of peer review is not dependent on a particular method of publication. They can communicate the lack of scholarly risk associated with publishing in open-access journals and depositing works in digital repositories.

Through their outreach and liaison activities, academic librarians can help authors understand the benefits open access can bring, not just to the larger academic community but also to individual scholars. Foster and Gibbons observe that what faculty members care most about is their research—and how they find and organize their resources, work with coauthors, and do their writing.[93] Through open access and, specifically, by self-archiving, scholars can

- make their own work easily accessible
- preserve their own digital items (publications, research data, creative works)
- provide online links to their work
- maintain ownership of their own work and control the use that is made of it
- free themselves from maintaining their works on a personal computer or departmental server

Libraries can equip their librarians to consult with authors—faculty, researchers, and students—about scholarly communications issues. One option is to prepare talking points for librarians to guide their conversations. Others are to draft issues papers for discussion with academic community groups, offer workshops, and sponsor campus-wide educational events. ACRL maintains a

"Scholarly Communication Toolkit" (http://scholcomm.acrl.ala.org/node/21) to assist librarians in engaging faculty and students in conversations about scholarly communications. It includes templates, flyers, and other resources that can be customized to a specific campus and library. Taking part in Open Access Week (www.openaccessweek.org) offers another opportunity to further education and conversation. Open Access Week is a global event that began as a single day in 2007 and is now held the last full week in October. The goal is to provide an opportunity for the academic and research community to learn about the benefits of open access and inspire participation in making open access a normal part of scholarship and research.

Another important role for librarians is advising and educating their communities about open-access policies and government and funding agency mandates. Librarians can help faculty members, researchers, and administrators understand the impact of these directives on their work. Many libraries and librarians have taken leadership roles in advocating policy changes at the local, national, and international levels that support the use of technology to advance scholarly communication. SPARC offers resources for librarians on campuses discussing the adoption of an open-access policy (www.sparc.arl.org/advocacy/on-campus).

Many large academic libraries have copyright information centers or scholarly communication offices. Smaller libraries may have an individual librarian charged with educating authors about copyright, fair use in education and research, and the changing scholarly publishing environment. One of the better known centers is the Columbia Libraries Copyright Advisory Office (http://copyright.columbia.edu/copyright). Its mission is "to address, in a creative and constructive manner, the relationship between copyright law and the work of the university in order to best promote research, teaching, library services, and community involvement." Another example is the Duke University Libraries Office of Copyright and Scholarly Communication (http://library.duke.edu/about/depts/scholcomm), which offers a website, personal consultation, and workshops and presentations on copyright and scholarly communication issues.

Open-Access Funds

An *open-access fund* is "a pool of money set aside by an institution to support publication models that enable free, immediate, online distribution of, and access to, scholarly research."[94] In other words, funds are provided by the author's institution to assist the author in paying gold open-access journals article processing fees. Many open-access funds are managed by libraries and jointly funded by libraries and other campus offices, such as the office of the provost or the office of the vice president for research. Terms of support and eligibility differ across institutions. Some institutions cover only submission fees to fully open-access journals; others also may reimburse, in part or whole, submissions to traditional subscription-based journals that offer an open-access publishing option (hybrid model).

An example of eligibility is found in the following description of the Harvard Open-Access Publishing Equity Fund, which is available to Harvard researchers who do not have alternative funding:

> The venue of publication must be an established open-access journal, that is, a journal that does not charge readers or their institutions for unfettered access to the peer-reviewed articles that it publishes.
>
> Journals with a hybrid open-access model or delayed open-access model are not eligible. To be eligible, a journal must meet these additional requirements:
>
> * Be listed in the Directory of Open Access Journals (unless the journal is too new for DOAJ eligibility),
>
> * Be a member of the Open Access Scholarly Publishers Association or adhere to its Code of Conduct,
>
> * Have publicly available a standard article fee schedule,
>
> * Have a policy to substantially waive fees in case of economic hardship.[95]

Tananbaum offers a practical guide to campus-based open-access funds, aimed at helping librarians and administrators understand the goals of a fund, the policies that govern it, how it is administered, and how to evaluate its results.[96] SPARC maintains a website (www.sparc.arl.org/initiatives/funds) with information for institutions contemplating a fund and those that currently have one.

Institutional Repositories

Libraries are responsible for most institutional repositories, although they may be jointly funded and sponsored through partnerships with other campus units. Placing a repository within the library's purview is logical because of libraries' responsibilities for facilitating discovery and preserving content. Jain offers recommendations for making institutional repositories more successful and enduring:

* comprehensive promotion and publicity of the benefits of institutional repositories to faculty and other stakeholders

- clear policies on ownership, institutional repository contents, quality standards, copyright issues, etc.
- strict institutional policies mandating deposit of all staff research outputs and student dissertations and theses
- recognition that institutional repositories are ongoing projects
- clear vision, strategy, and tactics
- a full range of academic and research support services including e-mail e-print requests and closed access deposit
- sustainable support from senior management and academia
- adequate resources (financial, technological, personnel)
- incentives to encourage faculty to deposit in institutional repositories[97]

Reiger proposes additional attributes for successful and sustainable repositories:

- clearly defined mandate and governance structure
- deep integration into the scholarly community and scholarly processes
- systematic development of content policies
- technology platform stability and innovation
- reliance on business planning strategies
- implementation of user-based strategies and feedback cycles[98]

In addition, creating high-quality metadata is an important component of repository infrastructure. These descriptive elements are critical for enabling discovery by campus users and search engines, so the repository and the descriptive metadata should be OAI-PMH-compliant. Staff in institutional repositories may create metadata for deposited materials or provide simple templates for depositors to use, or use a combination of these approaches.

Much library literature has focused on how to encourage faculty to deposit their scholarly works in institutional depositories.[99] In the absence of an institutional policy, legal requirement, or government mandate, several barriers deter faculty deposit. Kim found that age, copyright concerns and fears of plagiarism, and concerns about additional time and effort were negatively associated with faculty self-archiving.[100] The most significant motivations for self-archiving were altruism (the idea of providing open-access benefits for users), disciplinary norms supporting self-archiving, and a perception that archiving would have no harmful impact on promotion and tenure. A study in New Zealand identified the three leading motivations for self-archiving as meeting requests from the repository, making research available to colleagues and students, and increasing exposure of the research.[101] Barriers were similar to those identified by Kim, plus concerns about the risk of reducing the value of the peer review process and negative impact on the peer review process (perceived by younger faculty).

Librarians can increase self-archiving in institutional repositories by several activities, include these:

- improving content recruitment mechanisms
- tasking liaisons to reach out to individual faculty who may be likely depositors
- offering to deposit electronic materials for authors
- sending e-mail announcements
- recruiting early adaptor faculty to deposit content
- holding awareness-raising meetings and workshops

One technical solution to facilitate and increase deposit is automated harvesting of appropriate works. Work in this area is under way at the University of California, which passed an open-access policy in July 2013 covering all ten UC campuses.[102] Currently authors can manually deposit works in eScholarship (http://escholarship.org), the UC institutional repository and scholarly publishing service. The eScholarship website reports that it is focusing on work that will support automated harvesting of eligible manuscripts for deposit.

Until an option for automated harvesting is available, librarians can help their campus community understand what materials are appropriate for deposit in the institutional repository through a clear repository mission statement and guidelines that are consistent with this mission. "University Digital Conservancy Content Guidelines" from the University Conservancy, the institutional repository at the University of Minnesota managed by the University Libraries, illustrates a combined purpose and guidelines statement:

> The University Digital Conservancy (UDC) is a program of the University of Minnesota Libraries that provides long-term open access to a wide range of University works in digital formats. It does so by gathering, describing, organizing, storing, and preserving that content.
>
> Works produced or sponsored by the University of Minnesota faculty, researchers, staff, and students are appropriate for deposit in the UDC. Works might include pre- and post-prints, working papers, technical reports, conference papers, and theses.

Works produced or sponsored by administrative and academic units may also be appropriate for deposit in the UDC; see Regents' policy on University Archives. Works might include digital departmental newsletters, administrative reports, compilations of University data, meeting agendas and minutes.

The following statements are meant to guide contributors in determining appropriate types of submissions for the UDC.

The UDC welcomes works in most digital formats. Digital preservation support will be provided at different levels for specific formats as specified in the UDC preservation policy.

- Contributors must have authorization to place the works they deposit in the UDC.

- The UDC must be granted permission to distribute and preserve all works placed in the UDC. The author/original copyright owner retains copyright on all works.

- Works should be free from access restrictions and appropriate for open access by all users of the UDC.[103]

Discoverability and Access

Librarians can facilitate discovery and access by ensuring that finding open-access publications is easy for users. Options include open-access journals and books in A-Z lists and online catalogs. Collins and Walters examined the extent to which U.S. liberal arts colleges provide access to open-access journals through their journal titles lists (Serials Solution, Ex Libris, etc.) and their online public access catalogs.[104] They found that 57 percent of the thirty college catalogs examined provided access to at least 90 percent of the titles in their sample of 166 journals, but 20 percent of the colleges provided access to fewer than 20 percent of the journals. Using A-Z lists and adding records to online catalogs can require collections librarians to select the materials that will be included, a daunting task as the number of open-access titles continues to increase. Some libraries merely provide links from the library home page to OAIster and Google Scholar to simplify finding open-access resources.

Preservation

The collections librarian has a critical role as steward of the collection and its preservation. The issue of digital preservation is intertwined with issues of access.

Librarians can work to ensure that their institutional repositories are committed to providing long-term access to the digital works they contain, and that the repositories adhere to digital preservation best practices. These practices should support data accessibility through the use of persistent identifiers, stability (bitstream integrity), and usability (through format migration, emulation, and normalization) in perpetuity. Many institutional repositories have explicit preservation policies spelling out the commitment to perpetual access, along with policies about withdrawal and when it might be permitted. Just as collections librarians seek secure and safe facilities for print collections, they should aim for secure e-content storage, backup, and recovery services.

Publication

Many libraries are taking a proactive approach to changing the landscape of scholarly communication by creating new publishing venues. Library-based publishing is often closely connected with institutional repository services and may be a collaborative arrangement with another campus group, such as a university press. Services may be offered directly to campus researchers and departments or more widely to other institutions and professional societies and associations. The suite of services may include workflow management, copyright consultation, platform hosting, metadata, and archiving. More comprehensive publishing services may offer consulting on business models, content preparation, layout work, copyediting, web design, and delivery using subscription or open-access models.[105] Publications may be journals, books, conference papers, and more. A 2010 survey of North American academic libraries of various sizes found that 54 percent of responding libraries had or were interested in library publishing services; the percentage increased to 78 percent when respondents were limited to ARL members.[106] Morrison and Owen found that 55 percent of responding academic libraries in Canada were providing journal hosting services and another 24 percent were considering the provision of services.[107] This level of activity may be due to support provided by the Synergies project (www.synergiescanada.org), a partnership of Canadian university libraries and journals designed to allow small Canadian social science and humanities journals to publish online.

Some libraries use open-source software developed by and available from the Public Knowledge Project (http://pkp.sfu.ca), which aims to improve the scholarly and public quality of research. It operates through a partnership of Simon Fraser University, the School of Education at Stanford University, the

University of British Columbia, the University of Pittsburgh, the Ontario Council of University Libraries, and the California Digital Library. All software can be downloaded and installed on a local server or hosted by the Public Knowledge Project. Open Journal Systems (OJS) is a journal management and publishing system. Open Monograph Press (OMP) is software that manages the editorial workflow required to see monographs, edited volumes, and scholarly editions through internal and external review, editing, cataloging, production, and publication. Open Conference Systems (OCS) can be used to create a conference website, call for and accept papers, post conference proceedings and papers, post data sets, and more. Not all content published using Public Knowledge Project software is immediately open access, although Edgard and Willinsky found that 83 percent of the journals using OJS were offering immediate open access in 2009.[108]

Other publishing platforms exist. BePress's Digital Commons (http://digital commons.bepress.com), for example, is a proprietary, hosted software for institutional repositories. It supports creating and editing scholarly journals and other publishing initiatives such as e-only press imprints, conference proceedings, and student research. Digital Commons and similar proprietary systems are often used by smaller institutions with limited local technical capacity.

To support libraries operating publishing services or considering doing so, SPARC provides a website, "Campus-Based Publishing Center" (www.sparc.arl .org/resources/publishing), with information and resources for libraries, presses, and other academic units launching and maintaining campus-based publishing partnerships.

Engage in Shaping Public Policy

The previous paragraphs have focused on the role and responsibilities of academic libraries and their librarians in reshaping scholarly communication on individual campuses. All librarians have an opportunity to contribute to the conversation about open access. They can advocate federal and state policies that support barrier-free access to publicly funded research. Contacting elected officials when key legislative measures are being considered is an obvious option. The benefits of open access extend to all citizens. School librarians, special librarians, and public librarians can explain the issues to their communities and work to avoid misperceptions. The story of Jack Andraka that opens this chapter is a powerful example of why journal paywalls "have to go."

McKinney State University is a publicly funded research institution with an emphasis on science and technology. It has 30,000 students, of whom 5,500 are enrolled in professional and graduate programs or engaged in postdoctoral research. The university employs 1,800 faculty; an additional 2,500 employees are professionals engaged in scientific research. McKinney State receives an average of $250,000,000 annually in contracts and grants. With the support of these funds, faculty and researchers conduct research and publish their findings. The university library has managed an institutional depository for ten years, and library liaisons work with faculty, researchers, and academic departments to encourage deposit. Liaisons advise authors on their copyrights on an individual basis but have realized that many have little or no understanding of these issues as they relate to educational, scholarly, and classroom use.

The university librarian presented this problem to the provost, the vice president for research, and the Office of General Counsel, who agreed to jointly fund a new, continuing position that will focus on copyright information. They have also provided one-time funding to create a copyright information and resources website. The university library has just hired Geoffrey, who has both MLS and JD degrees. Geoffrey has been charged with identifying and developing content for the website and (initially) three, four-hour workshops for faculty. Faculty who attend these workshops will receive credits toward meeting the campus requirement for continuing education in responsible conduct of research; faculty must meet an annual education requirement to be able to submit grant proposals through the Office of Research, which manages grants for the campus.

Activity

Develop an outline for the copyright information website, identifying five or six topics to be addressed. The outline should include the primary topics and four or more subtopics. Where appropriate, list external resources to which the topical pages will link. Select the topics for the three workshops and prepare brief syllabi. Each syllabus should list the goals or expected outcomes for the workshop, a summary of the topics to be covered, and a bibliography of at least ten supplemental resources.

Notes

1. Jack Andraka, "Why Science Journal Paywalls Have to Go," *PLOS Blogs* (blog), Feb. 18, 2013, http://blogs.plos.org/thestudentblog/2013/02/18/why-science -journal-paywalls-have-to-go; see also Andraka, "The Virtual Human Right: Jack Andraka at TEDxHousesofParliament," TEDxTalks, YouTube video, 9:28, posted Nov. 4, 2012, www.youtube.com/watch?v=r55a0FapF2M.

2. Paul N. Courant, "Scholarship and Academic Libraries (and Their Kin) in the World of Google," *First Monday* 11, no. 8 (Aug. 2006), http://firstmonday.org/ojs/ index.php/fm/article/view/1382.

3. Karla L. Hahn, "Talk about Talking about New Models of Scholarly Communi- cation," *Journal of Electronic Publishing* 11, no. 1 (Winter 2008), http://hdl.handle .net/2027/spo.3336451.0011.108.

4. Courant, "Scholarship and Academic Libraries."

5. Amy Friedlander, "The Triple Helix: Cyberinfrastructure, Scholarly Communi- cation, and Trust," *Journal of Electronic Publishing* 11, no. 1 (Winter 2008), http:// hdl.handle.net/2027/spo.3336451.0011.109.

6. "Ulrichsweb: Global Serials Directory" (the subscription-based, online version of Ulrich's *Periodicals Directory*). The search, conducted Nov. 22, 2013, was limited to "active" and "referred/peer-review" and applied the "Edition Type" filter to isolate "Primary" editions, which removed counts for multiple formats.

7. Albert N. Greco and Robert M. Wharton "Should University Presses Adopt an Open Access [Electronic Publishing] Business Model for All of Their Scholarly Books?" in *ELPUB2008: Open Scholarship: Authority, Community, and Sustainability in the Age of Web 2.0: Proceedings of the 12th International Conference on Electronic Publishing, Toronto, June 25–7, 2008,* ed. Leslie Chan and Susanna Mornati, 149–64 (Toronto: ELPUB, 2008), http://elpub.scix.net/data/works/att/149_elpub2008. content.pdf.

8. Modern Language Association, *Report of the MLA Task Force on Evaluating Scholarship for Tenure and Promotion* (New York: MLA, 2007), www.mla.org/ rportsummary_taskfor.

9. Richard Fisher, quoted in Colin Steele, "Scholarly Monograph Publishing in the 21st Century: The Future More Than Ever Should Be an Open Book?," *Journal of Electronic Publishing* 11, no. 2 (Spring 2008), http://quod.lib.umich.edu/j/ jep/3336451.0011.201/scholarly-monograph-publishing-in-the-21st-century ?rgn=main;view=fulltext;q1=steele.

10. Phil Pochoda, "The Big One: The Epistemic System Break in Scholarly Monograph Publishing," *New Media and Society* 15, no. 3 (2012): 367.

11. Peter Suber, "Happy Birthday BOAI!" *Open Access News: News from the Open Access Movement* (blog), Feb. 14, 2008, www.earlham.edu/~peters/fos/2008/02/happy -birthday-boai.html.

12. Budapest Open Access Initiative, "Budapest Open Access Initiative" (Feb. 14, 2002), www.soros.org/openaccess/read.shtml.

13. "Bethesda Statement on Open Access Publishing" (June 20, 2003), www.earlham .edu/~peters/fos/bethesda.htm; "Berlin Declaration on Open Access to Knowledge in the Sciences and Humanities" (Oct. 22, 2003), http://oa.mpg.de/files/2010/04/ berlin_declaration.pdf.

14. Peter Suber, *Open Access* (Boston: MIT Press, 2012), http://mitpress.mit.edu/sites/ default/files/titles/content/9780262517638_Open_Access_PDF_Version.pdf, 4.

15. Peter Suber, "Gratis and Libre Open Access," *SPARC Open Access Newsletter* no. 124 (Aug. 2008), http://legacy.earlham.edu/~peters/fos/newsletter/08-02-08.htm.

16. *How Open Is It? Open Access Spectrum* (Washington, DC: Scholarly Publishing and Academic Resources Coalition, and Public Library of Science, 2013), www.sparc .arl.org/sites/default/files/hoii_guide_rev4_web.pdf.

17. Association of Research Libraries, "Principles for Emerging Systems of Scholarly Publishing" (May 10, 2000), www.arl.org/storage/documents/publications/tempe -principles-10may10.pdf.

18. Budapest Open Access Initiative, "Ten Years on from the Budapest Open Access Initiative: Setting the Default to Open" (Sept. 12, 2012), www.budapestopen accessinitiative.org/boai-10-recommendations.

19. Robin Osborne, "Why Open Access Makes No Sense," in *Debating Open Access*, ed. Nigel Vincent and Chris Wickham, 96–105 (London: British Academy, 2013), 97, www.britac.ac.uk/templates/asset-relay.cfm?frmAssetFileID=12663; see also Adam Mossoff, "How Copyright Drives Innovation in Scholarly Publishing" (April 2, 2013), George Mason Law and Economics Research Paper no. 13–25, http:// publishers.org/_attachments/docs/copyrightdrivesinnovation-mossoff.pdf.

20. Richard Poynder, "The Finch Report and Its Implications for the Developing World," *Open and Shut?* (blog), July 18, 2012, http://poynder.blogspot.com/2012/ 07/the-finch-report-and-its-implications.html; *Accessibility, Sustainability, Excellence: How to Expand Access to Research Publication* ([UK]: Research Information Network, 2012), www.researchinfonet.org/wp-content/uploads/2012/06/Finch-Group -report-FINAL-VERSION.pdf.

21. See, for example, Stevan Harnad, "Why the UK Should Not Heed the Finch Report," *Impact of Social Sciences: Maximizing the Impact of Academic Research* (blog), July 4, 2012, http://blogs.lse.ac.uk/impactofsocialsciences/2012/07/04/why-the -uk-should-not-heed-the-finch-report; Peter Suber, "Finch Group Report on OA in the UK," Google+ (blog), June 18, 2012, https://plus.google .com/109377556796183035206/posts/DsBAeSCofDX.

22. BIS: Department for Business Innovation and Skills, "Letter to Dame Jane Finch on the Government Response to the Finch Group Report: 'Accessibility, Sustainability, Excellence: How to Expand Access to Research Publications,'" (July

16, 2012), www.bis.gov.uk/assets/biscore/science/docs/l/12-975-letter-government
-response-to-finch-report-research-publications.pdf.

23. Research Councils UK, "RCUK Policy on Open Access and Guidance" (July
    2012), www.rcuk.ac.uk/documents/documents/RCUKOpenAccessPolicy.pdf;
    Research Councils UK, "RCUK Announces New Open Access Policy" (July 16,
    2012), www.rcuk.ac.uk/media/news/2012news/Pages/120716.aspx.

24. European Commission, "Communication from the Commission to the European
    Parliament, the Council, the European Economic and Social Committee, and
    the Committee of the Regions: Towards Better Access to Scientific Information:
    Boosting the Benefits of Public Investments in Research" (July 17, 2012), http://
    ec.europa.eu/research/science-society/document_library/pdf_06/era
    -communication-towards-better-access-to-scientific-information_en.pdf.

25. CARL-CRKN Open Access Working Group, "Implementing Open Access: Report
    of the CARL-CRKN Open Access Working Group" (Oct. 19. 2012), www.crkn
    .ca/sites/default/files/oawg.final_.report.121018.pdf; CRKN, "Joint CARL-CRKN
    Statement on Open Access" (Apr. 9, 2013), www.crkn.ca/communications/joint
    -carl-crkn-statement-on-open-access.

26. Bo-Christer Björk et al., "Anatomy of Green Open Access," preprint accepted for
    publication in *Journal of the American Society for Information Science and Technology*
    2013, www.openaccesspublishing.org/apc8/Personal%20VersionGreenOa.pdf;
    Alma Swan and John Houghton, "Going for Gold? The Costs and Benefits of
    Gold Open Access for US Research Institutions: Further Economic Modelling:
    Report to the UK Open Access Implementation Group" (June 2012), http://
    ie-repository.jisc.ac.uk/610/2/Modelling_Gold_Open_Access_for_institutions
    _-_final_draft3.pdf; see also John Houghton and Alma Swan, "Planting the Green
    Seeds for a Golden Harvest: Comments and Clarifications on 'Going for Gold,'"
    D-Lib Magazine 19, no. 1/2 (Jan./Feb. 2013), www.dlib.org/dlib/january13/
    houghton/01houghton.html.

27. Pochoda, "The Big One," 372.

28. Ryan C. Amacher, *Faulty Towers: Tenure and the Structure of Higher Education*
    (Oakland, CA: Independent Institute, 2004); Richard P. Chait, ed., *The Questions
    of Tenure* (Cambridge, MA: Harvard University Press, 2002); Frederick Rudolph,
    The American College and University: A History (New York: Knopf, 1962); American
    Association of University Professors, "AAUP's 1915 Declaration of Principles"
    (Dec. 31, 1915), www.campus-watch.org/article/id/566.

29. Diane Harley et al., "The Influence of Academic Values on Scholarly Publication
    and Communication Practices," *Journal of Electronic Publishing* 10, no. 2 (Spring
    2007), http://hdl.handle.net/2027/spo.3336451.0010.204.

30. Diane Harley et al., *Assessing the Future Landscape of Scholarly Communication: An
    Exploration of Faculty Values and Needs in Seven Disciplines* (Berkeley, CA: Center
    for Studies in Higher Education and University of California Press, 2010), http://

escholarship.org/uc/item/15x7385g, ii; see also Diane Harley and Sophia Krzys Acord, *Peer Review in Academic Promotion: Its Meaning Locus, and Future* (Berkeley, CA: University of California Berkeley Center for Studies in Higher Education, 2011), http://escholarship.org/uc/item/1xv148c8.

31. Friedlander, "Triple Helix."

32. Brian A. Nosek and Yoav Bar-Anan, "Scientific Utopia: I: Opening Scientific Communication," *Psychological Inquiry* 23, no. 2 (2012): 217–43.

33. Peter Suber, "Ten Challenges for Open-Access Journals," *SPARC Open Access Newsletter* no. 138 (Oct. 2, 2009), http://legacy.earlham.edu/~peters/fos/newsletter/10-02-09.htm#challenges.

34. Bo-Christer Björk and David Solomon, "Open Access versus Subscription Journals: A Comparison of Scientific Impact," *BMC Medicine* 10, no. 1 (2012), www.ncbi.nlm.nih.gov/pmc/articles/PMC3398850/#B3.

35. OpCit Project, "The Effect of Open Access and Downloads ('Hits') on Citation Impact: A Bibliography of Studies," http://opcit.eprints.org/oacitation-biblio.html, provides an annotated list of studies on this topic. See also Alma Swan, "The Open Access Citation Advantage: Studies and Results to Date," *Technical Report*, School of Electronics and Computer Science, University of Southampton (2010), http://openaccess.eprints.org/index.php?/archives/716-Alma-Swan-Review-of-Studies-on-Open-Access-Impact-Advantage.html; A. Ben Wagner, "Open Access Citation Advantage: An Annotated Bibliography," *Issues in Science and Technology Librarianship* 60 (Winter 2010), www.istl.org/10-winter/article2.html.

36. Suenje Dallmeier-Tiesseet al., "Highlights from the SOAP Project Survey: What Scientists Think about Open Access Publishing" (Jan. 20, 2012), http://arxiv.org/pdf/1101.5260v2. Note that data from the SOAP survey is freely available under a CCO license (Creative Commons license with no rights reserved).

37. Harley et al., *Assessing the Future Landscape*, 23.

38. "San Francisco Declaration on Research Assessment" (May 2013), http://am.ascb.org/dora/files/SFDeclarationFINAL.pdf.

39. United States Copyright Office, *Copyright Law of the United States and Related Laws Contained in Title 17 of the United States Code*, Circular 92 (Washington, DC: 2011), www.copyright.gov/title17/circ92.pdf.

40. Elizabeth Gadd, Charles Oppenheim, and Steve Probets, "RoMEO Studies 1: The Impact of Copyright Ownership on Academic Author Self-Archiving," *Journal of Documentation* 59, no. 3 (2003): 243–77.

41. See Scholarly Publishing and Academic Resources Coalition, "Author Rights," www.sparc.arl.org/initiatives/author-rights, for the U.S. SPARC author addendum and the Canadian SPARC author addendum in English and French.

42. GNU Operating System, "GNU Free Documentation License," www.gnu.org/copyleft/fdl.html.

43. Stevan Harnad and Tim Brody, "Comparing the Impact of Open Access (OA) vs. Non-OA Articles in the Same Journals," *D-Lib Magazine* 10, no. 6 (June 2004), www.dlib.org/dlib/june04/harnad/06harnad.html; John Willinsky and Juan Pablo Alperin, "The Academic Ethics of Open Access to Research and Scholarship," *Ethics and Education* 6, no. 3 (2011): 217–23.

44. John Houghton et al., *Economic Implications of Alternative Scholarly Publishing Models: Exploring the Costs and Benefits* ([UK]: JISC, 2009), xxii, www.jisc.ac.uk/publications/documents/economicpublishingmodelsfinalreport.aspx.

45. David Wiley, "Defining the 'Open' in Open Content," http://opencontent.org/definition.

46. Wikipedia, "Wikipedia: Copyrights," http://en.wikipedia.org/wiki/Wikipedia:Copyrights.

47. Suber, *Open Access*, 138.

48. Peter Suber, "No-Fee Open Access Journals," *SPARC Open Access Newsletter* no. 103 (Nov. 2, 2006), http://dash.harvard.edu/bitstream/handle/1/4552050/suber_nofee.htm?sequence=1.

49. David Solomon and Bo-Christer Björk, "Publication Fees in Open Access Publishing: Sources of Funding and Factors Influencing Choice of Journal," *Journal of the American Society for Information Science and Technology* 63, no. 1 (2012): 98–107.

50. Suber, *Open Access*, 143.

51. Heather Morrison, "Dramatic Growth of Open Access 2013 First Quarter: Comparisons," *Imaginary Journal of Poetic Economics* (blog), Apr. 3, 2013, http://poeticeconomics.blogspot.com/2013/04/dramatic-growth-of-open-access-3013.html.

52. DOAJ, www.doaj.org/.

53. Ross Housewright, Roger C. Schonfeld, and Kate Wulfson, *Ithaka S+R US Faculty Survey 2012* (New York: Ithaka S+R, 2013), www.sr.ithaka.org/sites/default/files/reports/Ithaka_SR_US_Faculty_Survey_2012_FINAL.pdf.

54. Jingfeng Xia, "A Longitudinal Study of Scholars Attitudes and Behaviors toward Open-Access Journal Publishing," *Journal of the American Society for Information Science and Technology* 61, no. 3 (2010): 615–24.

55. Jeffrey Beall, "Predatory Publishers Are Corrupting Open Access," *Nature* 489 (Sept. 12, 2012), www.nature.com/news/predatory-publishers-are-corrupting-open-access-1.11385; see also Beall, "Predatory Publishing: Overzealous Open-Access Advocates Are Creating an Exploitative Environment, Threatening the Credibility of Scholarly Publishing," *Scientist* (Aug. 2012), www.the-scientist.com/?articles.view/articleNo/32426/title/Predatory-Publishing; Beall, "Predatory Publishing Is Just One of the Consequences of Gold Open Access," *Learned Publishing* 26, no. 2 (Apr. 2013): 79–83.

56. Declan Butler, "The Dark Side of Publishing: The Explosion in Open-Access Publishing Has Fueled the Rise of Questionable Operators," *Nature* 495, no. 7442 (March 28, 2013): 433–35; Michael Stratford, "'Predatory' Online Journals Lure Scholars Who Are Eager to Publish," *Chronicle of Higher Education* (Mar. 4, 2012), http://chronicle.com/article/Predatory-Online-Journals/131047; Kent Anderson, "'Predatory' Open Access Publishers—The Natural Extreme of an Author-Pays Model," *Scholarly Kitchen: What's Hot and Cooking in Scholarly Publishing* (blog), Mar. 6, 2012, http://scholarlykitchen.sspnet.org/2012/03/06/predatory-open-access -publishers-the-natural-extreme-of-an-author-pays-model.

57. Heather Morrison, "Dramatic Growth of Open Access 2013 First Quarter: Comparisons," *Imaginary Journal of Poetic Economics* (blog), Apr. 3, 2013, http://poet iceconomics.blogspot.com/2013/04/dramatic-growth-of-open-access-3013.html.

58. E. S. Hellman, "Open Access E-books," in *The No Shelf Required Guide to E-book Purchasing*, ed. Sue Polanka, 18–27, *Library Technology Reports* 47, no. 8 (Chicago: ALA TechSource, 2011).

59. Michael Jensen, "Presses Have Little to Fear from Google," *Chronicle of Higher Education* (July 8, 2005), http://chronicle.com/article/Presses-Have-Little-to- Fear/25775.

60. Robert B. Townsend, "Gutenberg-e Books Now Available Open Access and through ACLS Humanities E-book," *AHA Today* (blog), Feb. 13, 2008, http://blog .historians.org/publications/454/gutenberg-e-books-now-available-open-access -and-through-acls-humanities-e-book.

61. Gary Hall, "Towards a New Political Economy: Open Humanities Press and the Open Access Monograph," presentation at OAPEN Conference 2011, Humboldt University, Berlin, Germany, Feb. 24–25, 2011, http://openhumanitiespress.org/ Hall_24_feb_11_OAPEN.doc.

62. Stevan Harnad, "1. Overture: The Subversive Proposal," in *Scholarly Journals at the Crossroads: A Subversive Proposal for Electronic Publishing: An Internet Discussion about Scientific and Scholarly Journals and Their Future*, ed. Ann Shumelda Okerson and James J. O'Donnell, 1–2 (Washington, DC: Association of Research Libraries, 1995), www.arl.org/bm~doc/subversive.pdf; Stevan Harnad, to American-Scientist- Open-Access-Forum, "Re: When Did the Open Access Movement 'Officially' Begin," June 27, 2007, http://users.ecs.soton.ac.uk/harnad/Hypermail/Amsci/ 6519.html.

63. Open Archives Initiative, "The Open Archives Initiative Protocol for Metadata Harvesting," Protocol Version 2.0 of 2002-06-14, Document Version 2004/10/12T15:31:00Z, www.openarchives.org/OAI/openarchivesprotocol.html.

64. OCLC, "The OAIster Database," www.oclc.org/oaister.en.html?urlm=168646.

65. SHERPA/RoMEO, "RoMEO Statistics," www.sherpa.ac.uk/romeo/statistics.php.

66. David Nicholas et al., "Digital Repositories Ten Years On: What Do Scientific Researchers Think of Them and How Do They Use Them?" *Learned Publishing* 25, no. 3 (July 2012): 195–206.

67. Consultative Committee for Space Data Systems, *Reference Model for an Open Archival Information System* (Washington, DC: Consultative Committee for Space Data Systems Secretariat, 2002); International Organization for Standardization, *Space Data and Information Transfer Systems: Open Archival Information System (OAIS): Reference Model*, 2nd ed., ISO 14721:2012(E) (Geneva: International Organization for Standardization, 2012).

68. Charles W. Bailey et al., *Institutional Repositories*, SPEC Kit 292 (Washington, DC: Association of Research Libraries, 2006), 13.

69. Peter Suber, e-mail message to the author, March 8, 2008.

70. Raym Crow, *SPARC Institutional Repository Checklist and Resource Guide* (Washington, DC: SPARC, 2002), www.sparc.arl.org/sites/default/files/presentation_files/ir_guide__checklist_v1.pdf; Raym Crow, "The Case for Institutional Repositories: A SPARC Position Paper," *ARL: A Bimonthly Report* 223 (Aug. 2002), www.sparc.arl.org/sites/default/files/media_files/instrepo.pdf.

71. Clifford A. Lynch, "Institutional Repositories: Essential Infrastructure for Scholarship in the Digital Age," *ARL: A Bimonthly Report*, no. 226 (Feb. 2003), www.arl.org/bm~doc/br226ir.pdf.

72. Primary Research Group, *The Survey of Institutional Digital Repositories, 2012–13 Edition* (New York: Primary Research Group, 2012).

73. "SHared Access Research Ecosystem (SHARE): Development Draft" (June 7, 2013), www.arl.org/storage/documents/publications/share-proposal-07june13.pdf; see also Association of Research Libraries "SHARE Tenets and Overview" (Oct. 23, 2013), www.arl.org/storage/documents/publications/share-tenets-and-overview.pdf.

74. Richard W. Boss, "Institutional Repositories" (paper prepared for the Public Library Association, April 29, 2006).

75. OpenDOAR, "OpenDOAR Charts—Worldwide: Most Frequent Content Types," www.opendoar.org/find.php?format=charts.

76. Data retrieved from OpenDOAR: Directory of Open Access Repositories, www.opendoar.org, Nov. 2013.

77. Jennifer Howard, "The Road from Dissertation to Book Has a New Pothole: The Internet," *Chronicle of Higher Education* (Apr. 3, 2011), http://chronicle.com/article/The-Road-From-Dissertation-to/126977; Marisa L. Ramirez et al., "Do Open Access Electronic Theses and Dissertations Diminish Publishing Opportunities in the Social Sciences and Humanities? Findings from a 2011 Survey of Academic Publishers," *College and Research Libraries* 74, no. 4 (July 2013): 368–80.

78. American Historical Association, "American Historical Association Statement on Policies Regarding the Embargoing of Complete History PhD Dissertations" (adopted July 19, 2013), *AHA Today* (blog), July 22, 2013, http://blog.historians .org/2013/07/american-historical-association-statement-on-policies-regarding-the -embargoing-of-completed-history-phd-dissertations.

79. See, for example, Rebecca J. Rosen, "You've Spent Years on Your Ph.D.: Should You Publish It Online for Free?" *Atlantic* (July 23, 2013), www.theatlantic.com/ technology/archive/2013/07/american-historical-association-universities-ought -to-embargo-dissertations-from-the-internet-for-6-years/278024; Scott Jaschik, "Embargoes for Dissertations?" *Inside Higher Ed* (July 24, 2013), www.inside highered.com/news/2013/07/24/historians-association-faces-criticism-proposal -embargo-dissertations; Stacey Patton, "Embargoes Can Go Only So Far to Help New Ph.D.'s Get Published, Experts Say," *Chronicle of Higher Education* (Aug. 1, 2013), http://chronicle.com/article/Embargoes-Can-Only-Go-So-Far/140603.

80. Julia C. Blixrud, "Scholarly Communication and Public Policies: The Experience of the Association of Research Libraries," *Journal of Library Administration* 51, no. 5/6 (2011): 543–56.

81. U.S. Congress, Consolidated Appropriations Act, 2008, Pub. L. No. 110-161 Div. G. Titl. II Sec. 218.

82. National Institutes of Health, "The Omnibus Appropriations Act of 2009 Makes the NIH Public Access Policy Permanent," http://grants.nih.gov/grants/guide/ notice-files/NOT-OD-09-071.html.

83. Ray English and Heather Joseph, "The NIH Mandate: An Open Access Landmark," *College and Research Libraries News* 69, no. 2 (Feb. 2008): 82–85.

84. Michael W. Carroll, "Complying with the National Institutes of Health Public Access Policy: Copyright Considerations and Options: A Joint SPARC/Science Commons/ARL White Paper" (Feb. 2008), www.sparc.arl.org/sites/default/files/ NIH_Copyright_v1.pdf. To deposit with the NIH, see National Institutes of Health Public Access, "Identify Submission Method," http://publicaccess.nih.gov/ submit_process_journals.htm.

85. Harvard University Library, Office for Scholarly Communication, "Harvard Faculty of Arts and Sciences Open Access Policy" (voted Feb. 12, 2008), https:// osc.hul.harvard.edu/hfaspolicy.

86. Andy Guess, "Harvard Opts in to 'Opt Out' Plan," *Inside Higher Ed* (Feb. 13, 2008), www.insidehighered.com/news/2008/02/13/openaccess.

87. Memorandum for the Heads of Executive Departments and Agencies by John P. Holdren, Director Office of Science and Technology Policy, "Increasing Access to the Results of Federally Funded Scientific Research," Feb. 22, 2013, www.white house.gov/sites/default/files/microsites/ostp/ostp_public_access_memo_2013.pdf.

88. Canadian Institutes of Health Research, "CIHR Open Access Policy" (Jan. 1, 2013), www.cihr-irsc.gc.ca/e/46068.html.

89. International Federation of Library Associations and Institutions, "IFLA Statement on Open Access—Clarifying IFLA's Position and Strategy" (April 18, 2011), www.ifla.org/files/assets/hq/news/documents/ifla-statement-on-open-access.pdf.

90. Alma Swan, *Policy Guidelines for the Development and Promotion of Open Access* (Paris: United Nations Educational, Scientific, and Cultural Organization, 2012), http://unesdoc.unesco.org/images/0021/002158/215863e.pdf.

91. Maria Carpenter et al., "Envisioning the Library's Role in Scholarly Communication in the Year 2025," *portal: Libraries and the Academy* 11, no. 2 (Apr. 2011): 678.

92. Rachel Radom, Melanie Feltner-Reichert, and Kynita Stringer-Stanback, *Organization of Scholarly Communication Services*, SPEC Kit 332 (Washington, DC: Association of Research Libraries, 2012).

93. Nancy Fried Foster and Susan Gibbons, "Understanding Faculty to Improve Content Recruitment for Institutioanl Repositories," *D-Lib Magazine* 11, no. 1 (Jan. 2005), www.dlib.org/dlib/january05/foster/01foster.html.

94. Scholarly Publishing and Academic Resources Coalition, "Campus-Based Open-Access Publishing Funds," www.sparc.arl.org/resources/funds.

95. Harvard University Library, Office for Scholarly Communication, "HOPE Fund," https://osc.hul.harvard.edu/hope.

96. Greg Tananbaum, *Campus-Based Open-Access Publishing Funds: A Practical Guide to Design and Implementation* (Washington, DC: Scholarly Publishing and Academic Resources Coalition, 2010), www.sparc.arl.org/sites/default/files/oafunds-v1.pdf.

97. Priti Jain, "New Trends and Future Applications/Directions of Institutional Repositories in Academic Institutions," *Library Review* 60, no. 2 (2011): 125–41.

98. Oya Y. Rieger, "Assessing the Value of Open Access Information Systems: Making a Case for Community-Based Sustainability Models," *Journal of Library Administration* 51, no. 5/6 (2011): 502.

99. See, for example: Adolfo G. Prieto, "From Conceptual to Perceptual Reality: Trust in Digital Repositories," *Library Review* 58, no. 8 (2009): 593–606; Brigitte Burris, "Institutional Repositories and Faculty Participation: Encouraging Deposits by Advancing Personal Goals," *Public Services Quarterly* 5, no. 1 (2009): 69–79; Tomasz Neugebauer and Annie Murray, "The Critical Role of Institutional Services in Open Access Advocacy," *International Journal of Digital Curation* 8, no. 1 (2013): 84–106.

100. Jihyun Kim, "Faculty Self-Archiving: Motivations and Barriers," *Journal of the American Society for Information Science and Technology* 61, no. 9 (2010): 1909–22.

101. Rowena Cullen and Brenda Chawner, "Institutional Repositories, Open Access, and Scholarly Communication: A Study of Conflicting Paradigms," *Journal of Academic Librarianship* 37, no. 6 (Nov. 2011): 460–70.

102. University of California, Academic Senate, "Open Access Policy for the Academic Senate of the University of California" (adopted July 24, 2013), http://osc.universityofcalifornia.edu/openaccesspolicy/OpenAccess_adopted_072413.pdf.

103. University of Minnesota Digital Conservancy, "University Digital Conservancy Content Guidelines," http://conservancy.umn.edu/pol-content.jsp.

104. Cheryl S. Collins and William H. Walters, "Open Access Journals in College Library Collections," *Serials Librarian* 59, no. 2 (2010): 194–214.

105. Ji-Hong Park and Jiyoung Shim, "Exploring How Library Publishing Services Facilitate Scholarly Communication," *Journal of Scholarly Publishing* 43, no. 1 (Oct. 2011): 76–89.

106. James L. Mullins et al. "Library Publishing Services: Strategies for Success: Final Report" (March 2012), http://docs.lib.purdue.edu/purduepres_books/24.

107. Heather Morrison and Brian Owen, "Open Access Journals Support in Canada," presentation at Canadian Association of Learned Journal Meeting at Congress, Montreal, June 1, 2010; see summary at https://circle.ubc.ca/bitstream/handle/2429/32106/OAJSSLAIS%20proposalfinal.pdf?sequence=1.

108. Brian D. Edgar and John Willinsky, "A Survey of the Scholarly Journals Using Open Journal Systems," *Scholarly and Research Communication* 1, no. 2 (2010), http://src-online.ca/index.php/src/article/view/24/40.

Suggested Readings

Albitz, Rebecca S. "Copyright Information Management and the University Library: Staffing, Organizational Placement, and Authority." *Journal of Academic Librarianship* 39, no. 5 (Sept. 2013): 429–35.

Archambault, Éric. "The Tipping Point: Open Access Comes of Age," in *Proceedings of ISSI 2013 Vienna: 14th International Society of Scientometrics and Informetrics Conference*, ed. Juan Gorraiz et al, 2:1665–80. Vienna: Austrian Institute of Technology, 2013. www.issi2013.org/Images/ISSI_Proceedings_Volume_II.pdf.

Association of Research Libraries, Digital Repository Issues Task Force. *The Research Library's Role in Digital Repository Services: Final Report of the ARL Digital Repository Issues Task Force* (Washington, DC: Association of Research Libraries, 2009). www.arl.org/storage/documents/publications/repository-services-report-jan09.pdf.

Bankier, Jean-Gabriel, and Irene Perciali. "The Institutional Repository Rediscovered: What Can a University Do for Open Access Publishing?" *Serials Review* 34, no. 1 (2008): 21–26.

Bernius, Steffen. "The Impact of Open Access on the Management of Scientific Knowledge." *Online Information Review* 34, no. 4 (2010): 583–603.

Björk, Bo-Christer. "The Hybrid Model for Open Access Publication of Scholarly Articles: A Failed Experiment?" *Journal of the American Society for Information Science and Technology* 63, no. 8 (2012): 1496–1504.

Branin, Joseph. "Institutional Repositories." In *Encyclopedia of Library and Information Sciences*, 3rd ed., ed. Marcia J. Bates and Mary Niles Maack, 2785–96. New York: Taylor and Frances, 2010.

Bresnahan, Megan M., and Andrew M. Johnson, "Assessing Scholarly Communication and Research Data Training Needs." *Reference Services Review* 41, no. 3 (2013): 413–33.

Brown, Josh. "Collection Development and Institutional Repositories." In *Collection Development in the Digital Age*, ed. Maggie Fieldhouse and Audry Marshall, 149–62. London: Facet, 2012.

Burns, C. Sean, Amy Lana, and John M. Budd. "Institutional Repositories: Exploration of Costs and Value." *D-Lib Magazine* 19, no. 1/2 (Jan./Feb. 2013). www.dlib.org/dlib/january13/burns/01burns.html.

Campbell-Meier, Jennifer. "A Framework for Institutional Repository Development." *Advances in Library Administration and Organization* 30 (2011): 151–85.

Cassella, Maria, and Licia Dalvi. "New Journal Models and Publishing Perspectives in the Evolving Digital Environment." *IFLA Journal* 36, no. 1 (2010): 7–15.

Clarke, Roger, and Danny Kingsley. "E-publishing's Impacts on Journals and Journal Articles." *Journal of Internet Commerce* 7, no. 1 (2008): 120–51.

Cope, Bill, and Angus Phillips, eds. *The Future of the Academic Journal*. Oxford, UK: Chandos, 2009.

Copeland, Andrea J., and Deborah Barreau. "Helping People to Manage and Share Their Digital Information: A Role for Public Libraries." *Library Trends* 59, no. 4 (Spring 2011): 637–49.

Crawford, Walt. *Open Access: What You Need to Know Now*. Chicago: ALA Editions, 2011.

Cryer, Emma. "Incorporating Open Access into Libraries." *Serials Review* 37, no. 2 (2011): 103–107.

Dillon, Dennis. "Hand Wringing in Paradise: Scholarly Communication and the Intimate Twinges of Conscience." *Journal of Library Administration* 52, no. 6/7 (2012): 609–25.

Dunlap, Isaac Hunter. "Going Digital." In *Digitisation Perspective*, ed. Ruth Rikowski, 131–44. Rotterdam: Sense Publishers, 2011.

Emmett, Ada, et al. "Toward Open Access: It Takes a 'Village,'" *Journal of Library Administration* 51, no. 5/6 (2011): 557–79.

Eve, Martin Paul. "Before the Law: Open Access, Quality Control, and the Future of Peer Review." In *Debating Open Access*, ed. Nigel Vincent and Chris Wickham, 68–81. London: British Academy, 2013. www.britac.ac.uk/templates/asset-relay .cfm?frmAssetFileID=12661.

Fernandez, Leila, and Rajiv Nariani. "Open Access Funds: A Canadian Library Survey." *Partnership: The Canadian Journal of Library and Information Practice and Research* 6, no. 1 (2011). https://journal.lib.uoguelph.ca/index.php/perj/article/ view/1424/2084.

Ferreira, Miguel, et al., "Carrots and Sticks: Some Ideas on How to Create a Successful Institutional Repository." *D-Lib Magazine* 14, no. 1/2 (Jan./Feb. 2008). www.dlib .org/dlib/january08/ferreira/01ferreira.html.

Ferwerda, Eelco. "New Models for Monographs—Open Books." *Serials* 23, no. 2 (July 2010): 91–96.

Fitzpatrick, Kathleen. "Giving It Away: Sharing and the Future of Scholarly Communication." *Journal of Scholarly Publishing* 43, no. 4 (July 2012): 347–62.

Furnival, Ariadne Cloe. "Open Access to Scholarly Communications: Advantages, Policy, and Advocacy." In *Towards Greater Information Accessibility: Proceeding of the 3rd International Conference on Libraries, Information and Society (ICoLIS2010) 9–10 November 2010, Petaling Jaya, Malaysia*, ed. Abrizah Akdullah, 15–30. Kuala Lumpur, Malaysia: Library and Information Science Unit, Faculty of Computer Science and Information Technology, 2010. http://dspace.fsktm.um.edu.my/ bitstream/1812/1072/1/P1T1_FURNIVAL_UK.pdf.

Galloway, Patricia. "Digital Archiving." In *Encyclopedia of Library and Information Sciences*, 3rd ed., ed. Marcia J. Bates and Mary Niles Maack, 1518–27. New York: Taylor and Frances, 2010.

Gargouri, Yassine, et al. "Self-Selected or Mandated, Open Access Increases Citation Impact for Higher Quality Research." *PLoS ONE* 5, no. 10 (2010). www.plosone .org/article/info%3Adoi%2F10.1371%2Fjournal.pone.0013636.

Getz, Malcolm. "Open Access Scholarship and Publishing." In *Encyclopedia of Library and Information Sciences*, 3rd ed., ed. Marcia J. Bates and Mary Niles Maack, 4008–19. New York: Taylor and Frances, 2010.

Giesecke, Joan. "Institutional Repositories: Keys to Success." *Journal of Library Administration* 51, no. 5/6 (2011): 529–42.

Gilman, Isaac. *Library Scholarly Communication Programs: Legal and Ethical Considerations.* Oxford, UK: Chandos, 2013.

Guédon, Jean-Claude. "Mixing and Matching the Green and Gold Roads to Open Access—Take 2." *Serials Review* 34, no.1 (2008): 41–51.

Guibault, Lucie, and Christina Angelopoulos, eds. *Open Content Licensing: From Theory to Practice.* Amsterdam: Amsterdam University Press, 2011.

Hahn, Karla, et al. *The University's Role in the Dissemination of Research and Scholarship: A Call to Action.* Washington, DC: Association of American Universities, Association of Research Libraries, Coalition for Networked Information, National Association of State Universities and Land Grant Colleges, 2009. http://eric.ed.gov/?id=ED511357.

Hahn, Trudi Bellardo, Mariann Burright, and Heidi Nickisch Duggan. "Has the Revolution in Scholarly Communication Lived Up to Its Promise?" *Bulletin of the American Society for Information Science and Technology* 37, no. 5 (June/July 2011): 24–28.

Hall, Gary. *Digitize This Book! The Politics of New Media, or Why We Need Open Access Now.* Electronic Mediations 24. Minneapolis: University of Minnesota Press, 2008.

Harnad, Stevan. "Open Access to Research: Changing Researcher Behaviour through University and Funder Mandates." *JEDEM: Journal of Democracy and Open Government* 3, no. 1 (2011): 33–41.

Harris, Sian. "Moving towards an Open Access Future: The Role of Academic Libraries: A Report on a Roundtable Commissioned by SAGE, in Association with the British Library" (Aug. 2012). http://dfdf.dk/dmdocuments/Library-OAReport.pdf.

Houghton, John W., and Charles Oppenheim. "Proposition: The Economic Implications of Alternative Publishing Models." *Prometheus* 28, no. 1 (Mar. 2010): 41–54.

Jantz, Ronald C., and Myoung C. Wilson. "Institutional Repositories: Faculty Deposits, Marketing, and the Reform of Scholarly Communication." *Journal of Academic Librarianship* 34, no. 3 (May 2008): 186–95.

Kennan, Mary Anne. "Learning to Share: Mandates and Open Access." *Library Management* 32, no. 4/5 (2011): 302–18.

King, Donald W. "An Approach to Open Access Author Payment." *D-Lib Magazine* 26, no. 3/4 (Mar./Apr. 2012). www.dlib.org/dlib/march10/king/03king.html.

King, Donald W., and Carol Tenopir. "Some Economic Aspects of the Scholarly Journal System." *Annual Review of Information Science and Technology* 45, no. 1 (2011): 295–366.

Laakso, Mikael, and Bo-Christer Björk. "Anatomy of Open Access Publishing: A Study of Longitudinal Development and Internal Structure." *BMC Medicine* 10, no. 124 (2012). www.biomedcentral.com/1741-7015/10/124.

Lewis, David W. "The Inevitability of Open Access." *College and Research Libraries* 73, no. 5 (Sept. 2012): 483–506.

———. "The Role of Subsidy in Scholarly Communication." *EDUCAUSE Review* 48, no. 3 (May/June 2013): 60–61.

Li, Yuan. "Institutional Repositories and Digital Preservation: Assessing Current Practices at Research Libraries." *D-Lib Magazine* 17, no. 5/6 (May/June 2011). www.dlib.org/dlib/may11/yuanli/05yuanli.html.

Little, Geoffrey. "Solutions in Search of Problems? The Challenges and Opportunities of Institutional Repositories." *Journal of Academic Librarianship* 38, no. 1 (Jan. 2012): 65–67.

Lorimer, Rowland. "Libraries, Scholars, and Publishers in Digital Journal and Monograph Publishing." *Scholarly and Research Communication* 4, no. 1 (2012): 1–18. http://src-online.ca/src/index.php/src/article/view/43/117.

Mabe, Michael A. "Scholarly Communication: A Long View." *New Review of Academic Librarianship* 16, no. S1 (2010): 132–44.

Malenfant, Kara J. "Leading Change in the System of Scholarly Communication: A Case Study of Engaging Liaison Librarians for Outreach to Faculty." *College and Research Libraries* 71, no. 1 (Jan. 2010): 63–76.

Markey, Karen, et al. "Institutional Repositories: The Experience of Master's and Baccalaureate Institutions." *portal: Libraries and the Academy* 8, no. 2 (Apr. 2008): 157–73.

Marshall, Catherine C. "Rethinking Personal Digital Archiving, Part 1." *D-Lib Magazine* 14, no. 3/4 (Mar./Apr. 2008). www.dlib.org/dlib/march08/marshall/03marshall-pt1.html.

———. "Rethinking Personal Digital Archiving, Part 2." *D-Lib Magazine* 14, no. 3/4 (Mar./Apr. 2008). www.dlib.org/dlib/march08/marshall/03marshall-pt2.html.

Maughan, Perry, Anali et al. "Libraries as Journal Publishers." *Serials Review* 37, no. 3 (2011): 196–204.

McCabe, Mark J., Christopher M. Snyder, and Anna Fagin. "Open Access versus Traditional Journal Pricing: Using a Simple 'Platform Market' Model to Understand Which Will Win (and Which Should)." *Journal of Academic Librarianship* 39, no. 1 (2013): 11–19.

Mercer, Eric T. *Splashes and Ripples: Synthesizing the Evidence on the Impacts of Digital Resources.* London: JISC, 2011. http://papers.ssrn.com/sol3/papers.cfm?abstract_id=1846535.

Mercer, Holly. "Almost Halfway There: An Analysis of the Open Access Behaviors of Academic Librarians." *College and Research Libraries* 72, no. 5 (Sept. 2011): 443–53.

Mercer, Holly, et al. "Structure, Features, and Faculty Content in ARL Member Repositories." *Journal of Academic Librarianship* 37, no. 4 (July 2011): 333–42.

Morgan, Cliff, Bob Campbell, and Terri Teleen. "The Role of the Academic Journal Publisher and Open Access Publishing Models." *International Studies Perspective* 13, no. 3 (2012): 228–34.

Morrison, Heather. *Scholarly Communication for Librarians.* Oxford, UK: Chandos, 2009.

Mukherjee, Bhaskar. *Scholarly Communication in Library and Information Services: The Impacts of Open Access Journals and E-journals on a Changing Scenario.* Oxford, UK: Chandos, 2010.

Mullen, Laura Bowering. *Open Access and Its Practical Impact on the Work of Academic Librarians: Collection Development, Public Services, and the Library and Information Science Literature.* Oxford, UK: Chandos, 2010.

Nabilou, Hossein. "A Response to Prof. Shavell's 'Should Copyright of Academic Works Be Abolished?'" *Review of Economic Research on Copyright Issues* 7, no.1 (2010): 31–44.

Nariani, Rajiv, and Leila Fernandez. "Open Access Publishing: What Authors Want." *College and Research Libraries* 73, no. 2 (Mar. 2012): 182–95.

Nykanen, Melissa. "Institutional Repositories at Small Institutions in America: Some Current Trends." *Journal of Electronic Resources Librarianship* 23, no. 1 (2011): 1–19.

Odlyzko, Andrew. "Open Access, Library and Publisher Competition, and the Evolution of General Commerce." *Social Science Research Network* (Feb. 4, 2013). http://papers.ssrn.com/sol3/papers.cfm?abstract_id=2211874.

Peterson, A. T., Ada Emmett, and Marc L. Greenberg. "Open Access and the Author-Pays Problem: Assuring Access for Readers and Authors in a Global Community of Scholars." *Journal of Librarianship and Scholarly Communication* 1, no. 3 (2012). http://jlsc-pub.org/cgi/viewcontent.cgi?article=1064&context=jlsc.

Pinfield, Stephen. "Is Scholarly Publishing Going from Crisis to Crisis?" *Learned Publishing* 26, no. 2 (2013): 85–88.

———. "Paying for Open Access? Institutional Funding Streams and OA Publication Charges." *Learned Publishing* 23, no. 1 (Jan. 2010): 39–52.

Potvin, Sarah. "The Principle and the Pragmatist: On Conflict and Coalescence for Library Engagement with Open Access Initiatives." *Journal of Academic Librarianship* 39, no. 1 (Jan. 2013): 67–75.

Prieto, Adolfo G. "From Conceptual to Perceptual Reality: Trust in Digital Repositories." *Library Review* 58, no. 8 (2009): 593–606.

Primary Research Group. *Institutional Digital Repository Benchmarks.* New York: Primary Research Group, 2013.

Rausing, Lisbet. "Toward a New Alexandria: Imagining the Future of Libraries." *New Republic* (Mar. 12, 2010). www.newrepublic.com/article/books-and-arts/toward -new-alexandria#.

Reinsfelder, Thomas L. "Open Access Publishing Practices in a Complex Environment: Conditions, Barriers, and Bases of Power." *Journal of Librarianship and Scholarly Communication* 1, no. 1 (2012). http://jlsc-pub.org/jlsc/vol1/iss1/10.

Richard, Jennifer, Denise Koufogiannakis, and Pam Ryan. "Librarians and Libraries Supporting Open Access Publishing." *Canadian Journal of Higher Education* 39, no. 3 (2009): 33–48.

Salo, Dorothea. "Innkeeper at the Roach Motel." *Library Trends* 57, no. 1 (Fall 2008): 98–123.

Shavell, Steven. "Should Copyright of Academic Works Be Abolished?" *Journal of Legal Analysis* 2, no. 1 (2010): 301–58. http://jla.oxfordjournals.org/content/2/1/301.full .pdf+html.

Shorley, Deborah, and Michael Jubb, eds. *The Future of Scholarly Communication*. London: Facet, 2013.

Solomon, David J. "Digital Distribution of Academic Journals and Its Impact on Scholarly Communication: Looking Back after 20 Years." *Journal of Academic Librarianship* 39, no. 1 (2013): 23–28.

Vincent, Nigel. "The Monograph Challenge." In *Debating Open Access*, ed. Nigel Vincent and Chris Wickham, 107–19. London: British Academy, 2013. www.britac .ac.uk/templates/asset-relay.cfm?frmAssetFileID=12664.

Wacha, Megan, and Meredith Wisner. "Measuring Value in Open Access Repositories." *Serials Librarian* 61, no. 3/4 (2011): 377–88.

Walters, William H., and Anne C. Linvill. "Characteristics of Open Access Journals in Six Subject Areas." *College and Research Libraries* 72, no. 4 (July 2011): 372–92.

Xia, Jingfeng, et al. "A Review of Open Access Self-Archiving Mandate Policies." *portal: Libraries and the Academy* 12, no. 1 (Jan. 2012): 85–102.

Waters, Donald. "Open Access Publishing and the Emerging Infrastructure for 21st Century Scholarship." *Journal of Electronic Publishing* 11, no. 1 (Winter 2008). http://hdl.handle.net/2027/spo.3336451.0011.106.

Weller, Martin. *The Digital Scholar: How Technology Is Transforming Scholarly Practice*. London: Bloomsbury Academic, 2011.

Willinsky, John. "Toward the Design of an Open Monograph Press." *Journal of Electronic Publishing* 12, no. 1 (2009). http://quod.lib.umich.edu/j/jep/3336451.0012.103/ toward-the-design-of-an-open-monograph-press?rgn=main;view=fulltext.

Professional Resources for Collection Development and Management

Selected Journals

Titles described here are those of greatest interest to collections librarians. Many more journals publish occasional pertinent articles, so this list is not intended to be comprehensive. Information about each journal below was taken from Ulrichsweb, journal websites, and the journals themselves. When available, ISSNs are provided for print and e-versions of titles. The rapidly changing nature of journals and the identity of publishers means that information becomes dated quickly and should be verified by those seeking to consult the titles listed here. Only the most recent titles of publications are listed.

Against the Grain: Linking Publishers, Vendors, and Librarians. Charleston, SC: Against the Grain. ISSN: 1043-2094.

Provides news about libraries, publishers, vendors, and subscription agents; covers library-vendor and publisher-library relations, acquisition business, publisher profiles, prices, studies, and collection development.

Bookbird: A Journal of International Children's Literature. Baltimore, MD: Johns Hopkins University Press, for the International Board on Books for Young People. ISSN: 0006-7377 (print), 1918-6983 (online).

A peer-reviewed journal containing news, reports, and analysis and debates on topics of international children's literature.

The Bottom Line: Managing Library Finances. Bingley, UK: Emerald. ISSN: 0888-045X.

A peer-reviewed journal providing practical information on planning, budgeting, managing cash, purchasing, investment, cost analysis, new technology, and other financial tools and techniques.

Collection Building. Bingley, UK: Emerald. ISSN: 0160-4953.

A peer-reviewed journal dedicated to all aspects of library collection development and maintenance from the practical to the theoretical. Coverage includes resource development, new information formats, technology, and valuation of electronic resources and collection development policy issues.

Collection Management. Philadelphia: Routledge. ISSN: 0146-2679 (print), 1545-2549 (online).

A peer-reviewed journal covering all aspects of collection management and development, including building, administering, preserving, assessing, and organizing library collections. Articles address sharing and providing access to resources, creating digital collections, preserving both traditional and digital library resources, applying technological developments to managing collections, training and developing staff, and managing and analyzing administrative issues associated with building collections such as usage, licensing or rights, access, and finance.

Horn Book Magazine. Boston: Horn Book. ISSN: 0018-5078.

Features articles on children's and young adult literature and book reviews. Covers fiction, nonfiction, poetry, and picture books.

Insights: The UKSG Journal. Newbury, UK: UKSG. ISSN: 2048-7754.

An online journal published by UKSG (formerly United Kingdom Serials Group) that aims to facilitate communication between the many stakeholders in the global knowledge community; contains a mix of topical articles written by librarians, publishers, vendors, and other industry experts, along with conference reviews, editorial comments, and features on people in the global knowledge community.

Journal of Electronic Publishing. Ann Arbor, MI: University of Michigan Press. ISSN 1080-2711.

An open-access, online journal covering all facets of publishing material in an electronic environment and the impact of those practices upon users; publishes both invited contributions from experts and practitioners and longer articles (some peer-reviewed) from scholars, publishers, and others writing about electronic publishing.

Journal of Electronic Resources Librarianship. Philadelphia: Routledge. ISSN: 1941-126X (print), 1941-1278 (online).

A peer-reviewed journal covering the presentation and discussion of current research, evolving work-related processes and procedures, and the latest news on topics related to electronic resources and the digital environment.

Journal of Interlibrary Loan, Document Delivery, and Electronic Reserve. Philadelphia: Routledge. ISSN: 1072-303X (print), 1540-3572 (online).

A peer-reviewed journal covering interlibrary loan, document delivery, and electronic reserve, including articles on cooperative collection development, shared virtual library services and digitization projects, library consortia, networks, cooperatives, and other multilibrary collaborative efforts.

Journal of Scholarly Publishing. Toronto: University of Toronto Press. ISSN: 1198-9742 (print), 1710-1166 (online).

A peer-reviewed journal for authors, editors, librarians, marketers, and publishers covering publishing and the new challenges resulting from changes in technology and funding, including articles on the future of scholarly publishing, scholarship on the Web, digitization, copyright, editorial policies, computer applications, marketing, and pricing models.

Library and Archival Security. Philadelphia: Routledge. ISSN: 0196-0075 (print), 1540-9511 (online).

A peer-reviewed journal addressing security planning, policies, procedures, and strategies dealing with libraries, archives, and other information centers, including security and safety of materials and people, vandalism, information ethics, data and communications security, relevant legislation, and disaster preparedness and recovery.

Library Collections, Acquisitions, and Technical Services. London: Elsevier. ISSN: 1464-9055 (print), 1873-1821 (online).

A peer-reviewed journal covering acquisition of books and serials in academic, public, school, and special libraries, cataloging and authority control, outsourcing of technical services operations, electronic publications, gifts and exchanges, microforms and other nonprint media, document delivery, networking, resource sharing and access, and pertinent library automation projects.

Library Resources and Technical Services. Chicago: Association for Library Collections and Technical Services. ISSN: 0024-2527 (print), 2159-9610 (online).

The official journal of the Association for Library Collections and Technical Services; a peer-reviewed journal covering bibliographic access and control, preservation, conservation and reproduction of library materials, serials, and collection development and management.

New Review of Children's Literature and Librarianship. Philadelphia: Routledge. ISSN: 1361-4541 (print), 1740-7885(online).

A peer-reviewed journal covering the management of library services to children and adolescents; collection development and management; critical assessments of children's and adolescent literature; book and media selection; education issues affecting library services; user education and the promotion of services; staff education and training; and research in literature and library services for children and adolescents.

Publishers Weekly: The International News Magazine of Book Publishing. New York: PWxyz. ISSN: 0000-0019 (print), 2150-4008 (online).

A trade news magazine of interest to publishers, booksellers, literary agents, and librarians covering publishing trends, mergers and acquisitions, other trade news, and book reviews.

Restaurator: International Journal for the Preservation of Library and Archival Material. Munich: De Gruyter Saur. ISSN: 0034-5806.

A peer-reviewed journal that focuses on the conservation of library and archives materials including technology, practical experience, and organization. Many articles deal with the development of new preservation techniques and the improvement and better understanding of established methods.

Serials Librarian. Philadelphia: Routledge. ISSN: 0361-526X (print), 1541-1095 (online).

A peer-reviewed journal covering serials selection and acquisition, bibliographic control, cataloging, staffing and department management, serials control systems, subscription agencies, publishers, and computerization problems.

Serials Review. Oxford, UK: Elsevier. ISSN: 0098-7913 (print), 1879-095X (online).

> A peer-reviewed journal covering the practical aspects of collecting, managing, and publishing serials, and emerging and theoretical issues of importance to librarians, publishers, and others in the serials community.

Technical Services Quarterly. Philadelphia: Routledge. ISSN: 0731-7131 (print), 1555-3337 (online).

> A peer-reviewed journal covering new developments and future trends concerning the technical operation of libraries and information centers. Articles address technical services, automation, networking, document delivery, information technology, library instruction and information literacy, reference and bibliography, case studies, cost analysis, staffing, space, organizational behavior and leadership, and collection development and management.

Electronic Discussion Groups and Blogs

ACQNET. www.acqweb.org/acqnet.html

> A moderated, archived list that facilitates the exchange of information, ideas, and solutions to common problems in the areas of acquisitions and collection development and management.

CCBD-Net. www.education.wisc.edu/ccbc/ccbcnet

> A moderated, archived list that encourages awareness and discussion of ideas and issues critical to literature for children and young adults. The list focuses on a new topic each month.

COLLDV-L: Library Collection Development List. www.infomotions.com/serials/colldv-l

> A moderated, archived list directed to collection development librarians and others (including publishers and vendors) interested in library collection development and management.

Collection = Connection: The Library Collection Management Blog. www.collectionconnection.alcts.ala.org

> A blog sponsored by the Collection Management Section of the Association for Library Collections and Technical Services that seeks to present new ideas about library collections and to provide a forum to discuss changes in the practice of collection management and development.

CoOL: Conservation DistList.
http://cool.conservation-us.org/byform/mailing-lists/cdl

An interdisciplinary, moderated, archived list open to conservators, conservation scientists, curators, librarians, archivists, administrators, and others whose worklife touches on the preservation of cultural property.

LIBLICENSE-L. http://liblicense.crl.edu/discussion-forum

A moderated, archived list for the discussion of issues related to the licensing of digital information and other topics central to the creation, publication, distribution, and economics of scholarly electronic information.

LM_NET. http://lmnet.wordpress.com

A moderated, archived list for school library media specialists worldwide and others involved with the school library media field.

PADG-L: The Preservation Administration Interest Group.
http://lists.ala.org/wws/arc/padg

A moderated, archived discussion list sponsored by the Association of Library Collections and Technical Services Preservation and Reformatting Section, concerned with preservation issues.

PUBYAC. www.pubyac.org

A moderated, archived discussion list concerned with the practical aspects of children and young adult services in public libraries, focusing on programming ideas, outreach and literacy programs for children and caregivers, censorship and policy issues, collection development, administrative considerations, and other pertinent services and issues.

SERIALST: Serials in Libraries Discussion Forum.
www.uvm.edu/~bmaclenn/serialst.html

A moderated, archived list intended to serve as a forum for most aspects of serials in libraries; topics addressed include collection management and development, serials budgets, and pricing.

VIDEOLIB. www.lib.berkeley.edu/MRC/vrtlists.html

A moderated, archived list devoted to copyright and intellectual property issues, evaluation of materials, collection development policy issues, selection methods, acquisition concerns (locating hard-to-find materials, library/vendor relations, etc.), and issues related to evolving video technologies and libraries.

Professional Associations

American Library Associations (ALA): Divisions, Sections, Committees, and Interest Groups within Those Divisions

American Association of School Librarians (AASL). www.ala.org/aasl

> The mission of AASL is to advocate excellence, facilitate change, and develop leaders in the school library field. AASL works to ensure that all members of the school library field collaborate to provide leadership in the total education program, participate as active partners in the teaching/learning process, connect learners with ideas and information, and prepare students for lifelong learning, informed decision making, a love of reading, and the use of information technologies. AASL publishes *Knowledge Quest*, ISSN 1094-9046 (print), 2163-5234 (online).

Association for Library Collections and Technical Services (ALCTS), Collection Management Section (CMS). www.ala.org/alcts/mgrps/cms

> CMS supports library professionals who perform collection management and development while selecting and evaluating all types of library materials in all types of institutions.

Association for Library Collections and Technical Services (ALCTS), Preservation and Reformatting Section (PARS). www.ala.org/alcts/mgrps/pars

> PARS focuses on preservation and reformatting of library materials in all types of institutions and the application of new technologies to assure continued access to library collections.

ALCTS has several interest groups that focus on different elements of collection development and management:

- Chief Collection Development Officers of Large Research Libraries Interest Group. www.ala.org/alcts/mgrps/cms/grps/ats-cmdchi
- Collection Development Issues for the Practitioner Interest Group. www.ala.org/alcts/mgrps/cms/grps/ats-cmdcolldevp
- Collection Development Librarians of Academic Libraries Interest Group. www.ala.org/alcts/mgrps/cms/grps/ats-cmdcolldev
- Collection Evaluation and Assessment Interest Group. www.ala.org/alcts/mgrps/cms/grps/ats-cmdigcea

- Collection Management and Electronic Resources Interest Group. www.ala.org/alcts/mgrps/cms/grps/ats-cmdigcmer
- Collection Management and Development in Public Libraries Interest Group. www.ala.org/alcts/mgrps/cms/grps/ats-cmddgcodes

Association for Library Services to Children (ALSC). www.ala.org/alsc

ALSC is dedicated to the support and enhancement of service to children in all types of libraries and committed to a better future for children through libraries. ALSC publishes *Children and Libraries*, ISSN 1542-9806.

Association of College and Research Libraries (ACRL). www.ala.org/acrl.

ACRL is dedicated to enhancing the ability of academic library and information professionals to serve the information needs of the higher education community and to improve learning, teaching, and research. ACRL has several sections (e.g., Asian, African, and Middle Eastern Section; Science and Technology Section) focusing on various disciplines and geographic areas, which are of interest to subject specialists. ACRL publishes *College and Research Libraries*, ISSN 0010-0870 (print), 2150-6701 (online).

Public Library Association (PLA). www.ala.org/pla

PLA exists to provide a diverse program of communication, publication, advocacy, continuing education, and programming for its members and others interested in the advancement of public library service. PLA publishes *Public Libraries*, ISSN 0163-5506.

Reference and User Services Association (RUSA), Collection Development and Evaluation Section (CODES). www.ala.org/rusa/sections/codes

CODES provides a venue for reference and user services librarians and staff from all types of libraries to discuss the rapidly changing landscape of collection development, readers' advisory, and publishing.

Reference and User Services Association, Cooperative Collection Development Committee (a joint committee of the Collection Development and Evaluation Section and the Sharing and Transforming Access to Resources Section). www.ala.org/rusa/sections/stars/section/cooperativecollectionde velopmentcommittee/ccd

This committee is charged to study, promote, and support cooperative collection development and related user services.

Reference and User Services Association, Sharing and Transforming Access to Resources Section (STARS). www.ala.org/rusa/sections/stars

STARS addresses the interests of librarians and library staff involved with interlibrary loan, document delivery, remote circulation, access services, co-operative reference, cooperative collection development, remote storage, and other shared library services as well as providers of products and services that support resource sharing.

Young Adult Library Services Association (YALSA). www.ala.org/yalsa

The mission of YALSA is to expand and strengthen library services for teens. Through its member-driven advocacy, research, and professional development initiatives, the association builds the capacity of libraries and librarians to engage, serve, and empower teens. YALSA publishes *Young Adult Library Services*, ISSN 1541-4302.

North American Serials Interest Group (NASIG). www.nasig.org

NASIG is an independent organization that promotes communication, understanding, and sharing of ideas among all members of the serials information community.

Canadian Library Association (CLA): Divisions and Interest Group

CLA has several divisions that address issues of importance to collections librarians:

- Canadian Association of College and University Libraries. www.cla.ca/AM/Template.cfm?Section=CACUL
- Canadian Association of Public Libraries. www.cla.ca/AM/Template.cfm?Section=CAPL2
- Canadian Association of School Librarians. www.cla.ca/AM/Template.cfm?Section=CASL2
- Canadian Association of Special Libraries and Information Services. www.cla.ca/AM/Template.cfm?Section=CASLIS

Collection Development and Management Interest Group. www.cla.ca/AM/Template.cfm?Section=Collection_Development_and_Management&Template=/CM/HTMLDisplay.cfm&ContentID=10285

This CLA interest group represents the interests of librarians involved in collection development and management, arranges opportunities for continuing education, provides a means of communication among librarians involved in collection development and management, and raises the awareness of the library community at large with regard to the issues of concern to librarians involved in collection development and management.

International Organizations

International Association of School Librarianship (IASL). www.iasl-online.org.

The IASL mission is to provide an international forum for those people interested in promoting effective school library media programs as viable instruments in the educational process. IASL has a Children's and Young Adult Literature Special Interest Group, with several objectives, including the exchange of information about current developments in the field such as collection development, author awareness, and publisher access and issues.

International Federation of Library Associations and Institutions (IFLA), Division of Collections and Services. www.ifla.org/VII/d5/dcs.htm

This division of IFLA focuses on acquiring information for the improvement of collection building of specific types of materials such as rare books, serials, newspapers, and government publications.

International Reading Association (IRA). www.reading.org

IRA is in a nonprofit, global network of individuals and institutions committed to worldwide literacy. Its members are involved in teaching reading to learners of all ages and dedicated to promoting high levels of literacy for all by improving the quality of reading instruction, disseminating research and information about reading, and encouraging lifetime reading.

Selection Aids

Many of these tools are updated through new editions and supplements, and many are available in electronic format. Generally, ISSNs listed here are for the print versions. Collections librarians should consult the most recent resources available and be aware that publishers and publications cease, merge, and change names over time. For example, the print editions of several standard Bowker and H. W. Wilson publications are now available from Grey House, while Bowker and H. W. Wilson continue to offer the online versions. This information was verified in Ulrichsweb, WorldCat, and pertinent websites as of 2013.

Bibliographies, Online Lists, and Directories

Allyn, Pam. *Pam Allyn's Best Books for Boys.* New York: Scholastic, 2011.

American Book Publishing Record: Arranged by Dewey Decimal Classification and Indexed by Author, Title, and Subject. Amenia, NY: Grey House. ISSN 0002-7707 (monthly).

American Library Association, Gay, Lesbian, Bisexual, and Transgender Roundtable. "Over the Rainbow List of LGBT Books for Adult Readers." www.glbtrt.ala.org/overtherainbow/archives/category/final-bibliographies (annual).

American Library Association. Video Round Table. "Notable Videos for Adults." www.ala.org/vrt/notablevideos.

American Reference Books Annual. Santa Barbara, CA: Libraries Unlimited. ISSN 0065-9959 (annual).

Association for Library Services to Children. "Core Collection of Graphic Novels." www.ala.org/alsc/compubs/booklists/grphcnvls (annual).

———. "Great Web Sites for Kids." http://gws.ala.org.

———. "Notable Children's Books." www.ala.org/alsc/awardsgrants/notalists/ncb (annual).

———. "Notable Children's Recordings." www.ala.org/alsc/awardsgrants/notalists/ncr (annual).

———. "Notable Children's Videos." www.ala.org/alsc/awardsgrants/notalists/ncv (annual).

Association of American University Presses. "University Press Books for Public and Secondary School Libraries." www.aaupnet.org/news-a-publications/aaup-publications/university-press-books-for-libraries (annual).

Barr, Catherine. *Best Books for High School Readers, Grades 9–12.* 3rd ed. Santa Barbara, CA: Libraries Unlimited, 2013.

———. *Best Books for Middle School and Junior High Readers, Grades 6–9.* 3rd ed. Santa Barbara, CA: Libraries Unlimited, 2013.

Barr, Catherine, and John E. Gillespie. *Best Books for Children: Preschool through Grade 6.* 9th ed. Santa Barbara, CA: Libraries Unlimited, 2010. See also Barr, Catherine. *Best Books for Children, Preschool through Grade 6: Supplement to the Ninth Edition.* Santa Barbara, CA: Libraries Unlimited, 2013.

Barstow, Judith Riggle, and Leslie M. Molnar. *Beyond Picture Books: Subject Access to Best Books for Beginning Readers.* 3rd ed. Santa Barbara, CA: Libraries Unlimited, 2007.

Bluemel, Nancy Larson, and Rhonda Harris Taylor. *Pop-Up Books: A Guide for Teachers and Librarians.* Santa Barbara, CA: Libraries Unlimited, 2012.

Books in Print. Amenia, NY: Grey House. ISSN 0068-0214 (annual with supplements).

Books Out Loud: Bowker's Guide to Audiobooks. Amenia, NY: Grey House. ISSN 0000-1805 (annual).

Bowker's Complete Video Directory. Amenia, NY: Grey House. ISSN 1051-290X (annual).

Carstensen, Angela A. *Outstanding Books for the College Bound: Titles and Programs for a New Generation.* Chicago: American Library Association, 2011.

Children's Book Council. "Outstanding Science Trade Books for Students K–12." www.cbcbooks.org/outstandingscience (annual).

Children's Books in Print: An Author, Title, and Illustrator Index to Books for Children and Young Adults. Amenia, NY: Grey House. ISSN 0069-3480 (annual).

Children's Core Collection. Amenia, NY: Grey House. ISSN 2160-4673. (annual).

The Complete Directory of Large Print Books and Serials. Amenia, NY: Grey House. ISSN 0000-1120 (annual).

Crosetto, Alice, Rajinder Garcha, and Mark Horan. *Disabilities and Disorders in Literature for Youth: A Selected Annotated Bibliography for K–12.* Lanham, MD: Scarecrow, 2010.

"Current Cites: An Annotated Bibliography of Selected Articles, Books, and Digital Documents on Information Technology." http://currentcites.org (monthly).

Directories in Print. Detroit, MI: Gale. ISSN 0000-1120 (annual).

El-Hi Textbooks and Serials in Print: Including Related Teaching Materials K–12. Amenia, NY: Grey House. ISSN 0000-0825 (annual).

Fichtelberg, Susan, and Bridget Dealy Volz. *Primary Genreflecting: A Guide to Picture Books and Easy Readers.* Santa Barbara, CA: Libraries Unlimited, 2010.

Fiction Core Collection. Amenia, NY: Grey House. ISSN 2155-0808 (quadrennial).

Film and Video Finder. Albuquerque, NM: National Information Center for Educational Media. ISSN 0898-1852 (irregular).

Forthcoming Books. Amenia, NY: Grey House. ISSN 0015-8119 (quarterly).

Fulltext Sources Online. Medford, NJ: Information Today. ISSN 1040-8258 (semiannual).

Gale Directory of Databases. Farmington Hills, MI: Gale Research. ISSN 1066-8934 (annual).

Gale Directory of Publications and Broadcast Media. Farmington Hill, MI: Gale Research. ISSN 1048-7972 (annual).

Graphic Novels Core Collection. New York: H. W. Wilson (online).

Guide to Microforms and Digital Resources. Berlin: De Gruyter (annual).

Guide to Reference. Chicago: American Library Association (online).

Guide to Reprints: Subjects. Munich: De Gruyter Saur. ISSN 1439-2755 (annual).

Guide to U.S. Government Publications. Detroit, MI: Gale Research. ISSN 0092-3168 (annual).

Hysell, Shannon Graff, ed. *American Reference Books Annual.* Santa Barbara, CA: Libraries Unlimited. ISSN 0065-9959 (annual).

———. *Recommended Reference Books for Small and Medium-Sized Libraries and Media Centers.* Santa Barbara, CA: Libraries Unlimited, 2013.

Index to Current Urban Documents. Westport, CT: Greenwood. ISSN 0046-8908 (quarterly).

"Infomine: Scholarly Internet Resource Collections." http://infomine.ucr.edu.

International Directory of Little Magazines and Small Presses. Paradise, CA: Dustbooks (CD-ROM or online). ISSN 0092-3974 (annual).

International Reading Association. "Teachers' Choices Reading List." www.reading.org/Resources/Booklists/TeachersChoices.aspx (annual).

———. "Young Adults' Choices Reading List." www.reading.org/Resources/Booklists/YoungAdultsChoices.aspx (annual).

International Reading Association and the Children's Book Council. "Children's Choices Reading List." www.reading.org/Resources/Booklists/ChildrensChoices.aspx (annual).

Internet Scout. "The Scout Report" (annotated descriptions of Internet resources). http://scout.cs.wisc.edu/report/sr/current.

Jones, Cherri, and J. B. Petty. *Multiethnic Books for the Middle-School Curriculum.* Chicago: American Library Association, 2013.

Kalen, Elizabeth F. S. *Mostly Manga: A Genre Guide to Popular Manga, Manhwa, Manhua, and Anime.* Santa Barbara, CA: Libraries Unlimited, 2012.

Law Books and Serials in Print: A Multimedia Sourcebook. Amenia, NY: Grey House. ISSN 0000-0752 (annual).

Lima, Carolyn, and Rebecca L. Thomas. *A to Zoo: Subject Access to Children's Picture Books.* 8th ed. Santa Barbara, CA: Libraries Unlimited, 2010. See also Thomas, Rebecca L. *A to Zoo: Subject Access to Children's Picture Books, Supplement to the 8th Edition.* Santa Barbara, CA: Libraries Unlimited, 2012.

Lynn, Ruth Nadelman. *Fantasy Literature for Children and Young Adults: A Comprehensive Guide.* 5th ed. Santa Barbara, CA: Libraries Unlimited, 2005.

Magazines for Libraries. Ann Arbor, MI: ProQuest. ISSN 0000-0914 (annual).

Martinez, Sara E., ed. *Latino Literature: A Guide to Reading Interests.* Santa Barbara, CA: Libraries Unlimited, 2009.

Matthew, Kathryn I., and Joy Lowe. *The Neal-Schuman Guide to Recommended Children's Books and Media for Use with Every Elementary Subject.* 2nd ed. New York: Neal-Schuman, 2010.

Medical and Health Care Books and Serials in Print: An Index to Literature in Health Sciences. Amenia, NY: Grey House. ISSN 0000-085X (annual).

Middle and Junior High Core Collection. Amenia, NY: Grey House (quadrennial).

National Council for Social Studies and the Children's Book Council. "Children's Choice Book Awards." www.cbc.org/ccba (annual).

———. "Notable Social Studies Trade Books for Young People." www.social studies.org/notable (annual).

———. "Outstanding Science Trade Books for Students K–12." www.cbcbooks .org/ outstanding-science (annual).

The Newbery and Caldecott Awards: A Guide to the Medal and Honor Books. Chicago: Association for Library Service to Children. ISSN 1070-4493 (annual).

Oxbridge Directory of Newsletters. New York: Oxbridge Communications. ISSN 0163-7010 (annual).

"Parents' Choice: Reviewing Children's Media since 1978." www.parents -choice.org.

Public Library Core Collection: Nonfiction. Amenia, NY: Grey House (every two years).

Reference and User Services Association. "Best Free Reference Web Sites." www.ala.org/rusa/sections/mars/marspubs/marsbestindex.

———. "The Listen List: Outstanding Audiobook Narration." www.ala.org/ rusa/awards/listenlist (annual).

———. "Notable Books List." (fiction, nonfiction, and poetry books). www.ala .org/rusa/awards/notable books (annual).

———. "Outstanding Business Reference Sources." www.ala.org/rusa/sections/ brass/brasspubs/outsandingbusrefsources/outstbusrefsources (annual).

———. "The Reading List." (outstanding genre fiction). www.ala.org/rusa/ awards/readinglist (annual).

Resources for College Libraries. New Providence, NJ: Bowker (online).

Safford, Barbara Ripp. *Guide to Reference Materials for School Library Media Centers.* 6th ed. Santa Barbara, CA: Libraries Unlimited, 2010.

Senior High Core Collection. Amenia, NY: Grey House (quadrennial).

Serials Directory. Birmingham, AL: EBSCO Publishing (online).

Standard Periodical Directory. New York: Oxbridge Communications. ISSN 0085-6630 (annual).

Subject Guide to Books in Print. Amenia, NY: Grey House. ISSN 0000-0159 (annual with supplements).

Subject Guide to Children's Books in Print. Amenia, NY: Grey House. ISSN 0000-0167 (annual).

Thomas, Rebecca L., and Catherine Barr. *Popular Series Fiction for K–6 Readers: A Reading and Selection Guide.* 2nd ed. Santa Barbara, CA: Libraries Unlimited, 2008.

———. *Popular Series Fiction for Middle School and Teen Readers: A Reading and Selection Guide.* 2nd ed. Santa Barbara, CA: Libraries Unlimited, 2008.

Ulrich's Periodicals Directory: International Periodicals Information. Ann Arbor, MI: ProQuest. ISSN 0000-2100 (annual, with supplements).

United State Government Printing Office. "Catalog of United States Government Publications: New Titles." http://catalog.gpo.gov/F/SE234X66KEP3QP UL94J91UPEY8I37CRCX6TBIPAGVA6AF15B59-50211?func=file&file _name=find-net&local_base=NEWTITLE.

Videohound's Golden Movie Retriever. Detroit, MI: Gale. ISSN 1095-371X (annual).

Welch, Rollie James. *A Core Collection for Young Adults.* 2nd ed. New York: Neal-Schuman, 2010.

Young Adult Library Services Association. "Amazing Audiobooks for Young Adults." www.ala.org/yalsa/amazing-audiobooks (annual).

———. "Best Fiction for Young Adults." www.ala.org/yalsa/best-fiction-young -adults (annual).

———. "Fabulous Films for Young Adults." www.ala.org/yalsa/fabulous-films (annual).

———. "Great Graphic Novels for Teens." www.ala.org/yalsa/great-graphic -novels (annual).

———. "Popular Paperbacks for Young Adults." www.ala.org/yalsa/popular -paperbacks-young-adults (annual).

———. "Quick Picks for Reluctant Young Adult Readers." www.ala.org/yalsa/ quick-picks-reluctant-young-adult-readers (annual).

———. "Readers' Choice." www.ala.org/yalsa/readers-choice (annual).

———. "Teen's Top Ten." www.ala.org/yalsa/teens-top-ten (annual).

Zbaracki, Matthew D. *Best Books for Boys: A Resource for Educators.* Santa Barbara, CA: Libraries Unlimited, 2008.

Review Sources and Guides to Reviews

Audiofile: The Magazine for People Who Love Audiobooks. Portland, ME: Audiofile. ISSN 1063-0244 (bimonthly).

The Best Children's Books of the Year. New York: Bank Street College. ISSN 1523-6471 (annual).

Billboard: The International Newsweekly of Music, Video, and Home Entertainment. New York: Prometheus Global Media. ISSN 0006-2510 (weekly).

Bookbird: A Journal of International Children's Literature. Baltimore, MD: Johns Hopkins Press for International Board on Books for Young People. ISSN 0006-7377 (quarterly).

Book Links: Connecting Books, Libraries, and Classrooms. Chicago: American Library Association. ISSN 1055-4741 (bimonthly).

Booklist. Chicago: American Library Association. ISSN 0006-7385 (bimonthly, 22 times a year).

Bookmarks: For Everyone Who Hasn't Read Everything. Chapel Hill, NC: Bookmarks. ISSN 1546-0657 (bimonthly).

Book Review Digest: An Index to Reviews of Current Books. Amenia, NY: Grey House. ISSN 0006-7326 (monthly except February and July; annual cumulation).

Book Review Index. Detroit, MI: Gale Research. ISSN 0524-0581 (three times a year, with annual cumulation).

Bookwire: The Book Industry Resource. New Providence, NJ: Bowker. ISSN 0000-1759.

Bulletin of the Center for Children's Books. Baltimore, MD: Johns Hopkins University Press. ISSN 0008-9036 (monthly except August).

The Charleston Advisor: Critical Reviews of Web Products for Information Professionals. Denver, CO: Charleston. ISSN 1525-4011 (quarterly).

Children and Libraries. Chicago: American Library Association. ISSN 1542-9806 (three times a year).

Children's Magazine Guide: Subject Index to Children's Magazines and Web Sites. Westport, CT: Greenwood. ISSN 0743-9873 (nine times a year).

Children's Technology Review. Flemington, NJ: Active Learning Association. ISSN 1555-242X (monthly).

Children's Video Report. Princeton, NJ: Children's Video Report. ISSN 0883-6922 (eight times a year).

Choice: Current Reviews of Academic Books. Chicago: Association of College and Research Libraries. ISSN 0009-4978 (monthly, except bimonthly in July/August).

Chronicle of Higher Education. Washington, DC: Chronicle of Higher Education. ISSN 0009-5982 (weekly, 49 times a year).

College and Research Libraries News. "Internet Resources." Chicago: Association of College and Research Libraries. ISSN 0099-0086 (11 times a year).

CM Magazine: Canadian Review of Materials. Winnipeg: Manitoba Library Association. ISSN 1201-9364 (biweekly).

The Comics Journal: The Magazine of Comics News and Criticism. Seattle, WA: Fantagraphics Books. ISSN 0194-7869 (monthly).

Counterpoise: For Social Responsibilities, Liberty, and Dissent. Gainesville, FL: Civic Media Center and Library. ISSN 1092-0714 (quarterly).

Down Beat: Jazz, Blues, and Beyond. Elmhurst, IL: Maher Production. ISSN 0012-5768 (monthly).

EContent: Digital Content Strategies and Resources. Medford, NJ: Information Today. ISSN 1525-2531 (10 times a year).

"Educational Media Reviews Online." Buffalo, NY: University at Buffalo Libraries. http://emro.lib.buffalo.edu.

The Electronic Library: The International Journal for the Application of Technology in Information Environments. Bingley, UK: Emerald. ISSN 0264-0473 (bimonthly).

Film and Video Finder. Albuquerque, NM: National Information Center for Educational Media. ISSN 0898-1582 (irregular).

Five Owls: A Publication for Readers, Personally and Professionally Involved in Children's Literature. Marathon, TX: Jara Society. ISSN 0892-6735 (quarterly).

Gay and Lesbian Review Worldwide: A Bimonthly Journal of History, Culture, and Politics. Boston, MA: Harvard Gay and Lesbian Review. ISSN 1532-118 (quarterly).

Government Information Quarterly: An International Journal of Information Technology Management, Policies, and Practices. London: Elsevier. ISSN 0740-624X (quarterly).

HNS Magazine. Starcross, UK: Historical Novel Society (quarterly). Reviews available online at http://historicalnovelsociety.org/reviews.

Horn Book Guide to Children's and Young Adult Books. Boston: Horn Book. ISSN 1044-405X (semiannual).

Horn Book Magazine: About Books for Children and Young Adults. Boston: Horn Book. ISSN 0018-5078 (bimonthly).

The Independent (covers film and video). New York: Independent Media Publications. ISSN 11557-5799 (quarterly).

Instructor. New York: Scholastic. ISSN 1532-0200 (eight times a year).

Jeunesse: Young People, Texts, Cultures. Winnipeg: University of Winnipeg Centre for Research in Young People's Texts and Culture. ISSN 1920-2601 (semiannual).

Kirkus Reviews: Adult, Young Adult, and Children's Book Reviews. Austin, TX: Kirkus Media. ISSN 1948-7428 (monthly).

Knowledge Quest. Chicago: American Library Association. ISSN 1094-9046 (five times a year).

Lambda Book Report. Washington, DC: Lambda Literary Foundation. ISSN 1048-9487 (quarterly).

Library Journal. New York: Library Journal. ISSN 0363-0277 (20 times a year).

Library Media Connection: Magazine for Secondary School Library Media and Technology Specialists. Vandalia, OH: Linworth. ISSN 1542-4715 (seven times a year)

Literature Film Quarterly. Salisbury, MD: Salisbury State College. ISSN 0090-4260 (quarterly).

Magazines for Libraries: For the General Reader and School, Junior College, University and Public Libraries. Ann Arbor, MI: ProQuest. ISSN 0000-0914 (annual).

Microform and Digitization Review. Munich: De Gruyter Saur. ISSN 2190-0752 (quarterly).

"Movie Review Query Engine." www.mrqe.com.

"Mystery Ink." www.mysteryinkonline.com.

New York Review of Books. New York: New York Review. ISSN 0028-7504 (20 times a year).

New York Times Book Review. New York: New York Times. ISSN 0028-7806 (weekly).

New Technical Books: A Selective List with Descriptive Annotations. New York: New York Public Library. ISSN 0028-6869 (bimonthly).

Notes. Canton, MA: Music Library Association. ISSN 0027-4380 (quarterly).

Publishers' Weekly: The International News Magazine of Book Publishing. New York: PWxyz. ISSN 0000-0019 (weekly).

Quarterly Review of Film and Video. Philadelphia: Routledge. ISSN 1050-9208 (five times a year).

Rolling Stone. New York: Rolling Stone. ISSN 0035-791X (biweekly).

SB&F: Your Guide to Science Resources for All Ages. Washington, DC: American Association for the Advancement of Science. ISSN 1533-5046 (bimonthly).

School Library Journal. New York: Media Source. ISSN 0362-8930 (monthly).

School Library Monthly. Kettering, OH: Libraries Unlimited. ISSN 2166-160X (eight times a year).

Science Books and Films: Your Guide to Science Resources for All Ages. Washington, DC: American Association for the Advancement of Science. ISSN 1533-5046 (bimonthly).

Serials Review. Oxford, UK: Elsevier. ISSN 0098-7913 (quarterly).

SF Site: The Home Page for Science Fiction and Fantasy. www.sfsite.com.

Sing Out! Bethlehem, PA: Sing Out Corp. ISSN 0037-5624 (quarterly).

Small Press Review (online). Paradise, CA: Dustbooks. ISSN 1949-2731 (bimonthly).

Teacher Librarian: The Journal for School Library Professionals. Lanham, MD: Scarecrow. ISSN 1481-1782 (five times a year).

Technology and Learning (online). San Bruno, CA: Newbay Media (monthly).

TLS: The Times Literary Supplement. London: Times Newspapers. ISSN 0307-661X (weekly).

Video Choice. Peterborough, NH: Connell Communications. ISSN 0896-2871 (monthly).

Video Librarian: The Video Review Guide for Libraries. Seabeck, WA: Video Librarian. ISSN 0087-6851 (bimonthly).

Voice of Youth Advocates: The Library Magazine Serving Those Who Serve Young Adults. Bowie, MD: E. L. Kurdyla. ISSN 160-4201 (bimonthly).

Sample Collection Development Policy Statements

Denver Public Library
Collection Development Policy

Last revised September 2012

1. Mission Statement

The Denver Public Library connects people with information, ideas, and experiences to provide enjoyment, enrich lives, and strengthen our community.

2. Purpose of Collection Development Policy

The Collection Development Policy, approved by the Library Commission, is one of the Library's fundamental policy documents. It outlines the philosophies that create and shape the Denver Public Library's unique collection, the practices that maintain it over time and the guidelines that help the collection respond to community needs while protecting the collection from societal and political pressures. The Collection Development Policy ensures that over time, the Denver Public Library's collection will remain on course, reflecting the needs of Denver's community, while creating unique experiences of meaning and inspiration for the individual customer.

3. Philosophy and Scope of the Collection

The Denver Public Library collects materials, in a variety of popular formats, which support its function as a major information source for the demanding needs of a metropolitan population. The collection also serves the popular and

Reprinted with the permission of the Denver Public Library.

recreational needs of the general public, and reflects the racial, ethnic and cultural diversity of the community.

Customer use is the most powerful influence on the Library's collection. Circulation, customer purchase requests and holds levels are all closely monitored, triggering the purchase of new items and additional copies of high demand items. The other driving force is the Library's strategic plan.

In addition to customer demand, selections are made to provide depth and diversity of viewpoints to the existing collection and to build the world-class Western History/Genealogy and African American Research Library collections. The Denver Public Library collects to the research level in the following areas: Western History, Genealogy, Federal Government Publications and African American History in Colorado and the Rocky Mountain West.

Inherent in the collection development philosophy is an appreciation for each customer of the Denver Public Library. The Library provides materials to support each individual's journey, and does not place a value on one customer's needs or preferences over another's. The Library upholds the right of the individual to access information, even though the content may be controversial, unorthodox or unacceptable to others.

Materials for children and teenagers are intended to broaden their vision, support recreational reading, encourage and facilitate reading skills, supplement their educational needs, stimulate and widen their interests, lead to recognition and appreciation of literature and reflect the diversity of the community. The reading and viewing activity of children is ultimately the responsibility of parents, who guide and oversee their own children's development. The Denver Public Library does not intrude on that relationship.

4. Scope of the Central Library

The Central Library contains the core fiction and nonfiction collections for the Library system and includes material of an enduring nature as well as current-interest materials.

Central Library collections include information in multiple formats and represent the diverse viewpoints and interests of the community the Library serves. The Reference collection contains current and historical non-circulating publications, including many periodicals, to support extensive and in-depth reference service for the general public, students and businesspeople.

5. Scope of the Branch Libraries

Branch libraries serve the needs of the communities in which they are located. Library staff regularly evaluate the collection to ensure its relevance. Collections of the branch libraries concentrate on materials of high interest and materials that support the Library's strategic goals. Branch collections are shaped, in part, by customer use through the floating collection system, in which items move freely among library locations rather than being owned by a specific location.

6. Scope of the Online Collection

The online collection represents the diverse viewpoints and interests of the entire community the Library serves. This collection includes citation and full-text databases; eBooks and other downloadable and streaming media; and instructional programs.

7. Scope of Special Collections

WESTERN HISTORY AND GENEALOGY

The Western History/Genealogy Department collects to the research level original and secondary materials in a variety of formats in the following subject areas: history of the trans-Mississippi West, genealogy, conservation and the 10th Mountain Division. The Department is also the repository of the Library's institutional archives. Other collections housed in the Western History/Genealogy Department include the Eugene Field Collection, the Ross-Barrett Historical Aeronautics Collection, the Douglas Collection of Fine Printing and Binding and Denver Municipal and Denver Regional Documents.

FEDERAL GOVERNMENT PUBLICATIONS

The Denver Public Library is a selective depository in the Federal Depository Library Program. The government documents collection provides information about the past and present operation and activities of the United States Government and public access to authoritative information from government sources. The collection level is aimed at a general audience consisting of engaged citizens and residents, businesspeople and students of all ages.

BLAIR-CALDWELL AFRICAN AMERICAN RESEARCH LIBRARY

The Blair-Caldwell African American Research Library collects materials on the history, literature, art, music, sports, religion and politics of African Americans in Colorado and the Rocky Mountain West. By collecting primary and secondary source materials such as archival papers, photographs, periodicals, artwork, books, and artifacts for the research collection as well as for the museum, the Library documents the African American experience from the Five Points neighborhood to the trans-Mississippi West.

8. Selection Criteria

Collection development staff use their training, knowledge and expertise along with the following general criteria to select materials for the collection:

* Relevance to interests and needs of the community
* Extent of publicity, critical review and current or anticipated demand
* Current or historical significance of the author or subject
* Local significance of the author or subject
* Relevance to the existing collection's strengths and weaknesses
* Reputation and qualifications of the author, publisher or producer, with preference generally given to titles vetted in the editing and publishing industry
* Suitability of format to Library circulation and use
* Date of publication
* Price, availability and Library materials budget

9. Customer Recommendations

Customers may request items the Library does not own. Each request is reviewed for inclusion in the collection or for loan through Interlibrary Loan. Staff determine the best method for delivery of materials using the selection criteria.

10. Requests for Reconsideration

The Denver Public Library selects material using established criteria and full consideration of the varying age groups and backgrounds of customers. Requests for removal of items from the collection may be made using a formal procedure outlined in Appendix 5.

11. Collection Management

PHILOSOPHY OF COLLECTION MANAGEMENT

The Library's collection is a living, changing entity. As items are added, others are reviewed for their ongoing value and sometimes withdrawn from the collection. Great care is taken to retain or replace items that have enduring value to the community. Decisions are influenced by patterns of use, the capacity of each location and the holdings of other libraries that may specialize in a given subject matter. Staff review the collection regularly to maintain its vitality and usefulness to the community.

RESPONSIBILITY FOR COLLECTION MANAGEMENT

The final authority for the Library collection rests with the Library Commission. Implementation of collection development policy and management of the collection is assigned to Library staff. The Denver Public Library disposes of materials that have been withdrawn according to the criteria for weeding and withdrawal outlined below. The Friends Foundation serves as an instrument for the Library, reselling and redistributing Library materials that are withdrawn from the collection or donated to the Library and designated by the Library for resale.

CRITERIA FOR WEEDING AND WITHDRAWAL

The following criteria are used in selecting materials for withdrawal:

- Damage or poor condition
- Number of copies in the collection
- Relevance to the needs and interest of the community
- Current demand and frequency of use
- Accuracy and timeliness
- Local interest
- Relevance to Denver Public Library's research collections
- Availability elsewhere including other libraries and online
- Deemed to be of an enduring nature

In addition, staff use the following guidelines for the withdrawal and sale of items from special collections:

- Legal restrictions, possession of valid title and the donor's intent
- Relevance to the scope of the special collections

When a statement of a donor's preferences accompanies an acquisition, any departure from it is carefully considered and negotiated with the donor or the donor's heirs or settled by appropriate legal procedures. For an item withdrawn from special collections including rare books, artwork, photographs, antiquarian maps, and archival materials, the Library will document its disposition.

Sale of withdrawn items will be carried out in the manner most advantageous to the Library. This may entail a relationship with a dealer, auction house or other institution. Staff will deposit the proceeds from the sale of items back into special collection funds. In accordance with Denver City rules regarding the sale of municipal property, Library employees cannot privately acquire materials from a special collection.

GIFTS

The Denver Public Library accepts donations of books and other materials. The Library retains the authority to accept or reject gifts. Library staff and/or representatives of the Friends Foundation make all decisions as to the use, housing and final disposition of donations. The Library does not evaluate or appraise gift materials for tax purposes.

APPENDIX 1

Statements Endorsed by the Library Commission

In August 2012, the Denver Public Library Commission reaffirmed its endorsement of the American Library Association Library Bill of Rights.

APPENDIX 2

Western History and Genealogy Collections

WESTERN HISTORY

The Western History Collection encompasses primary and secondary source material of the trans-Mississippi West with special focus on the Rocky Mountain region.

Primary sources include:

> *Manuscript Collection*—personal papers, family papers, records of organizations and architectural records

> *Maps*—primarily of the 22 contiguous states west of the Mississippi River, plus Alaska and Hawaii

Photography Collection—chiefly original negatives and photo prints of photographers who documented the West, with the primary focus on the Rocky Mountain region

Art Collection—primarily works of original art and other illustrative materials of historical interest to the Rocky Mountain Region, and secondarily work by artists who lived in Colorado or who came to Colorado to work. The Library also acquires representative works of contemporary Colorado artists

Denver Municipal and Regional Documents—publications produced by Denver City and County agencies, and Denver regional agencies including RTD [Regional Transportation District] and DRCOG [Denver Regional Council of Governments]

Secondary sources include books, pamphlets and government publications covering such broad subjects as exploration and discovery, trappers and traders, frontier and pioneer life, Native Americans, railroads, mines and mining, livestock and ranching, trails and roads and many other subjects of a local and regional nature.

GENEALOGY

The Genealogy Collection focuses on United States source and research materials and international how-to guidebooks. The Library collects regional, state, county and local histories, and primary and secondary source materials such as cemetery, mortuary, tax, probate, census and vital records, and passenger and immigration lists. Media include print, electronic, and microfilm resources.

CONSERVATION

The Library collects conservation materials as they relate to the politics and preservation of natural resources. This includes primarily manuscripts, but also photos, books and ephemera. The Conservation Collection is national in scope, with a focus on the western United States.

10TH MOUNTAIN DIVISION

In association with History Colorado, the Library acquires the personal papers and records of the men and units of the World War II United States ski troops. This relationship is called the 10th Mountain Division Resource Center.

ROSS-BARRETT HISTORICAL AERONAUTICS COLLECTION

Focusing on commercial and general aviation, the Library has collected books and other materials that document the history of aeronautics through World War II. The Library is not currently collecting actively in this area.

DOUGLAS COLLECTION OF FINE PRINTING AND BINDING

The Library has collected examples of craftsmanship in the art of bookmaking, including books representing the best work in typography, papermaking and decoration, unique binding, and hand bookmaking as an art form. The Library is not currently collecting actively in this area.

HISTORY OF THE BOOK

The Library collects examples demonstrating the history of writing and printing. This includes representative examples of papyrus, incunabula, vellum, and historical first editions. The Library relies solely on donations to develop and conserve this collection.

APPENDIX 3

African American Research Library Collections

The research collection at the Blair-Caldwell African American Research Library encompasses primary and secondary source material of the African American experience in the trans-Mississippi West with special focus on the Rocky Mountain Region.

Primary sources include:

> *Archival collection*—personal papers, family papers, business archives, and the records of civic, social and religious organizations

> *Photography collection*—original negatives and photo prints that document the African American experience in the West

> *Artwork and Museum collection*—art and artifacts that document and illustrate the history and contributions of African Americans in the trans-Mississippi West

Secondary sources include books, pamphlets, maps, government publications, and periodicals that support African American research and scholarship as well as genealogy and community programs.

APPENDIX 4

Federal Government Documents

The Denver Public Library has been a selective depository in the Federal Depository Library Program since 2009. Before that date, the Library was a regional depository for many years and has collected federal documents since the nineteenth century.

The base of the Library's selection profile is the *Suggested Core Collection* (Federal Depository Library Manual, Appendix A). Beyond these, item selections support the Library's general collection and fill the current and future needs of the community in formats that the Library can sustain. Priority is given to print and electronic formats in selection and retention decisions.

The Library selects items with documents in the following subject areas:

- Executive and legislative activities of the federal government, including hearings and annual reports
- Consumer protection
- Health
- Criminal justice
- Recreation, with an emphasis on Colorado and the Rocky Mountain West
- Historical monographs, with special emphasis on subjects included in the Western History and Genealogy collection
- Arts
- Energy
- Water issues
- Materials supporting the K–12 curriculum
- Materials about and of use to small business

Item categories that are not selected:

- Newsletters
- Directories
- Catalogs and bibliographies
- Forms (except IRS)
- Announcements
- Technical reports, notes, bulletins
- State-specific publications for states outside the Rocky Mountain West

Procedure for Request for Reconsideration

Library customers requesting reconsideration and removal of items in the collection may submit a Request for Reconsideration of Library Material form, which is available at any Library location. Staff review the request in relation to the Library's mission and selection criteria. The City Librarian reviews the request and replies within thirty days of receipt of the request. The item in question will not be removed from the shelf during the reconsideration process.

University of Minnesota Libraries
Collection Development Policy for the Institute on the Environment

Revised February 2010

Selector

[name and contact information]

Web Page

http://environment.umn.edu/

Primary Departments and Research Centers

Institute on the Environment (IonE)

Programs include: Dialogue Earth, Global Landscapes Initiative, Initiative for Renewable Energy and the Environment, NorthStar Initiative for Sustainable Enterprise, River Life

Other affiliations: Acara Institute
Environmental Sciences, Policy and Management (ESPM), www.espm.umn.edu

Degree Programs Supported

IonE

Sustainability Studies Minor, which includes a core course titled "Sustainable People, Sustainable Planet," interdepartmental electives, and a project-based capstone course. Graduate fellowships in the IonE are also awarded.

ESPM

Undergraduate degrees in the following tracks:

- Conservation and Resource Management
- Corporate Environmental Management
- Environmental Education and Communication

- Environmental Science
- Policy, Planning, Law and Society

Minors
- Environmental Sciences, Policy and Management
- Environment and Natural Resources Minor
- Corporate Environmental Management Minor

Background

The IonE focuses its research around three grand challenges: 1) energy, 2) food, land and ecosystems, 3) freshwater.

At this point, neither the IonE nor ESPM is the home to faculty members. The IonE has 20 part time faculty fellows who rotate in and out, and ESPM draws faculty from several College of Food, Agricultural, and Natural Resources Sciences departments. This means that much of the material in this area is purchased by other selectors.

Specific Areas of Emphasis

Algae
Bioenergy and bioproducts
Biofuels
Biomaterials
Carbon sequestration
Chemical catalysis
Conservation and energy efficiency
Environmental policy
Hydrogen production, storage
    and use

Land use and stewardship
Mississippi River
Next generation feedstocks
Policy, economics, and ecosystems
Renewable energy
Solar energy
Tools to analyze large datasets
Transportation fuels
Wind, hydro, and geothermal energy

User Communities

The IonE has strong ties to industry, and many of their projects have multiple industry partners. They also have a large community outreach component.

Areas Shared with Other Libraries

- Bio-Medical Library—public health
- Entomology, Fisheries and Wildlife Library—numerous
- Forestry Library—numerous
- Walter Library—environmental engineering, water, sustainability, green chemistry
- Wilson Library—policy, government documents, maps

Core Databases

- BIOSIS Previews
- CAB Abstracts
- Environmental Sciences & Pollution Management
- Geobase
- SciFinder
- Water Resources Abstracts
- Web of Science

Pennsylvania State University Libraries
Collection Development Policy

History

Latest revision: July 1, 2007

Principal Selector

[name and contact information]

I. Purpose and Programs Supported

The History fund provides primary support for the curricular and research needs of faculty and students in the History Department. The Department offers an undergraduate major and minor, and an M.A. degree en route to a Ph.D. The fund supports 40–50 faculty, 60–70 graduate students, and over 300 undergraduate minors in the History Department, as well as an indeterminate number of scholars in other disciplines whose research employs historical materials, including African-American Studies, American Literature, Classics and Ancient Mediterranean Studies, Communication Arts and Sciences, Comparative Literature, Film, History of the Book, Philosophy, Political Science, Science, Medicine, and Technology in Culture, and Women's Studies. The Religious Studies Program, administratively housed within the Department of History, is primarily supported by the Religion fund.

The History Department offers a broad curriculum of undergraduate and graduate courses, and sustains a robust program of faculty and student research. In addition to national and region-based history, subjects include:

> History of Religion, Diaspora Studies, Comparative Colonialism, Women and Gender History, Political and Diplomatic History, Cultural and Social History, Military History, Economic History, Labor History, Environmental History, and History of Science, Technology, and Society

Collection development is focused on acquiring materials that match Penn State's History course offerings and research interests. Current areas of Faculty strength include the early modern period, the US Civil War era, and modern society. The Department has also developed faculty concentrations in thematic areas which cut across geographical or chronological lines, such as gender, the African Diaspora (including Latin America and the Caribbean), and empire and colonialism. In conjunction with the Department of Classics and Ancient Mediterranean Studies, Penn State also has a strong emphasis on Ancient history. The history selector works collaboratively with other selectors to ensure interdisciplinary needs are met.

ADDITIONAL SOURCES OF SUPPORT

Many subject specialists acquire materials related to the history of the discipline they collect for (e.g., Medicine, Anthropology, Education). Additional materials of value to historians are acquired through communication and cooperation with selectors across the libraries, including: African and African American Studies, Archaeology, Art, Asian Studies, Classics and Ancient Mediterranean Studies, Comparative Literature, English, Ethnic Studies, Global Studies, Jewish Studies, Latin American Studies, Law, Lesbian, Gay, Bisexual, and Transgender Studies, Middle East Studies, Politics and Government, and Religious Studies.

In addition to subject-based funds, historians rely on material purchased by related Penn State libraries including the Business Library, the News and Microforms Library, the Social Sciences Library, the Maps Library, and the Special Collections Library. Certain history of science courses depend upon the science library collections.

II. General Collection Guidelines

Location of Materials: Physical collections acquired using [History] funds are ordinarily housed at University Park. The History subject specialist consults and cooperates with subject specialists at Penn State campus libraries to ensure coverage of needed research materials at all locations.

Languages: English is the most commonly collected language, with important primary and secondary works in modern languages collected including German, French, Spanish, and to a lesser degree, Italian and Russian. Works in Chinese and Japanese are often acquired in cooperation with the Asian Studies librarian (see the collection policy statement for Asian Studies). Other languages are selectively acquired in consultation with researchers working in these areas, with an emphasis on acquiring core works, reference materials such as directories, biographies, etc. . . . , and collections of primary source documents.

Chronological Guidelines: Acquiring recent in-print publications takes priority. However, older, out-of-print materials are frequently pursued to fill gaps in the collections as they are discovered. Ordinarily no preference will be given to original printings over reprints.

Geographical Guidelines: Collecting follows the University's research and teaching emphases, with significant current concentrations in Asia, Latin America and the Caribbean, Western Europe, and the United States. Collecting of materials concerning Eastern Europe, Canada, and modern Africa mirrors the evolving emphases of the Department. Materials related to Pennsylvania history are collected extensively.

Weeding and Deselection: By definition historians retain an interest in older materials long after they lose value in most other disciplines. To support historical research it is understood that acquired materials will ordinarily be retained indefinitely in the collection. In the event of de-selection, preference will be given to retaining works that are unique to Penn State (or held by few other libraries), and works in subject areas where Penn State has developed in-depth collections.

III. Types of Materials Collected

The collection is developed to support teaching and research in higher education. Regardless of format, academic publications are the focus.

Monographs form the largest portion of the collection and include university press books, trade publications, conference proceedings, etc. Facsimile reproductions, anthologies, and other collections of English-language primary source documents are collected selectively as needed for teaching. These materials may be collected in greater depth for languages other than English where we lack the original documents.

Journals: Scholarly journals publishing research throughout the sub-disciplines of History are acquired in all relevant languages. Subscriptions to new journals are initiated after careful review and in consultation with the History faculty.

Theses and Dissertations from institutions other than Penn State are acquired in limited numbers, typically on a case by case basis upon request.

Archival Materials including rare books, original manuscripts, broadsides, interviews, and other unpublished materials, which are not in microform, are the primary responsibility of Special Collections and are covered by separate collection statements.

Microforms including primary source materials, manuscript collections, periodical and newspaper backfiles, and other items unavailable or too expensive in hard copy are often acquired on microform (microfilm, microfiche, etc). Additional microform collections are purchased as funds permit. Often such purchases are possible only when additional funds are available through endowed library funds, Arts and Humanities Group funds, or other sources.

Government Documents are acquired and managed by the Government Documents Librarian. See the statement for the U.S. federal government Depository Program.

Maps and Atlases are primarily the responsibility of the Maps selector. Additional cartographic materials may be purchased on the History fund.

Historical News Sources are typically acquired on microfilm, or more recently, online. The Communications selector has primary responsibility for current newspaper subscriptions. History funds are used to acquire retrospective archives of older publications as funds permit. For online, databases that provide facsimile page images are preferred over those that provide text only.

Reference Works including bibliographies, dictionaries and encyclopedias, directories, indexes and abstracts are collected extensively in print and online to support faculty and student research.

Films are acquired primarily to support curricular interests in the Department.

Electronic Resources are acquired for most formats, particularly scholarly journals, reference works, and collections of historical documents such as *Early American Imprints* or *Eighteenth Century Collections Online*.

The following types of materials are not ordinarily collected: minor revisions and reprints of works, works on poor quality paper, and juvenile literature. Textbooks, anthologies, and popular level publications are acquired selectively when they relate to research and teaching in the Department. Genealogical materials are not collected excepting resources relevant to historical researchers such as the U.S. Census Manuscripts, or selected items documenting central Pennsylvania history.

IV: Other General Considerations

All selectors are guided by the Collection Development Guideline adopted by the Dean's Library Council in 2001. In addition the Collection Development Council has begun working on Core Principles to guide the overall development of the collection.

V: Collection Levels

The levels below reflect existing collection strengths, which are heavily influenced by the cumulative impact of prior collection decisions. It is not a statement of desirable future collection levels. These will evolve with the interests of historical scholars. Collecting patterns and strengths within the broad categories are in the "Comments" column.

(F = non-English language collection level; E = English language collection level)

Subject	Collection Level	Comments
Auxiliary Sciences of History	3	See also the appropriate collection policy statements for CC (Archaeology), CJ (Numismatics) and CN (Inscriptions, Epigraphy).
History, General	4E 3F	
Great Britain	4	
France	4E 3F	
Germany	4E 3F	
Mediterranean, Greco-Roman World		See the Statement for Classics and Ancient Mediterranean Studies. Modern history of the region is collected at Level 3E and level 2F.
Italy	4E 3F	See also the Collection Statement for Classics and Ancient Mediterranean Studies.
Netherlands & Belgium	3	
Eastern Europe, Balkans	3E 2F	Acquisitions relating to the Ottoman Empire have recently increased.

Subject	Collection Level	Comments
Russia, U.S.S.R.	4E 3F	
Northern Europe, Scandinavia	3	Emphasis on trade and relations in the early modern world
Spain	4	See also the Spanish Collection Development Policy.
Portugal	3	
Asia	4E 3F	Acquisitions have strengthened since the 1990s with an emphasis on China, Japan, and India.
Middle East	4E 3F	
Africa	4	
Indians, North America	4	
United States	4	All time periods, with an emphasis on slavery and the Civil War Era, African-American history, women's history
New England, Atlantic Coast	4	Pennsylvania history collected at near Level 5
Southern U.S., Gulf States	4	
Midwest, Mississippi Valley	3	
The West	3	Increasing emphasis since early 2000s in conjunction with new Latino/a Studies minor
Latin America	3	Areas closer to Level 4 include Mexico, the Caribbean, and topics such as African Diaspora, colonialism.
Canada	2	

VI: Priorities for Future Collection Efforts

- Continue to pay special attention to women's history and African-American history.
- Support new areas of interest in the Department such as Latino/a Borderlands Studies, and Ottoman History.

- Expand subjects collected at Level 3 and 4 in languages other than English.
- Continued purchase of microform and online primary source materials
- Expand upon current strengths in historical newspapers from the United States and Pennsylvania to include more international titles, and titles from minority populations in the United States.

VII: Related Collection Policies . . .

The Paideia School Elementary Library
Atlanta, Georgia

(Revised June 2012)

About the Library

PURPOSE OF THE LIBRARY

The Elementary Library program is a community-wide resource used by parents, teachers, and students. It supports children's independent reading and research as well as their classroom activities. The elementary school library curriculum emphasizes reading for pleasure and the metacognitive skills involved in reading comprehension. The program introduces children to the care and parts of books, reference sources, search skills, a wide array of fiction and non-fiction, the Caldecott and Newbery awards, the concepts of authorship and publication, and the role of libraries in a democracy. As students progress through the elementary school, they develop increasingly sophisticated approaches to research in a variety of media, both in the library and online. Most elementary classes come to the library on a weekly basis throughout the year. The upper elementary classes also come for specially focused units that include information literacy activities to foster effective, critical and ethical use of information. In addition to scheduled classes, individuals drop in throughout the school day for research and pleasure reading needs. Our goal is to prepare students to become lifelong learners who are confident users of information and who love reading for pleasure.

ROLE OF LIBRARIAN

Librarians need to be masters of every aspect of the school curriculum. They must be informed in all areas to keep teachers, administrators and students up to date on the newest and best in books, other materials and technological education practices. The library should be the showcase for information literacy, engaged learning, problem-based learning, and technology use in the everyday school. The librarian should demonstrate educational leadership in all areas of learning.

COMMUNITY DESCRIPTION

There are approximately 330 elementary students at Paideia who range in age from 5 to 13, plus 48 in the Half Day program, and the library collects with all

Reprinted with the permission of the Paideia School/Natalie Bernstein.

their needs in mind. Their skill levels range from non-readers to those who are reading far beyond the sixth grade level. The students represent a diverse array of learning styles, backgrounds, races and religions and come from neighborhoods throughout the Atlanta area.

COLLECTION DEVELOPMENT PLAN AND RESPONSIBILITY FOR SELECTION

The library collects materials to support the curriculum at all levels. Selection is based on extensive consultation between the librarian and the teachers; close communication is essential in developing a collection that is relevant to the curriculum. The library subscribes to multiple reviewing journals in print and online. The librarian is responsible for selecting materials, building and maintaining the collection.

CRITERIA FOR SELECTION

The following criteria will be used in consideration of the purchase of materials and the acceptance of gifts:

- objectives of instructional program
- timeliness and/or permanence
- relevance
- quality of the writing/production
- overall purpose
- authority
- reputation and significance of author/editor/artist
- reputation of publisher/producer/distributor
- format
- favorable review from professional reviewing aid
- developmental appropriateness
- favorable review from other media
- content-appropriate
- diversity
- requests from students, faculty and parents
- cost

The library uses the following reviewing sources in making selection decisions:

- *School Library Journal*
- *Horn Book*
- *Booklist*
- *Booklinks*
- *The New York Times*
- online reviewing sources from ALA and ALSC

COLLECTION DEVELOPMENT GOALS

Priorities for the current year include the following:

> building the science collection with help from resources of the National Science Teachers Association;

> deepening the collection of bibliotherapy titles for children and for adults: divorce, death, adoption, anxiety, learning disabilities, and mindfulness practices;

> adding to the graphic novels collection to meet demand.

I continue to seek books that reflect the diversity of our community, reviewing each outgoing order to ensure that it has a strong percentage of titles representing people of color, a strength of our collection.

Intellectual Freedom/Access Statements

The school library plays a unique role in promoting intellectual freedom. It serves as a point of voluntary access to information and ideas and as a learning laboratory for students as they acquire critical thinking and problem solving skills needed in a pluralistic society. Members of the school community involved in the collection development process employ educational criteria to select resources unfettered by their personal, political, social or religious views. Students and educators served by the school library have access to resources and services free of constraints resulting from personal, partisan or doctrinal approval. School librarians resist efforts by individuals to define what is appropriate for all students or teachers to read, view or hear. Library policies support free and open access to information.

Challenge Policy

Should a member of the school community object to the presence of any material in the library, the following steps will be taken:

> The patron will be asked to write a letter that includes a statement he or she has read the work in full and has read the library's selection policy; and which includes a specific description of what is offensive in the work.

> The Library Use Committee, comprised of an administrator, the librarians, two faculty members and the chair-parents of Friends of The Library will then review the work, considering carefully the written complaint.

If the work is from the Elementary collection, the Committee will then determine if the work should remain part of the elementary collection; be held on reserve in the elementary collection; be moved to the upper school collection; or be removed from the library. If the work is from the Junior High/High School collection, the Committee will then determine if the work should remain part of that collection; be held on reserve in the high school collection; or be removed from the library.

Confidentiality Statement

Circulation records and other records identifying the names of library users are confidential in nature. Every effort will be made to protect this confidentiality by staff and volunteers.

Access. The ability or right to gain entry to and use an electronic product or service.

Accrual accounting method. An accounting method that reports revenues and expenses when they are incurred, regardless of when cash is exchanged. *See also* **Cash accounting method.**

Acid-free. Materials with a pH value of 7.0 (neutral) or greater (alkaline).

Acquisition. (1) The process of obtaining and receiving physical library materials or access to online resources. (2) The organizational unit within a library that handles the acquisitions function. (3) The item acquired by a library.

Agent. An individual or company that acts as an intermediary between a library and a publisher in the purchase of materials, e.g., a subscription service that manages periodical subscriptions. *See also* **Vendor.**

Aggregated package. A package of content based on agreements between various publishers and the aggregator. The content is not necessarily stable; titles may change as agreements between the aggregator and publishers change.

Aggregator. (1) A third party that provides access to the full text of periodicals, articles, books, or media originally published by multiple publishers and provides online access through a common interface or search engine. (2) More broadly, an organization, individual, or application that gathers content from multiple sources for presentation elsewhere.

Aggregator database. The searchable collection of digitized materials produced by an aggregator.

Agreement. A legally binding understanding between two parties, often documented in a written contract. In the licensing context, this term may be capitalized (i.e., "Agreement"), in which case it refers to the contract (along with any appendixes, amendments, or exhibits) that codifies the parties' understanding about access to and use of the digital information resources.

Allocation. (1) The dollar amount distributed to fund lines in the budget. (2) The process of distributing financial resources.

Alternative literature. Publications not part of the dominate culture and not sharing the perspectives and beliefs of that culture.

Alternative press. A small, independent publisher. Alternative presses often address social issues and the interests of minority and diverse populations and publish innovative and experimental works.

Appropriation. Funds granted through formal action by a controlling or funding authority.

Approval plan. Method of acquiring library materials, usually books. The vendor supplies books automatically, according to a profile from the library, which may keep or return the books to the vendor. Some plans provide advance print or online notifications instead of sending the physical item. *See also* **Blanket order.**

Approval profile. *See* **Profile.**

Archivally sound. A nontechnical term describing a material or product that is permanent, durable, free of contaminants, and chemically stable. No formal standards exist that describe how long "archivally sound" material will last.

Archive. A repository of information. *See also* **Dark archive**, **Light archive.**

Archive copy. A copy of a work, in printed or digital format, preserved for future use.

Assessment. *See* **Collection assessment.**

Audit. The systematic evaluation of procedures, operations, and cash records to establish whether they conform to established financial criteria.

Authentication. A process by which a computer system verifies the identity of a user accessing the system or source of communication. Some common methods of authentication are passwords and user IDs, Internet protocol (IP) addresses, and public keys and digital certificates. In security systems, authentication is distinct from authorization. Authentication confirms that the individual is who he or she claims to be but does not address authorization.

Authorization. A process that gives or denies an individual access rights to an online resource based on his or her identity, which often is matched against a directory with various profiles granting various types of access. Most computer security systems are based on a twostep process: authentication, followed by authorization.

Authorized signature. The signature by a person with authority and power to represent and legally bind a party to a written agreement.

Authorized use. (1) The specific product use rights and capabilities authorized under the terms of the license; may also be referred to as "Permitted Use." (2) Use of copyrighted material in a way permitted by work's rights holder.

Authorized user. A person or entity authorized by the licensor to access and use an electronic product or service under the terms of the license. *See also* **Unauthorized user.**

Author-side fee. Fee charged by some open-access journals when accepting an article for publication to cover the costs of production. Fees are usually paid by the author's institution or employer, or through the grant funding the research. Fees may be waived because of financial hardship.

A-Z list. A listing of a library's electronic serials, databases, or e-book collections, usually available via the library's website and providing direct links from the entry to the item.

Back file or **back run.** Issues of a periodical that precede the current issue.

Backlist. A publisher's list of older but still available books.

Balanced scorecard. A performance metric used in strategic planning and management to monitor and improve various internal functions and their resulting external outcomes. The balanced scorecard attempts to measure and provide feedback to organizations to assist implementation of strategies and objectives; it is also used to report progress to stakeholders.

Banned book. A book that has been prohibited or suppressed by a governing or religious authority because its content is considered objectionable or dangerous (or both), usually for moral, political, or cultural reasons. *See also* **Censorship, Intellectual freedom.**

Bibliographer. (1) A subject specialist in a large library whose primary or sole responsibility is selecting for and managing a collection; may be used interchangeably with selector. (2) One who conducts research about books.

Bibliographic utility. An online service that provides a shared database of cataloging records created by member libraries. The database may be used for copy cataloging, interlibrary loan, selection, and bibliographic verification.

Bibliometrics. The use of mathematical and statistical methods to study the usage of materials and services within a library, or to analyze the historical development of a specific body of literature. *See also* **Citation analysis.**

Big Deal. A publisher's license agreement, often multiyear, that provides access to all or a substantial portion of titles from a single publisher at a cost less than the sum of the titles purchased individually. Usually, libraries have limited ability to select titles, and cancelling titles before the end of the contract period results in financial penalties.

Blanket order. An order placed with a publisher, vendor, or distributor to supply automatically all publications that match a profile. Blanket orders can be for a single publisher's series, all publications of an individual publisher, or all materials of a particular type or subject. Most blanket orders do not allow returns.

Book distributor. *See* **Vendor.**

Bookseller. A person or company in the business of selling new or used books and related materials to the retail trade. *See also* **Dealer, Vendor.**

Born digital. Materials that originate in digital form.

Brand. (1) The cumulative perceptions about an organization, company, or product. (2) A name, term, sign, symbol, or design used to identify a company, product, or service.

Breach. Failure to perform an obligation set forth in a contract.

Brittleness. Fragility of paper due to acid-caused deterioration. The standard test for brittleness in paper is whether a corner can withstand folding in each direction twice.

Budget. (1) A plan for the use of money available during a fiscal year, reflecting allocations, expected revenues, and projected expenditures. (2) A document reporting the total amount of funds available to meet an organization's projected expenditures over a fixed period of time. This budget document shows the amounts allocated to fund lines as well as fund balances and encumbrances brought forward from the previous year. *See also* **Materials budget.**

Bundling. (1) The practice of providing a group of serial or monographic titles to a library. (2) The practice of providing access to an online version packaged with subscription to the print version, or vice versa.

Cancellation. The termination of a subscription, standing order, or firm order.

Capital budget. A plan to finance long-term outlays, such as for fixed assets like facilities and equipment.

Capital expenditure, also **capital expense.** An expenditure made on a one-time basis, expected to benefit more than the current period, and recorded as an asset. Library materials expenditures are usually capitalized, except in the case of expenditures for the rights to access an online resource.

Cash accounting method. A method of bookkeeping that records transactions when a cash exchange has taken place, that is, when an account is paid, not when an expense in incurred.

Censorship. Suppression or prohibition of the production, distribution, circulation, or display of a work on grounds that it contains objectionable or dangerous material. Censored materials may be deemed objectionable on moral, political, military, or other grounds. *See also* **Banned book.**

Challenge. A request made by an individual or group that a book or other library material should be removed from the library.

Circulation analysis. Examination of statistics compiled on the circulation of library materials, usually broken down by classification, material type, category of borrower, time of year, and so on, to determine patterns of usage.

Citation analysis. A bibliometric technique that examines the works cited in publications to determine frequency and patterns of use. Two methods are counting the number of times a journal title appears in footnotes and bibliographies, and counting the number of times a title is cited by local faculty.

Clapp-Jordan formula. A method developed by Verner W. Clapp and Robert T. Jordan to calculate the total number of volumes required for minimum-level collection adequacy in an academic library.

Classed analysis. A format for collection analysis that describes the collection and, perhaps, current collecting levels and desired future collecting levels in abbreviated language and numerical codes, according to a classification scheme.

Client-centered. *See* **User-centered.**

Closed stack. A shelving area in a library to which only library staff members have access. Also called closed shelves and closed access.

Collection. A group of materials assembled by a library or individual. A library collection consists of both physical items held by the library and digital resources (local and online) selected and organized by the library and accessed by library users and staff members.

Collection assessment. Systematic quantitative and qualitative measurement of the degree to which a library's collections meet the library's goals and objectives and the needs of its users. *See also* **Collection evaluation.**

Collection-centered analysis. An analysis method that focuses on the collection itself, not on its users.

Collection condition survey. A detailed survey of the physical nature and condition of a collection.

Collection development. Originally denoted activities involved in developing a library collection in response to institutional priorities and user needs and interests—that is, the selection of materials to build a collection. Collection development was understood to cover several activities related to the development of library collections, including selection, determination and coordination of policies, needs assessment, collection use studies, collection analysis, budget management, community and user outreach and liaison, and planning for resource sharing. Now often used interchangeably with or in combination with collection management.

Collection development officer (CDO). The individual within a library charged with managing or overseeing collections-related activities. This person may also have an organizational title such as assistant university librarian for collection development, assistant librarian for collections, or collections coordinator.

Collection development policy, collection development and management policy, or **collection policy.** A formal written statement of the principles guiding a library's selection of books and other materials, including the criteria used in selection, deselection, and acceptance of gifts. It may also address intellectual freedom, future goals, and special areas of attention.

Collection evaluation. Systematic consideration of a collection to determine its intrinsic merit. Evaluation seeks to examine or describe collections either in their own terms or in relation to other collections and checking mechanisms (lists, standards, etc.). *See also* **Collection assessment.**

Collection management. Proposed in the 1980s as a term under which collection development was to be subsumed. In this construct, collection management includes collection development and an expanded suite of decisions about withdrawal, transfer, cancelling subscriptions, storage, and preservation. Collection development and collection management now tend to be used synonymously or in tandem.

Collection mapping. A technique for graphically representing the strengths and weaknesses of a library collection used primarily in school library media centers. The categories of the collection map usually are based on the curricular needs of the school. *See also* **Conspectus.**

Collection profile. A statistical picture of collection at one point in time.

Common good. A specific good that is shared and beneficial for all (or most) members of a given community. *See also* **Public good.**

Compact shelving, also **compact storage.** A storage area for lesser-used materials employing stacks that either are designed with narrower aisles and higher-than-normal shelves or are mobile and can be compacted by moving together. Compact storage accommodates more materials than conventional stack arrangements.

Concurrent use. The simultaneous use of digital information by more than one user.

Conservation. Noninvasive physical or chemical methods employed to ensure the survival of manuscripts, books, and other documents. *See also* **Preservation, Restoration.**

Conservator. A specialist with advanced training in the arts and sciences related to the theoretical and practical aspects of conservation who is able to prescribe and undertake various physical and chemical procedures and techniques to ensure the preservation of materials.

Consortium. Two or more libraries that have formally agreed to coordinate, cooperate in, or consolidate certain functions. Consortia may be formed on the basis of geography, function, type, or subject.

Conspectus. A comprehensive collection survey instrument, first developed by the Research Libraries Group, to record existing collection strengths, current collecting intensities, and intended future intensities. It is arranged by subject, classification, or a combination of these two and contains standardized codes for languages of materials collected and for collection or collecting levels. Sometimes called collection mapping or inventory profiling.

Constituency. The users and potential users of a library.

Content provider. A supplier—generally a publisher, aggregator, or full-text host—that offers content for sale or lease to libraries.

Contingency fund. An amount set aside, usually at the beginning of the allocation process, in a budget to cover unexpected or unplanned expenditures and emergencies.

Contingency planning. The process of preparing a plan of action to be put into effect when prior arrangements become impossible or certain predetermined conditions arise.

Continuation order. *See* **Standing order.**

Contract. A formal, legally binding agreement between two or more parties; the writing (including any appendixes, amendments, or exhibits) that details the terms and conditions of a formal, legally binding agreement between two or more parties. *See also* **Agreement, License.**

Cooperative collection development. Sharing responsibilities among two or more libraries for the process of acquiring materials, developing collections, and managing the growth and maintenance of collections in a user- and cost-beneficial way.

Copyleft. A type of license that grants the freedom to use, extend, and redistribute a creative work and all derivative works for noncommercial purposes without charge.

Copyright. A legal regime that grants for a limited time exclusive rights to authors of original, creative works that are fixed in a tangible medium of expression and provides exceptions to those exclusive rights under certain circumstances. Copyright gives the author, the author's employer, or anyone to whom the author transfers his or her right the legal ability to control who may copy, adapt, distribute, publicly perform, or publicly display his or her work, subject to certain legal exceptions. In the United States, the current federal law is the Copyright Act of 1976, which is codified at Title 17 of the United States Code (17 U.S.C. §101, et seq.). *See also* **Fair use.**

Core collection. (1) A collection intended to meet the basic information needs of a library's primary user group. (2) A collection that represents the intellectual nucleus of a discipline.

Course pack. Copies of materials that an instructor assembles for student use.

Cure period. The time within which a party to a contract has to fix a contractual breach.

Curriculum mapping. The process of documenting by teacher, grade, and class what is taught over an academic year; the structured overview usually contains a timeline, content, units or broad activities, and perhaps applicable standards and benchmarks.

Customer service representative. The employee of a publisher, vendor, subscription agent, aggregator, or other supplier of content and services who is responsible for solving problems and meeting needs on a day-to-day basis. *See also* **Sales representative.**

Dark archive. A repository that protects digital content as a failsafe measure and that is to be used only if the content is not available elsewhere. *See also* **Light archive.**

Database. (1) A large store of digitized information, consisting of records of uniform format organized for ease and speed of search and retrieval and managed by a database management system. (2) In libraries, usually used to refer to a set of records that provide bibliographic information from indexes and abstracts, and that may or may not include full-text articles associated with the bibliographic information.

Data logger. An electronic device that measures environmental factors, such as temperature and humidity, that can be downloaded to a computer.

Deaccession. *See* **Withdrawal.**

Deacidification. Processes that chemically reduce the acid content of paper to a pH of 7.0 (neutral) or higher. Deacidification also may deposit an alkaline buffer intended to neutralize any acids that develop in the future.

Deacquisition. *See* **Withdrawal.**

Dealer. A individual or commercial company in the business of buying and selling new books, used books, and rare books for resale to libraries, collectors, and other booksellers. *See also* **Bookseller, Vendor.**

Deed of gift. A signed document stating the terms of agreement under which legal title to property, such as a gift to a library or archives, is transferred, voluntarily and without remuneration, by the donor to the recipient institution, with or without conditions.

Demand-driven acquisition. *See* **Patron-driven acquisition.**

Democratic planning. A cyclic planning process in which all units are requested to formulate their plans for program development on a regular schedule. The source of ideas rests with individuals and individual units, and these ideas are assembled into a coherent plan for the larger organization.

Deposit account. A fund managed by a content provider into which the library deposits money and against which it draws during the year rather than pay individual invoices as they are issued.

Depository library. (1) A U.S. library legally designated to receive, without charge, all or a portion of the government documents provided by the U.S. Government Printing Office and other federal agencies to the superintendent of documents for distribution under the Federal Depository Library Program. (2) A library legally designated to receive without charge all or a selected portion of publications from an international governmental organization, foreign government agency, or U.S. state.

Deselection. Usually applied to the process of identifying materials for withdrawal or subscriptions for cancellation. *See also* **Withdrawal.**

Desiderata file. A list of materials needed and wanted by a library, to be purchased when money is available or when the item is located.

Differential pricing. (1) The practice of charging different rates based on the geographic location of the customer library or the number of users, or both. (2) The practice of charging different rates to institutions and individuals.

Digital object. A data structure whose principal components are digital material, plus a unique identifier for this material.

Digital repository. A library or archive where digital content is stored and made accessible to a user community. Digital repositories may be open to all or require authentication. *See also* **Disciplinary repository, Institutional repository.**

Digital rights management (DRM). Access control technologies used by hardware manufacturers, publishers, copyright holders, and individuals to limit the use of digital content and devices. DRM is intended to control access to, track, and limit uses of digital works.

Digitization. The process of converting analog materials to digital format.

Direct order. An order placed with a publisher instead of with a vendor or other supplier.

Disaster preparedness plan or **disaster response plan.** Procedures prepared in advance by a library to deal with an unexpected occurrence (flood, fire, earthquake, building failure, etc.) that has the potential to cause injury to people or damage to equipment, collections, and facilities. *See also* **Contingency plan.**

Disciplinary repository. A digital repository hosting the research output of a field or discipline. *See also* **Institutional repository.**

Disclaimer. A statement denying responsibility for a particular action. *See also* **Warranty.**

Discretionary purchase. An individual order for an item or items placed by library that is outside of any existing approval plan, blanket order plan, serial subscription, or other nondiscretionary purchase. *See also* **Firm order.**

Document delivery. The provision of documents upon request. Commercial document delivery services charge a fee to provide libraries or individuals with the requested item. The commercial service usually manages payments to publishers for copying rights.

E-book (electronic book). A digital object specifically designed to be accessible online and read on either a handheld device or personal computer.

E-book reader, also **e-book device, e-reader.** A handheld electronic device designed primarily for the purpose of downloading and reading e-books and e-periodicals.

EDI. *See* **Electronic data interchange.**

Eigenfactor. A technique for assessing the significance or influence of an article by using an iterative ranking scheme to weight top journals more heavily.

E-journal. An electronic journal; periodical literature that is made available as an individual title via an electronic medium.

Electronic data interchange (EDI). The transmission of data between organizations by electronic means; often used in the library environment to facilitate ordering and invoicing using the Internet and a library's integrated library system.

Electronic resources management (ERM) system. An automated system that tracks a library's e-content and manages details involved with its acquisition, including subscription and licensing, usage, cost, access tracking, and data gathering.

Embargo. A limitation on access to a resource, placed by the publisher on distributors of the publisher's data, usually to prevent the cancellation of individual subscriptions. For example, a publisher's own website provides current issues of their e-publications, but an aggregator's website provides only issues older than one year. The length of the embargo varies by publisher and is called a moving wall.

Emergency plan. *See* **Contingency plan, Disaster plan.**

Emulation. Techniques for imitating obsolete systems on future generations of computers and thus providing continued access to digital content.

Encumbrance. A recorded commitment of monies for an anticipated purchase. An encumbrance at the end of a fiscal year is carried forward into the next fiscal year as an outstanding commitment.

Endowment. A permanent fund consisting of gifts and bequests invested to earn interest. The interest can be spent, sometimes for purposes specified by the donors, leaving the principal intact to generate further income. *See also* **Fund raising.**

End user. An authorized individual or organization that accesses digital information for their own use.

En masse, also **en bloc.** Collected at one time or through a single purchase decision.

Entrepreneurial planning. A laissez-faire, individual approach to planning that relies on individuals to come forward whenever they have an idea for altering or expanding programs. Sometimes called opportunistic planning.

Environmental scanning. A method used to gather information and enhance understanding of an organization's environment and constituents. Its purpose is to detect, monitor, and analyze trends and issues in the environment, both internal and external, in which the organization operates.

Ephemera. Materials of everyday life not normally retained because they are perceived to have little or no permanent value. Pamphlets, leaflets, fliers, performance programs, and comic books often are considered ephemera. Sometimes called fugitive material. *See also* **Gray literature.**

Ethics. Principles of conduct or standards of behavior governing an individual or profession. These standards may be legal, moral, personal, or institutional.

Evaluation. *See* **Collection evaluation.**

Exchange. (1) An arrangement in which a library sends its own publications or those of its parent organization to another library and receives in return publications from the other library, or sends duplicate copies to another library and receives duplicate materials in return. (2) Any publication given or received in this manner.

Expenditure. A payment made during the current fiscal period.

Fair use. A legal doctrine, codified in Section 107 of the 1987 U.S. Copyright Act, that permits unauthorized use of copyrighted work for education, scholarship, teaching, news reporting, commentary, and research purposes. *See also* **Infringement.**

Farmington Plan. A federally funded program (1948–1972) intended to ensure that at least one copy of every book important for research, regardless of place of publication, would be available in at least one U.S. library.

Federal Depository Library Program (FDLP). A program established by the U.S. Congress to coordinate the federal depository libraries and to provide U.S. government publications to these libraries.

Firm order. A purchase order for an item submitted to a publisher or vendor. Money is encumbered for these orders, and the materials cannot normally be returned unless defective or damaged. Firm orders normally are placed for materials requested by the individual selectors. *See also* **Discretionary purchase.**

First sale doctrine. An exception to copyright that generally allows any person or entity who purchases an authorized, legal copy of a protected item to resell, lend, or give away that item. The first sale doctrine, which the Copyright

Act of 1976 codifies at Section 109(a) (17 U.S.C. §109(a)), is a recognized exception to the copyright owner's exclusive right to distribute protected works under Section 106(3) (17 U.S.C. §106(3)).

Fiscal year. A budget or accounting twelve-month cycle.

Fixed asset. Item with a determined and continuing value owned by the organization.

Focus group. A technique for gathering opinions and perspectives on a specific topic. A small group of people, with common interests or characteristics, is led by a moderator, who asks questions and facilitates group interaction on the topic being investigated.

Free balance. Money available for purchasing. The free balance is the allocation minus payments made and any encumbrances.

Fugitive material. *See* **Ephemera.**

Fund, or **fund line.** A self-balancing account in a budget with monies set aside for a specific purpose.

Fund accounting. A process of dividing an organization's budget into categories, usually according to proscribed regulations, restrictions, and limitations, used primarily by nonprofit or government organizations. In fund accounting, a fund is a self-balancing set of accounts, segregated for specific purposes.

Fund balance. The amount remaining in a fund that is the difference between assets (allocations or revenue or both) and liabilities (expenses and encumbrances). For most funds, a fund balance is available for additional allocation or spending.

Gift-in-kind. Charitable donation consisting of gifts, services, or property, but not cash or stocks.

Graphic novel. A book-length illustrated publication; a graphic novel can be fiction or nonfiction.

Gold open access. Open access through journals available online without financial, legal, or technical barriers.

Gratis open access. Access that is free of charge but not necessarily free of copyright and licensing restrictions. *See also* **Libre open access.**

Gray literature. Works such as reports, internal documents, dissertations and theses, and conference proceedings not usually available through regular market channels because they were never commercially published, listed, or priced. *See also* **Ephemera.**

Green open access. Open access through self-archiving in disciplinary or institutional repositories.

High-density shelving. Warehouse-style shelving in which materials are shelved by size to maximize storage efficiency. *See also* **Compact shelving.**

Historical budgeting. *See* **Incremental budgeting.**

Holdings. The entire collection of materials owned by a library or library system, usually listed in a catalog.

Impact factor. A tool for determining the importance of a journal in a subject field. Impact factor measures the number of times an article is cited within a given time period divided by the number of articles published during that time period.

Incentive planning. A planning model that views the organization in economic terms and has an incentive structure that rewards particular types of activities. Incentives are frequently financial—increased budget allocations or the opportunity to retain funds generated through various activities or operations. Also called responsibility-centered management.

Incremental budgeting. A process by which historical allocations are added to or subtracted from a standard amount or percentage.

Indemnity. One party's agreement to insure or otherwise defend another party against any claims by third parties resulting from performance under the agreement. It can, for example, provide for financial compensation should the warranties made in the contract prove false.

Infringement. A violation of law, contract, or right; unauthorized use of materials protected by copyright, patent, or trademark law, or contract.

Input. Resource (e.g., money, staff, collections) that provides a service or program.

Institutional repository. A library housing the digital objects created at a specific institution, intended for the purposes of collection, access, and preservation. *See also* **Disciplinary repository.**

Integrated library system (ILS). A group of automated library subsystems working together and communicating within the same set or system of software to control such activities as circulation, cataloging, acquisitions, and serial control.

Integrating resource. A resource that is added to or changed by means of updates that do not remain discrete but are integrated into the whole.

Intellectual freedom. The right granted in the First Amendment to the U.S. Constitution that permits a person to read or express views that may be unpopular or offensive to some people, within certain limitations. *See also* **Banned book, Censorship.**

Intellectual property. Products of the human mind, creativity, and intelligence that are entitled to the legal status of personal property, especially works protected by copyright, patented inventions, and registered trademarks.

Interface. The point or process that serves as an intermediary between two components of a data processing system, for example, the screen display that functions as intermediary between a software program and its human users.

Interlibrary loan, also **interlibrary lending (ILL).** Transaction in which one library requests and another library lends an item from its collections (a returnable) or furnishes a copy, either paper or digital, of the item (a nonreturnable) to another library.

Interoperability. The condition achieved when two or more technical systems can exchange information directly.

Inventory profiling. *See* **Conspectus.**

Invoice download. Electronic transmission of invoice data from a supplier's automated system to the library's system.

Jobber. *See* **Dealer.**

Journal. A serial that disseminates original research and commentary on current developments within a specific subject area, discipline, or field of study. Librarians distinguish between journals and magazines, but publishers and users often use the terms interchangeably; for example, *Ladies Home Journal* is considered a magazine by librarians. *See also* **Periodical.**

Knowledge base. A centralized repository for information; in library information technology, a machine-readable resource for the dissemination of information about content a library owns or has the rights to access. An OpenURL link resolver depends on the completeness and quality of data in the knowledge base to determine if an item (article, book, etc.) is available electronically and what the appropriate copy for a user is.

Lease. A contract by which one party grants access to or the use of real estate, equipment, or a resource for a specified term and for a specified amount to another party.

Liability. Legal responsibility for an act or failure to act. A limit of liability contractual clause sets out how much and what kind of damages will be paid for remedies. Many libraries have policies that forbid them from indemnifying licensors or holding them harmless to other parties.

Liaison. (1) Communication for establishing and maintaining mutual understanding and cooperation. (2) A librarian charged with liaison responsibilities. *See also* **Outreach**.

LibQUAL+. An online survey instrument within a suite of services that all types of libraries can use to solicit, track, understand, and act upon users' perceptions of library service quality.

Library binding. An especially strong and durable binding, usually conforming to the American National Standards Institute standard for library binding.

Library cooperation. Methods by which libraries and library systems work together for mutual benefit, including cooperative collection development, cooperative cataloging, exchange of bibliographic information, resource sharing, and union catalogs.

Library network. A mechanism that links libraries through shared bibliographic utilities or other formal arrangements.

Library survey. A written or oral question-and-answer instrument designed to elicit feedback from library users.

Libre open access. Access that is both free of charge (gratis open access) and free of a least some copyright and licensing restrictions.

License. A contract or portion of a contract that defines explicitly the rights to use a product or service that the licensor is granting to the licensee. A license to use digital information gives a licensee permission to access and use the information under the terms and conditions described in the agreement between the licensor and the licensee, usually in exchange for compensation.

Licensee. The party to a contract receiving permission or the rights to access or use an electronic resource.

Licensor. The party to a contract granting permission or the rights to use or access an electronic resource. If the licensor is representing the interests of copyright owners in a license agreement, it must have the financial means and legal authority to provide the services to which the parties agreed under the license agreement.

Light archive. A data storage site that can be accessed by authorized users.

Line-item budget. A detailed financial plan or method of tracking allocation and expenditures by categories.

Link resolver. Application software that uses the OpenURL standard to provide context-sensitive linking between a citation in a bibliographic database and the electronic full text of the resource cited (article, essay, conference paper, book, etc.) in an aggregator database or online from the publisher, taking into account which materials the user is authorized by subscription or licensing agreement to access.

Machine-Readable Cataloging (MARC). An international standard digital format for the description of bibliographic items developed by the Library of Congress to facilitate dissemination of catalog records.

Macro selection. Adding large quantities of materials to the library or access to numerous resources through a single decision. *See also* **Micro selection.**

Magazine. A popular-interest serial usually containing articles on a variety of topics, written by various authors in a nonscholarly style. *See also* **Journal, Periodical.**

Management report. A term used in libraries for statistical and informational reports, typically used in acquisitions and collection management activities, produced by vendors or locally by libraries.

Marketing. An umbrella term describing several activities: understanding an entity's market (in the case of a library—its present and future users), planning how best to serve that market, implementing the plan, and assessing its effectiveness.

Market segmentation. Dividing a market into distinct groups of buyers on the basis of needs, characteristics, or behaviors that might require separate products or marketing mixes.

Mass digitization. The scanning of print texts or images to digital format on a very large scale using user-operated equipment capable of scanning hundreds of pages per hour.

Master planning. Top-down planning that begins in the administrative offices of an organization.

Materials budget. The portion of a library's budget allocated for the purchase of books, media, serials, and other information resources. Some libraries include electronic resources, postage and service charges associated with acquiring materials, and conservation and preservation in the materials budget; others make separate allocations for these categories. Also may be called the acquisition budget, access budget, or collections budget.

Mending. Minor restoration of a book's condition, not requiring replacement of material or removal of the bound sections from the cover. *See also* **Rebinding, Repairing.**

Metadata. Literally, data about data. Structured data that describe the attributes of a resource, characterize its relationships, and support its discovery, management, and effective use in an electronic environment. MARC records are metadata.

Micro selection. Selecting titles to acquire or to which a library will provide access individually, one title at a time. *See also* **Macro selection.**

Migration. Transferring digital resources from one hardware or software configuration to another or from one generation of computer technology to another.

Monograph. Any nonserial publication, either complete in one volume or intended to be completed in a finite number of successive parts issued at regular or irregular intervals, consisting of a single work or collection of works.

Monographic series. A group of individual monographs that have a collective title applying to the group as a whole. Monographic series may be numbered or unnumbered; publication is expected to continue indefinitely.

Monographic set. A multipart title with a predetermined last volume; the date of the last volume may or may not be specified. Examples include encyclopedias and collected letters of historical or literary figures.

Multimedia. A combination of two or more digital media (text, graphics, audio, animation, video, etc.) used in a computer application or data file.

Narrative collection policy. A prose-based collection policy.

Needs analysis, also **needs assessment.** A systematic process that gathers information about a user community and then analyzes that data for planning.

Negotiation. The process of submissions, considerations, and reviews of offers between two or more parties that occurs until the licensee and licensor agree on terms and conditions (thereby codifying the agreement in a contract), or until the parties mutually agree to end this process without agreement.

Network. A hardware- and software-based data communication system consisting of interconnected computers, terminals, workstations, and other electronic resources used to support communication between each element. *See also* **Library network.**

Nondisclosure agreement. A contract or contract provision that contains a party's promise to treat certain information as confidential.

Nondiscretionary purchase. Any purchase that happens automatically. Examples are serial subscriptions, approval plans, and blanket orders. Nondiscretionary purchases imply a continuing annual commitment against the acquisitions budget.

Obscenity. Speech, writing, or artistic expression that appeals to prurient interests with no artistic, literary, or scientific purpose. The courts have had difficulty developing a legal definition of obscenity because of differences in what people find offensive. *See also* **Pornography.**

Open access (OA). (1) Condition in which scholarly content is made available to users without charge and free of needless copyright and licensing restrictions via the Internet. (2) The social-technical movement to promote this condition.

Open Archives Initiative–Protocol for Metadata Harvesting (OAI-PMH). A protocol defined by the Open Archives Initiative that provides a method for content providers to make records of their items available for harvesting by service providers.

Open source. A movement in which software developers make their source code freely available to anyone for use and modification.

OpenURL. A framework and format for communicating bibliographic information between applications over the Internet. The information provider assigns an OpenURL to an Internet resource instead of a traditional URL. When the user clicks on a link to the resource, the OpenURL is sent to a link resolver that resolves the OpenURL to an electronic copy of the resource appropriate for the user (and potentially to a set of services associated with the resource).

Operating budget. A budget allocated to meet the ongoing expenses incurred in running a library or library system.

Opportunity cost. In economics, the value of the best alternative forgone, in a situation in which a choice needs to be made between several mutually exclusive alternatives given limited resources. Assuming the best choice is made, it is the cost incurred by not enjoying the benefit that would be had by taking the second best choice available.

Order record. A record that includes information such as price, vendor, and invoice about the acquisition of an item.

Orphan work. An original work still protected by its term of copyright for which the rights holder cannot be found by someone who wants to use the work and is seeking permission to do so.

Outcome. Benefit to the user or user community as a result of a library's inputs and outputs; that is, the ways in which library users are changed as a result of contact with a library's resources and programs.

Out of print (OP). No longer obtainable from the publisher, who has no more copies in stock and does not plan another printing.

Output. Result from the library's inputs that can be measured quantitatively (e.g., numbers of books circulated).

Outreach. (1) A program that encourages the community to use library collections and services. (2) The act of reaching out or extending services beyond current or usual limits. *See also* **Liaison.**

Outsourcing. The contracting of library services formerly performed in-house to an external party. Examples of outsourcing are conservation and preservation (particularly binding and reformatting), purchasing catalog records in machine-readable form, purchasing cataloging for foreign-language materials, and acquisitions plans (approval plans, blanket orders, subscription agents, etc.).

Patron-driven acquisitions. A book purchasing model in which selection decisions are based on input from library patrons. MARC records for books, often matching a profile determined by the library, are loaded into the library's catalog. Once a specific book has been discovered and viewed by a predetermined number of patrons, it is automatically purchased for the collection. Also called demand-driven acquisitions, patron-initiated purchasing, and books-on-demand.

Pay-per-view. A per-transaction method of purchasing access to material at the point of use. This is the common means by which readers obtain an individual article or book (or chapter of a book) if they or their organization do not have a subscription to the resource containing the document. This service is provided by publishers and full-text hosts.

Peer review. (1) The process in which experts critically evaluate the work of an author prior to publication. (2) The process in which the job performance and professional contributions of a librarian or other library staff member are reviewed and evaluated by the individual's colleagues, who make recommendations about contract renewal, promotion, and tenure decisions.

Penalty. A specific cost or consequence to be assessed against a contractual party for breach of a term specified in the contract.

Periodical. A serial publication with its own distinctive title, containing articles, editorials, reviews, columns, short stories, poems, or other short works written by more than one contributor, sequentially numbered, issued more than once, generally at regular intervals of less than a year. Content is controlled by an editor or editorial board. Includes magazines, journals, and newsletters.

Perpetual access rights. Contractual rights granted to the licensee to access an e-resource after the termination of a license.

PESTLE. A technique for categorizing information gathered in an environmental scan as political, economic, social, technological, legal, and environmental in nature to inform planning.

Pittsburgh Study. A major study of the usage of library materials, conducted at the University of Pittsburgh by Allen Kent during the 1970s. It reported that approximately 40 percent of the materials purchased never circulated.

Pornography. Works of no artistic value in which sexuality is depicted with the conscious intention to arouse sexual desire. *See also* **Obscenity**.

Postprint. Any version of an article approved by peer review, regardless of whether it has been published.

Preprint. Any version of an article prior to peer review.

Preservation. A broad range of activities intended to prevent, retard, or stop deterioration of materials or to retain the intellectual content of materials no longer physically intact. *See also* **Conservation**.

Preservation needs assessment. Analysis of the condition of a library collection and the environmental conditions in which it is housed to determine what preservation treatments are needed.

Price index. A method of calculating and describing the inflation rate. It shows the effects of price change on a fixed group of items over a period of time.

Print-on-demand (POD). A technology, made possible through digital printing, in which new copies of a book are not printed until after an order has been received.

Profile. (1) A set of criteria prepared by a library for a publisher or agent that supplies materials on an approval plan or through a blanket order. The profile usually describes subject areas, levels of specialization and/or difficulty, languages, series, formats, price ranges, and so on. (2) A demographic study of the community served by a library or library system that measures economic, social, and educational variables.

Programmatic or **program budgeting**. A budget in which categories of funding relate to organizational goals or programs.

Provider. Individual or entity that provides access to information and delivery of services; includes traditional print and electronic scholarly publishers, trade publishers, information aggregators, vendors, and other electronic-only information disseminators.

Public domain. In copyright law, the total absence of copyright protection for a creative work (e.g., an article, book, painting, photograph, movie, poem, musical composition, or computer program). Works enter the public domain through either deliberate surrendering of the copyright by the creator of the work or the expiration of the copyright due to the passage of some legally stipulated period of time.

Public good. In economics, a good that is nonrivalrous and nonexcludable; that is, consumption of the good by one individual does not reduce the amount of the good available for consumption by others, and no one can be effectively excluded from using that good. *See also* **Common good.**

Purchase order (PO). An order placed by a library, authorizing a publisher, dealer, or vendor to deliver materials or services at a fixed price. A PO becomes a contract once it is accepted by the seller.

Qualitative methods. Analytical techniques that measure perceived success or goodness.

Quantitative methods. Analytical techniques that count things (volumes, circulation transactions, etc.).

Recasing. The process of regluing a book that has come loose from its cover.

Rebinding. The complete rehabilitation of a book too worn for mending or repairing. Rebinding usually entails removing the case or cover, resewing the sections or regluing the text block, and applying a new cover.

Refresh. The process in which digital information is copied to a new storage medium without changing the data's content or structure.

Remedy. The resolutions or corrections available to a party that has been harmed by a breach of contract.

Remote access. The access and use of digital content from a location other than where it is physically located or the primary site identified in a contract.

Repairing. The partial rehabilitation of a worn book or other item, including restoration of the cover and reinforcement of the hinges or joints. More extensive than mending but less extensive than recasing or rebinding.

Repository. A central place where data are stored and maintained; often used in place of digital repository.

Reprint. A new printing of an existing edition, with no changes in the text except, in some cases, the correction of typographical errors.

Request for proposal (RFP). A document listing the requirements for services along with the steps to be followed when submitting proposals to handle a library's account(s). RFPs typically are issued for services provided by, for example, monographic vendors, subscription agents, binders, and integrated library systems. Most public agencies use an RFP process in awarding contracts for services.

Resource sharing. Sharing of resources among a group of libraries. Resource sharing traditionally has referred to the sharing of materials through interlibrary loan.

Restoration. Returning a book, document, or other archival material as nearly as possible to its original condition. Restoration can include mending, repairing, rebinding, and deacidification. *See also* **Conservation, Preservation.**

Retrospective selection. The process of selecting materials to fill in gaps in the collection or to replace missing or damaged items.

Return on investment (ROI). A method to quantify and demonstrate the amount of income ("return") to the institution that a library contributes, compared to the monetary investment the institution makes in the library.

Rights. Powers or privileges granted by a contract or law.

Sales representative. An individual charged by a vendor, publisher, aggregator, or other content or service provider with selling products and services and with resolving general questions or concerns about the products or services already purchased. *See also* **Customer service representative.**

Scenario planning. The process of developing scenarios that describe alternative futures and formulating plans or strategies for the library in those various futures.

Scholarly communication. The means by which individuals engaged in academic research and creative endeavors inform their peers, formally or informally, of the work they have accomplished. *See also* **Peer review.**

Search engine. Software that searches a file, database, or network for a specific character string typed as input by the user.

Selection. The process of deciding which materials should be added to a library collection.

Selection criteria. The set of guidelines used by librarians in deciding whether an item should be added to the collection. *See also* **Collection development policy.**

Selector. One who selects materials for a library and, usually, makes decisions about collection management (e.g., what will be withdrawn, preserved, stored, transferred). *See also* **Bibliographer, Liaison, Subject specialist.**

Self-archiving. The practice of an author (or a publisher as part of the agreement with an author) depositing his or her work in free, open electronic archives or repositories, usually either disciplinary repositories or institutional repositories.

Serial. A publication issued over a period of time, usually on a regular basis with some sort of numbering used to identify issues, without a foreseeable ending date. Serials may be popular magazines, scholarly journals, electronic journals, or annual reports. The term serial is often used interchangeably with the term periodical to reflect the periodic nature of its publication.

Serials agent. *See* **Subscription agent.**

Server. A computer that provides some service for other computers connected to it via a network. A file server provides storage and retrieval capabilities; a printer server provides printing services via a remote printer; a communications server provides access to remote networks and databases.

Service charge. An amount added by a vendor, agent, or dealer on items with little or no publisher discount.

Service fee. A charge added by a subscription agent to the price of a subscription to cover the agent's costs in ordering and managing subscriptions for the library.

Shared E-Resource Understanding (SERU). A recommended practice of the National Information Standards Organization that allows libraries and publishers to forgo a license agreement and rely on a mutual understanding of widely accepted practices.

Shelf-ready. Supplied by a vendor and received ready to go to the stacks, usually in reference to books and similar materials. Shelf-ready items usually come already cataloged and processed (with spine labels, book plates, antitheft strips, etc.).

Signing authority, also **signature authority.** The authority to bind a party to, approve, or execute a contract on that party's behalf. If an individual signs a contract beyond his or her authority, that individual may be held personally liable for enforcing the contract or paying damages on the contract.

Simultaneous use. The limit of access to or use of an electronic product based on the number of simultaneous users.

Simultaneous users. The number of users who may access simultaneously a digital information resource.

Single-user model. Access model in which only one user may use a digital title at a time, with the user's access to that title expiring after a specified length of time.

Site. As used in a license, a physical location affiliated with the licensee where the licensee may permit access to digital information to authorized users.

Site license. A license granting official permission from the producer or vendor of an e-resource to use it, under specified conditions, on all the computers located at a specific location, a specific IP (Internet protocol) address, or a range of IP addresses.

Small press. A small independent publisher.

Social media. Mobile and web-based technologies used to create interactive platforms through which individuals and communities share, co-create, discuss, and modify user-generated content.

Social networking. A process through which people with shared interests link to each other via websites and other online tools.

Standardized Usage Harvesting Initiative (SUSHI). A National Information Standards Organization standard that defines an automated request-and-response model for the harvesting of e-resource usage data utilizing a web services framework.

Standing order. An order placed by a library with an agent or publisher to supply automatically until further notice each succeeding issue, volume, or part of a serial or series as published. Standing orders are billed as each volume is shipped and usually do not permit returns. Sometimes used synonymously with continuation order. *See also* **Approval plan.**

Storage. The transfer of less-used materials or rare, valuable, and fragile materials to areas with restricted access within a library building or to a remote facility. *See also* **Compact storage.**

Strategic planning. The systematic, broadly participative process by which an organization formulates policy objectives for future growth and development over a period of years. A strategic plan has an external focus and usually involves an environmental scan.

Subject or **area specialist.** A librarian responsible for selecting materials, managing a collection, and providing bibliographic instruction, reference services, and outreach to users in a specific academic discipline or field of study. *See also* **Bibliographer, Liaison, Selector.**

Subject-based packages. Collections of titles focused on a defined subject area.

Subscriber. The party to the agreement that is purchasing, leasing, or licensing a product or service; used in the context of an agreement, the subscriber may include all authorized users.

Subscription. An agreement or arrangement through which a library (or individual) receives a periodical or the rights to access a remote e-resource for a designated period of time or number of issues upon paying a fee to the publisher, subscription agent, or vendor.

Subscription agent. A company in the business of providing centralized subscription services to relieve libraries of the time-consuming task of dealing with publishers individually. Customers are required to pay a service charge, usually 5–10 percent of total annual subscription costs. Some subscription agents also provide access to bibliographic and full-text databases.

Surrogate. A substitute for an original item. In preservation, a surrogate is usually made in another medium that is more durable.

SWOT analysis. A technique for analyzing environmental factors in terms of strengths, weaknesses, opportunities, and threats to inform planning.

Term. (1) A period of time during which a contract is in effect. (2) A clause or agreement in a contract.

Termination. The cancellation or ending of an agreement.

Transfer. Physically move library materials from one location in a library to another.

Trial. A limited period during which a library may test a new electronic product or resource without paying a fee.

Trigger event. An occurrence that opens access to a digital archive of commercial content. Typical trigger events are when a publisher ceases operations and titles are no longer available from any other source, when a publisher ceases to publish and offer a title and it is not offered by another publisher or entity, when back issues are removed from a publisher's offering and are not available elsewhere, and upon catastrophic failure by a publisher's delivery platform for a sustained period of time.

Trueswell's 80/20 Rule. A circulation pattern, first reported by Richard W. Trueswell in the 1960s, in which 20 percent of a library's collection accounts for 80 percent of its circulation.

Unauthorized user. Any person or entity that does not have permission to access or otherwise use the digital information that is the subject matter of an agreement. Also, any user that the license does not explicitly define as an authorized user.

Unmediated borrowing. A process in which patrons directly place interlibrary loan requests for materials without staff mediation or intervention.

Usability. The effectiveness, efficiency, and satisfaction with which users can achieve tasks, using a particular electronic product.

Use. A licensee's right to operate the licensor's program, software, website, or other electronic environment in order to access the digital information the licensee is leasing under an agreement. *See also* **Authorized use.**

User. (1) A person who uses library materials or services. (2) Any person or entity who interacts with licensed digital resources or puts these resources into service. In a contract, the term *user*, whether in singular or plural, typically is synonymous with *authorized user*. *See also* **Authorized user, End user, Simultaneous users, Unauthorized user.**

User-centered. Focused on how a collection is being used and how well it meets user needs, applied to assessments.

Utility. In economics, utility is a measure or expression of an individual's expected or anticipated satisfaction.

Vendor. (1) A wholesale distributor through which the library obtains books, serials, other materials, and services, usually at a discount, instead of dealing directly with a publisher. Some vendors offer customized services such as continuation orders, approval plans, cataloging, and technical processing. *Vendor* is more common today and replaces the term *jobber*, which was more prevalent in the twentieth century. (2) A company in the business of providing access to one or more electronic resources. *See also* **Agent.**

Verification list. An extensive subject-based list of important monographs and serials against which a library's holdings are checked to evaluate the quality of a collection.

Waiver. The intentional or voluntary surrender of a known right or privilege.

Weeding. The process of selecting items in a library collection for withdrawal or relocation to storage.

Withdrawal. Removing an item from a library's active collection and removing the bibliographic record from the library's catalog.

Zero-based budgeting. A budgeting process in which all allocations start at zero and funding needs and requirements are estimated as if no previous allocation had been made.

zine. A small-circulation, narrowly focused, often irregular, noncommercial magazine, newsletter, or newspaper, self-published by one person or a small group and usually not available by subscription.

This glossary has been compiled from various sources, including these:

CNET: The Computer Network Glossary. www.cnet.com/Resources/Info/Glossary.

Harris, Lesley Ellen. *Licensing Digital Content: A Practical Guide for Librarians*, 2nd ed. Chicago: American Library Association, 2009.

Johnson, Peggy. *Developing and Managing Digital Collections*. Chicago: American Library Association, 2013.

Levine-Clark, Michael, and Toni M. Carter, eds. *ALA Glossary of Library and Information Science*. 4th ed. Chicago: American Library Association, 2013.

LibLicense: Licensing Digital Content. "Licensing Vocabulary." http://liblicense.crl.edu/resources/licensing-vocabulary.

Reitze, Joan M. "ODLIS: Online Dictionary for Library and Information Science." www.abc-clio.com/ODLIS/odlis_A.aspx.

Wikipedia. www.wikipedia.org.